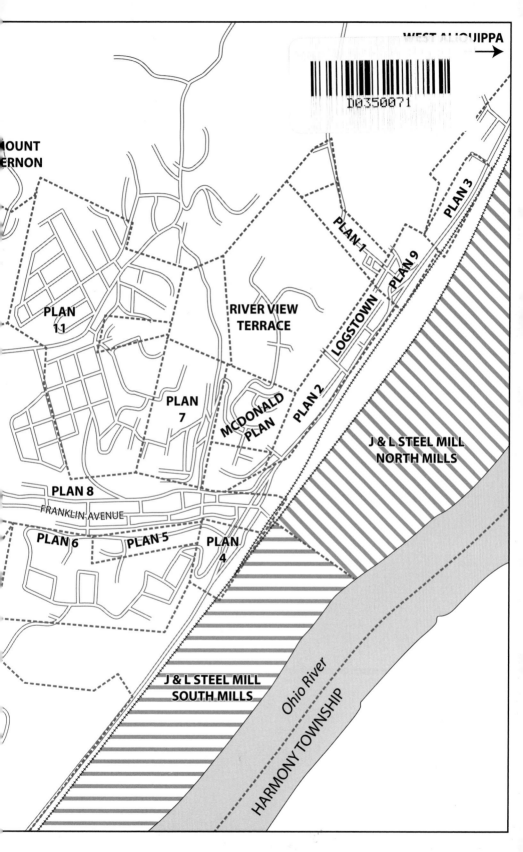

WEST ALIQUIPPA →

MOUNT
VERNON

PLAN
11

RIVER VIEW
TERRACE

PLAN-1

PLAN 9

PLAN 3

LOGSTOWN

PLAN
7

PLAN 2

MCDONALD
PLAN

J & L STEEL MILL
NORTH MILLS

PLAN 8

FRANKLIN AVENUE

PLAN 6

PLAN 5

PLAN
4

J & L STEEL MILL
SOUTH MILLS

Ohio River

HARMONY TOWNSHIP

PLAYING THROUGH THE WHISTLE

PLAYING THROUGH THE WHISTLE

Steel, Football,

and an American Town

S. L. PRICE

Atlantic Monthly Press
New York

For Fran

On and on the compact ranks,
With accessions ever waiting, with the places of the dead quickly fill'd,
Through the battle, through defeat, moving yet and never stopping,
    Pioneers! O pioneers!

—Walt Whitman, "Pioneers! O Pioneers!"

Contents

PART ONE

October 14, 2011

Once, years before, John Evasovich had come to the field with his mother in his pocket. It was an autumn evening much like this one, chill and damp, and only a practice session, but he is one of those men who prefer the routines, the purposeful quiet of football practice. Besides, Evasovich needed to do the woman one last service. She had seen her son play high school ball; she had seen John grinding it out young as a fullback and guard, his sharpest critic; she had seen every block and tackle he missed and always let him know. Later, after he moved back after sixteen years gone, he'd pick up his mother and her sister and her sister's husband on game nights and they'd all ride up together. Her first time had been in 1940. John knew what she loved.

Every game—week after fall week, decade after decade, come rain or snow or biting cold—Liz Evasovich had sat in the cracking concrete stands with her lips daubed Aliquippa scarlet, peering out from the 50-yard line with seven younger women in their black "Quips" sweaters, rattling cowbells long and loud. So twelve days after she died, her only son brought a small plastic bag filled with the cremated remains to Carl A. Aschman Stadium. He felt the weight of her on his hip the whole time: driving, walking down to the field, bullshitting in head coach Mike Zmijanac's office beforehand. . . .

When the team ran out of the locker room and the coaches began to bark, their breath forming clouds, he opened the bag in an end zone and tipped it and watched the gray dust settle into the grass. Nobody saw. Then he pinched it closed, walked out to the Indian head symbol in the center of the field, and, with tears running down his cheeks, tipped the bag again to let more of his mother go.

3

"You are where you belong," he whispered. "It's where you want to be."

Evasovich wasn't a young man then, and the five years since are five reasons more for any cold-hating, bandy-legged seventy-one-year-old to feel that drizzly ache, scan the low skies, and stay in for the night. But no, tonight Evasovich did what he has done nearly every fall Friday since: walk into the dining room, glance at the black-and-gray urn containing the last of Liz's ashes, and announce, "I'm going to the game, Mom."

Aliquippa High is unbeaten as usual, and one of its prime rivals, Beaver Area, is coming in undefeated, too. Every showdown between these two, it seems, conjures a classic; everyone's just a bit edgier. It's Senior Night, the last home game. Some boys will never play in "The Pit" again.

That's what it's called, oddly when you consider that the stadium squats, supreme and precarious, upon one of the highest ridges in town. But it's true: the New Deal genius who decided to wedge the 7,500-seat matchbox into hillside, just below the apex, created an effect—for opposing fans and players, at least—of descending into a particularly cramped and hostile corner of hell. The visitors' locker room is little more than a dank hole. The crumbly visiting stands feel like they could, at any time, pitch in one screaming entirety down the ravine behind. Most opponents don't come to Aliquippa these days thinking victory. They also know that you can't say you've played football in Western Pennsylvania—not really—until you've played The Pit.

One reason is that, in a week before a showdown like this one with Beaver, the game can feel like the only thing that matters. "I think Aliquippa will win," outgoing mayor Anthony Battalini said two days before. "They have to win. If they lose? Christ, the town'll cut up Mike—'The team's no good!'—like they lost their life. It'll be booming Friday night, believe me. It'll be booming."

Another reason is that, even in one of the most talent-rich regions in America, Aliquippa remains puzzlingly special. Usually places this small—27,116 souls, at its peak—can claim one, perhaps two, names a century that tunnel out to become nationally known. But something in the air or water or blood here didn't just produce NFL Hall of Famers like Mike Ditka and Tony Dorsett, but also basketball wizard Pete Maravich, major league baseball players like Tito Francona and Doc Medich, a U.S. Surgeon General, the National Guard's first black female general, one of the more famous CIA operatives in American history, an NCAA president, one of the *great visual effects artists in cinematic history, and Oscar-winning composer Henry Mancini.*

That roll enables locals to mix twenty-seven Grammy Awards and twenty-six Academy Award nominations in with the annual rushing totals, yet numbers hardly do the place justice. Obscure Aliquippa—"the ultimate melting-pot," as one of its sons put it—kicked off the Golden Age of American labor and crafted the arms that won two world wars. Four U.S. presidents have visited in the hope of winning its symbolic heart. Name the arena: the town has always punched well above its weight.

But Aliquippa has also been dying for thirty years now, its population in free fall, its downtown a drive-by stretch, mostly, of empty buildings and leveled lots. Legendary New York Giants general manager Ernie Accorsi made a point of visiting after he retired in 2007, and "I almost fainted," he says. "It looks like they just said, 'There's a nuclear war: get out of here.'"

Yet he wanted to—had to—walk onto the field and take in the stadium, too, because the place still churns out high-level players at an astonishing rate. Every fall, still, a handful of Quips will walk into some premier Division 1-A university with full football scholarships. Since 1990, four alums from Aliquippa High, enrollment 270, have been selected in the first round of the NFL Draft: All-Pro defensive lineman Sean Gilbert, three-time Super Bowl champ Ty Law, All-Pro cornerback Darrelle Revis, and wideout Jon Baldwin.

Only one other high school in America, California's Long Beach Poly, can match that, but its enrollment is seventeen times larger. Aliquippa High averages three dozen boys in its senior class, gets smaller by the day, but it defies logic. It refuses to buckle. The Quips have won a record thirteen Western Pennsylvania Interscholastic Athletic League titles, each year painted in white on the roof of the old field house, and will win a fourteenth this year, and a fifteenth the next. This is a growing concern. Soon, they will run out of roof. . . .

Through the window he could see black hills powdered with snow, an occasional coaltipple, rows of gray shacks all alike, a riverbed scarred with minedumps and slagheaps, purple lacing of trees along the hill's edge cut sharp against a red sun; then against the hill, bright and red as the sun, a blob of flame from a smelter. Ward shaved, cleaned his teeth, washed his face and neck as best he could, parted his hair. His jaw and cheekbones were getting a square look that he admired. "Cleancut young executive," he said to himself. . . .

—John Dos Passos, *The 42nd Parallel*

1

The Red and the Black

They came for the money. Years later, once purchase had been gained at the steel mill, early-twentieth-century immigrants to America would speak of luxuries like liberty or freedom of worship. But the prospect sketched by industry agents who fanned out, then, through Europe's destitute cities and farms had less to do with steeples and voting booths than the squat outline of blast furnace, powerhouse, and ore yard, high chimneys belching volcanic ash and endless fire. The pursuit of happiness? Being "happy" was never the point. Old-World peasants were near starving. The Serbs had a motto: *Čovek mora da radi:* A man must work. America had the work. America had money.

So they kept coming in that first decade and half, 15 million strong, most uneducated and unskilled and speaking no English, a constant flow of labor being drained from ancestral homes and hills and fields and streaming to the nearest big ports. Some were young boys, and alone. But they were mostly young men at first, cast out blindly by families like fishhooks, fleeing threat of war, natural disaster, the crumbling order of king and czar. They came from Italy, Germany, Russia, Poland, Hungary, Ukraine, Croatia, Serbia, Slovakia, Lebanon, Greece; they were Slavs and Roman Catholics and Jews and Eastern Orthodox sardined together into boxcars, sometimes legally. Other times the men hopped down and dissolved into fields at border crossings, crouching silent until the officials went away. The journey was tedium, filth, spasms of fear. They kept coming.

It was, too, the first era of movement for movement's sake, of speed as a virtue. The human rush was on: to cities, to empire, to battle, to getting wherever *there* was faster. Steel made speed possible. Expanding rail systems, rising skyscrapers, Henry Ford's automobile, and the buildup of European armies created a near-bottomless hunger for the light, flexible metal, made Western Pennsylvania an industrial behemoth and magnet for all the "mill Hunkies" filing then through New York's Ellis Island. Sent funds in 1903 by an older brother in Pittsburgh, Martin Zelenak, a twenty-year-old from the Czech-Slovak slice of the Austro-Hungarian Empire, set out for Hamburg; en route he was dragooned into the Austrian cavalry and shipped to the eastern frontier. Two years later, Corporal Zelenak arrived in New York and began walking the 370 miles West to his brother's home. When his shoes dissolved, he stole potato sacks off porches and wrapped his feet in the burlap and walked on.

In 1905 Pittsburgh's Jones and Laughlin Steel Company, founded in the 1850s by the self-made B. F. Jones and James Laughlin—or, as one observer quipped, an old firm "when Andrew Carnegie was still a telegraph messenger boy"—began buying up acreage twenty-six miles down the Ohio River: Crow and Hog Islands; the untouched farmland above sleepy Woodlawn; a small, adjoining manufacturing village, Aliquippa; and the remains of a once-bustling amusement park.

The original village name, applied randomly by a railroad company looking to entice customers in 1878, was lifted not from some local feature but from Queen Aliquippa, a pro-British Seneca chief who never set foot there and whom George Washington, when he met her miles away in 1753, tendered "a present of a match-coat and a bottle of rum, which latter was thought much the better present of the two." General "Mad Anthony" Wayne—en route to his victory at the Battle of Fallen Timbers—trained troops cross-river in the winter of 1794; legend has it that his soldiers rowed over so often to the Woodlawn whorehouse that Wayne had it leveled with a blast of cannon shot.

Now second in size only to Carnegie Steel, J&L had only recently come under full control of the next generation of the Jones family. Freshly incorporated, its ambitions increasingly squeezed in its South Side works, the company as pure business animal needed to expand to capitalize on the mushrooming global markets in tin, tube, and wire. But "The Family," as the Jones management entity came to be known, didn't only view the rolling expanse along the Ohio as a blank slate upon which to write their financial future. They had something more elevated in mind.

President B. F. Jones Jr., the only son of B. F. senior and Princeton-trained, and his more voluble cousin, vice president William Larimer Jones, considered themselves part of an enlightened subset of industrialists in that Darwinian era, touting a management bent as paternal as it was profitable. Tom Girdler, the mill's de facto superintendent from 1914 to 1924, never had a stranger job interview: W. L. Jones and he barely talked business. Starting with the *Mayflower*, Jones lectured Girdler on the nation's history of immigration, on the poorer, darker, oft-bewildered horde now pouring in, on the real estate and criminal interests that funneled them into shantytowns thick with typhoid and cholera. Aliquippa would be the corrective, Jones believed, a utopian machine designed to make citizens as well as steel.

"We can make a fresh start," Jones told Girdler. "When the plant is fully built the men who work there will constitute, with their families, the population of a good-sized town. We want it to be the best steel town in the world. We want to make it the best possible place for a steelworker to raise a family."

By then, the task of town-building was well under way. The first blast furnace had been fired up—or "blown in"—on December 1, 1909, and over time Woodlawn, the original Aliquippa (later named West Aliquippa), and the highland area known as New Sheffield would all be bound by the company's implacable will. Separated by railroad tracks, linked by a downtown viaduct—always known as "The Tunnel"—that later marked the divide between the North and South Mills, Aliquippa's work and living quarters rose together. By the end of 1912, three more furnaces were roaring, and the tin mill; rod, wire, and nail mill; blooming mill; open hearth; Bessemer converter; and beehive coke ovens began operation on a spread that would stretch a full seven and a half miles.

Across the tracks, through the tunnel, J&L sliced the town into 12 "Plans" that kept ethnic groups separate, reinforced old-country language, customs, and suspicion of outsiders, and—not incidentally—made any attempt at labor organizing that much more difficult. Its land company threw up a two-story house—hot and cold water, indoor plumbing, base price of $2,200—a day in 1908, built a half-dozen schools and a community pool, financed and laid out the bus lines. The central commercial district, Franklin Avenue, was built atop a channeled river, the Logstown Run, and anchored by a company store called Pittsburgh Mercantile. J&L owned the water company and 674 homes. Downtown streets were paved with brick. Residential streets glowed with fresh-laid macadam.

"It has every modern utility such as natural gas, electric light, a pure and potable water supply and ample police and fire protection," read a promotional brochure for the town in 1910. "Its opportunities for delightful home and neighborhood life are not equaled in this end of the state." City fathers in Vandergrift or nearby Midland, other model steel towns, might take issue with the claim. But in light of the day's industrial slums, it felt like true progress.

Serbs, Croats, Poles, Slovaks, and a small scattering of blacks were sent to Plans 1, 2, 4, and 9 along the tracks, making up much of what was known as Logstown. Plan 7 held Serbs and other Slavs, Plan 11 the Italians and some Poles. Jews held down Plan 8, along Franklin Avenue; Greeks and Lebanese settled at its eastern end, by the tunnel, in the area known as the Wye. Italians dominated West Aliquippa. The higher in the surrounding hills you went, the whiter, richer, and quieter it became. Plan 6, with its three clay tennis courts, was reserved for management: "cake-eaters," in the slang of the day. Anglos, Germans, and Nordics lived in Plan 12, spilling over the bridge into a neighborhood soon to be dubbed "Hollywood" because of its decadent parties, its wayward wives.

The line between each Plan was invisible but known to all. Crossing entailed risk. Each enclave transplanted Old-World rivalries along with food and music, and in rich precincts police jailed anyone who seemed out of place; if you worked at J&L, the cost of arrest—$10—came out of your pay. Class rules levied a different kind of sting.

"The fathers and mothers didn't allow you to talk to their girls," said steelworker Joe Perriello, a five-year-old when his family moved to Aliquippa in 1919. "If you wanted to date one of these Anglo-Saxons, you came to the door and even if you were a football player or a star or anything, they didn't give a damn. You knocked at the door and you asked for the girl, they said, 'Who the hell are you? Well, get out of here, you goddamn Dago, and don't you come back.' That's the way it was."

That first generation filling the Plans didn't argue—not when they were told where they couldn't walk or live, not when they were told how to work. Nothing mattered more than the job early on, both the job and the idea behind it. That a man could leave his parents, wife, and life behind in Vilnius or Minsk, ride steerage in a fetid steamship, and land employment that allowed for periodic returns back home, cash in hand, felt like salvation. So what if the cake-eater at the desk couldn't navigate the mash of consonants, and in seconds wiped out generations of family history by telling some proud Serb named Božidar Sučević, "From now on, your name is 'Mike Suder'"? You nodded. You took it. Complaint was a vice broken back on the docks of Hamburg.

Soon after the mill's opening, Martin Zelenak, the corporal, landed a job in J&L's boiler room, blacksmithing, swapping out pipes in 130-degree heat, inhaling coal dust and oil fumes. "Twelve-hour shifts in those days," said his son, Martin Jr., a boilermaker at J&L himself for thirty years. "He'd get carbon-monoxide gas from working in the boilerhouse. When we worked in there we had a gas mask and a meter; if there was too much gas we had to get out. But my father, they didn't have it. He'd get gassed, go out in the alley, lay down, and throw up—and go back in there and keep working. If he wouldn't, they would fire you."

In moments of repose, sipping a cup of home-brewed wine or puffing a pipe, older Italians would take in the thick woods slanting above Franklin Avenue and say that Woodlawn—the name officially changed to Aliquippa in 1928—reminded them of the Seven Hills of Rome. J&L built playgrounds, gave money to the Boy Scouts, bought neighborhood baseball gear. But good intentions aside, its main order of business was still filth-ridden, dangerous, and fully in line with a business ethos that saw ravaged hearing and scorched skin—or worse—as a fair trade for a day's pay.

"In the Aliquippa plant of the Jones & Laughlin Steel Company Eli Skylo, 22 years old, of Woodlawn, was injured in an accident at 11 o'clock Sunday and died shortly afterward," read an item in the July 15, 1913, *Pittsburgh Post*. "And in the evening Jack Reynolds, 17 years old, a water boy who resided with his mother in Woodlawn, was killed. Skylo was crushed in an ore dump and the boy lost his life beneath ladle cars."

Within a year, the Great War had changed the dynamic. Demand for barbed wire, shell casing, spikes, rails, steel sheet, and tin food containers had the mills running at full capacity, and fighting across Europe dammed the labor flow. Three thousand J&L workers would go off to fight; in Aliquippa, jobs abounded. Schools ran year-round. The air hummed with twenty-four-hour clamor by the river; every nine minutes or so, flashes of flame bleached the night sky. That was steel's signature, the Bessemer converter in blow, beautiful and monstrous and illustrating like nothing else the dazzling might of "industrialization."

In use since 1875, the Bessemer—egg-shaped, steel-plated, taller than two men—reshaped a craft once dominated by artisans into a mass production manned by unskilled labor. B. F. Jones may have been the first in Pittsburgh to experiment with the process, in 1864, but it wasn't until a decade later, when Andrew Carnegie introduced the method at his Edgar Thomson Works, that it became industry standard. By 1916, Aliquippa had three Bessemers online. Each blow was a small apocalypse—50,000 pounds of molten iron ore and carbon poured into the egg, colliding with 7,000 pounds of forced oxygen. A blossom of red, then yellow, then white flame exploded out of the top.

"It was a terrifying site, and hypnotic," author Stewart Holbrook wrote of the scene inside a Bessemer shed in Aliquippa. "The roar was literally deafening; and little wonder, for here was a cyclone attacking a furnace in a brief but titanic struggle, a meeting in battle of carbon and oxygen, cleverly arranged by the sweating gnomes whose red faces appeared white in the Bessemer's glow. Both carbon and oxygen would lose, each consuming the other, and men would be the winners by twenty-five tons of bright new steel."

All darkness above the mill, meanwhile, was obliterated by sheets of crimson and gold. "Hell with the lid lifted," is the line Charles Dickens borrowed to describe Pittsburgh, but it fit Aliquippa, too. Come the next morning, a film of soot and fly ash—"J&L pepper," "black snow"—was swept from countertops and porches all over town.

"Goddamn you!" one old Serb screamed at a complaining daughter. "You don't have that dirt? You don't have no food! Shut up, get a hose, clean it off!'"

Franklin Avenue offered dozens of bars to wash down the dust. Wages were paid in a mix of coupons, redeemable only at Pittsburgh Mercantile, and cash, snatched up by wives waiting outside the tunnel before their men could blow it playing cards or the numbers or shooting craps. "They called us 'Little Las Vegas,' if you please: gambling joints. Every other store was a gambling joint," said Joe Perriello, who came of age in Aliquippa in the 1920s. "When we got paid twice a month, they'd gamble from Friday to Monday. Everybody played for money. It was a money town!"

Debt was a constant. J&L deducted house, gas, and electric payments out of paychecks. To be fired meant eviction, and the loss of any mortgage payments made on a company home. Such power invited abuse: mill foremen demanded kickbacks—drink, cash, sex with a worker's wife—or else. The notorious Black Hand ran extortion schemes out of Plan 11; when an Italian fruit seller refused to pay $2,000, they blew up his downtown store and the whole three-story building that held it. More and more, the Family's Utopia had the feel of the Wild West.

"It is said that the region is largely peopled by uneducated foreigners, who invariably carry concealed deadly weapons; that murders are common," a state supreme court judge summarized in 1918. "And that when a quarrel ensues, the question as to who shall be the murderer and who is murdered is, largely, if not wholly, determined by the ability to draw such a weapon quickly."

But crime—in deed or mind—was a small chaos, and chaos was never good for the making of steel. Enamored with its own goodness, left militantly antiunion by Pittsburgh's savage Homestead Strike of 1892, terrified that its Slavic workers, in particular, would spread the infection of anarchism or communism, J&L surveyed the mess from the head office in Pittsburgh—and cracked down. Tom Girdler, its top official in town, fancied himself "an unofficial caliph, an American Harun al-Rashid obliged by my office in a big corporation to consider a whole community as my personal responsibility.

"There was in Aliquippa, if you please, a benevolent dictatorship. We policed it our own way and we policed it well. We began policing it because we had to—if we were to keep faith with the fine intentions of The Family."

As the implement deployed to shape such intention into day-to-day practice, The Family couldn't have chosen a more dangerous man. Not because Tom Girdler was inherently cruel, but because he was plagued by a limitless certitude. Because he was the hero of every story he told, no matter that it didn't always match fact. It takes a healthy dose of self-delusion to be solid money-born and management-bred, a fraternity man at Lehigh, yet look back from the prospect of old age and decide to call one's autobiography *Boot Straps*. But then, Girdler came of age in an era where every politician needed to be born in a log cabin—and every millionaire needed to start off as a version of Horatio Alger's Ragged Dick.

That Girdler was shrewd, and worked relentlessly, was never in doubt. He grew up mowing hay on his father's farm in 1880s Indiana, stacking endless dense sacks in the family cement plant, steeped in a narrative that marched in lockstep with the nation's own. Girdlers had fought the British in the Revolution, captained ships in the War of 1812, manned a ship alone in San Francisco Bay when the crew deserted to chase gold. Every Girdler man enlisted in the Civil War. "So, good or bad," Tom wrote, "every fiber of me is American."

His father bequeathed him a "feudal" approach to labor: those Indiana hands who produced without complaint were "good," and if any of them fell sick the elder Girdler looked after their families, guaranteed their credit, paid the doctor. If they were "bad," he kicked them out of town. Relations between boss and worker were man-to-man; nobody went on strike. In love with the furious clank of heavy industry, young Tom sprang out of college primed, ever conscious of his smallness, and—in a milieu populated by the tough and unlettered—vaguely ashamed of his considerable advantages.

To compensate, Girdler chewed tobacco; he became addicted to smoking cigars, and the wearing of brown hats. Balding, bespectacled, weighing no more than 150 pounds, he was never prouder than when he could take a bigger man down. Once, during his first days as foreman in a Pittsburgh area mill, a young Polish boltmaker cursed Girdler out. He stood three inches taller, forty pounds heavier.

"I hit him in the mouth, cutting my hand on his teeth," Girdler recalled in his memoir. "Instead of punching back he dived at me and when we hit the floor he was on top and my elbows (my sleeves were rolled up) felt as if they were on fire. He was grappling and pulling at my cheek as if he were drawing a chicken. That's when I began to wrestle and when I got on top I reached for his hair because this was rough-and-tumble. But he didn't have any hair; it had been clipped. I got hold of his ears. I hammered his head on the brick floor until I was sure nobody would be disposed to call the fight a draw. I stopped when he was out."

A year after Girdler's 1914 arrival in Aliquippa, J&L hired a brutal and canny ex–state trooper, Harry G. Mauk, as "Director of Plant Protection." The title included mastery of the company's "Coal and Iron Police"—a privately paid armed force, sanctioned by the state—de facto control of the town's municipal police department, and anything else that Girdler deemed vital. Mauk infiltrated bars and barbershops with spies, placed puppets on the city council, monitored worker mail. When a cadre of Finnish tin workers refused to buy Liberty Bonds in the fall of 1918, the law marked them as members of the Finnish Red Guard. After a J&L foreman ordered a gang of fellow workers to attack them, the Finns were hustled to the riverbank, stripped naked, tarred and feathered, and kicked forever out of town.

"They had local government, the county government, state, on their side," said J&L tin worker Michael Zahorsky, who was born in 1907 and began working in the hot mill at thirteen. "There was no such thing as 'challenging.' You had all these things going around in your mind that you were not able to challenge for fear you may be thrown out of the job. You may be run out of the country. You were declared an anarchist just because you raised your voice."

Come Election Day, Aliquippa always went Republican. To register—never mind vote—as a Democrat meant risking the loss of job and home; J&L goons made sure of it. "There were scarcely half a dozen registered Democrats," Girdler recalled of the town that, within eight years, would begin a seven-decade run as a Democratic stronghold. "Did that situation make it easy for me to run the Aliquippa Works? I'll confess! It did."

So went William Larimer Jones's "fresh start" for the lowly working class, a near-instant casualty of America's forever war between freedom and control. So it went, too, in industrial metropolises like New York, Chicago, Detroit, Pittsburgh, but a tight company town made surveillance easier and enforcement more intimate. The smaller melting pot brought its ethnic mix to a quicker, more furious boil. That alone might've been enough to make Aliquippa the epitome of a tough new class powered by grievance, toughened by fire, energized by a hope its fathers never knew. But they weren't the only outsiders settling in.

Finding escape from that tension, relief from the daily dirt and fatigue, wasn't hard in river towns like Aliquippa. Every Plan had its house of worship, whether the God was Methodist, Baptist, Roman Catholic, Russian, Serbian or Greek Orthodox, Jewish, African Methodist, or Episcopal. Immigrants opened every kind of social club, too: the Sons of Italy, the Lebanon Society, Serbian and Croatian clubs. In the summer of 1925, Italians transplanted from the village of Patrica initiated their annual two-day San Rocco Festa: music, fireworks, a grand parading of the saint through town, boys' and girls' footraces, and "for men, any size," a sack race, a bucket game, and a "slippery board contest." First prize, $5.

For those seeking distraction that didn't involve salvation or good clean fun, there was McDonald Hollow, a sliver of hillside—overlooked by The Family in its initial landgrab—that quickly grew to offer every kind of vice. "On any payday that was a noisy place," Girdler said. "Its

17

saloons were dives. There were brothels and gambling houses, jailbirds, prostitutes, and other outcasts."

The bars closed down with the enactment of Prohibition in 1920, but Aliquippa barely missed a drink. Moonshiners and basement vintners moved product, initially by strapping hot-water bags to women's legs and sending them into the streets in oversized black raincoats; when business began booming, the 'shine was delivered in five-gallon tins. The booze was stored in hidden "patents," some with elaborate funneling systems: under floorboards, in basement holes, along row house walls. One downtown soda fountain sold shots under the counter, 30 cents for two. Those caught paid a hefty fine, and spent a night in jail mulling over where to secrete their patent next.

The river provided fishing and swimming in the hot months and, on the backriver channel between Crow Island and West Aliquippa, ice skating in winter. After it acquired the island, J&L set aside fields for baseball and football, and distributed seed and thousands of "truck garden" plots to its employees. Because Crow Island sat in federal waters, it was exempt from Pennsylvania blue laws forbidding Sunday games and liquor. For a time, boys ferried fans back and forth across the channel in sixteen-foot rowboats. When that proved too risky, J&L had three barges lashed end to end, and Sunday outings to a game began with a stroll across the makeshift bridge.

Baseball was king in Pittsburgh then. The Pirates, a National League power, had won the 1909 World Series and starred local boy— and former twelve-year-old coal miner—Honus Wagner at shortstop. But the game's pastoral air, subtle details, and gunfighter showdowns between pitcher and batter harked back to an era of artisans and yeomen, its rhythm increasingly at odds with the nerve-racking pace of the machine age. Football was new. Football was obvious. Football, with its bone-snapping tackles, minimal protections, and masses toiling in syncopated fury, killed 330 American college men between 1890 and 1905. It channeled frustration, rewarded power. It fed and fed off the ethos of factory, mill, and mine. It demanded—like the production line and labor union—the sublimation of individual want to group need. Muddy, bloody, and raw, football felt more like the life now unfolding at ground level in Western Pennsylvania: bodies punished in a fight for the slightest edge, with money, so often, dictating the terms.

Professional football began in Pittsburgh. In 1892, the Allegheny Athletic Association publicly claimed that its supposedly amateur rival, the Pittsburgh Athletic Club, paid its top player and coach, William Kirschner. Both teams responded by seeking more inventive ways of making under-the-table payoffs, and in October the PAC offered Yale all-American William "Pudge" Heffelfinger and Knowlton "Snake" Ames $250 to play against Allegheny. The AAA countered with an offer of $500. Heffelfinger surrendered his amateur status, and stunned the PAC by showing up on game day in the opposing team's uniform.

"The AAA expense sheet provides the first irrefutable evidence of an out-and-out cash payment," says the official history at the Pro Football Hall of Fame. "It is appropriately referred to today as 'pro football's birth certificate.'"

Gamblers had bet so heavily on AAA that day that the contest was downgraded to an exhibition. AAA followers were furious that they couldn't collect on their bets; PAC fans publicly lamented their rival's use of "ringers," and privately fumed at being outfoxed. AAA manager O. D. Thompson crowed that he had just done "what the Pittsburghs tried to do. Only we were successful where they failed."

That mercenary tone filtered down to the prep level. The practice of hiring the city's best players, some in their early twenties, and sending them out to play high school football soon became so common as to be embarrassing. In response, four Pittsburgh schools combined in 1906 to form the Western Pennsylvania Interscholastic Athletic League, complete with age eligibility rules and membership standards for all sports; once WPIAL administrators actually began to enforce player bans—even when, as one local paper put it, "leading citizens found fault"—its membership began to spread outside the city.

The first serious challenge to the Pirates' civic supremacy emerged in 1914, when former Carlisle coach Glenn "Pop" Warner took over as head football coach at the University of Pittsburgh. Warner had coached the great Jim Thorpe. He never stopped tinkering with the game—inventing the screen pass, tackling dummies, the 3-point stance, and the single- and double-wing formations; numbering jerseys; and improving helmets. He instantly made Pitt a power—national champions in 1915 and '16—and defeated fellow coaching legend John Heisman and his unbeaten Georgia Tech team, 32-0, before 30,000 converts at Forbes Field, to seal a third title in 1918.

"You cannot play two kinds of football at once, dirty and good," Warner once said.

It took a while before Aliquippa even had the choice. What was then called Woodlawn High graduated its first class in 1913. Early forays into football resulted in four games over two years, four losses, and an abandonment of the sport by 1911. In the fall of 1914, just as Pop Warner's Pitt machine was picking up steam, Woodlawn tried again.

"Ha! Ha! At last!" begins the description in *Condor*, the school's 1915 yearbook. "The Woodlawn High School of 1914–15 holds the distinction of producing the first high school football team. Attempts in previous years to produce a football team were cut short by the advancement of permits, to be signed, and by the insufficient number of enthusiasts. But this year all above mentioned difficulties were easily effaced and our team was soon on the road to the Hall of Fame. In the meantime, football togs were furnished by means of a bake sale."

In its opener Woodlawn's enthusiasts beat Freedom, 6-5, for the program's first win. They then went 0-4-1, including a 100-0 loss to East Palestine, Ohio. "Our boys appeared to have stage fright, while playing on visiting grounds," the *Condor* continued. "As a whole, our team lacked experience. . . . Two-thirds of our boys never played football before; some of them never had a football in their hands until this year. Nevertheless, several star players have been located and will undoubtedly receive the best of attention next year."

But the 1915 season was little better. One site for a practice field in Plan 12 was rejected as "inconvenient." Its replacement was an overgrown lot between two buildings littered with refuse; workers spent a day removing all manner of brick and stone. "Some of the portly candidates displayed their superior ability by removing telegraph poles by hand," *Condor* reported. "Knighty showed his knowledge of farm implements by breaking a scythe or two in trying to mow the field before the stubbles were tramped down." The team didn't start practice until October. Only five players had experience. "The remaining six and the substitutes were new men. Now who would expect that a team so handicapped would witness anything but severe defeat?"

Yet even with such raw talent, in one respect Aliquippa was more sophisticated than any college campus, near or far.

Grading human despair is a fool's game, but it's hard to imagine a more pitiable lot than that of Gilded Age blacks in the American South. The masses crowding Ellis Island had fled lives of grinding poverty, but—pogroms aside—theirs was an escape from uncaring; they were "wretched refuse" made bold by a thousand years of neglect. The forces bearing down on the lives and families of former slaves, meanwhile, were sharp, savage, singularly directed. For many Southern whites, black freedom was a reminder of defeat; keeping the black man "in his place" was combat by another means. It made loss feel like victory.

Jim Crow laws, first enacted in Mississippi in 1890, spread across Dixie to ensure that blacks remained politically crippled. Sharecropping and tenant farming kept them economically subservient. A system of terror, endorsed by state and local authorities, threatened retribution for crimes big, small, or wholly imagined. Generations grew up carrying the marks of that world, physical and psychic: an internal flinch that never stopped.

"My mother was born in 1909," said Melvin Steals, whose parents moved from Alabama to Aliquippa in the 1920s. "When my mother was seven, she experienced a lynching in Greenville, Alabama. Her best friend, name was Tutta, her brother went North and came back and he was perceived to be 'uppity.' He said or did something that made the local whites so angry they grabbed him and drove him to this wooded area where there was an opening and in the center of this area was a huge tree. They tied this young man to the tree and every white man and boy who could hold and fire a rifle and pistol lined up. My mother was a little girl. She could hear—she and her classmates could hear—the gunshots echoing down through the woods."

The fathers of James Frank, college president and first black head of the NCAA, and Eugene "Salt" Smith, a longtime leader of Aliquippa's Democratic machine, both emigrated to town from Blakely, Georgia, where, in 1916, six black men were lynched. In 1919, the year that seventy-six blacks were killed by mob violence in the Deep South, Private William Little returned to Blakely from the battlefields of France and made the mistake of wearing his Army uniform in public. The first time he was caught, Little was beaten and forced to remove it. The second time, he was beaten to death.

Almost any alternative, then, would've been an improvement in the lives of Southern blacks. American industry dangled one. The coming of World War I slashed European immigration by two-thirds, and the resulting labor shortage amid high demand sent labor scouts scurrying below the Mason-Dixon Line, jobs and train tickets in hand. Some 500,000 blacks left Georgia, Mississippi, Texas, Alabama, and North and South Carolina between 1910 and 1920, the first wave of the "Great Migration" that remade a nation.

During the last few years of World War I, 12,000 new black workers appeared on the industrial rolls in Western Pennsylvania. In

Aliquippa, the main influx began after 1920, settling in the earliest days at the mill itself. Four wooden bunkhouses, Western style, had been erected on the J&L site, sleeping four to a room—actually, eight: When one man rose to start his twelve-hour shift, another ending his dove onto the still-warm pillow. Bedding was changed once a week. Workers made 33 cents an hour, paid $15 a month for room and board.

Enough white ethnics passed through the bunkhouses to make the arrangement seem less than segregated, and when black workers saved enough to buy a home they were first sent to the enclave—in their case, Plan 11 extension—reserved for them by the J&L-controlled land company, same as any Serb, Pole, or cake-eater. In truth, few first-generation arrivals—of any stripe—garnered much respect. Management looked down on Italians as a matter of policy during World War I, demoting and firing them for the least cause and threatening, as one investigative report stated, "to send them to Germany and have them shot." When J&L built its first community pool near the end of the war, a black man named James Downing Jr. recalled, his people weren't the only ones shut out.

"Italians, Polacks, Serbians, Lebanese, they couldn't attend that pool because when they went up there, they would tell them, 'Say, you're too hairy, you make the water dirty,' all this kind of stuff," Downing said. "So they told them: 'You have to go down and swim in the Ohio River.'"

But it was also fact that blacks arrived with two indelible marks against them. Racial prejudice, of course, was just as pervasive in the North as in the South. And the practice of using Southern blacks as strikebreakers in Pittsburgh, dating back to 1875 and recently reinforced by the tens of thousands employed during a national steel strike in 1919, left them even more isolated among the white rank-and-file. Thus blacks found themselves relegated to the worst jobs at J&L, the most filthy and dangerous; if they weren't working punishing twenty-four-hour shifts in the open hearth, where so many collapsed unconscious, they were the ones shoveling sizzling coke-oven muck and chomping wads of tobacco to flush their mouths of soot and fumes.

Such stratification served J&L well. A workforce divided, be it by resentment, competition, or prejudice, made for cheaper labor costs. Blacks sat at the bottom of the wage scale—the region's skilled and semiskilled steelworkers making an average of 60 cents an hour, compared with the 70 to 90 cents earned by their white and foreign-born counterparts—and the industry had no interest in making the workplace more equitable. When the superintendent of J&L's seamless tube insisted that not one of his 2,800 workers could be black ("I don't want no niggers working here"), upper management saw no need to challenge him.

Promotion—the hope of working one's way up and out—was not an option. Too quickly, newly arrived blacks had to stomach the realization that, though their families had been in America far longer, they seemed fated to be passed over in favor of even the newest arrivals. "Betrayed by Reconstruction and upstaged by steerage immigrants," as cultural critic Albert Murray put it, his generation, "the grandchildren of slaves freed by the Civil War," tamped down a cancerous resentment. Upon his arrival in Aliquippa from Georgia in 1927, James Frank's father, Willie Frank Sr., began a thirty-year stint as a blast furnace keeper, standing in unmeltable wooden shoes for hours in the breathless heat and opening a chute whenever the molten ore flowed. James himself worked two summers on a labor gang and in the blast furnace; in his family's time, he says, "I don't remember a black *ever* receiving a managerial job."

Coming North, meanwhile, didn't even provide refuge from Reconstruction's most harrowing symbol. In 1925, 25,000 members of the Ku Klux Klan marched, in full regalia, with flags waving, down Pennsylvania Avenue in the nation's capital. Perhaps it was inevitable that the arrival of so many dark, non-English-speaking immigrants, the societal shift from farm to city, and the preoccupation of Woodrow Wilson's administration with "100% Americanism" would spark a nativist backlash. But if the resurgent KKK's expanded brief against "mongrelization," alcohol, immorality, Jews, and especially Catholic foreigners gained deep traction in Northern states in the 1920s, its mission of white supremacy remained central. And Pennsylvania proved fertile territory.

Between 1920 and 1926, the KKK added anywhere from 250,000 to 300,000 new members in the state, a quarter of whom dwelled within the fifty-mile radius of Pittsburgh that included Aliquippa and surrounding Beaver County. Next-door Allegheny County and the four counties contiguous accounted for ninety-nine local chapters, or "klaverns"; Beaver County, with nine klaverns and a relatively small black population, appeared less invested. But the KKK made its presence felt. In July 1923, nine members kidnapped a black man in the town of Beaver and—accounts differ—either placed a rope around his neck as a warning before letting him go, or lynched him outright.

Aliquippa, just five miles away and soon to be Beaver County's commercial hub, had its own klavern, "The Ku Klux Klan of Woodlawn." It was announced in the spring of 1922 with a late-night launch of skyrockets, a burning cross above Plan 11, and a front-page letter in the *Woodlawn News*. Girdler, the mill superintendent, wrote about numerous local cross-burnings in the early 1920s, the KKK's attempts to organize, its circulated promise "to drive the colored people back to the South," and its demand that he fire a member of the J&L police force for anti-Klan actions. In typical fashion, Girdler painted himself as the tough who booted the KKK out of his office. Crosses continued to burn on area hills, he said, "but almost as quickly as those flames died the Ku-Klux Klan had burned itself out in Woodlawn."

But Girdler's concern seemed to center more on control than employee welfare. Many a night the town's young black men clambered up to the high, scrubby emptiness of Griffith Heights, the hill behind Plan 11, only to see a KKK flame ignite on another ridge. Between such displays and the mill's racist employment practices, they were primed for the black nationalist message espoused in a pair of Pittsburgh speeches by Jamaican expatriate Marcus Garvey. Attendance at the town's black churches dwindled. One black pastor, panicked by the way Aliquippa's 1,500 blacks had taken to Garvey's "Race First" rhetoric, warned the FBI of a coming race riot.

In 1923 Aliquippa grocer Matthew Dempsey tried to open a chapter of Garvey's Universal Negro Improvement Association; fifty black millworkers met secretly, and regularly, behind a curtain in Dempsey's store. Every J&L employee involved was fired, and soon all talk of black empowerment dissolved. In 1924, the year Girdler moved to J&L's head office in Pittsburgh, the Klan—far from being eradicated—was welcomed in "the regalia of their order" by town pastors, marched to the altar of one Presbyterian church while a choir sang "Onward, Christian Soldiers," and was celebrated with a "special sermon" at an evening Methodist service at Woodlawn High.

Within four years, courthouse revelations of corruption and infighting within the Pennsylvania Klan would decimate membership and mark its end as a political force statewide. But deep into the next decade, it still cast shadows in Aliquippa.

"Sometimes in the summer we would see crosses burning on the top of the hills late at night, two or three of them a night," said composer Henry Mancini, who came of age in the late 1930s. "We knew it was of course the Ku Klux Klan. Though there was a substantial black population in Aliquippa, there were very few black students in that high school of three thousand. I used to think about it and wonder why they weren't coming to school. And if the burning of crosses on the hills in the night gave *me* a chill, I couldn't begin to imagine what it did to them."

Some, like Emory Clark—father of jazz great Sonny Clark, up from Georgia to work the coke yards in Aliquippa Works—let the KKK drive him away to the coalfields east of Pittsburgh. But most blacks stayed, burying their bitterness beneath smiles or sighs. The game was rigged, South *and* North; they knew that now. Theirs was not a nation of healing and high theory, of "all men are created equal." It was a far harder reality, one annealed by the same simmering rage that fueled the

Boston Tea Party, Bloody Kansas, the Haymarket affair. They, too, in other words, had cause to fight.

Pitt and Penn State did not integrate their football rosters until the mid-1940s. But just two years after the Aliquippa team's inception, a *Condor* photo of the 1916 squad includes, for the first time, one unnamed black player. And it was no anomaly. Starting in 1919, every Woodlawn team for the next six years featured, without newspaper mention or yearbook comment, an unnamed black player.

The town—or borough, as it was called—was hardly color-blind. Black families had begun to move beyond Plan 11 extension, into mixed immigrant areas like Plan 11 and Logstown, but were still relegated to segregated sections in the downtown movie theaters and barred from entering shops and bars there. Blacks played on all-black mill teams and their own semipro baseball team—first named the Aliquippa Tarzans, then the Aliquippa Grays—though they did compete each season against the all-white Aliquippa Reds. The semipro football Aliquippa Indians, which began play on Crow Island in 1925, never allowed black players.

Still, the public high school—renamed Harding High for five years before finally settling on Aliquippa High in 1930—and its sports teams were allowed a social leeway granted almost nowhere else. It wasn't the only town in Western Pennsylvania to do so. While Aliquippa's anonymous black players were making a quiet mark at Woodlawn High, thirty miles south, in Washington, Pennsylvania, a black athlete named Charlie "Pruner" West was making history.

By his senior year at Washington High, the teen, who had reputedly outraced a horse and wrestled the family bull to the ground, had been named all-WPIAL in football, track, and baseball and led the Presidents—the "Little Prexies"—to a championship. In 1920 West enrolled at his hometown college, Washington & Jefferson, a football force then on par with Notre Dame and Michigan. In his first varsity game, he ran a kickoff back 65 yards for a touchdown and threw in another 46-yard romp. In the off-seasons he dominated in the pentathlon, proving talented enough to make the 1924 U.S. Olympic team.

Surrounding Washington County would, in the next six years, spawn seventeen KKK chapters, but West's presence on the roster caused no stir; "at least 95 percent of the local people," West felt, pulled for him because his integration was so seamless at Washington High. In 1921, a 98-yard run spurred the Presidents past Syracuse and made West a national star known for "ripping through would-be tacklers with high knee action"; Pop Warner called him the most formidable open-field runner in the country. Then West stepped in as starting quarterback and led the team to Morgantown for a showdown with West Virginia. When the Presidents' train pulled into the station, a waiting crowd chanted, "Kill the nigger!"

West, light-skinned and unknown enough that no one recognized him, debarked last and said, calmly, "We didn't bring him with us this time."

W&J won 13-0. At the end of the season, West traveled with only ten other players to take part in the 1922 Rose Bowl against the undefeated "wonder team" from the University of California. It would be the last time a small college would take part in the prestigious game, the only time the contest would end in a 0-0 tie—and the first time a black man would quarterback a team in Pasadena. Later, after graduating from Howard Medical School, West established a thriving practice in Virgina. Black kids all over Western Pennsylvania took note.

"He was an idol of mine since my earliest days," said Ray Kemp, who, with the Pittsburgh Pirates, an early iteration of the Steelers, was one of two blacks to play in the NFL during its first stab at integration, in 1933. "I wanted to be an athlete in football and track because of him. Back then, blacks had so few role models to follow that Dr. West stood out as the sort of man I wanted to become."

No councilman, mayor, school principal, or mill superintendent in Western Pennsylvania then explicitly made racial tolerance on public school teams a matter of policy. The numbers early on were tiny, just one or two black players every few years, with slots opened only to those too talented to ignore. But that crack in segregation became custom. In the late '20s, the black population at Aliquippa High produced football-playing brothers Norman and Albert Wilkens, and their Serb and Croat and Italian teammates made room. The rivalry between Aliquippa and nearby Ambridge had become overheated by then, and the fact that both head coaches, Nate Lippe and Moe Rubenstein, were Jewish paled next to the teams' ongoing feud. Winning mattered most.

"It was segregated, but not in sports," said Townsell "T-baby" Thomas, who arrived in town in 1925 and played basketball for Aliquippa High in the late '30s. "That's the one place where they didn't go over the line."

The melting pot has been a staple of American thought since Independence; variations on the metaphor include a smelting pot, a crucible, even a steelmaking blast furnace. It also becomes fashionable, once a generation, for intellects to question whether the process of blending ethnicities into one "society" is ever as complete as advertised, but in Aliquippa, anyway, one detail is clear: Sport is where the melt in the pot began.

2

Little Hell

Early in October 1934, a tall, lanky balding man with a strange handshake, soon to turn forty-six, drove his car twenty-five miles up from Pittsburgh to Ambridge. He slowed, parked, reached into his mouth, and removed his dental plate. Then he began the dusty four-mile walk to Aliquippa. Though his customary suit had been replaced by work slacks, a battered hat, and rough shoes, he was hardly slumming. Clint Golden had known dirt all his life. By seventeen he had worked a plow, driven mules, worked as a drill tender in a hillside mine, spent months wiping oil off engine parts, and fed locomotive tenders an endless gorge of coal. Yet something about Aliquippa's filth offended him.

It wasn't just that, after a day there, Golden's clothes came away with a new blackness all but woven into the wool. Or that in the short time between ordering a meal and receiving it, his hands would need scrubbing all over again. When a dense fog mixed with the usual mill spew, the air became like some oily second skin, insinuating itself into the tightest creases. He could feel the stuff working its way inside. Back, each night, in his plush room at the Pittsburgher Hotel, Golden could still taste coal smoke on his tongue, thick like the tar of a cheap cigar, resistant to the onslaught of strong drink and the most savory dinner. When he woke, no amount of water could flush the inky grit out of his nostrils and throat. Getting Aliquippa out of your system literally took days.

It was as if the town couldn't bear to let you go—or sought, like a disease, to keep killing long after exposure. Union-minded men like Golden weren't surprised. Aliquippa was the hottest enemy turf going. Spies shadowed strangers. Company muscle itched for heads to crack. That's why he wore the shabby clothes, made his mouth a gummy shame: J&L's boys might overlook another shiftless tramp wandering in off Route 51.

Golden worked his way through the bars on Franklin Avenue, the streetcorner clots of men who chattered and fell silent when a cop passed. The idle in Aliquippa talked women, baseball, basement stills and basement wine, those organizers huddling in Ambridge who managed to sneak in. He listened, seemingly harmless. Some spoke of the fiery speech the governor's wife made in Ambridge five weeks before. Some took it further and spoke about the need for a union. And that's about the time when someone would inevitably say, "Well, you know what happened to Georg, don't you?"

Golden had some idea. He had heard the rumors. The place dubbed "Little Siberia" had been at fever pitch for months. Twenty steelworkers who'd just been to Pittsburgh to testify against J&L to the National Steel Labor Relations Board were so scared to return home that the governor had sent state police to protect them. Then there'd been the desperate letter sent to the state capital by an Aliquippa housewife, but her story had seemed almost *too* incredible. But now, the wide eyes of the men, and the fear and near-awe that accompanied the news about Georg, all but confirmed that some new low had been reached.

Golden edged away from the clusters of men and shambled back to the borough line, one more bum trying to hit the bridge before sundown.

He reached his car, popped his teeth back in, and scribbled some notes. Then he returned to Pittsburgh, hoping to get clean.

What happened to Georg? Debris from a society cracking. Fallout from a fight between two forces certain that they alone represented American ideals. Georg was a small-bore culmination of a high-strung era, one that began well before the great stock market crash and its manic bank runs. Things never should have gone as far as they did with the broken mill Hunky, but the logic of fear, the momentum of ever-escalating extremes, made it almost seem preordained.

To see this, though, one must first know that the distilled image of the 1920s—amoral flappers swanning about a sea of bathtub gin—is but a dim caricature of a nation unnerved. The 1917 victory by Communists in Russia, and their stated aim of fomenting global revolution, touched off America's first Red Scare. Anarchists tried twice to blow up Attorney General A. Mitchell Palmer. Management successfully painted the 1919 strikes by coal miners, steelworkers, and the Boston police as Leninist plots—and smashed them all. Race riots erupted in thirty U.S. cities.

This is how the "Roaring '20s" began: On New Year's Day 1920, more than 6,000 people nationwide were arrested, and hundreds deported, in so-called Palmer Raids. The Attorney General then spent the winter warning of a domestic Communist revolution set for May 1: it didn't happen. But on September 16, hundreds were injured and thirty-eight killed when anarchists exploded a bomb on Wall Street. Later that year, Irish poet William Butler Yeats published "The Second Coming," summing up in a line—"Things fall apart; the centre cannot hold"—the sense that life in the West was unraveling fast.

Many credit F. Scott Fitzgerald with inventing the "Jazz Age," but his best rendering of moneyed ephemera and romance also captured upper-class unease and a determination—personified by Tom Buchanan in 1925's *The Great Gatsby*—to respond with a clenched fist.

"The idea is if we don't look out the white race will be—will be utterly submerged. It's all scientific stuff; it's been proved."

"Tom's getting very profound," said Daisy, with an expression of unthoughtful sadness. "He reads deep books with long words in them. What was that word we—"

"Well, these books are all scientific," insisted Tom, glancing at her impatiently. "This fellow has worked out the whole thing. It's up to us, who are the dominant race, to watch out or these other races will have control of things.'"

"We've got to beat them down," whispered Daisy, winking ferociously toward the fervent sun.

Life in Aliquippa was never so subtle, so arch. The town had acted out the republic's industrial boom, its migratory ebbs and flows, in crude and broad strokes; by 1920 its five blast furnaces, four 250-ton tilting open hearths, and three Bessemers were churning out 900,000 gross tons of pig iron and 900,000 gross tons of steel ingots a year—and its struggles were becoming increasingly emblematic. U.S. Steel's control of half the world's steel market ensured industry preeminence, and by 1924 Bethlehem Steel had edged past J&L to become No. 2. But the company's harsh tactics and glib superintendent lent it outsized stature among fellow "Little Steel" independents like Republic Steel, Inland Steel, and Youngstown Sheet and Tube, and partisans pro and con.

"Girdler," wrote Communist Howard Fast of J&L's Aliquippa superintendent, "was the front, the testing ground, the trial balloon of the most reactionary forces in American capitalism."

And once Girdler's J&L deputy, Harry Mauk, had his own deputy, the teetotaling, equally ruthless Michael "M. J." Kane, installed as Aliquippa police chief, the populace was caught in a uniformed squeeze.

Kane had ridden with John "Black Jack Pershing" in Mexico, vainly chasing down Pancho Villa: pursuit in a compact town, five thousand residents but growing fast, couldn't compare. The chief rumbled about on his motorcycle, sidecar attached. He and his officers ransacked apartments, broke up dances, fraternal meetings, boardinghouse card games; if a discussion seemed the least bit suspect, Kane would gun his motorcycle through the kitchen door, shouting, "Break it up, you Hunkies!" He had his reasons. Crime. Union. Threats of any kind.

"Woodlawn is governed and regulated by Fear. The self-constituted Bosses, of whom we spoke in our last editorial, are afraid," began a remarkable front-page screed in the March 30, 1923, *Woodlawn News*, not least because the paper was owned by one such boss, J. A. C. Ruffner, the town's premier banker, tax collector, and chair of the local Republican Party. "They shrink from the light of public opinion. They want certain news suppressed. We know that well. They want free and honest discussion restrained. . . .

"On the other hand, a large portion of the population are victims of fear. They fear that their means of livelihood will be snatched from them if they do not subordinate their self-respect to coercion and restraint. They sense that they are being shadowed by spies and gumshoers. They recoil in sullen submission, feeling helpless to combat the hidden menace which casts its shadow over their homes."

Four days later, the newspaper spoke of a network of J&L "informers" that "the former Kaiser, at the height of his glory, certainly would have envied." It mentioned operatives planted in barbershops, pool halls, railroad stations, mill furnaces and floors, their ears pricked for any talk of union and any complaint, eyes gauging each worker's actions for "loyalty."

That was, at the time, the most incendiary word in the nation's discourse, applied as it was to immigrants, KKK critics, leftists, and anyone else whose patriotism was called into question. Loyalty—not the eight-hour day or six-day workweek—became the issue when the steel industry first executed its so-called American Plan, in 1919, to smash the Amalgamated Association of Iron, Steel, and Tin Workers' bid to organize. More than 350,000 workers nationwide walked out, only to be swamped by a propaganda campaign denouncing the action as Marxist-led and foreigner-dominated. Posters of Uncle Sam stared down from walls, pointing and shouting "Go Back to Work" in seven languages; public support for the strikers withered. By the time it was over, fourteen weeks later, twenty workers were dead and $100 million in wages had been lost. Labor won nothing.

In Aliquippa, though, The Family had gone about business as usual. The town's isolation allowed J&L a strict defense of its "open shop"—a workplace open to nonunion personnel—which theoretically gave workers "freedom of choice" but in fact drained unions of all bargaining power. Mauk's boys met organizers on the train platform and shadowed their every step; meeting with nervous workers proved impossible. The steel strike of 1919 shut down three-quarters of the mills in Pittsburgh, but not one department in Aliquippa. J&L's happy employees, Girdler boasted, broke production records throughout. "Open shop" meant a closed town.

"In that day you had to keep your mind shut," said Angelo Razzano, who began work as a laborer at J&L in 1924. "You were not a free man in that day because the company controlled the mills; the company controlled Aliquippa. You had to do what the company wanted you to do. You had to be a good jackass."

But J&L's power to just hire and fire or dump a family out of its home wasn't a case of overreach; it had the backing of federal law. The 1917 Supreme Court ruling that legitimized "yellow-dog" contracts—the kind that made hiring contingent on a worker's pledge to *not* join a union—also held that any inducement to join a union was a breach of said contract, and neatly split the rhetorical hair by ruling that the right to strike was not a right to *instigate* a strike. As one steel president, speaking for Girdler and every other steel executive, coyly put it: "We don't discharge a man for belonging to a union, but of course we discharge men for agitating the mills."

"Agitating" being the era's other incendiary word. What with the Great War, bomb threats, unrest, and the emotions stirred by the 1921 convictions of Sacco and Vanzetti and subsequent six-year death watch, the vast majority of Americans—the great middle that was neither hard-line management nor aggrieved labor, neither reactionary nor radical—had wearied of tumult. They wanted a return to the half-mythical prewar state of harmonic dullness that President Warren Harding termed "normalcy." Yes, Prohibition was an annoyance. But so long as there was money to be made—and the occasional bootlegger's bottle to cadge—most seemed willing to trade the loss of a few civil liberties for a bit of quiet.

Pennsylvania was one of the many states that passed a law against sedition—advocating violence to effect political or social change—after World War I; it became a handy bludgeon in Aliquippa. Pete Muselin, immigrant from Croatia at twelve and American doughboy at seventeen, returned home from the war a newly minted Communist. He held meetings in his barbershop, at the Croatian lodge, at the home of fellow traveler Tom Zima. One of the town's few registered Democrats, Muselin gave speeches, passed out literature, pushed publicly for workers to organize. "It wasn't so much union," said J&L tin worker Michael Zahorsky. "They were actually talking revolution."

Such talk was anathema in mainstream America, but Muselin wasn't living there. To him, Aliquippa was a "typical Cossack town," the kind he'd supposedly left behind when his family left Eastern Europe. From the dining room window of his mother's home he'd see Mauk's men, outside the building that once held amusement park dances, blasting away on a shooting range with pistols, rifles, machine guns. Mauk controlled the council that controlled the permits for gatherings. Cops ransacked Muselin's home, carted away his books, jailed him when he spoke out.

But Muselin countered that he had a constitutional right, outlined in the First Amendment: freedom of speech, of peaceful assembly. At one Aliquippa council meeting, he stood and began reciting, "When in the course of human events, it becomes necessary—"

A cop cut Muselin off. "That's communistic stuff you're reading," he said. Muselin resumed, making it to "all men are created equal" before the cop moved to arrest him. Aliquippa's new chief of police, Charles O'Loughlin, walked in.

"You dumb ——," the chief reportedly cursed. "He's reading the Declaration of Independence."

Not long after, in 1926, police broke up a meeting in West Aliquippa and arrested three dozen people. Most were released. Muselin and two others—Zima and Milan Resetar—were detained and charged with sedition. The prosecuting attorney was a volunteer: a longtime J&L lawyer. The next year all were found guilty—"though no evidence," according to the American Civil Liberties Union, "was produced at trial to show they ever contemplated violence"—and sentenced to five years' hard labor. In 1929 the men were sent to the state workhouse at Blawnox.

"One of the dirtiest, the toughest jails in Pennsylvania. The food was repulsive," Muselin said about Blawnox. "Any minor infraction of the rules, they'd put you in the hole. You'd get one or two slices of bread and one cup of water per day. With that one cup of water, you had the option of drinking it if you were thirsty, brushing your teeth, or washing yourself. And you slept on the floor, on a couple of boards nailed together. . . ."

Calling them "political prisoners," the ACLU took up the case just as the men's time behind bars began. More than two years passed. Resetar died there. Muselin's family went broke. Maintaining that he'd been framed, he refused an offer of early parole and demanded exoneration. Muselin's disgust with lack of support from the Communists' legal team made it easier to recant party membership, but that wasn't the only reason why the State Board of Pardons, in February of 1932, finally set the two men free.

Word had it that, behind the scenes, Cornelia Bryce Pinchot, wife of the governor, born rich but "hopelessly maladjusted to the butterfly existence my parents wanted for me," had charmed and pressured the board members to clear and release the men. Few noticed this as her opening strike at J&L. Soon enough, though, workers in Aliquippa and beyond would be calling her a modern-day Joan of Arc.

The Great Depression crippled American steelmakers. Production at J&L fell by two-thirds, and losses climbed to $4 million annually in the early 1930s. But in one sense the company's hand was stronger than ever. In Aliquippa, The Family opted against mass layoffs and instead slashed man-hours, a production stratagem with the added virtues of seeming magnanimity and tighter control. Eleven thousand workers now jockeyed to hold on to a shift a week. When one extra "turn" decided whether the kids ate meat or bullion or not at all, a man thought twice before spouting off.

"There was nothing," said Joe Perriello of the employment prospects when he left high school in 1932. "We did all kind of odd jobs, carried coal for a couple, twenty-five, thirty cents a ton, in the summertime hauled ice, shoveled snow—did whatever we could to make a buck."

Town merchants fired staff, or closed altogether. "Sometimes we would have a customer for the day, sometimes two," said Jesse Steinfeld, his forty-two-year-old father dead of a heart attack in 1931, his mother left to raise two boys and run a small notions shop in West Aliquippa. "It was not a store as we would think of these days; it was very, very poor. There was really no business."

Applying for work only reinforced one's place in the pecking order. Every day, hundreds of men lined up hours before the local employment office opened, and "they'd bring in maybe twenty or thirty of us in this room, lock the doors; and we'd sit in there for no reason until four o'clock," Perriello recalled of his 1932 application. Then they were told to go outside. "Every once in a while a company man would come out and say, 'Any Dagos, niggers, or Serbs wants greasers or wipers jobs, c'mon in,'" Perriello said. "You'd get sick because you watched the expression on their faces. They were ashamed."

Never was a crisis so aptly named: Like the nation at large, battered by 25 percent unemployment, Aliquippa's populace of 27,000 suffered now from an enervating lack of hope. The high school was so crowded it was running year-round—in two daily shifts—and graduating four classes each year: But into what kind of future? Belief in the capitalist model was being tested like never before, driving the beleaguered further left, delighting Communist Party recruiters. Then, in November 1932, Franklin D. Roosevelt was elected president. And what had been a series of labor-management skirmishes escalated into all-out war.

It's perhaps difficult, now, to understand the intense loathing held for "that man" by his fellow millionaires, especially after the first hundred days of FDR's term—replete with labor-friendly New Deal laws—confirmed their worst fears. Just before Black Monday sent the stock market plummeting, Tom Girdler, management's unapologetic id, left J&L to begin an even more notorious tenure as the chairman of Republic Steel. Word had it that The Family had wearied of his manner and method, but the Depression did nothing to reduce Girdler's belief in the primacy of American business.

"What my father thought of Franklin Roosevelt?" said Tom Girdler Jr. "I don't think it would be polite if I used the exact words. Father thought Franklin Roosevelt was a disaster to the United States."

The National Industrial Recovery Act (NIRA) of 1933—as weak and poorly administered as it proved, and as unconstitutional as it was declared two years later—signaled the coming flood. For the first time, the power of the federal government swung behind the concept of collective bargaining, its Section 7(a) guaranteeing workers the right to form unions. Open-shop entities like J&L tried to skirt the law by creating company-run "employee representation plans": workers who didn't participate were frozen out or fired. Emboldened union organizers stormed once-impenetrable industries and factories, every isolated mill and mining town.

Few had more symbolic value than the place called, on its best days, "Little Siberia." On its worst, they called Aliquippa "Little Hell." The Amalgamated's first two organizers arrived in July; unable to rent rooms or office space, they slept across the river in Ambridge, suffered a beating and a fine for disorderly conduct, and were gone in less than a week. The Amalgamated sent two more the next month, both hard-bitten after years of organizing miners. One, fifty-one-year-old John Mayer, was attacked by two thugs—"You wanted to sign me up in the union," one said. "How do you like it now?"—then jailed by Aliquippa police. Both he and his attacker were charged $5. J&L paid the attacker's fine. The presiding authority was Michael "M. J." Kane.

The man had risen some since resigning as Aliquippa police chief in 1925: now, Kane was Aliquippa's justice of the peace, and not the kindly, marrying kind. As state chairman of the "Constitutional Defense League," an antiunion strike force spawned by the "Americanism Committee" of the American Legion, Kane regularly made speeches advocating violence against anyone whom he regarded as communist, and publicly called upon "patriots" to "take 'em out and hang a few" or to "nail a few of them to the mast."

In October '33, the first full impact of FDR's election hit Western Pennsylvania, when 75,000 coal miners walked out and a steel strike spread through the Beaver Valley and out to Weirton, West Virginia, and Steubenville, Ohio. Though it often felt like Aliquippa's doppelgänger—a company town incorporated in 1905, settled by immigrant steelworkers and named for the American Bridge Company, a U.S. Steel subsidiary—Ambridge lacked the former's suffocating control. Its burgess—or mayor—P. J. Caul, was a former American Federation of

Labor plasterer, foe of Coal and Iron cops, and a Democrat. He would barely have been able to live in Aliquippa, much less run it.

One by one, Ambridge's steel mills had been organized, largely by a strong Communist Party cadre; one by one, its workers now took to the picket lines. There was strong talk about marching across the river on J&L. One of the organizers of the Ambridge action was Pete Muselin. When strikebreakers tried to enter the Spang, Chalfant and Co. tube plant on the morning of October 4, 1933, picketers beat them back amid clouds of tear gas.

On October 5, Kane and his successor as Aliquippa police chief, Charles O'Loughlin, organized a force of two hundred Legionnaires, detectives, teenagers, and J&L workers in Aliquippa and armed them with shotguns, pistols, clubs, tear gas, and machine guns; at least one had a bayonet fixed to his rifle. Their convoy of buses crossed the Ambridge–Aliquippa Bridge and approached a crowd of a few hundred strikers armed with sticks and stones. O'Loughlin climbed out of a car and demanded they drop their weapons. The strikers roared back, "Come and take 'em!"

But behind them, a hail of tear gas shells—and a hundred more Spang strikebreakers—emerged from the plant. Kane's army surged, clubs high; the strikers were caught in a vise. Dozens of shots were fired, and dozens were injured. A fifty-year-old confectioner named Adam Pietrusaki lay dead with a bullet in his neck. "It was probably meant for me," Muselin said. "My brother Tony was standing right next to Adam when he was shot. Tony and I looked almost like twins. They must have taken aim at Tony but hit Adam. I petitioned Governor Pinchot for a public hearing on the killing. . . . Some deputies were there who testified that they were gunning for me."

No charges were brought. The Aliquippa blitz ended the strike, the immediate threat to J&L, and warmed the hearts of city fathers disgusted by their softer counterparts in Ambridge. "One of the most wonderful things that ever happened in this valley," exulted the publisher of the *Aliquippa Gazette*, J. A. C. Ruffner. "They were picketing! Whenever three or four men gather and make remarks that could be resented by another person, they are inciting to riot."

When Amalgamated officers managed—while trailed by a J&L plainclothesman—to pick up their charter and open a local, Beaver Valley Lodge #200, on August 4, 1934, J&L only stepped up its campaign of what the National Labor Relations Board called "violent terroristic action." Stockpiles of arms, ammunition, tear gas bombs, and riot guns were stored at the Aliquippa Works; an inside bay was fitted out with beds and kitchenware to house workers for the expected strike. The union's top leaders were beaten, evicted, forced to establish headquarters at a hotel in Ambridge. Any pretense about The Family's noblesse oblige disappeared.

"We want you to get busy on those black bastards and stop them from joining the union," Harry Mauk said that month to an influential J&L employee, a deacon in one of Aliquippa's Baptist churches. "If you black sons of bitches want a job at the J&L mill, you will have to help the company break up this organization or we will send all you black bastards back south."

No one doubted Mauk's resolve. Ramrod posture, steely blue eyes, and great marksmanship made him the perfect personification of J&L might. "One of the most fearless, well-controlled people I've ever seen," said Tom Girdler Jr. "There was a time, in the thirties, when a fellow went berserk in the payroll department and starting shooting at the people in there, and he come out the side door of the main office with a revolver in his hand."

Screams, panic: Everybody ducked. Mauk held his fire. The man leveled his pistol, but Mauk didn't shoot and didn't move. He wanted no one to accuse him of killing in cold blood. Dying himself didn't seem an option.

"He shot at me and missed, and I shot him three times and didn't miss," Mauk told Girdler Jr. "The first time, when he didn't go down,

I thought to myself, *I must be getting old; I can't shoot.* I found the bullet hit a rib and slid right around his heart."

"Where did the other two go?" Girdler Jr. asked.

"About an eighth of an inch away," Mauk replied. "But they missed the rib."

Yet Aliquippa also moved to another lighter rhythm, dictated by the calendar and the daily rounds. There were the two Christmases to celebrate: Western Christian on December 25 and Eastern Orthodox on January 7. The staggered graduations upended the seasons: Some teens had "summer" vacation in January. Weekends, there were movies at the Strand, the Temple and the State movie theaters, your pick of Clark Gable or Shirley Temple or Jean Harlow. There was the success of Nate Lippe's Aliquippa High basketball team, and the high-scoring flair of Press Maravich; during the 1934–35 season Aliquippa would, for the first time, be good enough to dominate Moe Rubenstein's boys in Ambridge.

Sports was everywhere. No one swam in the river anymore, befouled as it was with sewage and chemical waste, but neighborhoods, churches, and various ethnic groups had leagues for all ages, season upon season. The Amalgamated #200 organized a baseball team almost the moment it came to be; a Logstown store, Friedman's, sponsored the Aliquippa Friedmans. There were endless intramural games in the J&L league—basketball, tug-of-war, the no-glove version of softball known as "mushball," baseball, South Mill vs. North Mill, Blooming Mill vs. Coke Works—with a few blacks sprinkled in among the Croats and Itals and Serbs, and nobody making a fuss about it, either.

How could they? Nate Lippe's 1934 Aliquippa High football team was one of the best the town had seen yet, and it featured the high school's first black star. Yet another transplant from Blakely, Georgia, tackle Major "Loggie" Powell was held in high enough esteem to be appointed cocaptain. With him anchoring both offensive and defensive

43

lines, Aliquippa posted a 7-1 record and, along with Frank Hribar and Frank Gnup, Powell was named all-WPIAL.

That Ambridge was responsible for the one blemish that season was only proper. Moe Rubenstein had long made it his business to torment Lippe. The two had been roommates and football and basketball teammates at Geneva College; a 1925 team photo shows Lippe glaring at the camera while the younger Rubenstein sits three seats away, grinning. He would always deny that their enmity arose from the much-trafficked rumor that he'd stolen Lippe's girl (Aliquippa partisans inverted the legend) and married her. But, said one former Bridger, Rubenstein "always told us we had to win THAT game because of his wife."

Age and player eligibility, for both, didn't seem high priorities. Since both Lippe and Rubenstein coached football, basketball, and baseball, they had all year to raid each other's rosters, tattle to WPIAL officials about transgressions, endure the resulting forfeits, and storm off court and field in a rage. "Intense to say the least," is how the *Pittsburgh Post-Gazette* described the men's mutual antipathy. "Their frequent conflicts have brought them before the decisions committee on previous occasions."

Their personal animus dovetailed with the civic. Both towns claimed to be "the best": Aliquippa boasted of having the county's largest employer and, at 27,023 and rising, population; Ambridge's 20,000 bragged that they'd built the gates of the Panama Canal, New York's Chrysler and Empire State Buildings, and the San Francisco–Oakland Bay Bridge. The two played their first football game in 1920, a 6-0 win for the Bridgers, but it took completion of the Ambridge–Aliquippa Bridge in 1926 to breed the familiarity needed for true contempt. And then the jealousy kicked in.

Football in the WPIAL, the nation's largest high school conference, was dominated then by the likes of Wilkinsburg, Washington, and New Castle, but when the league created a Single-A division for smaller schools in 1932, Rubenstein's Bridgers snuck in to win the inaugural championship. Aliquippa—it had no official nickname yet, but writers couldn't resist "Steelers," "Quips," "Red and Black," even the "Lippemen"—had never won a WPIAL title in any sport.

Thwarted ambition was Lippe's recurring theme. The Cleveland native wanted to be a doctor, but the University of Pittsburgh Medical School turned him down after it filled its Jewish quota, and after a few years of basketball barnstorming he settled into coaching. He would eventually win six Beaver County football crowns, but finish 3-15-4 against Rubenstein. Three times as a football coach, Lippe had the chance to go undefeated: each time, Rubenstein spoiled it. Perhaps the worst loss came in October 1934, when, on the eve of their showdown in Ambridge before fifteen thousand fans, Rubenstein revealed that star Aliquippa running back Mike Casp was over the age limit of twenty. Casp was disqualified, Ambridge won 14-0, and Aliquippa was knocked out of the title hunt. In 1935, Lippe finally beat Rubenstein for the first time—in an Aliquippa campaign made meaningless by four ties—but that only set up another excruciating result.

On September 24, 1934, an unnaturalized Slovak named Mary Isasky, mother of seven living on $7 a week, thirty-seven but looking two decades older, sat down in what a reporter would call her "squalid, three-room shack" on Beaver Avenue in West Aliquippa, and tried to find the right words in English. It was her third language. She took up a balky fountain pen, dipped the nib into ink, and in the top left corner of a cheap piece of lined paper wrote a simple address: "Mrs. G. Pinchot/ Harrisburg Pa." She took a breath. Then she began:

"Dear Madam: I am writing to you because I have no other one to look to for help. . . ."

In any other state, and especially at that time, Isasky's choice of savior would have made little sense. As the wife of Pennsylvania's Republican governor Gifford Pinchot, Cornelia Bryce Pinchot technically wielded no power. The nation's forty-eight First Ladies, like First Ladies in the White House, left matters of justice or politics to their husbands, whiling away their ornamental days at flower shows, teas, and other gatherings of well-heeled women.

But Pennsylvania politics then wasn't like any other state's. Gifford, the conservationist famed for his close alliance with Theodore Roosevelt and his work as the first chief of the U.S. Forest Service, clashed with the powers in his own party and publicly supported FDR's New Deal. And Cornelia was like no other First Lady, ever.

Her father had been a congressman, foreign minister, and advisor to Theodore Roosevelt; a grandfather had been mayor of New York; a great-grandfather founded Cooper Union. After shirking the Daisy Buchanan lifestyle envisioned for her by her Long Island parents, Cornelia Bryce leveraged a $15 million fortune—and its $300,000 yearly income—into a life marked by eccentricity and sobering purpose. By thirty she had made her name in New York as a suffragette, social service doyenne, and defender of working women; by 1914, when she married the forty-nine-year-old Gifford—after a three-week courtship amid his first senatorial race—the thirty-three-year-old heiress had gained a shrewd appreciation for the ways and uses of power.

"She had," said Teddy Roosevelt, "one of the keenest political minds that I have ever known."

Cornelia gave nine speeches a day during Gifford's senate campaign. A landslide loss did nothing to quell her enthusiasm: "At least he had dared," she said. But the Republican Old Guard was quick to sense the source of Gifford's ambition—and a substantial hunk of his campaign money. "Pinchot never *dared*," sneered one of the party's sharper analysts to the *New York Times*. "His wife did all the daring."

The 19th Amendment gave women the vote in 1920, and Cornelia turned them out in decisive droves during Gifford's run for governor a year later. "Women," she instructed him, "don't want generalities and hot air." As if in rebuke to the era's Red-baiting hysteria, she reveled in the color: red auto, red dresses, her 5-foot-10 frame topped by a signature sweep of dyed hair invariably described as "titian" or "copper" or—right to the metaphorical point—"flame." The state's party machine opposed the progressive Pinchot in the primary; he was given 100-to-1 odds, and knew exactly why he beat them. "It was due to Mrs. Pinchot and the women she organized—far more than any other single factor," Gifford wrote.

Cornelia moved into the Governor's Mansion in 1923 with three dogs, a pet parrot named Oscar, and an omnipresent bag of knitting. She pushed for labor reform, women's and children's workplace rights, the eight-hour workday, the setting of a minimum wage. No such laws were passed. But by the time the term ended in 1926, the state machine worried more about Cornelia's acumen than Gifford's considerable appeal; Gifford Pinchot, the joke went, is a politician's husband.

"All my speeches are extemporaneous and I love heckling," she said. "What is the fun of wasting campaign speeches on people already converted?"

Cornelia had gone to dancing school as a young girl with Eleanor Roosevelt; when the far shyer Eleanor moved into the White House in 1933, the standards—and limits—of an activist First Lady had been set. Mrs. Pinchot—everyone called her that—ran unsuccessfully for Congress in 1928, helped steer Gifford to his second term as governor in 1930, ran unsuccessfully again for Congress in 1932. With FDR's election she became only more vociferous, the most dynamic weapon in her husband's administration.

Gifford's hand was hardly untipped: He had officially abolished the owners' Coal and Iron Police statewide in 1931, and when NIRA's passage unleashed a wave of strikes in the summer of '33, he mediated coal negotiations and released relief money to striking families. But his wife crisscrossed the state, joining textile picketers in Allentown and Reading, visiting strikers in Philipsburg and Altoona, addressing the first labor meetings ever in the steel bastions of Vandergrift and Duquesne. That town's company-backed mayor once vowed she would never speak there so long as he was alive.

"Well," Cornelia said to the 3,500 people packing First Street to hear her. "Here I am."

In February 1934, she traveled to a Washington, DC, labor forum, made a speech calling FDR's National Recovery Administration "a grisly farce" and calling out its head, General Hugh Johnson, for discouraging strikers while offering union members none of the NRA's pledged protection. "I wonder if you ever stay awake at night, seeing the faces of the thousands of men and women who are pacing the streets of Pennsylvania towns, jobless and desperate—without resources, and with despair in their hearts," she said. "Because they had faith in your promises and went ahead and organized a union and, for so doing, lost their jobs—and never a finger in Washington lifted to help them."

Stung and bewildered by the vague nature of his unelected, unappointed, unprecedented attacker, Johnson blustered, "Who is governor of Pennsylvania?"

It wasn't an idle question: By late summer, petitions had gathered ten thousand names to nominate Cornelia as an independent candidate to succeed her husband. Management derided her as an "enemy of capitalism"; labor regarded her as one of its great voices. When Cornelia came to Ambridge to speak on August 25 on a vacant lot next to the U.S. Post Office, a crowd of 3,500 turned out. Many from J&L crossed the bridge to be there.

Mauk's policemen tried to stop them, failed, then followed. Mill bosses went, too, taking note of any J&L workers and standing out so conspicuously that Ambridge burgess P. J. Caul ended the proceedings by sarcastically calling out Mauk's "gumshoes" and warning that they—as well as communists or other subversives—have "no business on this side of the river." Back on the other side, they took action. "For only just one reason I was fired: I went to hear Mrs. Pinchot in Ambridge," said Joe Latone, an Aliquippa Works employee for twenty-six years. "My boss, he like me, I know it, but he had orders from the office."

Still, the fact that the First Lady could arrange and deliver a speech in Ambridge declaring the "need" for organized labor signaled a local momentum shift. J&L felt it. Union men were offered bribes to name members; company police went to the fired Latone and dangled a job for his son if he became an informer. Harry Mauk, accompanied by the Aliquippa burgess, called a meeting at Tony Ferro's Plan 11 barbershop—a noted union venue. Mauk's first words to the two hundred men gathered: "You black-handed mothers and son bitches, I am here to tell you if you don't soon try and bust this association of the Amalgamated we are going to bust you people up. . . ."

Three days later, Mary Isasky's husband, Georg, was beaten by Aliquippa police, kidnapped, and committed without his family's knowledge to the Torrance State Hospital, a mental institution east of Pittsburgh. His crime—his madness—was clear. He had been seen on Franklin Avenue, picking up union cards.

Georg Isasky arrived in the United States in 1910. He was eighteen years old, like many immigrants starting a life in which even the most basic facts refused to gel. Homeland? He was a German-speaking Slovak born in the soon-to-be-demolished Austro-Hungarian Empire, and his country would change its name three times before he died. Name? He was at various times called Iseaky, Issoski, Isosky, Isarski, and Isorski, managing after twenty years to take slight hold of the matter by adding an "e" to the end of his first name. In 1916 Isasky landed work as a laborer in an Aliquippa blast furnace. He found no stability there, either.

Nine months in, a scaffold beneath him collapsed and Isasky fell twenty-five feet into a steel pit. Spine wrecked, one vertebra crushed, he spent six weeks in the hospital. A J&L safety official dangled five hundred weeks of compensation—at $10 per—if he signed a piece of paper. Isasky signed. He received payment for only a few months; at war's end he was fired. J&L later made Isasky a steamfitter's helper, cutting his pay, but eventually tired of his complaints about back trouble and fired him again in 1930. The family survived on relief.

After the Amalgamated approached him in August about passing out pledge cards, Isasky gathered a large number of signatures. After a week, three company cops began to harass and frisk him. He kept gathering pledges. Four days later, two of Mauk's men came to his house in West Aliquippa, called Isasky outside, and berated him. Two days later, September 11, a company cop bought him a gin and a beer in a bar; then an Aliquippa policeman waiting outside arrested him for drunk and disorderly. He was last seen being hustled away, face thick with bruises. Upon arriving at the jail, he was beaten again.

Within days, the Aliquippa police chief, O'Loughlin, asked for a "lunacy commission" to examine Isasky. Wife Mary, a baby on her hip, went to the Beaver County Jail expecting to visit him, but was instead met by Dr. Margaret Cornelius—whom the state secretary of welfare would soon declare the possible possessor of "rather neurotic and pathological tendencies"—and told that Georg was "very crazy" and unavailable. Cornelius insisted that she sign a paper declaring her husband insane. When Mary refused, the doctor threatened to cut off the family's relief payments.

A week later, Mary received a letter from the mental hospital in Torrance that her husband had been admitted and "has been quiet and orderly and cooperates with the hospital routine." She wrote her letter soon after to Cornelia Bryce Pinchot. On September 29, the First Lady wrote back: She would be contacting the state's secretary of welfare immediately. She wanted to know how and by whom Georg was beaten. "Let me know about this," Cornelia wrote. "and I will do anything I can to help you and him."

But by then the wheels in Harrisburg had already started to turn. Clint Golden, one of the mediators under state Secretary of Labor and Industry Charlotte Carr, had been investigating stories of J&L intimidation for three weeks when the First Lady responded to Mary's letter. On October 5, the same day Mary wrote back with the requested details, Golden was wandering the town, dressed as a bum. The following day, he returned. This time he didn't go unnoticed.

"Talk about the way the workers and peasents [sic] were handled under the Czar—it had nothing on the way the J&L Steel Co. handled them in that town," Golden wrote to his wife that night. "I had no more than reached the outskirts today than I was spotted and followed."

But arriving, too, were the eight state policemen (a special, out-of-jurisdiction detachment from Butler, because Harry Mauk's own brother was the state police captain in nearby Greensburg) charged with protecting testifying workers. When Golden met with the corporal in charge, his shadows disappeared; late that afternoon, for the first time in memory, J&L ordered Mauk's police to confine themselves to company property. "You could almost feel the relief from the tension as you passed thro [sic] the darned town," Golden wrote.

Only then did he go to Mary Isasky's home and hear her story first-hand. The next day, October 7, Golden traveled the forty-one miles east to Torrance and found Georg Isasky to be "as sane as I am." When his report arrived in Harrisburg, Cornelia suggested the governor order an independent doctor's examination; two days later the doctor, along with the medical staff at Torrance, declared Isasky's mind perfectly sound.

Sure that J&L had had Isasky railroaded for union activities, Golden tried tracing the request for his arrest, commitment, and harsh treatment at the Beaver County Jail to Mauk's company police. He had no hard evidence, no paper trail, no witnesses willing to testify. And the company would deny any involvement. Meanwhile, Governor Pinchot, with a sane man sitting in one of his state's insane asylums, began exploring whether he possessed the legal or medical authority to demand Isasky's release.

But the First Lady was impatient. She wanted Isasky's martyr-dom known. She wanted to be able to accuse J&L now. Because unlike Golden, who could retreat to his hotel in Pittsburgh; or her husband, who could stay in the mansion in Harrisburg; or even Isasky, who for the moment remained safe from reprisal at Torrance, Mrs. Pinchot was heading into the belly of the beast. She was going to Aliquippa, and she intended to give its precious "Family" hell.

3

Free Men

Aliquippa's revolution began forty-five minutes late. It was getting on early evening, October 14, 1934, the air unseasonably chill; men moved to keep warm, feet stamping, shoulders hunched, hands jammed in pockets. A crowd of 1,500 sat waiting in the Polish Hall in Plan 11. Hundreds more milled outside. A few thousand lingered along Franklin Avenue, and even more down near the tunnel. Across the river, another cluster of faces—including Burgess P. J. Caul, the Amalgamated's vice president, three organizers, the bored, the curious—and scores of cars had gathered outside the Ambridge Hotel. Some had been there for hours. Some, in a sense, had been waiting for decades.

It was a Sunday. Mrs. Pinchot had given a speech earlier in New Kensington, an hour away, and those waiting understood that such events never went off on time—though then again, they knew, there was always the chance that someone had gotten scared and called it off. . . .

But now her car approached. A roar broke out and grew at recognition of it; and then her red hair and squared jaw inside; and then the fact that, yes indeed, it truly was going to happen, *now*, rippled through the assembled like an electric charge. Everyone scrambled into cars. In a line they pulled out toward the bridge, scores of autos with little American flags fluttering on fenders, out of windows.

When they arrived in Aliquippa minutes later, it was clear that something elemental had changed. Whether because of the eight state troopers, or the surety that the governor was paying heed, or the sudden leaning weight of massed men brave enough to flout J&L dicta—or all that, plus the fact that Georg Isasky's commitment was unraveling fast—the company had dialed back its presence. The bullies, for this one afternoon at least, seemed quite docile. "It was wonderful!" reported the *Amalgamated Journal*. Mauk's men, along with the Aliquippa police, politely directed traffic and, as the union account reported, "assisted in every way possible."

Cornelia, in a gold-spangled dress and red shoes, took her place at the head of a parade of workers that wound through town, past thronged sidewalks, protesting the denial of free speech and assembly. She led them all up to the Polish Hall, and with anywhere from 4,000 to 8,000 workers filling the seats and spilling outdoors and surrounding the building, and all of the proceedings being piped outside on loudspeakers, together they sang the first verse of "America." Then, after many shouts and "deafening" applause, she opened the first public and independent labor meeting in the town's history.

"Friends," she began. "I am glad you asked me here today. For some time I have wanted to come and talk to you—to ask if I couldn't help you in any way. I am with you in the fight you are making for decent conditions—for the right to live—for the chance to call your souls your own.

"I am against Jones and Laughlin first, last, and all the time— because of the brutal and un-American way they have been behaving towards their workers. . . ."

This came, one reporter wrote, "with a swish of her neatly coif-fured red head." Mrs. Pinchot did not mention Georg Isasky, not by name.

"I have only just been learning of the things that have been going on in Aliquippa," she continued. "It is a horrible situation. I wish you had told me about it sooner, for I would have been with you, fighting long before this. It's time that the Steel Operator should learn that the worker has some rights—that no employer . . . can set himself up above the law.

"I have come a long way to be here with you tonight—and one of the reasons for my coming is that I wanted to read you a paragraph from a document that is apparently unknown to the Steel Operator. 'Congress shall make no law . . . abridging the freedom of speech, or of the press; or the right of the people peaceably to assemble, and to petition the Government for a redress of grievances. . . .'

"I am told there is a man called Mauk, who needs to learn that the workers have some rights in America. If some of the stories that I hear are true, I believe that legal proceedings should be started. Perhaps if we can get this great man behind the bars he would have time to read the American Constitution, which he has evidently never heard of. . . ."

Cornelia Pinchot went on to lambast J&L's managers and "hired thugs" for a "reign of terrorism, brutality and oppression . . . that compares with the worst day of the Russian czars." She vowed that her husband would protect any threatened workers and any independent union with state police, sneered at the company-directed "unions," and said that the only way for workers to get their fair share was "a union that belongs to you." The state's First Lady also issued a threat:

"We will see," she said, "whether the J&L people can run this country forever or not."

When Pinchot finished, the Polish Hall thundered. She was handed two lovely bouquets: it was the least the Amalgamated leaders could do. They now had their legs beneath them. Ten days prior the membership of Beaver Lodge #200, exiled in Ambridge, had numbered two hundred. Within a month it would register near four thousand, half the mill's workforce. Years of grueling work and true courage by many had led to that surge. But no one questioned the final, legitimizing factor.

"Cornelia Bryce Pinchot," said Harold Ruttenberg, the influential research director for the United Steelworkers of America, who began his career investigating the town in 1934. "She came to Aliquippa and spoke and broke the strong control that the company police had on the community. . . . And the control of the companies over the unionizing meetings was broken."

In the movie version that never was—with Elia Kazan directing—Cornelia Bryce Pinchot's speech would've been the dramatic end of the steelworkers' struggle in Aliquippa, with shots of grimly determined men cheering in gritty black and white, with hard-assed workers walking tall, with a brassy, uplifting Leonard Bernstein score blaring as the screen goes black. Ruttenberg, speaking from the perspective of fifty-eight years later, had it mostly right: October 14 was a climax of sorts. It did mark the beginning of the end of the most blatant aspects of the "worker- and thought-control system" created by Tom Girdler, of the helplessness in the face of it, of the idea that no one in the outside world with any clout cared.

God knows, the giddiness that trailed the men out of the Polish Hall that night spread and lasted for weeks; it was one of those rare times when life *did* feel like some Hollywood production, not least for Cornelia. She left Aliquippa thrilled by that over-the-top moment and the thought of creating more of them—legality, decorum, or her husband's position be damned. Five days later she personally put up the $500 to bail out a striker in Allentown. Newspapers ate it up. Isasky's continued confinement presented the chance for a far wilder flourish.

"I had planned to kidnap him from the asylum in a very dramatic way," she wrote a month later.

Instead Governor Pinchot "knocked my plan galley west" by simply releasing Isasky. The freeing of the "small in stature and meek appearing" union operative on October 24—six weeks after Isasky's arrest—sparked national headlines, complete with photos of the suffering wife and kids. "You know what this is," Isasky said upon his release. "It's the crazy house." Charges flew about commitments of other sane union men in Aliquippa. The governor pledged to investigate.

But by then statehouse tolerance for loose-cannon dramatics had seemed to cool. Cornelia's initial contacts with Mary Isasky weren't revealed, and she saw the merit in stepping back. The night before Isasky's release, the First Lady telephoned a balky Clint Golden and demanded that he allow officials to publicize his role "as they saw fit." Why? "I want somebody's names besides those of a couple old women," she explained. Golden gave in. "What a person!" he wrote his wife that night. And so, the next day, he was credited with being the first to uncover Isasky's arrest.

Meanwhile, though J&L had been publicly humiliated twice in a month, the company refused to be cowed. A spokesman declared that the mill "had nothing to do" with the Isasky matter. J&L's political allies vowed to ignore any inquiry. "We can't believe what that damn fool governor says or what the newspaper prints," said the Beaver County district attorney. "If the governor wants to do anything let him do it with his attorney general or his state policemen."

The governor tried. Yet no one was prosecuted or lost their job because of Isasky's confinement. No pattern involving other labor men and asylum commitments could be proven; the hearings were so feeble that Isasky himself never made it to the witness stand. Harry Mauk—and his private armed force of nearly three dozen men—remained very much employed.

✻   ✻   ✻

Because it turned out, of course, that life in Aliquippa wasn't a movie. It was like life anywhere—slower, more complex, and more resistant to change than any cinematic dream. The mill still held the ultimate power, all the more pronounced at a time when Pennsylvania was suffering from 37 percent unemployment. And the drive for unionization did not preoccupy all. Beneath the hard-core activists rumbled a variably rousable populace, many concerned less with abstractions like "civil liberties" than with living in a place peaceful enough to raise kids, keep a stable job, and grab a few drinks in the new beer gardens.

Once Prohibition ended in 1933, bars had cropped up like mushrooms. "We had a happy town," Perriello said. "You didn't have much personal what you'd call *movement.* You couldn't do everything you wanted, but as long as you followed their rules—which was, 'Keep your mouth shut; don't talk against J&L; don't join any unions'—you were in good shape."

Indeed, even with Mrs. Pinchot and the Amalgamated and Isasky dominating the headlines, most workers were preoccupied with the scrounge for any loose shift, and worry over the ever-mounting debt with the Italian grocer. Everybody but bosses struggled; neighbors in mixed areas like Logstown learned to share the load. Blacks weren't allowed inside certain beer gardens or restaurants, yet sometimes skin color didn't matter a bit.

"If my mother was sick, the neighbors, they would come over and help out—even though the neighbor was an Italian woman, a Serbian woman, a Polish woman—they would come over here and they would do the washing," says James Downing Jr. "At that time, they washed it with a rub-board, you understand, wasn't no washing-machine, see. Then there'd be someone would cook. My father'd be working in the mill, he'd come home, you know . . . dinner would be ready."

By the fall of 1936, too, relations between the rival towns seemed almost fraternal. Ambridge had been a union haven and ally against J&L, and strikes, beatings, and speeches, all sealed with blood or job losses, had forged a solidarity that transcended borders. On Labor Day, two competing worker parades—one supporting the company union in the morning, one for the independents in the afternoon—filled Aliquippa's downtown. Fired J&L workers, followed by hundreds brandishing Roosevelt posters, finished the second by marching to the bridge and over the river into Ambridge for a massive flag-waving rally.

A month later, Aliquippa kicked off a new era when it opened its pristine new football stadium on the hill above the high school in Plan 12. Twenty-one rows of bench seating—all California redwood and steel brackets daubed black—backed up the hillside in five sections, framing the "deep rich green turf," said the *Aliquippa Gazette*. "It will be ideal to play on—dustless—comfortable—beautiful!"

Hundreds of workers, part of a Works Progress Administration program to erect forty-eight such facilities statewide, had finished the 3,400-seat (officially, anyway) jewel in less than a year—and now here, on October 24, came Ambridge, the perfect foil with which to christen the place. Both teams were unbeaten. Aliquippa had scored 61 points the week before and looked unstoppable. . . .

It didn't matter. Rubenstein escaped the stadium—packed with an estimated 12,000 locals—with a 0-0 tie. Aliquippa and Ambridge then ran out their remaining three games without a loss; the Quips didn't surrender another point all season. Aliquippa and Ambridge thus shared the 1936 county championship, lending the fractious days a rare and perhaps welcomed glimpse of harmony. Lippe's thoughts on the matter, though, have been lost to history.

No, J&L didn't give in. It couldn't. Thirty years earlier, the company had designed and built a town to make money, an entity that thrived on the feed of cheap, docile labor. This took a certain cool genius—one that even the NLRB conceded in summing up J&L as a "vast mechanism"—and genius rewarded rarely knows when to stop. The fact that, three

generations on, the company was still controlled and run by its founding family made it unique; that it had expanded without benefit of
merger or consolidation made it formidable. By the mid-1930s Jones
and Laughlin Steel had indeed become a machine of estimable reach.

Employing 22,000, valued at $3.2 billion in today's dollars, J&L's
operation extended well beyond Pittsburgh and Aliquippa and into
every stage of the steelmaking process. The industry lived off limestone, iron, and coal. J&L dug 40 percent of its limestone out of its
own quarries in Pennsylvania and West Virginia. It controlled or owned
mines in Michigan and Minnesota stocked with 60 million tons of
iron ore, and the quartet of steamships on the Great Lakes needed to
transport it. It owned mines in Pennsylvania stocked with 600 million
tons of recoverable coal, and the 10 towboats and 165 barges needed
to transport that.

J&L also operated its own railroad, complete with 49 locomotives
and 1,327 freight cars, and was the largest shipper on the corresponding
Pittsburgh and Lake Erie line. It owned warehouses in Chicago, Detroit,
Cincinnati, and Memphis. It pioneered the hauling of its finished steel
downriver to markets like New Orleans, in barges of its own design and
making, and shipped 240,000 tons a year down the Ohio and Mississippi Rivers. It operated steel fabricating shops in New York and New
Orleans. Through a wholly owned J&L subsidiary, it owned, leased, and
operated stores, warehouses, and yards for the distribution of equipment
for drilling and operating oil and gas mills, pipelines, refineries, and
pumping stations. It had sales offices in twenty U.S. cities and a wholly
owned subsidiary charged with distributing its products in Canada.

"The ramifications of the Jones and Laughlin Steel Corporation
are thus as broadly extended as the nation itself," the NLRB declared
in 1936. "It is impossible to isolate the operations of the Works in
Pittsburgh and Aliquippa or to consider them as detached, separate—
'local'—phenomena. These works might be likened to the heart of a
self-contained, highly integrated body."

J&L was never going to be as massive as U.S. Steel and Bethlehem Steel. But the Aliquippa Works had become one of the largest integrated mills in the world, covering every step of the process from conversion of iron ore to the production of custom-finished shapes, and Aliquippa was now the nation's largest steel company town. J&L owned the streetcar line, 128 acres of property, and 1,174 acres of farmland. Of its 30,000 citizens, 10,000 worked at its mill; factor in wives and children, and there was virtually no one in Aliquippa who didn't feel its weight.

"The company's opposition to a union was very simple," said Joe Perriello. "Would you want anybody interfering with your business if you had complete control over everybody that works for you? You tell them what to eat, you tell them where to live, you tell them how much water to drink, you tell them where to buy property, you tell them where to go to work. Now here comes a group of people who say, 'Wait a minute. That isn't all there is in this life. There also is a choice.'"

But almost as soon as that choice was established, it began to dissolve. FDR had been the first Democrat to carry the state since 1856, and the 1934 gubernatorial election of Democrat George Earle—and his running mate, a former official with the United Mine Workers— seemed to reinforce the climate's leftward tilt. Yet within two months, infighting at the Amalgamated gave J&L the legal opening to devastate the newly created lodge with a fresh offensive. Bosses and J&L police pressured employees to become stool pigeons and join the company-sanctioned union, threatening the loss of job and home.

"My uncle was fired. My brother was fired, blackballed," Perriello said. Three J&L policemen invaded Perriello's home and threw the sleeping twenty-year-old out of bed while his mother watched; then two of them pulled out blackjacks to administer a beating. But Perriello played football with the semipro Aliquippa Indians on Crow Island, and the third cop, a football fan, recognized him, "Leave him alone," he said. "I'll talk to him." The J&L men left. Perriello's bed was broken. His mother was so frightened that she had soiled herself.

In May 1935, the Supreme Court struck down the National Industrial Recovery Act, short-circuiting federal support for collective bargaining. Wage cuts slashed the average weekly pay at the Aliquippa Works from $19 to $17, and when Cornelia Bryce Pinchot returned for a speech on the eve of Labor Day that year, she met a crowd uncertain of lasting gains. "I have been reading over some of the cases of Jones and Laughlin men who have been discharged, suspended, and demoted in the last few months," she said. "Not a pretty story."

By the summer of 1936, mill timekeepers and J&L police were handing out flyers promising a shuttering of the Aliquippa Works if the push for an outside union continued. Fourteen of the sixteen men who attended a union meeting in town were fired. *Aliquippa Gazette* editorials characterized organizers as bloodsuckers, parasites, and mad dogs deserving of beatings. The number of members in Lodge #200, once hovering near 5,000, had dwindled to less than 100. But help was coming.

A year earlier, on July 5, 1935, FDR had signed the Wagner Act into law. The bill, technically known as the National Labor Relations Act, tied the right of independent unionization to the economy itself, protecting it as a matter integral to interstate commerce. It also created the National Labor Relations Board, with Clint Golden appointed as associate director of the Pittsburgh region. But all involved knew that only a constitutional nod by the Supreme Court could legitimate the Wagner Act. The lives of millions of workers would be affected; the test case needed to be airtight.

Four days after the president's pen hit paper, on July 9, J&L fired Martin Dunn, a charter member of the union, for leaving the key to his crane on a bench. Over the succeeding months, the company picked off Aliquippa union men one by one: Lodge president Harry Phillips, for failing to answer a whistle; vice president Angelo Volpe, for using his head and not his hands to signal while operating a crane; treasurer Martin Gerstner, after a nut fell off one of his inspected cranes; tractor driver Angelo Razzano—who had gone to see Cornelia Bryce Pinchot speak in Ambridge in 1934 and had signed up 1,500 members—for leaving open a mill door. Ten in all were fired, each a longtime J&L employee with an unblemished record, each for the most minor transgressions.

After his dismissal, on January 13, 1936, Razzano walked out of the superintendent's office and through the tunnel. He bumped into a friend who'd gone to law school. "Dominick, I'm finished," Razzano said. Then he told him why.

"There's a train at two-fifteen," Dominick said. "Get that train and go to Pittsburgh." He gave Razzano the name of a government attorney. Razzano climbed aboard, found the office. It took a while before the attorney called him in.

"I worked for J&L from 1924 to 1936," Razzano began. "I've got a good record. I'm always working; I've never missed work; I'm always doing more than what I'm supposed to do. The company is firing me, I guess, on account of the union activities. I can't prove it, but . . . "

When he returned that night, Razzano bumped into Eli Bozich, a laborer fired the same day for waiting for a boss to tell him what to do. Razzano gave him the lawyer's address. Soon he told Domenic Brandy, George Marell, Ronald Cox, and Royal Boyer, along with Dunn, Phillips, Volpe, and Gerstner—about the lawyer, too.

Boyer was the lone black in the group. This didn't seem striking at the time, at least beyond the NLRB's description of him as "a Negro" and as one of a subset of workers possessing "special qualities as leaders of particular groups—Brandy, the Italian, Boyer, the Negro." But his presence among the ten would give it symbolic heft, especially once John Lewis's racially enlightened Congress of Industrial Organizations replaced the obsolete Amalgamated in the drive to organize the steelworkers.

Relations between black steelworkers and organized labor had long been scarred by bigotry and mutual distrust. The American Federation of Labor, historically, either segregated its black members or excluded them outright, and the Amalgamated all but ignored black steelworkers in its membership drives. When steelworkers went on strike nationwide in 1919, management was only too happy to exploit the split. Some 30,000 newly arrived blacks—fresh from the Jim Crow South, unschooled in union aims, eager for a paycheck—were hired as strikebreakers and police deputies. The insults to supposed worker solidarity and white superiority sparked riots between white picketers and black scabs in Chicago; Gary, Indiana; and Donora, Pennsylvania, and violent attacks on blacks in the nearby Pennsylvania towns of Rankin, Duquesne, and Monessen. When the strike collapsed, the phrase "Niggers did it" caught on as the unofficial Amalgamated line.

Boyer came to J&L five years later, at eighteen, hired as a common laborer. After becoming a machine operator in Aliquippa's nail department in 1932, he quickly established himself as a union voice. He was one of the founders of Beaver Lodge #200 in Ambridge and signed up 250 of the mill's 800 blacks. His boss told him to stop. The threat was implicit. In January 1933, in the nearby town of Industry, Beaver County officials raided a party and arrested fifty-six black adults. Ten paid $2.50 fines and were released; the other forty-six were illegally loaded into trucks and dumped over the West Virginia line with no food. In 1933, a black man was killed by one of Mauk's policemen when he made the mistake of wandering into Aliquippa's Plan 6—the white enclave, the bosses' district—after dark.

Boyer was fired a month before Razzano, suddenly, for making bad nails. About that time, Mauk's police introduced a new tactic to sow division—pay or pressure blacks into assaulting white men around town, then release them while the outraged whites remained in custody.

On January 23, 1936, the Amalgamated filed a formal complaint against J&L on behalf of the ten men fired in Aliquippa. Calling the Wagner Act—and thus the NLRB—unconstitutional, the company refused to take part in NLRB hearings or to obey its order to reinstate the ten and cease hindering union organizers. The board petitioned for enforcement. Gambling that the Fifth Circuit Court of Appeals in New Orleans would rule faster, the NLRB got its wish—and nearly lost everything. On June 15, the court struck down the NLRB's order, and the Wagner Act, by backing J&L's contention that its employee relations were a local issue concerning manufacturing and production—not interstate commerce—and thus beyond the power of Congress under the U.S. Constitution's Commerce Clause. The federal government, in other words, had no power to regulate labor relations.

The next day, the CIO's Steel Workers Organizing Committee (SWOC) held its first meeting, in Pittsburgh, and sent one of its toughest organizers, Joe Timko of the United Mine Workers, into Aliquippa. On November 9, just after the town went Democratic—by a 2-to-1 margin—for the first time ever to help reelect Franklin Roosevelt, the Supreme Court agreed to take up *National Labor Relations Board v. Jones & Laughlin Steel Corporation*. On February 9, 1937, the court began to hear arguments. The decision would reconfigure the nation's political and cultural life for the next fifty years.

At noon on April 12, Chief Justice Charles Evans Hughes led the justices through a curtain and to their positions on the bench. In one account, the "silent intake of spectators' breaths all but caused a vacuum in the courtroom."

Equating employees' "fundamental right" to organize themselves with an employer's right to arrange its business affairs, and finding that the Aliquippa Ten had been fired for union activity and to discourage union membership, Hughes announced the Court's finding, 5–4, in favor of the NLRB.

"When industries organize themselves on a national scale, making their relation to interstate commerce the dominant factor in their activities," he said in the majority opinion, "how can it be maintained that their industrial labor relations constitute a forbidden field into which Congress may not enter when it is necessary to protect interstate commerce from the paralyzing consequences of industrial war?"

The decision, which essentially endowed Congress with new power to regulate labor relations under the Commerce Clause, had titanic impact. In the big picture, it effectively spelled the end of court challenges to the New Deal, reinforced Roosevelt's landslide reelection, and greatly expanded congressional might. One scholar calls *NLRB v. Jones & Laughlin* "a major turning point . . . for the whole course of American constitutional development." Another says the ruling "revolutionized industrial relations in the United States and climaxed more than a century of labor history. . . . There no longer could be any question of a union's right to exist. The very interference with its existence by an employer through unfair labor practices became outlawed."

J&L was ordered to rehire the ten fired men, with 18 months back pay; Royal Boyer received $2,040 ($34,215 today) and Angelo Razzano more than $1,000. J&L refused public comment. But reaction in corporate America, among Tom Girdler and his ilk, was hardly a secret. "I'm sure I know what it was," says Tom Girdler Jr. "I'm sure it was one of utter disgust and dismay."

But for most of Aliquippa the news, hitting just after the afternoon shift change disgorged thousands into the streets, sparked jubilation. Angelo Volpe cheered and ran to tell his wife. Eli Bozich stopped tending bar to give a speech. Soon a parade steamed up Franklin Avenue, led by two cars filled with the now-reinstated ten. One featured a sign that read, "We Are the Ten Men Fired for Union Activity by J&L, We Are Ordered Back to Work by the Supreme Court." The second read, "The Workers of Aliquippa Are Now Free Men."

"When I hear Wagner Act went constitutional, I happy like anything," said one steelworker. "I say, 'Good, now Aliquippa become part of the United States.'"

*　*　*

Yet it wasn't over. Still J&L refused to bend, never mind that its stand had become increasingly lonely. Revivified by Roosevelt's landslide win, organized labor—and especially John L. Lewis's CIO in its push to organize steel—began a chicken-egg cycle of victory begetting converts begetting victory. In February 1937, sit-down strikes by 192,642 workers paralyzed American industry; when Michigan's governor refused to evict the occupying force at a General Motors plant in Flint, GM caved. In April, even as J&L lawyers were attacking the Wagner Act before the Supreme Court, U.S. Steel chairman Myron Taylor came to terms with the Steel Workers Organizing Committee.

The move blindsided and enraged Little Steel operators like J&L and Republic. "I was bitter about this," wrote Tom Girdler, Republic's chief, in one of the era's great understatements. Taylor was soon deposed as chairman of the producers' federation, the American Iron and Steel Institute; Girdler took over. "My father made the famous statement that before he'd sign a contract with John L. Lewis, he'd go back to raising apples on the farm," said Tom Girdler Jr. "John L. Lewis, in my opinion, was a louse. And in his opinion, the same thing."

With the Supreme Court ruling, J&L shuttered its "Employee Representation Plan" and began tepid talks with the SWOC in Pittsburgh; it soon became clear that management had every intention of crippling the new steelworkers union, along with Aliquippa's freshly minted Local 1211, in its infancy. The company pushed for a vote to decide between a new company-backed plan and SWOC, with both sides certain that the union would lose. Union leadership refused. The Aliquippa Works readied for battle. A Clint Golden spy reported a J&L stockpile near one plant gate of "at least 150 holstered .38-caliber revolvers, all neatly stacked on shelves," ammunition for Thompson submachine guns, and "a great many" packages of what looked to be machine guns, tear gas, and ordnance.

On May 12, both J&L Locals—the old 200 and the new 1211—voted to walk out, and the Aliquippa air carried an unprecedented feel of possibility, of the old order crashing. By 10 p.m. a mass of picketers had clustered in front of the tunnel, along with a union truck loaded with weapons. At 11 p.m. workers arriving for their shift moved into the crowd, becoming part of the strike, like it or not. The tunnel was the main entrance, the cavernous symbol of every man's trudge into an oft-punishing job. Now the workers pinched it shut. J&L was under siege.

One of the Aliquippa 10, Angelo Razzano, had been back in the seamless tube mill only a few days when the strike officially began at 12:01 a.m. on the thirteenth. For a few hours he roamed about the mill grounds—cutting telephone lines in the machinists' shop, mulling whether to stuff his boss in a sack and hurl him into the river—finally emerging into the 4 a.m. bustle of a town transformed. He heard some strikebreakers planning to sneak into the mill via the railroad. In a frenzy, he chased one of them across the lawn of the Woodlawn Hotel, straight into the lobby.

"I beat the hell out of him," Razzano recalled. "I tore his shirt; blood all over the God-darn place, you know. I said, 'Now, if you want to go back to work, you'll have to go to work *now!*' So he didn't make any attempt."

Police, both municipal and company, tried breaking through the masses plugging the tunnel. They drove a bus nearly into the picket line, with hidden caches of tear gas and guns; the bus was pushed back. They tried to bull out from the inside, failed, and fired tear gas to clear a path. A cadre of women, out of the tin mill, didn't budge when set upon with fire hoses. And they were the first to challenge a suspect mail truck; workers overturned it and found it teeming with scab supplies. A fever took hold. Kids hurled rocks and tomatoes from hills at the strikebreakers lined up below. Everyone wanted to get their licks in.

"The strike is a rank-and-file affair," wrote SWOC staff member Meyer Bernstein. "SWOC may have called it, but it is now in the hands of anyone who can lead. It is a mob, not an organization. They have no more control than their lungs can command.

"Remember that Jefferson once said something about a revolution every twenty years or so being a blessing? The same is true of a strike. There is real solidarity now. And certainly no fear. . . .

"Of course there has been violence. Four or five old men who had no notion of what was going on tried to get through the picket line. They were stopped and led back, but the return was through a gauntlet. They were badly beaten and most of them were bloody. Even an organizer was just barely saved from an attack. . . . "

Daylight on the first full day, May 13, brought cold and pouring rain, dampening tempers, lowering the temperature. Rumors circulated that Girdler still couldn't resist taking a hand in Aliquippa; his Republic Steel, it was said, had shipped over its "gas pipe gang" and a contingent of company forces from Youngstown. Perhaps he sensed what few suspected: J&L's spine wasn't what it used to be. Girdler had taken two top executives with him when he left J&L in 1929, and the retirement of chairman George Laughlin in 1936 had ended "Family" control of top management. Executives with no vaguely exalted mission, no memory of Woodlawn, were running things now.

On the morning of May 14, Governor George Earle entered the tunnel in a car with strike leader Joe Timko, followed by four state police cars; the strikers let them through. Startled company police, waiting on the other end, greeted the governor with a phalanx of raised rifles. Recognizing him, they tried to hide the guns.

"Never mind: I've seen them," Earle said. "I don't want any trouble here. Let the company and the union get together and settle this peacefully."

And so it happened, with a whimper when all expected a roar. J&L negotiators called Timko and agreed to a settlement and an NLRB election. It took hours for the crowd of 20,000 outside the tunnel to leave: some workers wanted the feeling to last; some feared a trick. They also, Bernstein wrote, "wanted blood," the blood of strikebreakers who would eventually have to come out through the tunnel. Police didn't dare disperse the crowd. Finally Timko—the new power in town—hired a brass band, raised up an American flag, and began a parade that took them all away.

"J&L has been brought to its knees," Bernstein wrote. "Think of it. The toughest Corporation in America . . . has been forced to capitulate."

On May 20, the union swept the election in the J&L Works in Aliquippa and Pittsburgh by more than a 2-to-1 margin, 17,028 to 7,207. Five days later, J&L officially recognized SWOC Local 1211 as the workers' exclusive bargaining agent, and agreed to the new industry-wide standard: a forty-hour workweek and a $5-a-day minimum wage, with time and a half for overtime.

The victory was not contagious. For Tom Girdler and the rest of Little Steel, the hard line continued, savagely: on May 30, ten strikers were killed by police outside a Republic plant in Chicago, and the SWOC effort to unionize thirty other mills in eight states crumbled after five more violent months. Little Hell, though, took on a new texture. Some workers would call it dignity, some would call it freedom, and some would take a long time to believe that it had ever happened at all.

"Let us forget the tension of the past few weeks and cheerfully apply ourselves to our duties," read the coyly bland surrender statement issued by new J&L chairman H. E. Lewis, "as there is much for all of us to do with our order books better filled than for some time past."

4

Bootstraps

Still, the town seemed no better than most. It was like any factory city in Michigan, any textile hub in Massachusetts, any mining village on the Great Lakes, any of the dozens of mill feeders of Pennsylvania pinned along the shores of the Allegheny River, the Monongahela, the Ohio. After the buzz of the strike faded, once the reporters and organizers moved on, Aliquippa was known for nothing but steel, fire, and a brimstone sky. The mill's order books might have been "better filled"—though, due to a recession in 1938, probably not by much—but as it was, J&L was running a $6 million deficit.

Steelworkers like Achille Letteri felt lucky to land a single shift a week. When his wife and ten-year-old son, Joe, arrived from Italy in 1938 they found life "very, very hard," Joe Letteri said. "Very little food to eat. What my mother had to do, you wouldn't believe: She had to scrape. We made our own bread. We lived on soup and bread most of the time. My mother tried to sneak me stuff on the side because I was little."

The Letteris were typical. Achille had left everything behind—his wife, Agate; their hometown of Sulmona in the Abruzzi region of Italy—when he and his three brothers came to America after World War I. Every few years, after saving enough, he would travel steerage back to Sulmona for a few weeks, impregnate Agate, and return to America. Their two oldest sons sailed for Aliquippa first, then in 1938 Little Joe boarded the SS *Conte di Savoia*, third-class for the seven-day trip, got seasick, passed the Statue of Liberty, and shuffled through Ellis Island. He and his mom boarded a train in New York. When they stepped off at the West Aliquippa station, Achille Letteri was waiting.

"That's when I met him," Joe said. "I didn't know my father till I come to America."

They lived those first years in a company row house in West Aliquippa, the thirty-four-block enclave planted squat within the open hearth's shadow, atop the amusement park remains. The family picked tomatoes out of its plot on Crow Island, and come Sundays wandered over to the football field to watch the semipro Indians. The other six days, the men played the numbers, drank, cheered the high school teams that never won championships. The talk out of Europe was about Mussolini, Hitler, Neville Chamberlain; everyone here worried about family back home.

At night Joe would fall asleep to a piano's tinkling, the fingerings of a flute through the thin walls of the home next door. Already, fifteen-year-old Henry Mancini was known as a prodigy, playing for Aliquippa High and the Sons of Italy band. Sometimes Henry's gruff dad, Quinto, would invite the Letteris over for a glass, a chat about the old country, a listen to his gifted son.

"He used to play piano and we'd go over there and watch him," Joe said. "We didn't know what was going on."

Meaning that the Letteris, like everyone else in Aliquippa, had no sense that beneath the surface of things a subtle alchemy was at work. Through some combination of proximity, geography, friction, hardship, talent, conflict, drive—not to mention a loathing for steelwork—the town had stumbled on a knack for producing excellence. Its first examples, in fact, had just shipped out: Pete "Pecky" Suder out of Plan 7, and Press Maravich of Plan 2, teammates on Aliquppa High's 1933–34 basketball team, were off playing minor league baseball and college basketball, respectively.

No one, of course, would have predicted that Suder, a utility infielder buried in the Yankees system, would play thirteen years in the majors and with the '49 Philadelphia A's help set a record for double plays—218—that still stands. Or that Maravich would become a force as a college basketball coach in the '60s, winning conference titles and producing one of the game's most dazzling figures in his son. Who had that kind of foresight? American team sports weren't easily plumbed by immigrant parents—and besides, they had larger concerns. The coming of war in Europe changed Aliquippa, said Jesse Steinfeld, whose widowed mother ran a notions shop in West Aliquippa, "from a total disaster to a busy little town."

By the end of 1939, with the U.S. building ships for Great Britain, J&L's production had doubled and Achille Letteri had more work than he could handle. Soon his two oldest sons would land jobs at the Aliquippa Works, too, and start counting the days until they could move out, unaware that they were fleeing something rare. Mancini's music—encompassing everything from "Moon River" to the *Pink Panther* theme—would win him twenty Grammies and four Academy Awards. And though little brother Joe Letteri never made it past seventh grade, his own oldest son, Joe Jr., would go on to win four Oscars for visual effects in blockbuster movies like *Avatar* and *Lord of the Rings*.

"That's eight Oscars coming out of that one row house in West Aliquippa," said former Aliquippa postmaster, and Beaver County historian, Gino Piroli.

Half a mile up Beaver Ave., meanwhile, Silvio "Tony" Ciccone, the youngest son of a mill-working immigrant from Pacentro, Italy, had just turned seven; he'd later move to suburban Detroit, become the only one in his family to graduate college, and father the pop star Madonna. A few blocks over from the Letteris and Mancinis, Jesse Steinfeld was getting restless. Every day brought another anti-Semitic slur. The older Henry always looked out for him, and in the early '40s the two would pay their nickels and together ride the bus from West Aliquippa up to the high school. "He was very smart," Steinfeld said. "A great guy to have as a friend."

Mancini left town in 1942, and Steinfeld, after graduating Aliquippa High at sixteen, was gone a year later. He, too, rose to the top of his field, becoming the eleventh surgeon general of the United States in 1969, and one of the most effective; Steinfeld was an early voice warning about the effects of violent TV on children, and proved far more outspoken than any of his predecessors against cigarette smoking. His superiors in the Nixon administration pressured him to back off, but Steinfeld had no choice: His antipathy ran all the way back to Aliquippa.

"My mother hated it," he said.

Steinfeld's father had chain-smoked from the moment he woke, and between his exhalations and the putrescence billowing from the nearby stacks, there was little good air for the boy to breathe. Indeed, the most cursory scan of wartime Aliquippa's newspaper—rife with stories about gambling raids, wildcat strikes, men suffering horrific burns at the mill, a man killing his father with an ax, the occasional shooting—reveals an era far more complex than the sepia-toned, "Greatest Generation" caricature so beloved by nostalgists.

Too often, the idea of small-town America then gets reduced to a quaint admirable mush. But even the now-adored 1946 classic *It's a Wonderful Life* portrayed two sides: the light, wholesome Bedford Falls and the noirish Pottersville, staffed by bartenders serving "hard drinks for men who want to get drunk fast." Aliquippa had both. It was a cheek-by-jowl, working-class universe—family-centered, intensely clannish, busy, and warm: You knew your neighbors. Kids could roam. Time was marked by the steam whistles mounted on the mill's massive boilerhouse stacks, blowing the noon and midnight shift changes, signaling the arrival of the new year, the end of war.

"I grew up in Plan 11: it was wonderful," said Gilda Letteri, Joe Sr.'s wife. "I went to the Jones School, and ended up teaching there. I grew up on Third Avenue because our relatives all lived there. There were sections where all the Italians lived, all the Polish, all the Slovaks. We had a mix of all these different people who became all our friends. . . ."

But it could also be grimly Hobbesian. Work in the mill took arms and hands, polluted bodies fast and slow; three men a year died in the Aliquippa Works, and the town's above-average indices of infant mortality, respiratory death, and heart disease would hold for generations. You could smell J&L in the tap water and rising off the skin, its coke and chemicals defying the strongest soap. Few complained. The airing of grievances, large or small, received little sympathy from officialdom or the culture at large. The job, the cops, and the times were all tough, and the combination fostered a hard—even brutal—sensibility.

In 1937 fourteen-year-old Steve Zernich, a future beloved surgeon from Aliquippa, began work at his parents' tavern downtown, one of the first to get a liquor license. Massive rats occasionally swarmed the basement; ferrets were brought in, but the rats killed the ferrets. When business was slow, "our sport consisted of turning off the lights, then quietly going down the basement stairs," Zernich later wrote.

"We waited until we heard the rats racing across the shelves. Then we snapped on the lights and stabbed the rats," he went on. "I caught one, pinning his leg to a board. At first, he spun around the ice pick like a propeller. He then started to chew off his leg until I finished him with my other ice pick. . . ."

Many who lived in Aliquippa then can't help but list only its virtues. But steel-town nostalgia is never just about drugstore egg creams and Sunday night dances at the Sons of Italy hall. It's about the challenges that made its inhabitants tough—or broke them whole. Survival carried its own reward.

"A wonderful experience—in retrospect," Steinfeld said. "But I don't look back on it fondly at all. Unfortunately, there was nothing fond about it. We were not in the winning circle, so to speak. Not football players, basketball players—or any kind of players. It was just a question of keeping going."

On February 21, 1941, the newly named football coach at Aliquippa High School, irked by a dawning sense that fans and boosters and one particularly anxious drum-beater from the *Aliquippa Gazette* nicknamed "The Armchair Athlete" expected a savior, allowed himself a flash of temper. "Rockne is dead. Let's forget this Superman buildup," Carl Aschman snapped. "I've got a tough enough job on my hands now without any buildup."

He was thirty-seven years old, of Austrian descent, and had never before said anything so colorful for public consumption—or even admitted to being aware of Notre Dame's legendary Knute Rockne or any comic-book hero—and never would again. But such was the anxiety surrounding the program then. Coach Nate Lippe had won only eleven football games in the previous three seasons, and had resigned amid dimming prospects. "The varsity grid cupboard is bare," wrote Richard Amper in the *Gazette*. "The entire squad is gone. A few straggling reserves are around but do not amount to much."

Landing Aschman had been a major coup. As Lippe faded, "King Carl" had shined: building previously unheralded and tiny Brownsville into a WPIAL power, going undefeated his last three years, winning the 1940 AA championship. And Aschman had seemed happy at Brownsville, saying just two months before that he had "hit the jackpot" as the top coach in the Monongahela Valley. Yet like Lippe, like many high school coaches, he was in charge of all Brownsville's major teams, and when the Aliquippa school board dangled a county-high salary of $3,500 ($59,000 today) to coach only football—with a much bigger talent pool—Aschman jumped.

He was hardly met with a parade. Germany had overrun France the summer before, and the nation's first peacetime draft was register-ing, examining, and inducting Beaver County's young white men; the week Aschman agreed to terms, German planes were bombing London. Everyone had an eye on the old country. Women had learned to keep mourning wear—black dress and beads—handy for those killed back home and for Aliquippa friends who'd lost family elsewhere. Children's voices, singing patriotic songs like "Over There," wafted every other day out school windows.

Still, that last peaceful fall, Aschman made an impressive debut. His was a traditional, down-the-throat offense, and the team local pa-pers dubbed the "Steelers" opened the season grinding out thirteen first downs and crushing Freedom 39–0. Aliquippa allowed only two touchdowns in winning its first five games, seemed poised for a title run, shoehorned nearly 8,000 into Aliquippa Stadium when Ambridge came calling . . . and Moe Rubenstein walked out with a 21–0 win. It was Aschman's first loss in four years; Bridger fans couldn't have been more delighted. Welcome to the neighborhood, King Carl.

Aliquippa finished the season 8–1. Late in 1941 a young couple with two boys, drawn by the boom in war work, moved up from Carnegie. The twenty-three-year-old breadwinner, Ukrainian with a bit of Pole mixed in, had been born Mike Dyzcko, but he didn't wait for some boss to change his name; ever bullheaded, he did it himself—his way. One brother had changed his name to "Disco," another to "Discoe." Mike liked the spikiness of "Ditka" better. He worked as a "burner" for the Aliquippa & Southern Railroad, which serviced the mill, repairing cars with an acetylene torch. Nightly he'd come home with his clothes full of holes, arms and hands scorched raw by the spitting fire.

War eats steel. The '38 recession evaporated fast; J&L logged a
$10.3 million profit in '40, and after Pearl Harbor the workforce, pro-
duction, and money only grew. In spring of 1941 Aliquippa schools
led the county in enrollment, with the high school at 1,279 pupils; the
following year alone, 407 students dropped out to seek war work. The
ever-increasing, ever-shifting demand in the ensuing months and years
kept J&L engineers scrambling. Hot and cold rolled steel, tin plate,
wire rope were needed for all manner of machine parts, ship plate, tank
armor, sprockets, gun barrel tubes, gun mounts, food containers, bombs,
bullet jackets, blood plasma cans, and submarine construction. J&L's
furnaces ran literally full-blast, twenty-four hours a day, breaking nearly
a thousand production records in 1941, and five hundred more in '42.

Over the next four years some 6,000 of Aliquippa's young, most
of them white men, but soon enough blacks and some women, went off
to fight. The inducted got a union hall party, a Bible, a parade, waves,
backslaps, and tears. It became customary for a crowd to accompany the
departing soldier out of his Plan, the place he grew up, the mile or so
to Aliquippa's train depot. "The men would congregate and we would
all walk down to the train station while the young men would get on
the trains, to go to war," said Gilda Letteri. "Friends, the families: We
all got together and walked down. Following them."

Aschman's second season began even better than his first. Aliquippa
outscored its first three opponents, 93-6, edged Ambridge, and rolled
unbeaten into its first-ever WPIAL title game, against four-time champ
New Castle. With no fields available in Pittsburgh, the WPIAL decided to hold the game in, yes, Ambridge; no one knows if Rubenstein
played a part in the decision. The stadium filled with 11,000 people
on Thanksgiving Day, most from right across the river, but New Castle
won 25–0, the Quips' offense unable to muster a first down until the
final two minutes.

"Power by Jesse Gunn, Negro fullback, and snake-hip sprinting
by swift-cutting Robert (General) E. Lee, Negro left halfback, featured

77

their final scholastic work in New Castle's deserved triumph," read the *Pittsburgh Press* account. "Time and again the Quip backs, especially Mike Devonar and Nick Odivak, tried their utmost to get somewhere, but with no avail. New Castle was just too tough, rugged and alert."

By then service flags were hanging in windows, a blue star signifying a family member in the military, gold signifying the dead. Mothers and wives paled at the sight of the Western Union man. Blackout drills were held every few days, older men in Civil Defense hard hats and armbands toting flashlights, inspecting houses for the merest leaked light. Benefit dances raised money for the Red Cross, and scrap drives for steel, rubber, and rags allowed everyone to feel a part of the war effort. But with only radio, newsreels, and sometimes-months-late letters bringing home just snippets of news, the faraway fighting felt almost unreal. Only once did Aliquippa get a first-hand taste of carnage.

At 5:10 p.m. on December 22, 1942, a bus carrying war workers just off their shift at J&L was heading south on Constitution Boulevard at a spot opposite the coke ovens. The steep cliff above, softened and split by freezing rain, loosed a forty-foot-wide avalanche of stone and dirt, some two hundred tons, onto the bus below. Twenty-two of those inside, most heading back to Pittsburgh, died instantly. "There was no warning," said Joseph Manko, a metallurgist, who crawled out a rear window. "Just the crash. Not so loud either. After that just silence and darkness."

Bystanders arrived to a scene of mangled bodies and crushed heads. Men clearing the debris came home speechless and faint. Four more of the injured would die, their names soon lost among the era's millions.

Life and the war and the mill went on. Women poured into jobs vacated by men gone away; new lifts and conveyors allowed the most diminutive to swing unfinished shells and bombs into position. Afterward, there were movies to take in at Abie Rosenthal's theater next to Steinfeld's home, springtime baseball games played in the community league. Some nights, fifteen-year-old Joe Letteri, struggling still with his English, would hit West Aliquippa's Saxer Field to take in a ball game. Tonino "Toats" DiNardo pitched for the Panthers Athletic Club when he wasn't anchoring the Aliquippa High staff.

"I watched him play all the time," Joe said. "Nice guy. Real quiet. Never bothered anybody."

Nate Lippe didn't leave town with Aschman's arrival. He continued coaching Aliquippa High basketball and baseball, and in the spring of '43 DiNardo beat Ambridge twice and led the Lippemen to the WPIAL semifinals before losing—despite tossing a three-hitter—2-0. That would be his last high school game. In December of '43, before his senior season, the eighteen-year-old DiNardo began basic training at Camp Wolters, Texas. He was sent overseas and, like 128 other Aliquippa men in World War II, died there.

"He never made it back," said teammate George Suder. "What a great kid, too. Oh, my God: people get killed or they die and then they were all 'good guys,' but this guy really was a helluva man. He was going to be *the* pitcher on the team. Right-hander, and he had everything."

In January 1944, J&L—which had already scooped up fifty-two more Aliquippa High boys, age sixteen and up, for war work—put out the call for more. The job required a six-hour workday, five days a week, and bent the schedule around the school day. For most, it was voluntary duty. For Joe Letteri, sixteen now and flailing in seventh grade, there wasn't any choice. Both his older brothers had left in '42, one to serve as a gunner on a supply ship in India, the other in the antitank corps in Europe. Joe's dad sent him down to the mill to do grunt work weekends and holidays, at 68 cents an hour. When the school year ended in June, he dropped out and began a forty-year stint at J&L.

"My father had just got through the Depression and we had a tough time until my two brothers went to the service and I was the only one left," Letteri said. "I went to work to help out. We didn't have nothing."

He took home $21.76 for his first pay, for four days of work, and handed his father the envelope. Achille Letteri handed Joe back a dollar. From then on, every two weeks, the routine was the same. "I didn't even open it," Joe said. "He'd give me whatever he felt like giving me. I didn't take my first pay until 1946, when I went into the service. I stuck the pay in my pocket and left."

World War II was as much a war of production as a battle of wills, and Roosevelt's "Arsenal of Democracy" now hit full stride. In March 1943, Aliquippa's blooming mill rolled a world-record 171,440 tons of ingots (individual molds filled with molten metal weighing from hundreds of pounds to hundreds of tons); a single crew rolled an unprecedented 512 during one eight-hour turn. J&L's three main works fabricated beams and channels for ships and submarines, the walls and decks of the LSTs—landing ship tanks—for the assault on Europe. But only the Aliquippa Works could produce the Navy-designed "Steel Box"—a lightweight, 5-by-7-by-5-foot watertight container of impressive versatility. First used as portable piers in that year's invasion of Sicily—allowing troop landings where none had been possible—Steel Boxes could also be used as troop causeway, ferry for supplies and men, containers for precious water.

Steel mills don't get the Medal of Honor, but in 1943 the Aliquippa Works was awarded its equivalent: the Army-Navy "E" for excellence, "for distinguished service on the first line of defense." A pennant was raised over the grounds, and every worker received a silver "E" lapel pin. "This war is not merely the Army's war and the Navy's war," said Lieutenant Colonel John S. Swauger in a January speech to 5,000 workers. "It is being fought right here in Aliquippa, with milling machinery and engine lathes, calipers and micrometers, open hearths, blast furnaces and rolling mills."

Beyond the tunnel, the streets and air hummed with comings and goings. Early in 1944, Wes and Myrtle Dorsett arrived from Pittsboro, North Carolina, and moved into Aliquippa's Mount Vernon pocket, in a house just wide of the borough line. The local draft board reclassified Pete Suder—three years a mainstay with the Philadelphia Athletics, wintertime hand in the blooming mill, father of two—"I-A": available for unrestricted military service. High school halls and rosters were decimated by the steady departure of eighteen-year-olds, the last cluster leaving Lippe particularly shaken.

At the end of January, Lippe had walked another group of soon-to-be-soldiers to the Aliquippa train station. His basketball team had gotten off to a 4-0 start, with a game looming against Moe Rubenstein across the bridge. When Lippe tried to say some comforting words, the boys cut him off. "Don't worry about us," they said before boarding. "Just beat Ambridge."

The night of the game, Lippe gathered his Quips in the locker room and gave a teary-eyed speech relating the trackside scene, the young soldiers' words, his fierce emotions, the need to win. Then his team walked out onto Rubenstein's court and played passionately and well—and lost another heartbreaker, 56-54.

Take your left hand, palm up, cupped as if holding sand. Hold it against your gut and look down. This is your relief map of downtown Aliquippa in the spring of 1944. Riding along the ball of your thumb is Franklin Avenue, rounding past St. Titus Church. Veer off to the right, and rise to the top of your little finger, and you come to the highest point in town: the seventeen-year-old high school, jammed with students, and its seven-year-old football stadium. Stay left on Franklin and follow the lifeline for less than a mile, past the stately library built by company largesse, the five-story company store, the three dozen bars, overflowing. Aliquippa, population pushing 30,000-plus, was like any other place in America then. Everybody was waiting for the endgame.

The war in Europe had turned for good, it seemed, but the final push promised horrific losses. No blue-star family could escape the dread; a son's or father's or husband's fate hinged on timing, location, or the mocking lottery of pure dumb luck. In June of 1944, Mike Ditka of the A&S Railroad turned twenty-six: eligible even with a wife and two sons—four-year-old Michael and three-year-old Ashton—to be drafted. He went into the Marines, spent the rest of the war mostly at Camp Pendleton near San Diego, sent home $100 a month.

"He didn't get in the war," said his wife, Charlotte. "He got a vacation from me and his kids."

Without Toats DiNardo, Aliquippa High's baseball team tried to make do. Pete Suder's brother George, the youngest of thirteen, was a lank and feisty shortstop invited more than once to work out with the Pirates at Forbes Field; by summer he would be cursing out a badgering Honus Wagner (Wagner laughed) and meeting with Dodgers owner Branch Rickey in Brooklyn. Coming off two also-ran finishes in the WPIAL playoffs, "Juke" (everybody had a nickname) smelled a chance for the school's first-ever title in anything. He went to Nate Lippe and offered to move to the mound.

"You ever pitch before?" Lippe said.

"Never in my life," George said.

"What makes you think you can?"

"I've seen the rest of your pitchers."

Suder carried Aliquippa that '44 season, yet the coach made all the difference. Even with Moe Rubenstein retired from coaching baseball, Ambridge remained the most vexing puzzle—and here, at last, Lippe had the answer. In the season's second game, the Bridgers crushed Aliquippa, 8-0, the go-ahead run coming from left fielder—and Aliquippa High dropout—Alfred Sullivan. Suder started the next game, one-hitting Beaver Falls, and didn't give up the ball the rest of the season, winning seven of the Quips' final eight games. However, in his best performance, he struck out 16 yet lost, 2-1—to first-place Ambridge, of course.

In most other years, that would've ended Aliquippa's shot at a sectional title, much less bragging rights. But Lippe cannily filed a protest—the umpire wrongly awarded an Ambridge player first base after he'd been hit with a pitch on a swinging third strike—and got the result tossed. Ambridge coach Jack Burns confidently agreed to replay the game. But two weeks later, Lippe struck again, tipping off WPIAL officials to an open secret: Sullivan had never left Aliquippa; the home address he gave in Ambridge was a vacant lot. Caught, Ambridge High declared Sullivan ineligible, and forfeited two wins—including the 8-0 romp over Aliquippa—to concede the season. It may not have come on the field, but few of Lippe's victories tasted more delicious.

Not that the town noticed much: Sports hadn't yet assumed an outsized place in American life, and weren't about to gain much purchase with a war on. Suder's parents didn't see Juke play once that season. The team had nothing close to state-of-the-art gear; players wore jerseys emblazoned not with "Aliquippa," but "Celtic" or "Red"—hand-me-downs from the local Celtic Reds social club. Aliquippa entered the WPIAL playoffs 6-1, but even the most intense players knew that their preoccupation was a secondary thing, just one playful piece in a world dominated by the mill and the union, the bars and churches, the endless parsing of overseas news.

Juke had two brothers off in Europe—Pete, the oldest, building pontoon bridges in the engineering corps, and Ted, two years younger, serving in one of George S. Patton's tank destroyer units. Buddies like Nick "Ninnie" Vuich, first baseman on the '42 Aliquippa team, and DiNardo were somewhere fighting, too. "I'd wait for a letter from them," Suder said. "I was writing to two or three of my friends in the service that got killed. I remember one, getting a letter back and it was stamped on there, 'DECEASED.' That's the way I found out that he was gone."

Suder threw a three-hitter with eight strikeouts to beat Leetsdale, then gave up just two hits to shut down Mt. Lebanon in the semifinals.

In the two weeks before stepping onto the mound in the championship game at Forbes Field, against Charleroi, he took his Navy physical and passed. The game was set for June 5; a reporter for Aliquippa's *Evening Times* promised Suder front-page coverage if the Quips won.

There was no team bus. Gas and tire rationing were in full swing, so players cadged rides into Pittsburgh in individual cars. Usually they dressed at home, but this was the championship, a major league park: They brought their uniforms and changed in the Pirates clubhouse like big leaguers. Aliquippa second baseman Jack Cable had lost his cleats en route, sparking a mini-crisis, but Pirates All-Star infielder Frankie Gustine happened to be knocking around Forbes that day. He lent the kid a pair.

The Pirates' thirty-five-year-old home field was, by then, a beloved if creaky venue, its cavernous dimensions accentuated by the expanses of empty seats. The public address system wasn't used for high school title games; the hand-operated scoreboard sat untouched. "The only insignificant phase of the proceedings was the fact that the fray was played in comparative secrecy," wrote *Evening Times* scribe Nick Wallace. "Barely 200 fans had mammoth Forbes Field to themselves."

The turnout, Wallace added, "points up, as never before, the complete lackadaisicalness of local sports followers." It's like Joe Letteri said: *We didn't know what was going on.* No one figured this for the beginning, the moment when the town's talent began to show like some gleaming pocket of ore.

It didn't matter. Suder took the mound cocky; pro scouts had come to watch him. "First guy up was probably the second baseman, he must've been five-foot-two, and I said, 'Hell, I'll blow this fastball by him. . . .'" Suder recalled. "I throw that ball in there: *vooom!* He hits a line drive single. Next guy come up, he wasn't no bigger. Same thing— another line drive single. I said, 'Oh God, here we go. . . .'"

Aliquippa won, 9-1. Suder ended up having the game of his life: hit two doubles, went the seven-inning distance on the mound, struck out three, and limited Charleroi to five hits. For the final out, he easily fielded a slow roller and trotted to first, where his buddy Rudy Neish was waiting. Suder could've stepped on the bag himself, but why not share the wealth? He flipped the ball to Neish and the Red and Black, the Quips, the Steelers were WPIAL champs at last. There were a couple handshakes, maybe a hug, but no dogpile on the field. That wasn't done.

Instead, the team stayed in Pittsburgh to celebrate and take in a show at the palatial, blazingly lit Stanley Theater. Schmaltzy showman Ted "Is Everybody Happy?" Lewis and his orchestra performed one of his most famous bits, a soft-shoe rendition—with a black man imitating, in perfect synchronization behind him, his every step—of "Me and My Shadow." Nobody found it offensive: The top-hatted duet brought down the house.

When the boys straggled home to Aliquippa that night, there was no crowd waiting. Next morning the championship was an afterthought: News from Normandy was all over the radio, and the above-the-flag headline of that afternoon's *Evening Times* screamed, "CONTINENT INVADED." The only mention of the win was buried within a wrap-up story on the city: "Next to the invasion, the most discussed subject in town today is Aliquippa High's WPIAL baseball titlists. 'At last we broke the ice,' seems to be the general consensus of opinion.'"

Two days later, Aliquippa's catcher, Joe Branchetti, left for the Navy. Suder spent his summer waiting for orders, working some at J&L. The town's latest losses trickled and then rushed in over the harried months: The first local D-Day casualty, John Kaurich, a former Quips football player, died on June 7. Late in July came news that Ninnie Vuich, the first baseman, died of wounds suffered in a glider crash in France. Toats DiNardo was still alive then, with the 94th Infantry Division, readying to plunge across France in a tank with Patton's Third Army. By year's end he'd die, too, blown apart by a shell inside his tank at the Battle of the Bulge.

Still, even as families braced for the worst kind of telegram, everybody knew what D-Day meant. It was the last corner turned: The war would be won, maybe even soon. Meanwhile, people were suddenly eating well, flush with money. War work had swelled the population by 6,000; one prediction had Aliquippa hitting 50,000 if enough housing could be built. In July of '44, J&L announced it would spend $7.5 million to build 106 by-product coke ovens and increase capacity by 50 percent.

For decades, most townfolk had been told where to work and live and what to think by forces more powerful than they; now Aliquippa bristled with a pent-up, jazzy vim. The American Century was about to hit its stride. Teens began believing that, unlike their fathers and uncles, they just might control their fate. The dank streets seemed almost lovely. "Oh, my God: what a beautiful place," Suder said. "It was great. Honest, we used to go down on Franklin Avenue just a few blocks from where we lived, walked up and down and ordered a bag of peanuts maybe, stop for some ice cream or something. Every night we would walk up and down the avenue. Every store was booming. It was a boom town."

And soon all the bad war news, all the faraway killing and dying, would stop. The best days were coming. You could feel it.

PART TWO

October 14, 2011

. . . . *So there's an ESPN crew here tonight, a few local scribes, a writer from a national magazine, and a stream of a few thousand people ignoring the day's lashing rain. The reward is Aliquippa's biggest home game of the season, a glimpse of sun, a suddenly blueing sky. It's getting past 6:30 p.m., pregame drills just finishing, when defensive co-ordinator Dan "Peep" Short—massive, alert, poetically profane, and wielding a menacing five-foot staff of polished oak—pops out the field house door and into the home end zone.*

Standing there is Tommie Campbell, the latest Quip to make good. In 2005, Campbell was the area's Athlete of the Year, winner of the state title in the 100-meter dash, a can't-miss speedster with a full scholarship to play football at the University of Pittsburgh. Then he slept his way out of Pitt, blew a second chance at a smaller college, and ended up swabbing toilets as a night-shift janitor at Pittsburgh Airport before, essentially, waking in the nick of time. Now, just turned twenty-four, Campbell is a Tennessee Titans rookie with a four-year, $2.09 million contract, come back home to bask some.

Everyone knew Campbell would be here. Short, though, seems oddly startled. Campbell played for him, even wore the number 29 in honor of his coach's own uniform number at Pitt. Yet, at the sight of him, the coach cuts the volume on a persona usually set on full blast. It's a remarkable reduction of self: You could spend a year in Aliquippa and never once hear Peep Short described as shy. Then again, in a town where nearly every person can claim a bond of blood or circumstance with the next, no relationship may be more complicated than Campbell and Short's.

"How you feelin', Tommie?" he says.

Campbell keeps his eyes fixed on the field. He doesn't smile. The voice, when it comes, is full of ice. "Like a million bucks," he says.

Quips are trotting off the field now. They brush past the two men, their socks and gloves colored, for one night, fight-against-breast-cancer pink. Mess with the team's traditional black, red, and white? It seems sacrilegious, at least in the awkward silence that has now gone on three beats too long. "Why're you wearing pink?" Campbell says finally.

"Times change, Tommie."

Campbell stares at the emptying field as if it's on fire. "Man," he says, "Aliquippa ain't changed for fifty years. . . ."

"No," Short says. "It's changed."

Campbell takes another shot, a sharp, quick jab. "Same defense," he says.

"Why change the defense?" Short says. "We keep winning championships."

Short turns, follows the last straggler inside. Benches, battered steel lockers: Fifty-eight large young men jostle about, brewing up that fine sporting stench of polyester, sweat, and nerves frayed to hair-trigger sensitivity. Players pass around a Sharpie to scrawl memorials on the white tape choking their wrists." RIP Mom"; "RIP DLR"; "RIP Gram"; "T.D.W," "BDB," "WOO." Some players are jabbering, some stare at the floor; one senior is crying. Now a coach grunts. The players stand as one and, ignoring the central door leading straight out to the field, file out a side entrance for the presentation.

"The only time we go out that door," says assistant coach Timmie Patrick, nodding at the portal below the handmade wooden sign WE RULE OUR HOUSE, "is to kick someone's ass."

Aliquippa is a young team this season, its most talented cohort the tenth-graders who've been studied and pushed by the town since they began playing Little Quips ball at five years old. Game nights, it has long been school tradition that the starters' names be called by the public address announcer, punctuated by the school band's drumbeat—three hits—and cymbal crash, as the player runs on-field with a cheerleader on his arm. As much as its old-time offense, this is the nearly all-black, rap-animated squad's firmest connection to Aliquippa football's square, white roots. No one calls it corny. In fact, this moment—those three drumbeats, especially—remains the siren call for any youngster toting a ball on Aliquippa ground.

"We called it 'dunt-dunt-dunt,'" says Mike Warfield, a former Quips quarterback. "It's unspoken, but everybody wanted to get called out with the cheerleader." Lately, the expression has expanded beyond football. Drug dealers, cops, anybody who's been raised in town knows it as shorthand for recognition, respect, Aliquippa's be-all and end-all. "I get my dunt-dunt-dunt whenever I drive into the city," says incoming mayor Dwan Walker. "Swear to God, goose bumps on my arm. I ride down Franklin Avenue, I see the City Building, I feel like I'm getting my dunt-dunt-dunt."

There's no cheerleader on the arm tonight. Each senior runs out alone onto the field, crashing through a paper banner at midfield, where, on the other side, parents or sisters or brothers wait to bid him goodbye. "It's nice," says assistant head coach Sherm McBride, standing at the 5-yard line. He had his own such moment back in 1980, and for a second, watching them pass one by one, he seems unusually touched by the sight. Yes, someone agrees, it is kind of beautiful.

"No," McBride says. "Just seven seniors. THAT's nice." In other words: forget tonight, fool. Tonight's nearly past. Seven seniors means we're stocked deep for next season.

The PA announcer directs the crowd's attention to one corner, where Campbell, in a blue checked shirt and preppy shoes, stands now with Jon Baldwin, a rookie with the Kansas City Chiefs. "Two former Quips," the voice booms, "making their mark in the NFL!" Baldwin wears all black—jeans slung below his ass, T-shirt, baseball hat tilted at a rakish angle. He, too, is known for the path just missed: A derailed football career set his dad adrift for years on Aliquippa's mean streets; his half brother is serving twenty to forty years in prison for the 2001 murder of an Aliquippa police officer. The two pros grin and wave. Their mothers rise amid cheering, eyes wet, feeling something like victory.

When the team files back into the field house for its final pregame prep, a senior, Davion Hall, sits on a bench, drops his head in his hands, and doesn't move. One by one, his teammates pass, placing a hand on his head, his back. McBride leans into his ear, whispers, "This is your last game. Play hard. Go hard like you do. . . ."

Just before game time, head coach Mike Zmijanac—sixty-nine years old, 6-foot-1 when he doesn't stoop, walrus-mustached, with a mop of white hair and a habit of christening his players with lifelong nicknames like Sauce, Mouth, City, Dreads, The Big Russian, and Pimp—calls for the team to gather in. Players circle and drop to a knee; Coach Z draws himself up, towering now like a lighthouse in a sea of black. The walls thrum with the band's relentless drumming. The expanding bustle of the crowd, louder by the second, sounds like high tide coming in.

"The reason all these people are here today is not because of you," Zmijanac says, *voice deep and oddly self-echoing, as if rising from the bottom of a well.* "It's because of all the people who came before you—and all the people you owe for what you wear on your shirt. I keep reminding you: You want to make your own legend, you want them to come back because of you and what you did? It's strictly up to you and us to do it: make our own legend. Play hard, take care of the ball, pay attention to what you're doing and play the game the right way—the Aliquippa way. That's why it says that on your shirt. Play hard. Get after their ass. . . ."

"Come on, baby!" *McBride shouts.* "It's on! It's on, it's on, it's on!"

Zmijanac lowers his head. "Our Father . . . ," *he begins, and dozens of voices chime in,* ". . . who art in heaven, hallowed be thy name . . ." *and the prayer rushes as always to its mumbling end, followed by players shouting,* "Quips on three: one, two, three . . . QUIPS!"

Now they pour out the main door, each throwing up a hand to slap the sign. A man dressed as an Indian rides a horse named War Eagle to the center of the field and flings a flaming spear into the turf. War Eagle delays kickoff by dropping a shit on the grass, but no one in the stands seems to notice. Old, young, white, black, monied or desperate, criminal thinking about a score, ex-steelworker with aching knees, ex-teacher wondering which students will survive: it doesn't matter. In the final seconds before kickoff, they're all charged with that same old thrill. John Evasovich wanders up the sideline, eyes wide.

"You'd think, coming to games here since 1948, I wouldn't get excited— particularly having played," *he says, throwing up his hands.* "But I do. . . ."

The good things are football, kindness, and jazz bands.

—George Santayana

5

A War Game

Jackie showed him how. Jimmy Frank had heard of the man, of course; by the time June rolled around, Jackie Robinson's day-to-day shredding of baseball's color barrier had become part of the national conversation. And that was the general idea when Jimmy's oldest brother took him to his first-ever major league game at Pittsburgh's Forbes Field: to live the phenomenon, see the social pioneer. Witnessing the first display of Robinson's unmatched daring was a bonus.

It was June 24, 1947. Jimmy Frank was sixteen then, old enough to know what the ballplayer faced. By then he'd learned to sit in the balcony of Aliquippa's theaters, separated from the whites in the prime seats below. He'd already been driving his dad's truck for years, delivering coal and ice, cleaning trash out of the shops on Franklin Avenue—the Kroger, the Giant Eagle—hauling bushel baskets of ashes out of the basement of the tony Woodlawn Hotel down near the train station. In winter, they'd sprinkle ash on icy streets and sidewalks for traction. He would eat at the Station Lunch. It was the only restaurant downtown where blacks were allowed.

"You accepted those things," Frank said. "We couldn't stay at the Woodlawn Hotel: we could clean it up and clean the ashes and all, but we couldn't stay there. But we didn't protest, we didn't try no counter-sitting. We just accepted those things."

By 1940, some 3,200 blacks lived in Aliquippa, making up just under 12 percent of the population, their place in the social order like it was in the nation at large: they were third-class citizens, behind the WASP and northern European bosses, the immigrants whose white skin and shortened surnames made assimilation just a matter of time. Still, pejoratives like "Hunky," "Yid," and "Mick" flew as commonly as "Spade" or "Spic" or worse, sometimes among friends. Indeed, among Aliquippa whites, it has become an article of faith that the town's hardships discriminated against no one.

"I never grew up prejudiced," said Mike Ditka, who entered high school in 1953. "I knew black people were different than white people, but what the hell was the difference? Their dad worked right next to mine in the mill. It wasn't like we had anything they didn't have. So I could never understand that."

"Everybody was equal," said Aliquippa High football coach Mike Zmijanac, who graduated from the school in 1960. "All of us—Polish and Serbians, Lebanese and blacks—we grew up together because we all made the same money. All the parents worked in the mill, and they all worked together. There were really no prejudices. I learned to swear in Lebanese and Italian and Greek."

But if he himself was unaffected by bigotry, Ditka wasn't deaf or blind. The area was "very prejudiced," he wrote in his autobiography. "Whether you were a Polack or a Hunky or a Jew or a Dago or a Wop or a cake-eater or colored—we didn't use the other slang word for blacks—it was prejudiced." But then Ditka, by his own admission, led a fairly proscribed existence. One of his high school classmates, Gust

Avrakotos, who would later gain renown as a CIA operative guiding Congressman Charlie Wilson in his "war" to aid the Afghan rebels against the Soviet Union, kept much later hours.

"Each of the Plans had a gang, and they fought like cats and dogs," Avrakotos once said. "Each Plan fought among itself, but when the niggers came we all banded together. You had to be very fucking practical."

In other words, skin trumped ethnicity, push come to shove, and to be black in Aliquippa was to know that you were on your own. Until the mid-1950s, black workers at J&L almost invariably went through the tunnel and took a left toward the North Mill's dirty and sulfurous jobs in the blast furnace and 14-inch bar mill; whites turned right, toward the South Mill's cleaner shifts in places like the seamless tube mill. Restrooms were segregated. White leaders were known to look after whites first, in both the offices of management and at Steelworkers Local 1211, shunting blacks away from clerical or union work to lower-paying, unskilled positions like maintenance and service.

"I knew there was no future," said Eugene "Salt" Smith of his initiation into a ten-year stint at J&L in 1957. "When I got hired, they hired four people—two blacks and two whites. The two blacks were high school graduates, the two whites were nongraduates. One of the blacks was a football star, Richard Blackson; they sent he and I to the labor gang, and sent the two white guys to the special department. They started making, like, thirty-five, forty cents an hour more than us. Right away I said, 'Something's not right.'"

Options were limited. Jimmy Frank—future college president— had just finished his sophomore year and wasn't thinking about college. If a black kid wasn't obviously studious then, the guidance counselors at Aliquippa High directed him toward the trades; Jimmy Frank was taking the "electrical course." He loved basketball and baseball, but big-time sports in the mid-1940s was white-only. His path was heading straight to, as Frank put it, "the hottest place in the world"—a J&L blast furnace.

But then there he sat—with his big brother, Robert, who had followed their dad into the mill—taking in an afternoon ball game on a June Tuesday. They were hardly alone in the right-field stands; 35,329 others had crammed into Forbes Field, too. Robinson was playing first base, as he would all that season, and it was something to see in person—the way Jackie had of walking that line between aggression and control, the lone spot of black in an expanse of green grass, brown dirt, and white faces, without apology.

"He was the crack," Jimmy Frank said. "That gave us impetus, that gave us inspiration, that gave us hope. Jackie Robinson gave us hope that it could happen."

But hope's an abstraction. For a sixteen-year-old kid, nothing provided a more immediate, visceral thrill than Robinson's guts. Pittsburgh pitcher Fritz Ostermueller, a forty-year-old lefty, had fired a rising fastball at Robinson's arm five weeks earlier, a warning shot that drew rallying curses and threats from the Dodgers dugout. Now the score was tied, 2-2, in the fifth inning, with Ostermueller on the mound and Robinson dancing off third base. With the count 2-1, Robinson bolted; Ostermueller flinched and there Jackie went, sliding safe under the mitt of a Pittsburgh catcher named—perfectly—Dixie Howell, with what would prove the winning run. Looking back, no play better summed up Jackie Robinson, Ballplayer, than stealing home. He did it nineteen times in his career. Jimmy Frank was there to see the first.

"The image is very vivid today. I'll never forget," Frank said, sixty-five years later. "He's my hero."

Yet, in truth, what Jimmy Frank and Aliquippa had to learn from Jackie or Branch Rickey or major league baseball was more symbolic than practical. Because even with the racial and ethnic lines and tensions, when it came to the high school and its sports teams the town remained markedly color-blind.

Come summer, you'd see some divisions bubble as high school athletes drifted back into their various social hubs—the Serbian and Ukrainian Clubs, the Sons of Italy, the Celtic Reds for whites, the Quippian Club for blacks—to play for neighborhood and clan. But even there, teams raided each other for talent, looking to field the best lineup regardless of race. Jimmy Frank was tutored in the fine points of baseball by a white Italian, the manager of the MPI (Musical Political Italian) Club team, who didn't even ask him to play. He just wanted to make Jimmy better.

Each fall about a dozen black boys and girls enrolled at Aliquippa High, and when it came time for square dancing in Miss Elizabeth Carver's gym class, blacks were not allowed to dance with whites. For many, that was the first time they'd feel what some dubbed "a racial": blatant prejudice. "She would pick five white boys and five white girls and they would form a circle—and when she gets to the blacks, she would pick five black boys and five black girls," said Salt Smith. "Say there was two black males standing and one white female? You didn't dance." But if you could play—and help Aliquippa beat other towns—neither your color nor the Plan you lived in mattered. You played together.

Within a year after seeing Jackie steal home, Jimmy Frank had developed into a superb infielder himself. He was the only black that summer on Aliquippa's American Legion team, and when it hit the road for a game in Uniontown, Pennsylvania, "we went to this restaurant and they wouldn't feed us because of me," Frank said. "Everybody got up and left." A teammate was a teammate: against outsiders Aliquippa backed its own.

By then, too, sports had regained the heft it had lost in the war years. Peace meant a refunneling of the tribal urge, and the United Steelworkers was consolidating its newfound clout; wars had been won, home and abroad, by the workingman. The town wasn't J&L's alone anymore. Now it belonged to the workingman's sons, too, and investing in the high school football, basketball, and baseball teams was the easiest way to show that ownership, cheer that change. The shift in sensibility was one that some Ellis Island alums couldn't grasp. Sports? A game? Who cares? A job: that's what matters.

Frank Marocco would be the only boy in his family of fourteen to graduate high school; in the early '50s his father, Eleutero, kept pushing him to follow his ten older brothers and drop out and go to the mill or carve tombstones in the family's Logstown memorial shop. But the oldest son, Dominic, a boilermaker, sensed a way for Frank to break out, get an education. For two years, Frank hid the fact that he was playing football. "My father thought I played in the band," Marocco said. "He found out because my junior year, they had my picture in the paper. And my aunt sees me, says, 'Frank's picture!' and calls my dad. My dad says, 'He don't play football, he plays in the band.'

"A boy drove my aunt down to my father's, shows him the picture. I come home from school and my dad: 'Hey, how was band practice tonight?' and my dad was upset and then it was, 'Send him down to the mill! Go to work.' But Dominic told my dad, 'I'm the oldest of the family. He's going to go to school, and if you don't like it he'll come live with me.' And my father backed up."

Jimmy Frank's father wanted him working, too, especially winters, when he'd run the truck out twenty miles to Clinton, Pennsylvania, pick up a load of coal, drive back, and deliver it to homes all over town. "My dad wasn't too much on us playing ball," Frank said. "But of course when we started winning and got some notoriety, then he would tell people he taught me everything. But to keep him happy? If we had basketball practice on a Saturday morning, I would get up five o'clock in the morning, go to the coal mine, get a load, come back and deliver some, go to practice—then after practice continue delivering the coal."

The spring of 1949 showed just how important sports had become. Led by Frank, a cocaptain with his high-scoring teammate, Mickey Zernich, Aliquippa's basketball team went 29-0, easily claimed the WPIAL title, and traveled to Philadelphia to face York for the town's first state championship. Nate Lippe just missed out: After two decades of coaching—and three losing trips to the WPIAL finals—he had resigned the year before over a salary dispute, handing basketball, his first love, over to assistant Sam Milanovich.

Unlike the all-but-ignored '44 baseball champions, for this title shot the town turned out. The *Beaver County Times* sent four reporters, an editor, and a photographer to Philly's venerable Convention Hall, and estimated that more than 2,000 residents traveled east by private cars, chartered buses, and a fifteen-coach special train for the game. A plane was chartered to fly in sixty high rollers, including mill executives, politicians, and bank officers.

Two fans—"Timber" Mayconich and "Scratch" Chalfa—blew long horns to lead cheers, and everybody sang:

Let me tell you, friends of mine:
Aliquip-pa's team is fine!
They're the best in Section Three,
And will go down in his-tory!

The only notable absence, considering that he would attend every big Aliquippa High game for the next fifty years, was Joe Letteri. He'd done his time in the Army, after turning eighteen in 1946, but when he came back home the old rules still applied. Achille was king in his house, Joe's pay went into his pocket, and the job trumped all else. "My father wouldn't let me go," Joe said. "Because if I missed the train or bus, I might miss a day's work. They were that tough in those days."

Jimmy Frank scored five of the first seven points in the 63-51 win, and came home a hero. The players were feted in a Sunday parade featuring fire trucks rolling along Franklin Avenue; 30,000 people packed sidewalks on either side. The next day of school was canceled. The only thing Frank could compare it to was May 8, 1945—V-E Day, when Germany surrendered and he, only fourteen years old, had driven his dad's people-laden truck through streets filled with honking cars, screaming adults, an uncontainable joy.

"We didn't expect that kind of turnout," Frank said. "Sitting on top of the fire truck going down Franklin Avenue and the streets lined with people, waving and hollering and all? Heady experience for an eighteen-year-old."

It didn't make sense that winning a basketball game could feel like the end of the bloodiest war in history, but what was a young man to do? Jimmy Frank waved back.

Such fervor, though, has a way of curdling into expectation, impatience, and soon Aliquippa's nearly led to a big mistake. Carl Aschman was blunt, honest, a daily churchgoer, could boast of a championship from his previous stop, would work into darkness to teach a kid the proper technique—had all the qualities, in fact, that you could want in a head football coach. Except one: he had forgotten how to win. Since being crushed in Aliquippa's first shot at a WPIAL title in '42, the forty-seven-year-old Aschman had kept his teams hovering at just above .500—and, worse, had beaten Ambridge only once. When the 1950 season began shaping up as another mediocre stew, the knives came out.

"They were going to fire him," said town historian Gino Piroli.

No wonder. That year's loss to Moe Rubenstein's final Ambridge team might've been the most embarrassing yet in the schools' rivalry: Not only did Aliquippa surrender the winning touchdown with just twelve seconds left, but on the previous play a substitution error had left Aschman's defense a man short. Some members of the school board tried convincing players to sign a petition backing the coach's dismissal, hoping to replace him with an outsider or an assistant coach. But Aschman had built up plenty of goodwill—running out nightly to fight blazes as a volunteer fireman, cultivating the town booster group known as the "Curbstone Coaches"—and, most important, had never lost the faith of his players.

"They called us into a room in study hall to can Aschman," said Lou Mott, a center on that team. "We all voted to keep him."

Relieved or exultant, the coach didn't show it. His son, Carl Jr., recalls his father being worried about his job, but, he said, "he never discussed things like that, too much, with the kids." Aschman was of a piece with his generation of men, the hard cases who had survived wars, a deadly influenza epidemic, a child's journey into the unknown. Born in a small town outside Istanbul in 1903, son of an Austrian glassblower, he grew up in nearby Charleroi after his father went to work in the factory there. Carl thought he wanted to be a forest ranger, but proved a tough football center, and played well enough at Washington & Jefferson College to earn a spot in the then-prestigious East-West Shrine Game in San Francisco.

He liked to remind his players of that, clapping his hands and, just before squatting into position to demonstrate some nuance, growling happily, "You should've seen your coach when *he* played!"

But heart trouble also ran like a curse in his family, killing his mother and sister young and, years later, his daughter at the age of thirty-one. "Paper heart," the Aschmans joked, but never in public. If anything, Carl carried on as if his were made of steel.

"Some people thought he was nuts, constantly on edge, ranting, raving," said Don Yannessa, who graduated Aliquippa High in 1957. "When I played for him he was an absolute screaming maniac, lunatic. He wasn't physical, but talk about verbal abuse—he could make you feel like a piece of crap and never use a foul word. He'd cut you: 'You don't want to play this game. You don't have any guts—that's your problem!' And you'd just tore a knee cartilage and were still playing and couldn't figure out what he was talking about. He made you feel horrible because you didn't perform well in that practice or that last game. He knew how to push buttons."

But if there was plenty of grumbling about his record, no one complained about Aschman's style. His way—full of arbitrary, wide-ranging authority and dictatorial abuse—was *the* way for coaches then. Press Maravich, the hotshot basketball star for Aliquippa High in the 1930s, returned home to coach his alma mater and teach physical education in 1954, and his strict rules—backed up in class with public smacks delivered by a three-inch-wide paddle—included something called the "Crewcut Club": if you didn't have one, you didn't play.

Frank Marocco was a senior when Maravich took over the team. His hair was already short; dad Eleutero refused to pay for another trim. "Come here, you!" Maravich snarled when he saw Marocco and another player's unshorn heads. Frank protested that his dad wouldn't budge. Press kicked them out of the gym. "So we didn't play basketball," Marocco said. "I hated him for that."

No parent complained. Rough, top-down, sometimes incomprehensible discipline had saved the world, hadn't it? Press had been a Navy bomber pilot in World War II, and the American military, starring outsized egotists like Douglas MacArthur and soldier-slapping George Patton, had conquered Hitler and Tojo, and was now fighting communism in Korea. Its place in American life had never been more celebrated. Soon General Dwight Eisenhower, a former running back and linebacker at West Point who once tackled Jim Thorpe, would move into the White House.

Aschman sensed that connection earlier than most, and wasn't shy about linking his sport—and methods—with a model based upon following orders. "Today's football is a war game and there's no getting around it," Aschman said during a football banquet speech in January 1945. "All that the game is, is a mere forecast of the bigger one yet to come against the enemy.

"America's deadliest disease at the present time is fatigue. People simply tire out too fast and refuse to do anything about it. Yet because of America's love for sports, our boys over there are pressing ahead, ahead and ahead."

Indeed, football could make that analogous leap far more nimbly than basketball or baseball: mud was mud, whether you were a dogface slogging through the Bastogne or a tackle grinding down after down against New Castle. "Show me a line," Aschman would say, "and I'll show you a football team." His ideal offensive line would be filled with "ugly men"—there was no higher compliment—two-hundred-pound human plows who keyed the three-yards-and-a-cloud-of-dust attack that so resonated in a town sustained by three daily shifts of filthy toil.

"When I was a kid you had to be tough," said Marocco, a freshman at Aliquippa in 1951. "Get your ass kicked, you got back up again. You never cried. You didn't complain about being hurt; you went home hurt and cried down in the cellar. That was one of the things: never let people know you're hurt."

He takes a finger, smushes his nose against his left cheek. "I broke my nose in the Ellwood City game, 1954," Marocco said. "We didn't have face masks. Go to block a punt, the ball hit me in the nose, and I blocked it and went in the end zone. I come out bleeding, and my nose is over here and I know because I can *see* it. And [teammate] Pete Fuderich says, 'Shit, you broke your damn nose! Hey, Coach!'"

Aschman approached. "What happened to you?" he asked.

"I blocked the punt with my nose," Marocco replied.

Aschman reached out, centered the nose between his thumbs, and squeezed. Marocco nearly passed out. Aschman told someone to slap gauze on the break, and sent him back in. "So I went back in the game," Marocco said. "That's the way Aschman was."

Not always. Away from the field, he liked the quiet of fishing, an occasional tune; in the weeks before Christmas Aschman was known to trail behind the school's Bach Choir as it made its rounds caroling through the halls, loudly singing along. And he never brought home a loss or a win. When his only son stopped playing football after one fall of junior high ball, Aschman didn't make a fuss. "He didn't push me. He knew I couldn't play," Carl Jr. said.

Jimmy Frank worked for Aschman for four years as the football team's manager. "I didn't think he was the greatest guy," he said. "But my brother loved him."

Four years younger, Willie Frank was born in Aliquippa, too. For his first job, he worked as a towel boy/lifeguard at the colored pool in Plan 11. "I gave my dad my paycheck, twenty-some dollars and fifty cents—and he gave me the fifty cents," Willie said. "He was trying to teach me a lesson: *You go down to the company store down on the main drag, buy your two pair of shoes—one for Sunday and one for the school year? Dad gets ready to get paid and sees three X's. That means the company store got it all.* Man, was I upset about that."

In August 1951, Willie Frank headed to his second preseason camp with the Quips. The team trained at nearby Raccoon Creek State Park, on the remnants of a Civilian Conservation Corps campground, and that two weeks alone on "Camp Site 9" was a test: wood cabins, no fans, bunks with a couple overhead lights, outhouses featuring a wooden plank with five holes. Guys took shits side by side, talking football. A shower was an inverted hose with a sprinkler head.

"Like *Stalag 17*," said John Evasovich. "We would get there and walk down the field and pick out the bricks and rocks and throw them aside. You may have had two or three blades of grass for a while; the rest was mud. Sleep in the cabins—had mattresses that were all of two inches thick; outhouses and a shower. You had nowhere to hang your clothes, no change of clothes, and we would have sweatshirts from the years before for practicing. And they might have six different names on them, scratched out: 'Jones,' 'Yannessa,' 'Pesky,' then your name: 'Evaso-vich.' That was your sweatshirt for the year.

"They'd give you a couple pair of woolen socks that fell down two minutes after you put 'em on. Pair of shoes, canvas pants, and a helmet that weighed three thousand pounds. You practiced twice a day, chalk talk at night. Water was taboo. We'd get it once—line up, and we had this big galvanized thing with a stainless-steel ladle that we would all drink out of. You didn't wipe it off. You didn't bless it. That was your water for the day. Clothes you could barely put on by the third day, they stunk so badly. I think we got a change of clothes the second week—got 'em washed that weekend, put 'em on again. And we wore those goddamned clothes all year."

New players got to join Aschman's "Ghost Battalion"—a sexy name for the squad whose job was to get trampled, day in and day out, by the starters. "Aschman served breakfast, a big bucket of Mother's Oats," Marocco said. "He'd throw it in a dish and a couple pieces of toast, that was your breakfast. Then a sandwich and bowl of soup for lunch. In evenings the Quarterback Club would come out and cook us spaghetti. If you was at the football camp and really hated it? You didn't have the guts to say I'm going home, because the other guys would kick your butt."

Willie Frank had the guts. He did like Aschman better than his older brother, but unlike Jimmy he was less inclined to "accept those things" when he felt slighted by some white person in authority. Willie had gone to camp in 1951 intending to beat out fellow sophomore George Sarris and win the starting quarterback job, and felt good about his chances when Aschman suddenly switched him to halfback. Frank didn't protest. He kept working, felt he was being the ultimate good soldier until, in a meeting, Aschman stunned him by snarling something about "that prima donna Frank over there . . ."

That did it. Frank called his big brother, Robert, and said, "Come and get me. I'm finished." An assistant coach found out, and told Aschman he was about to lose one of his star players. In his later, more secure years, the coach would ignore kids who walked away from his program, no matter how talented. Not then. Aschman pulled Willie aside to explain himself. "I had to find somebody that could take it," he said. "I figured you could take it."

That, too, was an Aschman trait. He seemed attuned to some archaic form of fairness, and if he couldn't roar at students the way he could at players, anyone who came to his ninth-grade history class with notions of being a star there was quickly disabused. "He was a good teacher," said Carl Jr. "He kicked me out once or twice for not having my work done."

A generation later, the shifting of black players away from quarterback to other, more "black" positions came to be seen as one of football's less subtle forms of racism. But Willie Frank, who doesn't hesitate to critique Aschman for playing favorites when it came time to push his kids for college scholarships, thinks need—not race—was the impulse behind his switch to halfback and Aschman's insult. "Black players under Carl Aschman, I think they all got a fair shake," Frank said. The coach was hardly progressive. But he did play at Washington & Jefferson just two years after Charlie West quarterbacked the Presidents in the Rose Bowl, and his results-first attitude in Aliquippa helped bend white sensibilities in a new direction.

"I played my whole life, went to a Catholic grade school, we didn't have one black kid in school," said Ditka. "Went to Aliquippa High, played football, basketball, baseball, and all the (black) guys—Bob Rembert, Johnny Moore—were good athletes, better athletes than I ever thought I'd be, and we never had a problem. A lot of that was because Coach Aschman would say, 'I don't care what color your skin is: Everybody bleeds red.' I can still remember him saying that early on, and I thought, *He's right.*"

So Frank took it, and stayed, and in 1952 ended up anchoring Aliquippa's first great football team. Sarris had a whip arm and in tight end Ernie Pitts a huge, fast-moving target; for the first time in his life, Aschman would see the virtue of putting the ball in the air. But Willie Frank, quick and deceptively strong, led the team in scoring out of a traditional T formation; Zmijanac, who was in fourth grade then, says Frank was as good as any running back he's ever seen. Some, including Willie himself, say he was better than Tony Dorsett.

"They're comparable," Evasovich said. "Willie in his day was bigger than Dorsett and stronger, probably not as elusive and not as fast. But given the style of pro football then, if Willie played he would've been a star as a pro."

The Quips rolled Erie Tech 40-0 in their first game and never looked back; after seven games they'd outscored their opponents 292-19. Against Ellwood City Frank went off tackle and took a helmet to the thigh; the piercing pain left him sprawled on the field. Next thing he knew Aschman was looming over him. "Son, you can run!" Aschman rasped. "Get up!" Aschman then called the same play. Frank shambled some thirty yards for the touchdown, and then limped to the sideline. "I said, 'That's it,'" Willie recalled. "I didn't get in the rest of the game."

Though early crowds were sparse and skeptical, the first half of the season was still unlike anything Aschman or Aliquippa had ever produced, a culminating triumph of the town's ad hoc "system": each Plan's elementary school funneling talent into the all-encompassing hopper of Aliquippa High. The kids—with names like Gill, Tomko, Metropoulos, Monahan, Trbovich, Pitts, Sarris, and Passodelis—had played against, and with, each other all their lives. The familiarity bred far more comfort than contempt. "Once we got to high school we all came together," Willie said. "It was like a family. That's what made that '52 team as great as it was."

But as idyllic as memory can make such things, that team—now dubbed the "Indians"—flirted with danger, too. Late in October, seventeen-year-old Willie Frank took the wheel of his brother Albert's packed Studebaker after a night at the V-2 Club in Aliquippa. Heading up windy Monaca Road, Willie veered onto a soft shoulder, panicked, tried to wrench the wheel back. "The car flipped twice," he said, "right over my head." Frank insists that he didn't start drinking alcohol until the following year. Nobody was hurt; the Studebaker was totaled. "I'm still paying for that," Willie said, laughing. "Every time Albert wants to give it to me, he still lets me know."

Aschman visited him in the hospital, but Frank was clearly fine. Nine thousand people crowded into Aliquippa's stadium to see him open the scoring against Beaver Falls and its star halfback—and future New York Jets head coach—Joe Walton with an 80-yard run; the Quips won 28-7. The next week, Frank rushed for 102 yards and scored two touchdowns against New Castle and Aliquippa won its ninth straight, 18-7. Eight thousand fans filled the stadium for that one, and not even a five-car pileup in the ensuing traffic jam—two dead, eleven injured—could dampen the excitement. An estimated 12,000 filled Ambridge's home to see Aschman get back at the Bridgers, with Ernie Pitts, the gimpy workhorse Nick Passodelis, and Frank all scoring in a 27-13 comeback win.

Aschman had his superstitions. He was Catholic, and if the meatless dinner he ate—macaroni and cheese, fish—before the first game of the season resulted in a win, that was the family's meal for every game night the rest of the year. He wore the same uniform—khakis and a rumpled brown Army parka—on the sidelines, his movie star hair and lined face captured always by photographers in an expression of harried sadness. He didn't dare change a thing for the 1952 WPIAL Class AA—then the league's largest—championship game in Pitt Stadium.

Some 8,000 showed up in the 32-degree cold on November 29 for the Quips' battle against Washington's Little Prexies, Charlie West's old high school team. The chill air and rock-hard field made it anything but the expected blowout; Aliquippa dropped easy passes, found it hard to move the ball, and headed for the locker room at halftime with the game tied, 6-6. Midway through the fourth quarter, fullback George Trbovich, on his third straight rush at the slot over right guard, bulled into the end zone for the go-ahead score. Then Ernie Pitts—the team's best all-around athlete, a 6-foot-3, 205-pound track and baseball star who ran a sub-10-second 100-yard dash and would turn down offers from the Boston Red Sox and Philadelphia Phillies to play college football—caught the conversion that sealed the game, 13-12, ensuring the town's first WPIAL football title.

And with that, Aliquippa's singular take on success began to surface. Because it is neither those scores, nor the fumbles recovered by Aliquippa tackle George Hrubovchak and center Dick Fusco, nor the last-minute, game-tying extra point attempt that Hrubovchak and Fusco broke through to block, that townspeople recall and celebrate now. Instead, when you ask about the '52 team, someone always mentions Willie Frank and how, in the second quarter, he took a handoff on Washington's 28-yard line, ran right, and churned through at least five tacklers to score Aliquippa's first touchdown. It doesn't matter that Frank's ensuing mistake—a bobble while taking the snap on the extra point attempt—prevented the Quips from taking the lead. The idea of unalloyed toughness, of one man fighting off a gang almost single-handedly, jibed best with the town's burgeoning self-image. *One-on-five? We're Aliquippa. We'll take those odds. But you might need a little help.*

"On film I saw eight guys absolutely make solid contact," said Evasovich, who was a twelve-year-old watching in the stands that day. "They couldn't hold on to Willie. Eight guys, we know for sure, hit him. I don't know how the hell he got in the end zone."

There was a parade for that first-ever football championship, of course. "That one year turned it all around," Lou Mott said. Aschman never worried about his job again; that's how it worked in Western Pennsylvania. His was now the biggest name in town. "He was untouchable after that," Yannessa said.

As a baby, as a toddler, into his early teens, Mike Ditka was scrawny. He was the oldest child, and in his first years at the St. Titus Catholic school his mom, the former Charlotte Keller, doted on him, gave him free rein, dressed him like a little lord. The family lived in a four-room row house, an early version of what would later be called "projects," or government-subsidized housing. The joke in the Linmar area was that you visited your neighbor by opening the medicine cabinet.

The kid didn't know how good he had it. Because then World War II ended, and the force that would make Ditka into the football legend, Da Coach, the Hall of Famer, hit his world like a cyclone: His father returned to Aliquippa. "I didn't even know him until I was five years old," Ditka said. "Then when he came home? Shit, I really got to know him with that Marine belt."

The family revolved around the man. Big Mike, just 5-foot-9 but bearing a chippy authority that would serve him well in his thirty-one years as president of Local 1432 of the Transport Workers Union of America, worked daylight shift repairing cars for the Aliquippa & Southern Railroad, the mini-line dedicated to servicing J&L's seven-and-a half-mile-long facility along the Ohio. He'd stop for a drink at Savin's on his way home, and Charlotte kept dinner—and the two boys, Mike and little Ashton, two years younger—waiting. No one sat down to eat until Dad sat down. Little Mike would take in the scars on his father's hands, the burn holes on his sleeves and pants, the daily round of soot on the neck of his T-shirt.

"When he got done, he got up," Ditka said. "We didn't leave: We had to do the dishes, wash and dry. Then we were allowed to go out, but had to be home asleep by seven o'clock. The neighbors would be outside hollering and we'd be up in the bedroom. That's just the way it was. Those were his rules."

But Little Mike had this quirk: he knew the rules. He respected rules. He felt better in a world with rules. Yet he was constantly breaking the rules anyway, seeking out mischief, taking beatings in return. He went to St. Titus for elementary school, served as an altar boy—but there was also the time he stole a Christmas ornament off a tree at the nearby library, the day he beaned a buddy over the eye. Blood, six stitches: The nuns found out, Big Mike found out, the belt came out.

Tomatoes thrown at houses, garbage cans turned over, a kid's glasses broken: Big Mike always found out.

"Nearly burned the woods down," Ditka said. "My dad smoked Luckies, so I stole a pack and with a couple of my buddies, we were in a cement cul-de-sac, woods all over, and we were sitting in there. Smoke Lucky Strikes when you're seven years old and you're dizzier'n . . . So that goes into the weeds and there go the woods. We tried to put it out, the wind's blowin' . . . Finally they did get it out. . . . Firemen came.

"My dad's sitting there having dinner and looks up and says, 'What happened to the woods?' My mother said, 'You'll have to ask your son.' That was it. Boy, I got my ass *whipped.* That was the worst one I ever got. I don't think I've smoked a cigarette since." Ditka paused. "But I do smoke cigars."

The safest place for such a soul, one needing a bit of mayhem mixed into the comfort of defined parameters, is sports. It was a perfect fit: Anything that smacked of competition, Little Mike played with a bottomless fury. Little League officials announced that they'd bestow a ball autographed by Pirates legend Pie Traynor to the first kid to hit a home run? Ditka smacked one in his first game. During a Pony League game, brother Ashton was pitching and Mike catching; after a few walks Mike stalked out and made them switch positions. Then when the shortstop made an error, he took that kid's place, too. Another time, playing Legion ball, Ashton—who'd go on to a fine college baseball career at Bucknell—dropped a game-winning fly ball in center field. Little Mike chased his little brother out of the stadium, jumped the center-field fence, ran him down, and thrashed him before they got home.

"I tell you: It was bad," Ditka said. "And I never felt like I was doing anything wrong—never, ever. I knew others didn't feel the way I felt, but I had tunnel vision. I don't know where you get that competitive feeling; I don't know where it came from. But growing up it started with marbles and all that stuff, playing tag, touch football, stickball—and I hated to lose at whatever it was. You know why? I expected to win. I didn't ever expect to lose. Never. That's why losing was so hard."

That was a new attitude for a town that, by the time Ditka entered high school in '53, had just had its first taste of football glory. Baseball had brought the school's first WPIAL crown, and its basketball teams would regularly compete for WPIAL titles. But Aschman's pulverizing style—the gridiron call for manic, fist-in-the face toughness—resonated with mill families like no clean single or give-and-go ever could, and winning made it irresistible. Football was now preeminent. Just making the high school team became a badge of honor.

"Why? Because that was part of what you were and part of what you were meant to be," said Evasovich, who played a year behind Ditka. "Why would a guy my size be a starting guard in Division III football? I'm not that goddamn good. It's because if you weren't, you'd be embarrassed to come home. I would not come home and tell my father I didn't make first team. Whatever it took—and it took me until my senior year in high school, my senior year in college—that's what *had* to be done. And there were many of me out there.

"You didn't dare embarrass your family, your uncle, your friends, or your neighbors. And they didn't care if you got your ass kicked: *Johnny got his ass kicked, but boy he gave that kid all he had!* That's what it took. And you still hear that, all the time: 'That kid's tough.' 'Tough player.' 'That's Aliquippa.' That's the difference between Aliquippa and Hopewell and Center and some of these other schools. And it's a big difference."

Then again, if you were a skinny, unimposing freshman like 5-foot-7, 135-pound Mike Ditka, no one was really pushing you to join the football team. Little Mike was projected to be a baseball player. But come Friday nights, he could see the stadium lights blazing from his row house on the hill at Linmar: football players were the town's biggest winners. Ditka played third string on the freshman squad. Sophomore year, he was one of the last players chosen to go to camp at Raccoon

Creek State Park, and on one of his first series a lineman leveled him so brutally that his helmet went flying. Aschman, sure that he was going to get hurt, didn't let Ditka practice the rest of camp. He spent his time cleaning the latrines.

That season, Little Mike played jayvee or on the Ghost Battalion, "getting run over like dirt," Ditka said. He'd get up crying, but they weren't tears of surrender. "He cried a lot," said Marocco, a senior star that year, "but when he cried he got meaner."

Ditka would rise up snarling, "Come on, hit me again!" He didn't have to ask them twice.

Aschman liked that. "You could tell," Marocco said. "When Aschman liked you, he would chew you out every day." But Ditka hadn't been around long enough to know the signs; in the spring, he told Aschman that he was quitting to focus on baseball. Aschman responded by saying that he saw something special in him. "You can play," Aschman said. Coming from King Carl, that was encouragement enough.

Ditka worked out endlessly the next eight months, running the hills to and from school, gulping down wheat germ, shaking the house with push-ups. He added thirty-five pounds, pulled some size from Charlotte's side of the family, and pushed past six feet. His curfew was 9:30 p.m. now, and he circled his dad warily—less from fear than a growing distaste. He would later write that Big Mike "was tough with my mom . . . rough with me and my mom. When you see that as a kid, it bothers you. But then in retrospect you understand that he was raised like that, and that's what he knew. I blamed him for a lot. I didn't like him, basically, until I went off to college and lived away from home."

Charlotte didn't like Big Mike's heavy hand, either. "I would've stopped it more if I could," she said. "I would always hope that there was less 'correcting.'" It bothered her just as much when, in the summer of 1955, she saw Aschman lashing into her boy at football camp.

Ever after, Charlotte would be remembered as one of the few in Aliquippa to publicly take on the coach. "What are you always yelling at my son for?" she said.

"Don't worry," Aschman replied. "You'll find out someday."

It didn't take long, actually. By junior year, Ditka had improved enough to become a starter at offensive end and linebacker—an Aschman project made good. "It was all him: he was a magnificent coach, a magnificent man," Ditka said. "When he switched me to end, I hadn't caught balls. So he took me out, made one of those quarterbacks come, and we'd go for half hour to an hour after practice, and he'd throw me routes and teach me how. But it wasn't all catching balls. I was on that two-man sled, the one he called the 'cropper machine.' And I had to block that thing. I blocked it and blocked it, because he ran the ball a lot. He taught me how to block, how to use my body, how to cross-body block—put the dummies up and go.

"He did everything, and he did it over and over. I think about it, and I don't know if there was anybody else with us, just him and I and one other quarterback sometimes. He didn't have to do that. But he did. Whatever he saw in me? I'm glad he saw it."

Still, on a team that sent virtually its entire starting lineup to Division I-A schools like Kentucky, North Carolina State, Toledo, Arizona State, and Southern Illinois, Ditka was considered average. He stood 6-foot, weighed 160 pounds, and didn't score once all year. The star receiver on the '55 team was 6-foot-4 Bob Rembert, who had stepped in to save the freshman Ditka's hide once when a teammate tried to punch him out; and anytime Aschman needed variety, he had quarterback Johnny Sakal fire the ball to the more agile Willie Smith. Ten Aliquippa players would be recognized as all-WPIAL: every starter, that is, except Little Mike.

Publicly, Aschman didn't expect much from the '55 season. With just nine letterman back from a 6-3 campaign, he called out his Indians as "terrible" in the local paper before the opener against Westinghouse, and dismissed their character. "They haven't the desire," he said. Or maybe that was just good coaching. Aliquippa tore Westinghouse apart, 35-0, then beat McKeesport in the rain when Rembert caught a flea-flicker—"32 Crossfire"—touchdown pass from halfback Johnny Moore with ten seconds to play. The Quips cruised from there: 32-6 over Ellwood City, 23-6 over unbeaten Rochester despite a mid-game blackout at Aliquippa's stadium, easy wins over Sharon, Beaver Falls, and Duquesne to set up the usual showdown.

Ambridge came to Aliquippa Stadium on November 11 with all the elements in place for the Bridgers to ruin everything: the WPIAL's leading scorer in Joe Guido, an 18-10 series record against the Quips. But Moe Rubenstein wasn't there anymore. Ten thousand fans jammed in to see the Indians score nineteen straight points in the 26-12 runaway, then lift Aschman up and carry him off the field. All that was left was a meeting with Mt. Lebanon for the WPIAL championship.

It took a while getting there. A three-inch snowfall dropped on the area and postponed the game a week, past Thanksgiving to November 26. Though Mt. Lebanon had been rated higher than Aliquippa all year, the delay gave everyone enough time to figure out that Aschman's roster and his shuttling of two quarterbacks and what he termed an "eight-man backfield" was now unstoppable. Aliquippa was named 13½-point favorites. Which only made it that much more stunning when the Mounties took a 13-0 lead into the fourth quarter.

Sakal then engineered the team sixty yards in five plays, and Ditka had his big chance. He caught a short pass near the end zone but was tackled at the 1-yard line; six decades later he was still hearing his teammates' catcall: "Why didn't you *score?*" But Jimmy D'Antonio grabbed that prize with a 2-yard run, and the rest of the day's heroics unfolded in a most predictable way. Down 13-7 with three and a half minutes to play, the Quips lined up at their own 22-yard line. Six thousand Aliquippans filled the stands at Pitt Stadium, many of them sharing the same thought: *McKeesport.* Sam Milanovich, coach of Aliquippa's

'49 basketball champs and now the town's superintendent of schools, peered down from the press box.

"This is the time for the 'Crossfire' pass," he said.

Aschman complied. Again Rembert took off streaking down the left sideline, again Sakal pitched, again Johnny Moore took the ball, ran right, stopped, and hurled it across the field. Estimates figured the pass for at least fifty-five yards in the air. Rembert gathered it in at the Mt. Leb 39-yard line, shrugged off two defenders, and rumbled into the end zone. Willie Smith coolly kicked the point-after for the 14-13 lead. Fans flooded the field and tore down the goalposts, with time remaining on the clock. They had it right, though. Play resumed, Aliquippa's defense held, and the undefeated Quips had their second WPIAL title in four years.

"I don't think I have a fonder memory of high school," Ditka said.

The team rolled home from Pittsburgh on a bus through all the river towns, all the accompanying cars with their lights on, beeping away. As they passed through Ambridge, en route to the bridge and the river separating it from Aliquippa, the players hung out the windows to rub it in, shouting, "We're the champs!"

Aliquippa High was indeed the undisputed heavyweight champ of Beaver County. It had the area's largest population, its biggest employer, its most accomplished high school, and now the best football program. Students from next-door Hopewell High had grabbed a chunk of goalpost in the after-game melee at Pitt Stadium: The following Monday, they showed up at Aliquippa's pep rally and presented it as tribute. With three titles in hand, Aschman was now truly the WPIAL's "King Carl." The town was flush enough to reward him with a new 1955 Plymouth—painted, of course, Quips red and black.

"Even with the victory celebration, trouble was at a minimum," the *Beaver Valley Times* reported that late November afternoon. "Aliquippa police reported very few disturbances over the weekend." The place had reached a moment of civic equipoise, a rare balance of ambition, security, and achievement. Some might have called it peace.

6

Father Backs Up

Consider the phrase "Workers' Paradise." For most it's a contradiction that, throughout communism's decidedly earthy run, was impossible to take seriously. Yet perhaps the final irony of Karl Marx's vision, the ideal that spawned the Paris Commune, Lenin, Stalin, Mao, Castro, endless Red Scares, Senator Joseph McCarthy, and the Vietnam War, is that for a time nowhere came closer to realizing it than profit-driven company towns like Aliquippa.

Most there, of course, would have paled at the notion. Yes, postwar Aliquippa was hard-core Democratic, thick with New Deal true believers. But for four years the town had pumped out the weaponry and sent off its youth to die for the American Way; as late as snowy January 1949, sacrifices like Johnny Reft were still coming home in sealed coffins. To suggest any link with the Cold War foe whose iron curtain had clanged down over their relatives' lives, who then claimed 37,000 more American war dead in Korea, was to invite a punch in the face.

Yet this was the era when locals began describing J&L fondly, and downtown as "lovely"; the idea of smoky, clamorous Aliquippa as a blue-collar standard was taking hold. In 1953 the domestic steel industry, with J&L its fourth-largest producer, employed 650,000; J&L was spending $676 million in a decade-long drive to expand capacity by 35 percent. By the end of the '50s, the Aliquippa Works employed some 15,000 employees—13,550 of them hourly, unskilled to semiskilled workers whose entry qualifications were little more than a clean police record and the ability to endure monotonous, hazardous work.

Aliquippa's population stabilized at just over 26,000 after World War II. After the close of Ellis Island as the prime immigrant gateway in 1954, the best place to find a cross-sample of the nation's newest citizens was on a shop floor; locally run, union-backed "Americanization" programs, mandated in more than thirty states, only sped the melting pot's boil. Saturdays at Aliquippa High, five instructors taught immigrant children and adults English and "the customs and ideals of a new land," and prepared them for the naturalization exam. Runoff from the war—the broken and displaced—flowed for years.

"Between 1946 and 1950 there was a dramatic influx of Europeans," wrote Aliquippa schools superintendent Lytle Wilson of his system's population. "Americanization classes were filled to capacity. Young boys and girls from Europe came at the rate of four and five a month. They came from Italy, Greece, Yugoslavia, Czechoslovakia, Syria, Rumania, and Portugal. Three came from concentration camps. Evening classes were comprised of adults over forty years of age. From 1949 to 1950 the classes prepared for citizenship two hundred immigrants between the ages of nine and sixty-two. Twenty of these had come from German concentration camps; many had a fine educational background, and were lawyers, teachers, engineers, architects. They represented Russia, Hungary, Germany, Italy, Greece, Poland, Czechoslovakia, Yugoslavia, and Ukrania."

But this was a headier, more cynical mix than the one that had built the town two generations before, and decidedly less docile. Indeed, the war only completed what labor's New Deal victories had begun. Gone was J&L's iron grip over the town's politics, police, and planning, as well as any sense of noblesse oblige. In its despotic prime, the company had built streets and infrastructure, a quaintly gorgeous library, a slew of ball fields and recreational facilities. Then, in 1940, chairman of the board H. Edgar Lewis announced in the *Aliquippa Gazette*, "The days when J&L would build swimming pools, homes and public buildings and present them—complete and wrapped in an attractive package—to the people of Aliquippa are over."

Meant as an on-high pronouncement, Lewis's statement was actually an acknowledgment of a new reality. The combination of progressive politics, the Supreme Court, and national emergency had forced American industrialists to accept a partnership—often hostile, and increasingly unequal—with labor. War's end unleashed grievances bottled up by years of no-strike pledges, and a wave of industrial walkouts nationwide. In January 1946 some 750,000 steelworkers struck for an 18½-cent-per-hour wage hike. Three weeks later, management caved.

In June of the following year, a Republican Congress tried rebalancing the scales. Enacted—over President Harry Truman's veto—as a corrective to the Wagner Act's wholly pro-union provisions, the Labor-Management Relations Act sponsored by Ohio Senator Robert Taft and New Jersey Representative Fred Hartley outlawed union practices such as secondary strikes and the "closed shop" requiring union membership for employment, and banned communist leanings in union leadership. Most dramatically, Taft-Hartley empowered the president to step in, with the legal might of strikebreaking injunction, if an impending or ongoing strike was deemed a threat to national interest or safety.

Union heads declared Taft-Hartley a "slave-labor law," and spent much of the next decade fruitlessly pushing for its reform or repeal.

But their rhetoric was continually undermined by an age of prosperity: Between the rebuilding of Europe and Japan, steady U.S. military spending, and a booming U.S. auto industry, the demand for steel I-beams, welded tubes for water lines, seamless tube for oil and gas pipe, wires for bedsprings and field fencing, tin cans, pails and nails, fenders, tailpipes, and other car parts seemed limitless. For steelworkers the end of every three-year contract brought another nationwide strike, and victory. Their six-week action in 1949 won funded pensions and health care. A fifty-three-day walkout in 1952, marked by Truman's illegal seizure of the steel industry, landed significant wage and benefit hikes and recognition of the union shop. Thirty-four days out in 1956 earned the rank-and-file 45 cents more per hour and guaranteed 80 percent pay a year during layoffs.

J&L, meanwhile, had come a long way since the kidnapping of Georg Isasky. Its new chairman, Admiral Ben Moreell, had made his name as commander of the "Seabees," the Navy combat construction battalion legendary for its harried production of airstrips, docks, and roads in the Pacific Theater, before taking over J&L in 1947. Though deeply conservative, Moreell welcomed unions, considered unilateral management corrupting, and called United Steelworkers president Philip Murray "a true friend." Because the current labor situation was "so bad that we must experiment," Moreell once wrote, he was even open to some form of worker participation in management—the so-called Scanlon Plan of tying labor incentives and bonuses to company performance. Big Steel leadership and J&L's executive committee—suicidally, it would turn out—had no interest.

It's no coincidence that J&L workers often say that their strikes in the '50s were directed less at the company than the industry at large. During Moreell's eleven-year tenure, J&L emerged as a far more benign force in Aliquippa and, despite all its tough declarations, never ceased being a benefactor. Indeed, the company is universally remembered warmly today because it managed, in its retreat from absolute power, to create a sense that it cared about its workers as more than mere employees.

"J&L made us all middle class," said Gino Piroli, who began his twenty-two-year stint at the Aliquippa Works in 1946. "I always say they were our big brother, because if you needed a bandstand for the Italian festival? They built it. Memorial Day? They built the bandstand for the ceremonies. You needed a flagpole; they'd give you the flagpole. They really looked out for the people. After the union got in, they were more generous to the people. They weren't a 'benevolent dictatorship' then."

Nothing better demonstrated that the two antagonists could unite for a common good than the building of Aliquippa Community Hospital. Pushed by the indefatigable Nick DeSalle, an Italian immigrant and former J&L steelworker, the company agreed to sell the town thirty-three acres of land for $1 and give another $1 million in matching funds if DeSalle could first come up with the base. Each payday for the next twenty-five months, J&L workers pitched in whatever amount they could. Some 13,934 hands made donations totaling $2.3 million. In May 1957, the hundred-bed facility opened, but not before thousands lined up to tour the gleaming halls and rooms to see what, exactly, they'd all pulled off together.

And why not? It was a civic triumph, truly collaborative, and hard proof that J&L wasn't the only entity capable of making the town better. Labor's rise as the town's countervailing force was now cemented on a hill in New Sheffield. It seemed there was nothing that collective action couldn't accomplish—ensuing hospital additions would expand capacity to 204 beds—nor any reason to think that the good times would end. And thus, for one short generation, the worker class in Aliquippa, and nationwide, would have its golden age.

At first glance, such a dreamy term hardly seems apt. Yet when you hear whites, especially, speak of the town then as "wonderful" or "beautiful," they're not describing how it looked. They're talking about how Aliquippa made them feel. This is not just because of its three dozen bars, or the money to be made, or the friendly face of the old waitress, Crystal, at the Mill City Inn—though that all helped. You didn't need to take the ride into Pittsburgh for a wedding dress or jewelry anymore; Aliquippa was the de facto capital of Beaver County. And it hummed.

Paydays felt like Times Square on New Year's Eve. On weekends couples descended upon Franklin Avenue from the different Plans. They'd drop kids at the library, get their fishing gear at Sol's, gold rings at Eger's, shoes from S&S, all of it on the car-jammed main street laid out atop the old Logstown Run, where rainwater from the hills gathered into the main sewer line under their feet. In the late '50s Franklin Avenue accounted for 60 percent of the county's retail sales. There were the three movie theaters, a G. C. Murphy, a Dairy Queen, restaurants, drugstores, and soda fountains.

"That drive down there was pretty nice," Ditka said. "I remember when you'd get your car, you'd *cruise.* Just like any other kid in America: You'd cruise in the car, and see chicks, and whatever. . . . We all went through it. My buddy Bobby Joe Rockwell, he was the first one; his dad let him drive the Oldsmobile before anyone had one. Billy Glass: I remember these guys, drive around in those cars. Aah, we thought we were the goddamned cat's meow. We didn't know how many people were laughing. . . ."

It was hardly a life of ease. Strikes drained bank accounts and jangled nerves. The rotation many workers had to make between the day's three eight-hour shifts, or "turns"—one week working 8 a.m. to 4 p.m., the next week 4 p.m. to midnight, the next midnight to 8 a.m.—ravaged sleep and wrecked marriages. The attendant chemicals later unloosed cancers and ills that guaranteed a shorter, compromised life. Yet, for the first time a particular type of man and woman—lower middle class, lacking college education, and with little more to offer than a foreign accent, muscle, and sweat—could stick out a steel-toe boot and gain a foothold on the American Dream. They weren't disposable. They weren't at war with the community; they were a vital part of it. A workingman could make enough now to buy a four-bedroom house for $12,500, take vacation without fear of losing his job, buy a boat, plot retirement. He could send kids to college without needing a loan.

Looking back, Ditka says he came to understand that his dad's discipline instilled a work ethic and self-discipline he otherwise might never have had. Big Mike Ditka, smaller than his oldest son by the fall of 1956, had always seemed satisfied with what was a fine lot. "You have a job with A&S," he'd say, referring to J&L's railroad, "you're set for life."

But that was just the fallback plan. Big Mike's own father had been a burner; he didn't want his four kids working the mill, too. He pushed his son to keep his grades up, keep playing, in hope of a scholarship. The future "Iron Mike" didn't have to be told twice. A high school tour of J&L killed any interest in a job there—and he wasn't alone. In Aliquippa, what was once a ripple had become a tidal change of attitude. Even as the high school population boomed, enrollment in vocational shop courses kept dropping. A mill job was seen less as an end than a means, and the message at home was clear: *I work here, so you don't have to.*

"My dad was what they called a 'scarfer,'" Evasovich said. "They had these large ingots, solid ingots maybe fifteen, twenty, thirty feet long, and they'd come out red-hot and my dad would have to stand there—with wood shoes and clothing that was fireproof and the mask—and if there was any separation he would weld it together with an electric torch. If there was no separation but there was some scrap metal in there, he had a little air hammer and had to dig it out. He was only allowed to work twenty minutes at a time because of the heat and the smoke, the smoke always coming up underneath the mask."

Evasovich's dad went into the mill at twenty-three and left for good at sixty-two. There was no Ambien or Tylenol PM then; Big John would take the edge off with "Mr. Ditka"—as John still calls him—with beers and shots at Savin's, and Johnny would have to go fetch him home sometimes. For burns and wounds—for anything, really, ranging from a paper cut to pneumonia—the half-Serb, half-Croat family would spread on a thick black salve that was thought to cure most any ill. Into his senior year, Johnny was in bed by 9 p.m. He made honor roll or he didn't play ball. He was going to get a scholarship somewhere, his dad said. Johnny worked the wire mill for one summer during high school. That was enough.

"The nail mill, you could only work by signals," Evasovich said. "You'd stand a foot apart and scream and you couldn't hear each other. You would have to put stuff in your ears and if you didn't, you ultimately would be deaf. Dirty, noisy: I began to understand why my dad didn't want me there. I went down to where he worked and was maybe fifty feet away and I was shielding myself from the heat."

The next day, his dad came home from work and John said, "I don't know how you do it."

"That's why you're not going to do it," Big John said.

In the summer of '55, as Ditka was preparing for his junior year of high school, Frank Marocco was readying for his freshman year at North Carolina State. This alone was a family miracle; not only had Frank graduated high school, but he'd be the first male to go to college. To ensure Frank wouldn't give in to fear and, God forbid, stay home, big brother Dominic, a boilermaker high in the union, arranged a miserable summer job sealing oven caps in J&L's tin mill. First day in, Frank opened his lunch box to find his meal melted. After a week of streaming sweat and shoveling endless piles of sand, going away didn't seem so bad.

Frank had had his heart set on playing for Duffy Daugherty at Michigan State—had even been squired around campus there by all-American guard, fellow Pennsylvanian, and future hotheaded coach Frank Kush—but Carl Aschman wouldn't hear of it. A former Aliquippa player, Bill Smaltz, had just become an assistant in Raleigh. "You go down there with Bill," Aschman said. "He'll take care of you." Marocco didn't argue: You did what the coach said. But immediately it seemed like a mistake—too Southern, too few girls—and when Marocco found out that N.C. State planned on redshirting him, that he wouldn't even be playing football for another year, he bummed enough money to buy a one-way plane ticket home.

Smaltz phoned Dominic. When Marocco walked off the plane into Pittsburgh Airport, he was startled to see all thirteen of his brothers and sisters there to greet him.

"What are you doing here?" Dominic said.

"I quit," Frank said.

Dominic held out his hand. "Here's a ticket," he said. "Get back on the goddamned plane at five o'clock and go back down to school. If you don't, you ain't got a family."

Marocco got back on the plane.

Mike Ditka eventually caught that dream like a fever, even if he bristled at the source of it. Nights, he'd come home and tell Charlotte, "Boy, Mom, one of these days I'm going to have four cars, and a big house with a pool. You'll be able to drive it but Daddy can't."

He was different. He was, in truth, a bit crazy. How else do you explain a force like Ditka? There were better athletes, smarter football players, stronger kids to come out of Aliquippa High long before and long after he left, but he was the first to be named first-team all-America in college, the first drafted No. I by an NFL team, the first to score a touchdown in the Super Bowl, the first to coach a Super Bowl–winning team, the first inducted into the Pro Football Hall of Fame. "Ditka set all the standards," Yannessa said. "There's a perfect example of a guy who has this much ability"—he held up two forefingers, five inches apart, and then, grin widening, opened his arms as far apart as possible—"and plays that big."

Ditka had a tough dad? Who didn't? Hell, Ashton had a tough dad, too, and if that was enough to earn him a scholarship to play college ball, it didn't turn Mike's younger brother into a raging clone. No, Mike was sui generis. Aliquippa had the usual share of bad losers, but

Mike treated each setback like the death of a mother. Press Maravich was Ditka's basketball coach from 1954 to 56, and the best player on the court was Press's scrawny son. "A little shit!" Mike said of the future Pistol Pete. "He'd shoot the ball better than anybody on our team when he was eight, nine years old." Press's hard-core methods were, for Ditka, like fuel pumped into an overflowing tank. He'd had the crewcut his whole life.

"Did you ever see a lion jump through a hoop of flames?" Press Maravich said to a New Orleans newspaper in 1986. "That's how Mike was."

And basketball wasn't even his sport. When Ditka showed up at Raccoon Creek State Park for camp his senior year, you could see the difference. The season before, he'd been just another player on the '55 championship team. But now he'd grown two inches, put on twenty pounds. Aschman took one look at Mike's nearly 6-foot-2, 185-pound frame and switched him to fullback. Between the previous year's passing drills and all his running in the fall of 1956, the foundation for Ditka—the man who would revolutionize the position of tight end from a blocker to a dynamic, game-changing pass receiver—was being laid. "I didn't think he was very good until his senior year," said Evasovich, a junior in '56. "Then I thought: *Who the hell is* this *guy?*"

But already Ditka was known as the guy who, when a teammate had his leg broken on a clean hit against Beaver Falls, walked into the opposing team's huddle and threatened to kill them all. Aschman loved that, of course, because such passion couldn't be faked. Some tried. Gone from the '55 team were four of the "ugly men" Aschman so dearly prized, and in the second game of the '56 season Aliquippa traveled to McKeesport and got hammered, 25-6. Ditka began tearing the locker room apart afterward, screaming, berating himself, smashing lockers, throwing anything he could lay his hands on. The rest of the team began doing the same.

Aschman consoled Ditka. The others, he ripped. One boy tried sobbing, "I didn't do a good job! I didn't play hard enough!"

"Don't worry," Aschman snapped. "You won't be in there next week." The message was clear: *Ditka does this. The rest of you don't even try. You're not him.*

The Indians won their next three, but the season was a struggle. Ditka played even better on defense—inside linebacker—burrowing in on every tackle, never quitting. "Oh, my God," Yannessa said. "Mike was a pain in the ass to play with." Down 20-19 to Sharon with little time left and Sharon punting, Ditka was sure that a complicated, rarely used set, where the defensive linemen would somehow crunch the offensive linemen's shoulder pads and neutralize them, would result in a blocked punt, a recovery, a win.

"It was the goofiest thing," Yannessa said. "It only worked in practice and only if the other guy was passive. So Ditka was the linebacker behind us and he's telling us, 'You pull him! And you pull him! And I'll go through there! I'll block that punt!' Well, we don't block the punt, and with forty-eight seconds left we get the football and we don't manage anything and we lose. Now he's on the field, bitching at everybody, bitching at me; he wants to take it into the locker room and I'll never forget, I finally told him: 'Mike, fuck you. You think you're the only guy that hurts when we lose?'" And Ditka glowered, and growled, and finally stalked away.

He wasn't all intensity, though. Ditka was named "Most Popular" in the class of '57—along with his future wife, Margie Dougherty—and was alternately president, vice president, and treasurer of his homeroom, and a member of the astronomy, conservation, fishing, and hunting clubs. As a student he got Bs in English and social studies and Ds in French and math. Two weeks later, on the night before the Duquesne game, Evasovich drove Mike up to Plan 12 to see Dougherty. Ditka tried showboating with a flip off the back porch and ended up tumbling forty feet down a grassy ravine. The next day, sore before the 28-12 loss even began, he still made 80 percent of the team's tackles.

"Might've been the best game I've ever seen a high school kid play," Evasovich said.

But it couldn't save the season. The Quips lost four games in 1956, including an embarrassing, 53-13 finale against Mike Lucci–led Ambridge, with Ditka swarming, taunting, tackling every available Bridgers jersey—only to walk away from his final high school game furious and convinced that the Quips had given in. Scouts were watching. Aschman played favorites, and if he liked a player he would make the calls, cultivate the coaches, pull any string to get colleges interested. If he didn't like a kid? Well, he just didn't. "I was okay, but I had fifty offers—because of him," Ditka said. "Because if Coach Aschman recommended you, everybody would give you an offer. Clemson, Miami, Minnesota, Michigan State, Penn State, Pitt, Notre Dame, everywhere—because of him, not me. Pretty crazy stuff: that's how much he was respected."

The recognition did nothing to diminish Ditka's fire; what's remarkable was just how little such outward signs of success would register. His dad might've looked at sports as a way out, but for Ditka "it was personal," he said. He simply had to be better than everyone else, always, and when his high school football career ended Ditka moved on to basketball. During one game his senior season, with Press Maravich gone on to college coaching, Mike missed a layup, punched the wall in a rage, and broke his wrist. In the summer, when one might have expected him to ease up, to protect his body and psyche for college football, Ditka poured himself into American Legion baseball.

"I was there the day he chased Ash over the center-field fence," said Mike Zmijanac, on a local ball team for the first time then at the age of thirteen. "He scared the hell out of me. He was so big and tough, I was such a skinny little kid. We were playing Beaver Falls late in the year. I was the last guy, probably batting twelfth—last out of the game, couple runners on. If I make an out, we lose; if I get a hit, we win. He told me: 'If you don't get a hit, I'm killing you. I'm ripping your ass.' I'm a right-handed hitter, hit a little looper over the first baseman's head. I was never so glad of anything in my life."

Ditka's parents loved Penn State, if for no other reason than the beaky charm of head coach Rip Engle's top recruiter, Joe Paterno. Mike had committed to the Nittany Lions for the fall of '57 and, up to just a few weeks before the semester began, intended to enroll there. Though Mike was only an average science student, Aschman had latched onto the idea that he should dedicate his college studies to a future spent jamming those meathook hands into people's mouths. "He wanted me to be a dentist," Ditka said.

The idea has been a source of delight ever since. "Mike Ditka as a fucking dentist?" Yannessa said. "You got a better chance of seeing Jesus pulling teeth. Start bitching about the fact he's hurting you and he'll punch your lights out."

Yet dentistry was the hook that the Zernich brothers—Pitt boosters all, including Mickey, the star of the '49 basketball team—used to pry Ditka loose from Paterno. Mike wasn't thinking about playing pro football yet; the idea still was to use sports to pay for college. On August 18, thinking he'd be going to Happy Valley, Ditka joined Aschman and the rest of the Quips at Raccoon Creek State Park for training camp, looking to get in shape for freshman year of college ball. Paterno showed up and stayed three days in the cabins with the rest of the coaches, ostensibly to advise Aschman on some new offensive wrinkle. But everyone knew: He was keeping tabs on his prize.

"And guess what? At the last minute, the Zerniches told him, 'We'll guarantee you we'll get you into dental school if you go to Pitt,'" said Yannessa, the future Aliquippa coaching legend who was then a senior tackle. Paterno was livid. It would be twenty-eight years before he set foot in town again. "Let me tell you something about Joe," Yannessa said. "I've been to Joe's house; that's how close I was with him. He's an

Italian, Sicilian-Calabrese mix from Brooklyn, New York. He held a vendetta against Ditka and Aliquippa ever since."

But for the town, losing a pipeline to Penn State was a small price to pay. Eventually Ditka's success at Pitt and beyond, along with that often-unbearable, somehow comic, always unflagging intensity, would slowly become the prime example of the Aliquippa way: *Yes, you work hard, and yes, you win. But you also have to be a bit larger than life. You have to succeed in a way that the whole county, state, nation will be forced to notice.*

"Everybody in my family worked in the mill; that's what we knew," Yannessa said. "It wasn't until I was a junior and Mike was a senior that some people said, 'If you get your grades in order, you can get a scholarship playing football'—and then so many of our guys did get scholarships. That's the first time the light came on: *maybe I can escape.*"

In 1953, Gino Piroli—future Aliquippa postmaster, future Aliquippa historian, forever devoted partisan of Aliquippa High sports—moved to Hopewell. That's what you did in Aliquippa then, given the chance. Piroli had been married four years, had worked as a pipefitter at J&L for eight, and now he was making enough to leave the row house life, the ever-more-cramped neighborhoods in West Aliquippa or Logstown or Plan 11. It wasn't like his dad's time anymore—come through Ellis Island, live so close to the mill that you could feel its daily heave like a beast breathing until the day they cart you away in a box. Housing developments were springing up all over the former farmland surrounding the borough, out in townships like Center, Independence, Raccoon, and, of course, Hopewell: a man could carve out some *space* there, some quiet at last. Hadn't they had enough excitement?

After all, in 1944, at eighteen Piroli had gone to Pittsburgh and chose induction into the Navy with his buddy, Juke Suder. He served on a Fletcher-class destroyer, the USS *Irwin*, at the bloodbath of Okinawa in the spring of 1945, with Japanese kamikazes plummeting like hellfire out of the sky; Gino's ship was right there on July 29, 1945, when one Zero tore into the fire control deck of the USS *Cassin Young* and killed twenty-two men. Only three of the nine Fletchers at Okinawa survived untouched. His was one. Sometime that year, nineteen years old, he was sorting through a batch of letters. "I guess you heard what happened to us . . . ," his sister began. His father, Oreste, a railroad worker at J&L for three decades, had been crossing the street to work when he was hit by a car and killed.

When Gino returned, his mill job was waiting. "On the employment card when I got hired again, they had name, address, age, and had a thing that said, 'Nationality,'" Piroli said. "And they put 'Italian.' I said, 'Hot damn, I've been in the war for two years and I'm still not an American?'"

Moving to Hopewell was the most tangible reward for the promise people had fought for: a better life. In Hopewell you could get away from the street noise, the bars, the casual ethnic tension; you could count a day's cars on Brodhead Road on one hand, raise kids in peace. At least nine other veterans moved onto Gino's street in the new development, Crestmont Village, with its three-bedroom bungalows, $13,000 apiece—living room, kitchen, maybe a basement. Many of their children would graduate high school the same year. All the men drove to the mill now, coming in from Hopewell or Center or even from as far away as Moon Township. Vince Calipari, of Coraopolis, the father of future Kentucky basketball coach John Calipari, commuted into Aliquippa as a young man to work in the blast furnace, sweating off five pounds every eight-hour turn. He lasted a year. Driving later on Route 51 with his son, Vince would point to the blazing fire skimming along the horizon. "You see that red line?" he'd say. "I used to work right beside that thing. If I'd stayed, I would've died."

For those who did stay, the compensation carved out by the union—an average wage of $24 a day, pensions, an hourly minimum of $1.96—enabled steelworkers to put some distance between work and home, take a step up the social ladder. And Aliquippa was just a small sample: starting in 1950, eighteen of the nation's twenty-five biggest cities began a thirty-year slide in net population; U.S. suburbs, meanwhile, grew by 60 million people. "Nobody blames them," Zmijanac said. "It was just natural. . . . You do what's best for you and your family."

Still, Hopewell was just a place to lay your head then. Downtown Aliquippa was home. The men went there to work, to pick up school supplies or groceries when the whistle blew, to drink. The whole family went back for big days like January's Orthodox Christmas or the San Rocco Festival in August—a weekend of parades, the Sons of Italy and Musical Political Italian Club bands, the bishop of the Pittsburgh diocese waving—to honor the patron saint of Patrica, home village to so many Italian clans. They went on weekends to visit Mom and Pop, who just refused to move, and Sunday nights the unattached—or not—would drive in for the weekly dance in West Aliquippa, up on the second floor of the Sons of Italy hall. Cost a quarter admission: somebody spun records, and the hardwood floors squeaked from all that shoe leather and sweat.

In later years you went to Villa's Lounge, the nightclub on the upper end of Franklin Avenue, to see Diana Ross and the Supremes, Dionne Warwick, Ike and Tina Turner when they were all obscure and hungry, or to watch Dr. Steve Zernich, fresh from the operating table at Aliquippa Hospital, carousing with his latest dazzling woman. Closing time, they'd often end up—entertainers and all—at the good doctor's house, where the party only picked up steam.

"Those were the wild days," said Joe Letteri. "After that you settle down."

Joe married up. He'll be the first to tell you, when he landed Gilda Cappella, a schoolteacher at Jones Elementary in 1955, his life took the turn that made everything good happen. Except for the war, he'd work the same operation for thirty-nine and a half years: J&L carpenter shop, building scaffolds and platforms and doing the latest odd repair. "Only five, six years of schooling, but I had a pretty good job," Joe said. "My two brothers were both bosses, foremen; I wasn't that lucky. They come up through the ranks."

But he was lucky too. After marrying at twenty-seven, Joe moved out of his father's home in West Aliquippa, built a 24-by-24-foot home on a concrete slab behind his father-in-law's house in Plan 11. The money he'd been paying his parents for a decade? His mother had saved it all, and presented it back to him when he married. Joe and Gilda and the kids wouldn't make their big move out of town for another eight years, but the eight-room house they'd later build in Center was on the horizon. Aliquippa gave them that. "It wasn't a perfect Eden," Gilda said. "But you could make a living."

And there, in the simplest terms, was the small-bore miracle at work in the country then. Few stopped to wonder at the historical anomaly that allowed for it; indeed, in the future many would mistake the era for a national birthright meant to last forever. After the war, the U.S. had emerged as the world's preeminent power, virtually unchallenged as an industrial colossus. With Britain exhausted, Europe and Japan flattened, and China and South America still in their economic infancies, America accounted for 64 percent of the planet's steel production.

Management concessions through the 1950s could be seen as repayment for past sins or an overdue sharing of the wealth, but they were actually the result of a market misread, the idea that any wage and benefit increase would be passed along to industries—particularly automotive and construction—that were dependent on steel. That devastated countries like Japan could ever rebuild enough to seriously challenge American primacy seemed beyond imagining, yet the evidence kept mounting. By 1950, the U.S. was producing 46.6 percent of the world's steel; a decade later it accounted for 25 percent. Averse to innovation and engulfed in a "malaise," as former J&L vice president Harold Geneen once described it, that they would never quite shake, by the mid-fifties steel management had grown fat, happy, and slow.

In retrospect, of course, the trend lines all but begged for agility. Endless union demands meant ever-higher employee payouts. Large-scale investment was needed to replace facilities ravaged by wartime production; the introduction of the far more efficient basic oxygen furnace overseas had rendered America's classic open hearth and Bessemer converters obsolete. The price of steel, meanwhile, wasn't keeping up with costs. "The handwriting was on the wall," Geneen wrote. "Many could not see it at the time, and those who could see into the future seemed powerless to do anything about it."

The bosses, later, would bear much of the cultural blame for the resultant crash, if only because steelworkers would bear the most horrible scars. But with their relationship poisoned by decades of mistrust, violence, and zero-sum posturing, it's near impossible to imagine either camp having been capable of recalibrating for the long term. Labor-management partnerships in the face of job losses and shrinking market share were decades away; for the moment the two sides were determined to slice whole pieces off the other, get "concessions," and "win." And labor was winning a lot.

Indeed, the pendulum swing had been so laudable, the improvements for the worker—from the winning of what Piroli calls "dignity" to safer conditions and sane hours to the lifting of an entire multitude into middle-class pay and values—so patently "productive" for the culture, that no one could mark the exact moment when it tripped into excess. J&L workers never committed anything so extreme as the kidnapping of Georg Isasky, but late in the '50s they began—like all of American labor—edging into a mind-set that would, later, have many declaring that they too had gone too far.

"To the other extreme," said Paul Radatovich, a commander with the Pennsylvania State Police who grew up, the son of a steelworker, in nearby New Brighton and studied political science at Pitt. "You could argue that the steel industry actually started to die right after the Second World War *because* we were the only major power not domestically devastated. Our dollar was artificially inflated; labor in Europe was cheap. So we go over there and companies that were really domestic at that time—U.S. Steel, Gulf Oil—became diversified, international; they were investing in Japan and Germany.

"So if we're building these automated plants in the early fifties in Japan and Germany, how is J&L—where the furnaces are built in 1901, 1903, 1905—able to compete with an automated plant in Germany or Japan that's also paying one-third the labor cost because their workers don't have thirteen weeks vacation, and don't get time and a half to work overtime? All these things the union fought for, at some point actually became the knife that slit their own throat."

Abuses in a plant the size of the Aliquippa Works had gone on since it opened; stories are still told of men, in the '30s and '40s, who came to work drunk and somehow remained employed. But what began as union rules to protect workers from employer abuse, from arbitrary firing because the boss wanted to hire his brother-in-law or a willing wife's husband, over the next few decades would ossify into rules for the sake of rules, a labor force interested less in producing competitive, quality steel than in preserving hard-won gains. "The biggest concern for unions in those days," Piroli said of the 1970s, "was protecting people who didn't want to work."

But the first glimmers at the Aliquippa Works could be seen long before. John Evasovich came back one summer in the late '50s to work the wire mill, "and I wanted to do more work and wasn't allowed to do it because that was not in my job description," he said. "I was a laborer in the wire mill and when they would make this one kind of wire they would have scraps, and my entire job was to sweep up the scraps and dispose of them. When that was done, I volunteered to do other things and was not permitted. That amazed me."

It was inevitable that the union hall would become a power center: control a man's job, and you all but control the man. Union connections could make all the difference; Yannessa had uncles in the local, so a summer job at the mill during high school and when he came home from playing football at New Mexico State was always a lock. Even those benefiting, like carpenter Melvin Kosanovich, who worked more than two decades as a general griever for Local 1211, found it disturbing. "The union had very much power, a lot of power at times, too much power, because most of the things we done we had a lot of power," he recalled. "We had a lot of hiring."

J&L was producing more steel annually than at any other time in its history, and in 1959 set new records for sales and income; its second-quarter revenues, $316,384,000, put the steelmaker on pace for a billion-dollar year. But the way Kosanovich tells it, union officials were now given nearly the same due as Mauk's policemen in the '20s. "Whatever we wanted they gave us, because they were making money," he said of J&L management. "Things got slacked and they couldn't afford to pay those things, but, yes, we had too much power. At times I think the company had too much power, but I think union had more power."

"You know what?" said Yannessa, whose father worked as a crane operator at J&L for forty years and whose many uncles all worked there. "Everybody says, 'You got that steel-mill mentality. People that work in the mill are tough.' Yeah, they were tough guys, a lot of 'em, but a lot of 'em were lazy, laid-back, didn't do a good job on the job. They ended up union employees and a lot of it led to the demise of the steel industry in America."

At 11:25 p.m., July 14, 1959, a large parade of members of Local 1211—with 12,000 members the largest local in the state, and third biggest in the nation—marched behind a cluster of picket signs and American flags down Franklin Avenue toward the Wye, the tunnel, the mill. All had been drilled weeks before in their strike duties, and then again at 7:30 this night; near J&L the marchers efficiently broke ranks, spreading wide to cover the five entrances of the Aliquippa Works. Some 2,000 men and women from the midnight shift stopped on their way out to take in the scene, but by 12:45 a.m. only two gate pickets were left. "This Plant Is On Strike," read the sign. "Aliquippa Local 1211."

It would be the longest American steel strike yet: 116 days of banked furnaces, 500,000 idle steelworkers, and 250,000 more in secondary industries. Industry losses totaled $248 million a week; in Beaver County alone workers lost $45 million in wages. Some, like Joe Letteri, had a working wife and barely felt the pain. "I didn't have a problem with it," he said. "I just laid around and didn't do nothing. Go on a picket line once in a while, and that was it." But the walkout savaged most workers' savings. Aliquippa's local was flush enough to give out weekly turkeys and sponsor a thumb-nosing, community-wide party on Labor Day; a food bank supplied struggling families with flour, rice, dry milk, and powdered eggs.

Concerned with the long strike's threat to both the economy and defense, in early October President Eisenhower unleashed Taft-Hartley by asking for a board of inquiry; informed that there was no chance of a settlement, he ordered the steelworkers back to work. Arguing that Taft-Hartley was unconstitutional, the union went to court and lost at every level, capped by a November 7 decision by the Supreme Court that upheld a district court injunction forcing workers to return to their jobs for an eighty-day "cooling-off period." The 8-1 ruling effectively put the strikers on the wrong side of the law and became a landmark of antiunionism; it had been more than two decades since labor had felt so bullied. Management wasn't happy, either: steelmakers were outraged that Ike had taken so long to act.

Workers filtered back to J&L slowly, unsure whether they'd be back on strike when the eighty days expired. But the prospect of fresh paychecks with Christmas coming was a relief, and besides, Aschman had fielded another distractingly superb team. Aliquippa won its first ten games, beat a still-maturing Joe Namath of Beaver Falls and Ambridge handily, and came within two points of winning another WPIAL championship when Charleroi edged the Quips in the final, 13-12. It felt good to get back to the routine.

And when a deal got done on January 9, 1960, it seemed the union had walked away with another win. One of the union men back from signing the pact with J&L was on the front page of the *Beaver Valley Times*, grinning. "Best we've ever gotten," he said, and if it wasn't quite that, the contract was still pretty good: a raise of 39 cents an hour spread over the next thirty months, automatic cost-of-living increases for the first time, increased pension and health benefits.

But that was just money; it would take time for the less obvious losses to reveal themselves. As the Wagner Act had been cemented by the '37 strike, so Taft-Hartley was now actualized by Eisenhower's action and the Supreme Court's decision. Worse, with their mills quieted for four months, America's steel firms had turned to Japanese and Korean sources to fill any shortfall in their orders. With no drop-off in quality—and U.S. steelworkers averaging $3.10 an hour and the Japanese about 50 cents—the benefits of offshore manufacturing had been made tantalizingly plain. In 1959, for the first time since the turn of the century, U.S. steel imports exceeded exports. No one knew it yet. But the underbelly had been exposed.

7

Crossfire

Mike Zmijanac graduated from Aliquippa High in 1960. Five decades later, when asked to explain the bubbling cocktail of factors—ambition, genetics, pain, work ethic, and a constant pressure to excel amid a landscape of failure—that makes Aliquippa unique, his first stab is an offhanded: "If you aren't from here, you can't understand." But if we're being precise, the man who ended up being the greatest football coach in Aliquippa history—surpassing Aschman, his freshman history teacher; Yannessa, his smoother, far more popular mentor; and Marocco, Aschman's decorated but bitter heir—has less claim on the place than most. Zmijanac never played football, wasn't born in the state—much less the town—and moved from Aliquippa to Hopewell in 1969. Today he lives even farther away, in Mt. Lebanon, where he can plant tomatoes and plot his next trip to the racetrack in peace.

Distance, in fact, is central to the Zmijanac pose. With sheepdog bangs hooding his eyes, a sardonic grin flashing like a shield, his default mode falls in the same dismissive-to-flip range assumed by many bruised romantics—i.e., English teachers—who spend their adult lives corral-ling all manner of teenage bullshit. He shrugs often—his generation's version of "whatever"—and whether the subject is another game won or player lost, it's easy to wonder how much he truly cares. Yet in time served alone, few have devoted more to Aliquippa kids.

The convert may exceed those born to the faith, but it takes a while for Zmijanac to make his zeal plain. "The single greatest thing that ever happened to me," he said finally, "was growing up in this town."

He was sixteen when he graduated—a skinny, quick-on-the-draw wiseass, most comfortable with adults, left too often to his own de-vices. That had always been the way. Zmijanac's father, Stan, had been a master sergeant with the Marines in World War II, fought on Okinawa and Iwo Jima; his mother, Bette Swan, was the daughter of a Welshman who came to America at fourteen to dig West Virginia coal and drifted up to Aliquippa for millwork. Yes, Aliquippa is in Mike's blood: His parents met at Aliquippa High and graduated in the class of '41. He was born on the Marine base at Parris Island, South Carolina. When Stan deployed, Bette took the baby home to wait out the war on the family farm, bustling as it was with her parents and four ex-footballing brothers. By the time she brought five-year-old Mike and his little sister back for good in '49, moving onto Wade St. in Plan 12, the marriage was over. Bette began long hours waitressing, downtown at Della's Lounge.

That was August. Within a few days, Bette sent Mike out the door. "School's down there," she said, gesturing in the direction of Laughlin Elementary. "Go tell them we moved in." Maybe that prompted Zmi-janac's first shrug. He wasn't six yet. First day, Mike walked himself to school.

Summers, he would head back to his grandfather's farm, fifty acres up near where the interstate and Center Township would be one day. The land was the clan's second job. All the Swan men worked shifts, full- or part-time, at J&L—seamless tube, hot mill—and divvied up the endless chores at home. "He bought that farm as insurance against the Depression and the mill going down, and they raised everything on their own: chickens, a couple of cows," Mike said. "Sold potatoes. People would come with washtubs and go down to the bottomland, down by the creek, and they could get a washtub full of potatoes for fifty cents, fill up a colander full of eggs for a dime.

"They taught me how to work. For breakfast my grandmother called me: 'Butch, go down to the henhouse, get a dozen eggs, get a pail, milk the cow, go out in the field, get me a box of tomatoes. . . .' Pick some berries, this and that. She made everything from scratch; the only thing bought in the store was salt and pepper. Breakfast would be three, four pork chops. They raised pigs, bacon: that was the big meal of the day. When you went out to work you got a cold-cut sandwich delivered to the fields at lunchtime. Then a big dinner."

Sports opened up the town for him. His uncle Jimmy took nine-year-old Mike to the '52 WPIAL championship in Pittsburgh, where Willie Frank and that epic 28-yard touchdown run became Mike's template for what an Aliquippa running back should be. He has been at every Aliquippa title game since. But basketball was his love, not least because it was all the rage among Slavs; between Press Maravich's drive and Mike Ditka's fire, a half-Serb like Zmijanac had plenty of role models. But he didn't play for Aliquippa High; he wasn't good enough. So this became personal. Zmijanac made playground hoops, with its unstated codes and obscure triumphs, his proving ground. It was still basketball, but his way—held, like everything else, at a remove.

So on warm days there were endless pickup games down at Morrell Park: dozens lined up on the fence rails waiting for "Next," the cocky lift you got from taking on all comers—including the ringers back from Duke or LSU or Iowa and expecting to rule—and holding the court for hours. But Mike would find as much joy dribbling in the snow, a solitary figure endlessly shooting, knuckles purpled and the soggy, backspun ball splitting his fingertips like a razor. Get him in a gym, and he had his routine: a thousand shots, tote up numbers after each hundred; hit fewer than nine hundred and you start all over again. Therapy, he calls it now. "I don't miss playing organized, because those are better memories. That was great shit," Zmijanac said. "It kept me from being lonely. It solved a myriad of teenage problems. I would go play."

He made himself a name, too. "Mike was one of the best sandlot shooters I ever saw," said Robert Pipkin, an Aliquippa all-state selection who went on to play for the University of Idaho. "I don't know about a whole-court game, but, oh, he had a shot that was unbelievable. I'll give him his props for that."

Mostly, though, Zmijanac served time as the shyer, less accomplished sidekick to George Suder—son of Pecky, nephew of Juke—a handsome cock of the walk who earned himself, in 1961, a full-ride scholarship to play basketball at the University of Maryland. Together George and Mike were Batman and Robin, with Suder always at the center of the action, in a bar or on the court, reeling in women like honey draws flies. Zmijanac would be off to the side, of course, grinning. "Look at you," he'd say. "Ain't you fucking somethin'?"

Once, during a 3-on-3 tournament at Laughlin Elementary, Zmijanac got tangled up with Pipkin, and the two started yapping. "I remember punching him right in the mouth," Pipkin said. "He was bitching about something and I just hit him." Zmijanac didn't fall, and he didn't hit back. "No," laughed Pipkin, "I would've beat the crap out of him.

"That guy just rubbed me the wrong way. It was something about his arrogance. He was a crybaby. If you touched him, he cried. If he shot? 'You fouled me!' There was something about his spirit that I just didn't like."

Still, in the two of them—Mike whip-smart and roiling, George charming and self-destructive—you could see the Aliquippa elements at work, could see the charisma and brains and drive and self-destruction feeding off each other. George would die too soon, after all. And it's Mike who revels still in the civic self-image summed up to him when he was just a boy by Sam Milanovich, coach of the '49 hoop team: *We don't stab you in the back here. We tell you to turn the fuck around so we can bury it in your chest.*

"My current wife, been together twenty-some years, has said to me—and she grew up in the suburbs: 'There's something different about you guys from Aliquippa,'" Zmijanac said. "'All the ones I know are pretty bright, pretty charming, but you have these rough edges that I can't explain.' And there is an edginess to us. We have this 'veneer of education.' But we'll 'motherfuck' you in a minute."

Never mind that such hair-trigger machismo has caused more than its share of pain, and that Zmijanac knows this. He still finds it admirable. The town's decline has been so publicly detailed, its criminals and knaves are so much a part of an increasingly small social fabric, that any hypocrisy or spin gets called out fast. Why bother trying to cover up the feckless dad, the mother in jail? Why not be straight up? His weekly game plans make the attitude flesh: No trickery, no flash, just an unrelenting ground attack. Opponents know what we run, he says. We're Aliquippa. Try and stop us.

His critics, of course, use any loss as an excuse to carp about Zmijanac's supposed "lack of imagination," his reliance on the town's endless supply of fresh legs, its pure hunger, to overcome a musty playbook and mostly outclassed opponents. And if his pride makes for blind spots, they aren't limited to football. Zmijanac is described, by blacks and whites alike, as a fair, challenging, color-blind presence in classrooms and locker rooms, but his loathing of self-promotion or the slightest hint of a hidden agenda—his full-body embrace, that is, of the Aliquippa stance—left him blind to the cancer corroding the town even in its best days. Racial tension was percolating as Zmijanac grew and graduated. That it had to surface just two years later, in 1962, when Robert Pipkin made it a football issue for the first time, offends him still.

"That piece of shit!" Zmijanac yelled when he heard the name. "Bobby Pipkin. He's such a phony piece of shit. This was horrible, and fuck Bobby Pipkin, he was such a coward; he quit the football team. You know what? It's fuckin'. . . He is Al Sharpton, and I call him that to his face. He's fuckin' Al Sharpton: he's made his life out of being black. . . .

"There was always tension. But see, this is one of the reasons I have no respect: Bobby Pipkin was one of those guys who egged it on for no reason. This town was completely unbiased. It was artificial bullshit. The football team was three-quarters black, the basketball team was all black. But there weren't any black cheerleaders? Oh, fuck you. I'm blaming guys like that for exacerbating the whole situation. It was unnecessary. It was all artificial."

All artificial? No. But Zmijanac isn't alone in believing it so. Many whites who grew up in Aliquippa during the 1940s and '50s like to recall it as a haven where races and ethnicities bonded by labor wars endured the mill's hardships together. Older blacks, too, remember whites and blacks living side by side—and peaceably—in the two areas, Plan 11 and Logstown, given to color-blind housing. They speak fondly of the years before the African-American family unit, especially, went to smash. But when she hears white people voicing the notion of Franklin Avenue, then, as some kind of idealized Main Street, Carolyn Browder, class of '64, has to laugh. "Yeah," she said. "For *them*."

Browder grew up, too, in the wake of World War II—when racism on the job was blatant and there seemed little to do but take it. "It was terrible," George Stokes, hired in 1949, once said of his early years working on the A&S Railroad at the Aliquippa Works. First day, a foreman told him that he'd never advance past the job of track repairman, and "I had to accept that because I wanted the job," Stokes said. "I accepted it, but I knew I had a high school education. I wanted something else, too: I could do my math, took the test like everybody else. I passed all the tests they gave us down there. I said I want more, and I got more—but not from that guy. Not from him." Because train crews were white then. Blacks worked the tracks.

"And why did that occur?" said Stokes, who stayed at J&L for thirty-three years. "It's proven that our society is very racist. The whole mill was like that: they had certain bathrooms that blacks wasn't allowed in. They had big parties that blacks wasn't allowed. That was 1949. . . . The tin mill had no blacks, the carpenter shop, none of the trade units had any blacks. Electricians, none of the crafts. We got the labor jobs. Like he told me: *You'll be a laborer when you leave.*"

But there were, even then, glimmers of pride, agitation: In 1946, the school board received a petition asking that a "colored" janitor be hired for Jones Elementary School in Plan 11. Two years later, a black delegation presented another petition asking for an inquiry into a "pattern of alleged discrimination at Jones School." Decorous or not, that took guts. The town's small—4,175; 15.9 percent—black population had no political clout and plenty to fear.

Melvin Steals—future PhD, future Aliquippa junior high principal—grew up in postwar Aliquippa with a widowed mother scarred by memories of an Alabama lynching. "So my mother would beat me," Steals said. "Whenever my brother or I did something wrong she would strip us down to our underwear and we would have to lie on the bed while she beat us, and as she beat us she would always say, 'I would rather see you dead than in the white man's jail.'"

Steals recalls the first time he went into a store on Franklin Avenue. He was eleven or twelve. The white merchant called him a "nigger." Steals spoke back, and the man's face twisted and he unleashed a spew of graphically detailed threats. "It hurt me so much that I kind of blocked out the memory," Melvin said. "But I never blocked out the anger that I had. For some reason he just called me a 'nigger'. . . . The feeling of rage—and it was a rage that I could not act out, because my mother conditioned my twin brother and me to a point where we would accept second- or third-class citizenship."

Slurs, of course, provided the rawest reveal of one's "place," but it wasn't hard to pick up on more subtle forms. "You could see the economics of racism as well," said Barron Harvey, Aliquippa High class of '65, now dean of the business school at Howard University. "People say, 'Well, everybody was making the same money'? No. You might've *started* with the same money, but you weren't going to move up at the same money. The white guy who, when I was in elementary school, was living on my same block? Before I got out of elementary school, he was already gone—even though his father was at the same level as the other men on that street. But he had gotten advanced. He had moved up. . . . And then he's *gone*.

"There was a huge economic vitality there—but we didn't participate in it. We couldn't live where we wanted to live. We couldn't go to the stores we normally wanted to go and work where we needed to work, even though we were part of the unions as well. That really clouds how you see the world. We know how they saw the world: as privileged, and had everything accessible. But for us, it was looking up. Always looking up."

And never forgetting. Each new incident—large and small—built upon the previous. One day brought a snarled insult. The next, you fumed when a white person behind you in line was waited on first. Or you, a sixteen-year-old girl, became one of the first blacks hired at the C&L Supermarket, but were kept out of sight while the other, lighter-skinned black girl was brought up front to work the register. And all of it piled up, heavy in the collective gut. "It was brewing," said Salt Smith. "Even when I was coming up, you didn't have no black cheerleaders, no black majorette: *You can't even try out.* They made sure of that. And you'd resent that."

Small explosions vented some of the rage. In 1956, the existence of a black-only washroom at J&L's 14-inch mill ended only because black steelworker Matthew Strong, a reverend at New Hope Baptist Church, attacked the black washroom wall with a sledgehammer.

Tensions built, fistfights flared at the high school in 1955, '56, '57—evidence of a slow burn that, to the town fathers, seemed under control. "It wouldn't be all the whites and blacks, just a couple blacks and a couple whites," said Yannessa. "Come on. The undercurrent of racism has been in this country since they brought the slaves over from Africa. You always had something would be a bone of contention and something negative would come out of it and there'd be some volatility. It never had a long shelf life. But the undercurrent was always there."

By 1960, the continuing influx of black workers from the South began to tip the balance; now the percentage of blacks in Aliquippa had risen to 21 percent. But on the surface, it was as if little had changed. Downtown still bustled, and Aliquippa's population held steady at 26,369. The San Rocco Festival still went off each summer like clockwork, and on July 4th weekend, 1960, the Italians in West Aliquippa had an even more famous reason to be proud. Film composer Henry Mancini, thirty-six years old, was coming home.

He was still a few years away from winning his first two Academy Awards, for *Breakfast at Tiffany's* and *Days of Wine and Roses*, but Mancini had already made a mark: he'd been nominated for an Emmy, Grammy, and Oscar, and was famous for his infectious scores for the TV shows *Mr. Lucky* and, especially, *Peter Gunn*. So a "Welcome Home" banner was stretched across Franklin Avenue for "Henry Mancini Day," and Mancini flew in from Southern California. Thousands lined the street for his motorcade as it wound from the Wye up toward the high school. Mancini sat waving from the backseat with his wife, Ginny, and there in the front, taking the day off from the carpenter's shop at J&L, was the grinning face of the chairman of the organizing committee, Toats DiNardo's big brother, Phil. Way back when, he and Mancini had known each other in West Aliquippa.

It was, actually, a two-day affair, Mancini's homecoming and a 4th of July celebration combined—and so obviously a commentary on the American Dream that no one felt the need to mention it outright. Instead there were bicycle, go-kart, and homemade-wagon races; motorcycle, archery, and parachute-jumping exhibitions; two luncheon banquets; a testimonial dinner. Mancini conducted the community band in a concert, and it all ended in fireworks and cheers. Quinto Mancini, back in Aliquippa for the first time since his boy moved him out to California, had come to the country alone and poor and twelve years old in a boat. Now the New World was calling his boy a success.

"I just can't believe it—that it should happen to my son," Quinto said when it was over. "I wish it could happen to all fathers, so they could have the feeling that I have. I only wish his mother were here to see it, too."

In the fall of 1962, Robert Pipkin, a senior, sweet-shooting, 6-foot-3 leading scorer for the Quips basketball team, decided to go out for football. He'd had Aschman for history and thought him fair, and besides, Pipkin said, "Everybody wanted to play for Carl Aschman." Bob made the team, started the first two games at defensive end . . . but found himself distracted. He kept hearing complaints from black girls about the lack of black Aliquippa cheerleaders. Word was, there might've been one back in the late '50s, who would've been the town's first and only. But there were certainly none now.

His antennae for racial slights were well primed: In junior high, Pipkin and two girls made a point of walking into an Aliquippa whites-only deli and ordering water—and actually got served. The 1962 football team was a softer target; the Aliquippa roster featured more than a dozen black players and slipping morale. Aschman had had disastrous seasons in '60 and '61, began the '62 campaign 0-3, and for the first time found his program—long the symbol of a wholesome civic unity—racked by racial division.

Few noticed at the time. Aliquippa football that season had become the trigger for a far more public and random type of crime; cops used to dealing with bar fights and domestic tragedy found themselves fighting turf battles, juvenile delinquency, and random assaults on bystanders. The growing hostility between Aliquippa's black and white fans actually eased during home games, because the focus would shift to the visitors. "We always had other people to fight with after the game," said Barron Harvey. "That was Ambridge or Westinghouse."

A clutch of Aliquippa teenagers stoned the Westinghouse buses after the home opener, and after the next game at Aliquippa Stadium, a 20-0 loss to Sharon, nine juveniles were arrested for assaulting ten people in the exiting crowd. All the suspects were identified as living in Plan 11, home to many blacks, and Sam Milanovich, now schools superintendent, may well have been referring to race when he declared, "A rowdy minority group of so-called wolf packs has caused considerable trouble to people en route to their homes following the contests. . . . Some of our patrons were attacked after leaving the stadium. When arrests were made the attackers were found to be carrying knives, blackjacks, and other lethal weapons."

Milanovich decreed that the rest of the home slate would be played on Saturday afternoons. The problem wasn't unique to Aliquippa: By then games played by North Braddock and McKeesport, as well as some schools in Pittsburgh, had been moved from Friday night to Saturday for similar reasons. Already, the arbitrary violence that would mark the 1960s—flip side to psychedelia and peace marches—had begun to bare its teeth.

Four days after Milanovich's announcement, Pipkin played in his final football game—the Quips' first win of the '62 season, 13-7 over Ellwood City before a crowd of just 1,600 at the daylit stadium. The post-victory buzz didn't last long. During a practice in the ensuing week, "I talked to all the black football players and said, 'Listen. We need to quit until they get some black cheerleaders,'" Pipkin said. "About seventy-five percent of the players decided to quit. We protested."

For the white players, though, it was hardly that simple. Pipkin's agitation did prompt some seniors to bolt—estimates range from four to eight—but it's not clear if they quit or were forced out. "Some of us went to the coach and we said, 'There are black players right now that are creating a lot of problems and we'll walk out ourselves, off the football team, unless you get rid of so-and-so number,'" said Gene Yannessa, Don's younger brother, tight end, class of '64. "And we got rid of a whole bunch, and Pipkin was the leader."

The relatively quaint question behind Pipkin's strike—if a black man can serve as class president, as Howard Herring would in 1963, why can't a black girl lead cheers?—dovetailed with the more militant stance rising among young blacks nationwide. For weeks, the national news had been led by James Meredith's legal push to become the first black to enroll at the University of Mississippi; the night of Pipkin's last game, after it became clear that Meredith would succeed, rioting erupted at Ole Miss—cars burned, two dead. The next morning, escorted by four hundred U.S. marshals and a thousand federal troops, Meredith integrated the outraged heart of Dixie amid clouds of tear gas.

Even without football, Pipkin had plenty to protest that school year: the lack of black teachers, the town's segregated pools, and the unspoken rule that no more than three black basketball players could take the floor at a time for Aliquippa High. He went on to lead another demonstration protesting racial bias, as black students—Melvin Steals among them—marched out of the school building, up the path to the empty football stadium, and into the student section of the stands.

Yet despite being the locus of such tension, the school—and team—remained by far the town's most progressive institution. Star receiver Richard Mann, after all, was one of the black players who stayed on the team after Pipkin's departure, and he recalls the biggest racial clash of the 1962–63 school year, a seemingly inevitable fight between blacks walking down a path to town and a surrounding crowd of bristling whites with chains and bats, being defused only at the last minute.

"On both sides, man, it was lined with the white students and they were going to jump on us," Mann said. "The only thing that stopped 'em was the white football players. I remember that."

Such was the complex dynamic at the high school, and in the town and nation for that matter: Nothing—rivalries, racial division, friendships, fights—was ever as starkly black and white as later characterizations tended to make it. Mann agreed with Pipkin's stand, but considers many of the whites he grew up with as true comrades. Indeed, it was a white English teacher, Caroline Theil, whom Pipkin credits with believing in him most. He read just one book in high school—*Great Expectations*—but Theil kept insisting that he had leadership qualities, kept writing and encouraging him after he left town, even sent him money.

"She really gave me hope," Pipkin said. "That lady probably saved my life."

She wasn't alone. "Kindergarten up through twelfth grade I had only one black teacher—and he was a former football star at Aliquippa and played on the 1949 state basketball team," said Melvin Steals. "But I had some wonderful white teachers who saw my potential and really encouraged me." He rattles off a list, ending with Ivagean Ferry. "Mrs. Ferry taught us students about fairness," Steals said. "She was history, very proud to be an American. In fact, Mrs. Ferry taught me how to study."

But perhaps it was precisely the fact that Aliquippa High was less retrograde than other places that made it ripe for ferment. What with Martin Luther King's "Letter from Birmingham Jail," the killing of Medgar Evers, and the March on Washington, the following year, 1963, is widely considered the launching pad of the modern civil rights movement. But it was also a culmination. In places like Aliquippa, the transition from isolated spats to collective action had been gaining momentum for some time.

"Three years I went up there, and at the end of the school year there was always a riot in the school," said future Aliquippa mayor

Anthony Battalini, class of '64. "They would come down marching, on what we call 'The Paths'; you come out of the high school and there's a set of steps to go down to Plan 12. They'd come out singing that 'We Shall Overcome,' and then all hell would break loose. Teachers were out there and everything. I can remember when I was a kid in school, I was in shop class, carpenter's shop. And we knew: the blacks would be in carpenter's shop making these clubs and they'd have 'em in their locker. At lunchtime I went in all their lockers and cleaned 'em all out. . . ."

The black players that Pipkin led off the field in 1962 didn't return. Aschman never once spoke to him about the issue, or vice versa, but Pipkin never considered the coach himself racist. In fact, he points out, Aschman had no qualms about starting a black quarterback, Jethro McCoy, on his great team in '59. "He was a good man," Pipkin said, but "he was not going to beg you."

And he was not going to soften. Gene Yannessa separated his right shoulder during the Ellwood City game, "but you were fearful of saying anything to him," he said. "On Monday morning we had meetings; the whole football team would go an hour earlier before school would start and Aschman would go over and scream at us and bitch about what we didn't do right. I waited and waited—I hated to do this, but I had to go up to him: my shoulder was all fucked up."

After the meeting, Yannessa approached Aschman. "Coach, can I see you for a minute?" he said.

"What's your problem?" Aschman said.

"My shoulder, I hurt it in the game and I can barely pick up my arm. . . ."

Aschman grabbed Yannessa's arm, twisted it one way and then the other.

"There ain't nothing wrong with that goddam arm," he said. "Get the hell out of here and go to class!"

"And like an asshole, I didn't go to the doctor's or anything and eventually it healed on itself," Yannessa recalled. "But the pain was always there and there was a lump up there. Basketball season came and I went out, and the first time I had practice I went to take a shot from the foul line and I couldn't reach the basket."

After sitting out three weeks, Yannessa played the last three football games in pain. Though the Quips suffered humiliating losses to Beaver Falls and Ambridge, and finished the '62 season 2-6-1, Aschman never thought to use his clout to broker peace with the blacks. "He wasn't going to budge," said Aschman's son, Carl Jr. "He said, 'If they wanted to play, they could play. If they didn't, they could stay home'; he would use what he had."

Just days after the walkout, Aschman's outmanned boys, led by quarterback Frank Lalama's three touchdown passes, stunned the county by "beating" undefeated New Castle with a 19-19 tie. The upset was enough to knock New Castle's Red Hurricanes out of the running for a WPIAL title; their fans would be vowing revenge for years to come. Aschman eventually finished with 189 wins in all, and this wasn't one of them. But it was one of his great coaching jobs.

"We really jelled," Yannessa said. "Because we lost some of the people that were like a cancer, like Pipkin, and when that happened we came together more as a team, the blacks and the whites. I'm not sure we even knew how good New Castle was."

Surprisingly, news of Pipkin's walkout never became public knowledge. But the idea that a black player—and a wild card with poor grades, at that—would challenge the town's "king" and its crown jewel rankled elders even in the black community. One of them, the father of future Nebraska star tackle and Kansas City Chiefs draftee Bob Liggett, visited Pipkin at home one night to tell him he'd made a mistake, to ask him to apologize and lead the players back. Did he understand what he was taking on? Pipkin replied that he knew and, secretly, he was sure the school would give in. He would apologize for nothing.

"I rocked the boat," Pipkin said. "I went against the system that was the life of that community. *Who is this guy, sixteen, seventeen, to tell other black kids?* I just saw injustice: How come black girls couldn't be cheer-leaders? And nobody else saw it."

But the school didn't give in. Pipkin was hardly a unifying figure, even among fellow black athletes; it was lost on no one—including Zmi-janac—that the hoop star's seemingly principled stand was carried out in the context of an athletic lark. Pipkin wasn't seeking a future in football. "He played basketball," said Larry Stokes, a black sophomore who didn't strike that season. "I didn't walk out, because I just played football."

Such ambivalence—the idea that he risked little to make his point—rankles Pipkin still. After earning his education degree at the University of Idaho, he returned to Aliquippa and founded the Negro Youth Improvement Council to raise issues about black children in local schools. He later moved outside Pittsburgh and founded a branch of the NAACP in the northern suburbs, nagged by the notion that his hometown never gave him his due.

"From that day on I could never get a job in that community; I was more or less ostracized because I stood for something," said Pipkin, who, in fact, served as chairman of the board of Aliquippa Community Hospital before resigning in 2003. "To this day, I still think I have some resentment from black and white because of what I did."

Funny thing, though: If he was ostracized, it didn't happen right away. None of his actions affected Pipkin's status in school or with the basketball team. With football season's end came a reset; he began hoops practice, went on to lead Aliquippa to the WPIAL final in 1963, went on to score 27 points in the loss, went on to be named all-state. "He's great," his basketball coach, Frank Janosik, told the local paper after the season ended. "Just great."

But that, too, left Pipkin with a sour taste—though maybe it shouldn't have; Aliquippa, after all, was merely showing its priorities. One thing mattered more than racial strife or even Aschman's precious program. The football team had figured to be bad that season anyway. Basketball was a different story. That team had a chance to shine.

"I was the leading scorer," Pipkin said. "We'd just moved into a new gym. To them, winning was more important. Whatever happened, they forgave me."

And why not? The problem still seemed . . . *controllable.*

Didn't teenagers always get into fights? What ethnic group didn't run into trouble at some point? Blacks vs. whites? Hell, the Serbs and Cros still went at it from time to time: Such friction was part of the town's DNA. Besides, nearly everybody had a job. In late '62 the mill was still expanding—a new sinter plant in the blast furnace, a new electrolytic tin line, a new reducing mill, and burgeoning plans to double its landmass by filling in the river out to Crow Island—and the last labor contract had been signed without a strike.

Indeed, unions were on a roll nationwide, and could boast of having the best ally possible: the man in the White House was still smarting from a showdown with Big Steel bosses the previous spring. Eager to suppress inflation, President John Kennedy publicly accused U.S. Steel of a double cross in April 1962, when it tried, after agreeing to a no-increase contract, to raise its prices by $6 a ton. His famous quip then to aides—"My father always told me that all businessmen were sons of bitches, but I never believed it until now"—wouldn't go public for years, but his disgust was clear, and he soon forced industry leaders to back down. Kennedy had all the marks of a cake-eater, but to working stiffs he certainly had the right idea.

And now, a week after Aliquippa tied New Castle, 19-19, he was coming. On the afternoon of October 12, 1962, Kennedy flew into the state for a two-day campaign swing for the Democratic slate in the November elections, starting with a rally centered in a municipal parking lot downtown. About half the town—10,000 to 15,000 people—filled Franklin and Sheffield Avenues, spilling up onto the Plan 7 hillside, enduring hours of waiting and a late rain shower for the first visit ever by a sitting president.

Everyone, for once, was on their best behavior. The *Beaver County Times* would record a scene of civic tranquillity: kids tossing yo-yos, boys playing the Italian hand-game "Morra," women exchanging "recipes and pictures of their daughters' weddings." The apparel was a display of mingling classes—"work clothes, slacks, business suits, furs, haircurlers, headscarves, hats, Bermuda shorts, raincoats, Boy Scout uniforms, and dressy dresses"—and the cacophony a song of ethnic harmony: "They spoke many languages while they waited—English, Italian, Polish, German, Lithuanian, Russian, Croatian, Ukrainian and Serbian."

Aliquippa police officers were spotted on rooftops scanning the scene. Secret Service men eyed the crowd. They had nothing to fear. The *Beaver County Times* photo of Kennedy's arrival, with him standing in his convertible limo and shaking hands with someone as he steps out, is backdropped by a roiling sea of white and black hands waving, black and white faces mixed and grinning. "The crowd loved him," said Aliquippa mayor Clarence Neish after. "He's a dynamic personality. You have to see him close to appreciate his personal magnetism."

Kennedy took the stage near the old Pittsburgh Mercantile building at 4:05 p.m. He sat briefly in a rocking chair donated by a nearby department store, MISCO, then stood up behind a sign declaring, "Aliquippa Voters I Need You." Neish was right: to hear JFK unleash even this six-minute piece of campaign boilerplate was to feel a force subsumed by time, tragedy, and his own hypnotic glamor. Kennedy bit off the words and spit them out. He sounded like the last seconds before the first punch.

"This country has many responsibilities which it carries all around the world, but we cannot possibly carry them unless we are strong and vital and progressive here at home," Kennedy said, his microphoned voice booming. "A strong, free world begins here in this state, begins here in the United States, and we cannot have a strong United States if we sit still. . . ."

Kennedy never mentioned the town by name. No one cared. Aliquippa was a party stronghold, and here was its leader: defender of unemployment insurance and Social Security, steward of all the New Deal breakthroughs made a generation before. Standing in the crowd was Joe Casp, son of Ukrainian/Polish immigrants, high school dropout, tank commander at the Battle of the Bulge at eighteen—another piece of evidence of what mill and town were producing then.

Four Casp brothers had fought in World War II; one died in Germany, another was shot twice. Joe came home, drank away a year as a "52-20 man"—$20 from the government for fifty-two weeks—then went to work in J&L's wire mill. Mike Ditka served as altar boy, in 1950, when Joe married Ella Oskowski, and by the end of the decade they'd saved enough to buy a house on Irwin Street for $12,500. Casp could be harsh, small-minded, but he raised three nurses and a doctor in that house. He was also one of the founding members, in the early '60s, of the Quarterback Club, a booster organization that brought in college coaches to speak, that made sure every one of Aschman's seniors had a sports coat and slacks, and that met every Monday night at the Ukrainian Club to watch film of the previous week's game.

Casp lifted his eight-year-old son Bill, the future Princeton grad, up on his shoulders so they could watch JFK together. "Kennedy was Number One," Joe recalled later. "He had a tan that was out of this world. . . ."

Yes, racial rumblings and Kennedy's own callow performance during the 1961 Bay of Pigs debacle raised unsettling questions about America at home and abroad. But this was a bread-and-butter town, more than happy just to see the president jab the Republicans. Kennedy cited the fact that, when he took office, Pennsylvania had one of the nation's highest jobless rates—"nearly five hundred million people." Few noted the gaffe.

"Can you tell me how we can put them back to work," he asked, "if we have congressmen and senators and governors who oppose all the pieces of social legislation so vital to our country in the same way that their fathers opposed it in the thirties, when Franklin Roosevelt was president of the United States?

Kennedy had been in office nearly two years, but it wasn't until his showdown with Big Steel the previous spring that he seemed to find both footing and voice. Perhaps he'd never deliver on his immense promise, but the ideal Kennedy personified—the street-smart patrician, the rich man who had adopted the workingman's vision of life, not vice versa—was now giving a full-throated vow to keep it alive.

"How can the people of Pennsylvania who live with this problem in the coal mines and the steel mills—how can they support a party which opposes progress in 1962?" Kennedy asked the town. "So I come here today and ask your help in electing men and women in this state and in this country who will serve the people, who believe in progress, who believe that the national government has a responsibility."

It had been only two weeks since teenagers attacked innocent fans outside the football stadium. But city fathers wondering if their town could behave had nothing to worry about. "No arrests were made," the *Beaver County Times* reported. "There were no unruly persons and no incidents of any nature reported." Kennedy's voice, then, crackled over the loudspeakers amid a rare moment of calm:

"Education, medical care for the aged, job opportunities, equal rights: those are the things that this country stands for, and we can get those things only if we elect men who believe in them."

"So I come today not as a candidate for office, but as one who, after twenty-one months as president, recognizes how important it is that this great country of ours be dynamic and progressive. . . ."

By 4:23 p.m., Kennedy was in his car again, riding toward Constitution Avenue. The crowd dispersed quickly, and a *Times* reporter recorded this exchange with a young boy walking away.

"'Who was that man?'" someone asked six-year-old Buster Smith after.

"'He's president of the United States.'

"'And what does he do, Buster?'

"Buster stood erect, rubbed his eyes and answered, 'I think he saves our world.'"

Two days later, a U-2 spy plane photographed clear evidence of nuclear missile sites being built in Cuba. Soon the world would be on the brink of nuclear war. But that October evening, the scattering steelmen, housewives, politicians, and cops could be forgiven for feeling that any trouble could be overcome. "What a glorious moment," Gino Piroli said. "One of our greatest days." Aliquippa hadn't just arrived. It belonged.

8

Mother's Oats

The king was growing weak. You couldn't sense it at first, because, hell, Carl Aschman wasn't about to let you. That bad family history, all the quiet talk around the table about a "paper heart," hung at the back of his mind, but in public he gave every sign of being the same unyielding force. Despite the down years, the nation's top coaches always took Aschman's calls, took chances on the players that he assured them could play. "Guys from Aliquippa went to college everywhere in America," Don Yannessa said. "I can tell you every kid that played in that era and where they went: Arizona State, Kentucky, Minnesota, Pitt, New Mexico State, Arizona, Tulsa, Wichita. . . . They went everywhere."

And long after they played for him, Aschman still held the men in his thrall. In 1960, Frank Marocco came home after a fine career at N.C. State—ACC title, an Orange Bowl berth earned and then forfeited after a basketball recruiting scandal, teaming with star quarterback Roman Gabriel—hoping to play pro ball. The Winnipeg Blue Bombers of the Canadian Football League had offered Marocco a tryout and, like a puppy dropping a ball at its master's feet, he phoned his old coach up at the high school to let him know.

"I'm going to Canada," Marocco said.

"No," Aschman replied. "Come up here and talk to me."

What could he do? Aschman had sent him to Raleigh and that had worked out. Now he was telling Marocco that Canada was no good, to get serious and come coach at Aliquippa. Marocco was newly married, but it wouldn't have mattered if he were a wild bachelor: he couldn't say no. He signed a contract to teach physical education and monitor Friday night dances for $4,200 a year, and coach junior varsity for an extra $200. It wasn't until Marocco told his father-in-law, owner of a fruit stand downtown, his salary that he realized he'd been railroaded. "Come work for me down at the store," Frank was told, "and you'd make that a lot faster."

Aschman was pushing sixty in 1962, but seemed as engaged as ever. He had never been the most exciting teacher, but then, everybody knew why he was there. It wasn't unusual for his history class, "Problems of Democracy," to begin with Aschman telling everybody to read a chapter. When they looked up from their books, he'd be diagramming plays, all kinds of X's, O's, squiggles, and arrows filling the chalkboard. Weekends, he might cruise by the New Sheffield School field to watch the savage pickup football games, no helmets or pads. Half to see if any of his players were dumb enough to play, and half to see if there was anyone good enough to play for him.

"Teams of maybe thirty on one side and thirty on another, and we would get hurt," said George David, a '65 graduate of Aliquippa High and the future sheriff of Beaver County. "You'd lose teeth. A doctor used to tell me, 'I hate Sunday afternoons,' because the emergency room would be full of kids that had a broken leg, broken arm, broken shoulder, black eyes.

"Coach Aschman? He used to find his football players playing sandlot with us, he'd smack 'em on the head, kick 'em out of there. . . . I remember him coming Sunday afternoons and mad as a hornet, because we were playing with his players: 'I told you guys! I need them! They got to play! You're going to hurt 'em!'"

Everything about him still screamed old school. Every player, no matter how good, was a grunt. None wore a uniform number lower than 50. His Neanderthal view of injuries never changed. "Very sarcastic," said former receiver Richard Mann. "He would shame you. You might get a stove finger, and he'd say, 'Let me see it, son. . . . Bring it here, let me see. . . .' and he'd act like he was spitting on it and say, 'Wee-wee on it, son! Wee-wee on it! *Little* finger hurting. . . .' He was that kind of guy: 'Now you're all right! Get back in there!'"

No one challenged him. For twenty-five years steelworkers had been pushing for safer working conditions, but their sons toiled on under the rules of the old industrial sweatshop: Get hurt? Lose your job. Coaches like Aschman were the spiritual heirs to Tom Girdler's "dictatorship," with the "benevolent" part something of a bonus. Given time and space, some players came to feel they'd been little more than interchangeable parts. "I look back and whatever respect I had for him diminished," Gene Yannessa said. "I don't think that he really cared about his players."

Or maybe it just depended. Early in the 1962 season, Marocco's wife, Marian, with a one-year-old daughter and another on the way, died of a heart attack. There had been no warning. She was twenty-two. "Took her to a party, she sat down and dropped over dead," Marocco said. Aschman checked on him constantly in the weeks after, phoning and dropping by the dazed assistant's home, told him to take as much time off as he needed. "He was very humble," Marocco said. "The next time I saw him like that was when his daughter died—and that crushed him."

By the fall of 1962, Marocco's former jayvee team had matured into a dazzling collection of college prospects, and he had risen with them to a spot as Aschman's defensive line coach. It wasn't a glorious promotion. "I said, 'Boy, I'm going to be a coach on the varsity!'" Marocco said. "Then I found out what it was like: you go to practice and he'd say, 'Defense!' All I did was warm up the line and get the players ready." Aschman called every set, every adjustment, while his staff took a knee and chewed on straw. After enduring one such season, Marocco had had enough. When the same dynamic began playing out again during training camp in 1963, he threatened to quit.

"I can't coach this way," Marocco said. "This is not what football is about."

"What are you mad about?" Aschman said.

"You don't even include us. I want to coach defense, I want the kids looking at me and saying, 'That's my defensive coach.' I want to be able to talk to my kids."

So then came the first sign: Aschman gave in. He stunned Marocco by handing him his defense—and an immediate test. Aliquippa opened the '63 season on the road against Steubenville, Ohio's storied "Big Red," a team that had finished seventh in the state the year before. It wasn't even close. Powered by backs Mann and Howard "Hiway" Herring, receiver Matt Giles, and quarterback John Tazel, with a huge line—maybe Aliquippa's best ever—anchored by future Cornhusker Bob Liggett, the Quips offense racked up 32 points. More important, Marocco's defense forced three fumbles and two interceptions and became the first team to hold Big Red scoreless in seven years.

You could feel it all over town after that: Aschman's machine was humming again. The fan fights had eased, and games had been moved back from Saturday afternoon to Friday nights—another sign that things were returning to normal. But few outside the program knew that a transition had begun: Aschman was really letting go. Another assistant, Frank Heinecke, had taken charge of the offense, and even convinced the old man to shuck the old high-top Riddells and let the players wear low-cut cleats. And fifteen minutes before the Steubenville game began, the team manager had pulled Marocco into the locker room. He found Aschman lying on a training table, pale as snow.

"I got nervous," Marocco said. "Because he was the guy who controlled me, basically."

Aschman tried coaching, but he was too weak. Midway through the contest he handed the team off to his staff. At the time everyone chalked it up to food poisoning or flu, but looking back most assume the episode was a minor heart attack. Aschman coached the rest of the '63 season, finished 8-1, but those close to him could see a difference. "He didn't do nothing," Marocco said. "He changed completely after the heart attack. He was not as demanding. He wasn't himself anymore. It just wiped him out."

His son noticed, too. Carl Jr. had come back home in 1963. He'd kicked around a bit after graduating: a few years studying at Pitt, a year in J&L's seamless tube mill. Then the draft caught up with him and he found himself in a two-year stint in the Army, met a German woman in Wiesbaden, Germany, picked up a trade in electronics fixing Nike missiles. They had two sons, transferred to a base in Kentucky. When his wife died, Carl Jr. brought the boys, Harald and Carl III, to live with him and his parents in the old house in Plan 6.

King Carl took his grandson, Harald, in hand. He brought the seven-year-old up to training camp in 1964, made him unofficial team mascot, and put senior Bob Liggett in charge of the boy. The public pools in town were segregated, but at Raccoon Creek State Park the football players swam together; no one seemed to mind. Still, it was a sight: a huge black kid, 6-foot-5, 250 pounds, splashing in the pool with a little white boy, hoisting him up on his shoulders. The only sour moment occurred during a scrimmage, when Harald was flopped on the sidelines and a play came his way, players tumbling out of bounds. Bodies flew; someone's shoe smacked the kid in the eye. It began to swell.

Aschman snatched up the crying boy, hurried him down to his car, and, dust kicking up behind, rushed off to find the nearest doctor. And for that short flurry, the years fell away; the old man almost moved like the player he once was. Everything happened so quickly, in fact, that it took a while before anyone realized that this was the first time in memory, stretching back to his arrival in town twenty-three years before, that King Carl had left camp for any reason at all.

When Robert Pipkin graduated in the spring of 1963, off to junior college and then a stellar basketball career at Idaho, his "walkout" had seemingly changed nothing. The tryouts for the following year's cheerleading squad—seven varsity and six jayvee—produced the same grinning white faces, the same white-sounding names: Hodovanich, Sherba, Como, Ceccarelli, Glucki, Kelliher. Black girls did try out, including one talented gymnast, Carolyn Williams. But as so often seemed the case involving election to the school's honor societies and political offices, the bar for blacks seemed higher. Or the white women in charge just kept moving it.

"We girls who kept trying out for cheerleading, we were talking about it: 'Why? I made the finals, and then I got a D on my report card? My grades were good!' and stuff like that," said Carolyn Browder, née Williams. "It was conspiracy."

No one in charge ever admitted as much, but the issue didn't go away. In early 1964, backed by the First Class Citizens Council—a black organization dedicated to equality in housing issues and the hiring of blacks downtown—Aliquippa High students, including some whites, began a month-long boycott of the cafeteria to protest the lack of black majorettes, cheerleaders, and food-service workers in the cafeteria. They brought in their own lunches, dubbing themselves "The Brown-Bag Brigade."

Compared with the fire-hose-and-attack-dog footage of Bull Connor's Birmingham, Alabama, seen on nationwide television the previous year, such slights at a Northern high school seemed decidedly minor. But for young Aliquippa blacks, the school's cheerleading squad was the richest symbol: glittery proof of the cancerous views lurking below.

"Negroes," it seemed, were good enough to tend J&L fires and run a football—but God forbid the borough feature any darkness on its public face, or allow blacks any voice in public life.

"It was not until 1966 that the black population began to gain sufficient political strength to make any inroads into the political structures" of Aliquippa, the state's Human Relations Commission stated in a 1971 report. "And at present blacks are only marginally represented in the community system of power relations such as the borough council, boards and commissions."

Blacks at the Aliquippa Works, meanwhile, remained stuck in unskilled or semiskilled jobs. Composing 8 percent of the workforce there in 1970, blacks had minuscule representation in white-collar and craft jobs: Four of the 982 officials and managers, four of the 154 technicians, eight of the 812 office employees, and eight of the 2,310 skilled workers were black. Departments like carpentry and bricklaying remained off-limits, and those seeking promotion into management or clerical work, or a spot in apprenticeship programs, met with discouragement and hostility from white workers.

Life outside the tunnel offered little different. Aliquippa's local hiring practices, the report stated, "reflect a rejection of blacks in substantial proportions in the community businesses such as automobile dealers, retail trades, food, wholesale trades and real estate. Black women are primarily working as maids, waitresses, laundresses and in the hospitals. Professional blacks have limited positions in teaching, social work and nursing."

That lack of public and private clout was galling, but the lack of cheerleaders struck an even more basic nerve. It seemed just another way of saying that black skin, black people, would always be considered substandard, ugly even, when compared with white. "We have been referred to and treated like objects much too long, and the time has come that we are not going to take it anymore," said an unidentified black resident quoted in the commission's report. "For us to be constantly referred to 'them,' 'those,' 'they'—as objects rather than human beings: this is one of the reasons for the problems that we are having in Aliquippa. . . . To us blacks we are black, and to the whites the matter is that you don't consider us human beings."

So while the Brown-Bag Brigade started with far smaller slights, down to even the cafeteria's serving of fish on Fridays, its '64 boycott became a pivotal wedge. Whites—and older blacks—had no choice but to confront a lifetime of norms.

"It caused the entire community to start looking at other things that didn't make sense," said Barron Harvey, the future business school dean, a junior that year. "The white students had buses. We didn't. We had to walk the mile and a half, two miles through the snow down one hill, up another hill. As a function of that, buses started—even though they were coming real, real early."

Harvey's father, Henry, a bookkeeper in Ambridge, was president of one of Aliquippa's most venerable black institutions, the Quippian Club. He attended one of his son's protest meetings, and Barron was sure that his dad would echo his contemporaries. "All the rest of the older generation's saying, 'You're making fools of yourselves, you're making things worse than what they're going to be, you shouldn't be doing that. . . .'" Barron said.

Instead, when the meeting concluded, Henry said, "You're right. You can count on our support. I'm going back to my group and see what we can help with—and we're going to look at other things as well." Barron didn't see his dad again until the next night, at dinner. They didn't say a word about the meeting, but Barron couldn't help but stare a bit. He had never been more proud of the man.

Slowly, then, change started to come. All of it—the Brown-Bag Brigade, the glaring lack of black cheerleaders, the coverage in the press—began to be an embarrassment. "We had one meeting at the

500 Club, with the NAACP and the First Class Citizens and some of the school board and the superintendent and the principal and they asked [the cheerleading sponsor] why don't she ever pick black cheerleaders?" said Carolyn Browder. "And she said, 'Because they didn't have any rhythm.' Everybody in there cracked up laughing and she walked out and resigned as the cheerleading sponsor. And I had loved her dearly. Martha Mooney: she was my neighbor."

Browder was a senior in the spring of 1964. Late in April, without mentioning race or acknowledging a change in policy, the new cheerleading squads were announced for the following school year. No blacks made varsity, but they were in the pipeline at last: Judy Toliver, Rachelle Wingate, and Josephine Dudley were named to the junior varsity squad, and rising ninth-grader Cassandra Blue made the junior high team. Browder remembers seeing the names posted on a bulletin board. She was proud of the breakthrough, but it hurt.

"Too late for me," she said.

Browder stayed in Aliquippa. She didn't have much choice. "I was raped at eighteen," she said. "Graduation party, and I drank for the first time and he took advantage of the situation. And I felt like, *Here goes another bad thing in my life . . . but this child didn't ask to be born.* I wasn't going to give her up for adoption. My mom and dad told me, 'We'll raise her; you go on to California and go to college.' I said, 'No, I'm going to get a job and take care of her.' She ended up with cerebral palsy."

Browder married in 1969, and raised three daughters and a son. Her second, Carletta Browder, went to Aliquippa High and made the varsity cheerleading team. In her senior year, 1987–88, she was named captain.

Was Aschman too hard? Perhaps. But for the boys he coached, in the town he worked, the choice life laid out was as stark as could be. Richard Mann felt the chill on his neck, every day: father never around, mother unable to work, food and clothes supplied by what used to be called "public assistance." Raised by his grandparents in Plan 11, and later on Fourth Avenue, Mann watched his grandfather ready himself, year in and year out, for his shift on the by-product coke ovens with all the other black men, watched him come home filthy and spent, marked the pink burn scars on his legs and hands from a molten spill that had killed a man. At some point, too, the old man had lost a finger down at the mill. *Little finger . . . wee-wee on it, son!* But Grandpa didn't complain.

During a training-camp scrimmage in Donora before the '64 season, Mann felt his right shoulder crunch and pop—and knew almost instantly that he was done. Dislocation, muscle tear, the whole horrid deal: He could barely walk, the pain was so bad, and even then he was bent double and shuffling. A doctor in the hospital there wanted to operate immediately, but his grandfather drove up and got Richie discharged and hustled him home before they could do even more damage. This was his senior year. He needed an Aliquippa doctor, one who understood the stakes involved.

"If I didn't play the rest of the year, I wouldn't get a scholarship," Mann said. "And I just knew if I didn't get a scholarship, that was it for me. Nobody was going to give me money to go to school."

Enter Dr. Mickey Zernich, one of those crucial background figures—lubricants, really—that keep towns and high school powers running. A member of Aliquippa's '49 state-title basketball team and prime steward of its recruiting pipeline to Pitt, the Quips' jocular team doctor was an orthopedic surgeon with an unorthodox bent. He once took a box of M&M's candies as payment for surgery. He lived all his adult life next door to his brothers—and fellow doctors—Steve and Wally, and their sister, Nadine, in a compound in Center Township. Zernich had the run of Aliquippa Hospital. And Hippocratic Oath be damned, he knew that Mann—a quick and sticky-handed, 6-foot-3 talent—was right: He needed an Aliquippa doctor.

So Zernich made sure word got around to the hospital staff: *Loosen the rules a bit here.* Mann spent the season's opening week enduring hours of therapy, but some buddies also snuck in a pair of sneakers; the nurses looked the other way when Mann slipped outside to run in a field behind the building. At the end of the week, Dr. Mickey walked in with a ball of tape in his hand.

"How's it feel?" he said.

"All right," Mann said.

Zernich tossed the ball of tape high, and Mann reached up and grabbed it. Zernich asked if it hurt. Mann said no. He was lying.

Mann asked if he'd damage the shoulder any more by playing the rest of the season.

"No," Zernich said, lying a bit too. "You can take the operation after. You can probably learn to live with the pain."

Mann came back in the second game of the year, a 16-0 win over Farrell. Zernich had rigged a thin chain, with one end attached to a wrap on Mann's rib cage and the other under his right arm, for Mann to wear beneath his uniform so that he couldn't fully extend the arm. A week later, against Sharon, he went up in the back of the end zone, covered by two defenders, caught a pass from quarterback John Tazel, and came crashing down hard on his side—but held on to the ball. Aliquippa won, 7-0. The next week, Mann, moved now from flanker to tight end, fell on a fumble in the end zone with two teammates for the first touchdown in a victory over Ellwood City. The next week against New Castle, he recovered another.

Midway through the season, Mann felt good enough to dispose of the rig under his jersey. "Eventually I just learned to deal with the pain," he said, "and eventually I forgot about it."

It became one of the strangest seasons in Aliquippa history. The team was stacked with talent, but couldn't have been more unpredictable. Defense—and a line keyed by massive tackles Bob Liggett and Joe Catroppa—made the Quips unstoppable in Class AA league play, but the offense had no rhythm. On October 23 Aliquippa stuffed Butler—with future NFL quarterback Terry Hanratty leading its

40-point-per-game attack—41-21 before a home crowd of 9,000; Mann, at right cornerback, intercepted Hanratty twice and ground up 102 yards on runbacks.

Two weeks later, Aliquippa played Hopewell High for the first time. The two schools sat just 3.2 miles apart, if you took the windy route up Sohn Road through Plan 6, but it may as well have been 100. The new school, opened in 1940, was dismissed throughout the county as Aliquippa's smaller, softer stepbrother, populated mostly by the children of white couples who'd fled town in search of breathing room. Hopewell's mail still had an Aliquippa zip code, even though residents lived outside the borough limits, and the Class A high school didn't even have a football field; the Vikings borrowed Aliquippa's stadium for their "home" games on Saturday nights.

But on November 7, in the opener of a series played for a new trinket called the Steel Bowl Trophy, the impossible happened. It was a damp Saturday evening—technically a Hopewell home game—but 8,000 fans still poured into Aliquippa Stadium expecting the true home team, and its legendary coach, to romp. "We had nothing to lose," said George Medich, Hopewell's junior quarterback that night. "Everybody expected us to get our brains beat in. But we had a bunch of tough kids on that team. I think we surprised 'em."

Indeed, Hopewell's offense did nothing different than it had all year, yet Aliquippa somehow allowed halfback Chuck Blaney—whose dad, Larry, insultingly enough, taught biology at Aliquippa High—to canter all over them for 167 yards. In the second quarter fullback Clyde Fuller bulled in from the 1-yard line to provide the game's only score. "I thought we held him out of there, man," Mann said fifty years later, "but they called it a touchdown."

Medich, who would go on to earn a football scholarship to Pitt, attempted only three passes all night, muffed an extra-point kick, and hurt his ankle; his enduring memory is of the cleat marks the speedy Blaney left on his back when he ran over him from behind. None of it mattered. "Doc" Medich, as he'd later be known, would go on to win 19 games for the New York Yankees in 1974, while studying to be an orthopedic surgeon. He notched 124 major league wins overall, twice went into the stands during games to save heart attack victims—and ended up going into practice for a time with Mickey Zernich. Eventually, an addiction to painkillers would cost him his medical license.

But before all that, good and bad, Medich had one pure moment by which to measure every big event in his life: the night he, a Hopewell kid, helped take down the toughest guy around. "It was a big deal," Medich said. "Everybody was really surprised that we won. Everybody. Even the guys on our team were surprised that we won. Because we thought that they were tougher than that, really."

Who didn't? "In the annals of Beaver County football—and indeed the WPIAL—there has been no greater upset," the *Beaver County Times* announced the following Monday. It had been twenty-five years, Aschman declared, since he'd been so stunned by a loss. "Aliquippa fans, who had watched their team humble six league opponents as the top contender for the WPIAL Class AA crown, sat silent, waiting for the next miracle," the *Times* went on. "Their expressions would not have changed if the earth had opened up and swallowed Quip Stadium. Some, no doubt, would have welcomed it."

In other words, the loss couldn't have been more humiliating for school and town—and yet, oddly, it didn't matter at all. Aliquippa's two losses had both been nonconference affairs, uncounted in the WPIAL standings, and the following week the team zigged again, crossing the river to crush Ambridge 20-0. Mann intercepted a pass and ran it 23 yards for the final Quip touchdown. Fans tore down the goalposts. Though three other AA teams had posted undefeated seasons, the playoff-less WPIAL still relied on a long-controversial "Gardner Points" tiebreaker system to rate schedule difficulty and dominance. Aliquippa, with a league-high 146 points, was tapped to play Monongahela for the championship in Pitt Stadium.

Critics howled. But in what ended up being the supreme distillation of the Aschman style—smothering defense, punishing ground game, an utter disdain for flash—the Quips suffocated Mon City in the blustery cold, 7-0. The Mon offense racked up a measly 20 yards total in the game, completing just three passes to their own receivers and throwing three interceptions. One of them belonged to the "redoubtable" Mann, as the *Times* called him, the capstone of his high school career. No mention was made of the fact that he'd caught it wincing.

For the impartial spectator among the 9,109 present, everything about the frigid November day was ugly. On the sideline, the sixty-one-year-old Aschman—bags under his eyes, skin crosshatched with wrinkles—wore a hood to protect himself from the cutting wind. There was but one heart-stopping moment: near the end of the second half, on third and 14 on Monongahela's 22-yard line, Tazel hit Mann on a slant; the Mon defenders converged, Mann fumbled, and the ball squirted toward the Mon end zone. After a mad scramble Aliquippa halfback Ed Hauser fell on it at the 1-yard line. Tazel then ran the ball in for the only score. The second half was all trench warfare: young men trading small chunks of territory, accomplishing little.

The minute the clock ticked to 0:00, though, all tension and cold seemed to vanish. The Aliquippa players screamed and hoisted coaches on their shoulders; the massive Catroppa picked up Frank Marocco as if lifting a child. Aliquippa fans rushed the field. A goalpost came down. When Aschman was asked what it meant to win the town's third title, his fourth overall, he gave a perfectly clichéd answer about each one being "equally satisfying." But once he'd tunneled through the crowd of reporters and parents to the players gathered in the tumultuous locker room, his stoicism dissolved; Aschman saw his players, arms locked, posing for photographers, and rushed in, embracing every one he could. The room hushed. For a moment Aschman's head was hidden, face crushed and shaking against a shoulder pad.

Later that night, at the American Serbian Club in Aliquippa, Aschman came the closest anyone could remember to crowing. "Let 'em look that up in the records," he said, "if they don't think we belonged in that game."

On Monday, classes were cut short for a celebratory assembly. Aschman told the cheering students that he was just "a rocking-chair coach," able to coast because of his gifted assistants. No one took him seriously: He'd just pulled off the greatest turnaround of his career. Aliquippa had gone from suffering its most embarrassing loss to one of the most dominating defensive performances in WPIAL history. Aschman gave a nod to the wake-up call sent by "our good neighbors" from Hopewell, but didn't want anyone to misunderstand.

"You are never," he said, "going to see a defense like that as long as you live."

Mann never did get that surgery on his shoulder. "To this day it sticks up," he said. "I've coached receivers all my life, and now I get pains in it because I've got older. I get shooting pains up in there. That's all part of growing old, you know. . . ."

It was worth it. That '64 season, indeed, changed his future. Mann did get a scholarship to play football at Arizona State, where he graduated with a degree in elementary education, and he went on to coach receivers for thirty years at major colleges and in the NFL, helped to make talents like John Jefferson, Mark Clayton, and Keyshawn Johnson into stars, won a Super Bowl with Tampa Bay in 2002. In 2013, the Steelers, his seventh NFL team, brought the sixty-five-year-old Mann back home at last when they hired him as wide receivers coach.

But before all that, during the summer of 1966, Mann had one last crisis to work through. At Arizona State he played for head coach Frank Kush—the militaristic, merciless son of a Pennsylvania coal miner who, for his entire career, tapped Beaver County for kids who'd been raised to take it. During training camp, Mann slammed his right arm onto the turf; fluid seeped into that same shoulder, and he felt the pain all over again. He couldn't hold a tackling dummy, much less practice. He didn't dare go to the trainer, and that bone-deep Aliquippa ethos kicked in: *Get hurt, lose your job.* So Mann quit. He packed, left camp, began hitchhiking to Phoenix just as a thunderstorm broke. He figured he'd fly home. The mill was waiting.

He never made it. The first car along was a newspaper reporter, sent out by Kush to fetch him. Mann returned to camp, soaked, and a trainer gave him a shot of cortisone. Two days later, he was scrimmaging again. He ended up starting three years at flanker and tight end for Kush, the coach who was eventually fired in 1979 amid charges that he physically and mentally abused his players. Mann, though, never found him all that demanding.

"You grow up in Aliquippa, you can make it anywhere," Mann said. "Trust me: What we did in that Raccoon State Park? When I went to Arizona State I was way ahead of most of the guys.

"And a lot of kids I played with in the sixties that came from California? They had never gone to school with whites. I had. We'd had some problems, but I went to school with 'em. I remember the first time I ever saw an over-easy egg, out at Raccoon State Park. Joe Marchionda, we became real good friends—good fullback from West Aliquippa: when I saw him put that fork in and I saw that . . . running? I had never seen that in my life. I grew, from being around a different race. It made me grow as a person."

Mann didn't know it, but he had emerged from the tail end of something rare—a small moment of balance in the unending struggle between tradition and progress, order and chaos. Back home, the traditions and institutions that gave him the tools to work with, the social norms that kept tempers from overheating, were beginning to buckle. The town's old guard could sense it slipping away. The '64 championship was Aschman's last: he suffered what was publicly called "a minor coronary" during a fishing trip the following summer, and in mid-July 1965, the day he checked out of the hospital, he sent the school board his letter of resignation.

"I am forced to take this action because of the condition of my health," Aschman wrote. "It was a matter over which I had no control."

He apologized for any inconvenience, and thanked the board for "the opportunity to coach for so many years at Aliquippa. . . . The enthusiastic support and cooperation I have received from my colleagues, my coaches, my squads, the entire student body and the Aliquippa football fans will always live in my memory." He signed the letter, "Regretfully yours, Carl Aschman."

As ever, he didn't issue a public statement or call a press conference to explain himself. Aschman had been in Aliquippa twenty-four years, brought the town titles, built a vessel for pride that would forever define its identity. Yet no one seemed to find his quiet fade the least bit remarkable. His work was done, wasn't it?

Two days later, the *Times* published a farewell editorial lauding Aschman not only as "a master" of his game but as "a gentleman and a believer in the ideals which characterize the American way of life." It seems a curious addition, that last salute, unless you were alive then and taking stock, and worried about what came next.

PART THREE

October 14, 2011

. . . . *It is, suddenly, a perfect night for football: 51 degrees, a near full moon, the wind a whisper. At 7:02 p.m. the kickoff sails end over end. Beaver, it turns out, is more primed to play than Aliquippa; the Quips miss easy tackles, fall behind 10-0, and even when they do find the end zone late in the second quarter, miss the extra point. Zmijanac stalks along the sideline, eyes bulging. "We can't even do the simple fuckin' things," he yells.*

It doesn't help that the announcer keeps issuing updates from the nationally televised Hopewell–Central Valley game. Both nearby schools—richer, bigger, populated with the descendants of Aliquippa millworkers—are loathed. Central Valley formed in 2009 as a merger of Center and Monaca's dwindling school districts, a voluntary move taken, many suspect, to prevent the state from ever forcing their suburban white souls to merge with Aliquippa. As ninety-year-old Dan Casoli, a fixture at The Pit since 1946, said this afternoon from his bed at an extended-care facility, "I hope they both lose!"

A handful of his contemporaries are tucked now into the only shelter in the place: a roof extension jutting from the backside of a concession stand, marked with the stained white sign—"RESERVED SENIOR CITIZENS." Some two dozen black and white faces, carved by age and the mill's heated demands, huddle below in thick coats and scarves, as if on duty. For eighty-four-year-old Joe Letteri, though, the overhang smacks of surrender; he stands all game with the younger men, on an exposed, crowded slab next to the press box. And when the PA announces that Hopewell is winning, the snarls and groans rise as one from both cadres, old and young, and betray the vital truth.

It's always Hopewell Township, encircling the 4.5 miles of Aliquippa like a golden horseshoe, that earns most of the hate. It's Hopewell High that, today, staged a front-page press conference for running back Rushel Shell, the most coveted recruit Western Pennsylvania has seen in years, so he could declare that he'll be attending Pitt. It's Hopewell that has a new stadium and a weight room that doesn't smell like a root cellar—and a team that still can't win as much as the Quips. And it's Hopewell, most maddeningly of all, that shrinking Aliquippa High may have no choice but to embrace someday, perhaps soon, sacrificing history and bloodlines to a place regarded as forgetfully arrogant. . . .

"Rushel Shell's mother? She lived right behind the bar on Main Street here," says Quips assistant coach Sherman McBride. "But you want to say because your kid's going to Hopewell that you're better? We were fine for you when you were here, but you move a little to the left or right and your shit don't stink now?"

Besides, Aliquippa fans figure, they've got one even better than Shell—though the world doesn't know it yet. Around town, they're calling Dravon Henry "The Chosen One" or, better, "The Next One," but since he's only a sophomore, the explosive and elusive tailback has yet to light up recruiters' radars. That's how playing for Aliquippa works against you, early on: the team is so dominant that Zmijanac usually pulls his starters midway through. Henry is near unstoppable, but he hasn't racked up eye-popping numbers—or gotten anything close to Shell's press—because he's so often sitting down.

So Beaver has done everyone a favor. Down 4 points at the half, the Aliquippa players stream into the locker room angry, fully awake. "Time to see what we made of," says lineman Emanuel Williams. "Now we at the other end of the scoreboard. We running this ball. It's over. We RUNNIN' it." But Henry can't see this yet; he's miserable. The team's longtime doctor, Pat Sturm, nudges him. "It's a good thing," he says. "Now you get to play the second half."

Beaver opens with the ball. Aliquippa forces a fumble, but surrenders a safety; the grumbling in the stands slackens only upon word that Hopewell is now losing by 11. And it's here, abruptly, that Aliquippa finds a rhythm, grinding at last down the field: nine plays, 82 yards, Henry bulling in for the touchdown. This time the kick is good: 13-12, Quips.

At that the night sky, without warning, begins to explode. There are oohs and pointing, the childlike fascination with fireworks. Dwan Walker, standing at his usual perch atop the stands, glances up with a grin: His doing. In May, Walker defied the town's Democratic machine and all expectations by crushing Battalini in the mayoral primary; with no Republican running, that meant the election. The next day, he walked into A-Rocket Fireworks on Route 51 and paid $5,800 to lock down a display for every Quips home game. That's traditionally the Democratic Committee's preserve, but the campaign had been so vicious that Walker wasn't leaving anything to chance. It was also a way to stick it to the machine, one more time.

Come November, the thirty-six-year-old Walker will be sworn in as the first black mayor in Aliquippa history. His race, age, and inexperience make it easy to frame the moment as either a civic cry of desperation or a paradigm shift. But it's also a sign of football's centrality, the way the program keeps expanding to fill a vacuum once occupied by family, church, mill, or union. Walker and his twin brother, Donald, who won a seat on the city council, played for the Quips before graduating in 1994, coach Little Quips teams, and made Aliquippa football ties a subtext in their vague but emotional pitch—dubbed "One Aliquippa"—to revitalize the community.

It was a shrewd strategy. Even his fiercest critics can't question Walker's love for Aliquippa or its football players, given his good reason to despise both. In 2009 his sister, Diedre, was murdered in front of her twelve-year-old son by James Moon, a running back with the 2003 state title team. Walker found his nephew in the police station, covered in blood. The killing made Walker run for office. No one, he says, had believed in him more than D.

Now the mayor-elect returns his gaze to the field. When the Beaver band breaks into the sports arena chestnut, "Rock and Roll (Part 2)," he leads a chant: "Hey! You suck! We're gonna beat the hell out of you!" But Henry doesn't need any help. He intercepts a pass with six seconds left in the third quarter, and in the ensuing drive Zmijanac calls his number all seven plays, 54 yards of up-the-gut offense that Beaver expects and just can't stop. What had been a sloppy affair becomes inevitable: Aliquippa's line is driving Beaver backward, yard by muddy yard.

"Man," says Mike Warfield just before Henry breaks loose for the 25-yard score. "He is just pounding them."

Warfield came alone tonight, sitting his unmistakable, 6-foot-5 frame in the stands where everyone respectfully gives him room. The Pit is regarded as sacred space, a bubble *that gang conflict and crime almost never penetrate. But if one of the program's more talented quarterbacks, class of '87, draws plenty of nods, he gets his share of glares, too. It doesn't matter. "I refuse to NOT go back," he says of The Pit. "I'm going to go to football games; I'm going to go hang out. I refuse to hide and duck, because I'm doing something I think is right."*

Five months earlier, Anthony "Ali" Dorsett, nephew of Dallas Cowboys great Tony Dorsett, was sentenced to thirty years in prison for running Beaver County's biggest crack and cocaine ring, out of Aliquippa's Linmar Terrace. Warfield grew up in Linmar; his wife had kin in the ruthless crew. Yet, as a state trooper assigned to the Drug Enforcement Administration, he spearheaded the four-year federal and state investigation dubbed "Operation Enough Is Enough" that turned Ali Dorsett from kingpin to snitch, resulted in more than a dozen convictions—and broke, for the moment anyway, a fever of gang-and-drug-fueled gun violence that had gripped the town for more than a decade.

So this night, at least, the only breaking news is Dravon Henry. He's racked up 128 yards in the second half alone, 191 total, along with one interception and a drive-killing pass deflection that seals the 21-12 win. The crowd counts down the final seconds; someone sets off an orange-and-black popper in the stands: Halloween is coming. Afterward Zmijanac tries to deflect the media toward his seniors—and away from the fifteen-year-old sophomore who has just announced himself. "He'll have his time," Zmijanac pleads. But talent doesn't follow a schedule. It arrives when it's ready, and the world is the thing that adjusts. . . .

I can't get no satisfaction.

—The Rolling Stones, 1964

It's like a jungle sometimes it makes me wonder
how I keep from going under.

—Grandmaster Flash and the Furious Five, 1982

9

Mr. Lucky

At the time, it felt like the future. Early in 1964, the most striking benefit yet negotiated by the United Steelworkers began hitting mills all over America: thirteen weeks of vacation. Conceived by labor as a way to create jobs, touted as a hedge against automation and a transitional stage into retirement—and, since it came in lieu of wage hikes, seen by management as a clever way to hold down labor costs—the new perk had a crystallizing power that no dime-an-hour concession or term like "pension" could match. Two decades later, when the U.S. steel industry cratered, the steelworker with thirteen weeks of paid vacation would come to symbolize labor overreach almost as vividly as the Reaganite trope of welfare queens in Cadillacs. Depending on the color of your collar, it summed up unionism's impact at its best or worst.

Yet as the thirteen-week bonus began hitting the shop floor in February of that year, the only people concerned with its larger implications were social scientists—amateur and pro—curious to see how workingmen and their wives would handle the endless hours at home. Untroubled workers reveled in the chance to take long trips to Florida, to see their kids' plays and ball games, but for most the idea of a three-month "weekend" signaled a new and perplexing "Age of Leisure"—one of those cultural predictions that, in retrospect, had about as much chance of coming true as the vision of skies packed with flying cars.

"The above-average man, the aspiring young executive who not only puts in a long week at the office but takes home a briefcase full of reports to ponder after dinner and on weekends, may easily wind up working longer than did the old 12-hour-a-day steelworker," intoned *LIFE* magazine in a warning-shot article titled, "The Emptiness of Too Much Leisure."

"All the old rules of who enjoys the most leisure have been turned topsy-turvy in our modern society. . . . Today the richer and more prestigious a man is, the less leisure he is likely to have. . . ."

The piece, spread over twenty pages and bristling with experts, keelhauls the topic exhaustively, but the most pointed question commands a thick subheadline a quarter of the way along: "What is a steelworker going to do with a 13-week vacation?"

Joe Letteri built his dream house. He was thirty-six in 1964, and the 24-by-24 home they'd framed on the slab in the back of Gilda's dad's home in Plan 11 had gotten small, fast. Joey was born in Aliquippa in '57, and then bam-bam-bam they came: Bobby in '59, Richard in '60, Barbara in '61. The couple bought adjoining lots—for $4,400—a mile north out of Aliquippa through Hopewell and into Center Township, off Chapel Road. Joe assembled it the same way he'd built his first one, the way most workers at J&L did: everyone pitched in.

That was the formula: Go to the lot after work and on weekends, and use any carpentering, pipefitting, ditch-digging skills learned down at the mill to hammer and frame and saw for a few hours when what you really wanted was to sprawl on a couch. Maybe subcontract out the electric or plastering or plumbing, but the rest of the men from J&L

did plenty—and for free. Because someday soon, be it next month or next decade, the call to pay them back would come.

"The house I grew up in, my dad paid a guy to dig the foundation," said Doc Medich. His father, David, who ran the J&L carpenter shop, moved his wife and only child out to a house he built in Hopewell in 1954. "But he knew somebody that laid block and did cement work, and they did that. My uncle did the electricity and my godfather and my other uncle did the plumbing, and my dad did the carpentry. It was almost like the Amish: Then you'd go help somebody else build *their* house. He would come home from work, eat, put his clothes back on, and grab his tool kit and go back out the door to work on somebody's house. He did that an awful lot."

Joe's first thirteen weeks came in the summer of '64. Few in the general public knew that the benefit was neither awarded to all nor taken annually: The paid extended vacation was for the most senior workers, taken every five years, and most managed to take only one before hitting retirement. But Joe was younger than most. For eight weeks, his brothers and Gilda's father and guys from the carpenter shop showed up daily with their tool bags and crafted the bones of an eight-room house. When he got his turn working steady daylight—8-4—Joe would head out afterward and hammer away until nine o'clock. The Letteri family moved in August '65. "It was time," Joe said. "There was no more room in Aliquippa."

But in one sense, they never left: Joe still went into the mill, cycling month by month as always through the daylight, then the 4-midnight, then midnight-8 turns—and Gilda was in her twelfth year teaching in town. The Letteris remained, in other words, about as "J&L" as a couple could be. Even after their kids rose through the Center school system, with Joey valedictorian at Center High and Robert and Richard playing football there, and even though most of their new neighbors—Aliquippa exiles themselves—were all too happy to switch allegiances, Joe and Gilda never did. Friday nights would find Joe standing at the

Quips' stadium or wherever Aliquippa played, no matter how far—hands in pockets, half-grin on his face. "Near every game for the last forty years," he said.

Even when her kids entered high school, Gilda still knocked her neighbors' noses out of joint by hanging a massive "Go Quips!" banner outside her Center home. "I know these people didn't like it," she said, laughing. "But I don't care."

Much later, after Joe Jr. had gone to Cal Tech and Berkeley and Hollywood and started winning Oscars for visual effects, local reporters would write and broadcast that he grew up in Center. When he travels back from his home in New Zealand now, the homecoming stories essentially tout Joey as one of the most, if not *the* most, accomplished people to hail from that small slice of Beaver County. And it's essentially true. But Gilda always corrects them. "He is from Aliquippa," she says.

You could always tell. The Letteris taught their kids to attack the world, and leave the niceties to those with clean fingernails. When Joey later saw fraudulence in a last-minute switch of the qualification rules for valedictorian, expanding things so that *eight* seniors were given the honor, he stood up at his Center High graduation and gave a biting speech condemning it. He had become an astronomy nut by then, brainy in a way Joe Sr., the eighth-grade dropout, could barely comprehend: the boy spent hours each night with his telescope, intending to study cosmology and physics when he got to college.

And wasn't that how it should be? The son doing better than the dad? Joe Sr. felt no resentment. When Joey was eleven, he had needed a perch above the ambient light to mount his first telescope. Joe climbed into the attic with hammer and saw and cut open a door near the peak, through the joists and plywood and shingles, one giant hole in all that fine work begun over his first thirteen-week vacation. So what? That was part of the formula, too: Raise up your kids, punch a hole in the goddamn roof, and let them reach for the stars.

* * *

Frank Marocco got word just before Aschman checked out. The Quips' head coach had been in Pittsburgh's Mercy Hospital nearly three weeks in July of '65, everyone in the know waiting for him to retire when he summoned his young protégé. Marocco made the thirty-minute drive into the city alone. He wasn't the most logical pick to succeed Aschman; only the King's blessing would give him a chance. "They're going to give the job to Pete Fuderich," Aschman told him. "But you stay and help him."

"Okay," Marocco said. "Whatever you say, I do anyways."

On paper, such a safe move made sense. Training camp was beginning in less than a month. Fuderich, a former Quips player himself, had been Aschman's assistant for sixteen years. But the head coach's sudden departure revealed a lack of conviction in Aliquippa's school board and boosters, a deficit of the daring that had landed the WPIAL's hottest property twenty-four years before. When he resigned, Aschman had been in the midst of a five-year coaching contract paying $2,000 a year. Fuderich was given a one-year deal, paying $1,400—and his tenure soon justified the pay cut. He went 1-8 his first season, and his contract was renewed. He went 2-7 his second, and it was renewed again. Aliquippa won four games under Fuderich in three seasons, lost twice to Hopewell, began a descent so deep that the program almost didn't survive.

But Aschman's sudden departure, disastrous as it seemed, carried one seed for the future. Indeed, if he hadn't quit when he did, the modern history of team and town would have been wholly different. Because up until that moment, Don Yannessa couldn't land a coaching job anywhere—and was about to give up. He'd been out of New Mexico State two years, teaching at Aliquippa Junior High and applying for any assistant opening that came up. Rochester, Monaca, and Midland turned him down. Aliquippa High was stacked. "It was a closed shop," Yannessa said.

By the summer of '65, he'd had enough. A buddy from Aliquippa lived in Detroit, and Yannessa took a job in labor relations at Chrysler for $10,000 a year—more than twice what he was earning at the junior high. In July he was settling into an apartment in Detroit, enjoying the idea of a new career, when he heard the low rumble of Aliquippa schools superintendent Sam Milanovich on the other end of the phone.

"You still want to coach football?" Milanovich said. "Get your ass back here. Aschman had a heart attack, they're going to hire Fuderich, and he's going to need a junior high assistant. Fly back and interview with him this weekend. I'm setting it up."

Yannessa paid $40 for a round-trip ticket on Northwest Orient Airlines. Now he and Marocco were together, and if they weren't close, if they were too different—Yannessa whip-smart, eyeing every angle, seemingly unfazed by anyone else's opinion; Marocco dogged and half-sure the world was out to get him—to be full allies, they knew they could help each other. Fuderich's doleful tenure ended with the '67 season. "We got our ass kicked," Yannessa said, "and we all got fired."

Marocco was again passed over for the Aliquippa head coaching job in the summer of 1968. The board cycled through three more hapless coaches—Richard Jeric, Jack Laraway, and Dave Strini—in four years, touching off a fatal spiral of losses begetting declining interest begetting more losses.

But the problem was bigger than coaching. Rising take-home pay made migration to bedroom communities almost mandatory; for the first time in its history, Aliquippa's population shrank in the '60s, declining 16 percent to 22,277. Meanwhile, football's my-way-or-the-highway ethos wasn't resonating as much with kids; black-booted legend Johnny Unitas of the Baltimore Colts, a Pittsburgh product who'd worked the summer of '56 as a "monkey man" on an Aliquippa Works pile driver, was their dads' quarterback. The boys who played now increasingly modeled themselves after brash types like Beaver Falls' Joe Namath, the upstart Jets passer who sported white cleats and would soon guarantee a Super Bowl win over Johnny U's Colts. Be it in the NFL or locally, old-guard values were losing their grip.

It came as no consolation that Aliquippa's twin, archrival Ambridge, had hit an equally disorienting patch. Marocco applied for the Bridgers head coaching job, but found himself spinning on the same merry-go-round. "It was the funniest thing," Yannessa said. "First, they hired a guy named Miller from Wilkinsburg who'd won a WPIAL title—new head coach and Marocco's going to be an assistant there. Miller keeps the job three, four days and reneges on it. Go through the process again: I'm running over there with Marocco all the time politicking, trying to get him the job, because I know there's going to be in it something good for me.

"Guy named Rip Scherer gets the job: Marocco's out again. Frank's going to be an assistant for *him*. And I'm going to get stuck working for Jeric, back at the junior high level in Aliquippa, and I want to move up. Then Scherer keeps the job three, four days and *he* reneges on it; job open again, and it's the end of July. They're going to camp in two weeks, and so embarrassed over there they hire Marocco to a three-year contract. I become first assistant, go over there and teach English and economics, work for Frank. I'm delighted. Great opportunity."

Theirs were pure career moves, leaving to work for their historic enemy. The era's tensions and social stresses had yet to surface on Franklin Avenue; though 1967's long hot summer was marked by racial violence and upheaval in 150 American cities, Aliquippa had remained calm. "Beautiful," Yannessa said. "It was where you wanted to be."

That didn't last. For the next four years, he and Marocco worked just across the Ohio, close enough to see the cracks widening in their hometown. "There were times," Yannessa said, "we chuckled and said, 'We got out of there just in time.'"

If Mike Ditka was the town's template for success, the snarling trailblazer for the line of football greats to come, there had to be a pioneer for promise squandered, too. Because that, too, is the Aliquippa fate.

The scouts, journalists, fans, and fellow coaches who've seen them come and go for decades take a twisted delight in saying that for every wonder who made it, three others came home muttering, "Woulda, coulda, shoulda. . . ." Georgie Suder might've been the first.

He had the bloodlines. His dad, "Pecky," had squeezed everything out of his own talent: flanked thirteen years of major league ball around service in World War II, managed a couple more years in the minors, and then came home to work as a guard at the Beaver County Jail. In November of 1964, Pete was named deputy warden there, and his son had begun to slide.

Georgie had inherited the Aliquippa disdain for status and authority, too; just as his uncle had once cussed out Honus Wagner, Georgie loved taking the world's winners down a peg. When some hotshot home for the summer would show up at the Morrell Park game, wearing his big-time college colors and declaring, "I got next," Georgie was the one snapping, "Motherfucker, go back to Hopewell. You ain't got next here!" It was even better if the guy pointed at his shirt and sputtered, "But I play at LSU. . . ." Then Georgie slammed the door. "You can't play here," he'd say. "Get out."

His talent lent him the authority: Suder was a superb second baseman, having led Aliquippa's baseball team to the 1960 WPIAL final, and an even better basketball player. "One of the greatest athletes I've ever seen," Zmijanac said.

"I'd go along with that," said his uncle, George "Juke" Suder. "He was terrific. God, to see him play? If you weren't awake he'd hit you in the face with the ball. He was so smooth out there. Oh, what a kid. What a waste. Baseball player? Basketball player? Anything."

In 1961 Georgie's high-scoring shooting led Aliquippa's coach, Frank Janosik, to predict that "he'll keep the name of 'Suder' in the limelight for a long, long time." But Georgie hadn't come of age like his dad and uncle, laden with immigrant fear and Great Depression values that regarded the waste of anything—food, soap, talent—as a kind of sin.

He landed a scholarship to Maryland, led the Terrapins freshman team in scoring, and was bounced his second year because of failing grades. In 1963 he came back blazing—17 points against West Virginia, 16 against Georgetown, double figures against N.C. State and Clemson—to lead the young Terps varsity. "George Suder Is Star at Maryland," proclaimed the *Beaver County Times*. But that was the high point.

Georgie led Maryland with 13 points per game that season, but the young team limped to a 9-17 record. Then his chance to star in the storied Atlantic Coast Conference slipped away. "Was going to start—got thrown out of school for stealing," Zmijanac said. "Had offers from the Red Sox, New York Mets—turned 'em down, didn't want to play baseball. Ended up going to Youngstown State, walked on the court the first day, and the coach said something to him that he took as demeaning. Georgie said, 'Do you know who you're talking to?'"

Suder would experience the occasional shiver of regret, but he wasn't good enough to bounce back into form whenever he pleased. He tried out for the Pittsburgh Pipers before the team's inaugural American Basketball Association season in 1967, but was cut after three days. In truth, he seemed more interested in gambling at cards, or the small-bore victories he'd carve out with Zmijanac as they barnstormed around the area throughout the mid-sixties, playing for the "Aliquippa Atkinsons" in the Sewickley YMCA league, or dominating games for Aliquippa's entry in the Serb National Federation Basketball Tournament in Canton, Ohio.

"Just wasted his life," Zmijanac said.

Zmijanac came from the other direction: Nobody ever considered him can't-miss. He had graduated from Edinboro State College, up near Lake Erie, in '64, received his draft notice a day later, and rushed home to take a job teaching English at Aliquippa Junior High. "Either that," he said, "or go to Vietnam."

The new war was hanging over all young males by then. Kennedy's escalation had placed 16,000 U.S. troops in Vietnam by the time of his death in 1963; by the end of 1965, President Lyndon Johnson would raise the commitment to 184,000. In May 1965, the first of fourteen Aliquippans lost in the conflict died in a combat plane crash. But plenty would survive, too, and some even seemed to find purpose in the military.

One, a classmate of Zmijanac's at Aliquippa High named Edward Surratt, was a fixture of black Aliquippa. His father, Arthur, had worked tirelessly at different jobs all his life, risen from butler to J&L hand to owner of a successful refuse-hauling business; every year, at a time when few black families had cars, Arthur would buy a brand-new Chevrolet convertible. "Had it all: Surratt was an only child," said Salt Smith, who grew up a block away in Plan 11. "His mother and father were middle-class when there was no such thing as a black Aliquippa middle class."

But Eddie was twice arrested his senior year of high school, for loitering and prowling, and broke a policeman's nose resisting one of the arrests. Drafted into the Army in early '64, he faced charges while in the service for incidents involving assault, reckless driving, an unregistered gun, and going AWOL, and had another charge, for prowling, dismissed. But in mid-1965, the local paper featured a photo of a grinning, helmeted Surratt; he had completed airborne training. After leaving the Army with an honorable discharge in 1965, he enlisted in the Marines the following year, and by late 1967 was engaged in search-and-destroy missions to flush enemy fighters out of tunnels and shelters. He was promoted to platoon sergeant, and returned three years later with a Purple Heart and the Republic of Vietnam Cross of Gallantry.

Zmijanac, safe at home all the while, was smart enough to know how good he had it. His mother still lived in Aliquippa, remarried now and hearing daily about the rising racial division in the schools, about the cheerleaders and the Brown-Bag Brigade. "You have to get out of there," she kept telling her son. But Mike was enjoying himself. He was in his twenties, with money in his pocket—$4,700 a year—and twice-a-week pickup games across the bridge in East Liverpool.

"If there were a hundred fuckin' guys there trying to play, there were five hundred—up on railings, everywhere—watching," Zmijanac said. "Nobody keeping score except us. Nobody called any fouls. Connie Hawkins and Jimmy McCoy, a legend in Farrell, and Simmie Hill would pick up. Fifteen guys'd get to play. The only two white guys within ten miles of the place were me and Georgie."

Hawkins was a high-flying New York playground legend with massive hands—Dr. J before Dr. J—not to mention an innocent railroaded out of an NBA career after a nonexistent point-shaving scandal during his freshman year at the University of Iowa. He would eventually be cleared, and later gain a spot in the Basketball Hall of Fame. But in 1966 and '67, after a stint with the Harlem Globetrotters, Hawkins was living with his wife on Pittsburgh's North Side, broke, waiting out his lawsuit against the NBA, and playing games all over the area to stay sharp. One summer night at the Zernich compound in Center, he and Georgie and Zmijanac engaged in an epic run of five-on-five, then drank and swam until well past midnight.

At twenty-seven, Hawkins signed with the ABA's Pittsburgh Pipers for their inaugural season in 1967–68, and went on to lead the league in scoring, lead the Pipers to the championship, and be crowned the ABA's regular-season and playoff most valuable player. In the lovably chaotic way of the ABA, the Pipers moved to Minnesota the next season, then returned to Pittsburgh in 1969. And at some point after that first season, after a game in East Liverpool, Hawkins pulled Zmijanac aside and told him, "I got you a tryout with the Pipers."

Maybe it was because Georgie had been cut, and Zmijanac knew he was no better. Maybe it was because the Pipers were anything but a solid operation, and paying role players $1,000 less than his teaching salary. Maybe he was scared to fail.

"I didn't go," Zmijanac said. "Could I have made it? I don't know. I never regretted it. Just the fact that, in my heart, I know I could play with Simmie Hill and Norm Van Lier and Connie Hawkins—I could actually be on the same court and play and be good enough to play with them?—is enough."

✳ ✳ ✳

For a generation, the social fabric of Aliquippa had been left to expand, roil, and preen on its own. J&L had stopped telling people where to live in the '40s but, like a discarded glove retaining the form of a hand long removed, most ethnic enclaves remained intact. West Aliquippa was still Italian. Blacks still lived mostly in Plan 11 and Logstown. Whites still dominated Plan 12, where school and stadium sat. But the no-frills stock of low-income housing built for war workers—Linmar Homes, where the Ditkas lived, nearby Linmar Terrace, and Griffith Heights—was showing its age. Parts of town had sunk into squalor. Just off Franklin Avenue, above where crowds had cheered JFK, rose a narrow stretch of asphalt that newspapers termed "blighted" and the harsh called a slum. Whites now called it, simply, "The Hollow."

It wound up Superior Avenue toward the high old farmland once known as McDonald Heights, but the "superior" had grown more and more ironic. Now the district was just ratty apartments, cramped businesses, plenty of small-time and violent crime, and one church. "It was like *Gunsmoke*," Salt Smith said. In the early days, this slab of Plan 7 had been dominated by Slavs, but blacks had a presence that, with time, slowly grew. They called it "The Holla."

On the first working day in January 1968, the Beaver County Redevelopment Authority opened an office in town to help the 180 families soon to be displaced by a new housing project, built with federal funds, on twenty-seven acres in Plan 7. Superior Avenue would be widened and upgraded; The Hollow would be razed. Now a new, faceless, white-collar force, flush with cash, would direct where people would live: a $2.6 million low-income complex, with 120 garden apartment units and 82 row-type town houses, to be called "Valley Terrace." Urban renewal had come to Aliquippa.

Within a month, home appraisals began and the number of affected families rose to. Hearings, relocation, construction would all take years, but the neat racial boxes that J&L had constructed fifty years earlier slowly began to splinter. Melvin Steals, an aspiring songwriter just graduated from Cheyney State, came back to Aliquippa that summer to teach English in the junior high. He married in December of '68 and began shopping for a home, and "we couldn't buy a house anywhere," he said. "Except on Plan 11 or Plan 11 extension."

"At that time if you were black you couldn't buy a house where you wanted to buy: You were 'redlined,'" Salt Smith said. "The banks would only let you buy a house in, say, Plan 11—not Plan 12!"

As an open practice, redlining dated back to the early 1930s, when the Federal Housing Administration's lending arm ordered maps to determine the level of security for loans in 239 U.S. cities. The richest communities were designated "Type A" and outlined in blue. The poorest, high-risk and usually black, were labeled "Type D" and outlined in red. Private banks assumed the standards, which included instructions to avoid areas with "inharmonious racial groups," if only to guarantee FHA underwriting on their loans. Until the Fair Housing Act of 1968 outlawed it, redlining blocked the upward mobility of blacks cold. It cut them off from vital capital, ensnared them in declining neighborhoods no matter their worthiness or wealth.

But by the time the Fair Housing Act took effect, Aliquippa's blacks were already on the move. The purchasing of "Holla" properties by federal and state authorities had had an unintended effect. As a low-income project, Valley Terrace could be projected as a place where blacks would gravitate. But the lump-sum payments—in effect, the "loans" redlining had long kept out of reach—empowered those living paycheck-to-paycheck to buy anywhere in town, including Plan 12. It also empowered those waiting for an excuse to join the exodus out of town.

Money talked, and in the exchange one color-tinged term, "redlining," was replaced by another: "white flight." "Because now all the blacks got this money," said Salt Smith. "When the blacks got this money—say, twenty-five thousand dollars—the whites who were still living up there, that gave them a chance to fly. And now that the blacks had cash money, they didn't have to worry about the banks *approving*."

But the churn in housing was a slow, document-heavy process, experienced in quiet offices one family at a time. Aliquippa's junior and senior highs, on the other hand, were populated by hormone-charged teenagers and marked by what Melvin Steals would soon condemn in the *Beaver County Times* as "a corrosive and inequitable learning environment," caused by "the existence of a double-standard—one set of rules for white students and a harsher one for blacks—that is responsible for the past, present and future unrest among the black students who are daily made painfully aware of the fact that they are being discriminated against."

School hallways had become far more volatile since Robert Pipkin's walkout over cheerleaders seven years before. By the spring of '69, as Steals' first year of teaching neared its end, racially charged scuffles had become the norm. Blacks kids had tagged one white as the leader of a racist cadre. A white girl approached the twenty-three-year-old Steals, said she liked a black boy, and asked his advice. "It was the 1960s, and I said, 'Go for it,'" Steals recounted. "She came into the cafeteria one day holding this black boy's hand and the kids got all upset about it. I was changing the guard."

He also arranged for a talented young black deejay, "Brother Matt" Ledbetter, to pay a visit to the school. Something about the record-spinner's presence stirred resentment and empowerment, and a small frenzy of fighting broke out across the springtime grass. "Brother Matt's appearance became a racial incident," Steals said. "A riot broke out in the courtyard in the junior high and the police had to come. Outside in the courtyard . . . it was like a swarm of bees."

When Henry Mancini whipped up his breezy jazz tune "Mr. Lucky" in 1959—"I know I'm on a lifetime lucky streak/A lucky rainbow lights the sky"—there was never any indication that he was thinking of Juke Suder. But if anyone in his hometown deserved the title "Mr. Lucky," it was Georgie's uncle, Pecky's brother, the guy who pitched Aliquippa to its first WPIAL title the afternoon before D-Day.

Juke survived the war that teammates Ninnie Vuich and Toats DiNardo and 131 other Aliquippans didn't. He enlisted in the Navy just a few months after that championship game at Forbes Field, but while best friend Gino Piroli found himself in the terrifying soup outside Okinawa, Suder spent just twelve days of a two-year hitch on the water. "I wasn't involved in anything," he said. "The war ended before I went overseas. I was in on that big celebration in San Francisco." His two brothers did see action, especially Ted. They survived, too.

After five years of minor league ball, Juke returned to Aliquippa for good in 1950 and married an Italian girl, Josephine Spaziani; they would stay together sixty-one years. "What a wonderful woman," Suder said. "I thank God every night for every year that I spent with her."

He always had a job. When he was playing pro ball, he'd work winters on J&L's line and wire or electrical gangs, or in the shipping yard or seamless tube mill. When he quit baseball for good, he hooked on at the welded tube plant, and stayed thirty-four years. Josephine landed a job managing Linmar Homes, up where the Ditkas lived. About halfway through, Juke left the union and became a salaryman—lower management, lining up truck and rail shipments. That shot to hell his chance at the thirteen weeks off, but he couldn't say no. J&L had offered up the ultimate prize: "steady daylight"—no 4-to-midnight or midnight-to-8 a.m. shifts. Everybody wanted steady daylight. You could see your kids. Wives were happier. A worker could have a normal life.

Mr. Lucky was also Mr. Sunshine: it's no wonder that Honus Wagner laughed along when Juke Suder cussed him out. Always upbeat, almost sweet, he is one of the few residents lacking the Aliquippa tendency to see more darkness than light. He and Josephine raised two boys and un-like, say, Joe Casp, who made damn certain his son Bill worked the worst mill jobs when he came home from Princeton—so he'd hate it—Suder figured J&L could be counted on to reveal its nature without his help.

"I *wanted* them to work in the mill," he said. "It paid half their education. My first son was in the labor gang. and that was some rotten jobs, man. He was in the soaking pits, underneath the furnaces digging out the old bricks, wearing wooden shoes. He had enough bad jobs that he knew he didn't want to settle there." Suder makes it all sound easy, somehow. And it worked out. Both his boys went to college: one's the vice president of an insurance company, the other's a dentist. "They're both doing very, very well," he said.

That's why it's not surprising, really, to hear Suder say that he didn't notice any racial tension growing up in Aliquippa. He never needed a lock on his door in Plan 7, and in '44 he played with a black center on the basketball team without any sense of strain. If blacks were discriminated against in the mill, he said, it must've been before his time. Then again, Suder is also one of the few who found the mill enjoyable. When it finally closed, he said, "I felt like I lost a friend or something. A lot of people, they hated the place. But I didn't mind it, really."

Such a disposition is perfect for a bartender. So it's no shock, either, that as the '60s careened to a close, Juke found a spot pouring drinks at Savin's—the shot-and-a-beer joint up in Linmar on Penn Avenue, straight down from Woodlawn Cemetery. Ditka's dad, Big Mike, would show up most nights, after his shift with the A&S Railroad. "You sat in a bar with Mike, everybody really liked him, but ain't nobody was going to say anything to irritate him," Gino Piroli said. "Mike was tough."

It was a mill crowd, mostly, and white; guys like Piroli and Joe Letteri would stop in on their way out to Hopewell and Center. There was plenty to laugh or complain or wonder about: boys with long hair, LBJ and Richard Nixon, those black runners holding up their fists at the Mexico City Olympics, the assassinations of Martin Luther King and Bobby Kennedy, Vietnam. People argued sometimes, but nothing too serious. Juke Suder wiped down the bar, topped off glasses. Business was good, and the nights moved along.

10

Halls of Anger

On April 30, 1970, Richard Nixon, who'd won the presidency seventeen months earlier in part because of a promise to end the war in Vietnam, announced his decision to expand the conflict by ordering a bombing of enemy bases in neighboring Cambodia. He did so in a nationwide speech marked by a vision so bleak, so overarchingly apocalyptic, that it reads today like a cultural cry for help. And in a way, it was.

"My fellow Americans, we live in an age of anarchy, both abroad and at home," Nixon said. "We see mindless attacks on all the great institutions which have been created by free civilizations in the last five hundred years. Even here in the United States, great universities are being systematically destroyed. Small nations all over the world find themselves under attack from within and from without. . . ."

Such imagery, of course, was startling enough, but the self-analysis was even more unsettling—and resonated long after the war's details had been forgotten. "If," Nixon went on, "when the chips are down, the world's most powerful nation, the United States of America, acts like a pitiful, helpless giant, the forces of totalitarianism and anarchy will threaten free nations and free institutions throughout the world. . . ."

This was, of course, one man's alarmist justification for the stark reversal of a pledge, just ten days before, to withdraw 150,000 troops from Vietnam; and Nixon's core persona was marbled with darkness and paranoia. But he was also a brilliant politician with a career long sustained by shrewd readings of the national mood. One June 1970 poll had 59 percent of Americans supporting the Cambodia decision— end-of-days rhetoric and all—even with the virulent negative reaction it sparked in Congress and on campuses. Nixon wasn't alone.

It's impossible to pinpoint when, exactly, the white American center began doubting its core faith in political and social institutions, in the idea of the United States as an ever-renewable engine of progress; the transformative era known as "the Sixties," that eleven-year period between Kennedy's assassination in 1963 and Nixon's resignation in 1974, spawned so many wrenching events that each one has been cited as the moment when cynicism took hold as a mainstream attitude.

Yet the assassinations of John and Bobby Kennedy, Malcolm X and King, the prevaricating Vietnam maneuvers of Lyndon Johnson, the death of Mary Jo Kopechne at Chappaquiddick and Senator Ted Kennedy's subsequent silence, were but touchstones amid a broader landscape of urban unrest, a rising divorce rate, the "communication gap" between young and old—and outnumbered occasional mood-lifters like the 1969 landing of the first man on the moon. By the spring of '70 the old social compact—family ties, automatic respect for elders, the idea of "my country right or wrong"—lay in tatters. Few dared invoke the usual visions of America as a "city upon a hill" or the "last, best hope of earth." To many, both nation and notion felt unmoored.

Four days after Nixon's speech, National Guardsmen killed four students at Kent State University during a campus demonstration. That was White House chief of staff H. R. Haldeman's touchstone; thus began, he later wrote, the administration's slide into Watergate, presidential resignation, national disgrace. Four days later, in response to—and protest of—the Cambodian invasion, more than 4 million students walked out in the largest college strike in U.S. history. Some 100,000 protesters descended on Washington, D.C. Students and police clashed at twenty-six universities. Armed insurrection seemed possible; the military was called in to protect the White House.

White House counsel Chuck Colson recalled seeing troops from the 82nd Airborne sprawled in the basement of the Executive Office Building then and thinking, "This can't be the United States of America. . . . This is a nation at war with itself." On May 8, construction workers in New York City attacked student protesters. Just before dawn on May 9, Nixon—accompanied by his butler, Manolo—appeared unannounced among protesters camped at the Lincoln Memorial, looking, indeed, like a giant helplessly out of his element. Students gathered around to hear him ramble about the war, the plight of blacks, the wiping out of American Indians. Some were from Syracuse University; the president remarked that they had a good football team.

"Look at the situation," Democratic congressman Thomas "Tip" O'Neill said then. "No nation can destroy us militarily, but what can destroy us from within is happening now."

While wrenching, the centering of Vietnam protests on college campuses at least made for a bit of clarity. The media could point to a defining hub—complete with built-in, dramatic visuals—for an often amorphous "movement." Antiwar strategists could expect receptive audiences of teachers and students. And opponents could dismiss protesters as elitists who didn't speak for what establishment types called the "silent majority": the mass of Americans who liked the war and their nation just as it was.

But racial inequality was a far different issue, one lacking instantly recognizable targets like a president or soon-to-be-drafted eighteen-year-olds. America's "race problem" offered little in the way of battle-field "wins" and "losses," and presented nothing resembling an "exit strategy." There was no "silent majority" at a distance from the tumult. The war was here. They were the tumult. And their children were the first to feel the pain.

By the time bullets began flying at Kent State, Aliquippa, sitting just eighty-five miles southeast, was already a fortnight into its own violent crisis. It began with a growing sense of inequity in the schools; discipline for misbehavior and small-scale racial spats was increasingly falling hardest on blacks. Of the 174 Aliquippa junior and senior high students suspended during the 1969–70 school year, 162 were black; the five students expelled permanently were all black. Long-simmering tempers between the races began to snap.

"I remember you getting around a group of 'em, the whites, and they would say anything to you," said Chuckie Walker, a junior at Aliquippa High that year. "Teachers always played favoritism with 'em, in my time—always. Literally, they'd talk down to you."

On April 21, 1970, English teacher Melvin Steals took his junior high classes on a field trip into Pittsburgh. First stop was the Highland Park Zoo, and second was the Gateway Theater to see a new movie called *Halls of Anger*—an unflinching account of the travails of five dozen white suburban students bused into an inner-city Los Angeles high school populated by 3,000 blacks. It was a logical step: in his two years teaching, Steals had been a vocal critic of Aliquippa race relations—and "anathema," as he puts it, to many of his white colleagues and bosses. "We used to have meetings in Jones School and I'd dress like H. Rap Brown and we'd really exhort the crowd," Steals said. "There was a lot of tension.

"I would come into the men-teachers' lounge and they would get up en masse and walk out. And if I sat down in the crowded lunchroom at the table where the teachers sat with my tray, the others would get their trays and get up and walk away."

The film, starring soon-to-be-stars Jeff Bridges, Edward Asner, and Rob Reiner, depicts a high school with the reverse makeup of Aliquippa's, but the same explosive divide: fights, repeated mouthings of "nigger" and "honky," all-black and all-white lunch tables, a word-of-mouth assigning of "white-only" or "black-only" designations to water fountains. At Aliquippa High, meanwhile, another student boycott of the cafeteria over the lack of black cheerleaders was in full swing, complete with a new Brown-Bag Brigade.

In a letter to the *Beaver County Times* two weeks later, Steals denied that his trip to the theater had anything to do with the subsequent unrest. In fact, he wrote, the school principal and his fellow teachers— "impressed by the good results" of the "properly motivated" group he had first taken to *Halls of Anger*, "and perhaps fearful of the growing unrest within their classes"—the *next* week led a field trip of five hundred Aliquippa junior high kids to watch the same film at the State Theater in downtown Aliquippa.

"Obviously," Steals wrote, "the students attending this showing were not properly motivated."

In the days following that second field trip to *Halls of Anger*, black students reportedly designated water fountains at the junior high school "white-" and "black-only," and refused to sit in assigned seats unless they were next to a "soul brother."

"We went to the show, and it was like a white movie, how they disrespecting blacks, calling them 'niggers' and whatever," said Sharon Casterlow, a junior high student then who would go on to marry fellow student Chuckie Walker and raise Dwan Walker, Aliquippa's first black mayor. "So when we went to school the next day, you were mad as hell.

"Somebody white looked at you and said something? You were pissed about that movie; it was in your mind. *You going to disrespect me?* So you automatically jumped off."

Soon word spread: Blacks intended to make Friday, May 1, a "Halls of Anger" day in the junior and senior high schools by starting a riot. Some white kids told their parents and tried to beg out of going to school. Other whites met at the Eat'n Park restaurant the night before to make a plan to stow baseball bats under the steps outside Room 29 in the high school. By the time Friday's first bell rang, nerves had been rubbed so raw that the fear became self-fulfilling. "The white parents began to take their kids out of the school," said Steals, "and finally there was nothing left but black kids—who rioted."

An unnamed teacher later described a scene "of utter chaos at the junior high, a disintegration of law and order and no respect for authority." Windows were broken. "It happened in this hallway," said Zmijanac, a junior high teacher then, speaking one morning in what is now the Aliquippa High football office. "I remember the girl, Vera Motten, threw a big rock through that window over there. I taught in that hallway down there, and it was horrid. As bad as you can picture."

Quickly, the mayhem spread a half-mile down the hill, to the high school. Down on the ground floor there, in Room 29, the sound of rumbles and crashes from the floor above seeped through the ceiling. A white sophomore, Bill Casp, was sitting through homeroom period when a black student named Fred Peake, a rising track star and football player, suddenly said, "We got to get out of here." Peake led the mixed class of some twenty-five blacks and whites into an empty home economics classroom nearby. They locked the door from the inside, and could hear the rampaging on the floor above. Everyone hidden in the home ec room emerged unharmed.

"Why'd you do that?" Casp asked later.

"Because you're my friend," Peake replied. "I didn't want anybody to get hurt."

"That's the way we were," Peake said. "The class of '72 was close-knit, did a lot of things together. There were times when you were not going to let stuff happen—white or black, green or yellow."

Administrators sent students home early that day. A group of forty high school "youths"—and reportedly some adults—then ransacked a local A&P supermarket, overturning displays and causing thousands of dollars in damage. The arrival of a police car scattered the crowd; when it gave chase up Monaca Road, a brick crashed through the windshield. As the officers tried to step out, they were hit with a hail of rocks from a crowd estimated at two hundred.

Schools opened as usual the following week, but on Tuesday, May 5, the conflict reignited in the high school cafeteria, where the moment the bell rang to end the second lunch period, two black girls and a white girl began fighting. "It started as a sit-down situation in the cafeteria," Chuckie Walker said. "A fight started and then everybody jumped up and chairs started throwing." Within seconds the melee expanded to more than 270 students. Lunch trays went flying. Girls were seen backed against the walls, screaming.

"Then it went from the lunchroom up into the classrooms, out into the parking lot, up toward the junior high," Walker said. "Kids were coming out, and I remember one of the little kids coming down holding his head, saying a guy hit him in the head with a stick."

Rocks flew. A knife flashed. Police arrived: five white high school students were found to be carrying chemical Mace, hoses, a physician's scalpel, and a blackjack. Some whites reported seeing blacks with knives, but police found no weapons on black students. When the *Beaver County Times* asked the cause of the rioting, school board president William Zinkham said it had been building for two decades, and "the kids finally exploded."

Pressed for specifics, Zinkham could come up with only one. "Some people want to know why the school can put five black students on a basketball court and nine of eleven on a football team but don't have a black girl on the cheerleading squad," he said. In fact, he was wrong: that year's varsity cheerleading squad did feature one. But her uniqueness made nearly the same point. "It's harder for a black girl to become a cheerleader," Zinkham continued, "than it is for her to be named to the National Honor Society."

The crisis went deeper, of course, than cheerleaders or a movie. A sense that the town's white leadership didn't seriously account for black concerns, didn't truly *listen*, had been building for generations. Blacks accounted for 42 percent of Aliquippa's school population, yet students were now on their third boycott in eight years regarding cheerleader representation—with one girl to show for it. When they went home to Plan 11 and its declining housing stock, they heard parents complain about redlining and the lack of mobility at J&L, saw them diverted at every turn from that upward path to the middle class—and saw no reason to think that anything would change. And the nation outside hardly looked better: hundreds of U.S. cities had been buckled by race riots since 1965.

Classes across the city, in all Aliquippa schools, were canceled for the rest of the week, then again for a day the following week. Sheriff's deputies were brought in to patrol the halls, and seven junior high students were arrested after thirty whites attacked a group of blacks. That same May morning, a group of fifty black students gathered at the high school, demanding to talk to the superintendent, and then rushed to Room 225, interrupted a class, and injured some of the white students.

All the closings, reopenings, "cooling-off periods," and rumors of closings ravaged the school calendar. In all, nearly the entire month—fourteen school days—of instruction was lost. For the rest of the spring, and into the summer of 1970, administrators suspended classes intermittently—but refused to shut the doors for good. Attendance plummeted. "They tried to keep the school going," said Zmijanac, who was teaching eighth- and ninth-grade English then. "I have a grade-book here somewhere that shows the exact date where the kids stopped coming to school.

"And out there, outside that door? National Guard stood out there, with guns, for six weeks. And every day the kids who wanted to come to school? There were some. One black girl would come every day and sit in my classroom. Just one girl. I wish I could remember her name. . . . And we used to talk. She'd say, 'My father says I have to have enough courage to come here. He drops me off and picks me up.' I used to give her books to read, that kind of thing."

But such quiet acts gained little notice. King's message of passive resistance had lost its cachet among many younger blacks; the militant message of Malcolm X and Huey P. Newton's Black Panther Party advocated empowerment and armed revolt, loud and extreme. For centuries blacks had endured slavery, lynchings, third-class citizenry, discrimination in housing, jobs, and schools—often quietly, often nobly. But this was a time of violence, at home and abroad, televised nightly into American living rooms. Grievances, large and small, would not pass unanswered. Everybody, it seemed, was dead set now on making a statement—or else.

"It was tough," said Carl Legge, a ninth-grader at the junior high in 1970. "I grew up with a lot of black people and they were all my friends all my life, then all of a sudden they turned cold on me. I questioned a guy one time, down the mill, later on in life: I say, 'Hey, we grew up together and you wouldn't even talk to me when we went to junior high and high school.' He says, 'There was a lot of pressure on us. If we were seen conversing with white, it'd have repercussions.'"

Battle lines were drawn. Positions were hardening fast.

"White student threw an apple and struck a black student. Black student demanded white student be identified and expelled," read one passage of the state report detailing the school clashes. "Fifty-one white students held; when questioned, eight said they would be willing to get killed fighting blacks. The black student Ad Hoc Committee expressed a similar sentiment about white students."

Amid the upheaval, a ghost continued to make his rounds. Since he had retired in 1965, weathered, frail Carl Aschman was seen at the school, St.

Titus Church, the firehouse, the football field—but rarely heard. It was as if, stripped of his vocation, he had lost that part of himself he'd indulged only as a coach; the man didn't have a harsh word for anyone anymore. He kept busy substituting as a teacher in the area, showing up in Aliquippa one week, Ambridge the next. Don Yannessa would give his old coach a ride sometimes, pick him up at home and take him over the river.

"He was a bigger-than-life figure, the way I thought about him: constantly on edge, screaming, ranting, raving," said Yannessa, who was teaching and coaching at Ambridge then. "It wasn't till I got older and came back from college that I got to know him really good. I would pick him up in Plan 6 and drive him to work. I got to know him in a different perspective. He was gentle and . . . a nice guy."

Doctor's orders had something to do with it. Word circulated that Aschman had been told to stay away from Aliquippa games because the emotion would tax his heart. But he also knew that his presence would put pressure on the school's succession of struggling coaches, that fans would always ask what he thought of the new guy. He would show occasionally at Aliquippa's training camp, but cut short any talk about football. If a sportswriter got him to say, about some opponent, "They wouldn't have run that against us. . . ." it was considered a coup.

The other factor, of course, is that Aliquippa football had sunk to a heartbreaking low. The Quips won just six games in the five seasons after Aschman finished coaching and then, during two-a-day workouts at Edinboro State College in August of 1969, junior Aliquippa tackle Ron Vincich collapsed and died. "It was one of those days when it was just too hot; he overheated, hyperventilated, and we couldn't cool him down," Peake said. "We couldn't rescue him. He was a really big kid. That hurt us real bad."

The combination of racial problems and coaching ineptitude, meanwhile, shot the roster full of holes. Hopewell, Beaver Falls, Ambridge: Everybody beat up on Aliquippa during the fall of 1969, and the team went 0-10. Worse, almost no one seemed to care.

So come Friday nights, Aschman wouldn't go to Aliquippa Stadium. He'd ride instead to Ambridge, cheer his old archrival, watch his protégé, Frank Marocco, make a go of it as head coach. The football was better and, besides, he needed the distraction. One night in 1968, Aschman's thirty-one-year-old daughter, Susan, a home economics teacher and cheerleading advisor at the junior high, went to sleep and didn't wake up. No one ever knew why, but the family curse, that "paper heart," was always the prime suspect. Aschman's wife, Sarah, was devastated. It hit Carl even worse.

"It was very hard on my father, especially," said Carl Aschman Jr. "He just never really got over her dying."

Small consolation came in the knowledge that Susan passed away in bed, and never had to have her probable heart condition tested in the school turmoil of two years later. Indeed, when Aschman himself died of a heart attack at sixty-eight, on Thanksgiving Day 1971, it was easy to view him as a figure from a more fortunate, unquestioning era. The King had gotten out just in time, it seemed, untouched by the furies now roiling town and country.

But his family didn't go unscathed. In May 1970, Aschman's grandson, Harald, a seventh-grader at the junior high, was attacked by black students in a stairwell. Why? "He was the first one down the steps," said his father, Carl Jr.

"I happened to be white," Harald said. "I was by myself going to my locker and there was about eight or nine blacks down there. I only knew one of them; they weren't in any of my classes. I didn't provoke 'em or do anything. They threw me down the steps and started pounding on me."

And that was that. Carl Jr. pulled his son out the Aliquippa school system and sent him to St. Titus—where the waiting list had suddenly grown very long—for eighth grade, and then on to Quigley Catholic High in Baden. Harald played some football there, across the river. Soon the only thing in Aliquippa carrying on the Aschman name was the aging stadium up on the hill, and the boys inside who'd been left behind.

*　*　*

Aschman wasn't the only one. Ghosts were beginning to haunt heavy then. That's what happens when life gets harder: reminders of better days, of the way this town or family used to look and feel, mock even the most hard-boiled soul. And Tony Dorsett was hardly that. A mama's boy from the start, forever scared of his father's hard hand or his older brothers' jeers, young Tony assumed an eyes-wide cast so pronounced that his dad nicknamed him "Hawk." It stuck. But the best football player the place ever produced always felt more prey than predator, wary of what he might see next.

That quality made Dorsett. The skinny kid learned to juke, dodge, and corner so well—made near every rush, in fact, look like a hare fleeing a pack of wolves—that he went on to win the Heisman Trophy, a collegiate national championship, a Super Bowl title, and a place in pro football's Hall of Fame. To become great in a brutal sport can be a transformative act; for long stretches Dorsett could even convince himself that his career was about records or supremacy or fame, and not about a conquest of fear.

But ask him about his first years, and Dorsett will show you the truth. When he'd dress out for Pee Wee games, Tony would beg the coach not to put him in, then drag his pants in the dirt on the way home so the family wouldn't suspect. Once his brother Keith saw eleven-year-old Tony shrinking along the sideline, and screamed at him to get his hesitating ass out for kickoff. The ball, of course, came straight to him. "I took off like a rabbit," Dorsett said. "I was running up and down that field, went zigzagging because I was scared to death. I went about seventy-five yards for a touchdown the first time I touched the ball."

Then there was his maiden game against Aliquippa. He was in ninth grade, playing for Hopewell Junior High—high school ran tenth thru twelfth—and all week brothers Keith, Ernie, and Tyrone had been riding him at meals, at bedtime, between shots at the pool hall: *You'd better win. . . .* "Make sure you're at the game," fifteen-year-old Anthony—as he was known then—would answer, but he was hardly sure of himself. The older Dorsetts had starred for Hopewell, and everyone always said they were bigger and faster than Anthony was. And, besides, he was a wreck. Just a month before, he had watched their oldest brother die.

Melvin Dorsett never played for Hopewell. He dropped out of school, liked to drink wine, worked the mill some, had a heart condition: "My brother was a rough dude, man," Dorsett said. In August of 1969 Melvin was twenty-seven years old, and out of time. "That one morning, my brother—I think it was Keith—came running in, 'Mom, something's wrong with Melvin!' So they called the ambulance. I thought I saw him die in the house. They said he died at the hospital, but I *saw* him."

That it all happened so quickly—youth to death, promise to waste—was a shock; but then, the family always did move fast. Their daddy, Wes Dorsett, known to his family as "The Big Apple," had fine wheels himself and used to race beside his boys with a switch, goading and lashing at their legs. Ernie was known as "Speed Disease." Late in his career, a thirty-four-year-old Tony reportedly ran a 4.38 40-yard dash, and it's a measure of his younger self that many NFL peers believed it. But Melvin was the family legend. He'd run lightpole-to-lightpole races up on The Hill, everybody laying down bets. Challengers came in from all over Beaver County.

"He used to take their money," said Quips assistant Sherman Mc-Bride. "He was the fastest Dorsett. Tony didn't have nothing on Melvin."

"Talk about speed?" Tony said. "My brothers all had speed, but he was the one I'd watch at the park Fourth of July, everybody playing soft-ball, and it was amazing the stuff he'd do. He ran from left field to right field and caught a fly ball—the most unbelievable thing I've ever seen in my damn life. It was almost like he could play the outfield by himself."

After Melvin died in the family house, Dorsett found it impossible to sleep there. Moving in with his older sister helped, but he kept the light on all night. And now summer had turned to fall and it was time to play the Quips, their roster loaded with buddies like Fred Peake. In truth, Dorsett had far more friends on that team than on his own, so bragging rights were a worry, and his brothers were pushing him, so that was a worry—and he didn't know how he'd do, so that was a worry, too. But then the game started. Dorsett unleashed a breathtaking run, then looked up to the corner high in the stands where his family always sat. He saw his brothers. And then he saw dead Melvin.

"People always say they see visions," Tony said. "And what I saw was an image of my brother. I know people might think I'm crazy, but I made a great play, and I looked up to see my family and I saw him. I saw a vision, clear as could be. . . . He had a smile on his face."

Hopewell Junior High beat Aliquippa that day in 1969, and Hopewell Senior High beat their counterparts that season, too. No one was surprised. The tables had completely turned since Hopewell's shock win in 1964; the Vikings were the power, Aliquippa the pawn. That, more than anything, accounts for the persistence of a counterfactual query: What if Tony Dorsett had played for Aliquippa?

Hopewell folks dismiss the entertainment of this notion, of course, and it's true that no previous Dorsetts ever went to Aliquippa High. But talent-poaching is a constant of high school sports, and with Dorsett, it would've been easy. The boundary between Aliquippa and Hopewell runs through the middle—right through one home's kitchen, in fact—of the Mount Vernon housing project in Plan 11 where the Dorsetts lived, and hopping it for one school or the other is a time-honored tradition. McBride, for example, grew up in the '70s with his mother on the Aliquippa side and a dad wanting him to go to Hopewell; in eighth grade, Sherm moved in with his father in a house over the line. Sherman lasted just a few days at the school: a neighbor told on him.

He wasn't alone. Hopewell in Dorsett's day was known as "Whitey-land" to Aliquippa blacks, and its high school enrolled only a token handful. In the 1960s, Mount Vernon had been one of the first places to feel the effect of school busing as a way to ease desegregation; each day, black kids trooping out of their homes for the two-mile walk to Aliquippa High would look up to see a bus taking half their neighbors off to Hopewell. Tony grew up living the life of an Aliquippa black in Plan 11: his father worked the open hearth at J&L. His older brothers were part of a local gang called the Bugaloos, drinking beer, hustling. Tony ran some with the Baby-Baby Bugaloos, when they tried to stir trouble in Aliquippa.

And when it came to playing Midget League football—at the pivotal, high-school-deciding age of thirteen to fourteen—Dorsett wasn't even allowed to play in Hopewell due to hazy rules about age and weight limits. He and his best friend, Mike Kimbrough, played instead for the Aliquippa Little Steelers. In any other era, he was there for the taking.

But in the spring of 1970, just as the Aliquippa schools were becoming bedlam, Dorsett was a ninth-grader walking the calm, safe, football-happy halls of Hopewell Junior High. Even so, his mother, Myrtle, was taking no chances: she kept Tony home a few days when Aliquippa's rioting hit its peak. If Dorsett had once been a candidate to play for the Quips, that day had passed. In "1970, '71, '72, you didn't *want* to go to Aliquippa," Zmijanac said. "It was a terrible place to go to school."

Indeed, any Aliquippa football player with talent was looking to get out, too. "I almost attempted to do the same thing," said Peake, Tony's teammate on the Little Steelers. "It was a struggle playing for Aliquippa, even though it was my home. The chance to win a ball game every once in a while was zero to none."

So it is that many in Aliquippa today chalk Dorsett up as a hidden casualty of the era: the one that got away. Two years later Don Yannessa—all charm and gab and grins—would come back and begin the program's revival. Dorsett was finishing up his marvelous Hopewell career for coach Butch Ross then and, forty years later, the memory still stings. Yannessa has no doubt what would have happened if he had been in charge.

"I never would've let him play for Hopewell," he said. "I'd have got his ass. I never lost anybody to Hopewell; I used to get 'em *from*

Hopewell. I used to take their players. When I got the job in Aliquippa I never lost a player to Hopewell again."

Juke Suder was pouring drinks the night Aliquippa came undone. It was only a matter of time. The town had been edgy since blacks and whites began battling in the schools, and no subject stirs or reveals parents more than the fate of their kids. When children become the opening front in a war, escalation is near inevitable: now the future—no matter that the mill is booming and employing more than 10,000—seems at risk. So it was that, after years of seeing burning cities and fire-hosed black protesters on TV, after all the small-scale skirmishes and boycotts of their own, the two strains, national and local, finally merged. Aliquippa came to a moment of frightful clarity.

Just past 9 p.m. on May 21, 1970, Suder was behind the bar at Savin's in Linmar. Mike Ditka's dad, Big Mike, was sitting on a stool, as always, when the street outside Savin's and the nearby Linwood Tavern filled with restive members of a West Aliquippa softball league. Within minutes, they were battling a group of blacks from Plan 11 who, according to the next day's *Beaver County Times*, "had invaded the area and started a fight." Aliquippa's mayor, James Mansueti, immediately charged the blacks with planning the riot. "How else," he asked, "could such a large group arrive at Savin's at the same time?"

No one in the black community ever explained why so many had gathered then in the predominantly white area, and locals assumed the worst. "They were going to clean out the white people," said Charlotte Ditka, Big Mike's wife.

The Linwood Tavern was owned by West Aliquippa's Joe Battaglini.* "They were going to burn his bar down and one of the bartenders called down West and said, 'Hey, guys, there's a big riot starting up

---

* Battaglini spells his surname differently than the rest of the family.

here,'" said Anthony Battalini, Joe's brother, who served as Aliquippa mayor from 2003 to 2011. "That particular night, Battalini's Lounge softball team played the Panther Athletic Club, and they went up there and cleaned that place all up. They went up there with ball bats and everything—and from that, the blacks actually were so scared they shot all the streetlights out up in Plan 11 because they were afraid the whites were going to go up there and burn *them* out."

Police arrived and the blacks scattered, but not before a red Pontiac convertible sped through the area while a man inside fired a rifle at the police chief's car. Sniper fire, some random and some directed at police, was heard overnight and into dawn, but it wasn't long before the whites went on the offensive and did some "invading" themselves. Soon after, reports came in of bullets striking the low-income apartments at Linmar Terrace and windows being broken in the Plan 11 homes of blacks. Some blacks were evacuated for their own safety.

A swelling group of Linmar residents—armed with "clubs, chains, steel and iron tools and a machete"—became what the newspaper called "an angry charging mob of chanting whites," and were stopped from burning down a Linmar Terrace apartment building only when "police formed a human barricade and after taking much jeering and taunting by the group, managed to halt its progress and calm them down to a talking stage."

"'We're not going to let them [black people] cause trouble and run all over Linmar,'" one man shouted to the applause of the angry crowd. "We've put up with it long enough.'"

That night, four white Linmar residents were treated for injuries—two of them stab wounds—and seven people were admitted to Aliquippa Hospital. The following day the schools again closed, police arrested fifty people, and a citywide curfew of 7 p.m. was imposed. Cars were stoned. Sniper fire was reported. Blacks and whites were found cruising the streets with a total of 450 rounds of ammunition, clubs, bats, knives, revolvers, and "a home-made ball and chain attached to a billy-club type wooden handle."

The subtle and blatant lines of segregation, drawn up by J&L and cemented by decades of custom, were enforced now with bared teeth. Aliquippa—like Watts after thirty-four died in rioting there in 1965, like the 125 U.S. cities that exploded after King's assassination in 1968—became an armed camp. "The only time you were allowed up in the school [area], where the white people lived, was during school," said Sherman McBride. "We weren't allowed, and if you ran into a certain type you were getting jumped on. Vice versa for whites: if they were downtown, they were getting jumped on by black guys. And in the school, from what my brothers say, there wasn't a day you didn't have guys carrying switchblades."

Neighborhoods, split by the color line, organized vigilante patrols. "Both white and black citizens armed themselves in significant numbers," said the state report on the unrest. "In certain white communities, so-called 'walkie-talkie' groups organized, solicited funds and purchased electronic communications equipment."

In Plan 6, "King Carl" Aschman took his grandson Harald to a meeting on the old abandoned tennis courts, built in the elite area's 1920s heyday. "All these neighbors were getting real radical about pa-trolling the streets and saying, 'We should have guards at the two big roads,'" Harald said. "But even being the football coach and well known, he didn't say much of anything."

Vigilante whites in West Aliquippa, meanwhile, set up roadblocks on the bridge later named for Henry Mancini—the only way in and out of the area. Buses carrying workers to work the North Mill were stopped and searched, with the lunches of blacks checked for weaponry; there was a constant fear in West, the place where the original town was founded, of a black invasion. "Because our houses were so close together, we were worried about them throwing cocktail firebombs over and burning the houses out," Battalini said. "There was an old Jewish synagogue right there at the bridge, and a .50-caliber machine gun on top of that roof, protecting West Aliquippa. And we had a Catholic priest who went out and bought a Jeep and all the walkie-talkies for us to protect that town."

Blacks were no less trigger-happy. Larry Stokes, twenty-three years old and Richard Mann's best friend and teammate on the '64 champs, was arrested at an Aliquippa gas station with three others—but the concealed-weapons charge hardly did the moment justice. Stokes remembers "hand grenades and shotguns" in the car's trunk. Police informed the *Beaver County Times* then that the car held "one 12-gauge shotgun, a .30-30 Winchester rifle, a .32-caliber revolver, one bayonet and two bandoliers of live shells." Stokes, meanwhile, carried in his mind a mash of Black Panther and Nation of Islam rhetoric advocating violence against "blue-eyed devils."

"I was preparing myself to kill somebody," Stokes said. "That's what they told us to do. But I was so afraid."

Stunningly, during that tense summer no one ended up getting killed—not by racial shoot-out, anyway. George Medich, intent on becoming a doctor while he played pro baseball, had just graduated Pitt. He spent his time before the June amateur draft working as an orderly at Aliquippa Hospital, operating on high alert. "They always wanted me hanging around the ER . . . *just in case something happened*—whatever that means," Medich said.

In later years, residents found themselves downplaying the danger and playing up the Keystone Kops feel of those days: "sentries" with rifles dropping, asleep, out of trees. Or the goofy fear then in outlying townships like Hopewell, Moon, and Center. "Everybody was a nervous wreck that they were going to come up into Center and, 'Oh, what's going to happen next?'" said developer Mark Betters.

His brother Joe got so frantic that he fired a bullet through the floor of the family's home. "When these riots started, the guns were put out—loaded guns on tables in the living room," Mark said. "There was fear. We had a loaded gun in the living room and we always remember him fooling around or something and he shot a bullet right through the floor into the basement."

"Pistol," said another brother, developer C. J. "Chuck" Betters. "Joey was a fucking nutcase."

But the schools remained ground zero. On June 11, a hundred black students reportedly "invaded" Aliquippa High, breaking eighty windows and trashing the desks and chairs in two classrooms; seven windows were broken at the junior high, and seven students were treated for injuries at Aliquippa Hospital. Three unnamed white youths were arrested and charged with aggravated assault. When they weren't immediately released to their parents—like the several black youths arrested in earlier unrest—hundreds of furious whites descended upon the front of the Franklin Avenue police station and refused to leave.

Over the next three hours the crowd grew in size and outrage, like a spill of gasoline waiting for a spark. A smaller group of blacks gathered on Sheffield Avenue, the street running parallel to Franklin behind the station. After a gunshot was heard from up the hill, the "black turf" of Superior Avenue, Aliquippa police returned a volley of fire. The panicked white crowd surged into "Police Alley," the lane running perpendicular, and were beaten back. Sixty helmeted, billy-club-wielding members of the Beaver County Tactical Unit, a riot-police squad of officers from neighboring municipalities, then swept up Franklin Avenue, dispersing the mob with pepper and tear gas. In response to a shower of rocks from the hill, police fired another volley of buckshot into the dark.

To many, the melee downtown was Aliquippa's nadir, "the worst time," said Juke Suder. "The blacks are blocking up one side of the street and the whites were on the other side, and they were hollering back and forth, this and that, and some redneck from the white side yells, 'Let's go get 'em!'

"And they took off up the alley. . . . and both [groups] went up that Plan 7 hill. And the next thing you know tear gas is flying everywhere, man. Somebody was going to get killed: you knew that. It was burning your eyes like crazy."

By the end of the night, twenty-eight people had been arrested. One Plan 7 house was firebombed with a Molotov cocktail; no one inside suffered injuries. The following day, some five dozen police personnel ringed the campus of the junior and senior highs; only 29 of some 2,300 students showed and classes were canceled. Many families pulled their kids for the rest of the school year, never to return, and in the ensuing quiet tempers eased. Committees met, and administrators vowed increased dialogue and oversight so that blacks would become more integrated into school activities.

Still, the damage could hardly be undone. In physical terms, the havoc ravaged Franklin Avenue's status as a shopping destination; the opening, just three months later, of the hundred-storefront Beaver Valley Mall in Center helped guarantee the eventual shuttering of nearly three hundred downtown storefronts. Meanwhile, for more than fifty years black and white, rich and poor—not to mention Slavic, Lebanese, Italian, and Greek—students had arrived at the junior and senior high schools from segregated elementary institutions. Many became close friends. But now the cultural concept of a "melting pot"—in practice, at ground level—lost its allure.

"It calmed down," Steals said. "They eventually got control of the school, but from that point on white parents of means took their kids out of the public schools. Soon, every day there were about four hundred fifty, five hundred kids who were bused to private schools."

Because the new exodus folded into the decades-old migration of residents moving out to the spacious enclaves of Center, Hopewell, and beyond, it took time to realize that they weren't the same. The old was based on hope, and animated by the sense that Aliquippa was still home. The new one was based on fear, animated by the feeling that home was gone for good.

Yet if this was the time that Aliquippa's identity, its sense of itself as community, began, like some middle-aged body, to lose muscle mass, the bones remained strong. Fatherless homes, like the one Richard Mann grew up in, hadn't become common yet. Adults still hadn't cocooned themselves off from neighbors, so elders still felt a responsibility to discipline, advise, or cajole kids who were not their own. When Mann came home in the summer of 1970 from Arizona State—education degree in hand and heartbroken, his pro football dream destroyed by knee surgery—he didn't want to be anywhere near the game. He spent three months at his sister's house, steeped in self-pity, figuring he'd get some cushy work at a Pittsburgh YMCA.

But then George Stokes, the man Mann had watched every day growing up on Elizabeth Street heading off to work at J&L, took him aside. Maybe it was because his own son, Larry, had been arrested in the rioting of the previous spring. Or that George, an active member of Aliquippa's black leadership, could sense the slackness setting in, could tell that this wave of white flight would be taking with it, yes, some bald-faced racists, but also—bit by bit—the town's stabilizing voices. What would take their place? Here was a young black man with a degree. He needed every hand available.

"You need to go up to the school and help," George told the young and bitter Richard Mann. "You know football. You ought to go up and coach those kids."

Mann had had no intention of teaching math at Aliquippa Junior High, much less coaching. Just being on a football field—smelling the cut grass and that sour stink of used pads and tape and socks, or seeing a ball fly—twisted his gut like a knife blade. He missed the game too much. "I didn't want to be around it," Mann said. "I didn't want to do it."

But then he remembered how George Stokes, railroad worker, had bristled at the mill's daily reminder of all the higher-paying jobs he would never have because of his skin, but who showed up and worked hard anyway, every day, because that's what a man with a family does. And Mann just couldn't say no to Mr. Stokes.

When students returned on Tuesday, September 1, 1970, enrollment was already down two hundred students from the previous spring. Mann was starting his career teaching math at the junior high when he heard some startling news. It was starting again: White students planned to attack blacks. "It was 'Kill Nigger Day,'" Mann said. "My first day on the job. And they tried to start right in front of my building and I told 'em, 'Get the hell out of here!' I'm a young guy, had a big old Afro. If stuff got worse, I don't know what I'd done. But they moved on."

That was progress: The violence fizzled where, three months earlier, it would have flared. At the high school, too, junior Fred Peake noticed that his cousin Wanda had been elevated to varsity cheerleading. "Eventually they ended up getting there," he said. "In my time, there were a couple blacks who were cheerleaders." But such small steps barely registered: If the football team was any measure, town morale remained abysmal. Only twenty-nine boys showed up to play Aliquippa High football for new coach Dave Strini in August, and by late October the number was down to nineteen.

"He goes 2-7-1, and loses all of his white kids," Yannessa said. "All the white kids quit and there's nineteen kids playing; they're black. What a mess that was."

Parents, especially, couldn't shake a nagging dread. Every trend line seemed to be heading south. The just-reported 1970 census results showed that, even as Hopewell's population had risen to 14,056, Aliquippa's had dropped 15.5 percent, to 22,277. Drug use in the area was now among the highest in Western Pennsylvania. Even the vicarious pride taken in the town's famous successes—Ditka in the NFL, Mancini in Hollywood, Jesse Steinfeld in Washington, DC—experienced a chilling turn. On September 25, Ernie Pitts, in 1952 key to Aliquippa's first football championship and perhaps its greatest all-around athlete ever, a record-setting receiver for the Winnipeg Blue Bombers and a four-time Canadian Football League champion, and the father of six, was shot and killed outside his suburban Denver home by his wife.

"We were real close," said Willie Frank, Pitts's Aliquippa teammate. "He was out having a few, came home late, and knocked on the door. She thought it was an intruder and she shot him through the door."

Pitts's death—he was just thirty-five—was another first for Aliquippa. The too-early demise of America's best and brightest leaders, politicians, and movie stars would be one of the era's recurring themes. Now, in a year already soured by harsh division, the era's random cruelty had finally hit home.

Taken together, such hits couldn't help but have an effect. Don Yannessa had spent four years teaching and coaching at Ambridge, and during free periods he'd listen to the clipped voices on the police scanners—like a fan taking in radio play-by-play—describing the gunshots and unrest across the river. But he still wasn't prepared for what he found when he returned to his old high school to take over as head football coach in the summer of 1972.

"It was heartbreaking," he said. "When I came back to Aliquippa I didn't recognize it. It was totally different. I had never seen a community change so dramatically in a negative sense as I did in those four years I was gone. It was all racism, and it was white flight—all those bad things. It was ugly."

11

The Crack

Yet the town still possessed a certain beauty. Even as newspapers and TV stations now focused on the easiest story—public, emotional violence—to show and tell, even as Aliquippa in the 1970s became labeled a small-scale racial battleground, the old order and its undergirding rules did not vanish. Franklin Avenue still filled after each shift change. Mothers still demanded that homework be done. The ambition that drove families across oceans and up from the dying plantation South still burned.

In the summer of 1972, Mervin Steals was working the blast furnace at J&L. He didn't want to be there. But unlike his twin brother, Melvin, Mervin didn't stay long enough at Cheyney State to earn a degree, didn't have credentials to teach at the junior high. So he fell into the vocational safety net woven by the nation's manufacturing base, dipped into jobs at the Fesco plastic works in McKees Rocks and at American Bridge in Ambridge, then made a stab at selling insurance before finally heading through the tunnel for a six-year stint in the mill that killed his father.

That's how the family saw it. The twins were five years old when Thomas Steals died of cancer at forty-nine, and his three decades at J&L, especially those years spent steeped in the galvanizing fumes of the welded tube department, always figured in family lore as the reason. When Mervin first punched in, twenty years later, a supervisor took him aside to say that Tom Steals had been a wonderful man. Mervin worked seamless tube, then in the stockhouse, finally as a lorryman feeding the furnace. He thought about training to become an industrial engineer and passed an in-house test. But some other worker was chosen for the program. He wonders, still, if that wasn't because of the man's lighter skin.

Then again, everyone knew Mervin Steals wasn't looking for a lifetime at J&L. During breaks he'd go outside and stare at the river, munching a sandwich and trying to organize the music in his head. Eddie Holman, of "Hey There Lonely Girl" fame, had taught him much about songwriting at Cheyney State, but it was their one post-grad summer spent in Philadelphia—Tammi Terrell's friendship, the months spent working the low rungs of the city's soul circuit with master producers like Kenny Gamble, Leon Huff, and Thom Bell—that gave him and Melvin enough fuel to think that they, too, could write a monster hit.

Nothing shook that belief, not even when things started to crack in Aliquippa and his brother stood at the center of the racial strife and the family home on Green Street provided little refuge. In the spring of 1970, word got around that Melvin was involved in the shipment to town of a cache of guns. White friends passed along word of death threats; a group of black radicals declared that they were coming, armed, to protect him. Neither showed. But the twins spent those hot months convinced that law enforcement had placed a tap on their mom's phone.

Still, on off days, Mervin would noodle for sixteen hours at the secondhand piano on the first floor, sometimes alone; sometimes Melvin came home from teaching and they'd go a few hours more. Mervin's boss was a man's man named Al Harvan, a bluff white guy from West Aliquippa, and Mervin loved him. Harvan treated him fair, with affection even, and it didn't hurt that he had grown up friends with Henry Mancini. And Mervin was less political than Melvin; as a student he didn't grasp what the radicals at Cheyney were after. "A lot of my friends used to fly around the country creating all these problems— black militants," Mervin said. "I took one to the side and I said, 'Why're you doing this?'"

To Mervin, dwelling on skin color was a near-pointless exercise. Part of that's temperament: "You've got to learn to laugh," he likes to say. But the twins were also under contract then with Atlantic Records, and in his midweek trips to studios in Philly or Chicago Mervin learned that sharks come in all shades. He wrote a song called "Soul Power," for Archie Bell & the Drells, that was retitled "Green Power"—and never, he thought, was a change more fitting. Money was like music: it didn't matter what race you were so long as you could bring it.

So he absorbed the Holland-Dozier-Holland Motown songbook, Burt Bacharach's arrangements, Carole King's *Tapestry* album. Mancini tunes were all over movies and TV; the Aliquippa High band broke out "Mr. Lucky" at football games. Local lore had "Moon River" named for the crescent-shaped bend in the Ohio seen from West Aliquippa: During breaks at J&L, Mervin would stand staring at the filthy Ohio, hear its haunting strains in his head. And one summer day in 1972, it all came pouring back out.

He had the hook first—"Could it be I'm falling in love"—and Melvin sat down and, inspired by the courtship of his wife, Adrena, filled in the rest of the words. The song took about fifteen minutes to complete. "Could It Be I'm Falling in Love" went on to be recorded in December by the Spinners, and by the spring of '73 was the top-selling rhythm and blues record—and No. 4 song overall—in America. It has since racked up more than 4 million plays, appeared on the soundtrack of three motion pictures, and been covered by nearly a dozen recording artists. But its triumph goes beyond numbers.

The house on Green Street, after all, sat smack between the whites up in Linmar and the blacks in Plan I I, in a town poisoned by distrust and, often, raw hatred, at a time more suited to produce a plea like Marvin Gaye's "What's Going On." Yet there and then, a schoolteacher and a steelworker managed to conjure a lighthearted classic, a four-minute, thirteen-second rebuke to the world in which it was made.

I don't need all those things, that used to bring me joy
You made me such a happy boy
And honey, you'll always be the only one for me
Meeting you was my destiny-ee . . .

Melvin has been married to Adrena ever since. And for his brother, the song laid a sheen upon the mill, the era, and his hometown that will never fade.

"My mother always told me how she set me up to go to college," Mervin said. "Melvin, he went to school and was a teacher, and my reward since I didn't graduate was J&L. But you know what? I liked it down there. J&L was the backbone of America."

Even as he became known as a football prodigy, Tony Dorsett never lost his wariness. At Hopewell High he had a short temper, was quick to fight, even stood at the center of what he calls "a small riot" his sophomore year and got suspended from team sports for "a short time." But challenging his father was never the rite of passage it was for his brothers. At home Tony always had his ears perked, his internal radar alert to the subtlest shifts in the family air. Now you see him, now you don't: Tony the running back and Tony the miscreant were one and the same. "I could always see it coming down and I could always somehow disappear," he said. The whippings Wes Dorsett laid on his brothers were not for him. By the time his dad came looking for him, Tony was already gone.

Dorsett played his first Hopewell season as a 130-pound defensive back, more than enough time for coach Butch Ross to realize he needed his speed on offense. Dorsett moved to running back as a junior, scored forty-two touchdowns the next two seasons, and became the hottest recruit in college ball. His senior year, the Quips' only consolation was "holding" Tony to 103 yards rushing in a 26-12 loss. "I put a defense on him, a 44-stack monster, and had a good athlete mirror Dorsett," Yannessa said. "We blitzed right and left every snap. He carried the ball thirty-one times, the highest amount of carries he ever had, because they were so stupid, their coaching staff. If they'd have thrown the ball they could've beat us by fifty. But they just ran Dorsett, ran Dorsett—and we were there."

By then Dorsett had learned to enjoy the daily transition from black Mount Vernon to tranquil Hopewell and back again. Ross, the son of an Aliquippa steelworker himself, had a rep for relating to black players and, besides, Tony was no militant. He'd date white girls, if discreetly: come the end of the night, the girls would crouch on the floor of the car when Dorsett rode them back into Whiteyland, and then he and Mikey Kimbrough would haul ass out of there before any neighbors could see.

The world is full of treasure unearthed by unseemly traits like selfishness and greed. Cowardice, too. His mother, Myrtle, once said that Tony was different from all the other Dorsetts—"scared easier and cried easier"—and it may have saved his life. Acclaim and achievement—not to mention a furious training regimen at Pitt—armored up his confidence, but the fear never fully dissolved. From then on, Dorsett was running from failure, shame, even death, and lucky to have come late in the family line. Surrounded by cautionary tales, he was the only one sensitive enough to be able to read them.

The mill? Wes Dorsett told all his boys: "Come in this place, you don't know if you're coming out. And if you do you might be missing an arm or eye or leg. Do *something* for yourself." But his brothers, at one time or another, all ended up working at J&L. Only Tony listened. He never forgot the time, at sixteen, when he went to drop off keys at the mill and couldn't recognize his dad for the filth on his face. When summertime came and his buddies started trolling for jobs there, Tony refused. Football helped; Mickey Zernich paid him to come out to the family compound and mow grass and tend the pool. But it wouldn't have mattered.

"I wanted that money. They made good money down there," Dorsett said. "But I said, I'm never, *never* going to work there. Because of what my dad said: There's better things for me in life."

Dorsett was no saint. While a freshman at Pitt in '73, he had his first child out of wedlock—on the same day that he rushed for 103 yards in his first college game—and was hardly apologetic. But something kept him tethered to college when he got homesick and wanted to quit, beyond his mom's urgings and the soothing presence of assistant coach Jackie Sherrill. After starring for Hopewell in the mid-1960s, Dorsett's older brother, Tyrone, had gone off to junior college for one year before quitting—and his life spiraled down from there. His decline felt different than Melvin's, his waste of speed more wrenching than Ernie's, if only because Tony saw it all firsthand. Tyrone, he still says, was "The Original 'TD,'" his childhood hero.

"He was the brother that I always wanted to be like," Tony said. "Ernie and Melvin, I didn't get to know; I was so much a whippersnapper, a young cat. But I got to see Tyrone play. He was called 'the Sophomore Sensation,' because sophomores weren't playing a whole lot.

"Man, he was spectacular. He was a nice-looking guy, had some of the prettiest girlfriends that I've ever seen. The way I learned how to drive, he was back up on The Hill, playing cards—bid whist and spades and all that. I had these girls we were dating and had to take them back;

he grabbed the keys and threw 'em to me. I was like, *Yeah!* I jumped in that car, and I hadn't driven a day in my life. I took off driving. . . ."

He took off for good. At Pitt Dorsett couldn't have run harder, becoming the first college running back to amass 6,000 career yards, but his reach for the brass ring gave off a scent of desperation. Folks back home had smirked when he allowed a Pitt media official to change his name from Anthony to "Tony," but found it truly insulting when, returning from his Heisman ceremony in 1976, he altered the pronunciation of his name from DOR-sitt to Dor-SETT. Down at the mill, word got around that Wes wasn't pleased.

Indeed, such tinkering for the sake of—what? celebrity?—smacked of a man who didn't know himself, much less his roots; or, if you paid closer attention, of a man terrified that those roots would wrap around his feet and never let go. Dorsett went on to star for the Dallas Cowboys, but always seemed slightly at odds with success. He publicly complained about the Cowboys' legendary coach, Tom Landry, and how tough it was to be a black star in Dallas, and was never fully embraced by "America's Team" and its fans. He squandered money, liked to party in an era when partying often meant marijuana and cocaine, and if Dorsett insisted that he never did recreational drugs it's not like he was tucked in by 9 p.m.

Yet Tony never, like many of his contemporaries, allowed himself to go fully off the rails. He finished his twelve-year pro career with 12,739 rushing yards, remains one of the greatest running backs in NFL history—and he did it all for one reason. That didn't become clear until his Heisman night, December 1976, when Manhattan's Downtown Athletic Club gave him college football's highest honor. Because suddenly there was his daddy's face, all clean now, the way Tony always wanted to see it.

"My older brothers, seemed like they were closer to him because they'd got out of school and they used to drink with my dad," Dorsett said. "I wasn't doing that. Everything I did, that was for my dad to be proud of me. I'll never forget: when I won that Heisman Trophy, the smile that was on his face? Man: He looked like the proudest man in the world. I felt so good about it, that whole experience, him having to be there, being able to go to New York. Oh, man."

Yannessa was right: Aliquippa *was* different. By the time he came back home in the spring of 1972, the racial divide wasn't a matter of muttered slurs or phantom red lines drawn by faceless bankers. Outsiders now reduced Aliquippa to the broadest of images, and the town made it easy: When the meager crowds showed up for home football games on Saturday afternoon, whites sat on the home side and blacks sat across the field, in the seats reserved for visitors. The head coach gave his weekly chalk talks to two separate booster clubs, one night to the whites at the Ukrainian Club and the next to the blacks at the Quippian Club. When it came time for the annual team banquet, the Quippian would hold its at the end of November for black families and the Ukrainian would hold its a few weeks later, in December, for whites.

And the players were no different. When the thirty-one-year-old Yannessa walked into the Aliquippa High gym for the introductory meeting with his team, some five dozen boys were waiting. The whites sat in the stands to his left and the blacks to his right. He started pointing at faces. He asked each one his name, made him stand and move to the other side. Then Yannessa delivered the same pitch the previous four coaches tried: *You have to learn to trust each other. We can win here. We can get nighttime football back. We can do magnificent things.*

"They'd heard this bullshit before," Yannessa said.

The blacks eyed him, nodding, but he knew they didn't trust him: Aschman's boy, old-line Aliquippa white guy. And when, in the ensuing weeks, he made every effort to win over the most gifted black player, Larry "Bulldog" Jones, a natural leader who never complained and had a way of seeing through phoniness, the white players weren't shy with the main question: *Is he going to be close to the niggers?*

"I had to put a stop to that shit," Yannessa said. "That's how crazy it was, every day. It was a powder keg all the time, just waiting for somebody to light the fuse."

He almost didn't make it. During the team's training camp at Edinboro State, Yannessa thought he had Bulldog Jones in his pocket. The kid was key in every sense—a linebacker and fullback, member of the French Club, great student. But on August 24, 1972, during a scrimmage, the seventeen-year-old took a hit to the head short of the goal line, suffered a blood clot, collapsed in the locker room, and fell into a coma. The team trainer packed him in ice and sent him to a local doctor. He died a day later. "Football was his heart," said Jones's father, Johnnie Price, at the time.

Players wept openly. "The grief knew no color barrier," said the *Beaver County Times*. "Tears swelled the eyes of black and white players alike."

The Quips went 2-8 that year, winning two games less than the season before. But Yannessa's charm was irresistible. His instant recall of plays and games, massive smile, and ever-quotable natterings were catnip to teenage boys, gloomy alums, and sportwriters alike. Two years later, when a reporter asked his strategy for beating defending WPIAL champ New Castle—which hadn't lost in two years and hadn't lost to Aliquippa in a decade—Yannessa quipped, "You win the coin toss, catch the opening kickoff, and then run into the field house and lock the door."

But he had been telling his team all week that they could win, that all of Western Pennsylvania had them wrong—and then Aliquippa came out gambling and beat mighty New Castle, 17-8. On the game's first play, Yannessa lost his center to a broken ankle; twice on fourth down, he went for it instead of punting, and picked up a big gain or a touchdown. "This is the biggest thrill of my life," Yannessa crowed afterward. "Not just for me and this team, but for the town of Aliquippa."

That con man's flair made football fun and fans feel special; in time Yannessa would, indeed, return Aliquippa football to Friday nights, come up with the idea of shooting off fireworks before, during, and after games, inaugurate the pregame spectacle of an headdressed Indian riding onto the field and impaling it with a flaming spear. But his first year was the foundation. Word got around that Yannessa didn't play favorites. He visited black players at their homes, ignored the rats and roaches, cultivated their parents. During one visit some mother's pissed-off boyfriend was said to be coming soon with a gun. Yannessa made a point of staying until the danger passed.

Before all that, though, Larry Jones died—and black players especially noted how the ever-glib Yannessa took it. Even forty years later, it's the one subject that can render him speechless.

"We came home, and that threw a black cloud over everything we were doing," Yannessa began, but soon his voice grew thick, and quavered. He tried to clear his throat. "There was nothing good that came out of that, but . . . but the one thing about it was, those black parents and the black community, ahhh, they supported us . . . in that situation . . . and I developed some really strong relationships with people like Charlie Lay. People like that."

He stopped, tried again. "And, uh . . ." But then Yannessa went dead silent. Ten seconds passed. You could hear his wife, Elaine, moving cutlery in the kitchen. He tried one last time. "I can't breathe," he said.

But if the town's darkening mood, that "black cloud," seemed to be spreading, it was hardly universal. Through the tunnel, out on the mill floor, you could be forgiven for believing that life hadn't changed much. In 1968, James Ling's Dallas-based airline/electronics/sporting goods conglomerate, the LTV Corporation, bought 63 percent of J&L, but the acquisition terms and a tenacious J&L management enabled the company to operate for years after as a quasi-independent entity. Industry leaders and experts already knew that the Japanese had grown far nimbler than their U.S. counterparts in the embrace of cost-slashing new technologies like electric arc furnaces; by the end of the 1970s, a Central Intelligence Agency study would declare Japanese design and operation "the best in the world . . . the envy of the world's steelmakers."

But at first, anyway, the wave that economists and executives would later consider tidal crashed lightly on the Aliquippa Works. Constant expansion over the previous decade—new blast furnaces and continuous casting operations, a second basic oxygen furnace facility, the filling in of the channel between the mill and Crow Island—signaled only eternal permanence and growth. Jobs were plentiful. Detroit was still making cars out of steel. The unions, fresh off a 1973 agreement that traded a no-strike pledge for ironclad 3 percent annual raises and cost-of-living raises, were only getting cockier.

"Stuff started to happen that just didn't make sense," said Mark Betters, sitting with older brother C. J. "Chuck" Betters. "I would hear my friends, even into the seventies, telling me how they would go to work on the night shift down there"—and here both men shout—"and *sleep!*"

"For eight hours," Mark continued. "And somebody'd come over and wake 'em up and they'd leave and get paid for a whole day. It was the gravy train. And basically the union people, down at that Franklin Avenue union hall there, would protect that. And then [the workers] would vote 'em back in."

Meanwhile, J&L management, in contrast to the hard-liners at U.S. Steel and elsewhere, had regained a reputation for relatively enlightened leadership. In 1971, they even allowed a gimlet-eyed reporter, John Hoerr—who would later write the definitive autopsy of the U.S. steel industry—to roam for a full week through the works. He walked away impressed. "The Aliquippa plant seemed impregnable," Hoerr later wrote. "Some ten thousand people worked there. Retirees were still so attached to the company that every day one could see half a dozen or more sitting on a bench outside the plant, old fellows with arthritic hands and wrinkled faces for whom the mill was the center of life.

"It should not have been, of course, because the union had tried to give workers the wherewithal to do other things—travel, set up a small business, move to Florida as so many steelworkers did. But this older generation, men who had started their working lives in the 1920s or before, couldn't pull themselves away. . . ."

Hoerr just missed, by a year, Giuseppe Battaglini, who had survived, alone and sixteen years old, the sea journey from Italy in 1927 and quarantine on Ellis Island, who spent forty-plus years face-to-face with 3,000-degree molten steel in the open hearth—"working the hot-tops," as his son puts it—weighing 140 pounds going into his shift and 135 coming out, every day. Giuseppe retired in 1970 at fifty-nine, but never really left. "That place was his life," said Anthony Battalini. "For six months after he'd get up every morning and go to that mill. I'd tell him: 'Dad, the mill's going to be there. You don't have to check to make sure it's running.'

"I never knew he was sick. He developed a lump over here on his neck, and was taken to the doctor who diagnosed it as cancer. Six months later, he was gone. It spread, went in everywhere down."

Hoerr would later tell of an ever-widening gulf between supervisors and workers in the early '70s, due to everything from the drug culture to a new generation's seeming disdain for hard labor to the hiring of business school grads with no hands-on knowledge of steelwork. But in Aliquippa, this was masked by plans for another capital expansion, valued at $200 million, and steel's relative health in the wake of the 1973 oil crisis; the resulting dip in auto production was offset by a spike in domestic oil drilling and the ensuing demand for pipe and tubing. Like the Soviet nuclear arsenal, cheap foreign steel was recognized as an existential threat. But the changing face of the workforce pushed more immediate buttons.

"Let's face it, men, it's no longer a man's world," read a 1973 editorial explaining the name change of J&L's in-house bulletin from *Men & Steel* to *JALTeam Almanac*. "It was called to our attention that the name of J&L's employee magazine . . . didn't take into account the fact that we also have many women working for J&L and that more are on the way." Macho glibness made it easy to credit or blame "women's lib," but the truth was more mundane—and far-reaching. Inflation was making it harder for families to stay afloat on one income. At J&L the names of many positions were officially changed: craneman to crane operator, foreman to supervisor. Old Tom Girdler would hardly have known the place.

But the work remained brutal. Aileen Gilbert was twenty-two years old, with four children out of wedlock, when she went into the open hearth to work the coke oven manned, for forty years, by her father. It was 1974. She needed the money. Her dad had died three years before, "and they called me to work in the department my father had worked in—on the same battery that he worked on," she said. "Which really blew my mind."

Gilbert worked, essentially, atop fire. A battery, standing twenty feet high and fifty feet front to back, contained fifty or more ovens that baked as much as thirty-five tons of coal at 2,000 degrees for seventeen hours; on top were charging holes into which was dumped the coal for cooking. She wore flameproof clothing and gloves, a helmet with a face shield, a pair of wooden shoes. Waited with a long pole with a hook on one end, near the charging holes, for the larry car's approach. She used the poled hook to pull loose the steel charging hole lids, then slide them aside.

"These lids, God, they weighed about fifty pounds," Gilbert said. "Then I'd move out the way. The larry car would come and drop coal down into the holes and after it dropped coal down into the holes, it moved on to the next three. Then I had to go back out there and push those lids back on—because the fire's shooting up out of the hole after he puts the coal in—take this stuff, pour it around to seal the lid back on, because now it's got to bake. And then I've got to go to the next three ovens."

She lasted two and a half years. The job paid more than $10,000 a year, decent money—maybe—for a single, childless person then, but Gilbert carried burns on her arms, soot on her face and neck, and bone-deep exhaustion every time she walked out of the tunnel. "I couldn't take it," she said. "I quit. Or they might've fired me, actually, because I couldn't take it."

In 1976, Gilbert picked up her brood and left—first to nearby Moon, then to Hartford, Connecticut—taking a series of jobs, including one involving the clearing of rats out of low-income housing, which all seemed like vacations compared with the steel mill. She had no intention of going back. Gilbert had felt ostracized by Aliquippa. Even juggling three jobs there, she had had to apply for welfare, and she had the kids and no husband and everybody knew everybody else's business and felt superior enough to judge it. "People talked about me really, really, really bad," Gilbert said. Really, what did her hometown have left to offer?

Eventually, though, she would return.

Don Yannessa could sell. Everybody could see that, even amid the 2-8 wreckage of his first season in '72. The football stadium was renamed for Carl Aschman the September afternoon that Aliquippa played Sharon High, and they almost won that one. Butler—always motivated, always tough—barely squeezed out a 1-point win, and the players began to believe. But the players weren't enough. If Aliquippa was ever again to play night football—with its bigger, revenue-generating crowds—Yannessa needed the town to buy in, to stop turning games into rumbles, to assure opposing players and fans that their buses and cars wouldn't get stoned. To get the town to buy in, he needed the black community to buy in. And to get the black community, he needed an ally.

Charlie Lay was a thirty-nine-year-old Korean War veteran who worked in the 14-inch mill at J&L, but made his name as a constant hand in Little Quips football, Little League baseball, and any other kind of ball, it seemed, played by his two sons, two daughters, and every other Aliquippa kid. Yannessa began cultivating Lay as soon as he took over. On Sundays he'd go with his assistants to the Quippian Club and drink for hours, waiting for the moment to break out the classic fund-raising weapons—flattery and shame. "You should hear what the whites are saying," Yannessa would tell Lay. "They're saying, 'We do everything. The blacks: What do they do? They just take. They don't give nothing back.' That's how they see it, Charlie: 'All you guys do is take.'"

So when some parents spoke of wanting to give the players a spaghetti dinner at season's end, Lay volunteered the Quippian Club. Before anyone could argue, the plan was set.

"It was tremendous," one white parent, Jean Rossi, later recalled. "The blacks were so proud they were doing something for the team, that the whites were there in their neighborhood.

"Parents from both sides were there. The men were at the bar together bending their elbows. It didn't matter whether the next guy was black or white. I think we've grown from there."

It didn't happen overnight. Lay spent months and years setting up mixed meetings of boosters, players, and parents in white homes and bars, black homes and bars, buying drinks, laughing at bad jokes and good stories told for the umpteenth time. There was no shortcut. "We used to have so many meetings among white and black people . . . at my home, others' houses . . . meet at the black club, have drinks and talk, meet at the white club, have drinks and talk," Yannessa said. "People in Aliquippa, you'd better be able to stand at a bar and drink a shot and a beer. If you can't do that nobody's going to trust you."

The two men's aims were different. "Don, you've got to get more white kids on the team. An all-black team isn't good for the community," Lay once told Yannessa at his home.

"Charlie," Yannessa replied. "I'm going to play my eleven best."

But both men knew that football success and racial unity were mutually dependent; Aliquippa couldn't have one without the other. Once he got past that first year, and the wins started to slowly pile up, Yannessa allowed himself to get cocky. "That racial shit" was unacceptable, he'd tell both groups of players, and if he heard "nigger" or "honky" or anything like it from any player, they would be gone. "I'll win with you and I'll win without you," he'd say, flashing that Pepsodent grin. But the players knew that he meant it. Yannessa would be staring at them hard when he spoke and his eyes, like pieces of coal, wouldn't be smiling at all.

And if Yannessa would later receive most of the credit for the way football helped stitch the town back together, it's only because few high school programs ever had a better front man—and because Charlie Lay died before the stitch-up was complete. The stricken steelworker conducted Quarterback Club meetings as long as his strength held, even out of his hospital bed, before pancreatic cancer killed him in December of 1980. The coach knew better than anyone what had been lost.

"Just a wonderful human being," Yannessa said. "He was the catalyst."

Still, it took four seasons of groundwork before Lay and Yannessa could unify whites and blacks into one mixed Aliquippa Quarterback Club. The permanent move back to night games remained elusive: In '74, three Butler students were injured, one with a fractured skull, in a postgame melee with Aliquippa fans; in 1975 a rolling fight behind the home stands resulted in six arrests, flying rocks and bottles, a police officer having to be treated at a hospital, and spasms of vandalism in the surrounding neighborhood. In February '76, the *Beaver County Times* offhandedly referred to Aliquippa "people rioting before and after football and basketball games for several years now." The school's reputation in the region had sunk so low that a writer for the *Pittsburgh Post-Gazette* wrote that same month, erroneously, that someone had been killed in the skirmish following an Aliquippa football game, explaining, "I thought I remembered something about it happening."

The *Post-Gazette* published a retraction, but few outsiders would've been stunned if such a murder occurred. The high school seemed afflicted by problems beyond the skills of a mere administrator to handle. "I've got to have the most difficult job any man would wish to have," said Aliquippa High principal Jerry Montini, a member of the school's 1949 state championship basketball team, in February 1976. "It's hard trying to maintain my sanity, if I may say so. I go home at nights and for a couple of hours I find myself just sitting in a chair or on the floor just wondering what's going to happen the next day."

In October of 1976, Aliquippa High forfeited all its football and basketball games for the 1973 and '75 seasons for playing ineligible athletes. Yannessa had never been shy about importing good players into his district, but the use of one ineligible athlete in 1973 and three more in 1975 earned him two years of probation by state and WPIAL officials. In the community, that hardly hurt his standing; the team had been steadily improving—going 5-3-1 in both 1973 and '74, 6-3 in '75, and 8-2 in '76. Mere residency infractions were hardly enough to overshadow winning.

"Yeah, Don Juan would recruit kids," said Melvin Steals of Yannessa's wooing of talent near and far. And yeah: "They called him 'Don Juan.' And they called him 'God.'"

But even God couldn't control everything. One warm Friday, February 25, 1977, the shaky peace that had existed between whites and blacks shattered again. The *Beaver County Times* had one version—after a white student sold a black student a bag of "bad marijuana," the latter tried to get his money back—and those on the ground had another. "I was there," said Dan "Peep" Short, Aliquippa's High's current defensive coordinator, then a sophomore. "Two black guys tried to buy from a white guy. They took the weed, the boy who got his weed taken went back into the school and told his friends that these two black guys took his weed; they came out and there was a standoff.

"Four whites . . . and three or four black guys were getting ready to fight, and all of a sudden this black guy comes running out the door and he punched a white guy in the fucking face. He came running off the steps—I can see it clear as day—and sucker punches the guy. All hell breaks loose. I get pinned down by somebody who's beating the living shit out of me. He got me pinned—and that's the guy who ended up getting stabbed."

The white pupil on top of Short, Mark Petrie, rolled off after being knifed in the abdomen—"somebody," Short said, "trying to help me"—and Short and the rest scattered for the paths leading down the hill from the school. The conflict metastasized: current Aliquippa schools superintendent Dave Wytiaz, a junior at the time, was taking a standardized test in the cafeteria when a black pupil named Robert Williams rushed in, yelling, "This whitey knifed me!"

"The next thing you know, tables were being thrown," Wytiaz said. "I'd never seen anything like it: it went from stone silence to tables flying. Boom! Everyone started yelling and jumping up, with the panic that happens."

Petrie survived. Five students were arrested; sixty-five more were suspended. School was canceled the following Monday, but even when it reopened the next day few bothered to show. At the first hint of trouble—real or imagined—some teachers locked their doors and hid. Some didn't. "Frank Antonini was an assistant football coach at the time and our gym teacher—and Frank had no fear," Wytiaz said. "Another kid got on campus, puts a gun in the air in front of the high school, and Frank, having no fear, went right at the kid—grabbed the gun. Today that kid would've probably shot the teacher."

As always, the school served as the most sensitive gauge of the town's mood. The ensuing weeks and months made the '60s notions of a "Great Society," of racial progress, and of a "war on poverty" seem laughable. "Every day we'd come to work and every day here's somebody beating the shit out of somebody, a white kid and black kid, white girls getting beat up," Yannessa said. "One day I look out my classroom window and here comes about seventy-five, eighty, a hundred white guys down this way, they got baseball bats, chains, all kinds of makeshift weapons. And coming from the stadium area to meet 'em, here's the black contingent.

"And you know what? It changed everything. I was going to work and I had a calendar; I'd scratch every day off and I'd say, 'I didn't sign up for this. I've got to get out of here. This is never going to work. It's never going to stop.'"

Battle lines kept getting drawn and redrawn. The teachers went on strike but the coaches kept coaching, crossed the picket line in a union town, and felt plenty of hostility. School renovations split the 1977–78 school day and gave everyone too much time to burn. Football players had little choice but to take sides, the black ones siding with their friends from Plan 11 or Logstown—or from the projects of Valley Terrace, where, just two years after opening, shoddy construction and living conditions led to its being all but declared a slum and placed under federal control—and the whites with theirs from Sheffield or Plan 12.

"We had some selfish sons of bitches on that team," Short said. "It was all about 'me-me-me.'"

Like most black players, Short had risen through Aliquippa's Pee Wee football program, winning alongside white teammates like Dan Metropoulos, Bobby Babich, and Art Piroli, all of them, he said, "closer than close." Metropoulos, especially, was like a brother. They had won and lost and bled together, laughing at racial differences while the outside world couldn't even mention the issue without burning up. The all-white offensive line and the all-black running back corps called themselves "The Black Backs and the White-Line Fever"—and as twelve-year-olds they had traveled together to Fort Myers, Florida, for a Midget Bowl game, went to Disney World as a pack, and never split along color lines. Now that unity splintered.

"There was a divide in the football team—again—after the boy got stabbed," Short said. "Even though we were playing together and practicing together, the chemistry and the unity wasn't what it should've been." And, he said, "that shit didn't heal itself all of a sudden."

After the Quips suffered a gutting 20-19 loss to Blackhawk to finish the '77 season 5-5, Yannessa all but surrendered. He'd lost his players. The program was facing total collapse. He began talking and ended up making the speech of his life, perhaps the most important speech in Aliquippa since Cornelia Bryce Pinchot's forty-three years before. "This is not my team," Yannessa told them. "You've got to turn this thing around. You got scumbag black kids out there and scumbag white kids out there causing trouble—and they don't give a shit. They'll destroy everything here. They don't care. They have nothing to lose. You guys have got to care. Because you do have something to lose.

"You got to take ownership. We're the coaches, we're the adults, and there's teachers and administrators but goddammit they don't *own* this. You own it. When I played here, I was proud of who I was and where I was from and I wanted to have a future and this was a catalyst to my future. Same thing for you. This is your team."

Still, into the spring of '78—a full year after the stabbing—each side eyed the other warily. Notions like "teammate" and "winning" seemed quaint. The school year ended, and no one could say if Yannessa's words would have any effect at all. "A lot of us [blacks], *most*, chose to be on the side with the blacks," Short said. "And they [whites] chose to be on the side of the whites."

He recalls looking around at his childhood buddies in the locker room, at training camp the following August, in the hallways. He recalls looking at Metropoulos, his "brother." *Am I going to fight Danny? Can I? Are we all really going to fight each other?*

✳　✳　✳

With memory of the early-seventies riots still fresh, healing that rift would normally have figured as Aliquippa's primary mission. But Yannessa wasn't the only one waving a white flag. The understanding that race, rather than being an issue "solved" by marches or legislation or endless attempts at "dialogue," was a bone-deep stain that might take generations to remove had all but settled in. No one expected a quick fix. Besides, the county was in a state of panic.

Locks that had never been used were being oiled and thrown. Aliquippa's streets emptied at night, dogs went unwalked, and every strange face—and even those that weren't—was suspect. "All you knew," said Sherman McBride, "is that there was a killer."

Starting in October 1977—with the death of a seventeen-year-old boy named John Feeny and the disappearance of his girlfriend, Ranee Gregor, sixteen, on a lovers' lane in nearby Findlay—and continuing deep into the spring, a series of what would amount to eighteen murders—most accompanied by rape; committed by shotgun, knife, or blunt object; and occurring in Western Pennsylvania and Eastern Ohio—dotted the map around Aliquippa. There seemed to be no motive, no pattern, and for seven months no suspect. At least one psychic was called in to search for a missing body. The hunting-obsessed region starting stocking up, and didn't stop.

"I had a gun shop, and I ran out of guns," said Beaver County sheriff George David, then an Aliquippa police officer. "Rifles, shotguns, pistols: Everybody was going frantic. They wanted guns."

Yet Aliquippa remained spared, and why didn't become clear until 10:20 p.m. on June 6, 1978. Four days after a Columbia, South Carolina, man was bludgeoned to death with a baseball bat, a tip from the wife of thirty-six-year-old Eddie Surratt, of Montini Street in Plan 11, led six state policemen to the victim's station wagon, parked near the Aliquippa Works. Surratt, who had served combat tours in Vietnam with the Army and Marines, kicked open the passenger-side door, got out with his hands raised—and bolted into the mill complex. Then he leapt down a sixty-foot embankment and disappeared.

Three weeks later, the sleeping Surratt was arrested in the home of a family he was holding hostage near St. Augustine, Florida. But as sensational as that news was, as astonishing as the speculation that Surratt had eluded police in Aliquippa by either swimming the gamy currents of the Ohio or scrambling up the drainage tunnel beneath Franklin Avenue ("Uncle Sam trained him," Salt Smith said, "to be a survivor"), was the numbing idea that this was one of their own.

Eddie Surratt returned from Vietnam in 1970 with shiny medals and a new wife, Offia. Many claimed that the war had changed him, and stories he told of clearing Vietcong bunkers, being hit by shrapnel, being overrun in a foxhole by Vietcong, or seeing his buddy's arm blown off perhaps spoke to how and why. But there were also signs of normalcy: The couple had a son, and in the year before his arrest Surratt repeatedly visited with a school official to monitor the boy's progress. Ocie Patrick, an old teammate of Ditka's, would play cards with Surratt, and sometimes when Ocie would go to work his shift at the blast furnace, Eddie would come by and visit with Ocie's wife, Betty, at their home on Orchard Street.

The Patricks' young twin sons, Timmie and Terry, weren't old enough to go off to school then. "He was good friends with the family," Timmie said.

Just two days before the chase down at the mill, then–Ambridge head coach Frank Marocco, who'd known Surratt nearly his entire life, had chatted with him while working at his father-in-law's fruit stand in town. "A very liked gentleman, very respectful," Marocco said. "He'd come in and take the garbage out. I knew him because of his military background; we were very close there. We were all figuring, *Who can this guy be?* When it was Eddie Surratt, I couldn't believe it."

But for Ocie Patrick, the mystery sat closer to the bone: not just what did happen with Eddie Surratt, but what didn't. For decades he'd tell Betty, "He could've cut you up and put you in a refrigerator!"

And all of them, Timmie and Terry and the rest of the Patrick boys, would laugh then. What else could you do? The rest of the country had its share of spree killings after World War II, their names tattooed into the consciousness—Starkweather, Green River, Zodiac, Manson, Son of Sam. Maybe they had always happened. Maybe TV made such horrors available in a way they never had been before. But each one seemed like another piece of evidence that the culture had spun off its moorings.

Aliquippa had always been a place high on cause-and-effect: at the mill, in the streets, on the football field. You worked, you got paid. You hit somebody, you got hit back. With Eddie Surratt, though, its people came face-to-face with the inexplicable, the senseless, the random—and it had risen from their midst. That was a shift. After his rampage, little could come as a shock.

"Sometimes people just take a turn and you never know what happens," Timmie Patrick said. "Just like you can have someone come to your house and you didn't know they were a serial killer."

12

Darkness on the Edge

Now it was Peep's turn. The weekend before the '78 season opener, Short, McBride, Bob Babich, Dan Metropoulos, and three others, a mix of juniors and seniors, black and white, met in someone's basement and listened as Peep Short, never quiet, stood up and got even louder. "This has got to stop somewhere," he said, and he meant: *Here, now.* The next day, after the team entered the gym and, for the first time in years, divided itself into white and black factions, the seven players walked together to the center of the floor. "You're either with us," they announced, "or you're out."

"No one left that gym," McBride said. "Everybody came together as one."

And as the season unrolled—one win after another (except for that big loss to Butler) over Canon McMillan, then Montour and Moon and New Castle and, yes, Hopewell and Seneca Valley and Ambridge, too—some could feel a change in the Aliquippa atmosphere. The crowd at football games began to mix. Black and white players were seen double-dating, sometimes interracially; "Danny Metro" and other white players were seen at parties in Plan II, and Short and Co. were seen at white parties up near Brodhead Road. Suddenly, Yannessa said, "everything became a lot easier for us as football coaches."

It may have been too soon, when the American president hit town, to say that some corner had been turned. But it had. On September 23, 1978, Jimmy Carter, the soft-spoken Southerner whose election nearly two years earlier had been taken as a corrective to the lies of the Johnson and Nixon administrations, the cynical drift of Vietnam and Watergate, had not yet become a symbol of weakness. He came to speak at an Aliquippa High scrubbed, principal Jerry Montini said, to "its super-sparkling best": grass remown, halls polished, none of the tension that, the year Carter won, had Montini wondering if he was losing his mind. People thronged Franklin Avenue to watch the president pass, and nine hundred locals filled the auditorium for a fifty-minute question-and-answer session. Carter's first comments, after the usual thanks, were about the town's famous names.

"Anybody who cares about sports knows about Beaver County," Carter said. "As you know, Joe Namath was a great friend of my mother's when she was in Alabama, and still is. Pete Maravich played for our team in Atlanta, great athlete who began here; Tony Dorsett, another great athlete, as you know; Doc Medich and many others. I won't try to mention all of them that came from here. But there must be something special about the climate or the training, because you have set a standard for the rest of the country in athletics."

No one was impolitic enough to mention that not one of those men had actually played for the high school in which he stood; and, besides, Carter followed up by saying that "Moon River"—written by Aliquippa's own Henry Mancini—was one of his favorite waltzes: "Rosalynn and I like to dance to it."

The event had little in common with JFK's drive-by speech sixteen years earlier: people were far less awed by the White House now, and the first question from an Aliquippa woman named Evelyn Rosmini concerned the loss of "old-fashioned things—respect, management, and cooperation. We no longer have small-town lifestyles. Everything is deteriorating. . . ." Locals knew that Rosmini was speaking less of abstractions than of Aliquippa itself—sending up a distress flare from the nation's gut—but she was right to be polite: anything more specific might've split the room in two.

Then came a question from another woman—this one black, Etta Colbert of Logstown—wondering why redevelopment was making her neighborhood disappear; why, in fact, this concept of "urban development" that was supposed to save poor people had left her world in "critical, deplorable condition"? And Carter said he loved small towns and didn't have the answer, but that his Housing and Urban Development secretary would phone her soon (and, indeed, Colbert received a call at 5 p.m. that same day).

The remaining questions went big—prayer in schools, national health care, unemployment, energy, Middle East peace, the future of a domestic steel industry besieged by foreign imports. But the moment nobody forgot was when a fifteen-year-old girl from South Heights, Ambridge High sophomore Wendy Babiak, whose mother had died the previous Wednesday of cancer, asked Carter if she could give him a big hug and, before he could answer, ran to the stage and skipped up and got what she asked for and told the president, "I love you."

"This was not on the program," Carter said, grinning, hugging back. "I would ask all of you not to tell my wife about this until I can get home and explain it."

The crowd laughed, of course, and that was the bit that made the news: Tense, torn Aliquippa had gone warm and cuddly. It didn't hurt that Aliquippa High had crushed Moon, 40-0, the same day (it would go undefeated until the last game of the season). That Yannessa's team, *their* team, was humming again. That football was *the* thing again, with black cheerleaders—not just one token girl, but now three fully a part of the squad; any players or parents agitating against it came off as distractions from the new, winning way, and who wanted that?

The season ended, and Yannessa knew that this was the time: He insisted that the end-of-year banquets, the white one hosted by the Ukrainian Club and the black one hosted by the Quippian Club, be merged. The two clubs agreed, and Yannessa pulled every string to make the night first-class, luring every recruit-hungry coaching name in to speak. With each ensuing year, the arrival of such famous football men—Joe Paterno, Dick MacPherson, Lou Saban—would only certify that this way, Yannessa's way, was the right one. Someone still might mention "black" this or "white" that, but the other parents would shake their heads and say, "Shut that down!" or "We don't need that here" or just change the subject.

Early on, though, the players were key. The players, Yannessa knew, would be the ones who made the unity last. That's why that loss against Blackhawk on the last day of the '78 season, a Friday night home game no less, mattered more than a lot of the Aliquippa wins that would soon be piling up like change on a dresser.

It was one of those grind-it-out defensive battles, down to the last second, Blackhawk holding a 7-0 lead, winner goes to the playoffs.

Peep Short was a senior tight end on the team, playing in his last game. "I dropped the ball," he said, staring into space, watching it happen all over again. "Last play of the game, I caught the ball and had one guy to beat and if I made that cut, I know I'm gone. Mike Sutton from Blackhawk hit me and the ball went about twenty yards in the air. And I couldn't get to the ball because he was on top of me and all I did was lay on the ground and watch that ball, and all I could think was, *Damn. There goes my season.*"

But what happened after mattered even more.

"When we lost that game, in front of a packed house in Aliquippa, against an all-white team, Blackhawk, everybody would've expected: *There's going to be trouble now. There's going to be a fight, our kids going after their kids because these white kids beat us,"* Yannessa said. "That didn't happen. Instead, our guys ran over and shook their hands, congratulated the coaches, ran off the field and into the field house—and cried like babies."

Together.

For the youngest players in the room, such an outbreak of raw emotion was unsettling. As bad as they felt over losing, they couldn't join in the sniffles and sobs or slammed locker doors, couldn't dress with tear-streaks on their cheeks. They had barely played. They weren't dirty. But for one sophomore this was particularly hard, because he was a softie; tears were his refuge. And his life had been one long struggle to tamp that softness down, because tough guys didn't cry, but now the toughest guys he knew were weeping and no one was laughing or calling them "pussies." Who wouldn't be confused?

In truth, none of it—football, the town, life, fatherhood—was ever going to be easy for Jeff Baldwin to figure. Thick, strong, and with a mammoth capacity for work, he was the latest in the series of Aliquippans with big-time talent—another product brewed up, as Jimmy Carter put it, by "the water." Soon he'd be drawing Division I-A scholarship offers from all over the nation, be squired around Pitt's campus by defensive legend Hugh Green. But Baldwin had weaknesses. Maybe if he'd come up in a different decade—like Jimmy Frank or Ditka or Richie Mann—before drug use had become casual, before the black family began to implode, before Big Steel collapsed and the church and unions lost their clout, they wouldn't have figured so prominently. Weakness was nothing new. Maybe, like the lost or hot-tempered or unskilled souls who had preceded him for generations, he would have found his impulses channeled by the mill or stunted by societal norms. Maybe he would've earned a college degree, or come home to find a stabilizing spot at J&L. Maybe.

But as it was, Jeff Baldwin came up at a time when the old pillars were crumbling, and he wasn't strong enough to withstand the ensuing shock waves. Indeed, he was fated like few others to live out the dual nature of Aliquippa just beginning to emerge—its pride and pain, its talent and trouble—and to personify the year-by-year narrowing of its options until football and prison could seem, at times, the only two left. For him, even then, the narrowing had begun: Jeff Baldwin, the sixteen-year-old boy hurrying into his clothes in the Quips locker room that night, was already the father of a one-year-old boy named Jamie Mandel Brown.

Baldwin wasn't living under the same roof as his son then; he was still living as a son himself, on Washington Street in the Plan 11 house of his parents, Henry and Delois Baldwin. Henry Baldwin had come up during World War II from Richland, Georgia, and worked in the J&L wire mill for thirty-five years. Delois arrived from Georgia a decade later, baby daughter in hand, fleeing a teenage marriage in Florida. The rest of her life, she told anyone who'd listen, "Don't get married too early."

But Delois got together with Henry and bore him two kids, Norman and Jeff, moving to the Washington Street house in 1969, thinking all along that she had wedded him, too, until the truth came out. "He was already married and I didn't know it, so it's just like we didn't," Delois said. "So that's not counting. No, it's not counting. Henry lied to me. Yeah, he lied, so I never was married to him."

By 1978, Delois was working at the mill, too, in the monotony of the seamless tube department. "I'd sit there and take account of the pipe that they was cutting," she said. "I worked on the 'cutoff': the crane would go where the pipes are and pick 'em up and bring 'em over and sit 'em on the table? And those guys would cut 'em—and I would count the pipe, keep track of how many they'd cut. And at the end of the shift, I would take it in the office. That was my job for a whole year. It just made me so lazy."

Norman, the oldest, was the sports star then. When it came to pickup games in Aliquippa, he never wanted Jeff around; in elementary school Jeff was big and clumsy and, worst of all, scared. The sharks smelled his fear. "They used to always beat me up and jump me: I never fought back," Jeff said. "They'd take my toys and stuff. That's why I've got a hard-stone face. You can punch me as hard as you want and won't nothing happen to it. They'd get me to play football and hit me. They'd use me for the dummy."

Finally, at eight or nine, he'd had enough. Two kids called the "Bucky Boys" jumped him, spit on him, and Jeff went blind and started swinging and beat them both. There were a lot more fights to come; he lost plenty—but he never backed down again.

Always exceeding top-end weight limits, Jeff didn't play organized football until ninth grade. But the game gave him confidence like nothing else. By his sophomore year he was playing both ways, offensive guard and defensive end, a two-hundred-pound hunk making up for inexperience with raw strength and good hands. First to practice and last to leave, he ran five sets of stadium steps afterward, rain or snow or shine, alone. Toil and talent brought him along. The town's inbred competition did the rest.

"Growing up Aliquippa, you play with older people and I guess you get the rough, true story of it," Jeff said. "Because older people don't cut you no break; they play hard and learn you the hard way."

Henry tried instilling larger lessons. He brought the boy grocery shopping, so Jeff would see him budget and shop; he tried to teach the need to take care of bills and family. At the same time, the house on Washington Street was renowned for the violent sounds of Henry and Delois fighting. The sight of a police car out front wasn't unusual. Finally, twenty-six days after the season-ending loss to Blackhawk, on the morning of November 29, 1978, the phone rang at A-Ambulance Service, Delois on the other end. Someone had been hurt, she said. When crew members arrived, they found a body on the floor.

"My daddy was in an accident; he got killed," Jeff later said. "It was a . . . domestic accident." Asked what that means, he said, "I really don't want to discuss that."

The Baldwin family can be remarkably open when speaking about stumbles involving sex, gunplay or the criminal justice system, but not about this. When asked about her husband more than three decades later, Delois said, "Who? No, Henry, he died. He's dead. When did he pass? I don't know." Asked if the two were together when he died, she said, "In a way we was and in a way we weren't. I don't know. I don't think about all that back stuff, like the years and the date and stuff like that. I have to go look. I don't know what it was."

Pressed, Delois said, "He died accidentally." By gunshot? "Yeah," she said. In the house on Washington Street, here, in the home she still lived in thirty-four years later? Delois nodded, then, and laughed, nervously perhaps. "No, I don't know what happened to him. I really don't." So she just came home and there Henry was, lying on the floor? "And there he was. . . ." she said.

The November 29, 1978, edition of the *Beaver County Times* ran a story that stated: "An Aliquippa woman is being held in connection with the murder early this morning of her husband. . . . Delois Baldwin, 44, was taken into custody by Aliquippa police shortly after the shooting occurred. She was charged with the murder of her 58-year-old husband, Henry, during a quarrel."

No court record seemingly exists to say that Delois Baldwin served a day in jail for that crime, and her arrest, any kind of "charge," or her ever being cleared don't show up in a criminal records search. A death certificate dated December 4, 1978, in fact, states the cause of Henry Baldwin's death as "homicide," and notes, "Victim shot by wife." Yet, six months later—and in apparent contravention of Pennsylvania's Slayer's Act, which prevents a decedent's killer from receiving benefits from his or her passing—Delois was made administrator of Henry's meager estate.

The only traces of what happened that night remain, then, in the family's touchiness, and in the article printed that morning in the *Times*. The accompanying photo shows three Aliquippa policemen staring at a pistol and some bullet casings spread out upon what appears to be a white handkerchief. The story goes on to say that Henry's corpse, pronounced dead at the scene, was lying on its left side in the kitchen when police arrived. A police officer named Herman Cain "then noticed" a .38-caliber revolver lying on a nearby table. The gun contained one live shell. The four others inside had been, according to police, "spent."

Mike Zmijanac was in the locker room, too, after the '78 loss to Blackhawk, one of the few there with nothing to cry about. He'd just finished his first season as Aliquippa's defensive coordinator, and it had been a sterling run to the end. His unit had limited opponents to an absurd 3.6 points a game in the season's second half, had held Blackhawk to sixty-six total yards and just two first downs this night—an achievement all the more remarkable considering that, on paper anyway, he had no real business being there.

No, on paper Zmijanac wasn't a football guy, wasn't an organized-team guy, wasn't—despite his vague renown in pickup games—technically even a basketball guy. Yet he had a talent for cursing and that sarcastic tone that snaps male teenage minds to attention; he had a way of seeming to call bullshit on authority even when, as a demanding English teacher, he *was* authority. And, Lord, Zmijanac was cocky. Never played a down, but he had the gall to believe that the game wasn't all that hard to figure.

"Football and basketball are the same thing: It's the same exact game," he said. "When teaching a linebacker how to get into his drops, it's teaching a basketball player how to take away the baseline—exactly the same footwork. And when I would need someone to square up and shoot the ball? It's the same thing: Square up and block the guy. Absolutely the same game. So it was easy for me. It took me a year or two to figure out the terminology. But . . . same game."

Still, someone had to open the door. After his first season, in '72, Yannessa had a few staff openings and asked Zmijanac what he thought. *What he thought?* Zmijanac had been pressed into service as a junior high football coach for a few games when the '70 riots made everything an emergency, and he had been junior high basketball coach for two seasons before losing interest. So when Yannessa beckoned, in the summer of '73, Zmijanac's first response was bewilderment.

"Have you lost your fuckin' mind?" he said.

"Come on," Yannessa replied. "I'll teach you."

"You ain't got enough patience to teach me about football," Zmijanac said.

"Come on. Be the assistant junior high football coach. I'll pay you five hundred dollars. . . ."

"We probably drank more than five hundred bucks' worth of alcohol this weekend, but . . . okay. Why didn't you hire me last year?"

"I didn't need you last year," Yannessa said.

He needed him now. "Mike was a good teacher," Yannessa said. "When you're a good teacher, I don't give a shit if you played football: If you know it, you can teach it. Plus, he was no-nonsense. Mike isn't exactly a tough guy. He acts like he is but he's not. But he won't take any crap from those kids. And Mike will tell you: He's learned a lot from me."

So for five seasons, Zmijanac served as an assistant at the junior high and, then, in 1975, he joined Red McNie's basketball staff as an assistant, too. Yannessa loved his sharp scouting reports on opponents, and even sharper observations on his own team. Before long, Yannessa was sending a varsity assistant out to scout and keeping Zmijanac close. He made himself just as valuable to McNie, made himself a name in the process, but there was a problem. By the fall of 1977, Zmijanac had grown sick of nearly all of it.

First, there was the job itself: low pay, long hours, thousands of critics and no sign of advancement. Two days after the '77 season ended, he told Yannessa, "If I'm not going to move up to varsity, I've got to give this up. It's junior high football: fuck it." Then came a break; four assistants got furloughed, another moved up to athletic director.

Yannessa shuffled the deck, and during a meeting asked his assistants, some former D-I players, who wanted to take over as defensive coordinator. No one spoke.

Zmijanac looked around, raised a finger. "I'll do it," he said. He even got a raise.

Still, there was also the matter of the players. Zmijanac had become convinced that kids had changed in some basic way, that authority had snapped at home, and that the aftereffects were seeping into sports. Aliquippa's reputation, meanwhile, had been stained by fan fights and postgame crime, by ineligible players and probation, year after year. Yannessa's iron-fisted charm held that largely in check during football season, but players like Short and McBride played basketball, too. And McNie didn't wield the same control.

On December 29, 1978, nearly eight weeks after that peaceable Blackhawk loss, a brawl broke out between Aliquippa and Midland at the end of the Quips' loss at a Christmas basketball tournament at the Community College of Beaver County. Benches cleared, Short was seen chasing a Midland player into the stands, and at least two dozen fans waded into the fray: The *Beaver County Times* reported a full five minutes of "punching . . . kicking and stomping" by all involved. McNie had worked two years to improve players' behavior. "I thought we had the whole problem licked," he said after. "You work so hard and it just doesn't get through. The whole thing is just so totally unbelievable. . . ."

Zmijanac didn't share McNie's dismay: he was outraged. He had gone out on the court, tried to pull some players apart and finally gave up. He threw an arm over the shoulder of one senior, Eddie Palombo, and stalked off to the locker room muttering, "I'm done here."

"On the floor, everyone rolling everywhere, people coming out of the stands, fights: fucking horrid," Zmijanac said. "That night we got back here, in the gym, I told Red to stay and all the kids left. I finished the year: Red's a friend of mine. But I said, 'I can't do it.'"

He applied for two basketball head coaching jobs at other schools, and barely got a sniff. For the first time since he was very small, hoops was no longer a central part of his life. Zmijanac, suddenly, was a football man.

June 3, 1981. Jeff Baldwin, eighteen years old and a day away from graduation, eighteen years old and heading to Pitt on a football scholarship, eighteen years old with the dawning certainty that people found him special, stood angrily in his dress shoes and suit coat and V-necked shirt and watched a hand with a gun rise and stop. It was pointing at his stomach now.

The two boys weren't five yards apart. The strange thing was, this was a teammate from football, a sixteen-year-old scrub who knew even less than he. And what began as a minor spat had now escalated into madness.

The roots of it, like so much of what happened in town, went deeper than most knew. In 1974, John Evasovich, one of Aliquippa football's steady hands in the late '50s, had come back home after sixteen years away at college and a career in Virginia. Over and over he was warned, *Things've gotten bad there: Don't send your girls to Aliquippa High.* That was the word all over Western Pennsylvania, passed hand to hand and then hammered in place by newspapers and TV.

"I was in a black neighborhood in Sewickley going to school; some people were descendants of freemen, not slaves," said Reverend Chris Leighton, who moved in 1979 to All Saints Episcopal on Franklin Avenue. "They were our friends—we were the first white people to live in the house—and they were extremely alarmed when they heard I was going to Aliquippa. One woman with tears running down her cheeks said, 'They'll kill you over there because you're white.'"

Evasovich had heard such things. His wife was nervous. He first tried sending his daughters, Jonha and Mia, to Quigley Catholic; they couldn't have hated it more. The girls' mom was in the hospital recovering from an operation when her daughters came to visit. "Good news, Ma," they said. "We made varsity cheerleading. Bad news—to you: It's at Aliquippa."

Jonha, the oldest, was a junior, and didn't know any better. In Virginia things had been different: Kids were starting to mix; she thought nothing of going to black dances and parties. Game weeks, she and Mia would drive up to Plan 11 to do the customary decorating of the starters' homes—bedsheets painted with "Good Luck!" and a player's name. "We can't believe you little white girls are coming up here to decorate," the mothers said the first few times. "Aren't you scared?"

"Should we be?" Jonha said.

From nearly the first day, Jeff Baldwin had looked after her. They were buddies; he made it clear that anyone who bothered Jonha would answer to him. And until the day before graduation, no one—black or white, male or female—ever did. Sometimes she would be the cheerleader to take Jeff's arm and accompany him out to midfield for his pregame *dunt-dunt-dunt*, and she couldn't believe how much her protector would be transformed.

"I don't think I hit the ground with my feet," Jonha said. "I remember grabbing his arm and Jeff just, like, dragging me because he was so focused. Honestly, he would scare the living shit out of you on the football field, because he had such a fire behind his eyes. But the second he got to the sideline it was, 'Let's go, team, come on, you can do it.' He was super-nice to everybody in high school, a big softie. But on the field he was mean."

That Wednesday morning, the seniors emerged from graduation practice to find a line of parked cars vandalized. And Jonha's car—her dad's, a brand-new sedan—was the worst: smashed-out rear window, mirrors snapped, a headlight shattered. Word of who was responsible, a scrub, got around, and at football workouts that day Jeff confronted the kid and turned him in. Indeed, Jeff felt so righteous about it, and so much happened—a graduation party, a girl to charm—in the hours after, that it was easy to think that everybody had moved on.

But then Jeff had been leaving the girl's place on Return Street, heading home with the school year nearly over and the late night thick with promise and a hint of rain, and the scrub found him and there was a confrontation, mutual curses. And now that hand with the .32-caliber pistol was rising and he could see it clench, hear the trigger pulled: *click, click, click, click.* Nothing happened. Then it rose to chest level and. . . . *Click.* This time there was a flash. Baldwin felt something hit his neck. He fell back.

"It's crazy," Jonha said. "But that's what those guys do there: They just aim to kill."

Later, maybe a decade later, Jeff Baldwin ran into the guy. He didn't want to fight. But Jeff had to know: How many bullets were in the clip that night? He'd figured with all that clicking, there had to be just one. "All five," the scrub said. "They was duds." That's the first time Jeff knew how lucky he was—could've been gut-shot, or dead. As it was, the one live round nicked a channel along his neck. The doctor at Aliquippa Hospital needed twenty stitches to close the wound.

"You know what actually saved me?" Baldwin said. "My sister bought me a stainless-steel silver necklace for Christmas and I told her I would never take it off. I had that on and it ricocheted off the stainless-steel necklace. Half a millimeter more, it would've hit my jugular vein."

He had been in the newspaper just that morning, listed with the dozen other Aliquippa football players who'd received scholarship offers to small colleges, junior colleges, but also Ohio State, Kansas State, and Michigan State. The class of '81 had gone 12-1 in its final season, lost in the '80 WPIAL final to Thomas Jefferson, and was, in all, one of the most talented lineups the town had seen. And Baldwin was one of the best—first-team all-state, 230 pounds and 6-foot-3 now. He made it to graduation the following night, too, in dress shoes and suit coat, a thick bandage pasted to his neck.

The scrub got hauled off to juvenile court, and Pitt head coach Jackie Sherrill made sure to hustle Jeff out of town for the summer, had him working a horse farm in Canonsburg. Jeff loved Sherrill, his drive and loyalty. He'd gained ten pounds for the man by the time he got to camp, and Sherrill switched him to defensive tackle and Jeff played second-string freshman year. But when Sherrill left for Texas A&M that winter, he took Pitt's faith in Jeff with him.

The new coach, Foge Fazio, wanted to move Baldwin to the offensive line. He refused, slogged through his sophomore season as a backup, and, when it looked like his junior season would be more of the same, told Yannessa he needed to transfer. "Don," Fazio explained. "If he would just go over to the offensive side of the ball, he would start."

"The problem with Jeff Baldwin was that, defensively, it's a reaction game," Yannessa said, pointing to his eyes. "And by the time the information went from here to his feet, it was too late: it was past him. On offense, you always know where you're going; you don't have to react. If he'd have made that transition, he would've played." Yannessa shrugged. "He didn't."

Soon Baldwin's confidence was in tatters. He started two games in his three-year Panther career before dropping out. "I just lost the desire," Jeff said.

His son, Jamie Brown, was a kindergartner in Aliquippa then. He lived with his mother, but recalls seeing Jeff play at Pitt, recalls his dad giving him a football each Christmas, recalls intermittent attempts to pass on wisdom. Jeff wasn't around much to coach him, day in and day out, but he pushed six-year-old Jamie to play Little Quips football. The boy quit midway through his first season. "He put so much in me," Jamie said. "Told me to be the best at whatever I do. Stand up for what you believe in."

Still, even then Jamie could sense a regret that never faded. "I think he wishes he could've made it," Brown said. "And thinks he should have."

✳   ✳   ✳

On Thursday, August 6, 1981, readers of the *Beaver County Times* were fed the usual hefty diet—local and national updates, four nearby murders, features about the Pirates and Steelers, ads for watermelon ($1.79 and up) and "ground beef or meatloaf mix" ("$1.33 lb. for a 3-lb. pkg. or more"), news about a crackdown on teen drinking, and a wire story out of San Francisco predicting that computers would soon handle "daily accounting chores" in American households and "drastically change the way of life for businessmen."

Indeed, it's easy, while scanning those pages, to feel like you're happening upon a century-old advertisement for the maiden voyage of the *Titanic*. The mind screams at the innocent names set by typesetters and printed by presses long gone, *Watch out! There's disaster ahead. . . .*

Because there on page one, above the flag and under the banner headline "Reagan firing controllers; union claims strength," is a story about President Ronald Reagan's unprecedented decision to fire 11,345 striking air-traffic controllers. And inside, atop the lead editorial praising a new, innovative labor-management partnership at the Aliquippa Works, is another headline: "A Good Omen for the Future at J&L Steel." Looking back, the two pieces feel like updates from the camps of iceberg and ship.

At the time, of course, it was hardly clear that Reagan's hugely popular act would signal Big Labor's demise. The firing of the air-traffic controllers was in its early stages, and the fate of elite federal workers— striking illegally and with little support from fellow unions—didn't figure to affect life on the shop floor. In 1981 nearly 10,000 workers were still flowing daily through the tunnel in downtown Aliquippa. If anything, J&L's willingness to try initiatives like "Labor Management Partnership Teams" seemed proof of a new era of employer-worker cooperation—not some too-little, too-late stroke of desperation.

But the ills ravaging the U.S. steel industry—high-level strategic blunders, mid-level mismanagement, and low-cost competition—all decades in the making and well past the point of reversal, went deeper than anything "LMPTs" might fix. Reagan busted the air-traffic control-lers midway through a period, 1974–86, that saw a free fall in domestic steel production—from 151 million net tons of raw steel annually to 85 million—and the loss of 337,552 jobs. Steelworkers were facing an existential crisis well before federal and popular support shifted against union protections. The *Times*'s idea of the "future," of a blue-collar security that had held for two generations, was fading fast.

Perhaps some saw this all coming in 1968, when James Ling's LTV first acquired a controlling interest in J&L. "Ling's goal in doing this is not altogether clear," reads the definitive history of J&L, 1999's *Portraits in Steel.* "A desire to break into a 'bastion of the Eastern Establishment,' a lack of understanding about the nature of steel's peculiar ratio of assets to sales . . . a desire to get at J&L pension funds to help buttress LTV's shaky financial underpinnings, a desire to reorganize J&L as he had Wilson and Company have all been suggested. Whatever it was, it would be a gamble that would cost him his fortune and ultimately result in bankruptcy for both LTV and J&L."

By 1974, J&L was subsumed as a wholly owned subsidiary of LTV. Juke Suder was in his twenty-fourth year in the welded tube operation then, and told anyone who'd listen—and many who wouldn't: *This is the beginning of the end, fellas.* "They thought I was crazy; they said, 'No, LTV is a big organization, they're going to expand. . . .'" Suder said. "I said, 'Don't bet on it.' A lot of companies were buying places, then selling them off. And that's exactly what they did. They started selling stuff off."

But for a while, the Beaver Valley seemed just fine; the mills were still churning. Gary Grandstaff, then twenty-five, began work as a crane follower in J&L's seamless tube annex in 1978, the year that the steel industry, as Jimmy Carter crowed in Aliquippa on his visit, regained 24,000 jobs. Beaver County's unemployment stood at 5.1 percent, ahead of the 6.0 national average. "It was a workman's paradise," Grandstaff said. "You could literally leave one job and cross the river and go some-where else and pick up another job that day."

Perhaps, in the long run, it wouldn't have mattered how badly LTV mismanaged things. Historian Barbara Tuchman dubbed the twenty years preceding 1978 as a period of "collapsing assumptions" in America, but when the industries, jobs, and towns began to fall, too, the impulse to blame a single culprit proved irresistible. The notion of LTV being venal and incompetent, a bunch of outsiders with little firsthand knowledge of the industry, remains the most popular one—no matter that the job cuts begun in Aliquippa in 1980 were made with butter-knife measures like reduced man-hours and early retirement. But there were also larger factors—the unstoppable transition from steel to plastics and lighter metals in construction and car design, a push for better fuel economy—that conspired to demote steel, like the once-vital horse or train, to a less central role in modern life.

"We also lost a lot of competition to other parts of the U.S.; mills in Alabama and the West have been growing for many decades," said University of Pittsburgh labor economist Chris Briem. "But the real story is, the way we made steel changed between the end of World War II and now.

"Pittsburgh, Aliquippa, all these places had the large integrated steel plant making coal, coke, and iron ore, and you put all those to-gether with a lot of manpower, you make steel. What came around was the electric-arc mini-mill, and that makes steel a lot differently. It doesn't use coal and coke; it uses electricity. It doesn't use iron ore; it uses scrap steel. And each of those things changes the competitiveness of steel. This is a big coal region and that coal advantage went from being a very positive thing to not very helpful at all."

It's inevitable, perhaps, that conventional wisdom would blame labor nearly as much as management for J&L's demise. Prod many a union man and it's not long before he'll admit that at some point the unions lost their way. By the late '70s, there were too many abuses on the mill floor, too much featherbedding, too little interest in producing the finest product—and yet an average pay of $23 an hour for a USW steelworker, not to mention, every fifth year, that glorious, cartoonish thirteen-week vacation.

Grandstaff, who finished as a crane operator in the seamless tube annex, had come out of the Army, then served a stint as an emergency room worker, before joining J&L in 1978. His four years there, he says, were the best of his working life, but he found the aura, if not the fact, of laziness appalling. "People would work for six hours, then sit for two," he said. "And everybody had the attitude: that ain't my job. If they're sitting somewhere and there's a pile of garbage right next to 'em? They ain't going to touch it. *That ain't my job.* It was like that throughout the mill. And it was terrible. It truly was."

The garbage pile isn't apocryphal: Once, Grandstaff says, a foreman did approach a lounging thread operator and told him to sweep one up. The operator had worked hard that day—had, in fact, busted his ass to hit an incentive-rate of production: twelve hours' worth in just six hours. But that left two hours on his shift to kill, and he just laughed and said he was done working. And he wasn't alone; men were reading newspapers, exercising, or just kicking back in corners to kill time all over steelmaking America. And no colleagues complained about the sight, because that would reveal that the incentive rates were too low and hurt the less productive workers. But the fact of it only reinforced peer resentment and the traditionally hostile boss-worker divide.

"The foreman insisted," Grandstaff said. "That escalated to the shop steward in the union, then to the steward of seamless tube, which escalated to the vice president of the union to the president. And the president came down, walked into the seamless tube annex; everybody knew he was coming and everybody knew who he was." The president then lifted his safety helmet above his head, signaling a walkout—and the room drained of men.

"We weren't out more than forty-five minutes to an hour," Grandstaff said, and thirty years later, he still says it in a kind of awe. "But even the lights turned off."

But even in the worst cases, management didn't seem to mind that much. "The union would defend everybody even if they were in the wrong," said Bill Macroglou, who began as a laborer at J&L in 1949 and ended as a supervisor in the tin mill. "If a guy was a repeat offender, say, or just negligent at work, you'd reprimand the guy and the next thing you know you're at arbitration. And as long as the money was there, LTV was paying out. They didn't give a damn about the grievances, because they wanted a rosy atmosphere. You'd get a guy who actually damaged product and damaged the equipment and you'd try to straighten him out, and they'd come and hush us up: Just forget about it."

Yes, said Pete Eritano, president of United Steelworkers Local 1211 in Aliquippa from 1979 to 1985, "we've defended some people probably shouldn't have been defended. But we did that as a job, as required by the Labor Act; we were required to represent somebody even if they did wrong things. And we did, and usually those people were fired anyhow. A lot of times we got 'em back.

"My whole take on what happened: The men in the mill knew how to work that plant. They knew how to make the steel, how to do the coke works, the wire, the seamless pipe, the welded tube: they knew it all. And they needed those key people down there to do all that. But when LTV took over, they started changing everything. The union could've been better on quality issues, but LTV didn't seem to want our help. They didn't want to listen."

Ernest Hemingway's famous retort to the question "How did you go bankrupt?" ("Gradually, then suddenly") applies just as well to businesses and towns as it does to men. There's the same initial disbelief, the slow nibbling away of resources and faith, then the stomach-lurching drop into the abyss. It was the fate of Pete Eritano—class of '57, Ditka's opponent in midget ball, mill lifer—to preside over all of it: his first year, 1979, the Aliquippa Works employed more than 10,000 hourly workers. Then, in September 1981, the slow bleed began.

LTV shut down the rod and wire mill, slashing seven hundred jobs. "We feel the impact is going to be minimal," said communications manager Curt Miller, who also informed the *Beaver County Times* that the shutdown "is not indicative of the profitability of J&L's other departments."

Then, one by one, four of Aliquippa's five blast furnaces were idled. In March 1982, 950 more lost work when the seamless tube department was shuttered; by then 2,600 had been fired and tax revenue plummeted and the town couldn't pay its bills. The electric company threatened to turn off the streetlights. Aliquippa was not alone: the economy was in recession. One in three steelworkers in America was jobless.

And then it got worse. By the summer of 1982, with nationwide steel production and employment numbers their lowest since 1933, nearly half of the remaining 7,800 hourly workers at the Aliquippa Works were gone; more than 1,000 salaried workers had also been fired. Grandstaff, with a $650-a-month house payment, a wife at home, and a daughter on the way, walked in one morning, 7:45 a.m., sure that he had a job for life. He was told to clean out his locker. In the seamless tube locker room, 'the blockhouse,' he found hundreds of his fellow shift workers, all tough men, breaking down and crying.

A food bank had been set up at J&L, where the remaining workers deducted from $1 to $20 out of every paycheck to help out their brethren. On July 25, the phone rang in the Local 1211 offices. The secretary thought someone was playing a prank.

The White House was calling, wanted to know if Eritano would take a call from Ronald Reagan. "Which means—and they ask me— Am I 'going to be civil?'" Eritano said. "Of course. I respect the office, okay? I didn't tell them I respected him."

The next day, a Monday, the phone rang again. "You don't mind if I call you 'Pete'?" Reagan's voice asked. Eritano didn't. "God bless you all in Aliquippa for doing such an outstanding deed," Reagan said about the food bank. One president to another, he also told Eritano that the union was a good example for the nation because they were helping themselves. He sent his congratulations and said something about the "spirit of America."

The call lasted five minutes. Reagan said his economic policies wouldn't work overnight. "We're hanging on," Eritano told him. "And hoping the economy will turn around. But we won't be able to hang on much longer."

Reagan wouldn't hear of it. "He said, 'Oh, don't worry, Pete, this'll all work out,'" Eritano recalled. "'There'll be a good steel mill there when you're all done. It'll be leaner, but it'll be good. There'll be good jobs.'"

Fourteen months later, the number of laid-off workers in Aliquippa had climbed to 4,000. Eritano wrote a follow-up letter to the president. "Where have you been when our people needed you the most?" he began. He reminded Reagan of their phone call, his promise of a recovery being right around the corner.

"Our people have paid a high price in this game plan you call recovery," Eritano went on. "We have a 30 percent unemployment rate in Beaver County. . . . Most of the layoffs have been for a year or longer. Homes and dreams have been lost; marriages and families have been torn apart.

"We currently have 1,000 steelworkers at our plant who have run out of benefits. These people live on a $25 food certificate that we supply every two weeks. Our food fund of over $200,000 will be gone in three months. Where have you been?"

One by one, over the next two years, departments kept shutting down: the A-5 coke battery; ingot steel production; the blooming, billet, bar, and round mills. A total of 250 jobs gone in one round, 360 in the next, and—always—the threat of more firings to come. Crime in Aliquippa was up 40 percent since 1981; police were arresting men who'd never been in trouble. Wives found themselves being hit for the first time. In 1984, Jerry Malesky was in his eleventh year on the basic oxygen furnace. "They'd put in a new round caster and told us it'd be twenty-five years before we peaked because we were the only ones in America making this kind of steel," he said. "So I bought a house, two new cars; I was very high-paid. Six weeks later they shut the mill down. Ruined everything."

On January 3, 1985, LTV, fresh off a desperation merger with Cleveland-based Republic Steel—originators of the emblem seen each Sunday on Pittsburgh Steelers helmets—announced the close of Aliquippa's welded tube division, killing off five hundred more jobs. "I shut the welded tube down," said Juke Suder. "Shut the lights and locked the door. I felt so bad about the place, because I worked there for thirty-four years. I felt like I lost a friend."

On May 17, 1985, LTV delivered the coup de grâce, laying off 1,300 in Aliquippa's coke plant and steelmaking facility. Eritano was in the 1211 office when he received the notice in that day's mail. He held himself together the rest of the day. "I didn't want them to see it," he said. When it ended, the union boss packed up some papers, walked to the parking lot, got into his car, and drove home to Center. He walked through his front door and veered into his bedroom, chest heaving now, and closed the door. Then he broke down and wept.

Only seven hundred workers, in the 14-inch and tin plate mills, now occupied the hollowed-out, seven-and-a-half-mile tract along the Ohio. The scramble for jobs elsewhere, anywhere, left the streets desolate; within five years only 13,374 Aliquippans—down from 17,094 in 1980—remained. One, electrician Chuckie Walker, was laid off late in 1986 after thirteen years. When he made it back home to Plan 11 that night, Walker broke the news to his wife, Chedda; his daughter, Diedre; and his twin sons, Dwan and Donald, and then walked out to the front porch to get some air.

Dwan followed him. The evening sky was pitch dark His father looked so alone.

"Who cries when I cry, son?" Chuckie said softly. "Nobody."

PART FOUR

October 14, 2011

. . . . *The crowd troops slow and happy up the stairs to the parking lot. Coaches gather to gloat in Zmijanac's office while the players scatter, some walking home in their football pants. Soon only one remains. Davion Hall, son of a Quip who lost in the '88 state title game, nephew of a Quip who won the program's first state title in 1991, has just played his final game at The Pit. All his life, Hall heard that he had to win titles, uphold tradition, do the family proud. His mother died when he was two; his has been an all-male upbringing, dodgy and hard.*

"We have the town on our back," he says. "Days through the week, after practice, we see people on the streets and they ask: 'You have a good practice? Make sure everything's good. . . .' They think we can do it. But more than that, we think we can do it. The whole town, they're depending on us."

There are few things deader than a football locker room after. What had been, a half hour ago, a bustling hive of ego and brawn is thunderously still; Hall collects his things and bolts as if chased by a spirit. Who can blame him? Cold is overtaking all of it now: the pile of flung white pants, the pile of flung black jerseys, the floor littered with leaves, sod-clumped cleats, balls of sticky tape, a tipped bottle of Faygo pineapple-watermelon soda, Skittles wrappers, an abandoned black duffel, pink socks, a receiver glove, skewed benches, clods of waffled dirt.

America, of course, is the land of renewal. We don't fancy ourselves a past-haunted people and, at first blush, our new national pastime doesn't look back, either. Football lacks baseball's clockless, county-fair feel. It doesn't, like college basketball's March Madness, smack of a time when loyalty to city, state, region, or school mattered so much more. But amid all that kinetic flash and fury and TV-perfect pace, it's easy to miss that football, too, serves a fierce nostalgia, a need to address connections made or frayed or fading fast.

It's no coincidence that mill and mining towns produced so many great players. Heavy industry and football share the same DNA. Both depend on collective striving, on "the line" and its meld of various skill sets, on the numbing repetition of task. Both feature hierarchical organization, an eternal tension between management suits and product-producing grunts. Both depend on—even celebrate—the implicit trade of health for money. Football can cripple; that is clear. And each gnarled joint and concussed brain is but an echo of the sacrifices made, two and three generations back, by the real steelers, packers, and giants who lost fingers or hearing or lungs on the job.

Indeed, the Quips' locker room at season's end feels like nothing so much as the empty building standing less than a mile away on the Ohio River, the one structure left from the titanic mill that died thirty years ago. The rough concrete floor, the open locker doors, the scattered remains of a workforce of thousands—then hundreds, then dozens—remain within the immense, 260,000-square-foot shell where Jones & Laughlin Steel's seamless tube annex once clattered and hummed. The mill's end cut the town's legs off. Quips football has propped it up ever since, each season's wins and titles like the spidery tingling of a phantom limb, the vibration that almost, for small moments each autumn, feels like the thing that's gone.

At 10 p.m., sharp, floodlights towering over The Pit snap off. Soon there are footsteps: Murph, the school's burly, crewcut building manager, is walking up the parking lot to the only pickup truck left. He's wearing a New York Jets jersey with "REVIS" on the back but, no, it wasn't a gift from Aliquippa's latest famous son. "Nah," he says. "They get rich, and they get cheap."

He climbs into the cab, guns the engine, rolls down the window. "One of these days they'll build a new stadium . . ." Murph says, and then he steps on the gas, his last words mixing with the exhaust, ". . . or we'll merge with Hopewell!"

The engine's roar follows the headlights cutting up and away through the dark. The field and hills drop back into silence, and almost instantly it's as if no one had spoken, nothing had happened, ever. That's an illusion. In the hills beyond, in surrounding kitchens and bars and bedrooms, people are pouring drinks, ordering another, talking about what they saw here, what it means for next week and next year. The game will go on for a while yet.

We represent the struggle. The pain. The oppression. We represent the fight. This is Aliquippa.

—Sean Gilbert, 2010

13

You-Know-Who

Everything was shrinking fast now. By 1980 Aliquippa's population was down to 17,094, and the exiting stream never stopped; by '90 there would be just 13,374 left. Half the world that JFK saw when he spoke downtown had dissolved away. One by one, bars and stores boarded up their windows. Ambition withered. Postures sagged. It was not the time and place to think big.

Yet by force of will, personality, ego, delusion, or spite, that is all Don Yannessa did. He made Quips' home games—complete with fireworks, an Indian on horseback, the *dunt-dunt-dunt,* and increasingly winning teams—into community events; packed Carl Aschman Stadium (official capacity, 5,500; oft-reported standing room crowd, 9,000) and made himself the unofficial drum major for Western Pennsylvania football. Publicity for his seniors? One fall he sent out a photo of them posed around a gleaming black Corvette. Media guide? Instead of the usual mimeographed notes, Yannessa provided a booklet with records and results and photo after photo of the players and their wondrous coach. The local newspaper couldn't send a writer on the road? Yannessa rasped postgame comments into a tape recorder and made sure it got there before deadline. His slick quotes sounded more like those of a network color man than some small town ex-lineman, and that figured: he made no bones about wanting to work in TV someday.

After John Evasovich moved back to Aliquippa, he attended the occasional game. He and Yannessa had been teammates, but barely knew each other. After one win in '82, Evasovich made the mistake of stopping by to congratulate the coach.

"Johnny, you got to get more involved in the program," Yannessa said.

"Next year, Don, I won't be on the road as much," Evasovich said. "I'll be happy to."

The following Tuesday, Evasovich answered his phone.

"Don Yannessa," said the voice. "Congratulations. You were elected president."

"Of what?" Evasovich said.

"The Quarterback Club."

"What the hell am I supposed to do?"

"Raise money," Yannessa said. Then he hung up.

The team budget was $36,000 a year and ticket sales brought in $40,000; even as the town frayed, Yannessa's inky mat of hair, gleaming teeth, and sleek cars only seemed to get shinier. He was making $42,000, teaching English, halfheartedly, waiting for the final bell and practice to start. He had a "QUIPSI" license plate bolted to, yes, that black Corvette. It soon made way for a Cadillac.

By fall of 1984, the forty-five-year-old Yannessa had led the Quips to three of the four previous WPIAL title games—though he still hadn't won a championship—and become a semicelebrity. National Public Radio and CBS's Charles Kuralt dropped in to produce features. Aliquippa principal Jerry Montini quipped that Yannessa could've worked for Barnum & Bailey—closer to the truth than he knew. Yannessa fed reporters his sense of the absurd and astonishing recall; he made anxious parents feel their kids were special; he fed boosters inside dope. And the entire time, like a ringmaster eyeing both the leaping lions and gate totals, he was sizing everyone up for what he needed next.

Zmijanac, who learned all he needed to know about the game—and, as a far pricklier presence, half of what he needed to know about cultivating people—from Yannessa, watched his mentor navigate the tricky course through black fans, white boosters, stern administrators, fellow teachers, and needy sportswriters. "Ain't you fucking somethin'?" he'd say. Yannessa would laugh, too.

"The best politician I've ever known," Zmijanac said. "Beautiful."

In the fall of 1983, 20th Century Fox released *All The Right Moves,* a high school football film starring young Tom Cruise and set in a dying Western Pennsylvania steel town. At one point the head coach, played by Craig T. Nelson, said a potential coaching job is between him "and you-know-who from Aliquippa." Everyone in Western Pennsylvania chuckled, but the real inside joke was even better: Hollywood Don had finagled his way onto the production as a technical advisor, and appears in the climactic game as the opposing coach. ("I don't want to hear that bullshit. Block 'em anyway!") You-know-who was a natural.

Yannessa plugged his own terminology and plays into the film's game sequences, and has banged the drum so often about his behind-the-scenes maneuvers that (despite the inconvenient fact that the film was based on a magazine story about Duquesne, Pennsylvania, and filmed in the spring of '83 in Pittsburgh and Johnstown) many, including Yannessa himself, have come to believe that the movie's about Aliquippa.

Why not? The town's fictional name, Ampipe, is clearly based on Ambridge. And the way Yannessa describes it one fall day, pointing out production stills on the wall of his home office, you can feel how the screenwriter, Michael Kane, first fell under his rat-a-tat spell.

"Craig T.—the coach? He stayed here for a weekend," Yannessa said. "There's Tom Cruise. I was on location for eight weeks. . . . That was his girlfriend at the time, Rebecca De Mornay. She was pretty. See some pictures here of Craig T. and Cruiser. . . . That's me and Cruise, right there: tough kid. We put him in the hospital two times; he was pissing blood one time. And this guy here came to me and said, 'Tell him we're going to double the football scenes; he's going to have a double.' So I went to the hospital to tell him and Cruise said no. He said, 'If I do it, it has to be real.'"

Not even Joe Paterno could resist Yannessa. It had been more than two decades since the Penn State head coach, bitter over losing Ditka to Pitt, had washed his hands of the town. But in December of 1983, Aliquippa High had a bright receiver named Marques Henderson, and time and Yannessa's blarney and Joe Pa's own vaulting ambition made the old grudge seem, well, silly. He agreed to speak at Aliquippa's annual football banquet, to be held at the Serbian Club.

Late on a Saturday, December 3, Paterno's private plane landed at Beckett Aviation in Pittsburgh, and Yannessa was waiting. First, he took him to the Quippian Club, the black hub. Paterno took up residence at one corner of the bar, slapped down his first $20 bill. White and black faces crowded around; he bought drinks for the next forty-five minutes, and didn't the town hear about *that* for years? Yannessa always reeled in big coaching names, but few bigger than Paterno. And the blacks liked that Joe Pa came to their place first; no doubt Marques Henderson was made aware.

Then Yannessa drove Paterno crosstown to the Serbian Club, the white and black boosters from the Quippian trailing fast behind. Paterno bought more drinks, until everybody finally sat down. Joe Pa spoke, and per his deal with Yannessa, he was hustled off the dais so he could get back on the plane while everyone was still eating. At that point, Porky Palombo, Yannessa's uncle, handed Paterno a white envelope stocked with $400.

"Just something for coming," Porky said.

"Put it back in your kitty," Paterno said. "I didn't come here for that. I came here for Don."

Yannessa snorted. "You came here for Marques Henderson," he said, and even Joe laughed at that. He didn't take the money, though.

Still, after eleven years at Aliquippa, Yannessa had proven himself great in everything but winning. And no one wanted to hear the excuse that Aliquippa played "up" two classes. Yes, its tenth-to-twelfth-grade enrollment of 449 students technically placed the school in the WPI-AL's Class A division; two schools with *larger* enrollments, in fact, did compete in Class A. Yes, the Quips ignored reality altogether, skipped past AA (enrollment range 486–688), and insisted on slugging it out in AAA (but, hell, some still insisted that they could play with the big boys competing in the WPIAL's recently created AAAA division). And yes, Aliquippa was by far the smallest of the thirty-five schools playing in its section, up against Ambridge and its enrollment of 989 students, Hopewell with 917, and the largest, Moon, at 1,140.

Really, it was no shock that his teams had a habit of fading at season's end; by then, injuries and exhaustion made it impossible to hide Aliquippa's comparative lack of depth. The Quips kept losing in the WPIAL title game—to Thomas Jefferson in '80 (enrollment: 924), Steel Valley (770) in '82, Mt. Pleasant (848) in '83. "We've got the copper trophy three times now," Yannessa said. "I think I'm going to melt them down into bullets and shoot myself." Not to his face, of course (*Love the guy!*), but people were starting to compare him with Bud Grant, the Minnesota Vikings coach who went to four Super Bowls but never won.

Finally, in 1984, just as the shutdown at the mill was hitting another horrific peak—660 jobs slashed at the Aliquippa Works the previous summer—Yannessa broke through. Powered by the unstoppable Rapheal "Pudgy" Abercrombie, a 5-foot-5 butterball who churned his way to a record 4,606 yards at Aliquippa, and guided by quarterback

Vic Lay, the '84 Quips bulled through the regular season, losing just one game—by a single point—crushing Hopewell and Blackhawk, edging Ambridge. In the WPIAL AAA title game at Pittsburgh's Three Rivers Stadium, a November grudge match against Mt. Pleasant, Aliquippa found itself down by a point with seven minutes to play, facing sixty-three yards of empty.

Just as he had nearly thirty years before, as a sophomore backup on Aliquippa's 1955 WPIAL champs, Yannessa found himself praying on the sideline. With 5:53 left and Aliquippa facing a fourth-and-6 on its own 41-yard line, he had no choice but to go for it. Yannessa prayed harder. Lay, who hadn't completed a pass all game, coolly fired a 17-yard strike to Kevin Haley. Minutes later Abercrombie, who finished the day with 240 rushing yards, used the final 12 to score and give Aliquippa the win, 20-15. It had taken Yannessa a dozen years—and those last seven plays—to go from loser to winner. His wife cried.

Twenty years had passed since Aschman's last season, since Aliquippa had last won. Now the team took the same route home from Pittsburgh that it had in '55 and '64 with King Carl, north on the other side of the Ohio River, through the streets of Ambridge, across the bridge and into the guts of the old downtown. Yannessa, riding in the back of a van, nibbled on shrimp cocktail and sipped champagne. At one point he noticed Zmijanac, his defensive coordinator, riding in a nearby car. Yannessa, buzzing now, rolled down a window.

"Hey," he screamed. "What'd Aliquippa do tonight?!"

It wasn't the same as it had been, decades back. Still, some five hundred fans were waiting at Aschman Stadium. Men, women, and children kissed the coach, patted his back. Fireworks lit up the sky, and they all sang the alma mater and everyone yelled for him to speak. And stunningly, for perhaps the only time in his life, Hollywood Don said, "No words needed," and raised the trophy into the cool night air.

Two days later, Sunday's *Beaver County Times* spoke of how the win, "helped the townspeople forget their troubles, even if only for a few hours. Politicians weren't squabbling and insecure workers weren't thinking about their uncertain futures." One black man from Plan 11 said, "The community needed this."

Though Yannessa—spawn of a steelworking family, son of the borough—had told reporters just after the game how happy he was to lift the town's spirits, though he thanked God for letting him win the big one at last, nothing for him really changed. Something in his nature—call it an extra layer of what-the-fuck confidence—left him unaffected by the usual slings. Yannessa had never been that tormented by big losses, and the long-awaited win came less as blessed relief than *It's-about-time!* arrival. And he wasn't about to become complacent.

The next September, for the 1985 season opener, Yannessa arranged to have three parachutists drop out of the Pennsylvania sky and onto the 50-yard line. One held a sign that read "Fighting Quips," the second held one reading "1984 WPIAL," and a third sign read "Champions." No coach in the area—hell, nationwide—had the imagination and balls to pull off such a stunt. And that, as he said later that fall, was nothing. Yannessa was already roughing out a scheme for Opening Night 1986.

"I want to get the Indian and the horse to parachute out of a helicopter," he said. "See if they can land at the fifty-yard line and just gallop away."

You can't pinpoint an exact date, because the creating of a cultural icon is usually a matter of accretion, a layering of moments that stack up until, suddenly, everyone understands that the person in question matters far more than he or she should. It wouldn't be until January 1991, in fact, when *Saturday Night Live* premiered a sketch called "Bill Swerski's Superfans," that Mike Ditka arrived at that point of American fame where hero worship, ubiquity, and ridicule mingle and even the most oblivious get the joke, where he had become not just a football great but a *personality*, an archetype called "Da Coach": Eyes popping, mustache bristling, everybody's half-unhinged uncle wreaking havoc over Sunday dinner.

But by the end of '85, it had started to build. Since taking over as head coach of the Chicago Bears in January 1982, Ditka had proven himself the perfectly imperfect change-agent for the mustied franchise: hot-tempered, decidedly unslick, all but boiling with the need to win. He promised his players they'd be champions in three years, screamed, threw clipboards and headsets, broke his right hand punching a locker in '83 ("Go out and win one for Lefty," he commanded), lost the '84 NFC title game to the eventual Super Bowl champion 49ers, came back the next season to beat them on the road—and was picked up for drunk driving after celebrating on the team flight home. His players also happened to be catnip for sportswriters, and soon all the Ditka stories that had been told for years in Aliquippa bars, Pitt alumni gatherings, and NFL coaching offices began spilling into the mainstream.

Didn't you know? Ditka had knocked himself out hitting a steel blocking sled at Pitt, punched out two teammates in a huddle, and in his spare time—playing Pitt basketball—called Kentucky's legendary coach, Adolph Rupp, "an old goat" during an on-court argument. Ditka joined the Bears out of college, in his first game barked at veteran teammate Ted Karras "to get the lead out of your ass" (Karras took a swing at him), won NFL Rookie of the Year. The guy had pedigree, all of it hard-earned: he rampaged at the knee of legendary Bears founder George Halas, revolutionized the tight end position from blocking lump into offensive weapon, and in 1963 led Chicago to its first championship in seventeen years.

A few years later, after standing up to the old man in a contract dispute ("Halas throws nickels around like manhole covers," Ditka growled—thus proving himself outspoken *and* poetic), he got shipped off to the losing hell of Philadelphia. He drank too much there. Revitalized by a move to the Cowboys, Ditka once stood up before a play was called and punched a Vikings linebacker in the face.

In Dallas, Ditka played four years for another legend, Tom Landry. He caught a touchdown pass in the team's '72 Super Bowl win over Miami, but within the franchise was known for his frantic clashes with teammate Dan Reeves in racquetball, golf, and any other competition a bunch of overcaffeinated machos could dream up. "And it killed Ditka, because no matter what they played Reeves would win most of it," said longtime Dallas executive Gil Brandt. "Just absolutely killed him. They used to bounce golf balls: who could catch them between their thumbs, all kinds of stuff; used to play cards all the time, darts. . . ."

And when Ditka lost? "Coach Landry had us rooming together," Reeves said, recalling Ditka's first season in 1969. "When we got him, I was a terrible gin player and he was really good, but the cards were just coming my way. He tore that deck in two, took that chair and threw it, and the legs just went into the Sheetrock. I knew then: 'Holy mackerel, he's a competitor.'"

That Ditka possessed a rapid-fire intelligence got lost in the carnage, of course; why ruin so wondrously Neanderthal an image? After his playing career ended in 1972, he coached tight ends and special teams for Landry and besides one early, rogue decision to call for an onside—and botched—kick against the Giants ("You ever do that again without telling me," Landry said out of the side of his mouth, squinting straight ahead, "and you'll be looking for another job"), proved capable of folding himself within the dictates of one of the more buttoned-down regimes in NFL lore. Ditka even sparked a revival of one wrinkle—the shotgun formation, out of commission for twenty years by then—that remade the modern quarterback position.

"His IQ was off the chart," Reeves said. "In 1975, we had really struggled on third-down conversion and he was the one who mentioned to Coach Landry: Why don't we go to the shotgun?"

"Exactly right," said Roger Staubach, Dallas's quarterback then. "Ditka was really behind it. He said, 'Hey, when it's third-and-three-plus, ninety-nine percent of the time we throw the football, so why not get back there and do something different? It really was creative. Ditka was the one that pushed it. We put it in and everybody thought we were crazy."

It wasn't the only thing that worked for the Cowboys that season; the shotgun, after all, was used only on third-down situations or in the final two minutes. But it did prove to be a vital part of the Landry "flex" offense that turned Staubach and the Cowboys loose that year, helping to build its much adored/hated brand as "America's Team." Dallas improved from an 8-win club to 10-4 in 1975, made the playoffs, and then became the first wild-card team ever to reach the Super Bowl. That they lost to Ditka's hometown Steelers in the most exciting title game up to then was, it seems, only appropriate.

"Ditka's got a subtleness about him," Staubach said.

"I wish," Reeves said, "I was that bright."

But never mind that. Never mind the fact that, in Chicago, Ditka would manage some of the most spectacular egos ever assembled in one locker room and—while feuding with his genius defensive coordinator, Buddy Ryan; barely coexisting with his general manager, Mike McCaskey; and holding his nose over the antics of his punk-rock QB, Jim McMahon—led the '85 Bears to an 18-1 record and a Super Bowl championship. Notwithstanding the passel of Chicago trick plays, Ryan's delight in questioning Ditka's coaching acumen made it easier to pigeonhole "Da Coach" as a mere fire-breather. Maybe that's to the good. Ditka the legend made Ditka the man rich, after all—and, besides, there was almost no way to stop it.

Indeed, you could say that he was the right man at the right time, one of those figures who prompts folks to say, in an echo of Voltaire's gibe about God, "If Ditka didn't exist, we would have had to invent him." He was no slick-haired savant with larger "lessons" to teach. He was a loon, a football animal, and, best of all, someone who smelled like the real deal. That his hulking figure and beaver-pelt hairline made him resemble, yes, a bear, made it easy for writers to classify him as "a throwback," and most left it at that. How much baggage can one man carry?

But it's no accident that Ditka's popular appeal came at the same time as the collapse of American industry and the lower middle class. In his gum-chomping, unapologetic Ditka-ness, "Iron Mike" provided a weekly, televised reminder of the life his dad and so many others had fought and worked for. His was the nasally Slavic voice of those chirping now in unemployment lines, forced to uproot from mill towns and scatter—to piecemeal jobs, to the vague promise of Sun Belt Salvation, to sunny places that had never heard of J&L.

He raged like so many blue-collars raged, and if there was injustice that caused all that growling, you still couldn't help but laugh sometimes. Why didn't they change with the times? Couldn't they see they were only hurting themselves? Ditka was slapstick-funny, but didn't yet know it: In 1987 he fired a wad of green gum at a fan, leaving the field after a bitter loss to San Francisco, and then flipped her the finger. In 1988, he suffered a heart attack mid-season and promised to come back as "Mellow Mike." Two weeks later he was back on the sideline, erupting.

"You know, I did calm down for a while," Ditka said. "But my nature is my nature. I can't change that. I wish I could."

Many liked to say that Ditka was the perfect coach for Chicago, but he would've been perfect in Pittsburgh, Detroit, and Cleveland, too, perfect in any city where workers were scrambling and idled and scared. The *SNL* superfans would dream up absurd competitions—Da Coach versus, say . . . a hurricane!—and all would always agree that Ditka would win. The audience roared; such blind faith was a joke, and even more hilarious because of the sad reality outside. Ditka's constituency wasn't winning a thing, and Iron Mike's force was all but spent. In Chicago he had been king of a one-year dynasty. Fired there in 1992, he came back for an ill-fated three years in New Orleans. He never won another Super Bowl.

But in Aliquippa, his successes had eternal shelf life: His successes were theirs. No place could ask for a better spokesman (as late as 2014, a Canadian reporter asked if the NFL should add more teams to the playoffs and Ditka shot back, "What? Are they gonna be able to get Aliquippa High School?"). People weren't listening to Henry Mancini much anymore, and every union loss chipped away at the Wagner Act's legacy, but Ditka provided a safe caricature of the town's rough virtues. Bears—then Saints—gear invaded Steeler country while he coached, and each visit home to his parents in Linmar—*Ya hear? Mike's in town*—was a certifying event, a reminder that Aliquippa product could still stand among the nation's best.

And he came back every year. In 1986, Ditka initiated a golf tournament to raise money for scholarships for Aliquippa High kids, and over the next two decades pushed the total well over $200,000. By some estimates, Ditka personally donated "in excess of $50,000," according to the city in 2000, but one of the organizers, his old teammate John Evasovich, said that estimate is low. "I can account for—out of his pocket—at least sixty-five thousand dollars to the Aliquippa football program," Evasovich said. "And I can account for an excess of three hundred thousand dollars in scholarship money."

There was, too, some off-the-books action. One year, Aliquippa High graduated covaledictorians; one girl had been awarded $34,000 in scholarships and the other had been given no more than $5,000. When the latter came to his table, Ditka pulled out a rubber-banded wad of paper and bills and one crumpled check—and asked the girl to spell her name. He wrote it down, then wrote "$5,000.00" in the box to the right. "Honey, when you get successful, you do this for somebody else," Ditka said.

"Do I have the greatest respect for him? Yeah," Evasovich said. "Do I think he's a pain in the ass sometimes? Yeah. But is it overweighed by what he does good? Yes."

Ditka tried for years to get his parents to leave Aliquippa. But where would they go? When they visited their son in his last coaching stop, New Orleans, Big Mike kept complaining that the house was so big that he kept getting lost. So they didn't move when Big Mike was alive, and for more than a decade after Big Mike died in 1998 Charlotte didn't move, either. Little Mike tried to keep her comfortable, kept buying her cars, paid for her flights and walking-around money when she felt the itch to go gambling.

But she stayed in the house at Linmar, where the neighbors knew her and the police chief and the postman checked on her near every day. "That's why I like it here: you're close," Charlotte said in 2010. "I could move away, but I just know from my own children; they move into these new places and big homes and you don't even know your neighbors. Everybody's got to work to pay for the damn house, and they don't have time to socialize. So I'll stay right here."

For a long time, his mother's coffee table in the house in Linmar had a small crystal bear on it, inscribed with the words, "Tough times don't last. Tough people do." Mike had given it to her, long ago. The phrase has been credited to everyone from boxer Jack Johnson to actor Gregory Peck to televangelist Robert Schuller, but Ditka had barked it out so often, and with such conviction, during his most famous years that it became a kind of town motto. In Aliquippa, in fact, you'd be pressed to find anyone who thinks he didn't invent the very idea.

When Aileen Gilbert, who had fled Aliquippa after working her dad's old job atop a J&L coke battery, returned from Hartford with her kids in 1982, she intended the move to be temporary. At least, that's what she told herself—and her miserable oldest daughter. Diana cried at first sight of tiny Aliquippa, but after her tears dried and nothing changed she took to cultivating a classic teenage rage, primed to blow at the slightest provocation. Anyone—especially a gang-seasoned sophomore yanked out of her big-city high school—could see the future turning its back on the damn place.

"There was nothing here," Aileen Gilbert said. "Stores were closing. There was already a sense of *No Jobs*. People were leaving, whole
families were going, because they needed jobs. I only meant to stay a
year—just to reset myself and then move. I didn't know where, but I
knew I didn't want to stay here. But that didn't happen. . . ."

So Diana, the oldest of Aileen's five—followed by Mark, Sean,
Tamu, and Jamal, their three fathers scattered while Aileen raised them
alone—entered Aliquippa High for the first time in her junior year, the
fall of '82. She made an immediate impression. "She was horrible," said
Zmijanac, chuckling. "She was tough." There were fights.

Only her mom knew why she was so mad; it was about then that
Diana told Aileen that relatives had sexually molested her from the age
of six to the time the family left Hartford. "I'm going to write a book
and tell about it," Diana said. "I'm not going to tell you now. I was
angry. It's a good story.

"I never fit in here. A lot of people don't—didn't—like me because
they didn't understand me. I did: I knew why I was angry. But when
you're young you feel vulnerable and powerful. That was my way of
controlling my atmosphere."

Diana was also very fast, a sprinter good enough to draw interest
from colleges and—much later, when Sean was playing in the NFL—to
beat her big-time pro athlete brother in a footrace out in Moon. ("He
won't acknowledge that," she said. "I'm his big sister; I'm not supposed
to be beating him.") But Diana was also young, hotheaded, and didn't
care: Come senior year, she was kicked off the track team. One career
option, perhaps the best, was gone before she even knew it existed.

She left the summer after graduation, in 1984, to live with a cousin
and find work in Washington, DC—but Aliquippa had its hooks in. She
returned in the fall, just in time for the football team's first championship run under Yannessa, and soon was seen wearing a letter jacket to
games. She and the senior fullback, Darryl Revis, had found each other.
On July 14, 1985, she gave birth to their son, Darrelle.

A year later, her little brother Sean announced himself as one of the greatest players ever to walk onto the field at Aschman Stadium. Even as a sophomore defensive tackle, his gifts were clear: 6-foot-5, 270 pounds, able to sprint 40 yards in 4.8 seconds. He had all the agility of his older brother Mark, who earned a basketball scholarship to Duquesne, and just a hint of Diana's rebelliousness. "I love Sean Gilbert," Yannessa said. "I used to tell him: 'I've only known two guys in my life that loved to practice: you and Ditka.' He could've went the other way; he had a temperament as a ninth-grader, and a couple times we had to kick him in the ass. But he was smart and he trusted you. Made me a helluva coach."

The next season, Sean's junior year, Yannessa stood him up, made him an inside linebacker. The result was a glorious havoc. Gilbert instantly stood out, as the *Pittsburgh Post-Gazette*'s Mike White put it, like "a Cadillac in a lot full of Volkswagens." No one had ever seen such size and speed combined: Sean would've run down and crushed the young Ditka. Recruiters began their siege as the Quips went 12-1 and won their third WPIAL title in four years. Yannessa declared that the Chicago Bears would happily draft Sean as a high school senior. It didn't seem all that far-fetched.

By then, Yannessa's machine was starting to pick up where the mill left off. Money wasn't a problem, not with all the boosters; Ditka, after winning his Super Bowl with the '85 Bears, had even promised to donate $5,000 a year so long as Yannessa kept coaching. On the field the Quips were steamrolling the WPIAL: With Gilbert even better in 1988, his senior year—he had 91 solo tackles, picked up a fumble and ran 70 yards for a score, intercepted a pass and ran 47 yards for another—the Quips won their first fourteen games and found themselves ranked No. 2 in the nation by *USA Today*. The paper also named Gilbert the republic's defensive player of the year. The program had never been held in such high regard.

And somewhere, in all that winning, the town's racial split had quietly faded. Not that there wasn't plenty of prejudice, or that Western

Pennsylvania had become any more enlightened: The Quips' arrival for
games at predominantly white Montour in 1984 and '86 were greeted
by a burning cross behind the end zone. But with Aliquippa's population
now 31 percent black—and its football team's 70 percent—with the
'70s riots a constant reminder of the alternative, with football emerging as one of the few remaining pipelines out, an us-against-the-world
unity seemed the only choice.

"Growing up we watched Pudgy Abercrombie and Darrelle's dad,
Darryl, and we watched them all as one family," Sean Gilbert said. "You
didn't see racism. You saw your brother next to you, and it didn't stop
there. When the game was over, we were over in their area of town, they
were over in ours: it didn't matter. I spent the night at David Mike's,
our quarterback—go over there after film, go over all night. Milk at Ed
Gripper's house and, after, hang all night, hanging over there the next
day. His parents treated me just like I was their son.

"Had Joe Becker, left tackle, hundred seventy pounds soaking wet.
Anthony Barnett, Italian guy, hundred sixty pounds soaking wet, but
would jack your jaw. And you know what? You weren't leaving him out
there. I get chills telling you this. Because, man, we loved each other."

Gilbert paused at the thought, a cause for wonder even now. He
lives in North Carolina these days, but upon hearing someone describe
a recent visit to Aschman Stadium on a fall Friday night, his voice went
softer. "Did you get chills?" he said. "What football will do. Football's
a religion sometimes."

Summer nights, before he went off to play at Pitt, Gilbert would
run to the bottom of the hill and back, up the long, high grade to his
mother's thirteen-room house on Seventh Avenue. Aileen had grown
up there, her children too, and now her grandchild, Darrelle, three years
old and absorbing the chemistry of the town: its always rough honesty,
and the changes now making the men weak and desperate. Once, Diana
found her son sitting on the front steps, eyes fixed far off.

"I'm waiting for Uncle Sean," Darrelle said.

"Where's he at?" Diana replied.

Soon they heard the sound of her brother huffing, saw that steaming hulk looming. He ran up to Darrelle, touched him on the arm, maybe the shoulder or head, and then pivoted and headed back down the hill again.

"Let him stay right here," Sean said, over his shoulder. "I'm going to keep touching him."

It has always struck Aileen Gilbert as suspect, how people became nicer once she came home to Aliquippa with two highly athletic sons. After Sean's talent began to emerge, more than one area school tried to get her to move into their district—to the point, she says, of offering housing and jobs—and she wonders if Salt Smith's visit to ask her to fill a seat on the Board of Education was a slick way to keep the boy from leaving Aliquippa.

So radical a shift left a sour taste. Her love for the place can modulate by the second. "I do think it's special," Aileen said of Aliquippa. "I don't think it's *that* special, though. I think that God has me here. Because I should not be living here under normal circumstances—because I went through so much here.

"When Sean got drafted and I became 'Ms. Gilbert' for the first time, it was like, *Okay, now I got all these friends, people coming to my house, calling me on the phone?* Before it was, *I don't like her*—and I did nothing but work and take care of my kids. So I have wanted to move. But every time I would think about it, the thought would just leave. It's just God. Sean and them have tried to get me to come to North Carolina to stay for, like, three months. I'd say, 'I'll come stay a week or two, but I'm coming back home. . . .' I ain't going nowhere. I will die here."

And then, with Yannessa rolling and the stands packed and Gilbert playing like an apotheosis of all the fierce talent that had come before—all the Franks and Suders, Dorsetts and Ditkas, all that speed and power and decades of *push*, distilled—then, with the team riding as high as it seemingly could, the typhoon hit. Crack cocaine, the pebbled, cheap, highly addictive and smokeable version of the disco-era staple, first hit major urban areas in the mid-eighties. It took a bit longer for the drug to bite down on the small towns, but the damage might've been worse there. Because you couldn't avoid it. There was nowhere to run.

Not that Aliquippa had no experience with getting high. Family stills had long been a basement tradition in the Plans and West Aliquippa, and the children of the wet-your-whistle generation hardly ignored the '60s drug splurge. Marijuana smoke became a staple during breaks at J&L in the '70s, and cocaine and hallucinogens were as much a part of the borough's underbelly as the numbers rackets. "It just wasn't as noticeable," Aileen Gilbert said. "I remember years ago—they hadn't even started making crack yet—it wasn't just cocaine: there was so much heroin here it was crazy."

Yet as far as drug markets go, crack had an impact—in sheer speed and force of penetration and all the resulting social costs—like few others. Like the later confluence of Viagra and aging baby boomers, crack was that rare case of chemistry and demography converging at the perfect time. In isolated, single-employer towns like those dotting the Beaver Valley, each mill closure had left behind 20-plus-percent unemployment, broken marriages, a spike in suicides—desperate wounds ripe for infection. Those who could leave did. Those who didn't were left with few options.

"It snowballed," said future city councilman Donald Walker. "If people weren't killing themselves because they lost their jobs, they were turning to drugs and alcohol. At one time in Aliquippa, there was fourteen bars, probably more. Not to mention the privates: my uncle Perry sold alcohol out of his house, a dollar a cup. I witnessed that. That was the times. That's what you did."

"That's when everybody gave up," said Jamie Brown, eight years old when LTV went down in '85. "It seemed like everybody gave up for life. A lot of people were involved in drugging, trying to escape reality."

Ty Law was thirteen in 1987, the year his mother, Diane, became a crack addict. He lived by then with her dad, his grandfather, Ray Law, a millworker who'd put in thirty years and retired and had adopted and raised Ty as his own. Diane came and went at the house on Wykes Street in Plan 11 extension, the declining pocket west of Monaca Road. The boy absorbed Ray's lessons on the value of hard, often-thankless work, day in and out; he took in the havoc and stink of his mom's dependency, the clash of old and new. New was winning. And once the epiphany hit, once young Ty figured out why his mom was acting so erratically, he was never the same. He began seeing crackheads everywhere.

In the longest of views, such carnage was generations in the making. "I do think that history leaves its mark on a region," said Reverend Chris Leighton, who left Aliquippa in 1985 after seven years of ministering downtown. "There was a lot of oppression in Aliquippa, especially in the early days. I know about it; I have an ancestor who led the Western Federation of Miners. The U.S. government shot and killed unarmed people in those days. It's horrific—and that pain never goes away from the land. People may forget about it, and they come and go. But there is this residual effect."

In the short term, though, the result may be as simple as the very human impulse to fill a vacuum. It's as if, without the built-in need to keep a regular schedule or one's wits in a world of metal and flame, without the social framework of the timecard and the hope of steady daylight, the town had lost the one force big enough to countervail drugs' seductive call. Little by little, decade by decade, narcotics of varying strengths had worked their way from the fringes—plaything of the rich, tradecraft of the criminal, millstone of the poor—to the national mainstream. Now in its demise, labor itself, dirty and dangerous and boring, stood revealed as the last defense. When the work crumbled, all hell rushed in.

"When that mill went down it took everything down with it," Ty Law said. "And when the drugs came in, either you were going to be a user—and more people did that—or seller. And if you did try it—which, in a town like that you probably ain't thinking too much of it, because I know heroin went through Aliquippa before because my dad was on that back in the seventies and early eighties—the crack-cocaine thing was a totally different ball game.

"That hit everybody. Everybody wanted to try it, and they got hooked. And the dealers who knew what it was about? They were getting paid. So they became the new role models—unlike my grandfather and the old-timers who did it the right way: saved up and got a nice car through hard work, went and got it financed, had decent credit. But the new regime came in and it's drug dealers, and now it ain't about getting a Buick. It's a Mercedes. It's BMW. So now for kids it's a different perspective: that's *real* money."

The institutions of legitimacy, meanwhile, only continued to crater. In 1985, LTV's tax assessment was slashed in half—from $19 million to $9.5 million—and the shrinking tax base left the borough, like many steel orphans in Western Pennsylvania, unable to pay its bills; the 1988 budget carried a deficit at $350,000. On December 23, 1987, Aliquippa became the second Pennsylvania town to be "declared distressed" under Governor Bob Casey's new Financially Distressed Municipalities Act—Act 47—which, while placing a town's fiscal affairs under state oversight, also allowed it to receive tax money from non-residents. Going into Act 47, said council president Mary Alviani then, is "the best Christmas present I could have received." Weeks later, the state granted the borough a no-interest loan of $460,000. Aliquippa, in essence, had gone on welfare.

One of the first signs that things were tipping radically in a new direction—especially in housing projects like Griffith Heights and Linmar—came in February of 1988, when a group of armed men was arrested early one morning after surrounding a Valley Terrace apartment building. All drove rental cars, three possessed semiautomatic weapons, five were carrying guns with obliterated serial numbers, and five gave

Detroit as their home address: Outside interests were making their play. A year later, an estimated 80 percent of crime in the borough was drug-related. Aliquippa was fast becoming the drug capital of Beaver County.

Jamie Brown, the oldest son of former Quips and Pitt star Jeff Baldwin, was on the cusp of adolescence then. "You could see everything from Third Avenue, Plan 11, could see the drug dealers with their cars and jewelry," he said. "All the shiny things. My mother was on welfare, Dad wasn't ever there: all the stuff a kid wanted, I could see I could get it on the street." He remembers the first step he took.

"About '89," he said. "Crack cocaine had just hit the area. Somebody I knew had it and was hustling it, a little bit older. He got involved and he let me help him. It started on from there. I saw shiny things."

14

Up in Smoke

It wasn't the shine that snagged Jamie Brown's father. It was the murk, that new, anarchic haze. Not right away—Jeff Baldwin gave himself a chance or two: After leaving Pitt, he took a year off and then washed up at nearby California University of Pennsylvania in the summer of '85, playing noseguard, Division II ball, looking for one last shot at the NFL. But he missed four weeks that season after breaking an ankle, took his cast off too soon, played hard—and was never the same. The Philadelphia Eagles came to work him out, and the Steelers seemed interested. Nothing panned out. He ended up back home at the house on Washington Street.

The next path was the one blazed by scores of ex-footballers who fell short of the league, who saw policing as the next best thing, on paper anyway; there was the badge and uniform, after all, and instant respect and a chance to feel that same adrenaline high from the hit, the chase, the thrill of bringing some hyped-up badass down. Peep Short did it, from Pitt to the semipro Pittsburgh Maulers to the police academy to corrections officer in the county jail—and now he was rising fast at the county sheriff's, loud and proud. Baldwin enrolled in the academy at the Community College of Beaver County in 1986.

"Matter of fact, we started out, got hired part-time as Aliquippa police together," said future Aliquippa police chief Andre Davis. "We were friends, and were in the academy together. He didn't last maybe two years, if that. He had an addiction problem."

Baldwin wasn't much of a cop. During that stint he admitted to misdemeanor convictions for theft and unauthorized use of a vehicle—neither of which resulted in immediate dismissal. Eventually, Baldwin "informed me that he had a drug dependency problem," William Alston, the police chief then, testified in court fifteen years later, and was told to either resign or be fired. Baldwin denied that on the stand, saying he quit because police training interfered with his wedding, and has never publicly admitted to drug use. But his reputation plummeted. Those who knew him at his best saw disturbing signs.

One night in 1986 or '87, Don Yannessa recalled, he was woken up by a banging on the front door of his house in Center. It was a Friday night, into Saturday, 3 a.m. He reached for a gun, crept downstairs, and squinted through the peephole at a figure outside in the dark. "Coach!" a voice yelled. "It's Jeff Baldwin!"

"Jeff?" Yannessa said.

"Yeah. I got to talk to you."

Yannessa walked into the nearby bathroom, placed the firearm on the sink and closed the door. He turned off the house alarm. When he opened the door, Baldwin said that his brother was in a Philadelphia hospital, bad accident, probably wasn't going to make it. Delois was going crazy, he said, and he needed to get there. He needed $50 for gas.

The coach walked back upstairs. Elaine was standing in the hallway in her housecoat, and watched her husband go into the bedroom and rustle through his wallet. It had been years now, but still: his player. "Coach," Baldwin promised, "I'll get it back to you on Monday."

When he got back upstairs, the bedroom was dark. Yannessa was feeling pretty good about himself; he liked being the one they could depend on. He hurried out of his clothes, slid back under the covers, figuring his wife asleep.

"Don," Elaine said in the darkness. "Why don't you just put a MAC (automated teller) machine on the side of the house, so when they pull down the driveway they can get their money and not wake us up?"

That gave him pause. "Then I found out," Yannessa said. "Everybody—the principal, other teachers, other coaches—was saying he was making the rounds: one, two, three o'clock in the morning, giving everybody the same bullshit. And then we all [figured] Okay, he's on crack. There was times when I was coaching in Aliquippa and involved in a bar and restaurant when he would come into this bar and he would ask. And I'd say, 'No, Jeff. Don't ever come to me for money again. You get somebody else to give you that money, shove that shit up your nose, whatever you do with it.'"

By then the drug trade was leaking into the town's lifeblood, wiping out thickly drawn lines between legitimate and illegitimate businesses and behaviors. Police found themselves arresting not just young bucks, but ex-steelworkers, some in their sixties and seventies. Peep Short and Sherman McBride were best friends, had been part of the core that made Aliquippa's football team the model for racial coexistence in the late '70s. They remained close, and after college was done—Short at Pitt, McBride at Ohio University—returned home. They saw each other plenty. Holidays, weddings, dinners: Short treated Sherm's mom like his second mother; he ate plenty at the McBride home in Mount Vernon.

Sherman's oldest brother, Grover "Bobo" McBride Jr., grew up playing football against Tony Dorsett; after graduation from Aliquippa, he joined his father in J&L's 14-inch mill. A decade later, along with thousands of others in the early '80s, "he got laid off," said Sherm McBride. "And got into the 'pharmaceutical' business."

It didn't take long for word to reach Short, now an officer in the Beaver County Sheriff's Office: Bobo was distributing. Short knew Grover well. "I ate over there and he ate over my house," Short said. "We were close. I *told* him. It wasn't like I was warning him off, but I said, 'Look, man, you're in the fuckin' way.' I told Grover, I tell just about anybody: I'm not giving you any kind of information that I'm coming to bust you, or the detectives or the state police is coming to bust you. All I'm telling you: 'You're in the fuckin' way.' Which is code or a language for: *Stop doing what you're doing, bro—because if I know, everybody else knows.*

"Some guys listened, some didn't. And those that were in the way that didn't listen, I arrested."

In July 1988, Short took a ride to see Sherm's mother, Janice.

"Mom, it's never personal with me," Short told her. "I've warned him several times, but his name just keeps ringing."

"Peep," she said. "You have a job to do. No hard feelings."

Two weeks later, Short arrested Grover Jr. in the Bethel Baptist Church parking lot, charging him with possession "with intent to deliver" multiple packages of rock and powder cocaine. Grover Sr. paid $2,000—10 percent of the $20,000 bail—in cash to get his son out. One month later, Short again busted Bobo, this time at 1 p.m. on Todd Road, and found in his possession "44 packets of white powder substance, to wit—cocaine and 2 packets of rock form cocaine." Grover Sr. paid that bail in cash, too.

Grover McBride Jr., then thirty-one, pleaded no contest to two criminal charges of "possession with intent to deliver," and in August 1989 was sentenced to fifteen to thirty-six months in state prison. "His first offense," Sherm said. "The first time he'd ever been in jail."

You don't talk about Berwick. Absurd, isn't it? Sean Gilbert has nothing to apologize for. All-American at Pitt, third overall pick in the NFL Draft, all-rookie, Pro Bowl, eleven seasons with the Rams, Redskins,

Carolina Panthers, and Oakland, 146 pro games. He never played in a Super Bowl, so the painful losses piled up, year after year. But even after more than two decades, it's that 13-0 defeat to Berwick in the '88 Pennsylvania state title game, the last game of his Aliquippa career, that hurts the most.

It doesn't help that Gilbert, afterward, starred as a senior on the Quips' basketball team that won a state title. *USA Today* had ranked Florida's Pine Forest football team No. 1 in the country to Aliquippa's No. 2; a loss by Pine Forest and an Aliquippa win over Berwick, Yannessa had told everyone, would mean the national championship. Not to mention the first statewide football title: Until then, competition for Pennsylvania prep footballers ended at the regional level. No Quips team had ever played for higher stakes. Yannessa spoke dreamily about national championship rings. Even the Berwick coach, sandbagging or not, said that Aliquippa was good enough to win the Division III *college* national title.

"Don't ever mention that one to him," Diana said of her brother. "If you say that to him? They all freeze up, like, *Who? Berwick?* Don't even say that name."

Oddly, most folks do leave Gilbert alone about this. He lives in North Carolina and remains a distant presence when he returns home. Maybe it's the fact that a state title in his day had nowhere near the prestige of winning one WPIAL crown, let alone two. Or maybe it's because he became the first postmill superstar, the best to rise out of town since Dorsett, the best to come out of the school since Ditka, that Gilbert is given the rarest of passes. Because anyone connected with Aliquippa football? If you lose, you never live it down.

"You can't walk out here with no bullshit team," said Peep Short. "You can't walk out here with all these former players and people who've been around fifty, sixty years watching you. You don't pass that smell test? They'll let you know. In every coffee shop and newspaper stand and every corner, they'll let you know: *Them boys is playing like shit. What's going on up there?* I've had old players call me after the first game: 'What's wrong with you, Coach Short? We didn't punch nobody. . . . That guy got beat and you didn't yell at him or nothing. . . .'"

To his dying day, Short will still be seeing that ball fluttering out of his grasp, twenty feet in the air, that sure touchdown on the final play, the win against Blackhawk in '78—gone. But just to be sure, someone at the wake will be whispering a reminder in his ear. "Nobody has to tell me," Short said, voice rising. "I know it. I know where I messed up." But then the voice goes soft. "They remind me of it, sometimes," he said.

Even in Yannessa's lean years, there had been a standard. In projects like Linmar Terrace, the idea that football players were small gods took hold. Little Mike Warfield, raised alone by a single mother, would sit on the stoop and stare after the team's kicker on fall Fridays, equipment bag over the shoulder, on the way to get his *dunt-dunt-dunt.* But Warfield's timing couldn't have been worse: he grew up to be the starting quarterback of the '86 team, the one squad after Yannessa started piling up titles to come up empty—no WPIAL championship, and a season-ending loss to Ambridge besides.

"Oh, we're like dogs," Warfield said.

The next year, '87, Timmie Patrick, a senior starting fullback, was sitting in a corner of the locker room just before the home opener against Center. His dad, Ocie, with all those burns on his hands from thirty years in the blast furnace, had regaled his six sons forever about the game *he* played just weeks after getting his appendix removed. Timmie's older brother, Daryl, had played out the '83 season with a broken wrist, caught passes in a cast. Now, every time the door swung open, Timmie heard the band playing, the crowd buzzing. He can't remember which came first: the goose bumps or the tears. He was crying as he ran onto the field.

His first carry, a cluster of bodies fell on his left ankle, and Timmie Patrick heard it pop. He limped off the field and as the trainer, Art Piroli, was taping him, Patrick kept urging him, "Art, hurry up. . . ."

"Why?" Piroli said. Timmie didn't even look up at the stands. He knew.

"My dad's coming down here."

After a few seconds, Ocie's voice rolled in from behind the bench. "What the fuck are you doing?"

"I hurt my ankle," Timmie said.

"Get your ass out there!"

Timmie played the entire game. He played every game that season, limping, and never let a doctor check it out. "I'm sure I had a fractured ankle," Patrick said. "That's just what you do."

By then the mill had all but shut down; Ocie and most every other steelworker in town were jobless. A small band of retirees, dubbing themselves the "Tunnel Rats," spent more than a year outside the old J&L tunnel entrance protesting pension and benefits cuts by LTV. "The group of steel workers were arrested by local police for disorderly conduct," reports the town's official account. "There were tears in the eyes of some of the arresting officers as they were forced to handcuff their own family members."

Yet even after most cuts were restored, the men kept coming to the tunnel, each weekday, no matter how cold or hot or wet. It almost felt like work.

But with all the winning—maybe *because* of the winning, almost too much winning now—Yannessa began to smell something else in the air. Sure, there's always that human need to criticize. But more than one national network had been in to do pieces on the team, and *Rolling Stone*, too, and now he had a cable-TV show each week, cohosting *This Week in High School Football*—and when people said "Hollywood Don" these days there was sometimes this shake of the head, a knowing twist of the mouth: *Guy just loves to hear the sound of his own voice and 'at, don't he?*

So Yannessa took it all in: little things like the accusations of training-camp hazing that came and went one year, none of them holding water, or the school board members who believed he'd become too powerful, too big to control. That was rich, considering the results, but it only lined up with the fatalistic streak that ran beneath his sunny banter. "It's just the way it is," Yannessa said. "The more success you have, you will accumulate enemies. They'll be a silent minority, but they'll be there. We used to say they're like wolves in the forest: if you look, you can see the moon reflecting off their teeth. Because they're gnashing their teeth and looking for a vulnerable moment. Somewhere they can attack you."

So Yannessa sniffed around a bit, even threw his name out there when a combo coach/athletic director position opened at North Allegheny in '87. Maybe that would shake 'em a bit. Maybe not. Maybe they'd just figure, *Aliquippa guy? He won't ever be able to leave.* Because even after the '88 run with Sean Gilbert, all the way to No. 2 in the nation, the school board ignored the clause in Yannessa's contract that promised a salary bump for "superior performance," a raise for his assistants, too, and acted—where it mattered most, in the wallet—as if '88 had never happened.

At the same time, though Yannessa was teaching only four classes in seven periods by then—no homeroom duty, didn't even have to fill out report cards; he didn't want to deal with the hassle of instruction anymore. So there he was, feeling stale, a bit pissed off, and meanwhile enrollment was down to less than four hundred kids; the Quips had been dominating AAA schools that had four times that many students. The pressure, there for years, to drop the football team to AA was proving more and more irresistible. He felt it, too.

But the old man, King Carl, was always in Yannessa's head, had been there even in the late '70s when the losses were piling up and his own athletic director was pushing him to drop down. He imagined the fans muttering, even if he did go on to win at that level: *He couldn't stay where*

Aschman was, Aschmann played in the big leagues. . . . "I knew that," Yannessa said. "There were people just waiting for me to do something like that so they could criticize the move."

But now, with that semifinal win in '88 over Brownsville—Aschman's old school, no less—Yannessa had passed the King to stand alone as the all-time winningest coach in Aliquippa history, 142-45-5, with four of the last five WPIAL titles in hand. When Baldwin High came calling, offered the AD position and head coach, no teaching and an $18,000 raise, it seemed a no-brainer. What did he have left to prove?

Baldwin's offer of a $60,000 salary for a high school coach was an outrage, of course. A teacher with twenty years and a master's degree at that school was making only $46,000; his principal was making $63,000. "You have to question the educational priorities at Baldwin High," *Sports Illustrated* tut-tutted at the time. But in Aliquippa they understood. When Yannessa took the job on June 2, 1989, saying over and over, "It was time," nobody blamed him. Who would walk away from that kind of money?

Still, it felt like a vicious decade's departing shot. Football was the valley's game, Aliquippa's game most of all, perhaps, and Yannessa had made it so again against all odds. "This is almost as big as J&L closing," Aliquippa's athletic director, Bob Castagna, said. "This is a black day for Aliquippa." He wasn't referencing race. But black families felt the loss, especially; Yannessa had helped them feel accepted, important, *celebrated*—in a way few whites ever had; as a result, the thought of any racial division—in football, anyway—came to seem frivolous. "As far as having a good rapport with the blacks, I think it's better to say he had a good rapport with everyone," Salt Smith, the president of the school board, said then. "The community is one. And he is Aliquippa."

Take such a man out of such a town, and neither one could ever be the same again. Everybody felt that, no matter the money to be made. After the announcement, Yannessa and his wife went to the stadium and stood at the fence staring at the place where he had made his name as a player and coach, as a favorite son. Both cried, and on Sunday a photo of the two adults weeping was stretched across the top of the sports section of the *Beaver County Times*. "It's not the end of the world," Elaine said to him. But it felt like something close.

The children being born then, after the mill died, would live unburdened by the knowledge that the town had once been anything but sinking. Maybe that was better. Remembering could be a curse. The generation that grew up with dads hauling themselves off to work, that eyewitnessed Aliquippa's meltdown, couldn't help but dwell on the better days. Some got stuck there.

"Had a Sol's Sporting Goods downtown; bought a little football there," said future mayor Dwan Walker, son of Chuckie and Chedda, born 1975. "Woolworths, the grocery store: downtown was awesome. On Friday nights you'd go to the drive-in. Load up vans and trucks and go out there, softball games old versus the young, play down at the playground. Used to go blackberry picking and sell them to the older ladies on our streets. Crab apples. Used to go crayfish pickin' in the creeks. It was fun then. And we had older adults that would take us to those places, and took time with us. . . ."

He and his identical twin brother, Donald, went everywhere together, big and grinning and loud and looking so much alike that people gave up and took to calling them both "Twin." And the twins said "Yessir" and "No, ma'am." They weren't alone: All their friends, when some lady would call out, had been raised by parental belt and glare to stop cold in their tracks and respond, *"Ma'am?"* But they were the last of that breed.

Christmas '87: that's when the boys started feeling it. Before that, a spray of toys and gift wrap and sports stuff would roll out from under the big tree, covered two-thirds of their living room floor in Plan 11; as an electrician, Chuckie had been making $18.75 an hour at J&L,

base, with as much overtime as he could handle. In his best years, he was pulling in near $70,000 a year, money enough to buy a good car, a house, ride the family out to Oklahoma each summer, and even, once a week, take the whole brood to Long John Silver's.

But then that stopped: the Christmas booty dried up. There was maybe a board game and some small trinkets now, the merciless accounting of two twelve-year-old boys: *What? This is all we're getting?* And their father would drift out of the room, quieter than usual.

By the cold early days of 1989, ex–Aliquippa High football star Jeff Baldwin, twenty-six, was known for a certain kind of trouble. So on paper, of course, she would appear vulnerable, the weaker of the two: Tezmalita Pharr was a high school junior, just seventeen years old, when she took up with him. But even then, some say, the mismatch went the other way. Because Jeff was easy, a big softie. And no one ever accused Tez of being anything but sharp and hard as a blade.

Not that she had been all that experienced. On numbers alone, Tez wasn't, but poor percentages grew her up fast. "The first time I had sex: fourteen. Got pregnant with her," Tez said of her oldest daughter. "The second time I had sex? I had Jonathan. I thought I was safe; I was on the pill. Later my aunts said to me, 'We could see *that* coming. We all got pill babies.' I said, '*NOW* you tell me?'"

Tez's single mom, Harriet, tried to keep the girl in check. Until her eighteenth birthday, in fact, Tez had to be home in Plan 11 before dark. She didn't go to parties. But she'd been a mouthy tomboy growing up, fast enough to play in the boys' pickup football games and tough for even the best athletes to catch. So when Tez began to show again in the spring and summer of '89, all her football buddies started getting on her: *All gonna change now! No more games, running around . . . Whole life got to change. . . .*

"You watch," Tez would say, all that summer. "You just watch what I *create.*"

She delivered Jonathan on August 10, 1989, adding an infant to the toddler now making demands in Harriet's house. After six months of dull domesticity—and high school studies—Tez moved out and checked out of mommy duty. She was eighteen, didn't want to hear it from Harriet anymore. And Jeff was hardly a steadying influence.

"It was freedom: I'm going to do what I want to do. That didn't work too well," Tez says. "More or less just partying, something that I was not allowed to do. So I wanted to party and being young with children, I was like, *This is kind of fun.* But after a while, it was, *Oh, this is not good.* To this day I tell people: You can't raise a child from a bar. A child requires constant, everyday attention."

Now Ty Law was coming. He was going to be "The Next One," the heir to Ditka and Sean Gilbert. Anyone could see that, ever since the time that he was playing Midgets one wet day at Carl Aschman Stadium, a championship game no less, and his cleats got stuck in the mud and damn if the kid didn't run right out of his shoes, leaving them right there in the ground, and race 65 yards for a touchdown in socks. First year with the Quips, 1989, the swift, tough sophomore showed he could do just about anything—run, receive, patrol the defensive backfield—and new head coach Frank Marocco, home at last, won a AAA WPIAL title in his first season. Good omens all around: maybe Yannessa's leaving wouldn't be such a loss, after all.

But there were problems. Crack use was only growing, its acrid scent wafting through Linmar and Valley Terrace, the Plan 11 quadrant known as the "Funky Four Corners," the environs of Wykes and Davis Streets in Plan 11 extension, where Ty lived with his grandfather Ray. Family ties and old mores curdled with the seep of fast money and an even quicker high. Football and the drug trade had become the town's most thriving concerns, and it took no time for the line between them to blur.

Ty Law wanted a new pair of Air Jordans. He wanted cash in his pocket so he could buy girls ice cream, and feel cocky, make like he was something to see. Being a football star wasn't doing that anymore, not nearly as much as it used to. The dealers were getting all the play. "That's what was cool," Ty said. "That's what got the girls." In the summer of 1990, a cousin of Ty's fronted him some product so he could ride around in a car, and sell it out the window. He dealt crack for about a month.

But mostly, Law wasn't very sly or very good at it, because the whole exercise made him uneasy. First, there was the fact that his mother had turned their home upside down with her own drug use, and now here he was peddling the same poison to other guys' moms. And then there were those disquieting moments when some lady his mom's age would offer up sex for the drugs he was selling—*Come on, hook me up, give me a ride. . . . I'll take care of you. . . .* —which made the fifteen-year-old Ty Law queasy. Because then he had no choice but to wonder: *Is my mom doing that?*

It was hard, too, because in lucid moments Diane Law tried to be a parent. Once that summer, she stumbled across his stash of cocaine, and screamed at Ty and said that she'd flushed it all down the toilet, even left the container floating in the bowl to convince him. But deep down Ty knew. He didn't admit it to himself until years later but, intentionally or not, he'd actually supplied his mother. Much later, after she had gotten clean, Ty would ask Diane, "So did you *really* flush my drugs?" They could even laugh about it.

"Come on, man: Drug addict ain't going to flush no drugs," Ty said. "At the same time, you're an addict but you're trying to be a mother. It was horrifying to her, but she ain't flushed 'em. She says, 'Hell no, I ain't flushed it!'"

Then there was one hot night on Wykes, when a guy Ty was snapping at about something small—a girl, an insult—pulled a gun and jammed the barrel against his head. "Say something!" he demanded. And Ty didn't, but the shame of being made into a punk—*Big-time football player, huh?*—the cold fear that he'd been forced to feel: It made him crazy. Ty ran home to his grandpa's house, to the closet where Ray kept his hunting rifles and handguns, and grabbed a long-barreled pistol and headed for the door.

His grandfather chased him. Ray Law hollered and asked *Why?* and tried to stop him, but not too much because how, exactly, do you stop a 190-pound whirlwind of teenage muscle with a loaded gun? Ty bolted from the house. He fired the gun into the night air as he loped down Wykes Street, got two or three shots off before the guy crouched and fired back, and the sound wasn't tinny like Ray Law's old hunting pistol: It sounded like rockets vrooming past. *Oh, shit!* Ty thought, and he turned tail and got out of there fast.

But it wasn't the flying bullets, the nearness of death, that made Ty quit. It was his grandfather's shocked and fallen face, both when he pushed past him the first time and when he came home after. Ray had always been Ty's ally against Diane's addiction, but now the boy saw a new heartbreak in the old man's eyes. Ray did everything for him: spoiling Ty no end, talking him up in the neighborhood, bringing real ketchup to school for Ty to put on his lunch hot dogs, even. Because the boy was good—Ray just knew it—and the boy was going to *make* good, too. Theirs was an unspoken bargain, but absolute. Ray had had no idea that his grandson was dealing, no idea that he'd bottled up that kind of rage. But now he could see it clear: *one daughter down, and my grandson hitting the same path . . .*

"My grandfather was scared to death," Ty said. "It shocked him so much, because I'd never showed him any of those sides of what I might be doing or tried to do out on the street—out of respect for him. He'd never seen that. It did something to him."

Is it any wonder, then, that here—late in the '80s—the game got bigger? Once merely the vessel of local pride, football in Aliquippa now assumed deeper resonance, even greater import. It was as if those who remained sensed the worst: This is it. This is what is left. Football is the endgame, the gritty final distillation of the dream that our great-grandfathers came here to dream, the one systematic and proven process that can still result in a scholarship, a way out for the next generation, maybe big money.

There were a few dissenting voices. After giving up on songwriting, Melvin Steals became an English teacher at Aliquippa High and was named the city's Teacher of the Year in 1984. He spent most of the decade working on postgraduate studies in education. While researching a support system for high school student-athletes, Dr. Steals said, "I solved the major mystery: I began to realize the true *meaning* of a student-athlete.

"Aliquippa was a plantation system. And I stopped going to the games because I saw a lot of these kids. People said, 'Don could get a rock into college'—and he did. There was a kid whose nickname was 'Killer Rock'—and he got Killer Rock into college. But you would see them by the second or third game of the following football season, after they graduated from high school, they began filtering back into the crowds at the football game. Because they were not academically prepared to meet the rigor of a postsecondary learning environment."

For his 1989 doctoral dissertation at Pitt, Steals appended the Aliquippa school system's 1988 results on the California Achievement Test. "By the time the kids had reached tenth grade, 60 percent of the students, white and black, were reading below grade level—and 62 percent were performing below grade level in math," said Steals, who departed Aliquippa High in 1989 to teach in Pittsburgh. He vowed never to return. "The longer they were exposed to that curriculum, the more poorly they did," Steals said. "I cried the day I left Aliquippa."

But such bad academic news provoked little outrage at football or Yannessa or any other sport or coach in town. If anything, it only reinforced the belief that athletics was the prime ticket out, an all-or-nothing proposition that, incidentally, announced its winners and losers to the world each week in newspapers and on TV. And with such a zero-sum atmosphere settling in, the town assumed an all-in tone about the team, darker and meaner and more urgent than the chords that once thrummed around Ditka or Dorsett.

Losing was awful. It had always been awful. But for all involved before, it wasn't considered so heinous, if only because Aliquippa had other options. Now they were gone. Motivation usually teeters between a push for pride and the avoidance of shame, but now the balance tipped. Now when a season ended without a title, players were told by brothers and friends and mouthy fools, 'Y'all suck!', and it was more harsh, less joshing, than ever before. Because without winning, without that one reinforcing emblem of relevance, the era's reality—its ever-diminishing returns—stood starkly revealed. What else was there to cheer?

Ty Law would go on to play big-time college ball at Michigan, then become the best cornerback in the NFL after breaking in with Bill Parcells' New England Patriots in 1995. He would lose to Notre Dame and Ohio State as a Wolverine, would be the defender burned by Colorado's Michael Westbrook's miracle catch in 1994. He would lose pro playoff games that meant money out of his pocket. But nothing in his career ever hurt worse than the seven obscure losses that Law experienced in his three years at Aliquippa High.

"It's like you've lost *everything*," Law said. "Nobody in the damn neighborhood wants to talk to you. You're already feeling bad when you lose, but when you lose in Aliquippa and come home and think you're going to get a pat on the back talking about 'Good game!' or 'You'll get 'em next time'? No. It's rough: 'You lost to *them*? What the hell? You all suck!' And they ain't just fans. We used to go down to a friend's of mine's house, we called it the Fifth Quarter, go hang out after, drink a couple beers . . . and boy, if you lose? And you think you're going to come up in there and get sympathy or think you're even going to grab a beer? That's not happening.

"At Michigan, they treat you nice. Even in the pros, there was noth-ing they could say or do that I hadn't already seen or wasn't prepared for. Coach Parcells is known for always messing with the first-round guys; he tried to give it to me every day, and I'm like, *I've seen way worse than this.* I looked at Parcells, like, 'Who are *you?*'"

Still, during his senior year at Aliquippa, the world became all kindness and light. Law was named a *Parade* all-American while doing what even Sean Gilbert couldn't: leading the Quips to their first-ever state title. That was 1991, a year after administrators finally admitted reality and dropped to AA—but what of it? Balanced by irrepressible running back Chico Williams, Marocco's boys avenged an early-season loss to edge Riverside to win the WPIAL, then rolled over Forest Hills, 20-6, to set up a state title showdown with defending champion Ha-nover, winner of thirty straight, in Pittsburgh's South Stadium. But that challenge was nothing compared with the gut-wrencher Law had faced right before.

Because on that December Saturday morning, along with two teammates, Law was scheduled to take the American College Test (ACT) at Moon Area High School. And he had to pass, if he wanted to play Division I-A college ball. Georgia Tech, Pitt, every school with an eye on a national championship wanted him, but this was Ty's second try, and in his previous attempt he'd come up just short of the minimum score required for eligibility. "I had to make it on this one," Law said. "I don't pass? I don't go." And then, right after the test, there was a state title game to get to, fast.

Law finished the test after noon, and felt pretty good. (He passed. His two teammates didn't.) A police escort led them on the twenty-mile sprint into Pittsburgh, and the three players could see the teams warming up as they scrambled into the locker room. Law never had a chance to stretch. He was still tucking in his shirt while waiting for the opening kickoff; teammate Dorian Jackson fumbled, and the ball landed in Law's hands. He ran 61 yards for the touchdown. This time, he kept his shoes on. Aliquippa crushed Hanover, 27-0.

"Crazy, crazy day," Law said.

It was, but that was only appropriate. Marocco, who hadn't coached in eleven years when he took over the program, only found out that he got the job when school board chair Salt Smith, appearing on a local radio program, rang him up and offered it to him on the air. Marocco had grown up with blacks in Logstown, and his hugs and kisses and voluble openness made him beloved by black families. His us-versus-the-world mentality—less tired coach's act than residue of immigrant paranoia—resonated with boys armed with decade-long evidence that the world, indeed, was against them.

"When we went to football games, we were going to wars," said Donald Walker, who played for Marocco three years later. "We'd close the doors and he'd say, 'If you don't like what I've got to say? Get the fuck out. These motherfuckers are coming up here to our house and we're going to fuck them up! Italian and blacks! Go kick their ass!' That's how he talked. You looked at Coach Marocco, you just wanted to tear off your shirt and kill something. Anybody who played for him, those years: you wanted to kill for that man."

Winning the town's first state title, of course, killed off any last grumbling about his hiring. At fifty-four years old, Marocco achieved something that both King Carl, his overbearing mentor, and Hollywood Don, his overpowering rival, never did. Afterward, some fans in the crowd could be heard chanting, "Don Who?"

That the outside world sneered at Marocco and his like to the last made it even sweeter. In the days before the game, Marocco had heard that his opposing coach, Alex Kopacz, had dismissively wondered, "What's a Quip?"

And in response, Marocco looked to the center of the town name and said to the press, "A 'Quip' is the heart of Aliquippa."

Marocco and his players thought the comeback clever, but, to Marocco's eternal mystification, it rubbed Kopacz wrong. "The coach for Hanover, he was very bitter about Aliquippa," Marocco said. "So at the end of the game they all said, 'Coach, go tell him what the hell a Quip is!' But he wouldn't shake my hand. He ran off the field. He would not even shake our hands."

Later that month, one of Marocco's assistant coaches, Peep Short, rolled late at night through Plan 11 in a Beaver County Sheriff's cruiser. He recognized a tall figure, walking alone. Short didn't coach Mike Warfield when he quarterbacked the Quips in '86, but this was Aliquippa football: Everybody knew everybody. Still, Peep hadn't realized that Warfield was back, home for good after graduating from little Catawba College—having passed for nearly 7,000 yards in his time there—in North Carolina. And in a flash he toted it up: ex-baller, no father, bored and at loose ends. He knew the sequence well. The next step was usually trouble.

"Get in," Peep said. Warfield opened the cruiser door, and they sat talking under the dome light.

"What are you doing?" Peep said.

Warfield didn't know. There wasn't a plan. He hadn't been drafted by the NFL. He'd heard about some tryouts. . . .

"You want a job?" Peep said. "Come down and put an application in."

Warfield had long looked up to Short, but that's not what tipped him. He'd always wanted to be a cop. And there was something else. He hadn't been back much since graduating in '87, but word of Aliquippa's decline had still found him. "You would hear things: Friends I knew robbed a bank," Warfield said. "And it just started going downhill after that. People in a position to do things, policemen, weren't doing their job. Things just got out of control. And once it got out of control, it couldn't be reversed."

Now he was seeing the spiral firsthand, all around his mom's home, No. 254, up on Linmar Terrace. To outsiders it looked like shabby public housing—and worse by the day—but for Warfield it was still home. And he did need a job.

For the next eighteen months, Warfield worked at the Beaver County Sheriff's Office. Short was Marocco's defensive coodinator then, and many shifts Warfield would ride with him, serving search warrants, talking football. Short was loud. He used "motherfucker" as a term of endearment. His father had been everything: drummer for Lena Horne, loan shark, newsdealer, ladies' man. When Peep was young, his dad owned three legit businesses—and ran a numbers joint, besides—in the Funky Four Corners. They dubbed the boy "Peep" because he would peer around a corner when the adults were talking, peeking into business that wasn't his.

That never changed. Peep knew nearly every dealer, thief, and gangbanger on sight; some colleagues muttered that he knew them too well. He had a volatile temper, was never averse to throwing his bulk around; one story, perhaps apocryphal, had him punching one suspect so often with his badge that he left imprints in his face. Another story Short tells himself: In 1997, he got word that Anthony "Ali" Dorsett— Tony's nephew, son of Tony's brother Keith—was talking to Short's sixteen-year-old daughter, Kiki. Short also knew that Ali, then twenty, was already hustling drugs. He warned him to stay away.

Not long after, Short was riding down Kennedy Boulevard when something in the car ahead seemed familiar: the back of Kiki's head, rising above the passenger seat, and Ali behind the wheel. He pulled them over, walked up to the door, and punched Dorsett square in the face. "Knocked the shit out of him," Short said.

Ali complained to the Aliquippa police. His father, Keith Dorsett, and other Dorsett men and in-laws came down to the station, and in the parking lot Chief William Alston found himself trying to keep Deputy Short, a rising drug dealer, and one of the town's most famous families from all killing each other. "She's going to college. We ain't having this!" Short bellowed at the Dorsetts. "You want a war? Come on. You and your whole family."

Depending on the critic, Peep had too rigid or too flabby a sense of right and wrong. "There's a dichotomy about him," said one area police source, "that's off the charts." But even those who would later decide that Peep Short was all kinds of dirty will tell you: *He had guts.* No matter what kind of rough or desperate soul lay behind it, he was always known for going through the door.

"A lot of people would say, 'Short, man, you know me, you're my boy, we grew up together,'" Peep said. "I said, 'If you're doing something wrong, and you see me come through your door? Then duck.' Because I'm coming through there for business. I've arrested friends. Family. The fucking whole nine yards."

Many, especially one-parent boys like Mike Warfield, would look upon Short as a father figure. But then there's this: In September 1987, Della Rae Campbell gave birth to a son, Tommie, who one day would become yet another off the Aliquippa line to make the NFL. Short wasn't a factor in Tommie's early life, but rumors flew and Della wasn't shy about feeding them; after Tommie graduated high school, the *Pittsburgh Post-Gazette* declared Short "Campbell's father." At the same time many locals, including Della's longtime boyfriend Rick Hill, remained sure that Tommie's dad was the man the boy was named for: Della's ex-husband, Tommie Campbell Sr.

Sometimes Della let them believe that, too. But Tommie's patrimony remained a mystery for a simple reason.

"I don't know," Della said. "I don't. When I had married Tommie Campbell Sr., I was dating Peep Short at the same time. I only married Tommie Campbell Sr. because my mother was telling me that I wasn't grown, that I don't need to be going out every weekend. I'm, like, 'I'm 19 years old!' I just went and got somebody and got married. I didn't even know the man."

Later, while moonlighting as a security guard at Valley Terrace, A Building, Short would watch little Tommie compete with the other kids, "and if he wasn't crying he was fighting," he said. Yes, he admits, the boy reminded him of himself.

But when asked directly, Short won't confirm or deny that he's Tommie's dad. His discomfort, it seems, lies more in taking credit than ownership. "All I'll say is this: any man would be proud to be his father—and I told him that," Short said. "We discussed it, and I think that's all I'm going to say on it. Because the thing with that is, I don't like this Johnny-come-lately shit where all of a sudden he's in the pros and I'm his *dad*."

Ty Law began noticing in his senior year at Aliquippa, '91 or '92: His things were disappearing. One trophy gone, then another. Then a letterman jacket. Then another trophy. It took a while for it to sink in, if only because he was racing everywhere and, besides, why would anyone get into his Grandpa Ray's house. . . . and only take . . . *Oh*. That's how it hit him: Slow, like the dawn of a dreary day. *Oh, damn. She's selling 'em off.* . . . And then an understanding hit him, the one he'd been trying to bat away. His mother was peddling valuables to buy crack.

How could she? Sell off my stuff, when you're supposed to love me? I'm your son. You love this drug more than you love me. . . .

Worse yet, Ty would come to find, as it kept on the next few years, that Diane Law was selling his possessions, the totems of his growing name, to a local doctor, for God's sake, who could read her ravaged symptoms, a white man that Ty had long looked up to and to this day will not name. It was almost too cold to take in: the man was buying stock, getting in at crack-rock-bottom prices. "He thought I was going to do something with myself and he'd have some 'Ty Law' memorabilia," Law said. "Which was pretty messed, because you knew exactly what my mom was doing. You knew what was happening. And it went on through when I was in college: anything that he could get."

The only respite came two weeks each summer, when Ty flew down to Dallas to visit his distant uncle, Tony Dorsett, in Dallas. Then he and Dorsett's son, Anthony Jr., would work out endlessly with Tony and Cowboys stars like Everson Walls and Ken Norton Jr., and listen to the just-retired legend's tales, all the little backstories behind the nearly 13,000 NFL rushing yards and that surefire induction into the Pro Football Hall of Fame. More than once, Tony caught Ty staring at his Heisman Trophy.

"Man," Tony jabbed. "You got to be a *bad* boy to get one of them."

That was the carrot, leading Ty on every day. Not that Law thought he'd win the Heisman—he knew his future was as a cornerback, and corners don't win Heismans—but that here was an Aliquippa guy, one who knew what it meant to have an old man working the mill and a family with drug problems, and he had made it out. Gorgeous house, nice cars: It could be done. "Tony Dorsett saved me as well," Ty said. "Because after my grandfather, I was looking at him; I was, like, *This is where I want to be.* My grandfather was doing it the right way, I knew that. But I wanted more."

But it wasn't just want: Law needed more. By the time he'd enrolled at Michigan, he had seen enough of Aliquippa. He had become convinced that only money could end their problems, end his grandpa's worry, solve his mom's drug addiction. Going to Ann Arbor, he wasn't worried about getting a degree. Law needed to get to the league. He needed to get paid. "I'm thinking you can *buy* your way off of drugs," he said. "Come to find out that ain't the damn case. . . . "

But that understanding wouldn't land for more than a decade. No, even as he'd put off older teammates ("They couldn't stand me," Law said) for refusing to redshirt and bragging that he wouldn't be at Michigan long—and then became the Wolverines' first true freshman, ever, to start—even as he'd disappear from campus some days and race the four hours home to shield Ray from some episode of Diane's drug nonsense and then drive all night back and still make it to morning class, Law had no doubt. The money, surely, would fix everything.

✻   ✻   ✻

Normally, the second week is too early in a football season for high emotion: Teams are still working their way into form; teachers and students
are just hitting the post–Labor Day stride. But the WPIAL front-loaded
the drama upon Aliquippa in 1994. Not only was Hopewell coming to
play its archenemy at Carl Aschman Stadium that Friday night, but an
even more charged game was scheduled across the river at Ambridge. For
the first time since Yannessa bolted six years before, Hollywood Don
and his Baldwin High kids would make an appearance in Beaver County.

But at 7:03 the night before, September 8, police radios all over
the county began crackling with alerts about a horror in Hopewell
Township, less than a mile from the Aliquippa exit off Highway 60.
U.S. Air Flight 427 from Chicago, a Boeing 737-300 on descent into
Pittsburgh International Airport, had dropped in silence and exploded
near Green Garden Road. All 132 passengers and crew were feared dead.

With time, Flight 427 would gain a significance unusual even for
major plane crashes. The National Transportation Safety Board declared
that a design flaw in the widely used jet's rudder had caused the crash,
and then called for a fleet-wide repair that cost the airline industry bil-
lions of dollars. The treatment of victims' loved ones over the first hours
and days, especially, was so bureaucratically callous that President Bill
Clinton issued an executive order and Congress later passed the Disaster
Family Assistance Act. "I can't think of one accident that had more
impact on the NTSB, on the aviation industry, and more importantly, on
how families of all disasters are treated worldwide than the Pittsburgh
accident," said NTSB chairman Jim Hall.

But all that came later. For the locals, the impact was instant,
visceral. No one on the ground was hurt that Thursday night, but children playing on a nearby soccer field had watched the plane crash and
explode. Any and all law enforcement hands, like Peep Short, rushed to
the scene. Off-duty nurses and doctors, like Mickey Zernich, mixed with

growing crowds of onlookers and media streaming in from all over the country. Body parts dropped from the trees, littered the gouged earth; the stink of fuel filled the air. Veterans spoke of their worst day in Vietnam and declared this its equal. "The most horrible scene I've ever seen in my life," Zernich said then. "You can't describe it. The pieces—the pieces were unidentifiable. It's just indescribable."

School was canceled in Hopewell the next day, but, after some debate, opened as scheduled in Aliquippa. Friday's night's Aliquippa-Hopewell game—just twenty-four hours after the crash—was allowed to go forward. "We really needed this to take our minds off it," said Cindy Caldwell, whose daughter was one of the soccer players who had seen the plane fall. "We're all looking for a diversion. You can't get away from it on the television."

She said this while surrounded by an overflow crowd, more than 7,000 people jammed into Carl Aschman Stadium. None of Yannessa's carny touches were allowed this night. Instead, there was a moment of silence, the playing of "Taps," the lowering of a flag to half-staff.

There was a new fear in the wind: Flight 427 was the fifth crash for USAir, the largest carrier in Pittsburgh, in five years. For many in town who worked there, the airline, though it paled in terms of total number of local employees, was the next best thing to J&L. Marocco, Aliquippa-born and its football coach now, was quoted in the next morning's *Detroit Free Press* with a message for the town's young. "Get out of here," he said. "There's nothing here for them. If you don't get an education, what are you going to do?"

Aliquippa beat Hopewell that night, 15-6. It was Marocco's hundredth career victory as a head coach. Less than three miles away, in Ambridge, Yannessa and his Baldwin team won 31-7. And no one cared. For the first time, ever, the football games were played and no one with any sense cared at all.

15

Mauling Apollo

All kinds tried to convince Ty Law to play out his college career at Michigan, stay for his senior year. His name was only then becoming widely known; yes, he was a newly minted all-American, but NFL "experts" projected him as nothing better than a fourth-to-seventh-round draft pick, and urged Law to resist the temptation. A Wolverines strength coach tried to convince him, too, saying, "What are you going to make? Two hundred thousand? Three hundred thousand? And what's that after taxes? And then you buy a house, car. . . ."

But none of them knew. Law had been seeing all these strange bills when he'd go home to Aliquippa, and in his junior year he learned that Ray had filed for bankruptcy and lost the Wykes Street house after taking out a $5,000 loan. For him. To buy Ty that used Chrysler LeBaron for those journeys to and from Ann Arbor. The old man tried to assure him that things would be fine, but Ty was scared. *Two to three hundred thousand?* he thought. *Sounds good to me!* Besides, he'd seen the other, so-called top college defensive backs. He knew he was better.

"I had to leave," Law said. "I knew that if I worked out I would go higher than projected. I was, like, *I'm just going to prove it to 'em in the league in due time, but I'm going to get my granddad's house back and get my mom up off these drugs.* That was my only concern."

On April 22, 1995, at 4:12 p.m., the New England Patriots chose Law in the draft's first round, the twenty-third pick overall. With Sean Gilbert by his side, Law took in the news at Champs Sports Bar in Aliquippa. "I bet on myself—and I won," he said. His mother was there that day, and a newspaper's camera snapped and captured Ty as he closed his eyes and squeezed her tight. The experts were all wrong. The contract would be five years for $5.5 million—worlds more than he'd ever dreamed.

But what Law remembers most is grabbing Ray, his granddad—his ally, a weary man who'd grown up in Brookville, Pennsylvania, the only black kid in a segregated world playing on teams full of whites, a man who'd endured too much early and late, the grandfather who'd raised him like a son and never let him down. The two hugged hard. The world quieted and Ty held on, and the moment felt like it lasted forever.

That was a great story, for a day. But once the local writers filed their copy and the TV news aired the footage, reality settled back in. Ty Law? A once-in-a-generation talent hitting the lottery. The rest of Aliquippa? Minimally skilled, and realizing at last that the mill was never coming back. The slow exodus continued. Families tapped connections in Phoenix, the Bay Area, New Jersey, and soon their car was packed, their houses were empty, and they were gone.

The Walkers almost left, too. Chedda had a sister in Atlanta who said there were jobs to be had, but that would mean moving into the projects down there, the twins and Diedre hitting adolescence in a new, cramped, seemingly more troublesome landscape. She went back and forth on it. Everyone kept saying: There was more upside down South, in Detroit, anywhere but Aliquippa; there just had to be. So many neighbors were leaving. Yet something about the devil you know . . .

"I just made up my mind: We were going to raise our kids right here in Aliquippa, where we knew they would be safe," Chedda said. "Which, back in the day, they *were* safe."

"I thought about it a thousand times, because of the money," said Chuckie. "But we just couldn't do it. We were born and raised here. We could walk anywhere and everybody knew you."

Familiarity was thin provision, admittedly, but better than nothing. Because either way—stay or go—the family had embarked on the now-common reverse odyssey, a step-by-step devolution in security and status of America's Working-Class Man. Between 1945 and 1978, real earnings for manufacturing workers had risen by 95 percent; over the following three decades the number shrank by 2.3 percent. For the unskilled, especially, it was worse: jobs simply evaporated. By 2002, 72 percent of men over twenty-five with only a high school diploma were employed. Ten years later, the number would be down to 64 percent, and those jobs were increasingly unstable.

The family got by for a time on Chuckie's unemployment and Chedda's job as a line cook at Perkins Cake & Steak; Chuckie would stay home and play Mr. Mom, combing out Diedre's hair and getting dinner on the table. Four years after his departure from J&L, he began working the assembly line at Rockwell International in New Castle, rose to inspector. Then Rockwell closed up in '91 and moved the plant to Mexico. After that came a string of odd jobs, an eighteen-month stint of long-haul trucking, time as a janitor at FedEx.

In 1996, Chuckie found work again as an electrician, this time in the 14-inch beam mill that had opened on the riverfront site five years after the shutdown at LTV. The operation went by the name "J&L Structural," but had nothing to do with the old place; it felt off, somehow, like launching a new blimp called "Hindenburg." A scaled-down tin mill—owned by old adversary U.S. Steel—also operated in the now-desolate expanse. Together the two shops provided some 515 jobs in a place that once employed 14,000.

Chuckie managed to get out a few months before J&L Structural filed for Chapter 11 bankruptcy in July 2000. Then he hooked on for a four-year stint at the new, $112 million U.S. Gypsum plant that opened up on the old J&L mill site, spawned two hundred jobs, and produced the lightweight Sheetrock and ceiling material that supplanted plaster and steel in the making of homes and offices. George W. Bush, then running for president, showed up one April day on a twenty-minute campaign drive-by and praised USG's cleanup as a shining example of industrial reclamation. So went the cycle then: slight hope, then desolation. U.S. Steel shuttered the tin mill that October. Four hundred more jobs—and $70,000 in annual tax money for the town—vanished.

Then Chuckie fixed streetlights for the state: part-time, no benefits. Now he was driving school buses for Aliquippa mayor Anthony Battalini, working building maintenance for a rehab center in Moon.

He smiles when he speaks of his stops, saying more than once that "God blessed me." But, in truth, all of it took a toll on body and pride. Chuckie's blood pressure spiked during his years driving the truck, and if he kept his head high and determinedly set an example of the work ethic for his kids, the struggle that began when J&L closed never really ended. "I didn't want my sons working there, but I enjoyed the work," Chuckie said. "I loved the people I worked with. I really missed it. I really missed J&L."

For thirteen years, the son of a laborer from Oklahoma had achieved that most basic version of the American Dream: a foothold in the middle class. He wasn't alone: In 1971, 61 percent of Americans fit into many economists' definition—household income between two-thirds and twice the national median—of "middle class." By 2011, the number would shrink to 51 percent—and Chuckie Walker wasn't included.

After the age of thirty-five, in fact, he never again came close. Even as the culture's vague promise of progress, the echo of an earlier, optimistic age, kept insisting that a better life lay ahead, Chuckie found himself forever losing ground. His first job after J&L halved his hourly wage of $18.75—then it dropped again, falling to as low as $8.50 per. His three decades since have been one endless, demoralizing struggle to avoid poverty.

"Where I'm at?" Chuckie said. "I started at twelve dollars—and I'm up to thirteen now. You get thirty-five, thirty-seven cents raise a year. That $18.75 is the most money I did make, in the mill—and I haven't seen that since."

Despite the despair, all the disruption and loss caused by the crack trade, Aliquippa still clung to that old idea of itself—strong, proud, and tough, a place abiding by the idea, if not the strict reality, of family, respect for elders, right and wrong. Yes, more and more babies were being born out of wedlock, but still with a faint tinge of disgrace. You might not come out and *say* that it'd be better if the parents married, but the notion obtained. And there were deeds one didn't think about, much less do.

Then, just before 10 p.m. on the night of April 11, 1996, William "Hackensack" Samuel, forty-nine, opened the front door of his Plan 11 home to two young men who said they were returning a Sega video game to his sixteen-year-old son, Brian. William let them in. After the door closed, one of them, Traz Durham, opened fire with a 12-gauge shotgun.

The spray of bullets ripped into William's stomach and the back of his forty-seven-year-old wife, Tresa. The other gunman, Pete Schoonover, finished her off by shooting a Tec-9 model 9mm semiautomatic pistol at the back of her head. William stumbled outside. Durham followed, shooting him again in the neck. William collapsed and died over the hitch of his boat trailer, entrails hanging, blood staining the street.

The couple's popularity only compounded the horror. Soft-spoken Tresa and the outgoing "Hackensack," named after the New Jersey hometown he left to come work at J&L, had made plenty of friends at church and acquired plenty of customers for their home-improvement business. A neighbor needed a tow, a car dug out of the snow? Hack was there. The Samuels prized their sixteen-foot fishing boat and Winnebago camper, but liked to share. The previous December, in fact, when Ty Law made his rookie appearance at Three Rivers Stadium, Hack had eagerly rented out the camper, and he and Tresa shuttled nineteen boisterous Aliquippans, including Ray Law, into Pittsburgh for the game.

It was a win-win: the Steelers crushed the Patriots, but Ty gave up only one completion and, after just a month as a starter, was conspicuously avoided by the Pittsburgh passing game. Best of all, after Hack got everyone home safely that night, they all gathered at the Quippian Club, where, later, Ty made a surprise appearance. Drinks flowed, men told stories: It was one of those warm interludes, a moment of pure victory.

But now, Hack and Tresa were dead. Brian Samuel had been in the house at the time, and immediately fingered two acquaintances—one with a previous conviction for murder, the other Jeff Baldwin's son, Jamie Brown. This made sense, at first, if only because of Brown's rising reputation as a street thug. He was just 18, but his flight toward trouble seemed unstoppable.

"Friends, everybody, tried their best to break me," Brown said. "My mother would be on me, and I'd go to my grandma's, my mom's mother, my dad's mother—ping-ponging around." He'd deny to family that he was dealing, but never stopped. Fights and gunplay were a constant.

"You had to get that respect, to not be prey," Brown said. "That's the only way you can survive: If you're *known*, they know you're not prey."

But the arrests didn't hold: Brian Samuel's behavior after the murders—a shopping spree, speeding around Plan 11 in his red Geo

Tracker—got everyone's back up on Hack's street; soon police were field-ing calls saying that they had gotten the wrong men. A high school kid told Sheriff George David that he'd overheard Brian and two others plan-ning the murders, and police rounded up the new suspects at Aliquippa High. Peep Short had coached the eighteen-year-old Schoonover when he played for the Quips. Since he was not a minor, he could be inter-rogated alone—and Schoonover said enough to implicate himself and the others.

"I think why he told me what he told me is because of that rela-tionship," Short said. "I don't know if he fully understood that I was in my law enforcement hat."

As gruesome as the murder had been, the story behind it was, somehow, even more chilling. Brian Samuel, a slight child who been given every kind of bauble—a new dirt bike, a new computer—had begun in the months before to act out. He marked up a wall with graffiti, was caught carrying a .380-caliber handgun to school. He shed old friends, gambled and lost to new ones. Word spread that football players were shaking him down for money.

Meanwhile, Hack was getting fed up. Two weeks before, the *Times* reported, he had punched Brian in the face, asked police to mediate an issue of stolen cash, and had the kid's handgun destroyed. But his wife coddled Brian, and when the couple returned from a brief vaca-tion they found that the boy's grandfather had bought him that Geo Tracker. The night of the murders, Hack took the keys. He was sure: Aliquippa is not a place for showing weakness. The last thing you want to be there is prey.

"The father was like, *You can't be one of them motherfuckers who every five minutes somebody say, 'Go get me a hundred dollars' and you give them a hundred dollars because you scared!*" said Peep Short. "Hack was like, 'Hell, no, you ain't giving them any more money. Go get your ass whupped; I don't care.'"

Brian promised Durham and Schoonover $12,000 apiece to kill his father. Reports at the time had the boy standing passively by while the gunmen finished off his parents, but both Short and David state that Schoonover recalled Tresa saying, "We forgive you, Brian, don't do this. We forgive you. . . .' before Schoonover lowered the barrel of the Tec-9 to the back of her head and Brian told him, "She's still alive. Shoot her. Shoot her!"

After the arrests, as word of Brian's cold calculation spread through town, dismay filled the air like bad weather. "We have been violated," neighbor Stephane Griffin said then. "The community has been mentally raped."

"I'm sixty-four years old: I never heard of nobody killing their mommy and daddy" in Aliquippa, grocer Benjamin Lee said. "I don't know if this town will ever get over it."

As palace coups go, you couldn't have asked for one more cold or sudden or clean. One day Frank Marocco was the most important man in town, the new king of Aliquippa football, a winner beloved by his players. And the next? By the time he realized his head was on the block, it was rolling across the floor.

At 7:51 p.m., on a stormy June night in 1997 that made the machinations at an Aliquippa School Board meeting seem even more portentous, Marocco found himself stripped of his head coaching position and replaced by Mike Zmijanac. This despite the fact that Marocco had just won his third WPIAL title in eight years, had no desire to leave his dream job, and was backed by a raucous crowd of players, coaches, parents, and friends. Once the vote to replace him—7-1—was tallied, the outraged gathering shouted the meeting to a close and kept going until the police arrived.

"It was the most ugly thing in the world," Marocco said. Nearly two decades later, he still hasn't gotten a straight answer as to why he was sacked. Making matters worse was the fact that three of the board members voting against him—Art Piroli Sr., Dan Casoli, and Dan

Santia—were relatives. "They just took it away, and slapped me in the face," Marocco said. His older brother Dominic, who had stood up to their father and made it possible for young Frank to play for Aliquippa High, who had made Frank get back on the plane when he tried to drop out of N.C. State, was enraged. A week later, on June 27, he had a heart attack and died.

"I hate a lot of people for that," Marocco said. "It really hurt me. It hurt my family."

Led by president Dave Wytiaz—one of Zmijanac's former players—the board had built a bureaucratic wall around Marocco that left no room to maneuver. Publicly, its reasons were budgetary and educational. To make the Aliquippa job more attractive in 1989, Marocco had also been given work as "Director of Secondary Services"—in essence, the principal's assistant in charge of discipline—at Aliquippa Middle School. In May of 1997, after being told that his "Director" job was being eliminated—and that he'd lose benefits if he didn't retire—Marocco accepted an early-retirement plan. He still, however, intended to coach.

But the board's position, suddenly, was that the coach needed to be a full-time presence in the high school. At the time, no Aliquippa team coach except Zmijanac, who'd been teaching English there for thirty-three years and who, in his first year as head coach, had just led the basketball team to the state title, worked full-time in the building. And later in his football career at Aliquippa, when Zmijanac himself had retired from teaching but still coached, the idea of a "retired" teacher continuing to coach was hardly an issue, with Wytiaz or anyone else. If the board had wanted to keep Marocco as head coach in 1997, they would have. Instead, his job was posted the minute his retirement from the "Director" job was official. Zmijanac applied and was instantly hired.

"What's getting misinterpreted is that we honestly had no problem with Frank's performance," Wytiaz said, officially, at the time.

On one level, that was the only feasible thing to say. Marocco's 73-25 record at Aliquippa, not to mention the fact that twelve of his fifteen seniors from 1996 had landed scholarships to play college ball, was unassailable by the core standards of high school football. No one wanted to state publicly that Marocco had alienated many of the program's boosters, or that he had less than thirty players on his roster, with only a dozen underclassmen expected to return. No one wanted to state the true reason for forcing him out, if only because that would be an admission that what outsiders had been saying for years about Aliquippa and its players was all true.

"We had a lot of gang activity starting on the team," Wytiaz admitted years later. "You see how the team dresses now? Everything's set. That had all gone by the wayside—there were bandannas. There was no discipline. You always heard how tough of a guy Frank Marocco was: great football player. But he had no discipline."

In one sense, the sixty-one-year-old Marocco knew no better. He was like everyone else his age—and plenty younger—in Aliquippa then: mystified by the influx of crack cocaine in the '80s. By the early '90s, the closing of mental institutions and group homes—and the relaxation of age restrictions in residential buildings once reserved for the elderly—had turned once-low-rent havens into crime magnets. The projects at Valley Terrace, Griffith Heights, and Linmar, the narrow streets on The Hill and Plan 11 extension, were subject to prostitution and every kind of violence. Turf was carved up and contested by Crips and Bloods, and ancillaries like the Black Rags at Valley Terrace and the G-Pound Crew, or Green Rags, in Griffith Heights.

But the mayhem hardly stayed contained. Neighborhoods and buildings once thought inviolable had fallen into crime's orbit; even the B. F. Jones Library, the downtown jewel placed on the National Register of Historic Places in 1979, wasn't immune. On April 2, 1998, a Raccoon Township mother returning a book to the refurbished facility was killed after a crack user with a record of violence and sexual assault jumped into her truck. Suzanne Bold, forty-five, with a husband and three children at home, fought back against her attacker. The truck careened a hundred yards down Franklin Avenue before crashing into a steel utility pole. It was 7:45 p.m. Bold died of blunt-force trauma. Her purse held less than $100.

Fear and apathy, meanwhile, were nibbling away at social niceties. Donald and Dwan Walker, graduates of Aliquippa High in '94, found it most noticeable after they started coming home from college. Old folks had stopped chastising neighborhood children: indeed, the kids cursed out such elders, and often their parents did, too. "We saw young dudes walking around smoking weed—side by side with their parents!" Donald said. "I couldn't believe that. I was like, 'What the hell is going on?'"

Meanwhile, the sight of football players wearing red bandannas made it easy for whites in authority to conclude that the team, under Marocco, had been contaminated. A hair-trigger readiness to fight had long been a trademark of Aliquippa players, but his regime seemed edgier from the start. In 1990, Marocco's second season in charge, the Quips announced themselves in the AA playoffs by mauling Apollo-Ridge 24-0. After Quips running back Eze Jones was tackled hard into the fence behind the home bench at Aschman Stadium in the final seconds, four of his teammates descended on Apollo linebacker George Smith, stomping him while he lay defenseless on the ground. "One of the most disgusting scenes you ever saw," Wytiaz said.

Smith needed eight stiches to seal the wound under his left eyelid. With WPIAL threatening an outright ban on the Quips for the '91 season, the four players were suspended from all athletics for the school year and Marocco agreed to "institute a program" to prevent another such incident.

Problem was, Marocco wasn't equipped, professionally or personally, to reverse the trend. He lacked state certification as an educator and hardly ran the tightest ship. Stars like quarterback Mike Lundy knew they could miss practice with no real excuse and still start the next game, and Marocco's rapport with black players, though appreciated by their families, fueled a perception that he was more interested in winning friends—and games—than in instilling high values and proper behavior. "He'd gotten fired at Ambridge and had a losing record in eleven years there, so now, this was his opportunity," Zmijanac said, alluding to Marocco's 48-51-7 record with the Bridgers. "The only thing that mattered to Frank was winning. So he could have his day in the sun."

Many of Marocco's players deny that still. "He was one of the few coaches who cared if you were getting your grades right, always asking, 'How's you're mom doing?'" Ty Law said. "Cared about you personally, so you wanted to play for him. To this day, if I'm at home I'll stop by and see him and his wife. When I have cookouts or anything at the house I invite Coach over, because he lives right around the corner from my mom.

"One thing: Because everyone was comparing him to Yannessa, he had to make his own mark and coach his own way—and people thought that Frank would be soft. And he was anything but. He was stern, yet he was understanding of the situation that a lot of us grew up in: drugs, broken homes. He was a father figure to a lot of us."

But few players were as self-motivated as Law. And the middle school, where Marocco was charged with keeping order, had gone rogue; a street-gang ethos swamped the halls. Marocco had been there eight years when Melvin Steals returned for a four-year stint as principal in June, 1996. "In my first year on the job, there were many days when there would be as many as five fights by nine a.m.," Steals wrote after his departure in 2000. "During my second year, two of my middle school students robbed and murdered a young father of four. A few weeks before, the individual who had provided them with the gun had punched me in the hall."

In all, Steals spent thirty-six years in public education. "Aliquippa Middle School," he said, "was the most dangerous building in which I had ever worked."

Near the end of Steals' first year there, Wytiaz asked about Marocco. "I told him that if that man was going to be serving in that position the following school year, I would resign," Steals said.

That stand, by such a vocal, on-the-ground member of the black community, swung African-American support on the board to Zmijanac. From there, Marocco was all but defenseless. He lacked Hollywood Don's glib charm and had nothing on Zmijanac's sardonic wit and connections. The Samuel murders, meanwhile, were still fresh: The fact that members of Marocco's team had been shaking down Brian for money didn't help his cause.

"Remember, you're in a suburban inner city right here. Frank Marocco, for as many wins as he had, had no control over anything," Zmijanac said. "That's why they wanted to get rid of him."

Still, more than anyone wants to admit, the board's problem with Marocco was as much as anything a question of style. "They didn't like him: bull-in-a-china-shop personality," Yannessa said. "Everything [with Marocco] is paranoia and looking over your shoulder and resentment." Zmijanac himself had two players suspended from his basketball team just months before he was given Marocco's job. He would, indeed, rid the football team of bandannas and gang colors, and make players behave come game day, but he was no more successful than any other Aliquippa coach in remaking players into choirboys.

"From the outset they screwed Frank: simple as that," said Peep Short, who has been Zmijanac's defensive coordinator nearly every season since that time. "Who controls the kids in the community? We had kids down here four or five years ago involved in a gunfight—kids on the football team. We've had kids get in arguments and fights with coaches. I've been through all three coaches. And all three coaches have the same problem that Frank had—no more, no less."

"I loved that job: they were like my kids," Marocco said. "They're still my kids. I go to a lot of black funerals."

Fifteen years later, after Zmijanac had become the winningest coach in Aliquippa history (never mind that Yannessa partisans, led by his wife Elaine, dismiss any Quips record set, as she says, with a "Little Sisters of the Poor" AA schedule), he sat in the football office at Aliquippa High and fielded a question about his successor. "That's not my domain," he said, "and whoever it is—and I'm not saying this arrogantly—has a problem.

"Because you don't follow Bear Bryant. I'm trying to be modest, but you don't follow somebody who has that kind of record. The guy who followed Bear Bryant, the guy who's following Joe Paterno: those are tough. The guy that followed Aschman crashed. The guy that followed Yannessa crashed in his own way, because he didn't do it right."

Sure, that's another shot at Marocco, and if you spend any time around the seventy-two-year-old Zmijanac, it's to be expected. Coaches are always defining themselves in relation to their predecessors; the profession's reliance on scorekeeping demands it. But bluntness is also part of Zmijanac's public persona, the way he has always distinguished himself. He delights in being contrary, in deflating hype and the notion that coaching takes some kind of "genius," in telling truths no one wants to hear. When critics say he's not the schmoozer Yannessa was, or as warm as Marocco, he hardly takes it as an insult. He had no great ambition to coach in Aliquippa, he says. He could walk away from it anytime.

No one has ever said Zmijanac wasn't smart. Those same critics call him uncaring, distant, skewer him from the stands for his predictable play-calling. But his mind and sharp tongue, not to mention an impeccable sense of timing, keep most off-balance. Indeed, Zmijanac had turned down the Aliquippa football job when Yannessa left—and the head basketball job when legend Red McNie retired in '93—because he knew: *You don't follow Bear Bryant.* The fact that Zmijanac never played football or basketball on even a high school level was a black mark for any coach, anywhere, never mind one taking up the reins in Aliquippa.

So he waited. Zmijanac taught creative writing and American literature year after year, worked as Yannessa's assistant at Baldwin and kept an eye on Marocco. He knew that only a crisis, a moment when football knowledge was secondary, would be the right time. And then the right time came. In 1997, a year after the Aliquippa School Board handed Zmijanac the basketball job, it handed him the football program, too. Elsewhere in America the age of two-sport coaches—at least at "name" programs—had long passed; but that was the point. This was the desperate act of a desperate board in a desperate town.

Aliquippa was facing $12 million in bond debts, and an ever-shrinking tax base. Eighty-five percent of the 1,850 children in its school system qualified for free lunches, 300 were special education pupils requiring more teachers and funding, and 65 percent were black. Most of the visitors' stands at crumbling Aschman Stadium had to be closed because no money was available for repairs.

Local officials kept launching trial balloons about a merger with Hopewell: all floated away unanswered. Everybody in Aliquippa assumed that was a matter of race, of the white burghers of Hopewell trying to ensure that their daughters would never date a black boy. "They think they're better than we are," said Jon LeDonne, a white Aliquippa grid-iron standout who graduated in 2001. "What makes you better than me? A lot of them left Aliquippa so they wouldn't have to have their kids there; it's always been that way. I hung out with Hopewell kids; I dated a Hopewell girl in high school—and today I think that feeling has left me a bit. I want to see their teams do well. But you still have something down inside you that's like: *They thought they were better than us.*"

Then again, with all the news about crime and mayhem, it was hard to argue any upsides for Hopewell in a merger. The only sure thing on offer was Aliquippa's football talent. And reining in that team, making sure the players behaved, was the most visible way to show the world that the town was worth investing in, merging with, fighting for. The board needed a hard-ass sheriff to stand firm against any threat to the town's most visible asset.

Yes, Zmijanac could coach. It was unquestionable: His football defenses surrendered just 6 points a game for five years in the '80s, he'd just won the state title in his first year as Aliquippa hoops coach; hell, when he turned his hand to girls' basketball at Baldwin, they started winning there, too. More to the point, his teams—like his classes—behaved. You never saw a Mike Zmijanac team running up the score or swarming a prone opponent and stomping his face.

His first year, 1997, Zmijanac followed Marocco's WPIAL championship with a shutout loss in the first round of the playoffs. The next two years his Quips lost in the WPIAL semifinals. But long after he got rolling in football, plenty liked to say that *anyone* could win in Aliquippa. Whenever Zmijanac-coached teams fell short—even after he'd won his own state title and six WPIAL championships; even while headed, from 2008 to 2015, to eight straight WPIAL title games—you heard it: With the talent Aliquippa produces, with all those tough and swift players that keep Division I-A scouts coming, year after year, with all the fathers and uncles pushing them to defend the family name, a coach in Aliquippa doesn't have to do anything but keep 'em healthy and out of jail.

Few ideas chafe him more. Mention it, and Zmijanac will start off flip and end up on fire. "Well, this is my comeback for that—and I don't really have much of one because I don't really give a fuck what they think," he said. "But from '65 to '71, Aliquippa was 12-51-2. Same-type players. The difference between those teams and this team now is, there were six times as many kids in school, six times as many boys, and the same kind of kids. So you have to account for that somehow.

"I would be the first to tell you there's always players here. There were players when I was a kid, there'll be players here when I'm gone. That doesn't mean you win. There are players in Monessen and Charleroi, other traditional football towns, Wilkinsburg. Lots of coaches have good players, but no clue what to do with 'em. You can take a woman who's a five and make her an eight; you can't make her a ten no matter how hard you try. There's lots of motherfuckers who take nines and make 'em fours. I've taken eights and made them at least that. At least."

"Wilkinsburg" is a name that comes up often with Zmijanac. The borough just east of Pittsburgh, home of the world's first commercial radio station, thrived like many towns in Allegheny and Beaver Counties in the 1950s and was a WPIAL football power. Now the population is half the size, its schools are penniless, and crime dominates; the team is a Class A afterthought. Once, it seemed like anybody could win there, too.

"I wouldn't downplay the talent for a second," Zmijanac said. "*Anybody can win here?* Might be right. But not everybody can look right, act right, play right—*do* it right. They may very well be fucking right. I don't count our success in wins and losses. I count our success in those young men who talk to you, who know how to talk to you and have respect for their opponents and their teammates and all."

He brings up his basketball predecessor, Jim Deep, who coached from 1993 to 1996 and finished 53-30.

"Jimmy Deep won here," Zmijanac said. "Jimmy Deep came in from Ambridge and won in basketball here, his first year won the state championship. But at Christmastime that first year . . . I'm trying to think of the kid's name—he's in jail in Florida right now—they're in the gym practicing and Jimmy tried to throw the kid out. And the kid said, 'You'll fuckin' leave before I will.'

"Deep called the police. Police came, my friend Dennis Riggins came up, and the kid told him the same thing: 'You'll take him the fuck out of here before you take me.' And guess what? Kid never missed a second of playing time, they won a state championship. Is that what you want? If that's what you want, okay. We could be Wilkinsburg that fuckin' fast. We were *close* to Wilkinsburg. Until the right people, including me, took over."

Still, while Aliquippa's football standard was getting shored up and walled off, decline worked like acid on everything surrounding. The downtown hollowed. Arrests rose. Definitions, too, shifted: little by little, behaviors considered immoral or fringe or "crazy" edged toward the center. The town's idea of convention gradually split from the world's. To hear Aliquippa High assistant coach and Beaver County detective Timmie Patrick discuss murder, illness, corruption, or racism—even in the most personal terms—is to hear the flat tone of a man mulling tomorrow's weather.

Part of that is distancing, part immersion. Patrick's lifelong steep in Aliquippa's extremes numbed him to shock or alarm. Crazy became normal well before he started chasing criminals; his dad screamed at him to play on a broken leg, after all. But even he has a limit.

This was 1997. Patrick had moved into a house up on Sheffield Terrace, and was just climbing out of his car when he noticed activity on a roof two doors down. It took a few seconds to assemble—first one face, then another, then a third appearing amid the peaks and dips— because the figures up there were all moving. Fast. And then, just when he realized that he knew them, that it was the LeDonne boys—the twins Jon and Justin, whom Patrick was then coaching at Aliquippa Middle School, and younger brother Nathan—Patrick also realized what they were doing: playing tag, twenty-plus feet above the ground with no railing, nothing at all, to hold them back.

"And I mean, *aggressive* tag—as in, trying to push you *off* the roof," Patrick said. "They literally were hopping roof to roof, pushing each other. The funny part is, my dad pulled up behind me and I said, 'Look. What would happen if you ever seen us do that?' He said, 'Before you fell? Or before I jumped up there and killed you?'"

In describing it, Patrick's eyes shine and he's almost yelling. You can't overestimate the joy felt by a jaded soul when forced to recalibrate its standard for shock. He thought he'd seen everything. Fifteen years later, he's still shaking his head. "Just . . . *crazy*," Patrick said.

Because it was different. Because the scene he witnessed wasn't about desperation or defending turf or any of the clashing human sadness seen whenever a mill or an era ends. This was a vision of lunatic, male adolescent *fun* at a time when fun had supposedly left town, fun with a decidedly Aliquippan coloring; one slip, of course, and the LeDonne boys could be paralyzed or dead. Then again, that family had always been different.

For one thing, they were white in an increasingly "black" town. For another, Chris and Edwina LeDonne didn't bolt far when J&L shut down; Chris, a truck driver running routes all over Western Pennsylvania, just moved his wife and oldest boy, Brandon, and the newborn twins up to broader confines in Sheffield. They thought about moving one last time, when Jon and Justin were in elementary school; Chris and Edwina actually looked at homes in Hopewell and Center. But it felt wrong. Aliquippa was home.

And not just in a physical sense. The fact is, the LeDonnes could've fit in anywhere: the boys were handsome, superb athletes, highly intelligent. But with a wild streak that responded to the more worldly facts of Aliquippa life, the LeDonnes mixed comfortably with blacks and, most of all, thrived in the macho, off-the-books aesthetic that accounts, still, for much of the town's vibe. They had the rare temperament—the human gold sought forever by coaches and generals—that revels in discipline *and* mayhem.

Brandon quarterbacked the Quips his senior year in '98 to the WPIAL semifinals, and by then Jon, two years younger, had been coming to practice for years. He was a fifth-grade water boy the day Peep Short, outraged by some player's back talk on the practice field, literally tore off the kid's uniform—shoulder pads, cleats, socks, helmet, pants, all of it—and sent him to the locker room in his underwear. "That kid came back maybe a week later, apologized, and never stepped out of line again," Jon said.

"Another time, my brother was the quarterback, it was my sophomore year, Short had maybe five or six sophomores starting at the time—me, Josh Lay, Monroe Weekley, couple other guys—and we were in a huddle at practice and messed something up," Jon said. "Short started beating the hell out of all of us, punching us in the helmets with a forearm—and he got to Brandon . . . and just looked at him. He wouldn't hit him because he was the quarterback." Younger brother was not pleased.

"Hit his ass!" Jon yelled. "Hit his ass!"

It's not that he wasn't loyal. This was football, and when it comes to football in Aliquippa nobody—not family, not friend—gets off easy. Jon and Justin have always been close. The twins played together all their lives, up through their senior year—Jon a tight end and linebacker, Justin a center and defensive end. But when it came time to run the classic Oklahoma drill—one-on-one, two players colliding until one is driven to ground or out of bounds—everyone else was just a warm-up act. Siccing the LeDonne twins on each other was the show of the year.

"Like watching two pit bulls go at it," Patrick said. "I'd say, 'LeDonne on the right and LeDonne on the left!' And they lined up and couldn't *wait* to hit each other. It didn't stop after the whistle, either: they literally were beating the crap out of each other. You had to pull them off each other."

The first time Jeff Baldwin got shot, he was alone. The second time, his first son was beside him. It was June 27, 1999, a hot, rainy Sunday. The two men—Jamie Brown had just turned twenty-two—were idling around Brown's green Jeep Cherokee on Third Avenue in Plan 11. Jeff was in the driver's seat; Jamie stood outside the passenger door. A blue Mazda pulled up; thirty-year-old Steve Henry stepped out. Within seconds a spray of gunshots—at least nineteen, according to police—filled the air between.

"Words were exchanged," Brown said. "I got behind the car and got my gun out. He probably fired six. I shot probably nineteen. Two guys, shooting recklessly."

Some bullets ended in nearby cars, some in houses. One rattled through the cab of Jamie Brown's Jeep, like a hot popcorn kernel looking to settle. When Jamie jumped into the passenger seat, Jeff told him he'd been hit. "Oh, yeah!" Jeff said, when reminded of it thirteen years later. "I forgot all about that one. I got shot in the head: the bullet hit me on the side and fell out. It went through the windowsill, the dashboard, and that probably stopped the momentum. But I got, like, three stitches in the side of my head."

Both vehicles fled: Jeff, thirty-six, was the driver of his son's getaway car. Father and son had been reversing roles for a while then, a result of Jeff's growing weakness and Jamie's growing strength. If he doesn't admit to directly providing his father with drugs, Jamie knows that in a larger sense he was. "He was doing what I was selling," Jamie said of Jeff. "He had a lot of stuff going on, because of his addictions."

Father and son were picked up within days; the district attorney decided not to prosecute. But even after Henry was arrested two months later—then convicted and jailed—for trying again to shoot Jeff Baldwin, no one in law enforcement considered the latter exactly innocent. Later that fall, Jeff was arrested and faced charges ranging from conspiring to steal a truck to possession of drug paraphernalia; he pleaded no contest to unauthorized use of a motor vehicle and was sentenced to 18 months probation. Jamie Brown, meanwhile, was seen by area police as a particularly shrewd drug dealer, his ruthlessness reinforced, violently, by partner Anthony Tusweet Smith. And he was already being chauffeured about Aliquippa like a kingpin.

As for those who crossed him? Within fourteen months, Steve Henry would be dead, gunned down through his back door in Moon by an unknown assailant while microwaving a 4 a.m. snack. "Yeah, they got the guy," Jeff Baldwin said of Henry, though it's not clear if he's speaking of the police or someone else. "He's not living today. Somebody killed him."

The only thing certain is that Jamie Brown didn't pull the trigger. By then a far more innocent man was dead and Brown was charged with the murder and the prosecution was seeking the death penalty. It seemed to be, by every measure, an open-and-shut case.

The first time he wept, it caught Jon LeDonne like an ambush. There he was, a senior, all-WPIAL, 6-foot-1 and 190 sinewy pounds, 4.0 GPA, master of near every situation. But something about that *dunt-dunt-dunt:* just waiting for the three drumbeats, much less the actual sound, at Aschman Stadium early in the fall of 2000 left him rattled. He felt himself cracking during his last moments in the field house, clustered at the door with teammates before his name got called and the cheerleader took his arm. Because it was slipping away. Week by week, day by day, his time playing Aliquippa football was almost done.

"It was so emotional," LeDonne said. "A lot of players run out with the helmet in their arms, but there were times I would leave my helmet on because I thought I'd be scaring the cheerleader running out with me. Like, *This asshole's crying? What's he crying about?*"

It wasn't like he had nothing to look forward to. LeDonne would play four more years on a full-ride academic scholarship at Robert Morris University, earn a 4.0 in engineering, then grind out a master's degree and PhD in material science at Carnegie Mellon. But there's nothing like playing and winning for your hometown, alongside kids you grew up with forever. There's nothing like a racially mixed team—a dozen whites still on Aliquippa's thirty-man roster then, sons of the street and sons of the book lined up side by side, just as it had always been—sweating and weeping and winning together.

More than a decade later, LeDonne would complete his doctoral thesis while working for Bettis Atomic Power Laboratory in Pittsburgh, fine-tuning the wiry innards of nuclear propulsion systems for the U.S. Navy. His dissertation—"The Investigation of Length-Scale Effects of Layered Thickness on the Heterophase Interface Character Distribution of Copper-Niobium Robotic Composites"—is comprehensible to only a few. But in essence, it's about marrying two metals—the penny-dark copper and off-white niobium—into a blend capable of conducting tremendous power.

"We just take two pieces, put them together, and put a force on them large enough to make the metals bond together—and then two pieces become one," LeDonne said. "It's an alloy, but it's not intermixed. It's still copper and niobium, in layers. And the interface of the bonding material is where the material gets its strength."

LeDonne calls this "a simple idea," but a human metaphor might help. Think of the two metals as a town's two dominant racial elements, each with its own fierce identity and strengths. Layer the two together on a football team, knowing that they won't ever fully fuse, and bond them with the force of tradition and family expectation and, yes, love. . . .

In 2000, Zmijanac's Quips rose up to take hold of the WPIAL season. As one of the last great Aliquippa teams with a strong cadre of whites, it was in a sense Hollywood Don's last gasp, the final example of what the town's two dominant cultures—its past and future—could accomplish when interfacing under pressure. Led by perhaps the most talented quarterback in Aliquippa history, Josh Lay, and LeDonne, whom the blacks gave the ultimate honorific—"White Chocolate" (and then proceeded to baffle the uninitiated by shortening it to "Chocolate")—the Quips steamrolled the competition, won the league title, and took a 14-0 record into the state championship game.

But what made Aliquippa truly scary that fall was the rampaging figure of Monroe Weekley, one of those once-in-a-decade talents so clearly better than everyone around him, so seemingly born to play pro ball, that it seems almost unfair to the rest. As a senior Weekley was listed at 6-foot-3 and 240 pounds, freakish dimensions for someone

347

so fast and quick. In terms of pure athleticism, Weekley was in that subset of Aliquippa oh-my-Gods with Ernie Pitts, Tony Dorsett, and Sean Gilbert. "A number one draft pick, for sure," LeDonne said, "if he had just kept his head straight."

"Mo-Mo was unbelievable," said Anthony Peluso, Weekley's teammate in 1998–99. "He was so good, and I don't want to say this like it's bad, but he was, like . . . *crazy*. He had no regard for his body whatsoever. He'd just go in there like a crash-test dummy and throw his body on the line, didn't care. If you told him to go run as fast as you can and head-butt that wall without a helmet—and that would win us the game? He would do it. Fearless and athletic: that made him deadly on the football field."

And by deploying him at offensive guard and inside linebacker, Zmijanac took full advantage of Mo-Mo's taste for violence. "I love hitting people," Weekley said after he devastated Center in 2000 with thirteen tackles, a forced fumble, and another fumble recovery. "I can't be on the field without hitting people."

Big-time colleges slavered at the thought. Pitt, Notre Dame, Miami, Arizona State, Michigan, and Wisconsin offered him full scholarships. Of course, none of his prospective coaches knew that Weekley lacked the ballast to succeed in life, much less high-level sports. But once it fell apart for him a few years later—after Pitt flushed him in '01 for stealing from his roommate and after the University of Kansas flushed him in '03; after he hit the streets and killed a twenty-four-year-old over a $600 debt in 2010 by firing a bullet into his skull and was sentenced to decades in prison—no one who knew Monroe Weekley could say they were all that surprised.

But that senior season, LeDonne and the rest kept Mo-Mo's lunacy in check, hanging out daily with Weekley and Josh Lay, who never panned out either and later fell into drug trouble. LeDonne kept his hand on the books but reveled in the grit, and the Quips crushed near everyone in sight that fall, avenged themselves on Washington after two straight losses, held off Waynesburg even after Lay broke his hand to win the WPIAL title at Heinz Field.

Zmijanac likes to point out that he's the only coach to win a Pennsylvania state title game in football and basketball, and the only one to lose both, too. But players have it worse; too soon, for them, there's no more "next year" to seek redemption. As senior captain on the 2000 Aliquippa football and 2000–01 basketball teams, LeDonne twice played for state titles—and lost both, just three months apart.

His reaction is telling. The Quips' history of basketball success nearly equals its record in football, but to fans, most families, the local media, the fate of the basketball team is important, but hardly life-and-death. When LeDonne's basketball Quips lost the state championship to Camp Hill's Trinity in March 2001, Weekley punted the ball into the stands, and the team sat on the hardwood during the awards ceremony, exhausted and empty. It hurt, but LeDonne's eyes were dry.

But when, three months earlier, the Quips lost the state football championship, undone by Lay's broken hand and blown out 26-6 by Mt. Carmel? LeDonne couldn't stop crying as he walked across the field. A photo of him, with Zmijanac muttering comfort into his ear, was splayed across the front page of the *Beaver County Times*. "Tears were coming down," LeDonne said. "Because it's the end to your high school career. You're never going to don that Aliquippa jersey again."

16

Shiny Things

When, exactly, does a town pass its point of no return? For every Watts or Scottsboro, with their crystallizing moment of ugly truth, thousands experience only a slow fade of grace, along with a concurrent dawning upon the outside world that things aren't right there anymore. Aliquippa's reputation had been on such a wane for thirty years. Then, just after 8:14 p.m. on March 15, 2001, Aliquippa police officer James Naim, on foot patrol near a playground and community center at Linmar Terrace, was killed when a 9-millimeter bullet entered his skull behind the left ear.

Some saw it coming. For the previous seventeen months, the drug trade in Aliquippa had experienced a spike in murders: Four young men had turned up dead, three others had come close, and earlier that afternoon Pennsylvania State Police lieutenant Paul Radatovich and trooper Don Neill met with a drug addict and thief named Rayetta Jo Lee at a rehab facility in Center. Lee, aside from telling them that Jamie Brown, with whom she had been sleeping, had directed two of those killings—of Eddie Humphries and Marvin Steals—also stated that Jeff Baldwin's son had told her "repeatedly" that he was going to kill an area police officer because the cops were shaking down his dealers.

That struck an old nerve; suspicion of the Aliquippa PD had been part of the town's DNA since Harry Mauk deployed it as a tool of J&L tyranny. But the infestation of crack—and the new flow of dirty money—turned mistrust into open antagonism, a disrespect edging right up to the door of police headquarters. Early on, that just meant addicts creeping into the Franklin Avenue parking lot to snap off the cops' radio antennas for use as crack pipes. But six weeks before Naim's death, Aliquippa officer Sonya Carter relayed to colleagues the same rumor about Jamie Brown's "hit list" of police officers. In the days after, "they told us to be extra careful when you go out to your car," Carter said. "Because somebody in Valley Terrace could shoot down and have a direct target."

But the new police chief, Ralph Pallante, and his assistant, Andre Davis, dismissed her tip as idle threat. Day by day, cop by cop, the department dropped its guard; only James Naim, thirty-two years old and just fourteen months on the job, seemed unnerved. And he wasn't just worried about Jamie Brown.

On February 16, Naim met with a *Beaver County Times* reporter and told him about the hit list, plus rumors of an ongoing investigation of department corruption. The FBI, it later turned out, had been investigating Beaver County law enforcement for months, looking into a pattern of cash evidence discrepancies: criminal sources reported that, after some arrests, money seized from dealers by Aliquippa cops would shrink when filed as evidence—or maybe none of it would be entered at all.

Naim also told his mother and brother, Paul, that he believed that he was going to be "ambushed"—and that if, indeed, any harm came to him the Aliquippa Police Department should be investigated. "He said, '*When* I get ambushed,'" Paul stressed to Radatovich. "Not '*if.*'"

William Alston, Aliquippa police chief for thirteen years before retiring in 2001, testified that he never heard a word about corruption in his department—from Naim or anyone else. Anthony Battalini, then an Aliquippa city councilman, says he never believed that Naim's fear of his fellow officers was legitimate. But after he became mayor in May 2003, he tried to clean house. "I got rid of six policemen because I knew they were bad cops; I knew they were with the drug dealers," Battalini said. "There was no discipline in the police department. It was, like, haywire; guys did what they wanted to do. When I got to be mayor, I had several meetings with them, tried to win the confidence with the guys, try to do them right. But it was just a bad situation in Aliquippa. They were just, like, renegades. They did what they wanted to do."

Still, Naim's suspicions were just hearsay—and no evidence of what he alleged was ever unearthed. The only thing certain to those who loved him is that Naim, just two months from finishing his bachelor's degree at Geneva College, believed that he was in danger and believed that area cops—some from the Aliquippa Police Department some from the county at large—were the men he had to fear most.

"This is one day before he got killed," George David said, sitting behind his desk in the offices of the sheriff of Beaver County, the post he was appointed to for two years in 1996, and elected to in 2007. Naim had called him, and "he told me, 'If something happens to me, these are the guys that you look at,'" Sheriff David said. "He gave me the names and everything. He said, 'I feel this way because I witnessed things and they know I witnessed it—so if something happens to me these are the guys that did it to me.'"

David doesn't think that any law enforcement officer—none of the three men whose names Naim gave him, men he knows well—pulled the trigger on his cousin. But he finds it hard to believe that the events of the following day began and ended with Jamie Brown's "hit list." Even a decade later, the county's top law enforcement official couldn't help but wonder about its most infamous crime.

"There was more he wanted to tell me, but he didn't want to talk over the phone," David said. "Maybe he was on the car radio, somebody could've heard it. I don't know. Why would he have got killed the day after he told me?

"There could've been somebody with him. I'm thinking who was with him told Jamie Brown or Tusweet, 'This guy's going to talk.' You know what I mean? In my mind, there's a question. Because you tell me one day, and you're dead the next day? How else? What did he witness?"

Even amid Aliquippa's crime spree in early 2001, there was hope that Linmar Terrace, just an 80-yard Hail Mary from where Mike Ditka grew up, had reached a moment of calm. The ninety-four-unit, fifty-eight-year-old complex of brick buildings—with an average monthly rent of $181, and the vast majority of its mostly black families headed by single mothers—had been plagued by all manner of assault and theft the year before. But the infusion of a full-time, federally funded police substation in the complex had seemingly taken hold in the second half of 2000, resulting in a dramatic 66 percent drop in police-related incidents.

A half hour after Rayetta Lee told police about Jamie Brown's intent to kill a cop, Naim began his shift at the Linmar Substation. It was 3 p.m. The job entailed making a circuit around the apartment buildings; investigators believe the men who ambushed Naim waited near the northwest corner of the Linmar housing units. After the first bullet struck, Naim dropped into the wet grass. "My theory: Jamie Brown did do the shooting," said Sheriff David. "When you get shot in the head, you bounce and everything. The kid that was with him, Acey Taylor, said, 'Shoot that motherfucker again! He's still living.'"

The second bullet entered Naim's left temple, bored through bone and both frontal lobes. Naim was sprawled facedown, just a hundred feet from Apartment 265, when Aliquippa officers Shawn Young and Dan Cassidy spotted him. His service revolver was still in its holster.

Medical personnel arrived. As police scrambled to protect themselves, secure the area, and follow up on leads, more than a hundred Linmar residents poured out of their homes. The officers from differing commands, some off-duty, all scared and angry, were hardly gentle with crowd control; in the ensuing days residents spoke of being called "niggers" and "monkeys." At one point, Sonya Carter recalled, one of her Aliquippa PD colleagues shouted, "Shut up!" and "You niggers, get back!"

Still, what most struck Radatovich was the coolness of the Linmar citizenry. The mostly black residents there had considered Jimmy Naim one of the "nice" Aliquippa cops, yet in the first minutes and then the long, quiet hour after Naim was attacked, there was only silence. "Do you know how many people called 911?" Radatovich asked. "None."

He doesn't bother to invoke the name "Kitty Genovese." When the twenty-eight-year-old Queens, New York, woman was stabbed to death in 1964, the news that some three dozen people ignored or watched the attack without calling police became one more signifier of a community—an America—grown cold. The narrative later proved less provocative (one neighbor yelled at Genovese's attacker, driving him temporarily away from her, and two others did call police during the attack), but if "Kitty Genovese" remains shorthand for detachment from the most basic idea of "community," the hour after Naim's death signaled the shattering of trust between a people and its police.

"We're knocking at doors, you can see 'em at a window; they won't answer the doors to talk to us," Radatovich said. "Not one person even calls 911 to just say, 'I heard what I thought was gunshots'? Is that normal? No, it's not. That community is so unified with regard to sports, to pride in their teams and all that stuff. But there's a divisiveness about it in other aspects. Some of it's racial. Some of it, whether real or imagined, is in their perception of inequality in how things are done."

*　*　*

To the public, it seemed as if the police and prosecutors had the case quickly in hand. Within fifteen minutes of finding Naim's body, assistant chief Andre Davis asked the state police to assume control of the investigation. Within two days, two suspects had been charged with criminal homicide and conspiracy to commit homicide: Jamie Brown, with his "hit list" already widely reported, and a mentally challenged eighteen-year-old Linmar resident named Darnell Hines. A manhunt was under way, too, for Brown's partner in the drug trade, Anthony Tusweet Smith, who within six days would be charged with trying to kill a star witness. Once seventeen-year-old Acey Taylor was picked up on April 20, all the suspects appeared to be in custody. Witnesses were singing. Cases were being built.

The streets and hills and projects of Aliquippa, though, kept bubbling in a state of apprehension. The race riots of the '70s and the days of mass murderer Edward Surratt had produced paralyzing tension, but then the public viewed the police as at least nominal referees. Now—and especially among black families—most police were viewed at best as hair-trigger hotheads looking to avenge the murder of one of their own.

"I thought this town was going to fall apart," said Sherman McBride, an assistant coach at Aliquippa High since 1984, then working for USAir at nearby Pittsburgh International Airport. "They were kicking down doors of guys who didn't have nothing to do with it. You didn't know who to trust. Our kids, the drug dealers, the parents, the police—everybody was on edge. It was like the Wild, Wild West: who was going to pull out their gun first?"

On the Saturday after the murder, during the Quips' basketball win over Windber in the state tournament in Pittsburgh, a Windber fan behind Aliquippa's bench yelled for his team to "beat the niggers." Zmijanac shook off his first impulse to go into the stands himself. He called for a security guard to escort the man away.

"I'm sure there are people who think all of us are like the lowlifes who did that horrible crime," Zmijanac told a reporter then. "I think looking at us that way must make them feel superior. I feel sorry for them. They have a problem with their character."

On the morning of Tuesday, March 20, "Jimmy's Last Patrol" began at the Darroch Funeral Home in Aliquippa. A bagpiper played as Naim's casket emerged and was placed into a silver hearse. More than a thousand officers in more than four hundred patrol cars—some from as far away as West Virginia and Ohio—lined up behind. The parade of cars poured onto Mill Street, crossed over Brodhead Road slow and silent, rolled down Kennedy Boulevard. It went nowhere near Linmar. The classrooms of Aliquippa Elementary School had been emptied; children lined the fence in homemade paper police hats.

Residents waved small American flags outside the CVS on Brodhead Road. The line of trucks and cars and fire trucks and ambulances swung right into the former heart of town along Franklin Avenue, past a throng of pupils from St. Titus School. The cars rolled past the gorgeous and ever more incongruous library, past the spot where JFK spoke and the old J&L company store had stood. People stepped out of their homes and the few businesses, heads bowed. Naim's body was carried to the on-ramp of Route 51 just before the old J&L tunnel. Ahead was the funeral mass in Hopewell, a riderless horse at Mount Olivet Cemetery, an officer blowing "Taps."

"His funeral was beautiful," said Sonya Carter. But behind the scenes, the fissures long evident in town had begun to surface in the foundation of Beaver County law enforcement. Reputations of some cops began to crumble; news that a grand jury had been launched to investigate allegations of police corruption in town and county made wholesale disgrace a possibility. Suspicions against cops hardened, often along racial lines. In Aliquippa, Carter's name was the first to get stained.

Despite the fact she had been one of the first Aliquippa cops to complain about corruption and the first to raise an alarm about Brown's hit list, Carter instantly became a suspect figure. Because Naim wasn't originally scheduled to work Linmar that Thursday night; Carter was. But though her superiors confirmed that Naim himself had asked for the shift change, Carter now found herself frozen out. She had always been considered too friendly, it seemed, with the criminals in Linmar.

Seven days after the killing, Carter waived Miranda rights, submitted to polygraph testing, and denied any prior knowledge of the shooting. The examiner dismissed the results as "inconclusive" because she was still "too emotional."

She remained on the Aliquippa force for two more years. Some officers stopped talking to her; some never trusted her again. "I tried to do my job, and it just kept weighing on me," Carter said. "I was so paranoid. They kept saying 'Jamie Brown, Jamie Brown'; I'd hear his name on TV or read it and start sweating bad and getting all scared. It was so bad."

She wasn't the only cop under pressure. Pennsylvania deputy attorney general Linda Barr and the state police made a conscious decision to cut Aliquippa police, Beaver County's sheriff, and county detectives out of the investigation. The unstated reason: to protect its integrity should the grand jury later find corruption involving any contributing officers, and to rebuild the police-community bond with a distrustful populace. Problem was, nearly all the locals affected were black.

"It was crushing," said Timmie Patrick of the Naim slaying. "It divided a community, divided law enforcement; it was just an ugly mark in Aliquippa's life. You had a law enforcement officer, cut down in his prime; he had a family. You had people who were making it a racist issue and trying to cloud the investigation. Race, corruption—it was the whole gamut.

"And the one name getting stained was black law enforcement. I was under investigation by the state. You had high-ranking black law enforcement officers—ex-chief Bill Alston of Aliquippa; Peep Short of the sheriff's office, commander at that time; Timmie Patrick, county detective; Anthony McClure, county detective; state trooper Mike Warfield: we were all under investigation. And except for Short, we were cleared. We were vindicated."

And Aliquippa's football machine chugged on. Not long after Naim's death, in the spring of 2001, Diana Gilbert walked into Mike Zmijanac's office at the high school with her son. Darrelle Revis had just completed a dominant ninth-grade season of basketball at a Christian school in nearby Rochester, had been recruited by prep powers in Pittsburgh and from as far away as DeMatha Catholic High in Washington, DC.

All the other coaches and friends and family said Darrelle was a surefire star. "He's going to be an all-American," Diana said.

Zmijanac was still coaching both football and basketball then. He'd had Diana in his class, temper and all, and had coached her brother, Sean. Darrelle stood just 5-foot-10. Zmijanac looked her in the eye and said, "No, he's not."

Now Diana had another reason to send her boy away. They lived in town, but she had avoided Aliquippa's dodgy middle school, spent three years carting him to Beaver Valley Christian Academy. It didn't fully take. Darrelle always was willful, different, locked up a bit inside his own head. He loved the idea of interplanetary travel, sitting quietly on the porch on Seventh Avenue staring at the stars. He would tell himself, *I'm going to outer space one day.*

But local gravity had its pull. Darrelle kept up his grades, but after school would slip into trouble with a Plan II crew. His uncle Jamal, Diana's youngest brother, had a hand in that. "My uncle was older; I used to follow him around, and one thing led to another," Revis said. "It was kind of a sports thing and then it started getting into people jumping people, beating people up. I used to see my uncle smoke; I never smoked—as bad as I wanted to be an athlete? Nothing's standing in my way. Smoking is bad for you, drinking, all those things would be a hindrance. But we were in that crew and as we got older things started getting more violent, violent, violent.

"But as it got more violent and they wanted to use guns, that's when I backed out. I went my way and they was cool with it. They didn't beat me up or try to kill me, no. And some of them was my cousins, so they were like, 'It's cool. You got other things to do. You're probably going to be playing ball.'"

Soon Darrelle had options. He could play high school hoops in Pittsburgh, for his uncle Mark's old coach. Or at DeMatha, a breeding ground for many NBA players and near his father's home in Maryland. "I was scared," Revis said. "My mom was like, 'It's your decision,' and at that young age, you don't know nothing. Just going to school, trying to play sports; I'm kicking rocks, and all this stuff was coming. I don't know if that was the right move. Going to DeMatha: a great school. I thought, *This is getting crazy. . . .*"

But finally the lure of that family line, the idea of getting his *dunt-dunt-dunt* proved irresistible. From his stargazing perch on that porch, after all, young Darrelle had also seen the lights of Aschman Stadium. "I always wanted to bleed red, black, and white," he said. But not for football. Revis hadn't played that since Midget ball in Aliquippa, had little interest; he dribbled a basketball everywhere.

That's what Zmijanac found Darrelle doing, out on the street the summer before his sophomore year. Diana wasn't around this time. Zmijanac tried again.

"You don't know me well, but I coached your uncles, dad, cousins," Zmijanac said. "I'm sure you're a talent. You should come out for football."

"Naw," Revis replied.

But the hook had been set. Diana had just moved to a house in Plan 12, near the high school, and Darrelle's footballing friends would hang out in the days before summer practice began, urging him to play. "No, I'm straight basketball," Revis said. "It's my love."

On the third day of drills, Darrelle walked into the Aliquippa High gym. It was July, and broiling: Six dozen guys were heaving, sweating, running line sprints in a set that would go for the next two and a half hours. Zmijanac took his time, then sidled over and tried to make the question sound innocent. Neither imagined it would lead to the NFL, a Super Bowl ring, a $70 million contract, and a career as one of the best cornerbacks in the history of the game.

"What're you going to do to keep in shape?" Zmijanac said.

"I think," Revis replied, "I'm going to give this football a try."

Coach Z gave his usual shrug. "Get in line," he said.

Revis's experience was hardly rare: More and more, the choice for Aliquippa's young men was boiling down to football or the street. Both offered a form of celebrity, a path to big money. On one hand you had Ty Law, a national name after he ran back an interception back 47 yards for a touchdown in New England's 20-17 win in the 2001 Super Bowl, making millions in an All-Pro career with the Patriots. On the other, you had Jamie Brown and his confederates, flush and feared and selling a different kind of rush.

And though Zmijanac and his assistants succeeded in banning gang colors and thug-life behavior, the line between the program and the problems kept getting thinner. By the time of Jamie Brown's arrest and May 2002 conviction for Naim's murder, the fact that he was the son of a onetime Aliquippa football star was lost on no one, especially after Jeff Baldwin tried providing Brown's alibi for the night of the murder. "He's innocent and it's political," Baldwin said a decade later. "We was together. We went to the store. We were together from, like, six o'clock to like nine o'clock. He had a big Rottweiler and he wanted to get dog food and wanted me to help him. We was together from, like, six o'clock to nine-thirty, however."

But Jeff was a problematic witness at best: Two nights after Naim's death, Radatovitch, Baldwin's old classmate from the police academy, led a search of the Plan 11 home of Tezmalita Pharr—Jeff's longtime girlfriend and the mother of their son, Jonathan Baldwin. Jeff was ordered onto his belly; police say they found a crack pipe in his front pocket and, in the house, foil wrappers with scorch marks and traces of white powder and a clutch of Federal .40-caliber bullets.

"Aww," Jeff said, when he recognized Radatovich. "It's got to be you?"

Sometimes, the line between the two worlds became so blurred that it was hard to see where one ended and the other began. Zmijanac's coaching staff—stacked with as many as fifteen men, most of them ex-players volunteering their time—featured some who worked full-time in area law enforcement, some who had arrested relatives of players. At least two, running backs coach Timmie Patrick and longtime defensive coach Peep Short, were under state investigation in the wake of Naim's murder. But they never stopped working with the Quips, no matter the questions, no matter the dirt.

Still, none ended up taking a bigger hit than Peep Short. With a swift rise in 1999 to the rank of commander—the third-ranking officer—in the Beaver County Sheriff's Office, and impressive work as Aliquippa's defensive coordinator, by 2001 the forty-year-old Short had put himself on the short list to one day run the department and/ or become the Quips' head coach. Naim's murder, though, would mark the end of his police career. And it left Short carrying so much questionable baggage that any school risked a public relations nightmare in hiring him to mold young men.

Short's version of things is in keeping with his self-image as Aliquippa's lone teller of truths, no matter the consequence—in Peep parlance, *Come what may, motherfucker.* Because in the first days after Naim's murder, with every investigative mind all but convinced that Jamie Brown was the culprit, Short had put up his hand and said no. Again.

It was he, after all, who along with Sheriff George David had rightly derailed Brown's arrest for the Samuel murders in 1996. This time, Short felt information that he had uncovered on the Naim murder deserved attention. Two hours following the discovery of the body, an informant told Short that, just after hearing shots, a Linmar resident had seen a white man with a ponytail run by, get into a red pickup truck, and drive off. Short turned the information over to investigators. Nearly five months later, Short wrote a letter to the state's attorney general again detailing his findings. Investigators doubled back and confirmed the existence of both Short's informant and a conversation between them that night—but in their reports made no mention of a ponytailed white man.

"I think they had to discredit what I wrote in that report," Short said. "There was a clear contradiction there. I didn't make it up: They can go talk to the witness themselves. That's what the lady told me: It was a white male. But . . . see, everybody knows Jamie Brown didn't kill that cop. Everybody really knows who killed Naim. I was one who always said, 'Let's get the motherfucker who did it.' And motherfuckers know Jamie Brown didn't do this."

Actually, investigators did talk to Short's "witness." At 8 p.m. the day after Naim's death, Connie Walker related to state police that she had come home from shopping the night before and heard gunshots while retrieving bags from her car. No mention in that report is made of a ponytailed white man, or a red pickup. A decade later, Walker says she was never asked about that by the follow-up investigators—but it didn't matter. "I never seen a guy with a ponytail," Walker said. "I can't tell you nothing. All I know is, we liked that Officer Naim."

Short contends that his suggestion of an alternate version of the murder was enough to rile those in charge. Peers and superiors say it's not that simple; it never has been with Peep Short. Just before the one-year anniversary of Naim's death, Short was forced to resign his sheriff's position—and the stated reasons had nothing to do with Jamie Brown.

The first black mark occurred in April 2001, when a prisoner was allowed time to have sex with his girlfriend during a sanctioned visit to Aliquippa for his father's funeral. Short was not present, but the visit came under his authority—and so tawdry an example of special treatment sparked more allegations and investigations. "They had to make someone the scapegoat," said Timmie Patrick. "Peep got a raw deal but there are rules, and he broke those rules. But I've seen people who did more and got punished less; and there's things they pulled out of that investigation about other law enforcement officers—who were not African-American—that never came to light."

In February 2003, the two-year grand jury investigation sparked by Naim's slaying—expected to unveil widespread police misconduct—resulted instead in eight low-level arrests, the most prominent those of a Beaver County sheriff's deputy and four current and former county jail guards. And though Short, the highest-ranking police official tagged with misconduct, had resigned the year before, he remained a lively topic. One fresh—and reported—allegation was a 1995 incident that had two unnamed associates extorting a suspected drug dealer, Rick Hill, on Short's behalf; he allegedly wanted $2,500 a month to let Hill keep dealing in Aliquippa.

A month later, Short arrested Hill. While he was in jail, the same two associates and a future deputy sheriff allegedly told Hill's girlfriend that Short would drop the charges if she gave him $2,500 and agreed to have sex with him. She declined. Missing from the court papers and newspaper account was one key detail: Hill's girlfriend at the time was Della Rae Campbell. In 1993, after finishing off a five-year sentence for armed robbery of an undercover narcotics agent, Rick Hill had stepped in, paired up with Della, and raised Tommie, the future Quips star and NFL player, while Tommie Campbell Sr. and Short—the boy's two possible fathers—were nowhere to be found.

"Rick Hill is my father," said Tommie Campbell Jr. "He's been with me since I was five years old. When I scored my first touchdown he was there to pick me up. Biological? Who knows? It doesn't matter. He's the only father figure. He's the only true dad. I still call him 'Dad' to this day."

Short was never disciplined or charged with the alleged extortions—nor for misconduct while serving as a law enforcement officer. While Della insists that the published account is "exactly right," and both she and Hill say that they made their sworn accusations before the grand jury, they don't agree on the aftermath. Della says that the couple suffered no retaliation. Hill says that Short's maneuvering resulted in another stint in prison. "With him getting me out of the way, maybe he felt he could get back with her and have Tommie," Hill said. "Because everyone seen that Tommie as a child had great potential."

Short dismisses the entire scenario. "Nothing that Rick and Della are saying had any merit whatsoever," he said. Of Della's claim that he had demanded sex with her in exchange for Hill's freedom, he chuckled and said, "I'd already had sex with her many times before that.

"See, I recognize Della for who she is: a strange creature, man. Wasn't so much when I was [dating] her, but over the years she got to be. And Rick was just a drug dealer who was trying to save himself from going to jail for three years. This dude didn't have twenty-five dollars to rub together—let alone twenty-five hundred. He couldn't bring together twenty-five hundred dollars to save his fuckin' life."

By then, though, little Short said or did could make a difference. Naim's murder and the grand jury investigation, all the rumors and allegations, had balled together into one indelible conclusion. "Oh, yeah," said Sherm McBride, Short's longtime friend and Aliquippa's offensive coordinator. "A lot of people thought he was dirty."

The loss of high position, the airing of so many allegations, would've broken others. But more than a decade later, Short remains Aliquippa High's loudly defiant defensive coordinator, putting on a face that allows no one to think that the resignation, the asides from former cop colleagues, have had much effect. "Flip this, if you will," Short said. "If I was really such an asshole—and with all the people that I knew who worked for the state police, the state attorney general's office, the confidential informants, police officers, their methods—why wouldn't I be doing all that shit right now?"

He certainly had the chance—and personal reasons—to do so. Years later, a task force combining the U.S. Drug Enforcement Administration and the state police's Office of Drug Law Enforcement unleashed "Operation Enough Is Enough," the campaign against Aliquippa's largest crack cocaine ring that eventually resulted in the arrest of seventeen men. The investigation was led by state trooper Mike Warfield, the former Quips quarterback and Short's onetime protégé. The ringleader was Anthony "Ali" Dorsett, who had ignored Short's punch in the face and ended up marrying Peep's daughter, Kiki, in 2004. They had two children, and Short had to admit that Ali took good care of his family.

Warfield had tracked Ali Dorsett for four years; in the months leading up to the arrests his inquiry had blossomed into a high-profile, multipronged operation. And in truth, he was worried how Peep would take it. Warfield *thought* he knew: working under Short's wing in 1992 and '93, he had never seen one instance of favoritism, much less corruption. But this was family now, and he owed Short. Warfield wouldn't know anything until the shit started flying. "I didn't want to lose Peep's friendship, because of what he did for me," Warfield said.

Short had sources; he could feel what was coming. But repeatedly, he told Warfield about his son-in-law: "He shouldn't have been doing it. You do your job." His message was so emphatic, in fact, that before the feds made the arrests in December 2008, Warfield—after, notifying his supervisor and, he says, receiving approval—talked to Short about "Enough Is Enough." Peep could have sent out a warning, but "nothing has ever been leaked," Warfield said. "Nothing has ever been said—and these people are close to him.

"I changed his daughter's life. . . . But Peep didn't hesitate. He knew, to a degree, what [Ali] was doing to the community. And what he had taught me, as a police officer, was no matter who it is—family or not, friends or not—you do your job."

That coolness remains. To hear Peep Short, it's easy to think that none of this touched him. Those who know him know better. "He loved that job, his standing in the community," Patrick said. "I know it hurt him deeply. He talks about law enforcement sometimes, and you still see the passion. He wants to do *something*, but has to do it by other means. Coaching is one of them."

But even that can be complicated. The news of Short's alleged extortion of Rick Hill and his girlfriend went public before Tommie Campbell's junior season at Aliquippa. If the boy ever heard the news, no one could tell; Hill says that he didn't tell Tommie about the couple's testimony to the grand jury until after his high school career ended. And if he ever resented Short's supposed squeeze on Hill or his mom, Campbell never showed it. He played Short's own position—defensive back—under Short his last two years at Aliquippa, and later, at Pitt, even wore Short's number, 29. To honor Peep? "Yeah," Tommie said. "You can say that."

But he doesn't say anything more. Even a decade later, with Hill and his mother broken up, with Hill moved away to Kentucky and his ex-coach and maybe-dad now available to him anytime, Rick Hill remains the man Tommie looks up to. Peep? Campbell does play golf with the man when he comes home to Aliquippa. They see each other often. But, publicly, he calls him "Coach Short," and nothing else.

17

Last Ones Laughing

Western Pennsylvania, by the twenty-first century, had become legendary among football cognescenti for producing greatness—
quarterbacks Johnny Unitas and Dan Marino from Pittsburgh, Joe
Namath from Beaver Falls, Jim Kelly out of East Brady, Joe Montana
from Monongahela—with everyone crediting the area's steely backbone
and coal-dusted lungs, the dead or dying industries that somehow made
its kids hungrier, more desperate, tougher. But few places in in the state,
much less America, kept spitting out talent like Aliquippa. Its seeming
twin across the river, Ambridge, could claim just one NFL star, Detroit
Lions linebacker Mike Lucci, and he'd retired in 1973.

Just in 2003, Aliquippa had native son Ty Law starring for New
England's record-setting defense, intercepting Colts QB Peyton Manning three times in the AFC Championship game and winning his
second Super Bowl. Aliquippa had Sean Gilbert finishing up his solid
eleven-year NFL career with the Raiders, and so what if his teammate,
eight-year NFL vet Anthony Dorsett Jr., went to school in Texas? He

was born in Aliquippa, too, when his dad, Hall of Famer Tony Dorsett, was a high school freshman.

"All those examples helped me, because you see that *you* can make it," Darrelle Revis said. "It seems like you're attached to it when you see them play on Sundays, or you see Mike Ditka on TV. You're proud: *He's one of us. He's a Quip. He's an Aliquippian.* That's the best of the best, being one of the best football players in the world, doing one of the best jobs. And when you see somebody doing it, you say, 'I want to be like him.'"

Of course, Revis also had examples closer to hand. Uncle Mark Gilbert, a former Division I-A basketball player at Duquesne, was a force in keeping young Darrelle safe and sound and taught him plenty about playing high-level hoops. And Sean Gilbert, in summers or on the phone during his seasons with the Panthers and Raiders, had Darrelle churning hard from sophomore year on. "I remember plain as day my uncle Sean working me out, and talking me through stuff: how to *be* a football player," Revis said. "*Just try to be the best you can. If you give a hundred percent, then there's no regret when you're done.*

"He used to have me in some intense workouts, but I never shied away. If he walked in here now and said, 'Let's go work out'? I'd go. I always challenged myself to try and match his level. *My uncle, NFL player?* If he wants to work out, I'm going. So I can show him that I can keep up with him."

The Quips went 8-3 and 10-2 his first two seasons. By 2003, Revis's senior year, he owned the game. Running back, defensive back, kick returns: He did it all. Zmijanac had him two years in basketball; Revis was his backbone there, too. "Quiet, always worked hard, never missed practice," Zmijanac said. "Late once: went to get his tuxedo for the prom and I think he had a flat tire coming back. Totally apologetic. Darrelle Revis is the finest young man I've ever known. He is exactly what you see. There are young men I put in the same class, but I've never met one finer. What you see is him.

"Never, never, never did I see him act any way that I would be . . . well, there was *one* time . . . ashamed of him. The first game he played basketball for me, we played man-to-man full-court press the whole game. We were playing Hopewell, and down twelve, fourteen points in the first quarter; he called time-out on his own. I stormed to mid-court and we had a discussion: *You aren't running anything! We won before you got here and we're going to win after you leave. Don't ever do that again. We're going to press them until they submit.* We ended up winning by twelve or fourteen and he came after and said, 'I'm sorry.'"

His legend-making moment came in 2003. No one in Aliquippa history—not Ernie Pitts, Ditka, his uncle Sean, Josh Lay, not Monroe Weekley—has ever come close. In the state championship final in Hershey, Pennsylvania, against Northern Lehigh—a team that had allowed just 47 points all season—Revis rushed for 91 yards and three TDs, the last one the game-winner. He returned another kickoff 89 yards for the score. He recovered a blocked field goal and ran 69 yards for another. He scored five touchdowns in all in Aliquippa's 32-27 win, intercepted a pass and returned it 33 yards, and even completed a pass, for 39 yards. Oh, and he had five solo tackles, too.

"He played like Jim Thorpe," Zmijanac said then. "That's who he was like. He was Jim Thorpe."

"I don't know how I did that," Revis said. "People don't really know the inside-inside: that week of school? I was sick. I didn't practice the whole week; I was throwing up and everything. I went to school a couple days and they would tell me to go home, I was so sick. Our game was on Saturday and it snowed, so they gave us an extra day and we played on Sunday. And Saturday's when I started feeling better. Took medicine and . . . I don't know. It was awesome."

Two days later, Aliquippa was due to play archrival Beaver Falls in basketball. "There is no way I'm going to miss that game," Revis had said on the football field after the state title win. It's Aliquippa

S. L. Price

tradition for its best footballers to finish the season and instantly suit up for basketball: Ty Law, Josh Lay, and Darrelle's uncle Sean had done it. Zmijanac had just stopped coaching double duty, was no longer in charge of hoops; it would've been no shock to see Revis and the rest of the footballers sit out. Problem was, Beaver Falls supporters and players counted on that, and took to the Internet to crow.

"They got on AOL, later in the night, talking trash: 'We heard your starters are not playing. We gonna crush y'all!'" Revis said. "So we were like, *We're going to surprise 'em.*" He made sure that everyone went to class on Tuesday, to make sure the best team was eligible. "Everybody was in on it . . . and we came."

The home crowd, grateful for his football performance and expecting little else, gave him a standing ovation during introductions. And despite just one basketball practice—his first time on court in seven months—Revis then scored 36 points to lead Aliquippa to an 86-82 overtime win; alone, in a span of forty-eight hours, he had scored 66 points, won a state title; he received another standing ovation at game's end. He had done everything a high school athlete could hope to do, and afterward had just one thought: *Man, I'm tired.* Everyone else around Revis, though, was smiling, hollering, declaring him the greatest Quip yet.

Such glory is plenty seductive. But like few others, Revis recognized early the trap of being a hometown god, had seen too many former Quip stars return, year after year, to the familiar streets because—even when it horrifies—there's no place like home.

"I remember telling my mom one time, 'We're going to make it out of here,'" Revis said. "Because those guys on the corner talk the same stuff—*I was this good in football or basketball!*—and have nothing to show for it. I didn't want to be in the same position, sitting somewhere and saying, 'I could've done this or that.' Well, why *didn't* you do it? Why *didn't* you prepare yourself?

"I was motivated then, I still am now: to get out of a place I didn't want to be stuck in forever. That's Aliquippa. I love it, I will always go back, but I always had a bigger picture of life and where I wanted to go and do. I knew what I wanted and was determined to get it. If I didn't? Then I'd done the best I could. But I told my mom: I am not going to be stuck on this corner."

When Revis graduated in 2004, everything about Aliquippa was getting older and, worse, smaller; the demographic death spiral now seemed unstoppable. Total population was heading south of 10,000, 25 percent were sixty-two or older, 22 percent were living below the poverty line, enrollment at the high school—amid what would become a 50 percent plummet over the decade—had shrunk to 465. The pool of boys showing up for football in late summer kept evaporating, from the edges in. The best eleven Quips could still compete with anyone at AAAA—let alone their own Class AA—but one ankle twist could spell disaster. Talk of dropping to Class A didn't spark the same scorn anymore.

Size matters, of course. A shrinking tax base means slashed public services, which leads to increased crime, declining schools, shoddiness in the public square. The Aliquippa school system, saddled with a special education population of 20 percent, regularly finished near the bottom of the state's rankings in math, science, reading, and writing. "It's a national issue, illiteracy in the black community, and it's alive and well here," said Dave Wytiaz, Aliquippa's superintendent of schools since 2010. "I could show you the data, the test scores; there's no question why we've struggled academically. That's one of the things I've been trying to change. It's a literacy factor.

"Looked at objectively: You can see a community like Aliquippa in its entirety going away, like the dinosaurs. I don't know if I can picture Aliquippa forty, fifty years from now. I love the community. Will I miss it once my mother is gone? I don't know. There's really nothing to hold me here. What I do now is look at these kids—white or black and they're seven and eight years old, truly innocent—facing conditions

S. L. Price

and situations where it's not their fault. It's not fair. A lot of the worst isn't seen—some things that'll turn your stomach: living conditions, everything. And at the same time there's this will, this . . ."

Wytiaz stopped, clapped his hands together, loudly, then gripped them tight. "*Together*," he said.

And more and more, the entity serving as glue and haven and rallying point was football. But even that was no guarantee of safety, no predictor of success: kids who studied hard and avoided trouble were destroyed by Aliquippa's random swipes; others immersed in crime became caring, productive citizens. "Half of them make it, and half of them don't—and you never know which half it's going to be," Zmijanac said. "It's joyful, and then it breaks your heart—all in the same day."

The stakes made football's usual my-way-or-the-highway mentality useless. Zmijanac figures he loses a good half-dozen players to the street each year, and has a long history of benching stars. But the team keeps an open door. "If he wants to come back, we'll always bring him in," Sherm McBride said. "No matter how many times they fall. Our job is not to give up on them."

And on the most fundamental level, the team kept people going. At the turn of the century, McBride and the rest of the coaching staff on the ground in town realized that too many kids, with nothing in the fridge at home, were coming to school on empty stomachs. Only the subsidized lunches—more than 80 percent of the students were eligible—kept some from dropping out altogether. Athletes were no different.

"The football field was my sanctuary: I didn't have to worry about nothing," said Willie Walker, a star lineman on Revis's 2003 state championship team. "They fed me. That was pretty much the biggest issue growing up, just being hungry. They fed me, showed me love, and gave me discipline. I got a friend Eric Veney, our Most Valuable Player in 2003, and never missed a day, not one, in all of high school. I missed a lot of days because I was doing other stuff for money and I said,

372

'Eric, why not?' He said, 'Because I wasn't going to miss no food.' So it wasn't just me.

"Then I'd go to practice—and Aliquippa's some tough football—and I just didn't have the energy. I went to Coach one day and said, 'I'm starving.' And Sherm, Coach Z, Peep Short went and got me some food. I'd be sitting on the sideline eating a sandwich. They were the greatest. They understood. And they helped you get through by making light of the situation."

Every Monday, Tuesday, and Wednesday after practice, the coaches handed each player a hoagie, chips, a cookie, a piece of fruit, and a drink, just to ensure they were eating at least once a day. Every Thursday, the Quarterback Club set up a spread and grilled hot dogs or hamburgers. Sometimes a parent would show up, grab a paper plate, and get in line. No one asked why.

Walker's situation was, if not typical, hardly unusual: father dead, mother on crack. When a parole violation landed her back in jail his junior year, Willie started dealing to keep himself and his thirteen-year-old sister, Kerrie, afloat in their Valley Terrace apartment. His cousins, the Dawkins boys up in Linmar, were in the business. Walker did and saw some "unhonorable things" over the fall and into the spring of '03, one of the worst being the moment when a colleague's mother approached and bought drugs from her own son.

"I was just lucky enough to keep my head and not let it suck me in," Walker said. "Because that's what Aliquippa does. It's a monster, and if you don't tame it, it'll just swallow you up."

Soon after his mom was locked up, he went to see Zmijanac and McBride to tell them he had to quit football; if he didn't land work, legal or illegal, he'd lose the apartment. The coaches loaded a small fridge with food and had it delivered to Valley Terrace, arranged to get him some odd jobs. When Willie started dealing, he didn't let them know. The combination kept his sister safe. He stayed in school, graduated, and enrolled at nearby California University of Pennsylvania. He spent five years there, played well enough to get himself a tryout with the Cleveland Browns, relieved to be away from his hometown—yet missing it awful.

"It definitely is a love-hate relationship," Walker said. "Aliquippa causes you a lot of pain. But to this day—and I've been up with the pros, I've played at college—there is *nothing* like Friday night at The Pit. When everyone is there it's the most beautiful thing Aliquippa has to offer, that Pit. It might as well be a monastery, because that's the best thing going for Aliquippa. Football brings people together.

"I've seen it. I've seen guys who hated each other . . . but then you start practicing together and playing, you can't help but depend on each other, and that camaraderie builds something that is unexplainable. I've seen guys try to rip each other's head off because they're from two different parts of this small town, but the hostility fades and the next thing you know these guys are sitting on the bench sharing a hoagie and tea."

No one mistakes this for a kumbaya-style unity. Walker and all the rest know that the town's divisions can still rear up and cripple or kill the best-intentioned man or plan. Pull some stunt to make the Quips lose? All-conference linebacker Mike Lowe blindsided an opponent, drawing the penalty that killed a score and Aliquippa's chance at a WPIAL title in '99; one teammate, Anthony Peluso, still can't forgive him. *"Mike Lowe,"* Peluso said, as if speaking about a nightmare. "The bad part is, I had to go to college with him: we both went to Edinboro, and I never talked to him. I'd see him and talk when in team meetings—but never went out of my way to go hang out with him. Prior to that, we were real good friends. But after that he was like a leper."

No, that football tightness, the *"Together"* that Superintendent Wytiaz describes, is more about a common defiance that remains despite the rotting beams and frayed cuffs, a core of resentment at a world that left them to die, an us-against-everyone chip that figures to teeter on the collective shoulder until the "us" shrinks to nothing. And even then, it will carry on.

"I still feel that sense of pride—even now, at Carnegie Mellon, one of the top engineering schools in the country, if not the world,"

Jon LeDonne said. "I walk in there the same way I walk into Aliquippa High or anywhere else: with my Aliquippa T-shirt and hat on, and sometimes people look at me, like, *Is this the janitor?* But I'm not going to change who I am or where I came from for anybody."

Oddly, the moment that may best encapsulate that pride happened nowhere near The Pit. It was expected by few and seen by even less. The school's track program, after all, had long been the sports scene's bastard child, used mainly to keep footballers lean and busy. Despite its storied athletic history and reputation for speed, Aliquippa had produced just three individual state track champs, all in field events—and none in the previous forty-nine years. This seems less stunning once you know that the Quips haven't had a track to run on since 1960.

That's when the new middle school was built on top of the hill in Plan 12, wiping away a classic cinder oval. So in cold weather, the relay team practices exchanges in school hallways, using the walls as starting blocks. When it warms, runners train in the parking lot. "Other than that? It's these hills," said Quips offensive coordinator Sherman McBride, who has doubled as head track coach since 2003. "They're running hills, running steps; I got a sled during football season that harnesses these kids. Put weights on the back of the harness. Using my football coaching to do whatever it takes."

So every Aliquippa meet is a road trip. Small rosters make competing well at dual—rather than multi-school invitational—meets all but impossible. Speedsters like Revis and Tommie Campbell made McBride's first squads a sprint threat, good for individual WPIAL golds and silvers. But with next to no participation in field events like pole vault, shot put, and javelin, the thought of a team title was usually absurd. And in 2005, especially, it looked all but impossible.

"That put me on the map," said McBride, who, as an Aliquippa football and basketball assistant and track head, has had a hand in thirty-two other team or individual WPIAL and state champions. None were more gratifying.

Academic troubles and distractions had trimmed McBride's twenty-five-man track roster down to eight in the spring of '05; well-funded schools with all-weather tracks often arrive at States with a squad of fifteen to twenty. By mid-May, when it came time to qualify for the WPIALs, the Aliquippa team had lost three more athletes. The five remaining rode a van three hours east to Shippensburg, Pennsylvania, and climbed out with just their spikes and a baton.

The first four were dependable. Tommie Campbell had emerged in Revis's wake as Aliquippa's "Next One," an all-state wide receiver/safety who won a WPIAL title in the relay in '04 and WPIAL gold in both the 100 and 200 meters just weeks before. Mike Washington and Campbell had finished 2-3 behind teammate Desmond Patrick in their sweep of the WPIAL 100 meters in '04. James Sims, having just finished second in the WPIAL 400 meters, was a solid middle-distance threat.

The question mark was senior long jumper Byron Wilson. At the WPIAL championships, he had finished second in the long jump with a leap of 20 feet, 3 inches. He entered the state championship seeded twenty-first out of a field of twenty-four. "We didn't know *how* he was going to do," said Washington, a wide receiver and defensive back who went on to play at the University of Hawaii. "He had leaping ability. But we'd practice out here on concrete in our cleats and Byron would sit there and chill sometimes. Sometimes he wouldn't even show up."

"I ain't going to lie," Campbell said. "Going in, wasn't nobody really thinking Byron could win State at long jump."

He had never quite fit in. Unlike his teammates, Wilson didn't play football. He was known for being alternately quiet and hot-tempered—and the fact that his stepfather, Andre Davis, was Aliquippa's assistant police chief only complicated things. "Quiet kid. Well dressed," Davis said. "Has an anger problem when somebody bothers him. My wife's family is from the North Side of Pittsburgh, but I've been with Byron since he was three. So he grew up and graduated from here—but somehow the guys down here never accepted him as an Aliquippian. Isn't that something?"

Wilson fouled on his first attempt. "It wasn't like Byron had technique," Washington said. "He was just *running*." Indeed, Wilson was starting his sprint toward the pit a yard too close, then chopping his steps to compensate, and taking off a yard short. His second try, 21 feet and change, was better. But on his third and final attempt, with Westmont Hilltop's Brad Kanuch leading the field with a jump of 21 feet, 10 inches, Byron took off. His strides were long; his steps dropped as if choreographed. He hit the board perfectly.

"The prettiest jump," McBride said. "He looked like he was just flying. He jumped 22 feet, 3¼ inches. Personal best."

The win gave Aliquippa the maximum 10 points. Suddenly, a team title was more than possible. Problem was, Campbell had been so ill the night before that McBride drove him to a Walmart for NyQuil, and when he woke that morning Tommie nearly emptied the bottle trying to calm his nerves. Now his stomach was imploding—and he had five races to run. He almost quit. "If it wasn't for Byron winning that long jump, I probably would've given up," Campbell said.

Instead, seventy-five minutes later Campbell survived the 100-meter and then the 200 semis. At 12:15 p.m., he ran 10.65 seconds to win the 100-meter final, and Patrick's fifth-place finish and Washington's eighth gave Aliquippa 24 points. Then, with Wilson running second leg and Campbell anchoring, the Quips won the 4x100 relay championship to give Aliquippa 34 points. Now Campbell's gut was heaving. And he had to finish at least second in the 200 for Aliquippa to win the team title.

At 2:13 p.m., as he was setting his feet in the blocks, Campbell dropped his head and vomited. The gun sounded, and he staggered through the first turn; for a moment it looked like he might finish last. But then, with the words *Come in second, we're going to win* pounding in his head, Campbell summoned one last burst. "I ended up catching everybody," he said, and he's just about right. Kanuch leaned in to finish first at 22.33 seconds, with Campbell a quarter-step behind at 22.42.

"If we had to run five more meters, he probably would've caught me," Kanuch said then.

Campbell's second place gave Aliquippa 9 points and the AA state title, 43-41 over Westmont Hilltop. His effort seemed the stuff of Revis-like legend: Ill and spent, Campbell had accounted for more than half of his team's total. He's still given credit for the town's biggest upset ever. But everyone close to the team knows better.

"Byron's really why we won gold," Washington said.

The news spread fast. And to anyone desperate for good news, it settled like a small blessing. "It just showed us—and everybody around us—that just because we don't have anything, you don't make excuses," Campbell said. "Ain't no excuses in *anything*. It's one of my best moments, sportswise. Something nobody ever can take away from us."

Later that afternoon, vacationing in North Carolina, Byron Wilson's mother and stepdad received a call from their son.

"He couldn't believe it: You could hear it in his voice," Andre Davis said. "It was gratifying. To us, it meant: *Thank God. Now he knows that he has a talent. He realizes if you put your mind to it, you can accomplish something.* And I'm sitting here, as we speak, looking at his medal awards in track. We have them hanging off the corner of our dresser mirror, right in our bedroom. All of 'em."

By then, Darrelle Revis was gone. He had learned to carry himself at a remove from Aliquippa's worst elements, had graduated healthy and whole. Now he'd just finished his freshman year at Pitt, his full scholarship already justified: started eleven games, made 49 tackles, picked off a couple of passes, and averaged 10 yards returning punts. Day by day that "corner" was growing smaller in the rearview.

Still, the town had a way of asserting itself. On a visit home from school his sophomore year with the Panthers, Revis drove up to Cureton's Mini Market in Plan II to buy the latest Air Jordans. On his way in that afternoon, he exchanged pleasantries with a Linmar lookout type standing by the door. "Yeah," the guy said, "I see you ballin'." The vibe couldn't have been friendlier.

Minutes later Revis walked out, new shoes in hand. His half-brother Jaquay showed up with Byron Wilson. Revis knew Wilson, had run track with him in '04. He also knew that in the few months after that miracle state championship and graduation in '05, Wilson's life had begun to slip. A scholarship offer to run track at California University of Pennsylvania, under Olympic great Roger Kingdom, had come and gone. "He never got in trouble in high school: goofy guy, wasn't even negative," Revis said. "But as soon as he got out of high school, something just flipped."

Wilson was never connected to the warring gangs that had infested Linmar and Griffith Heights. But his sharp tongue had inflamed hotheads on both sides, and without drugs or turf in the mix, his few friends in Griffith Heights had little interest in protecting him. "A lot of guys wanted to kill him," Revis said. "After it started Linmar was like, 'We're going to kill him': you'd hear that all the time."

Willie Walker, the Quips lineman, had long been close to Byron. But he was also related to the crew—the Dawkins family, led by Billy Love Dawkins—who along with Anthony "Ali" Dorsett had taken control of the drug operation in Linmar when Jamie Brown and Tusweet went to prison. Soon one of Willie's relatives warned him to distance himself from Byron. They wanted him dead, too.

Now Revis stood chatting outside Cureton's with Wilson and Jaquay. "This is how fast this happened: I'm talking to them for a second and this white car came up," Revis said. "Guy just came out the car and started shooting, pistol. I got a bag of shoes in my hand, I jump behind this car, and the other lookout guy—he didn't have no gun—now me and him are laying on the ground looking at each other, face-to-face. My heart is beating so fast, I'm like, *What is going on!?* and you just hear the gunshots: *Boom! Boom! Boom!*

"So now I'm looking at the lookout and he's acting, like, *Oh, shoot*—like he doesn't know what's going on. And I'm thinking, *You know what the hell's going on. . . .*"

Down on the pavement, Revis began fearing that his brother might be dead. "Then I hear the car pull off. Nobody got shot. Byron got up and started shooting. I'm shaking. My car was shot up; it had a couple bullets in it. I get in my car and get out of there. I'm like, *I don't need to be no witness.*

"You got to understand: That happens all the time; everybody who got shot, there's been people around. But that's the first time I saw somebody try to shoot somebody in broad daylight. Usually it happens at night. Aliquippa people, we always say, 'These guys see each other all day, be chillin' on the same corner, and then when night falls it's like . . . werewolves.' Like: *Why are you shooting at him? You were just hanging out with him four hours ago?!* It's crazy. We don't get it."

For Aliquippa people, though, such illogic can create a bond that only seems bewildering to outsiders. Revis was just a sophomore in November 2004, still building a rep, when he broke through to block a field goal attempt in Pitt's blowout win over the University of Connecticut. The ball dropped right in front of him, and a long, wide-open path to the end zone beckoned. It was a cornerback's dream play, as clear a star-making moment as football produces. But just as Revis was about to scoop it up, he noticed teammate Josh Lay closing in. Lay, a Quips star when Revis first arrived, was a Pitt senior now, playing the final home game of his college career.

Revis pulled back. "Josh, get it! Get it!" he said. "It's your day!"

The startled Lay did as he was told. And the two hometown boys raced 71 yards down the sideline, Revis yelling, "Reel it in for the touchdown!" Lay scored and Darrelle gave him a happy shove in the end zone. The moment didn't fit a sports culture given to me-first preening, but in Aliquippa they understood. No matter how much you want to flee the place, you never quite leave it behind.

Indeed, even with a twenty-five-mile cushion, Revis couldn't help but feel the latest odd vibes from back home. That same year, his mother, Diana Gilbert, lost her job at the Beaver County Jail. She had been working as a guard there—had been publicly honored, in fact, in 2002 for "outstanding achievement" in successfully transitioning from welfare to full-time work—always unarmed, no nightstick or Taser, and rarely seeing any trouble.

"Forty inmates to one guard in the pod," she said. "I had a man-down button. The rovers—a team of guys on the shift—would come and subdue the person." She pushed the button a few times, she says, but "I don't think I had any really bad situations."

In 2005, Gilbert resigned after her bosses alleged that she'd had a three-week-long sexual relationship with a male inmate. Despite the fact that such a relationship is a felony, the warden, William Schouppe, elected not to prosecute because the alleged convict would not cooperate, according to the report issued after an independent investigation in 2007. George David, the jail's chief of security from 1999 to 2008, called investigators' attention to Gilbert's resignation and "expressed concern that the matter was not pursued criminally." He repeated that concern during a meeting with investigators—with Schouppe present.

"She was a good guard, though," David said.

Oddly, considering that seven other jail officials were interviewed about the alleged affair, there's no evidence that Gilbert herself was approached by law enforcement or independent investigators to give her side of the story. Asked if David's assertion was untrue, she only said, "I want to say: what Georgie David put out, he could've handled it better.

"I've moved on past the situation. It made me a better person today. And I'm the last one standing, laughing."

Gilbert's affair was allegedly not the only one. The 141-page report included allegations of drug use and trafficking by guards, inmate abuse, one instance of falsifying documents in an attempt to get an inmate released, and the forced resignations of "several" guards for having sexual relations with prisoners. Despite his longtime authority over the guards there, David was not held responsible. In 2007, he ran for sheriff and won.

"Me and her got along very well," David said of Diana Gilbert. "She just messed up."

Years later, when David, as Beaver County sheriff, was led out of the courthouse in handcuffs to face eleven misdemeanor charges— including obstruction of justice and terroristic threats that involved allegedly menacing a reporter with a revolver and vowing to a campaign volunteer that he'd cut off his hands and eat them—Diana Gilbert tried not to gloat. David was cleared of all charges, but lost his job in the next election.

"Karma is a mother," Diana said. "The list of his manipulations is so long. He has done so much to so many—and he still hasn't really gotten what he deserved."

18

When the World Opens

Forever, the school had been a refuge. After the racial strain of the '60s and '70s had eased, once white flight had exhausted itself and Aliquippa High had become mostly black, the high school on top of the hill, The Pit, and the football team that called old and young to return each fall Friday gained an immunity to the town's most fearsome extremes. Teachers, parents, and administrators toiled to make that so. Kids and criminals, dealers and gangbangers knew that anyone crazy or dumb enough to bring the street to the school risked universal censure.

Because the school was the one last pipeline to a future. The school meant academic and athletic scholarships, football stardom, a job someday. The school was pride and hope, the last bit of it, and even the worst could sense that if that flickered out, the earth could split open and swallow the rest and nobody would give a good goddamn.

Still, by 2009 you could feel a cancer nibbling, insinuating itself closer to the now-consolidated Aliquippa Junior/Senior High than ever before. Once the exclusive domain of whites, the fabric of Plan 12 frayed as longtime families moved away and slumlords rented the old houses to the poor and transient and suspect. The random cruelties of Plan 11, the Funky Four Corners, and both sides of The Hill began to filter in.

"When we first moved up here, it was *love-ly*," said Tezmalita Baldwin, who, with Jonathan and his older sister, moved from Plan 11 into a house in Plan 12 in the early 2000s. "My friends used to laugh at me because I'd always say, 'When I move, I don't want any black neighbors.' Them being white, they used to be, like, 'You know, you're a jerk.' And I said, 'You don't understand, it's not that I'm a prejudiced person. I just know what'll happen.

"I wanted to be where it's comfortable and you don't have to worry about the loud stuff and trying to raise the kids right. I wanted to be where they weren't in situations that were sitting right at their front door. And a couple years later, I was like, *What the hell? This is done turned into Plan 11: They EVERYWHERE.* I don't have a problem with my own people, but my own people seem like they have a problem with themselves. Insecure ways. Everybody wants to prove a point."

Random gunfire became an everyday hazard. In September 2009, while students were meandering home from school, five shots blazed from a black Dodge Durango on the streets of Plan 12, aimed at one juvenile but instead hitting twenty-one-year-old Shawn Kimbrough just behind an ear. Junior Kevin Johnson, a wide receiver on the Quips football team who would receive a full scholarship to Howard University, found himself caught in the crossfire en route to practice.

"Someone drove past me and just started shooting recklessly," Johnson said. "I ran and felt the bullets go through my pants leg, and then as I got to the top of the hill, out of the way, I checked. Went to see that I didn't have no marks on my legs. I was happy. I smiled and I was, like . . . *Yes.*"

Thirty minutes later, a car parked near the market went up in flames. Two days later, about a block away, a thirty-six-year-old man took a bullet in the leg.

Indeed, with the carnage becoming so common only the most senseless loss could cut through. And more than any drive-by, nothing crystallized parental fear over the encroaching "street" more than one bizarre auto accident. On May 22 of that year, just before midnight, Aliquippa ninth-grader Tiquai Wallace, fourteen, died after a parked and revving car jumped the curb on Meadow Street and hit him on the sidewalk. Wallace pushed a sixteen-year-old girl out of harm's way as the car bore down, and was pinned against a building wall as its wheels spun.

"The car hit him straight-on," said Della Rae Campbell, Tommie's mother, who was walking with her boyfriend, Rick Hill, when they saw the accident unfold. "Doing at least fifteen, twenty miles an hour. And it hit him—*Boom!*—and bounced back. Then, *Boom!* again . . . bounce back. Then it hit him, *Boom!*—and that's when it stopped. The driver was unconscious. They was just coming from a party, the passenger was alert, and he just threw the car in gear. He was, like, 'What did I do?' I'm, like, 'What did you *DO*? You just caused this car to go up in this boy.'"

Immensely popular in Plan 12, the goofy and competitive Wallace was nicknamed "Goldie" for his light hair and "Wall Street" as a play on his last name. Della Rae and her boyfriend unpinned the boy from the wall.

"His face was, like, leaning this way on top of the hood of the car and his eyes just looked up at me," Della Rae said. "I told him, 'Tiquai, you know what to do, baby. You come from a praying family. Right now is your time to pray. . . .' He was looking at me, like, *Somebody help me.* He couldn't say nothing; it was all in his eyes. I see those eyes to this day."

The girl suffered a broken wrist. Wallace was pronounced dead at 12:40 a.m.

The driver was seventeen-year-old sophomore Chaquille Pratt, the leading scorer on Aliquippa High's basketball team and by all accounts the best player in Beaver County. Pratt jumped out of the car and ran; the next day, he turned himself in and was charged with homicide by vehicle while driving under the influence. Few condemned him outright:

Pratt's family had long been friends of Wallace's. Tiquai had played on Aliquippa's freshman team. The two were friends.

In the following days, those who knew both boys wondered about the invisible hands that gave alcohol and car keys to a seventeen-year-old, the invisible forces that had eroded community and family will to the point where it seemed normal for a fourteen-year-old to be hanging out on a dicey street at midnight. "That one-block section by the high school where Plan 12 Market is?" said Plan 12 resident Donald Walker two years later. "It's a drugfest."

And it was worse in 2009. Word spread that Tiquai's last utterance was, "I can't fight no more," and that resonated for years: another youth worn out way too soon.

Later that night, after the ambulance took his body away and the crowd cleared, Della Rae Campbell went back to the wall where Wallace died and spray-painted a few words: "Tiquai," and his nickname, "Wall St." In time, other words would go up, a makeshift memorial: "God has another angel . . . Gone but not forgotten . . . We love you."

Dwan Walker, thirty-four-year former Aliquippa High receiver, son of Chuckie and Chedda, knew Wallace. His sister, Diedre, had a daughter who was at Meadow Street that night and saw the boy fall. Dwan was holding the weeping teen at the funeral service at Plan 11's Church in the Round. Plans were percolating to retire the number Wallace wore for Little Quips football: it didn't seem enough. Dwan wanted to say something. Diedre all but forced Dwan to stand up and speak: "Go ahead," she said. "Get up there."

Diedre had always pushed him. He had often talked, half-jokingly, about becoming mayor of Aliquippa, but she always insisted it could be so. Walker heaved up his big frame, and trudged to the front of the church crowd. The room was filled with high school kids, and younger.

"Now you all realize you're not supermen or superwomen: death can reach out and touch you," Walker told them. "You're all too young for it to touch you this way, but you got to realize you're our dreams, our hopes, our future. We see something in y'all that you don't see in yourselves. And when you lose your lives, that's a dream unfulfilled, that's a goal not met.

"You see his mother up here crying? You see his dad and their family? Now you know death is bad. Death ain't a good thing, especially if you can prevent it. Especially if you can stop being stupid and following the lead of other people and stop being Indians and become chiefs. Stand up for yourselves. . . ."

He went on like that for some fifteen minutes. When he finished, many stood. Many applauded.

"They're ready for you now," Diedre told him after. "You should run."

And she kept telling Dwan that, too, over the following months, whenever he would come back from scouting city council meetings, discouraged because only five people showed up. She was younger than he but had always acted older, always told Dwan he could do or be anything he wished. She pushed him to play football, pushed him until he graduated college—and now D was at it again. *I'm telling you,* she said. *This town is ready.*

When Darrelle Revis walked off the field in Hershey, Pennsylvania on December 7, 2003, after nearly single-handedly leading Aliquippa High to its first state football championship in twelve years, he told his principal, "We did this for the school and the community." Zmijanac praised the players for their class and poise, said he was prouder of how they conducted themselves than of how they played. The tough and relentless team was everything the town likes to believe about itself. Its players have been dying ever since.

The funerals, the mourning mothers, came with numbing regularity in the decade after. Wide receiver Deon Johnson, shot in the eye during a gun battle in Linmar in 2005. Defensive end Jordan "Ricky" Cain, cut down at age twenty by thirty rounds from an AK-47 assault rifle in 2006. Backup running back Darius Odom, shot to death at twenty-one in 2009. Quarterback Stephen Hardy, killed in 2010 by seven gunshots at twenty-two. Then, in 2012, defensive end Marquay Riggins, shot dead in Linmar Terrace at the age of twenty-five, and defensive end Eddie Carter, taken by a weak heart at twenty-six.

"Seven of my high school teammates have died," Revis said. "One day I come here in the off-season and talk to 'em, and the next thing you know you're getting a phone call and the guy is dead. Which is sad."

But no death had more impact on Aliquippa than the death of running back James "Larry" Moon. No. 22 wasn't the most dependable player or even a starter; Zmijanac kicked him off the team during that championship season for some forgotten misdeed. But football kept Moon grounded like little else, and Zmijanac allowed him back for the title game in Hershey because he'd come begging for a second chance. It didn't hurt that Moon also averaged 4.5 yards a carry. "He was sincerely apologetic," Zmijanac said. "I don't know if it's like that everywhere: here it's because we really truly care about the kids. Do I want to win? Fuckin'-A right."

Midway through the following season, during a home game his senior year, Moon became so irate over his limited playing time that he walked off the field and into the locker room, removed his Aliquippa High uniform, got dressed and walked off up the hill. He didn't come back. And the further Moon got from the game, the more unstable he became.

Moon had a close friend, Tony Gaskins. They had grown up together in and around Griffith Heights, the cracked curbs of Plan 11, rose through every level—Termites to Midgets—of Little Quips football in the same cadre with Revis and Tommie Campbell. Gaskins worked the trenches as a center, mostly, played in spurts his sophomore year. Then he realized he could do better elsewhere.

"What stopped me playing was I seen how fast guys were making money out on the streets," Gaskins said. His dad, Johnny Gaskins, had worked thirty years at J&L, in the simmering filth of by-products. When Johnny lost his job in the mid-eighties, he had little to offer but stories about how the town and the mill and he had it all humming once. "My parents weren't as fortunate, and I couldn't get nice things," Tony said. "You know, Jordans tennis shoes or whatever? I just saw the opportunity to make some cash and get the things that I wanted. I knew it wasn't the right way. But I went along and did it anyway."

Gaskins dealt drugs for five years in Griffith Heights; girls treated him like some kind of star. He did two stints in juvenile detention, the second for hitting someone in the face with a brick. Late one day in November 2005, he and Moon started throwing dice up in Griffith Heights. Gaskins kept winning, and when he left three hours later he carried off nearly $200 of Moon's cash. He picked up his girlfriend, visited a friend, walked outside.

"Next thing I know somebody blindsided me," Gaskins said. "He suckerpunched real good, but it didn't knock me out so I was able to catch myself and realize what was going on. He started beating me on my head again, talking about, 'I want my f-ing money back, you're going to give me my f-ing money back. . . .'" Moon pulled out a handgun, a .22. Gaskins told him the cash was in the car.

"And I just turned around, grabbed him, took the gun, and shot him," Gaskins said.

Moon took two bullets in the chest and abdomen, but lived. Gaskins, then eighteen, was arrested on November 21, 2005, and spent the next eleven months in the Beaver County Jail. Eventually Moon recovered, if you can call it that.

"If I would've killed him," Gaskins said, "that girl would still be alive."

Four years later, at 3:15 a.m. on September 5, 2009, the now-twenty-four-year-old Moon shot his way into Diedre Walker's apartment, No. 301, A Building, in the Valley Terrace apartments on the hill behind the police station. The two had been seeing each other a few months, having met when Moon was serving time in a halfway house for shooting at his child's mother. Moon suspected Diedre, thirty-three, of seeing another man. That man was hiding in the closet when Moon shot Diedre three times in the head and chest.

D's youngest son, twelve-year-old Romerize "Ro-Ro" Owens, had been sleeping on the couch when the door gave way and Moon stepped in. He saw Moon shoot his mom. He saw Moon sit down on the couch, turn the gun on himself, and pull the trigger.

Police found Ro-Ro covered in blood. An officer took the boy down to the police station. By then, Dwan—phoned by a cousin, Aliquippa High assistant football coach Vashon Patrick—had raced to the apartment. Police stationed at the bullet-blasted door wouldn't let him enter. He saw his sister's feet. He could hear the paramedics, hovering above, saying, "Diedre, stay with us. . . ."

Dwan walked around for the next half hour numbed, hearing nothing. Then a cop told him that his sister was dead. "That's when the world opened up to me," he said.

Dwan saw his aunt Brenda collapse. Heard his twin brother Donald yelling at the crowd of friends in the Valley Terrace parking lot: "She's dead gone!" Saw his dad Chuckie on his knees, howling; saw his mom Chedda reaching out when they brought D out in a body bag. Saw the crowd mass toward the second body bag when they carried it out, trying to tear James Moon apart. They hadn't known till then that he was dead, too.

At the funeral home the following night, the family gathered. They rolled Diedre in on a gurney. Her eyes were open, the way they stayed open when she used to sleep. She had a bit of blood on her face, and Dwan took a napkin and wiped it off before his mom could see. Then his mom walked up and started shaking and screaming, "Why, D!"

"That's when I fell apart," Dwan said. "Because this is the first time she really let out a cry—like, angry. My sister always loved the underdogs. She always liked the runts nobody else wanted, the stray dogs: *I'm going to fix 'em, change 'em.* That's our curse. We think we can change people—and they end up changing you."

All that killing didn't happen in a vacuum. The *Beaver County Times* reported every detail, and the Pittsburgh newspapers and TV stations came out if the damage was notably bloody or strange, and now there was Revis, an instant, All-Pro force at cornerback with the New York Jets, spotlighting some of the town's grimmer corners in the New York media. Soon Aliquippa's narrative had changed, locked in: the town was about great football and terrible crime or, better yet, great football *in spite of* terrible crime, and the crumbling Pit and boarded-up windows along Franklin Avenue provided the perfect visuals for what, exactly, its kids were up against.

No resident much liked it, being reduced to a Jekyll-Hyde tale, but there was no denying the facts. The steel mill and sports success that defined Aliquippa in its prime had been supplanted by a new duality, and for proof one only had to look at former Quips football star Jeff Baldwin. One of his sons was serving twenty to forty years for the town's most notorious murder, and the other was a 6-foot-5 receiver with a 42-inch vertical, a 4.4 time in the 40, great hands, and no fear. Now Jonathan Baldwin was Aliquippa's "Next One."

Jonathan was just eleven in 2001 when his twenty-four-year-old half brother Jamie Brown was arrested for the murder of patrolman James Naim, and so skinny that he couldn't make weight for Little Quips football. Jonathan looked up to Jamie. "Every day we'd basically see each other, play PlayStation with the NFL," Brown said. "Some days, I'd be riding past, and he always had a basketball or football. He would be playing close to where I was going, and I'd say, 'Go back in that house. . . .'"

Once Jamie was charged, any hope of shielding Jonathan dissolved. The boy would go to school with the trial and the guilty verdict and the sentence unfolding, and kids sneered, "Your brother's a cop-killer!" Fists flew. Jonathan began dreaming of playing pro ball, making big money, and using it to fund the appeal that would spring Jamie from jail.

"He started taking things more seriously," said his mother, Tez Baldwin. "So it was a disaster that turned blessing because Jonathan always has said, 'I want to be able to help my brother.'"

Jonathan was nearly thirteen when, in May 2002, a jury convicted his half brother of murder in the third degree and he was sentenced—with extreme prejudice—by Common Pleas judge John D. McBride. He'll be eligible for parole in 2021. "I intend to oppose any parole being granted before the expiration of the maximum sentence," McBride told Brown at the Beaver courthouse.

His father also faced a stiff jail term. Seven months earlier, Jeff Baldwin had been arrested on charges of robbery and aggravated assault; police said that he tried to rob two undercover officers with a knife during a drug buy. "Mistaken identity," Jeff said. "Some guy took my ten dollars and drove off and I thought it was the same guy the next three days when I see him. Because it was dark and I wear glasses. And it was the wrong guy. Turned out to be the attorney general going on a drug bust. And they got me for forty-two months for ten dollars. Honestly."

That version gained no traction, but the idea that Jamie got framed became a constant of Aliquippa life. "A lot of people know it," Jonathan said, "but there ain't really nothing that we can do right now."

News accounts of the verdict detailed Naim's pre-death allegations of Aliquippa police involvement—disallowed by McBride and thus unheard by the jury—and Brown's attorneys and family all declared him railroaded. A columnist in the next morning's *Pittsburgh Post-Gazette* labeled the case "a first-degree miscalculation." Brown has proclaimed his innocence ever since.

"Innocent: a hundred percent," he said in prison in Marienville, Pennsylvania.

"Some of my family members say I should lie. But if it means lying to get parole, I'm not going to do it. I'd rather say nothing before I lie to a person. If they tell me I must admit and show remorse for a crime I didn't commit, I won't. If they want me to show remorse for things I *was* involved with up until I got arrested, I can do that. But I can't own up to things I didn't do."

Maybe this is to be expected. With his appeals all but exhausted, Brown's lone hope for freedom before 2021 depends on convincing the outside world that he suffered an injustice. He has spent the years since poring over evidence, searching for holes in the prosecution's case. Five weeks after telling police that she had "no doubt" that she saw Brown on Linmar at the time of the murder—and that she feared retribution—Monica Horton faxed in a recantation, saying that she "came to realize that I had just testified against the wrong person." In 2005, Rayetta Lee, who told police the morning of Naim's slaying about Brown's intention to kill a cop, sent a notarized statement to Judge McBride, the Pennsylvania governor and Department of Justice, and the *Allegheny Times* stating that her testimony was "all lies."

"Jamie Brown never told me anything at all about the alledged [sic] crime against Office Naim nor any of hist other criminal activities," Lee wrote. She then apologized to the Brown family. "What I hope to come out of this true confession is that one day soon Jamie Brown will be set free."

Regardless, others placed Jamie Brown on Linmar the day of the murder. His codefendant, Acey Taylor, told state police that he saw Naim shot dead and identified the shooter as Brown. Pennsylvania law does not allow statements of codefendants to be used against each other at trial, so the jury never heard that, either. And the state's star witness, Darnell Hines, declared that he was just 20 feet away when he saw Brown fire several shots at Naim.

With a mumbling delivery that signaled impairment or boredom, Hines hardly cut a commanding figure on the stand. A staff psychologist at Aliquippa Middle School placed his reading at a third-grade level, his IQ in the upper 70s. He changed his story multiple times early in the investigation; Hines first told police he heard and saw nothing that night, then he said he just heard the gunshots. After 26 days in custody—during which he complained that he was being pressured "to lie" and say he saw "them shoot that cop"—Hines flipped and said that he did see Brown fire repeatedly on Naim. He then passed a polygraph examination. A decade later, he hadn't changed his story.

"I don't care what anybody says," Hines said in 2012. "I saw it."

Still, many in Aliquippa and Beaver County remain uneasy with the verdict. The Naim case became the town's unhealed wound.

"And it's *going* to be a wound: a lot of people feel he didn't do it," said Beaver County detective—and Aliquippa High running backs coach—Timmie Patrick, who helped track and arrest Brown forty hours after the crime at his girlfriend's Hopewell apartment. It always struck Patrick as odd that, with police swarming like never before, the No. 1 suspect hadn't run. When the cops came for him, Jamie Brown was having sex.

"Whether we got the right guy?" said Andre Davis, longtime Aliquippa assistant police chief and police chief from 2011 to 2013. "I mean . . . only God knows."

"No," said Quips offensive coordinator Sherman McBride—no relation to the judge. "I think it was cops."

"I just know the wrong guy's in jail," said Aliquippa mayor Dwan Walker. "Now, [Brown] ain't no angel. But I've walked and talked to him. Dude's intelligent. He's not just going to say, 'Man, I'm going to kill me an officer and I'm going to stay home and let 'em catch me.' If I knew somebody said my name? I'm gone. I would've got the hell out of here."

Was Brown capable of shooting someone? Few doubt it. He carried three convictions for aggravated assault, two as a juvenile, the first when he was fourteen for shooting at a rival. But his knack for sidestepping hard time helped feed two other popular feelings: that Brown was too smart to commit such a crime, and that long-frustrated authorities were looking to nail him for anything. "Jamie Brown was involved with some real heavy hitters," said Peep Short. "He was doing well—as far as getting the drugs, distributing the drugs, and making money. Why would Jamie bring all this heat on himself? Kill a cop? Nah: he ain't stupid. He was doing too well to do that."

Notwithstanding Judge McBride's vow, the trial's divided outcome ensured that conspiracy theorists would never lack for ammunition. Acey Taylor, described by the prosecution as Brown's "lookout and cheerleader," was acquitted on charges of murder and conspiracy. Although Brown was depicted during the two-week trial as a police-hater aiming to execute an officer to send a message, the jury found him not guilty of first-degree murder and conspiracy. Though Naim was shot from behind by someone lying in wait, after twenty-five hours of deliberation the jury could not bring itself to declare premeditation. By definition, "third-degree murder" is a random act of recklessness or maliciousness.

"Can I rationally explain their verdict to you?" Judge McBride said of the jury at Brown's sentencing. "No, I cannot, nor would I attempt to. In short, they did perform their duty as jurors."

Jeff Baldwin claims that his three-and-a-half-year stint at the state prison in Somerset was "great for me": he learned to be patient, to care for other people, to value life. But it did have its downside. He missed Jonathan's first two football seasons—and not just at Aliquippa High. Period. Jonathan never played a proper game in pads until 2004, the fall of his freshman year. Until then, all the boy's time and effort had pointed to a basketball career. Tez wouldn't let Jonathan lift a weight, but drilled him endlessly: push-ups on a pair of chairs; up and down the stairs, two steps at a time on his tiptoes, little sister on his back.

Jeff would call from prison: "Make sure you jump your rope!" Jonathan jumped.

It couldn't be helped: father's reputation filtered down to son. But if one person made mention of Jeff being a jailbird, too many others had their own family brushes with the law. So mostly they'd talk of how they'd seen Jeff play in his prime. Crime was one thing. But taking someone apart because they weren't half the player some relative was? Fair game.

"Yeah, you don't want to stop the tradition in your family and then hear, 'Well, he's nothing like his father,' or 'He's nothing like his cousin,'" Jonathan said. "That makes you play even harder. You don't want to stop the family tradition of someone who was a stud.

"Growing up in Aliquippa, everybody's competing. Everybody has to be the best. It feels like, if you lose, *everybody* talks about it: People gettin' on you. So you never want to lose because you don't want to have to go through that."

Soon enough, Jeff, directing strategy from prison, had Jonathan going to football camps, learning and showing off skills. It became clear that he'd soon have to make a choice. Basketball would remain a factor through high school—he'd get plenty of Division I-A scholarship offers for hoops—but by the time Jeff got out, everyone around Jonathan had it figured: the NBA was stacked with 6-foot-4 leapers. But the NFL? Football was his best chance to get paid.

"I started to get notoriety in football," Jonathan said. "Before you know it, I was sitting in an office with my parents and Coach Z and Sherman, and they were telling me, 'In football there's not ten people in the country who can do what you can. But in basketball you go to New York and there's twenty-five people who can do what you can.' When I thought about it like that and talked to my parents later on, I was like, 'They're right.' Obviously it was the best choice for me."

Tez and Jeff finally married in August 2005. Tez didn't think about leaving when he was locked up. "The way I was raised, you never kick somebody when they're down," Tez said. "If I was to walk away, it would be when he's at his strongest point—not his weakest. And when I say it was terrible? It was terrible. But I just couldn't see myself walking away. . . .

"And that's what Jonathan wants. He has it stuck in his head that we're going to be together forever—regardless of whether I'm happy or Jeff's happy. That's what makes him happy. We've had some down periods even once Jeff came home and I was, like, 'I want out.' And Jonathan just wasn't having it. Like: 'You got to work this out. You're my mom, I love you; that's my dad, I love my dad. . . .' He has a different kind of love for his dad."

It all helped. Jonathan became an all-state basketball star, a state titlist in the 4x100 relay, and one of the nation's top-rated high school receivers, ending his Aliquippa career in one of Western Pennsylvania football's greatest shootouts. In any other game, Baldwin's 180 receiving yards and three touchdowns would've been legendary; in Aliquippa's

2007 AA semifinal against Jeannette, it wasn't even close to good enough. With perhaps the greatest individual performance in WPIAL history, Jeannette quarterback Terrelle Pryor—who went on to star at Ohio State—rushed for five touchdowns and threw for two more; he totaled 421 total yards by himself, and also forced two fumbles as a defensive back, in leading Jeannette to a 70-48 win. No two WPIAL teams had ever combined to score more.

Jonathan followed his dad's trail to Pitt, caught 57 passes for 1,111 yards and eight touchdowns as a sophomore. Off-field life proved tougher: groping a girl's buttocks on a bus landed him in court for indecent assault; the charges were dismissed. And after his production dipped during his junior year, Jonathan fired off a bratty—and hastily recanted—text about the Pitt coaches' play-calling, speculating that they were "purposely trying to disrupt my draft stock."

By Aliquippa standards, such incidents were decidedly small-bore. If anything, believing that his brother and dad had been railroaded by police made Jonathan less willing to court trouble. "That's why, when I'm in Aliquippa—I have a son now—I really don't go out," Jonathan said in 2011. "I just stay in the house and try and be with my son as much as possible. Because you're walking that tightrope. Sometimes people may get jealous. You don't know how people are going to react. Very seldom you see me walking."

His son, Jaden, lived then in Linmar with his mother. Jonathan already had him "prepped and ready": Whenever he called "down-set," the boy would get into a wide receiver stance. When Jonathan called "hut," he would know to run. Still, sending Jaden outside made him nervous.

"You don't know," Jonathan said. "When people are mad, they don't care what's going on. If they're shooting in broad daylight and your kids are out they might get hit by a stray bullet. You don't want to be—it's God's will, either way—playing football and your son is outside playing and you get called that your son got shot. Now what?"

19

Iron Buttons

*N*ow *what?* More than ever, that is the Aliquippa question.

The old ones worry. Not about themselves: They had their run, the men who returned from World War II into a world of high wages and uniquely leveraged union muscle, the women who swept the porches of homes their forebears could never buy. What's lost can't hurt them now. No, the old ones worry about their kids who are well beyond being kids, the ones whose drifting lives and careers over the last thirty years reveal just how vital the vanished factory, mill, and mine were to America's idea of itself.

Nobody grew up with the dream to work such jobs. They were filthy, boring, exhausting grinds, a drain on health, a daily assault on the senses. Yet the value of a J&L becomes more apparent with each fleeing decade, even as the idea that the old industrial model can never return hardens into orthodoxy. Technology made manpower quaint: In 1980, it took 399,000 American steelworkers to produce 101 million tons of raw steel; in 2011, 97,000 American steelworkers produced 86.2

million tons. Manufacturing's share of U.S. Gross Domestic Product is now half—22.7 percent to 11.9 percent—of what it was in 1970. The remaining "blue-collar" jobs require more education, training, computer skills. The days when a thick accent and a set of calloused hands were enough to find high-paying, secure employment are history.

"Those types of jobs—if they exist at all—are a much smaller part of the economy," said University of Pittsburgh labor economist Chris Briem. "And those jobs aren't coming back."

Still, it's not enough to say that American big industry built the bridges and rails that propelled the greatest economy in history, the tanks and battleships that beat Hitler and Tojo and won the Cold War, the skyscrapers that signified modern ambition and wealth. The more mundane fact is that places like J&L also served as social catch basins, places where those lacking academic skill or interest could fix a toe into the American flank and start climbing. J&L gave the Aliquippa working-man dignity—not to mention income enough to own a home, raise a family, take a paid vacation—and thus a stake, like that engendered in the rich and educated, in keeping the entire system humming.

Today's low-wage, low-security service industry jobs offer little choice—much less pride—to the unskilled. The forked road offering careers in cut potatoes or crack, McDonald's or a meth lab, have led an increasingly dispossessed lower middle class off the American grid and into the wild. "I always think about: if the mill was still going my second son would've been satisfied," said Gilda Letteri. Her son, Bobby, born in '59, wasn't the student that his siblings were. He tried college for two years, at nearby California University of Pennsylvania, worked J&L for one, 1979, and then headed up to Bucks County. He's in his mid-fifties now, and still renting.

"There was nothing wrong with him, but he was one of these young boys who was very impetuous and did everything he wasn't sup-posed to do," she said. "And today—I still wish—if the mill was there, or some sort of factory, he would be fine. He's a carpenter now.

"Last year he didn't work very much at all. This year he's working. He's building a house with a contract, but no stability for him. I'm always on his back about this. There's another young man on our street, and the mother always tells me—now he has a job, he's working here and lives with his parents, but he's also fifty-two—the same thing. If J&L was here, he would have his own home and be different than he is now."

Perhaps. But for decades now, there has been an oft-floated notion that most Americans—no matter their lack of skill—simply find menial labor beneath them. Hence the need for, say, illegal Mexican immigrants: *They do the jobs no one else will.* That this is actually a logical by-product of the American Dream doesn't make it easy to discuss on the stump or at 4th of July celebrations. Who wants to be the lone voice saying that the nation's hallowed vision of itself, almost by design, makes each succeeding generation more prideful, less resourceful, lazier?

"You came to the country with a brown bag with your clothes in it, and the only thing you had in terms of asset was your body," Beaver County developer C. J. "Chuck" Betters said. "It's so vivid to me: each generation wanted to make it better for their kid, to the point where we're sitting today—in a country that doesn't know how to use a shovel. Or want to.

"I'm more of that generation than today's. I dug so many ditches with picks and shovels that people wouldn't believe it. I know how long it would take me to dig a ditch, put a gas line in. I look at guys with a shovel today, I want to fuckin' pick it up and beat 'em over the head with it."

Even Aliquippa's ironfisted avatar of the glory days, Mike Ditka— secure in his restaurants and TV work—admits to helplessness. Long before his own grown sons, Mike and Mark, began piling up drunk-driving arrests in Illinois, he'd sensed them being buffeted by the values of a flashy, leverage-as-you-go economy. "I've had a big house and a lot of cars, have a few hobbies like that," Ditka said. "But the only time you're a success is when you're happy and know it. I'm pretty happy right now. I don't owe anybody anything. Our country is stupid because of the credit-card thing and if you get caught up in that shit, you're going to die. I've got kids that're caught up in it up to their ass.

"Debt, mortgages: everybody has to have one. I mean, that was the American Dream: put so much down, buy a house. Hello! After a while some guy's unemployed. It's not his fault all the time, but there's no sympathy from society. You're caught in a trap and you can't get out and it's terrible."

Still, Ditka and his generation can't do much about it now. They're on the fade, losing day by day the energy needed to hector, guide, take a public stand. Once, in 2004, Ditka mulled running for the U.S. Senate in Illinois. That kind of ambition is gone. He works TV mostly, bringing gruff gravitas to NFL broadcasts, but even his famed competitive fire is flickering.

Soon Ditka's ninety-three-year-old mother, Charlotte, would be moving out of the old house in Linmar and into a nursing home in Beaver. Soon, she would die. "You see her getting all the IV shit and all that: it's terrible," he said. Then he shrugged. "But I'm going to go through it, too."

Such is the mean secret of progress: it depends on the self-delusion of youth, the sense that, somehow, all striving and achievement—any kind of victory—will somehow hold death at bay. Once that goes and the truth is accepted, there's no stopping the air from leaving the balloon. The only shock is that it doesn't pain Iron Mike to admit as much: to admit he doesn't care about winning anymore.

"You know what it is? It's apathy," Ditka said. "You don't give a shit. Because it's not going to define me at this point. When I was growing up, I thought it would define me. I don't compete on TV to be the best; I say what I think I should say and that's it.

"Up until a couple years ago I was a pretty good golfer, and I was really competitive; I really wanted to win. But now? I want to play. If I win, fine; if I don't, that's fine, too. I play cards: same thing. It doesn't bother me a bit. I laugh now. I don't miss it. You'll find out. When apathy sets in, you don't give a damn. And it's setting in."

A company town without a company is like a man past his prime; both become hollowed, age faster, without the regenerating charge of daily purpose. Such has been the Rust Belt affliction for the past forty years, but large urban economies like Pittsburgh at least had the scale and diversified infrastructure that help make reinvention possible. "Aliquippa's in a weird place: it's not the center of the region, it's not the city, it's not quite rural," Briem said. "What is the competitiveness of a lot of towns that used to have a reason for being that don't anymore?"

Ditka's heirs, meanwhile, have scattered. Unlike Iron Mike, they left Aliquippa unburdened by golden-age memories; the town gave them toughness and fuel, they know, but ultimately it was a place to escape. Sean Gilbert lives in North Carolina, Ty Law in Florida, and Darrelle Revis in New Jersey and Florida in the off-season. They come back for weekends here and there to see family, to show that they haven't forgotten their roots, to give kids a chance to see a local boy made good.

All have tried giving back. Gilbert started a nonprofit counseling program and construction of a Plan 11 church; Law funded a Head Start program in Plan 12, and ran a charity golf tournament and basketball game to raise cash for school supplies and computers; Revis holds an occasional football camp, funneled NFL-style Nike uniforms to the Quips program. But all are wary of pleas to refurbish The Pit or simply drop masses of money on the town because, first of all, no one knows whether Aliquippa High and the need for a football field will even exist in five years. And then, there is the largest unspoken question: *How much, really, do I owe this place?*

Years ago, Law was stopped by an elderly lady. "What are you going to do for us here in Aliquippa, Mr. Law?" she said. "What are you going to do?"

If he had known the woman, Law says, he would've lit into her. "You look at it," he said. "There wasn't nobody out there running with me at midnight, there wasn't nobody dealing with what I was dealing with at home. So I don't owe you anything. I owe my grandfather. I owe my mom. Because if I was out there selling drugs and end up going to jail, what are you going to do? You going to come bail me out?

"Unfortunately, that's the mentality for some because a select few of us made it. Even if we put all our money together, all our contracts, we cannot change the facts. We can make it look nice; we can probably go out and fix up a hundred homes around there to where they look real nice and pristine. But that's not going to change the environment with the drugs and the fact that there ain't no jobs. How you going to maintain it? It's going to get right back like it was before we fixed it up."

Revis, for his part, can't say enough about his hometown; "I love it to the utmost," he said. But even "utmost" has its limits. He's got a son and a daughter being raised in Beaver Falls, and the boy is another athlete in the making. Revis has no desire to send his son back home, for seasoning or grit or anything else. "I don't know about that," he said. "I don't want him in Aliquippa. If Aliquippa can pick their school up, and their coaches, and move somewhere else? Yes."

But that is impossible. Town and team are going nowhere. Any salvation, it seems, will have to be delivered by those left behind.

The first weeks after James Moon killed D were hell. Dwan Walker careened about the emptied streets, hoping that someone would cut him off so he could slam the brakes and jump out and hit flesh, bone, feel the blood on his fists. He woke each night at the hour Diedre died, begged God to bring his sister back. *For a second, a minute: Please. Just five minutes with her again.* Chedda, worried, made him come by the house. His dad kept saying he heard D's voice. "Sit quiet, son," Chuckie said. "You don't hear it because you still got a lot of pain."

In November 2009, two months later, Dwan started his campaign for mayor, knocking on doors. Primary Day was still sixteen months away, but he'd finish a shift at FedEx, tug on his Quips football sweatshirt, walk until the day turned dark. He talked about his vision, passed out T-shirts: "Remember What Aliquippa Was, Knowing What Aliquippa Can Be."

And he heard her voice clear, stepping off porches, trudging Aliquippa's streets for twenty-two weeks straight in winter's biting cold and the slow-coming spring. He knocked on every door in every Aliquippa neighborhood—5,100 homes in all, even in West, his opponent's bastion. "I told you!" Dwan heard her say after each good contact. He answered by pointing at the sky.

Word filtered back to Anthony Battalini, Aliquippa's mayor since 2003, that the kid was hustling hard. Walker was thirty-four, an ex-Quips player with no political experience. Battalini was a three-term incumbent backed by the local Democratic kingmaker, Salt Smith—former real estate agent and black Aliquippa's most feared and connected voice, a thirty-two-year member of the Board of Education, the longtime general manager of the Municipal Water Authority, and chair of the Aliquippa Democratic Committee. Smith controlled jobs and pols alike, and Democratic governors and senators had long depended on him to deliver the town's black vote. Aliquippa had been a Democratic stronghold since the 1930s. Nobody had ever challenged the machine's mayoral choice—and won.

It so happened that Smith's property backed up against Chuckie and Chedda's place: in the 1980s, Smith would invite the Walkers over for barbecues. His parents urged Dwan to pay respects. The meeting didn't go well. In Walker's version, Smith told him that he had no chance of beating the machine, that he should wait his turn, work an election or two and build political capital, and only then would he deign to "give me a seat."

"And I said, 'I don't want you to *give* me anything, Mr. Smith, because I don't want your hands in my pocket," Walker recalled. "'I don't want nobody to say I owed 'em anything, because that's how y'all work.

If I owe you something, you're always going to have that over my head: 'Man, you wasn't *nothing* until I put you on this ticket!'

"When I said that to him, he said, 'Mr. Walker? You can't win. We're a machine. We do it right.'"

Smith says he was hardly that emphatic. He says he merely told Dwan to speak to his own cousin, Aliquippa city councilwoman Lisa Walker, and learn the system: help those who came before you, and maybe you'll get a shot. "The selfish person's out there supporting himself," Smith said. "People get involved, they work the election, next election there's an opening: Who're you going to turn to? The ones who showed the energy. That's the way it happens."

Neither man budged. At the end Dwan shook Salt's hand and thanked him. "Okay, Mr. Smith," he said. "You're going to regret telling an Aliquippa kid he can't win."

More than a year later, Walker still hadn't backed down. He convinced his twin brother Donald and a friend, Mark Delon, to run for city council on his "One Aliquippa" ticket; it didn't seem to matter that none of them knew how to write a grant application or break down a city budget ("They're so fucking green," said developer Chuck Betters, "that you could dig a little hole, stick 'em in, and they'd start growing").

Fans saw Walker screaming in the stands at football games. Most knew his story: dead and gone, D was still working for him. His love for the place that he had every right to hate seemed so obvious that it short-circuited any charge of callowness. Who could question his sincerity? The downtown had flooded twice in the past four years. The mayor's job paid $175.42 a month, after taxes, with no health benefits. Dwan Walker was gaining traction.

In truth, that shouldn't have been surprising. If there was one thing that Aliquippa still could be counted on to produce—and respond to—it was an against-all-odds tale. Jesse Steinfeld, James Frank, Ditka,

Ty Law, and Darrelle Revis were stories the battered town kept telling itself for comfort, inspiration; Dwan Walker was just tapping in. *You're going to regret telling an Aliquippa kid he can't win.* And sure enough, just then, yet another local was pulling off an unlikely victory.

They always speak of "The Next One" in Aliquippa, but the position also casts a shadow. Because for every alum like Revis there's a Monroe Weekley—some gun-toting wraith whose talent isn't enough to stop him from killing or being killed, fast or slow: the next waste. The next, *Man, that's pathetic.* And by 2008, Tommie Campbell had just about completed his jump from "One" to the other.

Of all of the great athletes on that '03 state championship team, he might've been the most gifted. But Campbell flunked out of Pitt, lost a full scholarship after two years of missed classes, practices, and football meetings. His last-chance meeting with head coach Dave Wannstedt? Didn't show; didn't even call. Campbell had narcolepsy, tended to skip his medication, and never saw why the world couldn't soften up its pesky rules, schedules, commitments. "Like a lost little boy," he said. "I never had a plan. I just thought things were going to be handed to me."

Such entitlement was rarely discussed on the "Next One" side of the divide. If football presented Aliquippa's flashiest alternative to drug dealing and led to scholarships, too often its players went off ill-prepared and returned without a diploma—never mind a pro contract. Athletics might get them out, shield them for a time, but higher competition or injury exposed any weakness. And, paradoxically, successes like Ty Law and Revis could discourage those bumping up against the limits of their own skill or desire. Once a means to escape the steelworker's fate, football had evolved into an end in itself, a promise of riches and fame that made a mere bachelor's degree seem shabby.

"Some of our guys have been struggling," Wytiaz said. "Everybody can't play at Pitt, Penn State, Notre Dame, but you may be able to play at Grove City or Westminster. But they go to these places, and quite honestly it's a step down athletically—and they can't handle it. The kids are bright enough. There's nothing wrong with going to Westminster, Slippery Rock, Indiana University of Pennsylvania. Get your education."

Still, if it doesn't work out, Aliquippa—and its troubles—always welcomes them home. Josh Lay, the gifted Aliquippa quarterback who manned Pitt's other cornerback slot during Revis's sophomore season, the senior Revis escorted into the end zone after his blocked kick, had short stints with the New Orleans Saints and St. Louis Rams, played semipro ball, and then, in March 2011, was arrested after being stopped near Sixth Avenue in a car carrying a digital scale and thirty-one bags of marijuana. "He's as good or better than Revis," said longtime Quips booster John Evasovich. "But no work ethic. Had all the athletic talent you could possibly have. All of a sudden he doesn't have a job because he doesn't have a degree . . . so what do you do? There ain't no mill. So you sell shit."

The guessing game on who will end up good or bad starts early ("I guarantee you: next year three of these kids will be in jail," Evasovich said, scanning a Quips roster; "I just don't know which three") and can finish late. Some surefire successes curdle: Jonathan Baldwin became a first-round draft pick in 2011, signed a $7.5 million contract with the Kansas City Chiefs with a signing bonus of $3.9 million, but was out of the league within three years because of a lax work ethic, inconsistency, injury. And some surefire failures, at the last minute, reverse course.

After sleepwalking his way out of Pitt, Tommie Campbell played the '07 season at Division II Edinboro and then washed out of there, too, all the way back to his mother's couch in Plan 12. He started smoking, drinking, dropped twenty-five pounds, frittered away a year on PlayStation. One night Tommie rushed in, shaken from a run up to Valley Terrace. "He was over some girl's house and they stuck a gun to his head," said his mother, Della Rae. "They thought Tommie had money and wanted to stick him up because he was delivering, you know, back and forth. They put the gun to his head and it jammed. Tommie had tears coming down his face. He just knew that was going to be his last thing, right there."

Campbell won't confirm the details, but admitted, "It was a real scary moment, man. If that had never happened to me, I probably wouldn't be where I am today. I got scared straight, you could say."

No. Fear was only half the antidote. Next came shame: he was twenty-two years old with two sons, no future, no job. He tried to enlist in the Marines, but a slew of unpaid speeding tickets—$2,000 worth—ended that. He stayed on the couch, scared to go out and face people asking what the hell he was doing with his life.

A girlfriend's connection finally landed Campbell one of the only positions he was qualified for: janitor, at Pittsburgh International Airport's USAir terminal. His mom had been a janitor once, at Aliquippa Hospital: Tommie used to vow that he'd never clean up people's trash. But now, for the next six months he worked graveyard shift—changing can liners, scraping gum off the floors with a blade, spraying blue chemicals into toilets littered with piss and pubes and streaks of shit. Every two weeks, he took home about $460.

Every day men and women hurried past him without a second look, on their way to homes, careers, respect. You'd think his worst nightmare would be the sight of a pro football player—the realization of what Tommie, once, was sure he would be—walking past. "I saw something worse: one of my ex-teammates from the University of Pittsburgh coming through," Campbell said. That evening, he was pushing his cleaning cart in the terminal when he saw defensive back Elijah Fields approaching in his team-issued sweats. Tommie wanted to disappear. Fields saw him.

"It made me feel little," Campbell said. "I was real skinny and everything, and it made me feel little just as a human being. He came over to talk to me for a brief second. I told him I was proud for him because he was doing the right thing at the time. I told him: 'Listen, if you don't take care of what you need to take care of, you're going to be right here, too. . . .'"

Fields didn't listen. By 2010, he had been kicked off the team and out of Pitt in a haze of indolence and pot smoke. The chance meeting has lingered with Campbell ever since. "There's a lot of time to think while you're mopping that floor," he said. "Lot of time to think about what you could've done better—and if you'll ever get a chance again, what're you going to do?"

His daily round was filled with cautionary tales: Mom, Rick Hill, Peep Short, so many football teammates. Then there was Byron Wilson, the long jumper on that miracle track team of '05, son of the Aliquippa police chief. Two years after his title-clinching long jump, Byron plea-bargained a fifteen-month sentence after pulling up next to his Linmar enemies in a car and opening fire. In August 2009, while Tommie Campbell was gathering trash, Wilson stepped into the Hollywood Lounge during a Linmar birthday party and wounded two men with a .22-caliber pistol, got two years in prison.

Finally, Tommie Campbell reached out to Larry Dorsch—a white real estate developer living in whiter, quieter Cranberry Township whom he'd met just before going to Pitt. Dorsch put Campbell to work on one of his job sites, spreading mulch, stocking shelves at a local supermarket, gave him money to eat. But Dorsch also knew that any comeback had to start instantly. He invited Tommie to move in with him, his wife, and her eighty-three-year-old mother. Della didn't like it; she wanted her son to stay home. But Tommie knew this was his last chance.

He stayed there a year and a half. The Dorsches laughed when their neighbors did double takes at seeing a young black man come and go. They started calling Tommie, after the old TV comedy series, "The Fresh Prince of Cranberry." He took to calling Dorsch "Pops."

"He helped me in every aspect possible," Tommie said. "He is the father figure to me. I have a stepdad and he was always there for me, but everybody had a disagreement. Larry never gave up on me. If I was willing to do it, he would always help me try."

The cigarettes disappeared. The first time Campbell tried a timed, 40-yard dash he ran a 4.70—good for bragging at the Hollywood Lounge and little else. Then the meals and sleep and work kicked in, and the pounds began to stick. Campbell paid off the speeding tickets. He convinced a skeptical defensive coordinator at California University of Pennsylvania to give him a shot. Everybody in Western Pennsylvania knew what a motivated Tommie, back up to 220 pounds now, could do.

Campbell turned twenty-three during the 2010 season—his final year of college eligibility—that he played cornerback for the Vulcans, suddenly the old guy. He started four games, appeared in all twelve, finished with 29 tackles. He showed up for meetings. He did not over-sleep. He made sure to take his medication. "I quit putting blame on everything around me," Campbell said. "Because in reality it's your choice. You have a choice to get up in the morning or not. You have a choice to work out or not. You have a choice to go to class or not. You're reflected by the choices you make and I was making no choices at all—by sleeping. That's even worse. That was basically saying: *Bump you. I don't care what you all say or do, I'm going to do what I want to do, and what I want to do is go to sleep. Bump everybody.*"

But at Cal U and beyond, Tommie wanted to run again. He went to the Cactus Bowl All-Star Game, lit up NFL scouts' eyes and stop-watches with his 40-yard times of 4.33 and 4.31. Suddenly Campbell's past and age didn't matter. The Tennessee Titans drafted him No. 251, the fourth-to-last pick in the 2011 draft. A 90-yard, game-winning interception for a touchdown against the Bears in preseason sealed his rise. He signed a four-year, $2.09 million contract. He'd made the league at last.

Campbell played three years in Tennessee, another in Jacksonville, mostly on special teams and as a backup defensive back, countering niggling injuries with preseason heroics—an 84-yard kick return here, a 65-yard punt return there. He was never a starter, never broke out as a star. But he became a steady, tough, fully awake professional. That's more than most can say.

When he walks through an airport these days, Pittsburgh or any other, Campbell carries a fine bag, and the clothes inside are expensive and clean. He eyes the men pushing carts, the men with short brooms and dustpans. He may not say a word, but when he stops at a urinal and sees the blue water, it comes back: Tommie can smell his past. He used to be so careless with trash, leaving cups and wrappers where they'd fallen. Now, no matter how long it takes, he leaves no trace of himself behind.

On June 6, 2010, sixty-six years after D-Day knocked Aliquippa High's first champions off the front page, the *Pittsburgh Post-Gazette* ran a piece about historical salvagers picking through the dusty, soon-to-be-demolished offices of the old J&L tin mill. After reaching the third floor, they pushed open a door, and the day crashed in before them. "Last one to die," read a scrawl of white graffiti on one wood-paneled wall, "please turn out the Light."

Those offices are gone now. What remains on the seven-and-a-half-mile stretch that was once J&L is the U.S. Gypsum plant. employing 120; a building products concern, employing 72; the fifteen-year-old Beaver County Jail; and a few other minor industries. What remains, too, is sixty-five-year-old C. J. Betters, who controls most of the stricken land and whose son Charles II—armed with a $37,000 pistol-like instrument that can read the metal composition in the stingiest clod of earth—helped find a way to wring more cash out of it when no one else could. In nearly a century of operation, the blast and basic oxygen furnaces had produced some 200 million tons of slag—composed mostly of the residual limestone or dolomite used to purify iron—and dumped it into any available lot, crack, or stream. Half is recoverable. The other half lies under the Ohio River.

Betters' first foray on the site, a purchase of 1,200 acres in 1993, cost him $1.25 million; he meant to build a casino until, two years later, Pennsylvania lawmakers outlawed riverboat gambling. Slag was not even Plan C. But early efforts there netted $3.50 a ton and helped bankroll the scrubbing of the U.S. Gypsum parcel, and Betters figures that in the twenty years since, Beaver County Slag, Inc., has exhumed nearly twenty million tons. Hand-tooled, air-shattering, Rube-Goldberg-like machines sift and sort the stuff all over the old J&L footprint, and magnets extract the metals. Mills buy the scrap, melt it down for reuse. Construction companies buy the remaining crushed rock for cement and subbase on road and construction projects.

It has none of gambling's jingle or sheen: the work is dirtier, more unpredictable, and the chips are far bigger. Slag now averages about $9.50 a ton, up from the $7 per when Betters officially started—and by 2011 the business was racking up annual revenues nearing $5 million. Between all the slag, as well as a century and seven miles' worth of reinforced rebar, "blue concrete" blast furnace foundations dropping three stories deep into the earth, and the iron "buttons" (500-ton boulders left over, like solidified sugar in the bottom of a teacup, after a ladle pour) buried God knows where, Betters and his boys figure to have their hands full for years.

One November Saturday, Betters hopped out of his truck at the sight of one such dirt-caked, massive plug of iron, now worth near $200,000 apiece. For a time, they used to burrow past such hulks to reach $7 slag. "We bring 'em, we break 'em, we knock the slag off 'em," he said. "Then we sell these buttons to a steel mill. This product today is worth about four hundred dollars a ton."

Betters shrugged. "We do stuff nobody wants to do," he said. "It's ugly, nasty, dirty, and hard."

Then again, Betters' Lebanese grandfather, his hard-drinking, heavy-handed father, and most of his uncles spent decades working at J&L. The family moved to Center before Chuck went to high school; he says his classmates named him "Most Likely to Go to Jail." Betters took over his dad's plumbing business, built a small empire with construction projects as far away as Texas and Detroit. Aliquippa always loomed, in his mind, as reminder and opportunity.

Betters spent two decades shifting cash from other businesses to launch the slag concern, scrub the J&L brownfields, build state-of-the-art docks to lure industry back. When, in 2008, bankruptcy claimed Aliquippa Community Hospital—that beloved, $3.3 million monument to management-labor teamwork, and home to 270 jobs—he bought it for $250,000, tried a revival, then tore it down. He has amassed debt in the millions, thrown money at candidates for the state house and Congress.

Lately he's been buying up what he calls "yellow iron"—heavy construction vehicles for rent—to cash in on the natural gas boom, sure that the fuel giants will soon be harpooning acreage all over Beaver County. He's also angling to develop a long-term health care facility on the old hospital site—and as many residents trust his motives as don't. Betters does want to make money. He insists that isn't all. "There's something relative to my legacy, and my family's legacy, in this town, working in this mill," he said. "The day that I put USG over there? I felt real good about it. It didn't create a fraction of what used to be here, but there were three hundred direct jobs and several thousand indirect jobs. I felt pretty fucking good about that.

"I'm pretty comfortable; my kids are going to be okay. I'm worrying about my grandkids. Because I think about when I was growing up, the opportunities, and the lack thereof now, so I very much care about doing this. People tell you about air pollution: I lost a daughter, thirty-seven years old, from colon cancer who never smoked and drank. We have no history of that in our family. How's that happen, the cancers? Young kids getting these different diseases, and you wonder, *Is this environmental?* Believe me, that made a profound impact.

"But I also look what's out there, and the biggest employers are meth labs, trafficking drugs. I'm going to let you talk to a couple employees today. And you tell me when you leave, is it just monetary? Because no fucking person in his right mind would do what I've done."

He drove to the J&L site's northern tip, up a dirt grade onto a vast plateau: windswept, sun-washed, and empty but for two men. They were goggled, wielding acetylene torches amid a landscape of jutting rock and gnarled metal. A rusted ladle squatted ten feet away, unhinged, the kind they cut and buried when a worker fell screaming into the molten pour. Here—thirty years after it closed—the mill was producing product still, belched up through the crust like splinters working through skin. Up here, somewhere, serial killer Eddie Surratt supposedly dumped a body. Not far off, a dying Eddie Humphries was found.

The six-hundred-acre site was once considered so toxic that the state's Department of Environmental Protection ordered it capped with dirt, fenced, and padlocked; Betters' crew has been toiling away on it for more than a decade. As he approached, the two men dialed down their torches. The oldest, a forty-nine-year-old white man named Fred, stole once from Betters and served time; after his release, Betters rehired him. The second man was twenty-five-year-old Tony Gaskins, who shot ex–Aliquippa running back James Moon four years before Moon killed Diedre Walker and then himself. Though far younger than Fred, Tony seemed to be in charge.

"Did we hit it?" Gaskins said.

"Yes, you did," Betters said.

"I didn't know that till right now."

In September, Betters had dangled a proposal to Gaskins and his crew of thirteen: cut and sort seven thousand tons of pitscrap by the end of the year, and you'll get a $100,000 bonus to split among you. For men making $13 an hour, that $7,142.82 apiece would come in handy. Of course, Betters didn't bother telling the men they had hit their number the month before. That's good management, old school: If they're pushing hard, why give them reason to let up?

Gaskins didn't mind. Betters had saved him. After serving his sentence for shooting James Moon, Gaskins had fallen back into the old corner rhythm: hung out, hustled drugs. But the birth of his daughter,

Jayde, and the fact that "my buddies kept getting killed" proved a sobering combination. Gaskins took a job washing dishes at Betters' country
club. Walking away from the street's faster money wasn't easy.

"I've thought about it, don't get me wrong," he said. "But I can't
go that route, because I have a family. It's not about me anymore. When
I was out doing all that, I didn't have a kid or a girlfriend or wife or
whatever. I was by myself and I didn't have a caring bone in this world
but to make money and take care of myself."

Betters eyed Gaskins for months at the club, heard about his criminal record. Gaskins didn't pretty up the tale. Betters liked the honesty,
his intelligence and hustle. "White people in this town don't like to
give blacks a chance to show what they can do," Betters told him. "I'm
willing to give you a chance."

It was also one old man's chance to reset the American Dream,
wind it back to its roots: hand a desperate man a shovel and see how
much he digs. That was 2010. "It took a year to beat that jive-ass shit
out of him," Betters said. "But once he got past that I knew he was
going to fly." Gaskins has worked for him ever since.

"I stay there because I got things now in life that I thought I would
never have," Gaskins said. "I got a home I never had before of my own,
I've basically got my family going, getting ready to have another kid
here in February. My parents weren't that fortunate, but once I started
working for Chuck? Basically everything I ever wanted? I'm getting it."

20

Family Matters

It was late 2010 when Tony Dorsett started feeling the pull, and strong: Family. Roots. Blood. Part of it was his mother, Myrtle, mind honeycombed by dementia, rattling around in the house in Center that he'd bought with his rookie bonus check. He was flying in from his home outside Dallas nearly once a month now, the plane's approach sometimes taking him over the stadium in Hopewell that was renamed, in 2001, in his honor. Each time he found himself visiting old haunts—the childhood playground in Mount Vernon, the twelve-mile training route he used to run up Monaca Road, Jack Chapman's bar in Plan 11 where that window broke and everybody scattered. He recognized fewer faces. He was pushing sixty, starting to forget things, too. Often, he felt like he was the ghost.

"The thing I'm disappointed in?" Dorsett said one golden, leafstrewn September afternoon, gunning his Chrysler 300 up Fifth Avenue, eyeing the chunked asphalt, the crumbling curbs, the growth spilling between slats and pressing in from woods once beaten back. "I understand that it's hard to get jobs. But see the side of this hill? It's like the weeds are overtaking the community. People used to have a sense of pride about themselves, and it seems like that's diminished. My mother used to tell me: 'It's not what you got. It's what you *do* with what you got.'

"But see it now? It's never been like this, man." He rolled through the old heart of Plan 11, corner of Fifth and Jefferson, the sun-bleached lots that used to make up the Funky Four Corners. "There used to be stores and clubs. The city or somebody should be able to clean this up, but people just don't give a damn anymore. It's just gone, man."

He drove half a block. "That's the funeral home my brother was in," Tony said.

That, just a month earlier, may be the biggest draw. The death at sixty-one of the original "TD" stirred something in Tony, if only because any idol's fall will trouble the soul. The first time Tony noticed was during his playing days, a Cowboys road trip to Philadelphia: Tyrone's eyes glassy, attention shot. Tony started giving his brother money, pried him out of Aliquippa, got him placed in rehab in Dallas. Tyrone checked himself out. "Okay," Tony said. "Just stay here with me then."

But Tyrone had to get back to Aliquippa. "*That's* the problem," Tony kept telling him. "Don't go back."

"I can fight it," Tyrone would say.

He couldn't.

"It was hard to watch him decay," Tony said. "Here was my brother who'd been one of the best dressers, beautiful girls, nice cars. Then I see him go completely down, just don't even care, it seemed like. I had to force myself to understand what an addiction like that can do. I'm a mama's boy and I'll fight a herd of elephants for her. I couldn't understand why my brother was stealing from my mother.

"You've to understand the disease, what it does to people—because it's not really them. Ooh, I got this real bad feeling in my mind about my brother. I was never taught to hate. You know what I'm saying? I can't hate my brother. But I had a strong dislike for my brother because of what he was doing. I stopped giving him money, because I was, like, 'This is all you're going to do with it; I'm not going to feed that.' But he couldn't even see what I was talking about."

Now Dorsett was steering his way back down to Franklin Avenue. He went on to speak of the way his father died of a stroke at sixty, back in '84, how it broke him to see such a strong man, with that big, proud gut, helpless in Aliquippa Hospital. "Daddy, get up," he pleaded to the prone figure. "Get up. . . ."

But seeing Tyrone was worse. Tony's voice was a croak now.

"Those last days when I was here? I swear to God," he said. "I'm going to tell you the truth: The smell of, of . . . *him*. Because he was passing stool and I'll never forget . . . I'll never forget the day when the nurse pulled back the cover on him and was checking him. I was standing in the room and I had to turn away from looking. It was horrible, man. He was skin and bone."

Aliquippa could look that way, too. The hospital had been gone since 2009; of the 9,438 people still living nearly a quarter were age 65 or older and 36 percent of those below age 18 lived below the poverty line. Dorsett rolled past the police station, the monument "to the workers of the Jones and Laughlin Steel Corporation and LTV who made the impossible possible in the production of steel." He parked nearby, wandered the downtown's dustied emptiness, recognized some faces. "Man," he said to the men. "Everything's shut down."

"Only one thing that ain't shut down, Tony," one of the men replied. "The bullets."

Yet, during the days of Tyrone's funeral, for the first time Dorsett told his wife, "Let's look at some houses. I think I want to move back closer to my family." Maybe somewhere near Pittsburgh. Maybe someplace closer. He didn't trust the town anymore, not to live in anyway, but maybe being near would ease some of the ache.

"Every time I come back, the feeling's there more and more," he said, heading again up Monaca Road. "It hurts me to see it, but this is Aliquippa. This is me. This is where I got everything."

✻　✻　✻

Salt Smith and the rest of the Democratic establishment felt the threat rising. More people were talking about Dwan Walker as the May 2011 primary loomed. Maybe it was just words, but Walker never let up, never stopped the sell that didn't feel like selling; besides, maybe change alone could bring about change. The kid promised to try to bring jobs, start a lottery, be visible and accountable, to find options for kids besides football and drugs. He told reporters and citizens how he wanted to work with Chuck Betters—Mayor Battalini's longtime foe—to revive the mill site and town. Yet he didn't seem bought and paid for.

"I did not contribute one cent to that campaign—although I would've dumped a lot of money in it if somebody had come to me," Betters said.

Through the winter and spring of 2011, things got nasty. One rumor had Battalini calling Walker a racial slur; Dwan accused Battalini of lying and stealing. Despite the fact that his ticket was aimed squarely at his own cousin, councilwoman Lisa Walker, some wondered if Dwan's family ties to the likes of Vance Walker—whose sex-on-prison-furlough episode brought down Peep Short—and Ali Dorsett (cousin of his first cousin, Anthony Dorsett Jr.) would give criminals the run of City Hall.

The Democrats' dominance had long rendered the November general election a formality: primary day *is* Election Day. On May 17, 2011, Walker crushed Battalini, Smith, and the Democratic machine 1,604 votes to 805 to win. Battalini refused to endorse the ticket in the upcoming general election but, he said, "This kid: I give him credit. He worked. The white people didn't come out to vote. They just took for granted that I was going to win. I never thought that I'd see a black president; he's here now. And I'm probably going to be the last white mayor in Aliquippa. I think it's shocking."

And, then, for six months . . . nothing. It wasn't until election night, November 8, 2011, that D's prediction officially came true: Dwan

Walker, thirty-six years old, former Quips receiver, became Aliquippa's mayor. With no Republican opponent, he spent the day moving precinct to precinct, inviting folks to the victory party at Captain's Corner, the runty tavern down the road from where Big Mike Ditka drank and James Naim's body fell.

That night, Walker smiled and hugged everyone in sight. His grandmother Rose, seventy-seven, clutched his arm. "I lived to see it," she said. "I lived to see a black mayor."

Folks started leaving near midnight. Walker stepped into the parking lot; every few seconds, the bar door banged open and another face called out good night. He smiled at each, but soon his voice cracked: it was unbearable, really, how winning felt like loss. Then Mayor Dwan Walker began to weep.

"I was trying to be calm but . . . I miss her," he said. "I know she'd have walked in that door and been happy for me: *I told you you could do it!* There ain't nothin' in this world I want more: Have her put her arms around me and tell me, 'Brah, it's going to be all right. I'm with you.'"

Yet, even by then their accomplishment had become old news. Whether Walker's election could even slow Aliquippa's demise was the only question.

"Twenty-five years? At the rate it's going now, it won't be here in five years," Battalini said. "I should be maybe a bit fairer to this kid and give him a chance. I just see that he don't have a clue what he's talking about. He's got the wrong people behind him. He's got people that are worried about themselves. Chuck Betters has already got his claws in his back. Kid has no experience whatsoever: Betters is going to end up running this town."

Not immediately, though. Four months after Walker's election, in March 2012, Betters' holdings of more than 75 percent of J&L's old seven-and-a-half-mile stretch along the Ohio River were rejected by Royal Dutch Shell as the site of its new, $2.5 billion ethane catalytic cracking plant. Aliquippa, like much of Western Pennsylvania, sits atop both the Marcellus and Utica shale fields. Though the natural gas boom has far less community-building clout than Big Steel—the finished cracker plant calls for only a few hundred permanent workers—the project still would've provided an estimated 10,000 direct construction jobs and created a secondary market for perhaps 6,000 more. But Shell chose a site just a few miles away, on the Potter/Center Township line.

"I still think we're going to get some bounce-back," Walker said after. "We've got a pipe-coating plant that's looking to get some of that land, an ethynol plant. Only Aliquippa's got two miles of riverfront that's ready to go. The new docks are right there. So anybody that wants to come here, we're ready."

By then Walker had lost his marriage, his job at FedEx, and forty-two pounds, but he still bubbled with hope, tinged with a bit of desperation. "One thing I'm trying now, I got a production favor I've called in and I'm going to start making DVDs and sell my city to everybody who's interested," he said. "General Electric? I don't care who it is. I'm going to try to mass-produce fifty thousand copies and send 'em off to top execs and let 'em know that Aliquippa's here to do business, man. I don't know what they've heard before, but we're here now."

Walker spent the rest of his first year trying to craft a recovery plan that would move the town into solvency and shed, after twenty-five years, its Act 47 status as a distressed municipality—an uphill slog with ever-declining revenues. Meanwhile came this cosmic slap: in September 2012 Battalini hit on six scratch-off Pennsylvania Lottery tickets and collected $15,000; two months later, he won top prize—$300,000—in the state's "Trim the Tree" game. Sure, Aliquippa's new mayor was young and eager. But the loser had all the luck.

Meanwhile, the tragedy that pushed Walker into politics remained raw in Plan 12. More than two years later kids were still congregating on the corner where Tiquai Wallace died, and no one dared paint over the graffiti tributes. Up at the high school all eyes were on running back Dravon Henry, who each week took the field with a dedication, "RIP WALL," scrawled by a black Sharpie on the white tape strapped to his wrists.

The afternoon of his last day alive, Tiquai had played pickup basketball with Henry. He didn't have fun. The thirteen-year-old Henry's athletic gifts had already marked him as the heir to Law and Revis, and that Friday in 2009 he was having his way with Tiquai, a year older but starting to realize that the implied dominance of age was a lie. "I was winning and he was getting mad, kept trying to throw the ball at me, and I just kept going around him, scoring," Dravon said. "And then he told me, 'I'm going to go to this party. . . .'"

Now it was a November Sunday, 2011, and Dravon was sitting with his parents on a thick couch in the front room of the family home. His sophomore season was nearly done; he had proven himself an explosive offensive force, and an even more devastating ball hawk on defense. Aliquippa High would go on to win its fourteenth WPIAL football championship later that month, with Dravon more than redeeming himself for his two fumbles in the failed title game the year before: He would make the key crushing tackle on Jeannette's live-wire quarterback Demetrious Cox on fourth and 4 to set up Aliquippa's game-winning, 96-yard drive in the final three minutes; he would rush for 96 yards; he would intercept Cox's last-gasp pass with twenty seconds to play to seal the 14-7 win.

Already, recruiters from Alabama, Pitt, Penn State, Miami, and West Virginia were circling hard. They would hang there, of course, for the rest of his high school days as Dravon racked up 5,454 career yards rushing—the all-time Aliquippa record —and established himself as one of the nation's best prospects at defensive back. Talent was only one reason; Dravon hadn't gone with Tiquai to that party. His parents kept a tight grip. They had a firsthand feel for Aliquippa's dual nature.

Dravon's dad, Roland Henry, had won a WPIAL title in '96 as a tight end and a state title in basketball in '97, went on to get a business degree at Thiel College; his mom, Shanell Askew, grew up in Valley Terrace in a family fractured by drugs, jail, and death. She was fifteen, still a student at Aliquippa High, on the October day she had Dravon. Soon after, she took her baby to class.

"I didn't know what else to do; I had nobody to keep him," Shanell said. She kept going, too, even after school officials told her it wasn't allowed, and the following spring Aliquippa High gave in and opened a student day-care center. "So he's been in school *all* his life," she said. "Dravon, I believe, from day one to now probably missed five days of school. His attendance is perfect. That's what he knows."

It wasn't until the next morning, after he woke, that Dravon heard about Tiquai's awful end. Text after text filled his phone—*Wall St. died. . . . Wal died. . . . Wall is dead*—and Dravon panicked and ran out of the house and up the street, where his teammate, Jyier Turner, told him that it was true. "I just stood there," Dravon said. "Shed a couple tears."

He didn't go to the funeral. But before every Aliquippa game, Dravon would point to the sky, he said, "for all the people who've passed away in 'Quipp."

As he explained this, the sound of a motorcycle sputtering into silence could be heard outside. Footsteps fell, the front door cracked: David L. Askew III, Shanell's thirty-year-old muscled and smiling brother, appeared in the room. He was wearing a New York Jets jersey, No. 24, with "REVIS" stitched on the back. The Jets had won this afternoon, and Darrelle alone had forced three turnovers. Talk turned to Aliquippa's football genes. Shanell and David's dad played at Aliquippa High; their grandfather, Ossie Foster, became its first 1,000-yard rusher in 1979; an uncle, Chad Askew, was talented enough to earn some tryouts in the NFL. Not David, though.

"No, no," he laughed. "I just look like I played."

Still, he has more of a claim on local football lore than most. His son, Kaezon Pugh, a running back two years behind Dravon, has been tagged as the next "Next One." And in December 2010, Askew married Diana Gilbert, Darrelle Revis's mother, tying even tighter the bond between the town's once and future stars. That raised eyebrows in town, and not just because of the age difference.

In December 2002, Askew and twenty-seven-year-old George Horton—both aligned with Jamie Brown and Tusweet Smith, each fingering the other as the triggerman—pleaded guilty to the third-degree murder of Eddie Humphries, twenty-six, in August 1999. Humphries had been found up the hill on Tank Road, dumped over the border in Hopewell, dying of a gunshot wound to the chest and gasping the words, "George . . . David." The case languished for nineteen months, until the killing of Officer James Naim and the subsequent grand jury investigation flushed out three witnesses who saw Humphries on his final day with Horton and Askew.

"When the Naim case happened, the brutality of it, I reminded my boss of this previous homicide," said Timmie Patrick, the Beaver County detective who would go on to be Dravon and Kaezon's running backs coach at Aliquippa High. "I said, 'If we don't solve *this* case, we're going to have more bodies.' So my boss asks for cooperation from Hopewell police, they turn over their material, and I produced a material witness within two days that observed George Horton, David Askew, and the deceased getting into a van before he was found murdered."

Askew served seven years of a maximum fifteen-year sentence for the crime. "At first I tried blocking it out," Askew said of the killing of Eddie Humphries. "I blocked it out for four years, and tried to justify in my head that what I did was kind of right—because if I didn't do it he was going to get me. But I was in prison watching *Oprah*, and a lady there had lost her son in a fire—little boy died in a fire—and the look on the mother's face and the way she was crying, I was like, *I made somebody's mom feel like that?* That's the first time I really understood how big it was what I did. . . . And I still feel bad for what I did."

After he paroled out in 2008, Askew bumped into Revis's mom at an Aliquippa tire shop. Gone were the wiry frame and flamboyant braids of his criminal days; prison had bulked Askew up, lent him gravity. "He was different," Diana Gilbert said. "We went on a date and I could tell by the way that he talked, his demeanor. He was talking to me from his heart and I'm looking in his eyes and I was like, *He is so genuine.*"

Many are convinced that Askew has left his old ways behind. "Got caught in that spiderweb," said Sherm McBride. "Great guy now." Still, when Diana finally brought Askew to New Jersey to meet Darrelle, Revis's first question was, "How'd you hook up with *him?*" Later, Darrelle pulled Askew aside.

"The only thing I ask is that you don't hurt my mother," Darrelle said. "She's been through a lot. You treat her right."

Askew has spent his time since working as a personal trainer, cheering Revis and Dravon, monitoring Kaezon, critiquing Aliquippa's coaches, and posting the occasional pro-Quips rant on message boards. Sometimes he speaks at area schools, because few can testify more vividly about how Aliquippa's boys are, as he says, "born with one foot to success and one in turmoil, one foot on the field and one in prison." He hates the place nearly as much as he loves it.

"'Quipp got its own thing that don't nobody else got," Dravon was saying that Sunday afternoon. "It's something . . . I can't explain it."

"Like a mystique," Askew agreed.

Asked how the town would react if the population kept shrinking and Aliquippa High shut down or, worse, merged with Hopewell—if, that is, Aliquippa football disappeared for good—everybody stopped talking.

"I couldn't imagine it," Askew said finally.

"I couldn't imagine it, either," Shanell said.

"I don't know what I would do," Dravon said.

"For there not to be football, they would have to change the water system," Askew said. "It's in the water. If I give you a cup of water right now, you would run a forty in four flat!"

Everyone laughed except Dravon, but his mom wasn't surprised. She found out, long ago, that no punishment was harder on him than the slightest threat to move out of Aliquippa. "It's worse than a whuppin'," Shanell said. "You don't even have to put your hands on him." Even the idea of vacation hits Dravon like a horror; after his freshman year, when his parents went to a North Carolina beach for a week, he begged off.

"Aliquippa just do something to me, inside," Dravon said. "I went to Cincinnati, on the road my stomach was hurting and I was, like, carsick. But as soon as I saw that 'ALIQUIPPA' sign? I was smiling and happy as ever. There's something about the town."

Maybe it takes a native to see it. Because if you didn't grow up there—or, like Tony Dorsett, you'd been gone a while—the place looked exhausted, beaten. Once past the day-care center, the police station, the library, a minimart and gas station and a few bars, there remained a whole lot of empty on the old stretch heading toward the J&L tunnel. Truck after truck rolled through without stopping. Any new business gravitates to the commercial cluster up on Brodhead Road, closer to Interstate 376 and away from the flash floods that, twice in the past decade, left the county's onetime business capital under four feet of water.

"Franklin Avenue? The best thing that could happen is bulldoze it and push it into the river," said Chuck Betters. "Because its infrastructure is inadequate for today."

There were die-hards, of course. In the spring of 2012, there was still Uncommon Grounds, a Franklin Avenue coffee shop/ministry/arts showcase/halfway house planted in a ravaged storefront by an Australian missionary. Inside, addicts manned the register and poured drinks, and the warm vibe felt nothing like the world beyond. Weekly open-mic shows, usually on Thursday, provided the same rare, safe opportunity to gather that football does on Friday.

But even there, amid a jokey, biracial crowd of the amiable, the earnest, and the aging, light moments came tinged with a sense of foreboding. One March night, a teenage boy sang "Never Gonna Give You Up" as a girl gyrated inside a Hula-Hoop; a woman recited a screed against "Shallow America"; Stephen "The Poet" Suggs provided volcanic readings of his "Police Knockdown"—and the audience cheered them all. It felt like the junior college play you attend because your kid is cast.

Then a middle-aged black man edged toward the stage. The emcee announced Paul McDaniel, and the sight of him was a caution: drooping black pants, broken shoes, a baggy, soiled T-shirt. McDaniel took the microphone, squinted into the spotlight; one or two teeth remained. Humiliation seemed certain. Then the music began, and McDaniel opened his mouth.

The sound was so beautiful that, at first, it seemed like a lip-sync stunt, some cruel incongruity played for laughs. But the wondrous voice kept rising out of that shabby figure, high and raw, Billie Holiday and Marvin Gaye fusing into this hair-raising keen. Many in the place knew McDaniel's story: there was no greater singer in the county, maybe the state, but word was that you couldn't ever pay him a cent up front—because then McDaniel might never show.

"I always tell people: You never got it worse than the next man," Mayor Dwan Walker said a few days later. "But that dude got it worse than anybody, and he's a great guy. But Aliquippa'll catch you. It'll pull you back in with run-ins, or the people around you will pull you back in. Just the nature of this beast."

McDaniel raised his seamy hands to his face. By then the shock of that jarring sight and sound had faded some, enough to let the words made famous by Nina Simone sink in:

Everything must change
Nothing stays the same
Everyone will change
No one, no one stays the same. . . .

His face crinkled, mouth gaping like a tunnel, McDaniel wasn't just singing, but it wasn't exactly performance, either. He was being the song. He looked ready to weep.

> . . . *The young become the old*
> *And mysteries do unfold*
> *For that's the way of time*
> *No one, and nothing goes unchanged.* . . .

The audience went still. McDaniel sang on about winter's turn to spring, the healing of wounded hearts, rain followed by a warming sun. Hopeful ideas, but not when delivered as a dirge: McDaniel's fingers trailed down his cheeks, pantomiming tears. "Everything must change," he kept repeating, and there was nothing to do but sit there and take it.

Yet if the town seemed stuck, economically and demographically, if it couldn't—like many former mill and mining centers—retool or even reimagine a way out of its thirty-year rut, the knack for winning remained. Generations of steelwork, labor and drug wars, ethnic pride, and racial grievance had left a toughness—a cruelty, even—that endured well after the furnaces went cold; call it the final residue, hard and valuable as buried slag. More than any sport, football unearths, sorts, and refines that toughness, providing a continuity found nowhere else. And Aliquippa's impassioned network of grandfathers, fathers, cousins, uncles, and brothers who once played The Pit demands that each new generation maintain the standard.

So each fall Saturday 160 boys, ranging from five to twelve years old, come to Little Quips field at Morrell Park to suit up in pads and helmets. Each August former stars like Peep Short, Sherm McBride, and Timmie Patrick—along with a dozen other unpaid volunteers—show up to coach Aliquippa High, where 40 percent of the boys, and more than 60 percent of its seniors, play football. And each year the greatest link in the chain, the man who has attended every WPIAL championship football game in the town's history, who saw Willie Frank and knew Carl Aschman and learned from Hollywood Don, keeps coming back, too.

"This is why I do what I do," Mike Zmijanac said before each winning playoff game in 2011, and then again in 2012, when the Quips—led by dual 1,000-yard rushers Dravon Henry and Terry Swanson—cruised through the postseason and crushed Washington 34-7 to win its fifteenth WPIAL title. In September of 2013 Zmijanac turned seventy, but neither he nor his team showed signs of slowing. Another undefeated regular season unrolled, capped by Aliquippa's sixth straight appearance in November's WPIAL championship game, at Pittsburgh's Heinz Field.

All over America, then, the view of football was changing fast. That was the month Tony Dorsett revealed that he had been diagnosed with chronic traumatic encephalopathy (CTE), the latest retired NFL player in an ever-lengthening line to blame the game for memory loss, depression, thoughts of suicide. "Football caused this," Dorsett said during a spate of national interviews. "Football has caused my quality of life to deteriorate." A week later, the country's largest youth football organization, Pop Warner, reported that participation had dropped nearly 10 percent from 2010 to 2012, and cited fallout from the game's concussion crisis as "the No. 1 cause."

Even smashmouth icon Mike Ditka was going soft; soon he, too, would admit that he wouldn't let a young son of his play now. "I wouldn't," Ditka said on national television in early 2015. "And my whole life was football. I think the risk is worse than the reward."

But if such talk circulated back in his hometown, it wasn't very loud. There was still a waiting list to play on all four levels of Little Quips—Twerp (eight and under), Termite (ten and under), Mighty Mite (twelve and under), and Midget (fourteen and under)—and any criticisms of the game focused on Zmijanac's seeming inability, of late, to claim big titles. People began carping again about his run-first/run-more play-calling after Aliquippa failed to score four times from inside the 20-yard line and lost to Wyomissing, 17-14, in the 2012 AA state title game. Then came back-to-back defeats in the WPIAL AA championship to South Fayette in 2013 and '14.

It didn't matter that South Fayette's enrollment was twice as large; that with just over 300 students—138 boys—Aliquippa was a Class A school facing the second-largest school in AA. It didn't matter, either, that Zmijanac hadn't lost a conference game going back to 2009, or that he would run his regular-season winning streak up to sixty in 2015. For some parents and fans—and especially the Little Quips coaches who'd handled the players before they hit high school—it meant more that Aliquippa went into that 2014 clash averaging a Class AA–leading 50 points per game and scored just 22. To them, Zmijanac was too stubborn, too predictable: the second coming of old King Carl.

"I guarantee you, a Yannessa-coached team would have never gone to Heinz Field three times and only scored twenty-one points," said Mayor Dwan Walker, a longtime Little Quips coach, referring to Aliquippa's total output in the 2008, '09, and '10 WPIAL title games. "Frank Marocco? It would have never happened. But you see Zmijanac on our sidelines: everything *he* says goes. He doesn't listen to nobody but himself. This is a basketball coach being a football coach, and all these ex-players are there coaching with him—and you don't listen to them? To me, that's selfish."

Indeed, when things went wrong—even slightly—things got personal, fast. For some, Zmijanac would always suffer in comparison to his predecessors, and his standoffishness—summed up all too easily by his residency in tony Mt. Lebanon—only made questioning his methods easier. Most parents loved Coach Z's my-way-or-the-highway stance on grades and comportment, but a small faction complained that he didn't do enough to help second-tier players land scholarships. Never mind that more sophisticated high school scouting, a deeper talent pool, and the reduced size of college rosters had made Division I-A far more discerning since Yannessa's day. Or that a marginal player's marginal transcript usually overrides any coach's glowing comments about the kid's "character." It had to be him.

Zmijanac, typically, shrugged all that off. Privacy laws, not to mention his own discretion, prevent any comment about student test scores, and, frankly, he figures his string of D-I players speaks for itself. And X's and O's? For years he had stressed, publicly, how much he leans on assistants Sherman McBride and Peep Short; if people weren't ripping him for being a control freak, they were griping about him being little more than a figurehead. Which one was it? As for Aschman, Zmijanac says he overhauled the offense after Yannessa left—and, anyway, it doesn't matter. It's not his play-calling that wins or loses games, he says; it's the players' talent and drive, and the way his assistants monitor, teach, and keep them playing clean and tough.

"They think they're fuckin' Vince Lombardi," Zmijanac said of his critics. "The correlation between Little Quips and the high school team is like the one between the high school team and the fuckin' NFL. I'm not angry with those people when I say that, but that's typical. They want the credit. It's silly. And here's my real attitude: They want to make themselves feel good about it? Fine. I don't care."

Still, by the time of the 2015 season, the heat was on. If Zmijanac had nothing to prove, everyone else felt it. Civic pride mattered, as always, but more than ever football was seen as the town's clearest path to success—and suddenly, the path didn't even seem that tortuous. Dravon Henry and Terry Swanson had wasted no time breaking in at name-college programs, West Virginia and Toledo, respectively; in 2014, Henry was named a freshman all-American at safety and Swanson rushed for 732 yards. But the most dazzling example played Sundays: fresh off a Super Bowl championship with New England, Darrelle

Revis was back in uniform with the Jets under a contract guaranteeing him at least $39 million. His career earnings, at thirty, now totaled $124 million.

"I guess I have a golden ticket," Kaezon Pugh said one night in October, sitting on the porch of his dad's house in Plan 12. "God planned this for me, and I'm just taking advantage of it."

He was, indeed, The Next One: The previous Friday Pugh, a senior now, had rushed for 313 yards and two touchdowns as Aliquippa breezed to a 35-14 win over Quaker Valley. And that was an off night; his calves had seized up with cramps nearly from the start of the game. At 6-foot-3 and 220 pounds, with a 4.4 time in the 40-yard dash, Pugh was bigger than Henry and Swanson and just as fast. By then he had sorted through three dozen scholarship offers and all but decided to follow the Ditka-Revis pipeline to Pitt, where the coaches project him as a linebacker.

Not that Pugh cares where he lines up. "Growing up, I hated football," he said. And though Pugh would soon become the fifth back in Aliquippa history to gain more than 4,000 yards, though he was starting to talk now about how he has come to revere The Pit, he had warmed up to the game only a bit. Like Revis and Jonathan Baldwin, he had lived for basketball as a kid. Like them both, he realized that it didn't offer much of a future.

"To be honest, I'm only in love with football because I think that's my only way out," Pugh says. "Because I have to love it. You can't succeed at something you don't love; it's just not going to happen—you can't be great."

His father, the rarest of crossovers, pushed him here. Aliquippans are as guilty as any outsider of portraying the town as a battleground for competing ecosystems: its spiderweb of violence and drugs versus that network of family and ex-players pushing their boys to play. But sometimes the two worlds mesh—and never more seamlessly than in the person of David Askew.

Until the eighth grade, Pugh was happy living with his mother, Katia Pugh, and two younger siblings in Ambridge, getting all the playing time he wanted against lesser competition. But when, in 2008, David Askew was paroled out of prison after serving seven years for the murder of Eddie Humphries, he kept stressing to his son that a growth spurt was coming—and that Kaezon needed to take full advantage. "My dad broke it down to me," Pugh says. "Told me what I was going to become."

That Askew had long been like a big brother to Pugh's cousin, Dravon Henry, and was on his way to marrying Diana Gilbert and becoming Revis's stepfather, only gave his words more weight. Pugh was struck, too, by his father's determination to change, to serve as a cautionary tale. "They say jail is good for some people; you come out a whole different person. My dad was one of those who didn't want to go back," Kaezon said. "He's been down that road, and I know I've got to go in the opposite direction. That's a must. And that's what I'm going to do—take my ticket, the way I want to take it."

Pugh moved to Aliquippa. He started at linebacker his sophomore year and moved into the starting backfield his junior, amassing 1,626 yards and averaging nearly 11 yards a carry in 2014. His Quips running mate, Hopewell transfer DiMantae Bronaugh, rushed for 1,262 and a 9.3 average. The back-to-back losses to South Fayette in the WPIAL championship stung, and the two vowed to come back even stronger for their senior year.

But beyond the football field, a small crack had surfaced in the public bond between the football program and the community. For years, going back to Yannessa's days, the program had enforced a policy of withholding players' recruiting letters during the season. The practice helped tamp down runaway egos, kept the focus on team and the game at hand. But for those inclined to question Zmijanac, it also bred easy resentment.

In December 2014, a week after the Quips' loss in the WPIAL final, David Askew visited the football office and was given a box of dozens of letters—none of them hard-core scholarship offers. But one, he said, was from the U.S. Military Academy and addressed to "the parent of Kaezon Pugh," requesting permission for the player to visit West Point—for a game that was now past. Irate, Askew posted a three-minute Facebook video of himself sorting through the box, naming Zmijanac, and calling for "change" in the Aliquippa football program.

That led to a community meeting: Peep Short was invited and attended, and a petition was presented calling for Zmijanac's resignation. The *Beaver County Times* published a story, another player's mother criticized the coach's perceived lack of interest in getting her son a scholarship, a Pittsburgh TV station ran a report. Word spread online. "That guy don't like me," Askew said. Bad enough that a star player's dad had taken such a stand, but no one stated—publicly—the real curiosity: as Diana Gilbert's husband, Askew was part of Aliquippa football's most famous clan, two of whose members had been coached by Zmijanac. Perhaps Sean Gilbert and Darrelle Revis had no sway with David Askew. Maybe neither thought it worthwhile to cross sister or mother, and hoped that the issue would just die. But, publicly at least, neither Gilbert nor Revis said a word in Zmijanac's defense.

Regardless, the movement gained little traction with the public or school board. But the program's hard-line stand on recruiting letters did dissolve—players can now come by the office once a week to pick up any mail—and some wondered whether Zmijanac would bother returning. He and his staff never talked, publicly, about the letters or the petition—not even McBride, who had called the reformed Askew a "great guy now." But Zmijanac's longtime ally, schools superintendent Dave Wytiaz, said, "Mike had been under fire for various stupid things involving a guy who's been in prison much of his adult life. It all died down because it was bullshit. But I think that's driven him, too."

Four months later, in April 2015, Zmijanac signed a new three-year contract that projected him still on the sideline at seventy-four. For the upcoming season, Kaezon would require some deft handling, to say the least; and only one starter each was returning to the offensive and defensive lines. Still, Wytiaz said, "I see a renewed vigor in Mike."

Then, a week before the first game, Bronaugh was diagnosed with acute lymphoblastic leukemia and ruled out for the season. The tone shifted: Quips Nation rallied. Bronaugh stood on the sideline in the opener, began a schedule of nauseating weekly chemotherapy sessions in Pittsburgh. Blood drives were held, blankets were knit, T-shirts were sold. The senior class donated $600 in gas cards for his hospital runs. Messages of hope poured in from California, Australia, Iraq. Former Quips like Mark Washington and Jon LeDonne, now coaching at Hopewell and Shaler High, respectively, raised money at their schools, and every road opponent chipped in at halftime. The team kept winning. The fundraising total rose to $9,000. Week after week, the players kept saying they were doing it all for DiMantae.

"The support has been overwhelming," said Bronaugh's aunt, Aliquippa High teacher's aide Anita Gordon. "People I don't even know walk up to me and say how much they've been praying and hoping he gets better. The community has been wonderful."

By September's end, Bronaugh was in remission. His teammates vowed to win him a championship and Pugh, meanwhile, shouldered Aliquippa's offensive load. He didn't complain. Any awkwardness with Zmijanac from the previous winter was gone. Between his dad going to prison and a thirty-one-year-old aunt dying of cancer in 2013, Pugh had survived worse. "I have a certain motor that keeps me going through anything," he said. "Just straight ahead, no matter what."

After rushing for nearly 1,300 yards during the Quips' 9-0 regular season, Pugh hit another gear in the 2015 playoffs. He had plenty of help; with a fast-maturing line and quarterback Sheldon Jeter's passing providing variety that Aliquippa hadn't shown in years, Pugh shook off a concussion in their first-round win, romped for 253 yards against Seton-La Salle, and ran for 237 over Freeport. The Quips sailed into Heinz Field for their third straight WPIAL title shot against their recent nemesis, South Fayette—now riding a 44-game winning streak. Pugh ground out another 179 yards, but the game ended up being about nearly everything but him.

Five times the lead changed hands. Aliquippa held a 14-point cushion with less than six minutes left—and let it slip away. Then, facing a do-or-die drive on the South Fayette 47-yard line with the score tied 38–38 and 1:11 left, Zmijanac—who seemingly had no imagination, who seemingly had lost his big-game touch—answered his critics with a bang. Out came a trick play he hadn't run in four years: Jeter flung a first-down lateral to wide receiver Jassir Jordan—who had never thrown a touchdown pass in his life—who then fired the ball downfield to a wide-open Thomas Perry. Perry raced the final 15 yards to give Aliquippa the 44–38 win, and its sixteenth WPIAL championship.

"Those are the kind of plays where if they don't work you look stupid," Zmijanac said after.

"He has been in this business a long time," said South Fayette coach Joe Rossi. "That's why he's so successful."

But if the breakthrough meant another paint job on the field house roof, it provided no relief. Aliquippa kept living dangerously. Now seeking its first state title since 2003, the Quips came from behind in the fourth quarter to beat Karns City in the state quarter-finals, then trailed Central Martinsburg in the fourth in the semis. Pugh had been laid out twice in the second half with blows to his elbow and upper body; now he took over. He scored the game's next 16 points—two touchdowns and two conversions—to seal the 30–21 win and a trip to Hershey, Pennsylvania, for the championship. He finished with 160 yards on 28 carries—a bit below his playoff average of 192 yards per game. No one complained.

"This is not a giving-up team," Pugh said after. "I was sitting there hurting and said, 'No, I can't go out like this.' I just had to push—and keep pushing."

Why? Winning was part of it. Helping DiMantae was part of it. Getting to college and the NFL, making millions someday, was a big part, too, but not all. Pugh has a dream, one he doesn't talk about much. It involves the dodgy streets of Plan 12 and the corner where his friend Tiquai died, the crumbling Pit, his mom living up on a darkened street off Monaca Road. It involves, even, all the factors that pushed his dad to pull a trigger and go off to jail.

"My plans? If I ever make it, I want to talk to all the big celebrities that came from around here and together we'll just rebuild Aliquippa," Pugh said that night in October. "Make it new. Get it to start feeling, like: *I'm home again.* I would love that feeling. That would be the best—to have everybody who's made it out come back and just . . . enjoy ourselves. Like a family again."

A winter's chill was already in the air. He let the idea marinate a moment; a shaft of light spilled from the living room window onto the darkened porch, enough to see Pugh nod and smile. "I think it can happen," he said. "I'll make it happen."

The fight was four to one—four men with law on their side, to one wounded freebooter, half-starved, exhausted by days and nights of pursuit, worn down with loss of sleep, thirst, privation, and the grinding, nerve-racking consciousness of an ever-present peril.

They swarmed upon him from all sides, gripping at his legs, at his arms, his throat, his head, striking, clutching, kicking, falling to the ground, rolling over and over, now under, now above, now staggering forward, now toppling back.

Still Dyke fought. . . .

—Frank Norris, *The Octopus*

December 19, 2015

Now they have come east. Some nine hundred parents, sisters and brothers, other rela-
tions, friends, administrators, teachers, alums still there and alums who moved out to
Hopewell or Monaca or farther but never really left—roughly a tenth of Aliquippa's
remaining population—filled five charter buses or piled into trucks, minivans, or cars
to make the four-hour drive here. It is nearing 11 a.m. Their black-shirted team oc-
cupies half of a stadium field, split into squads, running through plays one last time.
All have come to Hershey, Pennsylvania, annual site of the state championship games,
seeking the perfect ending.

A win would mean a promise kept to DiMantae Bronaugh, the Quips running
back sidelined with cancer. A win would redeem the state-title loss in 2012 and silence
all the old Aliquippa players who wonder about this generation's steel. And a win would
provide a fitting close to the program's twenty-five-year run as a Double-A power; two
weeks before, in response to the state athletic association's decision to expand to six classes
in 2016, Zmijanac and school officials announced that Aliquippa would bump up
yet another level, to AAA, and resume its rivalries with Hopewell and Central Valley.

That decision ensured that the program's future would only become more difficult,
but few argued against it. No place, after all, does difficult better. For further proof, the
15-0 Quips were heading back to Hershey—home of the candy empire, a throwback
amusement park, the so-called Sweetest Place on Earth; and what better setting for a
fairy-tale finish?

But now a savage wind has kicked up in Hersheypark Stadium, twenty miles per hour slicing through the thickest coats and long johns, the pouchy handwarmers shoved into pockets and gloves. The temperature reads a sunny 35 degrees, but nobody believes it; throughout the stands shoulders are tightening into a defensive hunch. Mayor Dwan Walker hunkers in the front row, 50-yard line. Peep Short, reduced by hip pain to using a walker, glowers on the sideline. Nearby, somebody congratulates schools superintendent Dave Wytiaz on Aliquippa's sixth trip to the state title game.

"It's a miracle that we're here," he says.

Short-term, he was talking about DiMantae's absence, not to mention a state budget impasse, six months old now, that threatened to shutter schools across Pennsylvania. Only an emergency $2 million loan had kept Aliquippa doors open through the fall, and food and supply vendors were still waiting for their money. The buses to ferry the team here were paid with a credit card. "What else?" Wytiaz said. Long-term? Another two hundred residents had fled town since 2010, and the ever-shrinking tax base pointed to only one eventuality.

"We're dying," Wytiaz says. "Financially I just don't see it. At some point the small schools have to become part of the larger ones. . . . It's sad. You're watching a slow death."

By now all fifty-four players and fifteen coaches have filed past, down the stairs to their cramped confines under the Depression-era stadium. The mood there is hardly lighter. Short leans on a wall near a chalkboard, diagramming sets, shouting about meeting force with force; he bangs the wall with a fist and warns that they are all in for a long day. The smell of marijuana wafts in from an open window above the coaches' lockers; eyebrows lift. Zmijanac stands, begins edging his way to the back toward his players. "Taj Mahal of a football stadium?" he mumbles to himself. "The place is a fucking dump."

When he stops the boys gather around as they have forever, some taking a knee, others pressing in close with heads bowed.

"Nowhere else I'd rather be," he says. "Come on! Slide in here, get in here, everybody. Step on a chair. I want to see your faces. This will be the last time this team gets to be in this situation. . . ."

A voice calls in from outside: "Two minutes!"

"Coach Short said it right," Zmijanac continues. "Be quicker than they are, every position. Be quicker. It never gets out of style. It never gets old. THIS is the reason I do

this: because of what it says on the front of your shirt. That's all of us. We're all from there. No matter where you go in your life. No matter where I live or where I go: I'm from Aliquippa—and I make sure they understand that before we talk about anything else. Play that way. Think that way. Deal with the situation that way. . . . Let's get after this shit!"

Now there's a push from outside the pack, and a path opens up: DiMantae Bronaugh, smiling, Nikes unlaced, guided from behind by Sherm McBride, tunnels toward the center. At the sight of his frail, 5-foot-7 frame, Zmijanac's face changes. You can be years around the program and think you've seen every Coach Z: thoughtful, sardonic, angry, mournful, laughing, cocky, unreadably blank. But now he smiles. Now the jaw goes soft and his eyes catch a bit of light; Zmijanac pulls the kid into a tight hug, chin on a shoulder, looking at once very old and very happy. It lasts just seconds. When Zmijanac lets DiMantae go, his face has regathered itself, all the hard lines, and it's easy again to forget how much he cares.

Zmijanac tries to resume. "Let's get after it," he says softly, but the momentum's gone. A player's voice cuts in, begins "Our Father . . . " and they all mumblingly rush through the Lord's Prayer, finishing as always with "One, Two, Three, QUIPS!" Then they're standing en masse, making for the door. McBride grabs Kaezon Pugh by the arm, pulls his ear down to his mouth. "You understand?" he hisses. "We only go as far as you take us. You've got to be the man. You've already got a name; make a bigger name! You're the man. . . ."

By the door John Evasovich, seventy-five years old, watches them pass. As always, just before walking out the door, he told his mom's ashes that he was heading to the game.

"I'm going to need water, John, outside," Zmijanac says over his shoulder.

"I have it, Mike," Evasovich says.

For the coin toss Zmijanac sends out DiMantae, in street clothes, along with his four seniors. Earlier that morning the officials had told the coach that he'd be allowed only four Aliquippa captains. "Throw him off the field then," Zmijanac replied. The officials do no such thing. DiMantae had been to other games, but this is his first time all season at midfield. The five boys hold hands.

The opponent, Southern Columbia from the eastern half of the state, is also 15-0, equal in enrollment, and wholly unknown to Aliquippa. Winner of six Class A state titles, led by their own legendary coach, the Tigers have been playing AA for only two years. Every local expert has predicted a Quips win. When Pugh scores on the game's opening drive and Aliquippa recovers a fumble on the ensuing kickoff, it seems a lock that the Quips' redemptive season, Wytiaz's miracle, will indeed play out.

But now comes disaster, and in waves. Quips quarterback Sheldon Jeter, who threw just five interceptions in 138 attempts all year, gets picked off in the end zone; Southern Columbia drives, scores, and converts the extra-point attempt to take a 7-6 lead. Then Jeter throws another interception, and the Tigers drive and score. Then Jeter throws another, returned 39 yards for a touchdown; then he gets sacked and fumbles the ball away. Zmijanac gives Southern Columbia pause with a perfectly run trick play, a 44-yard hook-and-lateral and then a 2-point conversion that cuts the lead to 21-14. But the Quips can't stop making mistakes, can't stop the Tigers quarterback, and a 28-14 halftime deficit feels far bigger. Players and staff walk into the locker room, stunned.

Kaezon Pugh sits at his locker holding his left hand in his right. "This shit hurts," he says. On the game's second play Pugh felt something give there, became convinced a bone was broken; he still carried the ball 11 times for 47 yards. The trainer leans over him, lining up a makeshift splint, taping it in place. Pugh pops a few Tylenol, swallows, winces. "Damn," he says, then stands and steps toward the door.

"Hey, Kaezon," says a teammate, "It's our last game. Let's go." Pugh doesn't seem to hear.

"Nothing left to do," Zmijanac says, "but play it out."

But it gets worse. With Jeter's confidence shattered, Zmijanac has no choice in the third quarter but to revert to down-the-throat football. Play after play, he gives the ball to Pugh, who scrambles for eight yards, five yards, six yards, four, who takes a pitch left for three more, then breaks loose for twenty to put the Quips inside Southern Columbia's 30-yard line. King Carl would be proud. And for the first time in hours, there's light, hope: Aliquippa is only down by two touchdowns. All they have to do is keep grinding. . . .

A flag flies. Aliquippa is called for a panic penalty, the worst kind: twelve men on the field. Then, on second and 18, Jeter drops back to pass, gets leveled from behind, and fumbles again. The Tigers all but race down the field and score again, each successful play dissolving what's left of Aliquippa's will. Midway through the fourth quarter,

Southern Columbia leads 42-14 and the sky has gone gray and low; Hershey is a frigid nightmare. DiMantae Bronaugh is standing forgotten on the sideline, hood covering his face. Another fumble: the Tigers score again.

Zmijanac stares out at the action, past the point of frustration or rage. Now it's just absurd. "That's the way that goes," he says.

One by one, he begins pulling seniors in the final three minutes—out of respect. But in truth, it's a worse torment for them to stop moving, to watch and think and begin to know what the town will say. With forty seconds left, the Quips fumble the ball away one last time; Aliquippa's seven turnovers is a record for a state championship game. Southern Columbia's 49 points is the most scored on Aliquippa in eight years, and the 35-point loss is the school's worst since 1994. One defensive back doubles over moaning, as if gut-shot.

For two minutes Kaezon Pugh stands with tears flowing over his cheeks, mouth frozen in a silent wail. He finished with 109 yards, all of them nearly useless. Finally, the clock ticks to zero and he hollers, "We can't get a ring to save our life, man!"

After the lineup, the shuffling handshake with Southern Columbia ("Good-gamegoodgamegoodgame . . ."), players gather around Zmijanac one last time. He's crying, too. He says he's proud. "They beat your ass today. Guess what? They beat all our asses," he says. "That's what life is about. If the worst thing that ever happens to you is you lose a football game, you're going to live a really good life." Then comes a final "Our Father," and he tells the seniors to hurry over and collect the loser's trophy.

Reporters from Beaver County and Pittsburgh, local TV, form a semicircle around Zmijanac. Southern Columbia players and fans whoop nearby, oblivious to the scrum; his hard shell begins regenerating fast. If someone had seven turnovers against us, they'd be in trouble, too, he says. Back in '03, when Darrelle Revis led Aliquippa to its last win here, Zmijanac had said that he felt like the jockey riding Secretariat. Today? "Barbaro," he cracks. "That's the one they shot." A band starts playing, tubas and trumpets blaring a slow goodbye. "Losing sucks," Zmijanac says. "That's just the way it is."

But when he walks away from the pack of writers, his eyes tear up again. Part of it is the wind, blowing harder now. The rest is the day, the program, the town. Nothing lasts forever.

"I don't know how long it will go on, to be honest with you," he says. "I have two more years. I'm going to do it for two years, and then ride off into the sunset. It's time. My wife's time. We're getting older, our kids are grown up. It's time for us to be together."

He'll leave for good then, for the first time since he moved in as a boy during World War II. The high school's future? Zmijanac is sure of only one thing. "No one will ever merge with us," he says. "No one wants us. I don't know. We can go the way of Wilkinsburg, Duquesne, the mill towns that got so small that they can't sustain their school, their community. But I don't think so. Aliquippa's different."

He walks off, toward the idling bus. One of few left in the emptying stands, DiMantae Bronaugh leans over a rail near the stairs to the Quips' locker room, waiting for the last player. The team's devotion, its nearness, all season kept him going, he says. He's down to twice-a-month chemo sessions, and the nausea comes and goes; in a couple hours, in fact, his aunt will pull over on the way home so he can throw up again. But he has started training, insists he's coming back to play—and win—next season.

Twenty minutes later Kaezon Pugh stands alone in the locker room, littered now with plastic bottles, cheap flattened equipment bags, a jar of petroleum jelly, sucked orange rinds, plastic wrappers. He hoists a backpack over his shoulder, grabs his shoulder pads in one hand and the silver trophy in the other. He walks up the tunnel and into a surprising light; the sun has broken through again, on its way down.

Pugh is nearly at the team bus when, abruptly, he stops, pivots, pauses just long enough to take in the field and the scoreboard and the final score one last time. Then he spins back, high school jersey stuffed away for good, looking for a moment like any of the millions to ever play football for neighborhood or town or region and move on. You can't tell if the kid is hurt or whole. It makes it easier. You can watch him go and forget all you know, and think once again that it's only a game.

Acknowledgments

When I first arrived in Aliquippa in the fall of 2010, I had no idea that I would end up spending so much time there, mentally and physically, over the next six years. It is a lovely place to be. The citizenry makes it so, in good times and bad, making up for any diminishment in size or stature with an unmatched warmth and generosity. I don't know that adversity makes for better people. I do know that it makes for striking candor, stunning toughness, blunt humor, and a forbearance for nosy visitors. I do know that Aliquippa and its children deserve a better fate.

My introduction to the place, as it is for many, came through its high school football program. Head coach Mike Zmijanac, assistant head coach Sherman McBride and defensive coordinator Daniel "Peep" Short threw open their doors, put up with too many questions and impositions to count, and gave me carte blanche to write about their team, town, and lives. Except in matters involving student privacy, no subject was deemed off-limits. They have my profound thanks.

All the locals, ex-locals, county residents, and interested parties whom I met subsequently were equally insightful and patient, some putting up with hours of interviews, repeated follow-ups, and sudden impositions of time. They all took great pride in what Aliquippa was and is, and sensed its unique importance. Without the following, this book would not be possible:

Ernie Accorsi, Carl Aschman Jr., Harald Aschman, David Askew, Shanelle Askew Henry, Delois Baldwin, Jeff Baldwin, Jonathan Baldwin, Tezmalita Baldwin, Anthony Battalini, Marisol Bello, C. J. Betters, Charles Betters Jr., Mark Betters, Lew Bolli, Gil Brandt, Charles Brantner, Chris Briem, Carolyn Browder, Jamie Brown, DiMantae Bronaugh, John Calipari, Bill Casp, Joe Casp, George David, Della Rae Campbell, Tommie Campbell, Sonya Carter, Dave Casoli, Pat Colalella, Carl Davidson, Andre Davis, Lynda DeLoach, Marlin Devinshire, Rev. Lawrence DiNardo, Charlotte Ditka.

Mike Ditka, Anthony "Ali" Dorsett, Tony Dorsett, Larry Dorsch, Daphney Elder, Pete Eritano, Michele Equale, John Evasovich, Nick Francalancia, Dr. James Frank, Willie Frank, Reuben Fuller, Anthony Gaskins, Ernest Genes, Aileen Gilbert, Charlie Gilbert, Diana Gilbert, Mark Gilbert, Mark "Bird" Gilbert, Sean Gilbert, Greg Gill, J. R. Gilliam, Anita Gordon, Gary Grandstaff, Davion Hall, Mikal Hall, Barron Harvey, Tyrik Hayes, Dravon Henry, Roland Henry, Darnell Hines, Rick Hill, Don Inman, Rod "Hoppy" Jeter, Kevin Johnson Jr., Kaylan Kenney, Verquan Kimbrough, Erika Kreisman.

Fred Kuppinger, Ty Law, Jon LeDonne, Carl Legge, Rev. Chris Leighton, Gilda Letteri, Joe Letteri, Renee Lias Claffey, Brandon Lindsey, Dwight Lindsey, Rev. Ezra Lowe, Jerry Malesky, Bill Macroglou, Richard Mann, Frank Marocco, Carlton McBride, Grover McBride, Janice McBride, Roxianne McBride, George "Doc" Medich, Dan Metropoulos, Mike Milanovich, George Mistovich, Edward Mitchell, Lou Mott, Ed Murphy, Don Neill, Ralph Pallante, Timmie Patrick, Vashawn Patrick, Fred Peake, Anthony Peluso, Joseph Perciavalle, Robert Pipkin, Gino Piroli, Jonha Pollock.

Kaezon Pugh, Paul Radatovich, Dan Reeves, Darrelle Revis, Dequan Rupert, Eugene "Salt" Smith, John Stanley, Roger Staubach, Melvin Steals, Mervin Steals, Jesse Steinfeld, Dr. Pat Sturm, Larry

Stokes, George "Juke" Suder, Stephen "The Poet" Suggs, Larry Taddeo, Torrie Taddeo, Townsell "T-Baby" Thomas, Ed "Junior" Thornton, Nick Trombetta, Rich Unen, Bill Vidonic, Fred Vuich, Sharon "Chedda" Casterlow Walker, Chuckie Walker, Devon Walker, Donald Walker, Dwan Walker, Willie Walker, Mike Warfield, Mike Washington, Bob Williams, Emanuel Williams, Connie Willis, Mike White, Dave Wytiaz, Don Yannessa, Elaine Yannessa, Gene Yannessa, Samuel Zbihley, and Michelle Zmijanac.

Four of them—Joe Casp, Charlotte Dikta, Joe Letteri, and Jesse Steinfeld—have since died. Dr. Steinfeld, in particular, made a heroic effort to speak to me twice despite great physical difficulty. May they rest in peace.

There were many others who proved helpful beyond measure in what became, in essence, an attempt to write the biography of one 100-year-old town. It's only right, then, to give here my One Hundred Years of Gratitude:

To the indefatigable Linda Helms and Cindy Murphy, guiding lights of the B. F. Jones Memorial Library on Franklin Avenue. Their equanimity in the face of endless requests and one balky microfilm machine, care in the maintenance of invaluable archives that include the *Woodlawn News* and *Woodlawn Gazette*, as well as insights into the town, its dynamics, and its history, made research a thrill. Their facility, against all odds, remains Aliquippa's jewel.

To Alvin Gipson, principal of Aliquippa Junior/Senior High School, and firm presence over what has always been the great refuge, town symbol, and engine of change for untold generations. I also want to thank English teacher Cindy Feher-Cherico, for allowing me to disrupt class and rummage through her vast collection of yearbooks.

To Julie Mulcahy, director of Laughlin Memorial Free Library in Ambridge, for her sharp guidance and generous contribution of an invaluable copy of the *Amalgamated Journal* archive. To the staff at Pennsylvania State University's Special Collections Library, especially

James Quigel, head of Historical Collections and Labor Archives, for his wit, warmth, and hands-on engagement regarding issues of labor and Western Pennsylvania.

To the staffs at the Pennsylvania State Archives, Harrisburg; at the Library of Congress Manuscript Reading Room in Washington DC; and the University of Pittsburgh's Archives Service Center: my deepest admiration, along with gratitude. Anyone attempting a project like this learns very quickly that the librarians, researchers, and archivists in charge of America's various collections are nonfiction's unsung heroes.

To *Sports Illustrated*'s Mark Mravic, now executive editor of the *MMQB*, whose family is rooted in Aliquippa and who first suggested a story on the town for the magazine; to former *Sports Illustrated* managing editor Terry McDonell, who saw the book possibilities before anyone else, and to managing editor Chris Stone, who for many reasons is responsible for this book getting finished at all.

To Morgan Entrekin and Jamison Stoltz at Grove Atlantic, who provided rare and unstinting support and suggestions, waved off any delays, and made everything better. You can't ask for more from either editor or publisher. Thank you for keeping the faith.

To Josh Paunil, whose early research assistance and diligence proved invaluable; George Solomon, whose interest and intervention kept the project on track; and to fact checker/ notesmith extraordinaire, Alex Holt, whose exacting eye and inextinguishable fire helped bring the thing home, at last: Thank you.

To those who sustained me through the roadblocks, enthusiasm lags, and small victories inherent in such a project, who read the manuscript early and often, who provided bottomless encouragement: my son Jack Price; my great good friend Don Van Natta Jr., ESPN's estimable investigative ace; my longtime editor Chris Hunt, *Sports Illustrated*'s unequaled dean of longform; and my super-agent/partner in crime, Andrew Blauner. "Thank you" doesn't begin to do justice to their unqualified support.

Six years is a long time to work on anything. Often without knowing it, sometimes with just a word, Marilyn Price, Sue Price, Eric Price, Bruce Schoenfeld, Simon Bruty, David and Julie Hamlin, Dave and Katherine Martin, Ilene Landress, Townsend Ludington, Joel Drucker, Steve Flink, Barry Levinson, Stefan Fatsis, Andrew Lawrence, Cullen Browder, Sam Stephenson, Dan McGrath, Kelli Anderson, Theodore Petrosky, Jonathan Yardley, and Alex Viorst kept me going. Todd Price provided a lead that proved to be gold: Thanks much.

A writer isn't the only one taken prisoner by the book researched and written; an entire family gets locked up, too. For putting up with all the 1,000-yard stares, grunts, strange mood shifts, and endless basement hours—not to mention the ubiquitous question, "Do you know who's from Aliquippa?"—I thank my daughter, Addie, and son Charlie, for the trips to Pittsburgh and State College/Harrisburg, respectively. I've never had better company on the road.

And, most of all, to my wife, Fran Brennan, for all the sacrifices made, the burdens borne, the nights and weekends lost: I offer my inadequate love and gratitude. You are the reason this gets done. You always have been.

The Town, The Players

Rapheal "Pudgy" Abercrombie—Running back, Aliquippa High, 1982–84.

Carl "King Carl" Aschman—Head football coach, Aliquippa High, 1941–1964.

David Askew—Father of Aliquippa High/Pitt running back Kaezon Pugh; uncle of Aliquippa/West Virginia defensive back Dravon Henry; husband of Diana Gilbert and stepfather of NFL defensive back Darrelle Revis. Served seven years in prison for the 1999 murder of Eddie Humphries.

Jeff Baldwin—Lineman, Aliquippa High football, 1978–80; University of Pittsburgh, 1981–83. Father of Jamie Brown and Jonathan Baldwin.

Jonathan Baldwin—Receiver, Aliquippa High football, 2005–07; University of Pittsburgh, 2008–10.

Anthony Battalini—Mayor, Aliquippa, 2003–11.

Charles "Chuck" "C. J." Betters—Owner, C. J. Betters Enterprises. Beaver County developer/entrepreneur.

Jamie Brown—Son of Jeff Baldwin, half brother of Jonathan. Currently serving a 20-to-40-year sentence for the 2001 murder of Aliquippa police officer James Naim.

Tommie Campbell—Defensive back/receiver, Aliquippa High football, 2003–05. Tennessee Titans/Jacksonville Jaguars, 2011–15.

George David—Sheriff, Beaver County, 1996–98, 2007–15.

Andre Davis—Aliquippa police chief, 2011–14. Aliquippa Police Department, 1986–2011. Father of Byron Wilson.

Mike Ditka Sr.—Burner, Aliquippa & Southern Railroad; 31-year president, Local 1432, Transport Workers Union of America. Died 1998.

Mike Ditka Jr.—Tight end, Aliquippa High, 1952–56; NFL, 1961–72. NFL head coach, Chicago Bears, 1982–92; New Orleans Saints, 1997–99.

Anthony "Ali" Dorsett—Nephew of Tony. Son-in-law of Dan "Peep" Short. Arrested as result of "Operation Enough is Enough"; sentenced to 30 years in prison in 2011.

Tony Dorsett—Running back, Hopewell High, 1970–72; University of Pittsburgh, 1973–76 (Heisman Trophy, College Hall of Fame); NFL, 1977–88 (Pro Football Hall of Fame).

Pete Eritano—President, United Steelworkers Local 1211, 1979–85.

John Evasovich—Running back, Aliquippa High football, 1955–57.

James Frank—Cocaptain, 1949 Aliquippa High basketball state champions. President of the NCAA, 1981–83.

Willie Frank—Running back, Aliquippa High, 1950–52.

Anthony Gaskins—Center, Aliquippa High football, 2002. Shot "Larry" Moon, 2005; released from prison, 2006. Slag-cutter, C. J. Betters Enterprises, 2010–2012.

Aileen Gilbert—Mother of Diana, Sean and Mark Gilbert. Grandmother of Darrelle Revis.

Diana Gilbert—Mother of Darrelle Revis. Wife of David Askew, stepmother of Aliquippa/Pitt running back Kaezon Pugh.

Sean Gilbert—Linebacker, Aliquippa High, 1986–88 (USA Today High School Defensive Player of the Year). Defensive tackle, University of Pittsburgh, 1989–91; NFL, 1992–2003.

Tom Girdler—Superintendent, Jones & Laughlin Steel, Aliquippa Works, 1914–24.

Clint Golden—Senior mediator, Pennsylvania Department of Labor and Industry. Associate director, Pittsburgh region, National Labor Relations Board, 1935.

Dravon Henry—Running back/defensive back, Aliquippa High football, 2010–13; defensive back, West Virginia University, 2014–present.

Georg Isasky—Laborer, Aliquippa Works, 1916–1930; union organizer, 1934. Committed to and later freed from mental institution, 1934.

B. F. Jones Jr.—President, Jones & Laughlin Steel Company, 1900–1923; Chairman, 1923–28.

Larry "Bulldog" Jones—Fullback, cocaptain, Aliquippa High football, 1970–72. Died of blood clot, 1972.

Ty Law—Running back/defensive back, Aliquippa High, 1989–91. Defensive back, University of Michigan, 1992–94; NFL, 1995–2009 (three-time Super Bowl champion).

Charlie Lay—Steelworker, Aliquippa Works. Aliquippa High football booster. Died 1980.

Bernard "Josh" Lay—Quarterback/cornerback, Aliquippa High football, 1998–2000. Defensive back, University of Pittsburgh, 2002–05; NFL, 2006–07.

Joe Letteri—Carpenter, Aliquippa Works, 1944–1984. Father of four-time Oscar winner Joe Letteri Jr.

Jon "White Chocolate" LeDonne—Linebacker/tight end, Aliquippa High football, 1997–2000; linebacker, Robert Morris University, 2001–2004. Head football coach, Shaler High, 2014–present.

Bob Liggett—Defensive tackle, Aliquippa High, 1962–64; University of Nebraska, 1966–69.

Nate Lippe—Head football coach, Aliquippa High, 1927–1940; head basketball coach, 1927–47; head baseball coach, 1927–47.

Henry Mancini—Composer. Aliquippa High, class of 1942. Winner of four Academy Awards and 20 Grammy Awards.

Richard Mann—Receiver, Aliquippa High, 1962–64; running back/receiver, Arizona State, 1966–68. Assistant coach, Pittsburgh Steelers, 2013–present.

Harry Mauk—Director of plant protection, Jones & Laughlin Steel, Aliquippa Works, 1915-1953.

Press Maravich—Basketball, Aliquippa High, 1933–34. Head basketball coach, Aliquippa High, 1952–54.

Pete Maravich—Born Aliquippa. Basketball Hall of Fame.

Frank Marocco—Guard/linebacker, Aliquippa High, 1952–54; head football coach, 1989–1996.

Sherman McBride—Wide receiver/defensive back, Aliquippa High, 1977–1979; wide receiver, Ohio University, 1980–83. Assistant football coach, Aliquippa High, 1984–92; 1997–2010. Assistant head football coach, 2010–present. Head track coach, 2004–present.

George "Doc" Medich—Quarterback, Hopewell High, 1962–64. Major league pitcher, 1972–82.

Sam Milanovich—Head basketball coach, Aliquippa High, 1948–1954; principal, Aliquippa High/superintendent of Aliquippa schools, 1954–66.

James "Larry" Moon—Running back, Aliquippa High football, 2002–04. Killed Diedre Walker and self, 2009.

Ben Moreell—CEO and chairman of the board, Jones & Laughlin Steel Company, 1947–57.

James Naim—Patrolman, Aliquippa Police Department, 2000–01. Killed at Linmar Terrace, 2001.

Timmie Patrick—Beaver County police detective; assistant football coach, Aliquippa High. Fullback, Aliquippa High, 1985–87.

Cornelia Bryce Pinchot—Activist for organized labor and women's rights. First Lady of Pennsylvania, 1922–27; 1931–35.

Robert Pipkin—Forward, Aliquippa High basketball, 1960–63; defensive end, Aliquippa High football, 1962.

Gino Piroli—Beaver County historian/newspaper columnist. Pipefitter, Aliquippa Works, 1943–66. Hopewell Township commissioner, 1956–67. Postmaster, Aliquippa, 1967–88.

Ernie Pitts—Receiver, Aliquippa High football, 1950–52. Winnipeg Blue Bombers, 1957–69. Killed in Colorado, 1970.

Major "Loggie" Powell—Tackle, cocaptain, Aliquippa High football, 1931–34.

Kaezon Pugh—Outside linebacker/running back, Aliquippa High football, 2012–15. Committed to University of Pittsburgh, October 2015.

Darrelle Revis—Running back/defensive back, Aliquippa High football, 2001–03. Cornerback, University of Pittsburgh, 2004–06; NFL, 2006–present. (Four-time All-Pro; Super Bowl champion.)

Moe Rubenstein—Head football coach, Ambridge High, 1929–50.

Brian Samuel—Aliquippa High. Sentenced in 1997 to life in prison for conspiracy in the 1996 murder of his parents.

Daniel "Peep" Short—Tight end/defensive back, Aliquippa High football, 1976–78. University of Pittsburgh, 1979–83. Defensive coordinator, Aliquippa High, 1989–present.

Anthony Tusweet Smith—Confederate of Jamie Brown. Sentenced in 2007 to at least 50 years in prison for drug and assault convictions.

Eugene "Salt" Smith—Inspection Department, Aliquippa Works, 1956–67. Member, Aliquippa School Board, 1971–2003. General Manager, Municipal Water Authority of Aliquippa, 1979–2011. Chairman, Aliquippa Democratic Committee, 2002–2014.

Melvin Steals—Guard, Aliquippa High basketball; class of 1964. Songwriter, "Could It Be I'm Falling In Love," 1972. English teacher, Aliquippa Junior High, 1968–75; Aliquippa High, 1976–90. Principal, Aliquippa Middle School, 1996–2000.

Mervin Steals—Guard, Aliquippa High basketball; class of 1964. Songwriter, "Could It Be I'm Falling In Love," 1972. Seamless tube department, Aliquippa Works, 1966–1976.

Jesse Steinfeld—Aliquippa High, class of 1943. U.S. surgeon general, 1969–1973.

Larry Stokes—Tight end, Aliquippa High football, 1962–64.

George "Juke" Suder—Pitcher, Aliquippa High baseball, winner of 1944 WPIAL title. Welded tube department, Aliquippa Works, 1950–1984.

George Suder—Guard, Aliquippa High basketball, 1958–61; University of Maryland, 1961–63.

Pete "Pecky" Suder—Infielder, Aliquippa High baseball, 1931–33. Philadelphia/Kansas City Athletics, 1941–55. Assistant warden/ warden, Beaver County Jail, 1961–68.

Edward Surratt—Aliquippa High, class of 1960. Currently serving two life sentences in Florida. Suspected of killing 18 people in various states in the late 1970s; confessed in 2007 to the killing of six in Western Pennsylvania.

Sharon "Chedda" Walker—Aliquippa High, class of 1974. Mother of Aliquippa mayor Dwan Walker and councilman Donald Walker, and Diedre Walker.

Chuckie Walker—Aliquippa High, class of 1971. Electrician, Aliquippa Works, 1973–86. Father of Dwan, Donald, and Diedre Walker.

Diedre Walker—Aliquippa High, class of 1995. Killed by James "Larry" Moon, 2009.

Donald Walker—Wide receiver, Aliquippa High football, 1993. Aliquippa city councilman, 2011–present.

Dwan Walker—Wide receiver, Aliquippa High football, 1993. Aliquippa mayor, 2011–present.

Tiquai Wallace—Aliquippa High ninth-grade basketball player. Died May 2009, age 14, after being hit in Plan 12 by vehicle driven by AHS basketball star Chaquille Pratt.

Mike Warfield—Quarterback, Aliquippa High football, 1984–86; Catawba College, 1987–91. Trooper, Pennsylvania State Police, 1994–2004; attached to Drug Enforcement Agency task force, 2004–present.

Monroe Weekley—Linebacker, Aliquippa High football, 1998–2000. University of Pittsburgh 2001–02; University of Kansas, 2003. Sentenced in 2012 to a minimum of 24.5 years for a third-degree murder over a $600 debt.

Byron Wilson—Long jumper, Aliquippa High track, 2003–05. Stepson of Aliquippa police chief Andre Davis.

Dave Wytiaz—Guard, Aliquippa High basketball, 1976–78. Superintendent, Aliquippa School District, 2010–2016, business manager, 2003–10. President, Aliquippa School Board, 1993–97.

Don Yannessa—Tackle, Aliquippa High, 1955–57; head football coach, Aliquippa High, 1972–88.

Mickey Zernich—Cocaptain, 1949 Aliquippa High basketball team; prominent doctor and Pitt alumni.

Mike Zmijanac—Head football coach, Aliquippa High, 1997–present. Head basketball coach, AHS, 1996–2003.

NOTES

PART ONE

7 *Čovek mora da radi . . .* : Morawska, Ewa. *For Bread with Butter: The Life-Worlds of East Central Europeans in Johnstown, Pennsylvania, 1890-1940.* Cambridge, U.K.: Cambridge University Press, 2003: pg. 42.

7 *"15 million strong"* . . . :"Progressive Era to New Era, 1900-1929: Immigrants in the Progressive Era", Library of Congress, Washington, D.C., http://www.loc.gov/teachers/classroommaterials/presentationsandactivities/presentations/timeline/progress/immigrnt/.

8 *Sent funds in 1903* . . . : Vukmir, Rade B. *The Mill.* Lanham, Md.: University Press of America, 2011: 248.

8 *Began buying up acreage twenty-six miles down the Ohio River* . . . : "Aliquippa History", Piroli, Gino, B.F. Jones Memorial Library, Aliquippa, Pa., May 20, 2008; "Aliquippa Celebrates 100 Years." *Beaver County Times.* May 25, 2008; *"The Islands of West Aliquippa were a source of food, leisure"*, *Beaver County Times.* February 25, 2015.

8 *The original village name* . . . : Ireton, Gabriel, http://www.aliquippa.gov/history.htm.

9 *General "Mad Anthony" Wayne* . . . : Thompson, Donald B. "Requiem for a Steel Town." *Industry Week.* June 10, 1985. 55.

9 *Tom Girdler, the mill's de facto* . . . : Girdler, Tom M, Sparkes, Boyden. *Boot Straps: The Autobiography of Tom M. Girdler.* Charles Scribner's Sons, 1943: 161–166.

10 *The first blast furnace* . . . : Inman, Donald R., Wollman, David H. *Portraits in Steel: An Illustrated History of Jones & Laughlin Steel Corporation.* Kent, Ohio: Kent State University Press, 1999: 63.

10 *By the end of 1912* . . . : "Aliquippa, J&L Steel and the National Immigrant Movement: A History Lesson for Beaver County." *The Bridge.* 12.

10 *Across the tracks* . . . : Piroli.

10 *Base price of $2,200* . . . : "Steelmakers Turned to African Americans in South to Fill Employee Rosters." *Beaver County Times.* February 25, 2015.

10 *The central commercial district* . . . : Piroli.

10 *"It has every modern utility . . . ":* Ireton.

11 *Plan 6, with its three clay tennis courts* . . . : Vukmir, 310.

11 *"The fathers and mothers . . . ":* Interview with Joe Perriello, conducted by Blackside, Inc. on December 19, 1992, for "The Great Depression." Washington University Libraries, Film and Media Archive, Henry Hampton Collection.

12 *Soon after the mill's opening* . . . : Vukmir, 248.

12 *"In the Aliquippa plant . . . ":* "City Items in Brief." *Pittsburgh Post.* July 15, 1913: 7.

12 *Three thousand J&L workers would go off to fight* . . . : Wollman, David H., Inman, Donald R. *Portraits in Steel: An Illustrated History of Jones & Laughlin Steel Corporation.* Kent, Ohio: The Kent State University Press, 1999: pg. 81; *Of Men and Steel,* No. 9, September 1944: pg. 7.

13 *B. F. Jones may have been the first in Pittsburgh* . . . : Inman, Wollman, 42.

13 *"It was a terrifying site, and hypnotic . . . ":* Holbrook, Stewart H. *Iron Brew: A Century of American Ore and Steel.* New York: The Macmillan Company, 1939: Chapter 1.

13 *"Black snow"* . . . : Mancini, Henry, with Lees, Gene. *Did They Mention the Music?* Chicago: Contemporary Books, Inc., 1989: 13.

14 *"Little Las Vegas"* . . . : Perriello interview.

14 *The notorious Black Hand* ...: "Italian Terror Is Lured to His Death." *Pittsburgh Gazette Times.* August 7, 1911: p. 1.

14 *"It is said"* ...: *Commonwealth v. Zec,* 262 Pa. 251, 105 Atl. 279 (1918), Pennsylvania Supreme Court, Walling, Emory.

14 *"An unofficial caliph"* ...: Girdler, 166.

14 *"There was in Aliquippa"* ...: Girdler, 177.

15 *"So, good or bad"* ...: Girdler, 19.

16 *"I hit him in the mouth"* ...: Girdler, 97.

16 *When a cadre of Finnish tin workers* ...: "War Hero Makes Mob Kiss Flag." *Pittsburgh Gazette Times,* October 8, 1919, 1–2.

16 *"They had local government"* ...: Zahorsky, Michael J., interview by Kocherzat, Stephen, June 20, 1978, in the Beaver Valley Labor History Society Collection, 1909-1981, AIS.1981.08, Archives Service Center, University of Pittsburgh. Box 2, File 58, pp. 4–5.

17 *"There were scarcely half a dozen registered Democrats"* ...: Girdler, 177–178.

17 *Immigrants opened every kind* ...: "Ethnic Clubs Are Fading into Beaver County's Past", *Beaver County Times,* February 26, 2015.

17 *In the summer of 1925* ...: "Immigrant Workers Sought New Beginning in Area's Burgeoning Steel Industry", *Beaver County Times,* February 25, 2015.

17 *"On any payday"* ...: Girdler, 170.

18 *"Shine was delivered in five-gallon tins"* ...: Zernich, Dr. Stephen, *Dr. Steve.* Pittsburgh, self-published, 1992: 3–4.

18 *After it acquired the island* ...: "The Islands of West Aliquippa Were a Source of Food, Leisure", *Beaver County Times,* February 25, 2015.

18 *330 American college men* ...: Zimbalist, Andrew, *Unpaid Professionals: Commercialism and Conflict in Big-Time College Sports.* Princeton, N.J.: Princeton University Press, 2001: 8.

19 *Professional football began in Pittsburgh:* "Birth of Pro Football", Pro Football Hall of Fame, http://www.profootballhof.com/football-history/birth-of-pro-football/.

19 *"The AAA expense sheet"*...: ibid.

19 *"What the Pittsburghs tried to do"*...: ibid.

20 *"Leading citizens found fault"*...: "History of the WPIAL", Western Pennsylvania Interscholastic Athletic League, http://www.wpial.org/history.asp.

20 *"You cannot play two kinds of football"*...: "Glenn 'Pop' Warner", National Football Foundation, http://www.footballfoundation.org/Programs/CollegeFootballHallofFame/SearchDetail.aspx?id=10054.

20 *"Ha! Ha!"*...: *Condor*, 1915, Aliquippa, Pa., Woodlawn High School, 33.

22 *"My mother was born in 1909"*...: Steals, Melvin, author interview, February 1, 2013.

22 *The fathers of James Frank*...: Frank, James, author interview, May 14, 2012.

22 *...and Eugene "Salt" Smith*...: Smith, Eugene, author interview, November 28, 2011.

22 *Private William Little*...: "The Meanest Little Town ..." *The Early County News*, March 25, 2015.

22 *Some 500,000 blacks*...: Dickerson, Dennis C. *Out of the Crucible: Black Steelworkers in Western Pennsylvania, 1875-1980*. Albany, N.Y.: State University of New York Press, 1986: 31.

22 *During the last few years of World War I*...: Dickerson, 32.

23 *Workers made 33 cents an hour*...: "Steelmakers Turned to African Americans in South to Fill Employee Rosters", *Beaver County Times*, February 25, 2015.

23 *Enough white ethnics*...: "Aliquippa Housing Plans Show Journey of Immigrants", *Beaver County Times*, February 25, 2015.

23 *When J&L built*...: *Aliquippa: The Union Comes to Little Siberia, The Great Depression*, WGBH, Boston, prod., PBS, 1993.

24 *60 cents an hour*...: Dickerson, 50.

24 *Superintendent of J&L's seamless tube*...: Perriello interview, 462.

24 *"Betrayed by Reconstruction"* . . . : Murray, Albert, *Trading Twelves: The Selected Letters of Ralph Ellison and Albert Murray.* New York: Vintage Books, 2001: preface, cit.

25 *250,000* . . . : "The Ku Klux Klan in Pennsylvania, 1920–1940", Jenkins, Philip, *The Western Pennsylvania Historical Magazine,* Vol. 69, No. 2, April 1986.

25 *300,000* . . . : Loucks, Emerson Hunberger. "The Ku Klux Klan in Pennsylvania: A Study in Nativism." Harrisburg, Pa.: The Telegraph Press, 1936.

25 *Next-door Allegheny County* . . . : Jenkins, Philip, *Hoods and Shirts: The Extreme Right in Pennsylvania, 1925–1950.* Chapel Hill, N.C.: The University of North Carolina Press, 1997, 71.

25 *. . . Beaver County, with nine klaverns* . . . : Ku Klux Klan Kleagle Robe Reports 1924-25 (Series #30.19); Record Group 30, Records of the Pennsylvania State Police; Pennsylvania State Archives, Harrisburg.

25 *In July 1923* . . . : Jenkins, *Hoods and Shirts,* 67.

25 *. . . Ku Klux Klan of Woodlawn." It was announced in the spring of 1922 with a late-night launch of skyrockets, a burning cross* . . . : *Woodlawn News,* letter, April 28, 1922, p. 1; article, June 2, 1922, p. 5.

25 *"To drive the colored people"* . . . : Girdler, 179–180.

25 *Many a night the town's young black men* . . . : Cobb, Clark, interview, May 14, 1980, in the Beaver Valley Labor History Society Collection, 1909-1981, AIS.1981.08, Archives Service Center, University of Pittsburgh; Box #2, File 48, p. 35.

26 *In 1923* . . . : Dickerson, 81.

26 *. . . welcomed in "the regalia of their order" by town pastors . . . while a choir sang "Onward, Christian Soldiers"* . . . : *Woodlawn Gazette,* January 11, 1924, p. 1.

26 *. . . celebrated with a "special sermon" at an evening Methodist service at Woodlawn High* . . . : *Woodlawn Gazette,* February 26, 1924, p. 1.

26 *"Sometimes in the summer"* . . . : Mancini, 16.

26 *Some, like Emory Clark* . . . : Stephenson, Sam. "Sonny Clark, Part 2." *The Paris Review,* January 26, 2011, http://www.theparisreview.org/

blog/2011/01/26/sonny-clark-part-ii/. Based on Stephenson interviews with Sonny Clark's surviving family members and friends in Herminie No. 2, Pennsylvania.

27 *Reputedly outraced a horse* . . . : North, E. Lee, *Battling the Indians, Panthers, and Nittany Lions: The Story of Washington and Jefferson College's First Century of Football, 1890-1990.* Daring Publishing Group, 1991: 125–132.

27 *In the off-seasons* . . . : "Sport and Black Pittsburgh, 1900-1930", Ruck, Rob, ed., Miller, Patrick B., Wiggins, David K. Sport and the Color Line: Black Athletes and Race Relations in Twentieth-Century America. New York: Routledge, 2004: 12.

28 *A waiting crowd* . . . : North, 125–132.

28 *"We didn't bring him with us this time"* . . . : ibid.

28 *The first time a black man* . . . : "Meet the Presidents", Meyer, Walter G., *Pittsburgh Magazine,* October 30, 2014.

28 *"He was an idol of mine"* . . . : "Payoff: Pruner Makes Hall of Fame", *Washington Observer and Reporter,* Washington, Pa., April 17, 1979, 19.

29 *"It was segregated, but not in sports"* . . . : Thomas, Townsell, author interview, April 10, 2015.

30 *Though his customary suit had been replaced* . . . : Green, James, "Democracy Comes to Little Siberia", *Labor's Heritage,* Vol. 5, No. 2, Summer 1993, George Meany Memorial Archives, Silver Spring, Md.: 11; Brooks, Thomas R. *Clint: A Biography of a Labor Intellectual.* New York: Atheneum, 1978: 129.

30 *By seventeen* . . . : Brooks, 14, 16, 20.

30 *Golden's clothes* . . . : Golden, Clinton S., letter to wife Dora, undated (Tuesday P.M.), Clinton S. Golden papers (1565), Historical Collections and Labor Archives, Special Collections Library, Pennsylvania State University.

31 *The idle in Aliquippa talked women, baseball* . . . : Brooks, ibid.

31 *Twenty steelworkers* . . . : Cortner, Richard C. *The Jones & Laughlin Case.* New York: Alfred A. Knopf, Inc., 1970: 34.

32 *On New Year's Day 1920* . . . : Stevenson, David. *Cataclysm: The First World War as Political Tragedy.* New York: Basic Books, 2009: 440.

32 *The Attorney General then spent the winter* . . . : "May Day Death Plot Is Uncovered", *Tulsa Daily World*, April 30, 1920, p. I.

32 *But on September 16* . . . : "Havoc Wrought in Morgan Offices", *New York Times*, September 17, 1920, p. I.

33 *"The idea is if we don't look out"* . . . : Fitzgerald, F. Scott. *The Great Gatsby.* New York: Charles Scribner's Sons, 1925: Chapter I.

33 *By 1920* . . . : Inman and Wollman, 289-290; *The Iron Age*, January 2, 2013, American Iron and Steel Institute.

33 *By 1924* . . . : Inman and Wollman, 92.

33 *"Girdler"* . . . : "An Occurrence at Republic Steel", Fast, Howard, in Leighton, Isabel, ed., *The Aspirin Age, 1919–1941.* New York: Simon and Schuster, 1949, 399.

34 *"Break it up, you Hunkies!"* . . . : Davin, Eric Leif. *Crucible of Freedom: Workers' Democracy in the Industrial Heartland, 1914–1960.* Lanham, Md.: Lexington Books, 2012, 160.

34 *"Woodlawn is governed and regulated by fear"* . . . : *Woodlawn News*, March 30, 1923, p. I.

34 *Four days later* . . . : *Woodlawn News*, April 3, 1923, p.I.

35 *"American Plan"* . . . : Brooks, 49–50.

35 *Girdler boasted* . . . : Girdler, 175–176.

35 *"In that day you had to keep your mind shut* . . . : Razzano, Angelo, interview by Hoffman, Alice M., January 16, 1974, in the United Steelworkers of America Oral History Collection, Penn State University. P. 3. This interview is listed as being with "Angelo Rozzano." For the sake of historical consistency, I've chosen to use the name listed in U.S Census and Supreme Court records, as well as contemporaneous accounts.

35–36 *"We don't discharge a man for belonging to a union"* . . . : Brody, David. *Labor in Crisis: The Steel Strike of 1919.* Champaign, IL: University of Illinois Press, 1965: 89.

36 *"It wasn't so much union"* . . . : Zahorsky.

36 *"Typical Cossack town"* . . . : Davin, 160.

37 *"He's reading the Declaration of Independence"* ... : Muselin, Pete, "The Steel Fist in a Pennsylvania Company Town", in Schultz, Bud, Schultz, Ruth, *It Did Happen Here: Recollections of Political Repression in America*, Berkeley, CA: University of California Press, 1989: 69–71.

37 *"One of the dirtiest"* ... : Muselin, 72.

38 *"Hopelessly maladjusted"* ... : Spiniza, Judith Ader. "Women of Long Island: Cornelia Bryce Pinchot, Feminist, Social-Activist-The Long Islander Who Became First Lady of Pennsylvania." www.spinizalongislandestates.com.

38 *"There was nothing"* ... : Perriello interview.

38 *"Sometimes we would have a customer for the day"* ... : Steinfeld, Jesse, author interview, June 27, 2012.

38 *"They'd bring in maybe twenty or thirty of us"* ... : Perriello, interview.

39 *"What my father thought of Franklin Roosevelt"* ... : Interview with Tom Girdler, Jr. , conducted by Blackside, Inc. on December 22, 1992, for "The Great Depression." Washington University Libraries, Film and Media Archive, Henry Hampton Collection.

40 *One, fifty-year-old John Mayer* ... : Mayer, John S., affidavit, August 29, 1933, Clinton S. Golden Papers, Box 5, Historic Collections and Labor Archive, Pennsylvania State University; Green, William, letter to Pinchot, Gifford, August 30, 1933, Clinton S. Golden Papers, Box 5, Historic Collections and Labor Archive, Pennsylvania State University; Brooks, 128-129; Heineman, Kenneth J. *Catholic New Deal: Religion and Reform in Depression Pittsburgh.* University Park, Pa.: Penn State Press, 2010: pgs. 50-51.

40 *Publicly called on "patriots"* ... : "Probe Demanded by Legion speaker", *Pittsburgh Press*, November 13, 1935, pg. 38.

40 *In October '33* ... :"Insurgent Miners Fight Peace", *Pittsburgh Post-Gazette*, October 3, 1933, page 4.

41 *"Come and take 'em!"* ... : "Ambridge Riot Described By Eye-Witness", Baubie, James A., *Pittsburgh Sun-Telegraph*, October 6, 1933.

41 *"It was probably meant for me"* ... : Muselin, 74.

41 *"One of the most wonderful things that ever happened in this valley"* ... : Davin.

42 *"Violent terroristic action"*...: National Labor Relations Board ruling, April 9, 1936.

42 *"We want you to get busy"*...: Brooks, 133.

42 *"One of the most fearless, well-controlled people I've ever seen"*...: Girdler, Jr., interview.

42 *"He shot at me and missed"*...: ibid.

44 *"Always told us we had to win THAT game"*...: "Rubinstein Honored, Ambridge Pays Homage." *Pittsburgh Post-Gazette.* August 30, 1977: 6.

44 *"Their frequent conflicts"*...: "Casp's Age Challenged by Ambridge." *Pittsburgh Post-Gazette.* October 24, 1934: 16.

45 *The Cleveland native wanted to be a doctor*...: Mark Kriegel, *Pistol: The Life of Pete Maravich*, New York: Free Press, 2008: 17.

45 *Perhaps the worst loss:* "Casp's Age Challenged by Ambridge." *Pittsburgh Post-Gazette.* October 24, 1934: 16.

45 *On September 24, 1934, an unnaturalized Slovak named Mary Isasky*...: Mary Isasky, letter to Mrs. Pinchot, Sept. 24, 1934. Cornelia Pinchot papers, Collections of the Manuscript Division, Library of Congress.

46 *Her father had been a congressman*...: Miller, Char. *Gifford Pinchot and the Making of Modern Environmentalism.* Washington, D.C.: Shearwater Books, 2001: 177.

46 *Leveraged a $15 million fortune*...: Beers, Paul B. *Pennsylvania Politics Today and Yesterday: The Tolerable Accommodation.* University Park, Pa.: Penn State Press, 2010: 101.

46 *By 1914*...: Miller, 180.

46 *"One of the keenest political minds"*...: "Cornelia Bryce Pinchot (1881–1960)", Grey Towers National Historic Site website, http://www.fs.usda.gov/detail/greytowers/aboutgreytowers/history/?cid=stelprd3824418.

46 *"Pinchot never dared"*...: Bruen, E.J., "MRS. PINCHOT, BOSS; Pennsylvania Old Guard Regards Her as Warwick Behind Candidate", *New York Times*, August 27, 1922.

46 *"Women don't want generalities and hot air"*...: Grey Towers NHS website.

47 *"It was due to Mrs. Pinchot"* . . . : ibid.

47 *"All my speeches are extemporaneous"* . . . : Beers, Paul B. *Pennsylvania Politics Today and Yesterday: The Tolerable Accommodation.* University Park, PA: Penn State University Press, 2010: 103.

48 *"Well, here I am"* . . . : "Mrs. Pinchot Gives Mellon Word Licking", *Pittsburgh Press,* November 26, 1933, 12.

48 *"Grisly farce"* . . . : Bryce Pinchot, Cornelia, speech, February 28, 1934, "Just Wolves, Mrs. Pinchot Says of NRA", Associated Press, *The Daily Oklahoman,* February 28, 1934.

48 *"No business on this side of the river"* . . . : *Amalgamated Journal,* August 30, 1934, Vol. XXXVI, No. 1, "Great Meeting at Ambridge", page 1, column 1.

48 *"For only just one reason"* . . . : "Steel Town", Ruttenberg, Harold. *The Nation,* November 28, 1934.

49 *"You black-handed mothers"* . . . : Brooks, 133.

50 *"Neurotic and pathological tendencies"* . . . : Liveright, Alice J., memorandum to Gifford Pinchot, October 19, 1934. Cornelia Pinchot papers, Collections of the Manuscript Division, Library of Congress.

50 *"Quiet and orderly"* . . . : McKinniss, C.R., letter to Mary Isasky, September 20, 1934. Cornelia Pinchot papers, Collections of the Manuscript Division, Library of Congress.

50 *"Let me know about this"* . . . : Bryce Pinchot, Cornelia, letter to Mary Isasky, September 29, 1934. Cornelia Pinchot papers, Collections of the Manuscript Division, Library of Congress.

51 *"Spotted and followed"* . . . : Golden, Clinton S., letter to wife Dora, October 6, 1934, Clinton S. Golden papers (1565), Historical Collections and Labor Archives, Special Collections Library, Pennsylvania State University.

51 *"You could almost feel the relief"* . . . : ibid.

51 *"As sane as I am"* . . . : Brooks, 135.

52 *Oct. 14, 1934* . . . : ibid.

53 *"It was wonderful"* . . . : *Amalgamated Journal,* October 25, 1934, Vol. XXXVI, No. 9, page 7.

53 *"Friends", she began* . . . : Bryce Pinchot, Cornelia, October 14, 1934, speech to the Amalgamated Association of Iron, Steel and Tin Workers, Aliquippa, Pa. Cornelia Pinchot papers, Collections of the Manuscript Division, Library of Congress.

55 *"She came to Aliquippa"* . . . : Interview with Harold Ruttenberg, conducted by Blackside, Inc. on December 21, 1992, for "The Great Depression." Washington University Libraries, Film and Media Archive, Henry Hampton Collection.

56 *"In a very dramatic way"* . . . : Bryce Pinchot, Cornelia, letter to Roger Baldwin, November 16, 1934. Cornelia Pinchot papers, Collections of the Manuscript Division, Library of Congress.

56 *"It's the crazy house"* . . . : *Amalgamated Journal*, November 1, 1934, Vol. XXXVI, No. 10, page 3.

56 *"I want somebody's names"* . . . : Golden, Clinton S., letter to wife Dora, October 24, 1934 (est. "Wednesday P.M."), Clinton S. Golden papers (1565), Historical Collections and Labor Archives, Special Collections Library, Pennsylvania State University.

56 *"We can't believe what that damn fool governor says"* . . . : "More Lunacy Commitments To Be Studied", *Pittsburgh Post-Gazette*, October 26, 1934: 8.

57 *37 percent unemployment* . . . : Bezilla, Michael. *Penn State: An Illustrated History.* University Park, PA.: Pennsylvania State University Press, 1985.

57 *"We had a happy town"* . . . : Perriello, interview.

57 *"If my mother was sick"* . . . : Interview with James Downing, Jr., conducted by Blackside, Inc. on December 20, 1992, for The Great Depression. Washington University Libraries, Film and Media Archive, Henry Hampton Collection.

58 *On Labor Day, two competing worker parades* . . . : "Two Celebrations Mark Labor Day", *The Daily Times*, Beaver, Pa., September 8, 1936, pg. 1.

58 *Deep rich green turf* . . . : *Aliquippa Gazette*, September 25, 1936: 1.

58 *"Vast mechanism"* . . . : *N.L.R.B. v. Jones & Laughlin Steel Corp., 301 U.S. 1 (1937)*, U.S. Supreme Court, April 12, 1937.

59 *Employing 22,000* . . . : "Jones & Laughlin: Depressions & Mutations of a Mighty Dynasty: Work Change in Steel's 4th Largest", *The Bulletin Index*, April 9, 1936.

59 *"40 percent of its limestone"* . . . : ibid.

59 *60 million tons of iron ore* . . . : National Labor Relations board ruling, *Jones & Laughlin Steel Corporation and Amalgamated Association of Iron Steel & Tin Workers of North America, Beaver Valley Lodge No. 200,* April 9, 1936.

59 *"The ramifications of the Jones & Laughlin"* . . . : *N.L.R.B. v. Jones & Laughlin Steel Corp., 301 U.S. 1 (1937),* U.S. Supreme Court, April 12, 1937.

60 *"The company's opposition to a union was very simple"* . . . : Perriello, interview.

61 *"I have been reading over some of the cases"* . . . : Bryce Pinchot, Cornelia, speech, Aliquippa, Pa., September 1, 1935. Cornelia Pinchot papers, Collections of the Manuscript Division, Library of Congress.

61 *Martin Dunn* . . . : Cortner, 83.

61 *Over the succeeding months* . . . : ibid.

62 *After his dismissal* . . . : Razzano, Angelo, interview with Hoffman, Alice, January 16, 1974, page 8

62 *When he returned that night, Razzano bumped into Eli Bozich* . . . : ibid, page 9.

62 *Beyond the NLRB's description of him* . . . : National Labor Relations Board ruling, *Jones and Laughlin Steel Corporation and Amalgamated Association of Iron Steel & Tin Workers of North America, Beaver Valley Lodge No. 200,* April 9, 1936.

62–63 *Relations between black steelworkers and organized labor had long been scarred by bigotry and mutual distrust* . . . : Dickerson, Dennis C. *Out of the Crucible: Black Steelworkers in Western Pennsylvania, 1875-1980.* Albany, N.Y.: State University of New York Press, 1986: pg. 92.

63 *Boyer came to J&L five years later* . . . : National Labor Relations Board ruling, *Jones and Laughlin Steel Corporation and Amalgamated Association of Iron Steel & Tin Workers of North America, Beaver Valley Lodge No. 200,* April 9, 1936.

63 *The year before, in the nearby town of Industry* . . . : "Beaver County Official 'Bucks' Pinchot's Order", *Pittsburgh Courier,* September 9, 1933, pgs. 1, 4; *"Beaver County Officials May Face Grand Jury Probe In Shanghai Case",* Pittsburgh Courier, September 2, 1933, pgs. 1, 11.

63 *In 1933, a black man was killed* . . . : Ruttenberg, Harold. "Steel Town." *The Nation,* November 28, 1934: pg. 624.

63 *Boyer was fired a month before Razzano* ... : National Labor Relations Board ruling, *Jones and Laughlin Steel Corporation and Amalgamated Association of Iron Steel & Tin Workers of North America, Beaver Valley Lodge No. 200,* April 9, 1936.

63 *Mauk's police introduced a new tactic* ... : Golden, Clinton S., letter to Moser, Clarence, March 7, 1935, Clinton S. Golden Papers, Historical Collections and Labor Archives, Special Collections Library, Pennsylvania State University.

64 *"Silent intake of spectators' breaths"* ... : *Time,* Altman, Nancy J. *The Battle for Social Security: From FDR's Vision To Bush's Gamble.* Hoboken, N.J.: John Wiley & Sons, 2012.

64 *"When industries organize themselves on a national scale"* ... : Cortner, 164.

65 *"A major turning point"* ... : ibid, pg. VIII of preface.

65 *"Revolutionized industrial relations"* ... : Lieberman, Elias. *Unions Before the Bar: Historic Trials Showing the Evolution of Labor Rights in the United States.* New York: Harper & Brothers, 1950: 193-201; Green, 19.

65 *Royal Boyer received $2,040* ... : *Pittsburgh Courier,* April 24, 1937, page 4.

65 *And Angelo Razzano* ... : Razzano, Angelo, Hoffman, Alice interview, January 16, 1974, p. 15.

65 *"Utter disgust and dismay"* ... : Girdler, Jr., interview.

65 *"When I hear Wagner Act went constitutional"* ... : Kennedy, David M. *Freedom from Fear: The American People in Depression and War, 1929–1945.* Oxford, U.K.: Oxford University Press, 1999.

66 *"I was bitter about this"* ... : Girdler, Sr., 226.

66 *"My father made the famous statement"* ... : Girdler, Jr., interview.

66 *The company pushed for a vote* ... : Green, 19.

66 *A Clint Golden spy* ... : Clint Golden spy report, February 24, 1937, Clinton S. Golden papers (1565), Historical Collections and Labor Archives, Special Collections Library, Pennsylvania State University. Collection of Pennsylvania State University, Box 5, Folder 29.

66 *Both J&L locals* ... : Green, 19; Inman, Wollman, 108.

67 *At 11 p.m* ... : Inman, Wollman, 108.

67 *"I beat the hell out of him"*...: Razzano, Angelo, interview by Hoffman, Alice, January 16, 1974, p. 15.

67 *"The strike is a rank-and-file affair"*...: Inman, Wollman, 108, cit. Brooks, Robert R.R. *As Steel Goes...: Unionism in a Basic Industry.* New Haven: Yale University Press, 1940: 124-125, Green, 20.

68 *"I don't want any trouble here"*...: Inman, Wollman, 111, cit. Robert R. R. Brooks, 126.

69 *"J&L has been brought to its knees"*...: Pacchioli, David, "Forged in Steel", *Penn State News,* January 1, 1999, http://news.psu.edu/story/141007/1999/01/01/research/forged-steel.

69 *"Let us forget the tension of the past few weeks"*...: Inman, Wollman, 114., cit. *The J&L Steel Employes Journal 2,* no. 9, May 26, 1937: 1.

70 *A recession in 1938*...: Harvard Business School, Lehman Brothers Collection-Contemporary Business Archives, "Jones & Laughlin Industries, Inc.", http://www.library.hbs.edu/hc/lehman/company.html?company=jones_laughlin_industries_inc.

70 *"Very, very hard"*...: Letteri, Joe, author interview, May 11, 2012

72 *No one, of course, would have predicted that Suder*...: "Aliquippa Star Played 13 Years in the Majors", Bires, Mike, *Beaver County Times,* November 15, 2006; Elias Sports Bureau.

72 *"From a total disaster into a busy little town"*...: Steinfeld, author interview, October 14, 2012.

72 *"That's eight Oscars"*...: Piroli, Gino, author interview, May 11, 2012.

74 *Steam whistles*...: "New Year Brings Back Memories of Past Celebrations", Piroli, Gino, *Beaver County Times,* January 11, 2016.

74 *Three men a year*...: Estimate based off author interview with Piroli, Gino, May 11, 2012.

74 *"Our sport consisted of turning off the lights"*...: Zernich, 6.

75 *"Rockne is dead"*...: "Speaking of Sports", Bickford, Peter, *The Daily Republican,* Monongahela, Pa., February 28, 1941: 2.

75 *"The varsity grid cupboard is bare"* . . . : Amper, Richard, *Aliquippa Gazette*, February 21, 1941.

76 *The team local papers dubbed the "Steelers"* . . . : "Steelers Open Season with 39-0 Victory Over Freedom", *The Daily Times*, September 6, 1941, pg. 7.

76 *He worked as a "burner"* . . . : Ditka, Mike, author interview, November 16, 2010.

77 *J&L logged a $10.3 million profit in '40* . . . : Inman, Wollman, 116.

77 *1,279 pupils* . . . : *The Daily Times*, Beaver, Pa., April 18, 1941, page 2, column 3.

77 *407 students dropped out* . . . : "Aliquippa", The History of Beaver County Schools, Volume 1. Adams, Belle, ed. Beaver County Historical Research & Landmarks Foundation, printed by Closson Press, Apollo, Pa., 1982.

77 *J&L's furnaces* . . . : "Army-Navy 'E' Is Presented in Aliquippa", *Pittsburgh Post-Gazette*, January 7, 1943: 16.

77 *Over the next four years* . . . : B.F. Jones Library Holding: "General Marshall's Victory Report on the Winning of World War II in Europe and the Pacific", "Added Section Featuring the Contributions made by our Community toward the Winning of the War", 1945, U.S. Department of War, distributed by Aliquippa VFW Post # 3577.

77 *"The men would congregate"* . . . : Letteri, Gilda, author interview, May 11, 2012.

77 *"Power by Jesse Gunn"* . . . : "Too Much 'General' Lee-New Castle Easily Wins Class AA Title", Kurtz, Paul, *Pittsburgh Press*, November 27, 1942: 38.

78 *"There was no warning"* . . . : *"22 Killed When Bus Is Crushed by Avalanche"*, United Press, *Shamokin News-Dispatch*, Shamokin, Pa., December 23, 1942.

79 *"Watched him play all the time"* . . . : Letteri, Joe, author interview, August 2012.

79 *In December of '43* . . . : *The Evening Times*, February 9, 1945.

79 *"He never made it back"* . . . : Suder, George "Juke", author interview, June 6, 2012.

80 *In March 1943* . . . : Inman, Wollman, 124.

80 *But only the Aliquippa Works* . . . : ibid, 127.

80 *"Distinguished service"* . . . : "Army-Navy 'E' is Presented in Aliquippa", *Pittsburgh Post-Gazette,* January 7, 1943: 16.

80 *"This war is not merely the army's war"* . . . : ibid.

81 *"Don't worry about us"* . . . : Piroli, Gino, *Beaver County Times,* July 22, 2002.

82 *"He didn't get in the war"* . . . : Ditka, Charlotte, author interview, November 5, 2010.

82 *"You ever pitch before?"* . . . : Suder, George "Juke", author interview, June 6, 2012.

83 *In most other years, that would've ended Aliquippa's shot at a sectional title* . . . : "Coaches' Rivalry Began in College Days", Piroli, Gino, *Beaver County Times,* January 15, 2001, page A2.

84 *"The only insignificant phase of the proceedings"* . . . : "Quips Win First WPIAL Title," Wallace, Nick, *Aliquippa Evening Times,* June 6, 1944.

84 *"First guy up"* . . . : Suder, George "Juke", author interview.

85 *That afternoon's Evening Times* . . . : The Evening Times, Aliquippa, June 6, 1944, page 1.

85 *The only mention* . . . : *The Evening Times,* June 6, 1944, page 1.

85 *John Kaurich* . . . : Omaha Beach Memorial, http://www.omaha-beach-memorial.org/public/kia.php.

85 *Ninnie Vuich* . . . : *The Evening Times,* June 25, 1944.

85 *Toats DiNardo* . . . : *The Evening Times,* February 9, 1945.

86 *In July of '44* . . . : *The Evening Times,* July 17, 1944.

PART TWO

96 *"You accepted those things"* . . . : Frank, James, author interview, May 14, 2012.

96 *By 1940, some 3,200 blacks* . . . : *1940 Census of Population and Housing: Pennsylvania,* Washington, D.C., 1940.

96 *"I never grew up prejudiced"*...: Ditka, Mike, author interview, November 16, 2010.

96 *"Everybody was equal"*...: Zmijanac, Mike, author interview, September 23, 2010.

96 *"Very prejudiced"*...: Ditka, Mike, with Pierson, Don. *Ditka: An Autobiography.* Chicago: Bonus Books, Inc., 1986: 47.

97 *"Each of the plans had a gang"*...: Crile, George. *Charlie Wilson's War.* New York: Grove Press, 2003: 43.

97 *Until the mid-1950's*...: "Black Workers at the Aliquippa Works", *Beaver Valley Labor History Journal,* September 1979: pg. 5; Dickerson, Dennis C. *Out of the Crucible: Black Steelworkers in Western Pennsylvania, 1875-1980.* Albany: N.Y.: State University of New York Press, 1986: 52–53.

97 *"I knew there was no future"*...: Smith, Eugene "Salt", author interview, November 28, 2011.

98 *35,329 others*...: *Baseball Reference* box score, "Brooklyn Dodgers at Pittsburgh Pirates, June 24, 1947", http://www.baseball-reference.com/boxes/PIT/PIT194706240.shtml; Piroli, Gino, "Robinson's First Pittsburgh Game A Momentous Occasion", *Beaver County Times,* May 6, 2007.

98 *"He was the crack"*...: Frank, author interview.

99 *"Five white boys"*...: Smith, author interview.

100 *"My father thought I played in the band"*...: Marocco, Frank, author interview, January 4, 2012.

100 *"My dad wasn't too much on us playing ball"*...: Frank, Jimmy, author interview.

100 *Led by Frank*...: Piroli, Gino, "Aliquippa's Run Brought Back Memories of 1949 Basketball Team", *Beaver County Times,* March 29, 2015.

101 *Nate Lippe just missed out*...: Piroli, Gino, "Coaches' Rivalry Began in College Days", *Beaver County Times,* January 15, 2001: A2.

101 **The Beaver County Times** ...: Bires, Mike, "Quips Rekindling Memories of 1949 State Champs", *Beaver County Times,* March 20, 2015; Piroli, Gino, "Aliquippa's Run Brought Back Memories of 1949 Basketball Team", *Beaver County Times,* March 29, 2015.

101 *"Let me tell you, friends of mine"*...: Piroli, ibid.

101 *30,000 people*: ibid.

101 *"My father wouldn't let me go"*...: Letteri, Joe, author interview, May 11, 2012.

102 *"We didn't expect that kind of turnout"*...: Frank, author interview.

102 *"They were going to fire him"*...: Piroli, Gino, author interview, January 4, 2012.

103 *"They called us into a room in study hall"*...: Mott, Lou, author interview, February 17, 2013.

103 *"He never discussed things like that"*...: Aschman, Carl, Jr., author interview, February 28, 2012.

103 *Played well enough*...: Beaver County Hall of Fame, "Carl Aschman", http://www.bcshof.org/halloffamers/aschman1976.htm.

103 *"Paper heart"*...: Aschman, Carl, Jr., author interview.

103 *"Some people thought he was nuts"*...: Yannessa, Don, author interview, March 29, 2012.

104 *"Crewcut Club"*...: Kriegel, Mark. *Pistol: The Life Of Pete Maravich*. New York: Free Press, 2007: 48.

104 *"Come here, you!"*...: Marocco, author interview.

104 *"Today's football is a war game"*...: *Aliquippa Gazette*, February 1, 1945, Section 7, pg. 5.

105 *"When I was a kid, you had to be tough"*...: Marocco, author interview.

106 *"He didn't push me"*...: Aschman, Carl, Jr., author interview.

106 *"I didn't think he was the greatest guy"*...: Frank, Jimmy, author interview.

106 *"I gave my dad my paycheck"*...: Frank, Willie, author interview, October 31, 2011.

106 *"Like Stalag 17"*...: Evasovich, John, author interview, November 6, 2011.

107 *"Aschman served breakfast"*...: Marocco, author interview, November 12, 2010.

107 *"Come and get me, I'm finished"* . . . : Frank, Willie, author interview.

108 *"He was a good teacher"* . . . : Aschman, Carl, Jr., author interview.

108 *"Black players under Carl Aschman"* . . . : Frank, Willie, author interview.

108 *"I played my whole life"* . . . : Ditka, Mike, author interview, November 16, 2010.

109 *"They're comparable"* . . . : Evasovich, author interview.

109 *The Quips rolled Erie Tech* . . . : *Aliquippa Quips 1910–2010: Football History*, Aliquippa High School, Aliquippa, Pa., 2010.

109 *"Son, you can run!"* . . . : Frank, Willie, author interview.

109 *"Once we got to high school"* . . . : ibid.

109 *Late in October* . . . : "The Sport-Lite With Wally Fausti", Fausti, Wally, *Beaver Valley Times*, November 5, 1952.

110 *Nine thousand people crowded into Aliquippas stadium to see him open the scoring* . . . : "Aliquippa whips Beaver Falls, 28-7", Fausti, Wally, *Beaver Valley Times*, November 1, 1952, page 10.

110 *The next week, Frank rushed for 102 yards* . . . : "Quips Come From Behind To Whip New Castle, 18-7; For Ninth Straight Win", Fausti, Wally, *Beaver Valley Times*, November 8, 1952, page 8; "Two Die, Eleven Hurt In Crash", *Beaver Valley Times*, November 8, 1952, page 1.

110 *An estimated 12,000* . . . : "Quips Earn Chance At Class AA Title", Perrotta, Sal, *Beaver Valley Times*, November 15, 1952, page 6.

110 *Aschman had his superstitions* . . . : Aschman, Carl, Jr., author interview.

110 *Some 8,000 showed up* . . . : "Extra Point Gives Quips AA Title", Anderson, Bill, *Beaver Valley Times*, November 30, 1952.

111 *"On film, I saw eight guys absolutely make solid contact"* . . . : Evasovich, author interview.

111 *"That one year turned it all around"* . . . : Mott, author interview.

111 *"He was untouchable after that"* . . . : Yannessa, author interview.

111 *Dressed him like a little lord* . . . : Ditka, *Ditka: An Autobiography*: 46.

112 *"I didn't even know him until I was five years old"*...: Ditka, author interview.

112 *Big Mike*...: Ditka, *Ditka: An Autobiography:* 50–51.

112 *"When he got done, he got up"*...: Ditka, author interview.

112 *He went to St. Titus for elementary school*...: Ditka, author interview; *Ditka: An Autobiography:* 48–49.

113 *"Nearly burned the woods down"*...: Ditka, author interview.

113 *"I tell you: It was bad"*...: ibid.

114 *"Why? Because that was a part of what you were"*...: Evasovich, author interview.

114–115 *Sophomore year, he was one of the last players*...: Ditka, author interview.

115 *"He cried a lot"*...: Marocco, author interview, January 4, 2012.

115 *"You can play"*...: Ditka, *Ditka: An Autobiography:* 53.

115 *Ditka worked out endlessly*...: ibid; Ditka, author interview.

115 *"Tough with my mom"*...: Ditka, Mike, Telander, Rick. *The '85 Bears: We Were The Greatest.* Chicago: Triumph Books, 2015.

115 *"I would've stopped it more if I could"*...: Ditka, Charlotte, author interview, November 5, 2010.

116 *"It was all him"*...: Ditka, Mike, author interview.

116 *Weighed 160 pounds*...: Ditka, Mike, *Ditka: An Autobiography:* 53.

116 *The star receiver*...: ibid, 52.

117 *"They haven't the desire"*...: "Quip Cleaters Set for Opener", *Beaver Valley Times,* September 14, 1955, page 12.

117 *Aliquippa tore Westinghouse apart*...: *Aliquippa Quips 1910–2010.*

117 *Then beat McKeesport in the rain*...: "Aliquippa Eliminates McKeesport in AA, 18-12", *Pittsburgh Post-Gazette,* September 24, 1955, page 15.

117 *32–6 over Ellwood City*...: *Aliquippa Quips 1910–2010.*

117 *23-6 over unbeaten Rochester*...: "Aliquippa Ousts Rochester Gridders, 23-6", *Beaver Valley Times,* October 8, 1955, page 6.

117 *Easy wins* . . . : *Aliquippa Quips 1910-2010.*

117 *Ambridge came to Aliquippa Stadium* . . . : "Quips Bump Bridgers In Thriller, 26 to 12", Fausti, Wally, *Beaver Valley Times,* November 12, 1955, page 6.

117 *A three-inch snowfall* . . . : "Aliquippa-Mt. Lebanon Game Postponed", *Beaver Valley Times,* November 19, 1955, page 7.

117 *Aliquippa was named 13½-point favorites* . . . : "Quips Favored over Mounties", *Beaver Valley Times,* November 25, 1955, page 8.

117 *But Jimmy D'Antonio grabbed that prize* . . . : "Wild Finish Beats Mounties and Gives Aliquippa High its Second Class AA Grid Crown", Mitchell, Jack, *Beaver Valley Times,* November 28, 1955, page 4.

117 *"Why didn't you score?"* . . . : Ditka, Mike, author interview.

118 *"This is the time for the 'Crossfire' pass"* . . . : "Milanovich Calls Touchdown Play", *Beaver Valley Times,* November 28, 1955, page 4.

118 *"I don't think I have a fonder memory of high school"* . . . : Ditka, Mike, author interview.

118 *Students from next door* . . . : "Aliquippa Cheers Gridders", *Beaver Valley Times,* November 28, 1955, page 1.

118 *"Even with the victory celebration"* . . . : ibid.

119 *Sacrifices like Johnny Reft* . . . : "Obituaries", *Beaver Valley Times,* January 25, 1949, pg. 14

119 *37,000 more* . . . : "The Ghosts of No Gun Ri", *Chicago Tribune,* October 3, 1999.

120 *With J&L its fourth-largest producer* . . . : "CIO, Steel Only Six Cents Apart", United Press, *Madera Tribune,* Madera, Calif., May 15, 1953.

120 *Employed 650,000* . . . : American Iron and Steel Institute. *Annual Statistical Report.* New York, 1954: 24.

120 *J&L was spending $676 million* . . . : *Beaver County Times,* July 23, 1959; Hogan, William. *Economic History of the Iron and Steel Industry in the United States.* Lexington, Mass.: D.C. Heath and Company, 1972: 1,749.

120 *By the end of the '50s* ... : "Rise and Fall—The Death of a Steel Union", Bauder, Bob, *Beaver County Times,* December 21, 2003; Inman, Wollman, 171.

120 *Aliquippa's population* ... : "Census of 1950", U.S. Census Bureau.

120 *"The customs and ideals of a new land"* ... : "Aliquippa", *The History of Beaver County Schools,* Volume I. Adams, Belle, ed. Beaver County Historical Research & Landmarks Foundation, printed by Closson Press, Apollo, Pa., 1982.

120 *"Between 1946 and 1950"* ... : "Aliquippa", *The History of Beaver County Schools,* Volume I. Adams, Belle, ed. Beaver County Historical Research & Landmarks Foundation, printed by Closson Press, Apollo, Pa., 1982.

121 *"The days when J&L would build swimming pools"* ... : "No 'Ghost Town' Likely Here—Aliquippa's Future Bright Says Jones & Laughlin's President", Tilton, Al, drafts in Inman Collection; Inman, Donald R., Wollman, David H. *Portraits in Steel: An Illustrated History of Jones & Laughlin Steel Corporation.* Kent, Ohio: The Kent State University Press, 1999: 128.

121 *In January 1946* ... : "Locals Call Immediate Walkout", Fisher, C. Edmund, *Pittsburgh Post-Gazette,* January 19, 1946, page 4, col. 1.

121 *"Slave-labor law"* ... : "National Affairs: Barrel No. 2", *Time,* June 23, 1947.

122 *For steelworkers the end of every three-year contract* ... : Inman, Wollman, 157–159.

122 *Its new chairman* ... : Inman, Wollman, 134.

122 *"A true friend"* ... : Moreell, Ben, *Men and Steel* 6, no. 1, November 1952, page 7; Inman, Wollman, 148.

122 *"So bad that we must experiment"* ... : Hoerr, John. *And The Wolf Finally Came: The Decline of the American Steel Industry.* Pittsburgh: University of Pittsburgh Press, 1988: 287; Inman, Wollman, 148.

123 *"J&L made us all middle class"* ... : Piroli, author interview.

123 *Pushed by the indefatigable Nick DeSalle* ... : Murphy, Cindy, Murphy, Ed. *Images of America: Aliquippa.* Charleston, S.C.: Arcadia Publishing, 2013: 106; "Residents, Businesses Band Together to Help Build, Maintain Community Hospitals in Beaver County", Snedden, Jeffrey, *Beaver County Times,* May 19,

2015; "Mills Built Pennsylvania Towns, Fostered Families", Davidson, Tom, *Beaver County Times*, February 22, 2014.

124 *In the late 50s Franklin Avenue*...: "Aliquippa, J&L Steel, and the National Immigrant Movement: A History Lesson for Beaver County", *The Bridge*, page 14.

124 *"That drive down there was pretty nice"*...: Ditka, Mike, author interview.

124–125 *A workingman could make enough now to buy a four-bedroom house for $12,500*...: Casp, Joe, author interview, October 14, 2011.

125 *"You have a job with A&S"*...: Ditka, Mike, author interview.

125 *A high school tour of J&L killed any interest in a job there*...: Ditka, Mike, *Ditka: An Autobiography*, 50.

125 *"My dad was what they called a scarfer"*...: Evasovich, author interview.

126 *In the summer of '55*...: Marocco, author interview.

127 *"Boy, Mom, one of these days I'm going to have four cars"*...: Ditka, Charlotte, author interview.

127 *"Ditka set all the standards"*...: Yannessa, author interview, October 8, 2010.

128 *"A little shit"*...: Ditka, Mike, author interview.

128 *"Did you ever see a lion jump through a hoop of flames?"*...: "Coach: Ditka's Talent Showed", Mule, Marty, *New Orleans Times-Picayune*, January 21, 1986, page 24.

128 *But now he'd grown two inches*...: Ditka, *Ditka: An Autobiography*, 53.

128 *"I didn't think he was very good until his senior year"*...: Evasovich, author interview.

128 *But already Ditka*...: "Iron Mike: From Aliquippa to Chicago, Bears' Ditka All Business", Prisuta, Mike, *Beaver County Times*, January 10, 1986, page C1.

128 *In the second game of the '56 season*...: *Aliquippa Quips 1910–2010*.

129 *"I didn't do a good job"*...: Yannessa, author interview, October 8, 2010.

129 *"Oh, my God"*...: ibid.

129 *Down 20-19 to Sharon* . . . : *Aliquippa Quips 1910-2010*; Yannessa, author interview, October 8, 2010.

129 *Ditka was named Most Popular* . . . : Prisuta.

129 *As a student he got Bs in English* . . . : ibid.

129 *Two weeks later* . . . : Evasovich, author interview; *Aliquippa Quips 1910-2010*.

130 *An embarrassing 55-13 finale* . . . : Ditka, Mike, author interview, *Aliquippa Quips 1910-2010*.

130 *"I was okay"* . . . : Ditka, author interview.

130 *"I was there the day"* . . . : Zmijanac, Mike, author interview, September 23, 2010.

131 *Ditka's parents loved Penn State* . . . : Ditka, Mike, *Ditka: An Autobiography*, 58; interview.

131 *"Mike Ditka as a fucking dentist?"* . . . : Yannessa, author interview, October 8, 2010.

131 *"And guess what?"* . . . : ibid.

132 *After all, in 1944* . . . : Piroli, author interview.

133 *Vince Calipari* . . . : Calipari, John, author interview, February 9, 2011.

134 *Starting in 1950* . . . : Jackson, Kenneth T. *Crabgrass Frontier: The Suburbanization of the United States*. New York: Oxford University Press, 1985: 4.

134 *U.S. suburbs, meanwhile* . . . : Miller, D. Quentin. *John Updike and the Cold War: Drawing the Iron Curtain*. Columbia, Mo., University of Missouri Press, 2001: 43.

134 *"Nobody blames them"* . . . : Zmijanac, author interview.

134 *The whole family went back for big days* . . . : "Immigrant Workers Sought New Beginning in Area's Burgeoning Steel Industry", Cubbal, Kayleen, *Beaver County Times*, February 25, 2015.

134 *"In later years, you went to Villa's"* . . . : Zernich, Steve, Dr. *Dr. Steve*. Pittsburgh: self-published, 1992: 28.

134 *"Those were the wild days"*...: Letteri, Joe, author interview, May 11, 2012.

134–135 *"Only five, six years of schooling"*...: ibid.

135 *"It wasn't a perfect eden"*...: Letteri, Gilda, author interview, May 11, 2012.

135 *America accounted for 64 percent of the planet's steel production*...: "World's Steel Output Drops 8 Million Tons", United Press International, *Pittsburgh Press*, January 2, 1947, page 24. From American Iron and Steel Institute, Raw Steel Production Annual (Net Tons), 1860-2011.

135 *By 1950*...: "Fortunes of the Steel Industry", *CQ Researcher*, December 27, 1962.

135 *"Malaise"*...: Geneen, Harold, with Moscow, Alvin. *Managing.* Garden City, N.Y.: Doubleday and Company, 1984: 72.

136 *"The handwriting was on the wall"*...: ibid.

136 *"To the other extreme"*...: Radatovich, Paul, author interview, March 29, 2012.

137 *"The biggest concern for unions in those days"*...: Piroli, author interview.

137 *"And I wanted to do more work"*...: Evasovich, author interview.

138 *"The union had very much power"*...: Vukmir, Rade B. *The Mill.* Lanham, Md.: University Press of America, Inc., 2011: 357.

138 *And in 1959 set new records*...: "J&L, Crucible Steel Set Income Records", *Beaver Valley Times*, July 23, 1959, page 1.

138 *"You know what?"*...: Yannessa, author interview.

138 *At 11:25 p.m.*...: "Big Mills Close Quietly: Pickets March In County", *Beaver Valley Times*, July 15, 1959, page 1.

139 *"I didn't have a problem with it"*...: Letteri, Joe, author interview.

139 *Aliquippa's local was flush enough*...: "Strike Losses Keep Climbing Despite Reopening of Mills", *Beaver Valley Times*, November 9, 1959, page 1.

139 *A November 7 decision*...: "County Steel Mills Reopen", *Beaver County Times*, November 9, 1959, page 1.

139 *Came within two points* . . . : *Aliquippa Quips 1910–2010.*

140 *"Best we've ever gotten"* . . . : "Steel Firms Sign Up", *Beaver Valley Times,* January 11, 1960, page 1.

140 *U.S. steelworkers averaging $3.10 an hour* . . . : *Survey of Current Business,* U.S. Department of Commerce, Office of Business Economics, December 1959.

140 *In 1959, for the first time* . . . : "International Competition in the American Steel Market", Revis, Joseph S., Hardy, Rudolph W., *Business Horizons,* Volume 3, Issue 4, Winter 1960, pages 30–37.

141 *"If you aren't from here, you can't understand"* . . . : Zmijanac, author interview.

142 *"The single greatest thing that ever happened to me"* . . . : ibid.

142 *"School's down there"* . . . : ibid.

144 *"Mike was one of the best sandlot shooters I ever saw"* . . . : Pipkin, Robert, author interview, February 9, 2013.

144 *"Look at you"* . . . : Zmijanac, author interview, March 26, 2012.

144 *"I remember punching him right in the mouth"* . . . : Pipkin, author interview.

145 **"We don't stab you in the back here"** . . . : Zmijanac, author interview, March 26, 2012.

145 *"My current wife"* . . . : ibid.

145 *"That piece of shit!"* . . . : ibid.

146 *"Yeah", she said. "For them"* . . . : Browder, Carolyn, author interview, February 4, 2013.

146 *"It was terrible"* . . . : Vukmir, 406.

147 *In 1946 the school board* . . . : "Aliquippa", *The History of Beaver County Schools,* Volume I. Adams, Belle, ed. Beaver County Historical Research & Landmarks Foundation, printed by Closson Press, Apollo, Pa., 1982.

147 *The town's small—4,175; 15.9 percent—black population* . . . : United States Census Bureau, *1950 Census of Population and Housing: Pennsylvania,* Washington, D.C., 1950.

147 *"So my mother would beat me"* . . . : Steals, Melvin, author interview, February 1, 2013.

148 *"You could see the economics of racism as well"* . . . : Harvey, Barron, author interview, February 14, 2013.

148 *"It was brewing"* . . . : Smith, Eugene "Salt", author interview, November 28, 2011.

148 *Black steelworker Matthew Strong* . . . : "Worker: Aliquippa Mill in 1950s was Segregated", Cubbal, Kayleen, *Beaver County Times*, August 31, 2014.

149 *"It wouldn't be all the whites and blacks"* . . . : Yannessa, author interview.

149 *Now the percentage of blacks in Aliquippa had risen to 21 percent* . . . : *1960 Census of Population and Housing: Pennsylvania*, Washington, D.C., 1960.

149 *Aliquippa's population held steady* . . . : ibid; U.S. Census Bureau, "Census of 1960."

149 *On July 4th weekend, 1960* . . . : Mancini, Henry, with Lees, Gene. *Did They Mention the Music?* Chicago: Contemporary Books, Inc., 1989: 221–222; "Mancini Worried About His Ride", Legge, Norma, *Beaver County Times*, July 5, 1960, pages 1 and 4.

150 *"I just can't believe it"* . . . : "Mancini Worried About His Ride", Legge, Norma, *Beaver County Times*, July 5, 1960, page 4.

150 *"Everybody wanted to play for Carl Aschman"* . . . : Pipkin, author interview.

150 *"Aschman had had disastrous seasons"* . . . : *Aliquippa Quips 1910–2010.*

151 *"We always had other people to fight with after the game"* . . . : Harvey, author interview.

151 *A clutch of Aliquippa teenagers* . . . : "Fights Break Out After Grid Game", *Beaver County Times*, September 8, 1962, page 1.

151 *After the next game at Aliquippa Stadium* . . . : "Quips Switch 3 More Games", *Beaver County Times*, September 26, 1962, page 19.

151 *"A rowdy minority group"* . . . : "Aliquippa Abolishes Night Grid Games", Kramer, Brute, *Pittsburgh Post-Gazette*, September 26, 1962, page 27.

151 *The Quips' first win* ...: "Passes Conquer Ellwood, 13-7", Rose, Ed, *Beaver County Times,* October 1, 1962, page 15.

151 *"I talked to all the black football players"* ...: Pipkin, author interview.

152 *"Some of us went to the coach"* ...: Yannessa, Gene, author interview, February 17, 2013.

152 *For weeks, the national news* ...: "Meredith Registers at Bayonet Point", Kuettner, Al, United Press International, *Beaver County Times,* October 1, 1962, page 1.

153 *"On both sides, man"* ...: Mann, Richard, author interview, February 25, 2013.

153 *"She really gave me hope"* ...: Pipkin, author interview.

153 *"Kindergarten up through twelfth grade"* ...: Steals, author interview.

153 *"Three years I went up there"* ...: Battalini, Anthony, author interview, October 12, 2011.

154 *"He was a good man"* ...: Pipkin, author interview.

154 *"But you were fearful of saying anything to him"* ...: Yannessa, Gene, author interview.

155 *Though the Quips suffered humiliating losses* ...: *Aliquippa Quips 1910–2010.*

155 *"He wasn't going to budge"* ...: Aschman, Carl, Jr., author interview.

155 *Just days after the walkout* ...: "Fighting Quips Stop New Castle, 19 to 19", Schley, Tom, *Beaver County Times,* October 8, 1962, page 15.

155 *Aschman eventually finished with 189 wins in all* ...: Beaver County Hall of Fame, "Carl Aschman", http://www.bcshof.org/halloffamers/aschman1976.htm.

155 *"We really jelled"* ...: Yannessa, Gene, author interview.

155 *Surprisingly, news of Pipkin's walkout* ...: Pipkin, author interview.

156 *"He played basketball"* ...: Stokes, Larry, author interview, February 8, 2013.

156 *Such ambivalence* ...: Pipkin, author interview.

156 *Went on to score 27 points in the loss* . . . : "Quips Best, Big John Says", Mitchell, Jack, *Beaver County Times,* March 13, 1963, page 1.

156 *"He's great"* . . . : ibid.

157 *"I was the leading scorer"* . . . : Pipkin, author interview.

157 *In late '62* . . . : Inman, Wollman, 289-292.

157 *About half the town* . . . : "They Came: They Saw the President", Holovach, Nadine, *Beaver County Times,* October 13, 1962, page 1.

158 *"Recipes and pictures"* . . . : ibid.

158 **The Beaver County Times'** *photo* . . . : "Hands and Hellos", Shunk, Rudy, *Beaver County Times,* October 13, 1962, page 1.

158 *"The crowd loved him"* . . . : "Visit Came Off Without a Hitch", Rose, Ed, *Beaver County Times,* October 13, 1962, page 3, col. 8.

158 *"This country has many responsibilities"* . . . : Kennedy, John F., "Remarks at a Rally in Aliquippa, Pennsylvania.," October 12, 1962. Online by Peters, Gerhard and Woolley, John T. *The American Presidency Project.* http://www.presidency.ucsb.edu/ws/?pid=8949.

159 *Four Casp brothers* . . . : Casp, author interview.

160 *"Can you tell me how we can put them back to work"* . . . : Kennedy, John F., "Remarks at a Rally in Aliquippa, Pennsylvania.," October 12, 1962. Online by Peters, Gerhard and Woolley, John T. *The American Presidency Project.* http://www.presidency.ucsb.edu/ws/?pid=8949.

160 *"No arrests were made"* . . . : "Visit Came Off Without a Hitch", Rose, Ed, *Beaver County Times,* October 13, 1962, page 3, col. 8.

161 *"Who was that man?"* . . . : "They Came: They Saw The President", Holovach, Nadine, *Beaver County Times,* October 13, 1962, page 3, col. 8.

161 *"What a glorious moment"* . . . : Piroli, author interview.

162 *"Guys from Aliquippa"* . . . : Yannessa, Don, author interview.

163 *"I'm going to Canada"* . . . : Marocco, author interview.

163 *"Teams of maybe thirty on one side"* . . . : David, George, author interview, January 6, 2012.

164 *"Very sarcastic"*...: Mann, author interview.

164 *"He was very humble"*...: Marocco, author interview.

164 *"I look back and whatever respect I had for him diminished"*...: Yannessa, Gene, author interview.

164 *"Took her to a party"*...: Marocco, author interview.

165 *Aliquippa opened the '63 season*...: "Aliquippa Team Easily Clobbers Steubenville, 32–0", Schley, Tom, *Beaver County Times,* September 7, 1963, page 11.

166 *"I got nervous"*...: Marocco, author interview.

166 *Finished 8-1*...: *Aliquippa Quips 1910–2010.*

166 *"He didn't do nothing"*...: Marocco, author interview.

166 *His son noticed too*...: Aschman, Carl, Jr., author interview.

167 *"We girls who kept trying out for cheerleading"*...: Browder, author interview.

167 *"Brown-Bag Brigade"*...: "Residents Relate Their Struggle to Overcome Racial Prejudice", Bauder, Bob, *Beaver County Times,* November 8, 2002.

168 *"It was not until 1966"*...: Pennsylvania Human Relations Commission, *Investigatory Hearing Report,* Aliquippa, May 24–26, 1971.

168 *Blacks at the Aliquippa Works*...: ibid, page 31; Dickerson, 241.

168 *"Reflect a rejection"*...: Pennsylvania Human Relations Commission, *Investigatory Hearing Report,* Aliquippa, May 24–26, 1971.

168 *"We have been referred to and treated like objects"*...: ibid.

169 *"It caused the entire community to start looking"*...: Harvey, author interview.

169 *"We had one meeting"*...: Browder, author interview.

170 *Richard Mann felt the chill on his neck*...: Mann, author interview.

171 *"If I didn't play the rest of the year"*...: ibid.

171 *He once took a box of M&M's candies as payment for surgery*...: "Dr. Michael Zernich; Aug. 5, 1931–June 1, 2011; Orthopedic Surgeon Once Basketball Star for Aliquippa, Pitt", Butterfield, Sam, *Pittsburgh Post-Gazette,* June 4, 2011, page A11.

172 *"How's it feel?"*...: Mann, author interview.

172 *Mann came back*...: "Aliquippa Stuns Farrell, 16 to 0", Schley, Tom, *Beaver County Times*, September 19, 1964, page 13.

172 *The next week, Mann*...: "Aliquippa Tops Ellwood, 13 to 7, On Touchdown in Closing Seconds", Schley, Tom, *Beaver County Times*, October 3, 1964, page 11.

172 *The next week against New Castle*...: "Strong Defensive Play Keeps Quips in WPIAL Race", Schley, Tom, *Beaver County Times*, October 10, 1964, page 11.

172 *"Eventually, I just learned to deal with the pain"*...: Mann, author interview.

172 *On October 23*...: "Aliquippa Ousts Butler High, 41 to 21", Schley, Tom, *Beaver County Times*, October 24, 1964, page 13.

173 *Two weeks later*...: "Tight Aliquippa Defense Stymies Sharon, 7 to 0", Schley, Tom, *Beaver County Times*, September 26, 1964, page 13.

173 *But on November 7*...: "Hopewell Upsets Aliquippa, 6 to 0", Schley, Tom, *Beaver County Times*, November 9, 1964, page 17.

173 *"We had nothing to lose"*...: Medich, George, author interview, May 2, 2013.

173 *"I thought we held him out of there, man"*...: Mann, Richard, author interview.

174 *"Doc" Medich*...: Baseball Reference, "Doc Medich", http://www.baseball-reference.com/players/m/medicdo01.shtml.

174 *Twice went into the stands*...: "Pittsburgh Pitcher 'Doc' Medich Battles to Save a Cardiac Victim's Life", *People*, vol. 5, no. 17, May 3, 1976; "How I Spent My Summer Vacation", Wulf, Steve, *Sports Illustrated*, June 29, 1981.

174 *Ended up going into practice*...: Beaver County Sports Hall of Fame, "George 'Doc' Medich", http://www.bcshof.org/halloffamers/medich1987.htm.

174 *Eventually, an addiction to painkillers*...: "Medich in Drug Program", United Press International, *New York Times*, November 17, 1983.

174 *"It was a big deal"*...: Medich, author interview.

174 *"In the annals of Beaver County football"*...: "Hopewell's Vikings Pull Greatest Upset", *Beaver County Times*, November 9, 1964, page 1.

174 *The following week the team zigged again* ...: "Quips to Play For 'AA' Title", Thompson, Don, *Beaver County Times,* November 14, 1964, page 1.

174 *Aliquippa, with a league-high 146 points* ...: "Quips Battle Wildcats Saturday", *Beaver County Times,* November 17, 1964, page 15.

175 *Supreme distillation* ...: "Quips Stymie Wildcats For AA Title", Schley, Tom, *Beaver County Times,* November 23, 1964, page 21.

176 *"Let 'em look that up in the records"* ...: "The Defense Did it For New AA Champs", Thompson, Don, *Beaver County Times,* November 23, 1964, page 1.

176 *"Rocking-chair coach"* ...: ibid, page 4, col. 7.

176 *"To this day, it sticks up"* ...: Mann, author interview.

176 *Went on to coach receivers* ...: "Coach Richard Mann Returns to Pittsburgh", United Press International, February 14, 2013, http://www.upi.com/Sports_News/2013/02/14/Coach-Richard-Mann-returns-to-Pittsburgh/42551360872528/; Mann, interview.

177 *"You grow up in Aliquippa"* ...: Mann, author interview.

178 *"I am forced to take this action"* ...: "Fuderich Tapped for Quip Post", Patton, O.K., *Beaver County Times,* July 21, 1965, page 4, col. 3.

178 *Two days later* ...: "Aschman Resignation Marks End of An Era", *Beaver County Times,* July 20, 1965, page A6.

PART THREE

187 *Thirteen weeks of vacation* ...: Inman, Donald R., Wollman, David H. *Portraits in Steel: An Illustrated History of Jones & Laughlin Steel Corporation.* Kent, Ohio: The Kent State University Press, 1999: 172.

188 *"The above-average man"* ...: "The Emptiness of Too Much Leisure", Haveman, Ernest, *Life Magazine,* February 14, 1964, page 76.

188 *Joe Letteri built his dream house* ...: Letteri, Joe, author interview, May 11, 2012.

189 *"The house I grew up in"* ...: Medich, George, author interview, February 2, 2013.

189 *"It was time"*...: Letteri, Joe, author interview.

190 *"I know these people didn't like it"*...: Letteri, Gilda, author interview, May 11, 2012.

190 *When Joey later saw fraudulence*...: ibid.

191 *"They're going to give the job to Pete Fuderich"*...: Marocco, Frank, author interview, January 4, 2012.

191 *When he resigned*...: "Fuderich Tapped for Quip Post", Patton, O.K., *Beaver County Times*, July 21, 1965, page 4, col. 3.

191 *Fuderich was given a one-year deal*...: ibid, page 1.

191 *He went 1-8*...: *Aliquippa Quips 1910–2010.*

191 *He went 2-7*...: ibid.

191 *"It was a closed shop"*...: Yannessa, Don, author interview, March 29, 2012.

192 *"You still want to coach football?"*...: ibid.

192 *The board cycled through three more hapless coaches*...: *Aliquippa Quips 1910-2010.*

192 *Aliquippa's population shrank*...: *1970 Census of Population: Characteristics of the Population, Volume 1, Part 40,* United States Bureau of the Census, 1970.

193 *"It was the funniest thing"*...: Yannessa, author interview.

194 *In November of 1964, Pete was named deputy warden there*...: "Suder Named New Deputy Warden", *Beaver County Times*, November 5, 1964, pg. 4.

194 *When some hotshot home for the summer would show up at the Morrell Park game*...: Zmijanac, Mike, author interview, September 23, 2010.

194 *"One of the greatest athletes I've ever seen"*...: Ibid.

194 *"I'd go along with that"*...: Suder, George "Juke", author interview, June 6, 2012.

194 *"He'll keep the name of Suder"*...: "Aliquippa Still Cheers Suders: Pete Jr., George Hold Spotlight", Kramer, Brute, *Pittsburgh Post-Gazette*, January 29, 1961, page 26.

195 *"George Suder Is Star at Maryland"*...: "George Suder Is Star at Maryland", *Beaver County Times,* January 7, 1964, page 13.

195 *Georgie led Maryland*...: *2012–13 Maryland Men's Basketball Record Book,* University of Maryland, College Park, Md., 2013, pages 2, 24.

195 *"Was going to start"*...: Zmijanac, author interview.

195 *"Either that"*...: ibid.

195 *Kennedy's escalation*...: "Papers Reveal JFK Efforts on Vietnam", Bender, Bryan, *Boston Globe,* June 6, 2005.

195 *By the end of 1965*...: "What Led the US to the Vietnam War?", Reid, Robert H., *Stars and Stripes,* November 10, 2015.

196 *In May 1965*...: *"County Navy Pilot Killed", Beaver Valley Times,* May 27, 1965, page 1.

196 *Fourteen Aliquippans*...: Vietnam Veterans Memorial Fund, "The Wall of Faces", http://www.vvmf.org/Wall-of-Faces/search/results/HOME_RECRD/ALIQUIPPA.

196 *"Had it all"*...: Smith, Eugene, author interview, November 28, 2011.

196 *Drafted into the Army*...: "Edward Surratt: A Man No One Really Knew", *Beaver County Times,* February 25, 2007, page 6.

196 *"You have to get out of there"*...: Zmijanac, author interview.

197 *One summer night*...: ibid.

197 *Went on to lead the league*...: Basketball Reference, http://www.basketball-reference.com/leagues/ABA_1968.html.

197 *"I got you a tryout with the Pipers"*...: Zmijanac, author interview.

198 *"It was like **Gunsmoke**"*...: Smith, author interview.

198 *On the first working day*...: "'Valley Terrace' Office to Open", *Beaver County Times,* December 30, 1967, page A1.

198 *Within a month*...: "230 Families in Terrace Affected", *Beaver County Times,* February 8, 1968, page 1.

199 *"We couldn't buy a house anywhere"*...: Steals, Melvin, author interview, February 1, 2013.

199 *"At that time, if you were black"*...: Smith, author interview.

199 *As an open practice*...: Jackson, Kenneth T. *Crabgrass Frontier: The Suburbanization of the United States.* New York: Oxford University Press, 1985: 197-218.

199 *"Because now all the blacks got this money"*...: Smith, author interview.

200 *"A corrosive and inequitable learning environment"*...: "Not at Fault, Aliquippa Teacher Says", *Beaver County Times*, May 5, 1970, page A6.

200 *"It was the 1960s"*...: Steals, author interview.

201 *"I wasn't involved in anything"*...: Suder, George "Juke", author interview.

202 *"You sat in a bar with Mike"*...: Piroli, Gino, author interview, January 4, 2012.

203 *"My fellow Americans, we live in an age of anarchy"*...: Nixon, Richard M., "Address to the Nation on the Situation in Southeast Asia", April 30, 1970, American Presidency Project, University of California at Santa Barbara, compiled by Peters, Gerhard, Wooley, John T., http://www.presidency.ucsb.edu/ws/?pid=2490.

204 *Stark reversal of a pledge*...: Nixon, Richard M., *"Address to the Nation on Progress Toward Peace in Vietnam"*, April 20, 1970, American Presidency Project, University of California at Santa Barbara, compiled by Peters, Gerhard, Wooley, John T., http://www.presidency.ucsb.edu/ws/?pid=2476.

204 *One June 1970 poll*...: "Nixon's Support Grows After Cambodian Move", Lawrence, David, *Spokane Daily Chronicle*, June 10, 1970, page 4.

205 *Some 100,000 protesters*...: "Nixon Up Early, Sees Protesters", United Press International, *Beaver County Times*, May 9, 1970, page 1.

205 *"This can't be the United States of America"*...: *Nixon: A Presidency Revealed*, directed by Angio, Joe, History Channel, February 15, 2007.

205 *On May 8, construction workers in New York City*...: "War Foes Here Attacked By Construction Workers; City Hall Is Stormed", Bigart, Homer, *New York Times*, May 9, 1970.

205 *Just before dawn on May 9* . . . : "I Am Not A Kook: Richard Nixon's Bizarre Visit to the Lincoln Memorial", McNichol, Tom, *The Atlantic*, November 14, 2011.

205 *"Look at the situation"* . . . : "What the Nation Learned at Kent State in 1970", Nolan, Martin F., *Boston Globe*, May 2, 2000.

206 *Of the 174 Aliquippa junior and senior high school students suspended* . . . : Pennsylvania Human Relations Commission, *Investigatory Hearing Report*, Aliquippa, May 24–26, 1971.

206 *"I remember you getting around a group of 'em"* . . . : Walker, Chuckie, author interview, October 13, 2011.

206 *"We used to have meetings"* . . . : Steals, author interview.

207 *"Obviously the students attending this showing"* . . . : "Not at Fault, Aliquippa Teacher Says", *Beaver County Times*, May 5, 1970, page A6.

207 *"We went to the show"* . . . : Casterlow Walker, Sharon, author interview, October 13, 2011.

208 *"The white parents began to take their kids out of the school"* . . . : Steals, author interview.

208 *"Utter chaos at the junior high"* . . . : "Reel Life to Real Life", *Beaver County Times*, May 2, 1970, page 3, col. 6.

208 *"It happened in this hallway"* . . . : Zmijanac, author interview.

208 *"We got to get out of here"* . . . : Peake, Fred, author interview, May 7, 2013.

209 *A group of forty high school "youths"* . . . : "Situation Calms, Suspect Is Held", *Beaver County Times*, May 2, 1970, page 1.

209 *"It started as a sit-down situation"* . . . : Walker, author interview.

209 *More than 270 students* . . . : "Officials Hopeful of Solution", *Beaver County Times*, May 7, 1970.

209 *"Then it went from the lunchroom"* . . . : Walker, author interview.

209 *"The kids finally exploded"* . . . : "Racial Tension Closes Schools", *Beaver County Times*, May 6, 1970, page 4, col. 3.

210 *Blacks accounted for 42 percent* . . . : Pennsylvania Human Relations Commission, *Investigatory Hearing Report*, Aliquippa, May 24–26, 1971.

210 *Sherriff's deputies* . . . : "School Calm Upset Again", *Beaver County Times*, May 14, 1970, page 1.

210 *"They tried to keep the school going"* . . . : Zmijanac, author interview.

211 *"It was tough"* . . . : Legge, Carl, author interview, November 8, 2011.

211 *"White student threw an apple"* . . . : Pennsylvania Human Relations Commission, *Investigatory Hearing Report*, Aliquippa, May 24–26, 1971.

212 *"He was a bigger-than-life figure"* . . . : Yannessa, author interview.

212 *"It was one of those days"* . . . : Peake, author interview.

212 *The Quips won just six games* . . . : *Aliquippa Quips 1910–2010*.

212 *Everybody beat up on Aliquippa* . . . : ibid.

213 *That "paper heart"* . . . : Aschman, Carl Jr., author interview, February 28, 2012.

213 *"He was the first one down the steps"* . . . : ibid.

213 *"I happened to be white"* . . . : Aschman, Harald, author interview, May 8, 2013.

214 *"I took off like a rabbit"* . . . : Dorsett, Tony, author interview, September 24, 2010.

215 *"Make sure you're at the game"* . . . : Dorsett, author interview, September 24, 2010.

215 *Late in his career* . . . : "Gaston Green Makes Debut as a Ram Tonight: He Will Be on Same Field as His Longtime Hero, New Bronco Tony Dorsett", Dufresne, Chris, *Los Angeles Times*, August 3, 1988.

215 *"He used to take their money"* . . . : McBride, Sherman, author interview, November 20, 2011.

215 *"Talk about speed?"* . . . : Dorsett, author interview.

215 *After Melvin died* . . . : Dorsett, Tony, Frommer, Harvey. *Running Tough: Memoirs of a Football Maverick*. New York: Doubleday, 1989: 9.

216 *"People always say they see visions"*...: Dorsett, author interview.

216 *Hopewell Senior High beat their counterparts*...: *Aliquippa Quips 1910–2010.*

216 *The boundary between Aliquippa and Hopewell*...: "Another Kind of Golf Scramble", Piroli, Gino, *Beaver County Times,* October 8, 2001, page 20.

216 *"Whiteyland"*...: Dorsett, author interview.

216 *Mount Vernon had been one of the first places to feel the effect of school busing*...: Dorsett, Frommer, 8.

217 *His father worked the open hearth at J&L*...: Millman, Chad, Coyne, Shawn. *The Ones Who Hit The Hardest: The Steelers, The Cowboys, The '70s, And The Fight For America's Soul.* New York: Gotham Books, 2010: 171. Dorsett, author interview.

217 *His older brothers were part of a local gang*...: Dorsett, author interview.

217 *And when it came to playing Midget League football*...: "You Need a T.D. in South Bend", Underwood, John, *Sports Illustrated,* September 20, 1976.

217 *He and his best friend, Mike Kimbrough, played instead for the Aliquippa Little Steelers*...: Dorsett, Frommer, 8; "King of the Hill: Tony Dorsett Talks of Where He's Been, Where He's Going", Churovia, Bob, *Beaver County Times,* September 17, 1976, page 7.

217 *Even so, his mother, Myrtle*...: Dorsett, author interview.

217 *"You didn't want to go to Aliquippa"*...: Zmijanac, author interview.

217 *"I almost attempted to do the same thing"*...: Peake, author interview.

217 *"I never would've let him play for Hopewell"*...: Yannessa, author interview.

218 *Juke Suder was pouring drinks*...: Suder, George "Juke", author interview.

218 *"Had invaded the area and started a fight"*...: "Racial Unrest Turns Violent", Evushak, Ron, *Beaver County Times,* May 22, 1970, page 1.

218 *"How else", he asked*...: ibid.

218 *"They were going to clean out the white people"*...: Ditka, Charlotte, author interview, November 5, 2010.

218 *"They were going to burn his bar down"*...: Battalini, Anthony, author interview, October 12, 2011.

219 *A swelling group of Linmar residents* . . . : "Racial Unrest Turns Violent", Evushak, Ron, *Beaver County Times*, May 22, 1970, page 4, col. 2.

219 *The following day* . . . : "School, NAACP Meeting on Tense Racial Issue", *Beaver County Times*, May 25, 1970, page 1.

220 *"The only time you were allowed up in the school"* . . . : McBride, Sherman, author interview, September 25, 2010.

220 *"Both white and black citizens"* . . . : Pennsylvania Human Relations Commission, *Investigatory Hearing Report and Recommendations: Aliquippa*, Aliquippa, May 24-26, 1971.

220 *"All these neighbors were getting real radical"* . . . : Aschman, Harald, author interview.

220 *Vigilante whites* . . . : Battalini, author interview.

220 *"Because our houses were so close together"* . . . : ibid.

221 *"Hand grenades and shotguns"* . . . : Stokes, Larry, author interview, February 8, 2013.

221 *"12-gauge shotgun"* . . . : "Law Slams Lid on Tense Town", Evushak, Ron, *Beaver County Times*, May 22, 1970, page 26.

221 *"I was preparing myself to kill somebody"* . . . : Stokes, author interview.

221 *"They always wanted me hanging around the ER"* . . . : Medich, George, author interview, May 2, 2013.

221 *"Everybody was a nervous wreck"* . . . : Betters, Mark, author interview, November 19, 2011.

222 *"Pistol"* . . . : Betters, C.J., "Chuck", author interview, November 19, 2011.

222 *On June 11* . . . : "Aliquippa School Bells Ignored", *Beaver County Times*, June 12, 1970, page 1.

222 *"The worst time"* . . . : Suder, George "Juke", author interview.

223 *One Plan 7 house* . . . : "Quiet Night Marred by Minor Incidents", *Beaver County Times*, June 13, 1970, page 1.

223 *Just three months later* . . . : "Beaver County Mall", Beaver County Chamber of Commerce, *Beaver County Times*, December 1, 2005, page 47 (page 3 of advertising section).

223 *"It calmed down"* . . . : Steals, author interview.

224 *When Mann came home* . . . : Mann, Richard, author interview, February 25, 2013.

224 *When students returned* . . . : "Aliquippa Enrollment Off, Following Recent Patterns", *Beaver County Times*, September 2, 1970, page 1.

225 *"My first day on the job"* . . . : Mann, author interview.

225 *"Eventually they ended up getting there"* . . . : Peake, author interview.

225 *Only twenty-nine boys* . . . : "Aliquippa Stuns Central, 14–12: Quips Win After 15 Straight Losses", Evushak, Ron, *Beaver County Times*, September 14, 1970, page B4.

225 *And by late October* . . . : Yannessa, author interview.

225 *"He goes 2-7-1"* . . . : Yannessa, ibid.

225 *The just-reported 1970 census results* . . . : *1970 Census of Population*, United States Census Bureau, Washington, D.C., 1970.

225 *On September 25* . . . : "Ernie Pitts Shot Fatally", *Beaver County Times*, September 26, 1970, page 1.

225 *"We were real close"* . . . : Frank, Willie, author interview, October 31, 2011.

226 *"It was heartbreaking"* . . . : Yanessa, author interview.

226 *In the summer of 1972* . . . : Steals, Mervin, author interview, May 6, 2013.

229 *"A lot of my friends used to fly around the country"* . . . : ibid.

230 *"A small riot"* . . . : Dorsett, author interview.

230 *"I could always see it coming down"* . . . : ibid.

231 *Dorsett played his first Hopewell season* . . . : Dorsett, Frommer, 10.

231 *His senior year, the Quips' only consolation* . . . : "Strength, Ball Control Produce Viking Win: A Typical Quip-Hopewell Game", Rose, Ed, Jr., *Beaver County Times*, October 16, 1972, page C3.

231 *"I put a defense on him"* . . . : Yannessa, author interview.

232 *"Come in this place"* . . . : Dorsett, author interview.

232 *"I wanted that money"* . . . : ibid.

232 *While a freshman at Pitt* . . . : Millman, Coyne, 183.

232 *"He was the brother that I always wanted to be like"* . . . : Dorsett, author interview.

233 *First college running back to amass 6,000* . . . : Millman, Coyne, 186.

233 *Pitt media official* . . . : ibid, 183.

233 *He finished his twelve-year pro career* . . . : "Tony Dorsett", Pro Football Hall of Fame, http://www.profootballhof.com/players/tony-dorsett/stats/.

233 *"My older brothers"* . . . : Dorsett, author interview.

234 *When it came time for the annual team banquet* . . . : "Sports Bound Aliquippa Wounds", Cook, Ron, *Beaver County Times*, February 22, 1981, page A10.

234 *And the players were no different* . . . : Yannessa, author interview.

235 *But on August 24, 1972* . . . : "Aliquippa Grid Star Larry Jones Dies", *Beaver County Times*, August 25, 1972, page 1.

235 *The Quips went 2-8 that year* . . . : *Aliquippa Quips 1910-2010*.

235 *"You win the coin toss"* . . . : "Aliquippa Turns Red Hurricanes Blue", Rose, Ed, Jr., *Beaver County Times*, October 12, 1974, A8.

235 *But he had been telling his team all week* . . . : ibid.

236 *"We came home"* . . . : Yannessa, author interview.

236 *In 1968, James Ling* . . . : Inman, Wollman, 172–178.

237 *"The best in the world"* . . . : Central Intelligence Agency, *World Steel Market: Continued Trouble Ahead*, Washington, D.C., 1977, page 10.

237 *Fresh off a 1973 agreement* . . . : Inman, Wollman, 186; Hoerr, John P. *And The Wolf Finally Came: The Decline of the American Steel Industry.* Pittsburgh: University of Pittsburgh Press, 1988, chapter 12.

237 *"Stuff started to happen"* . . . : Betters, Mark, author interview.

237 *"The Aliquippa plant seemed impregnable"* . . . : Hoerr, 479.

238 *"That place was his life"* . . . : Battalini, author interview.

238 *But in Aliquippa, this was masked by plans for another capital expansion* . . . : Inman, Wollman, 190.

238 *"Let's face it, men"* . . . : ibid, 187–188; *JALTeam Almanac* 27, no. 4, Winter 1974, page 3.

239 *"And they called me to work"* . . . : Gilbert, Aileen, author interview, September 22, 2010.

240 *The football stadium was renamed* . . . : "Disappointed . . . But Not Discouraged", Emert, Rich, *Beaver County Times,* September 23, 1972, B3.

241 *"You should hear what the whites are saying"* . . . : Yannessa, author interview.

241 *"It was tremendous"* . . . : "Sports Bound Aliquippa Wounds", Cook, Ron, *Beaver County Times,* February 22, 1981, page A10.

241 *"We used to have so many meetings"* . . . : Yannessa, author interview.

242 *Before pancreatic cancer killed him* . . . : "Sports Bound Aliquippa Wounds", Cook, Ron, *Beaver County Times,* February 22, 1981, page A1.

242 *"Just a wonderful human being"* . . . : Yannessa, author interview.

242 *"People rioting"* . . . : "Will Aliquippa Get Last Chance?", Bechtel, Sam, *Beaver County Times,* February 20, 1976, page B1.

242 *The school's reputation in the region* . . . : "Aliquippa Denies Version of Melee", *Beaver County Times,* February 11, 1976, page A3.

243 *"I've got to have the most difficult job"* . . . : "Will Aliquippa Get Last Chance?", Bechtel, Sam, *Beaver County Times,* February 20, 1976, page B1.

243 *In October of 1976, Aliquippa High forfeited* . . . : "Quips Found Guilty in PIAA Investigation", *Beaver County Times,* October 27, 1976, page D1.

243 *Steadily improving* . . . : *Aliquippa Quips 1910–2010.*

243 *"Yeah, Don Juan would recruit kids"* . . . : Steals, author interview.

243 *The **Beaver County Times** had one version* . . . : "Classes Back in Session at Aliquippa", *Beaver County Times,* March 1, 1977, page A3.

243 *"I was there"* . . . : Short, Dan, author interview, October 13, 2011.

244 *"The next thing you know"* . . . : Wytiaz, Dave, author interview, November 11, 2011.

245 *"Every day we'd come to work"* . . . : Yannessa, author interview.

245 *The projects of Valley Terrace* . . . : "Project Problems Many, Obvious", Walker, Joe, *Beaver County Times,* March 12, 1977, page A1.

245 *"We had some selfish sons of bitches on that team"* . . . : Short, author interview.

246 *After the Quips suffered a gutting 20-19 loss* . . . : "Cougars Dunk Quips, Hamilton", *Beaver County Times,* November 5, 1977, page B2.

246 *"This is not my team"* . . . : Yannessa, author interview.

246 *"A lot of us"* . . . : Short, author interview.

247 *"All you knew"* . . . : McBride, author interview.

247 *Starting in October 1977* . . . : "Police Comb Woods for Date of Slain Youth", *Beaver County Times,* October 24, 1977, page A3.

247 *A series of what would amount to eighteen murders* . . . : "Serial Killer Admits to 2 Findlay Deaths in 1977", Harlan, Chico, *Pittsburgh Post-Gazette,* February 27, 2007.

247 *"I had a gun shop"* . . . : David, George, author interview, January 6, 2012.

247 *Yet Aliquippa remained spared* . . . : "State Police Hope Faint for Nabbing Slippery Suspect", Grotevant, Bob, *Beaver County Times,* June 8, 1978, page 1; "The Crimes and the Capture", *Beaver County Times,* February 24, 2007.

248 *Three weeks later* . . . : "The Crimes and the Capture", *Beaver County Times,* February 24, 2007.

248 *"Uncle Sam trained him"* . . . : Smith, author interview.

248 *Stories he told* . . . : "Edward Surratt: A Man No One Really Knew", *Beaver County Times,* February 25, 2007, page A11.

248 *"He was good friends with the family"* . . . : Patrick, Timmie, author interview, November 27, 2011.

248 *"A very liked gentleman"* . . . : Marocco, author interview.

249 *"He could've cut you up"* . . . : Patrick, author interview.

249 *"Sometimes people just take a turn"*...: ibid.

250 *"This has got to stop somewhere"*...: Short, author interview.

250 *"No one left that gym"*...: McBride, author interview.

250 *And as the season unrolled*...: *Aliquippa Quips 1910-2010.*

251 *"Everything became a lot easier"*...: Yannessa, author interview, October 8, 2010.

251 *To "its super-sparkling best"*...: "Aliquippa Plans Giant Presidential Welcome", Leherr, Dave, *Pittsburgh Post-Gazette,* September 23, 1978, page 3.

251 *"Anybody who cares about sports"*...: "Crowd Cheers Carter on Aliquippa Visit", Grotevant, Bob, *Beaver County Times,* September 24, 1978, page 1.

252 *It didn't hurt that Aliquippa High had crushed Moon*...: "Aliquippa Emerging as Title Contender", Cosgrove, Randy, *Beaver County Times,* September 24, 1978.

253 *"I dropped the ball"*...: Short, author interview, September 25, 2010.

253 *"When we lost that game"*...: Yannessa, author interview, October 8, 2010.

255 *"He was already married"*...: Baldwin, Delois, author interview, March 3, 2012.

255 *"They used to always beat me up"*...: Baldwin, Jeff, author interview, November 1, 2011.

256 *"My daddy was in an accident"*...: ibid.

257 *"Who? No, Henry"*...: Baldwin, Delois, author interview.

257 *"The November 29, 1978, edition of the* **Beaver County Times** ...: "Aliquippa Woman Held in Husband's Death", *Beaver County Times,* November 29, 1978, page A3.

257 *A death certificate*...: Beaver County Register of Wills, death certificate for Baldwin, Henry, December 4, 1978.

257 *Apparent contravention*...: Pennsylvania Slayer's Act, http://www.legis.state.pa.us/cfdocs/legis/LI/consCheck.cfm?txtType=HTM&ttl=20&div=0&chpt=88.

258 *"Football and basketball are the same thing"*...: Zmijanac, author interview.

259 *"Have you lost your fuckin' mind?"*...: Zmijanac, author interview, March 26, 2012.

259 *"Mike was a good teacher"*...: Yannessa, author interview, March 29, 2012.

259 *"If I'm not going to move up to varsity"*...: Zmijanac, author interview.

260 *"Punching ... kicking and stomping"*...: "What Now? Dome Brawl Leaves McNie Seeing Red", Vranes, Marc, *Beaver County Times,* December 31, 1978, page C6.

260 *"On the floor"*...: Zmijanac, author interview.

261 **Things've gotten bad there**...: Evasovich, John, author interview, November 6, 2011.

261 *"I was in a black neighborhood"*...: Leighton, Chris, Reverend, author interview, February 17, 2014.

262 *"Good news, Ma"*...: Pollock, Jonha, author interview, July 7, 2013.

262 *"I don't think I hit the ground with my feet"*...: ibid.

263 *"It's crazy"*...: ibid.

263 *"All five"*...: Baldwin, Jeff, author interview.

263 **The doctor at Aliquippa Hospital**...: "Ex-Area Grid Star Wounded", *Beaver County Times,* June 15, 1981, page A5; Baldwin, Jeff, interview.

263 *"You know what actually saved me?"*...: Baldwin, Jeff, author interview.

263 *The class of '81 had gone 12-1*...: *Aliquippa Quips 1910-2010.*

263 *Lost the '80 WPIAL final*...: "Last Lesson Painful One for Aliquippa", Bires, Mike, *Beaver County Times,* November 23, 1980, page C1.

263 *First-team All-State*...: "All-Staters; Quips' Baldwin, Shannon on UPI First Team", United Press International, *Beaver County Times,* December 11, 1980, page C1.

264 *"The problem with Jeff Baldwin"*...: Yannessa, author interview.

264 *"I just lost the desire"*...: Baldwin, Jeff, author interview.

264 *"He put so much in me"*...: Brown, Jamie, author interview, April 28, 2012.

265 *There on page one* . . . : "Reagan Firing Controllers; Union Claims Strength", United Press International, *Beaver County Times*, August 6, 1981, page A1.

265 *And inside* . . . : "A Good Omen for the Future at J&L Steel", *Beaver County Times*, August 6, 1981, page A6.

266 *From 151 million* . . . : Hoerr, 606.

266 *The loss of 337,552 jobs* . . . : ibid.

266 *"Ling's goal in doing this"* . . . : Inman, Wollman, 309.

266 *"They thought I was crazy"* . . . : Suder, George "Juke", author interview, June 6, 2012.

266 *24,000 jobs* . . . : Carter, Jimmy, news conference, September 24, 1978, *Public Papers of the Presidents of the United States, Jimmy Carter, 1978, Book 2: June 30 to December 31, 1978*, Government Printing Office, Washington, D.C., 1978, page 1,661.

266 *"It was a workman's paradise"* . . . : Grandstaff, Gary, author interview, August 26, 2013.

267 *"Collapsing assumptions"* . . . : Tuchman, Barbara. *A Distant Mirror: The Calamitous 14th Century*. New York: Alfred A. Knopf, 1978: xiii.

267 *"We also lost a lot of competition"* . . . : Briem, Chris, author interview, October 11, 2010.

268 *"People would work for six hours"* . . . : Grandstaff, author interview.

269 *"The union would defend everybody"* . . . : Macroglou, Bill, author interview, August 16, 2013.

269 *"We've defended some people"* . . . : Eritano, Pete, author interview, January 6, 2012.

270 *"We feel the impact is going to be minimal"* . . . : "J&L to Shut Down Rod and Wire Mill", *Beaver County Times*, September 15, 1981, page A1.

270 *In March 1982* . . . : "J&L Work Force Slashed", Wasko, Rick, Mayfield, Dave, *Beaver County Times*, March 18, 1982, page A1.

270 *Grandstaff* . . . : Grandstaff, author interview.

270 *The White House was calling* . . . : "Union Begs Reagan for Help", Musala, Jane C., *Beaver County Times*, September 14, 1983, page 28 (page 1 of Moon Township-Coraopolis Area section).

271 *Crime in Aliquippa* . . . : "Old Steel Town Hopes to Survive Recession", Robbins, William, *New York Times*, August 23, 1984.

271 *"They'd put in a new round caster"* . . . : Malesky, Jerry, author interview, September 24, 2010.

272 *On January 3, 1985* . . . : "LTV Idling 500 at Aliquippa Works", Bickert, Tom, *Beaver County Times*, January 4, 1985, page A1.

272 *"I shut the welded tube down"* . . . : Suder, George "Juke", author interview.

272 *On May 17, 1985* . . . : "LTV: Death of a Mill; Workers, Union Officials Bitter", Bickert, Tom, *Beaver County Times*, May 18, 1985, page A1.

272 *Only 13,374 Aliquippans* . . . : *Census of 1990*, United States Census Bureau, Washington, D.C.

272 *"Who cries when I cry"* . . . : Walker, author interview.

PART FOUR

279 *By 1980 Aliquippa's population was down to 17,094* . . . : *Census of 1980*, United States Census Bureau, Washington, D.C.

279 *By '90* . . . : *Census of 1990*, United States Census Bureau, Washington, D.C.

279 *Official capacity, 5,500* . . . : "Top Quip; Yannessa Brings Football to Life in Aliquippa", White, Mike, *Pittsburgh Post-Gazette*, October 25, 1985, page 16.

280 *"Johnny, you got to get more involved in the program"* . . . : Evasovich, John, author interview, November 6, 2011.

280 *Three of the four previous WPIAL* . . . : *Aliquippa Quips 1910-2010*.

280 *National Public Radio* . . . : "NBC Show to Highlight Aliquippa High School", Xander, Rick, *Beaver County Times*, October 8, 1985, page C5.

281 *"Ain't you fuckin' somethin'"*...: Zmijanac, Mike, author interview, September 23, 2010.

281 *In the fall of 1983*...: "Yannessa Decides to Retire", White, Mike, *Pittsburgh Post-Gazette*, October 31, 2008.

282 *"Craig T"*...: Yannessa, Don, author interview, March 29, 2012.

283 *"Just something for coming"*...: ibid.

283 *Yes, its tenth-to-twelfth grade enrollment of 449 students*...: "WPIAL Realigns Football Classes, Conferences", Dulac, Gerry, *Pittsburgh Press*, December 23, 1981, page B-5.

283 *The Quips kept losing*...: *Aliquippa Quips 1910–2010.*

283 *"We've got the copper trophy"*...: "Mt. Pleasant Pulls a Surprise", White, Mike, *Pittsburgh Post-Gazette*, November 28, 1983, page 20.

283 *660 jobs*...: "More Employees Furloughed at Aliquippa Works", Swauger, Bill, *Beaver County Times*, September 23, 1984, page AI.

283 *A 5-foot-5 butterball*...: "Ex-Quips' Star Looks to Impress Gladiators", Neupauer, Nick, *Beaver County Times*, May 13, 1990, page CI.

284 *The '84 Quips bulled through the regular season*...: *Aliquippa Quips 1910–2010.*

284 *In the WPIAL AAA title game*...: "Aliquippa Trades Silver for Gold", Perrotto, John, *Beaver County Times*, November 23, 1984, page CI.

284 *"Hey", he screamed*...: Yannessa, author interview.

284 *Still, some five hundred fans*...: "The Victors: Quips Bring Home the Gold", Weiss, Steve, *Beaver County Times*, November 25, 1984, page AI.

284 *Two days later, Sunday's* **Beaver County Times**...: ibid.

285 *The next September*...: "Top Quip: Yannessa Brings Football to Life in Aliquippa", White, Mike, *Pittsburgh Post-Gazette*, October 25, 1985, page 16.

285 *"I want to get the Indian and the horse to parachute out of a helicopter"*...: ibid.

286 *He promised his players*...: *America's Game: The Super Bowl Champions*, "#2. 1985 Chicago Bears", CBS, February 3, 2007.

286 *"Go out and win one for Lefty"* . . . : "Ditka: 'Basic Guy' Molds Uncommon Team", Berkow, Ira, *New York Times*, January 20, 1986.

286 *Lost the '84 NFC title game* . . . : Ditka, Mike, with Telander, Rick. *In Life, First You Kick Ass: Reflections on the 1985 Bears and Wisdom from Da Coach.* Champaign, Ill.: Sports Publishing LLC, 2005: 6-9.

286 *Came back the next season* . . . : "Ditka Convicted of Drunk Driving", *Los Angeles Times*, November 9, 1985.

286 *Steel blocking sled* . . . : "Ditka Made It with Intensity: 'Iron Mike' Image Suits Hall of Famer", Parascenzo, Marino, *Pittsburgh Post-Gazette*, July 28, 1988, page 27.

286 *Punched out two teammates* . . . : "Ditka Huffs and Puffs and Creates a Monster", Schmitz, Brian, *Orlando Sentinel*, December 2, 1985.

286 *And in his spare time* . . . : Ditka, Mike, with Pierson, Don. *Ditka: An Autobiography.* Chicago: Bonus Books, Inc., 1986: 65.

286 *"Get the lead out"* . . . : "Ditka: The Mentor of the Midway Has Mellowed Some but Inside, He's Still Aliquippa Steel", Downey, Mike, *Los Angeles Times*, December 30, 1985.

286 *Won NFL Rookie of the Year* . . . : Beaver County Sports Hall of Fame, "*Mike Ditka*", http://www.bcshof.org/halloffamers/ditka1977.htm.

286 *"Halas throws nickels around like manhole covers"* . . . : "Batting the Breeze with Buttram", *The Free Lance-Star*, Fredericksburg, Va., March 15, 1967, page 26.

287 *He caught a touchdown pass* . . . : "Super Bowl VI: Dallas Finally Lands Big One; Super Defense Dooms Dolphs", Miller, Norm, *New York Daily News*, January 17, 1972.

287 *"And it killed Ditka"* . . . : Brandt, Gil, author interview, November 2010.

287 *"Coach Landry had us rooming together"* . . . : Reeves, Dan, author interview, November 2010.

287 *"You ever do that again"* . . . : Ditka, Mike, author interview, November 16, 2010.

287 *Shotgun formation* . . . : Ditka with Pierson, 148.

287 *"His IQ was off the chart"* . . . : Reeves, author interview.

287 *"Exactly right"* . . . : Staubach, Roger, author interview, October 25, 2013.

288 *8-win club* . . . : Pro Football Reference, "1974 NFL Standings, Team & Offensive Statistics", http://www.pro-football-reference.com/years/1974/.

288 *First wild-card team* . . . : Pro Football Hall of Fame, *"History of the Wild Card"*, http://www.profootballhof.com/news/history-of-the-wild-card/.

288 *That they lost to Ditka's hometown Steelers* . . . : "King Steeler II", Bechtel, Sam, *Beaver County Times,* January 19, 1976, page A1.

288 *"Ditka's got a subtleness about him"* . . . : Staubach, author interview.

288 *"I wish", Reeves said* . . . : Reeves, author interview.

289 *In 1987, he fired a wad of green gum* . . . : "In California, It's a Sticky Situation", Royko, Mike, *Chicago Tribune,* December 17, 1987.

289 *"Mellow Mike"* . . . : "Really, It Is Almost Too Much to Bear: Mellow Mike Ditka", Wojciechowski, Gene, *Washington Post,* December 4, 1988.

289 *"You know, I did calm down for a while"* . . . : Ditka, author interview.

290 *"What? Are they gonna be able to get Aliquippa High School?"* . . . : Footballnation.com interview, January 30, 2014, *"NFL Playoff Expansion Is Stupid"*, http://legacy.footballnation.com/video/ nfl-playoff-expansion-mike-ditka-and-others-hate-i/1376/.

290 *In 1986* . . . : "Annual Ditka Benefit Tournament Set for Beaver Lakes", Bires, Mike, *Beaver County Times,* June 23, 2002.

290 *Well over $200,000* . . . : "The NFL's Forgotten Players", Murray, Ken, *Baltimore Sun,* July 2, 2006.

290 *"In excess of $50,000"* . . . : Mansueti, James B., City of Aliquippa proclamation, May 7, 2000.

290 *"I can account for—out of his pocket"* . . . : Evasovich, author interview.

290 *One year, Aliquippa High graduated covaledictorians* . . . : ibid.

290 *"Do I have the greatest respect for him?"* . . . : ibid.

291 *"That's why I like it here"* . . . : Ditka, Charlotte, author interview, November 5, 2010.

291 *"Tough times don't last"* . . . : ibid.

292 *"There was nothing here"* . . . : Gilbert, Aileen, author interview, September 22, 2010.

292 *"She was horrible"* . . . : Zmijanac, author interview.

292 *Only her mom knew why she was so mad* . . . : "Mother's Love, Delivered Without Hug", Crouse, Karen, *New York Times,* September 9, 2007.

292 *"I'm going to write a book and tell about it"* . . . : Gilbert, Diana, author interview, September 22, 2010.

293 *6-foot-5* . . . : "Gilbert Receives Top Honor, Shows Skill as Running Back", Perrotto, John, Wolverton, Lee, *Beaver County Times,* December 4, 1988, page C4.

293 *Able to sprint 40 yards* . . . : "Star Linebacker Feels the Recruiting Blitz", Caldwell, Dave, *Philly Inquirer,* January 23, 1989.

293 *"I love Sean Gilbert"* . . . : Yannessa, author interview.

293 *"A Cadillac in a lot full of Volkswagens"* . . . : "Pick Play: Recruiting War Leaves Quips' Gilbert with Battle Fatigue", White, Mike, *Pittsburgh Post-Gazette,* February 8, 1989, page 13.

293 *Recruiters began their siege* . . . : *Aliquippa Quips 1910–2010.*

293 *Yannessa declared* . . . : "Pick Play: Recruiting War Leaves Quips' Gilbert with Battle Fatigue", White, Mike, *Pittsburgh Post-Gazette,* February 8, 1989, page 13.

293 *Ditka, after winning his Super Bowl with the '85 Bears, had even promised to donate $5,000 a year* . . . : "Aliquippa Crowns Ditka King for a Day", Bires, Mike, *Beaver County Times,* March 9, 1986, page C1.

293 *91 solo tackles* . . . : "Star Linebacker Feels the Recruiting Blitz", Caldwell, Dave, *Philly Inquirer,* January 23, 1989.

293 *Picked up a fumble* . . . : "Rams and Raiders Make It a Big Day", Downey, Mike, *Los Angeles Times,* April 27, 1992.

293 *The Quips won their first fourteen games* . . . : *Aliquippa Quips 1910–2010.*

293 *Found themselves ranked No. 2 ...:* "Quips Have Company in Best All-Time Debate", Equels, Jim, Jr., *Ellwood City Ledger,* December 12, 2012.

293 *The paper also named Gilbert ...:* "Quips' Gilbert Honored for Defense", White, Mike, *Pittsburgh Post-Gazette,* December 22, 1988, page 26.

294 *The Quips' arrival for games at predominantly white Montour ...:* "Cross Burning at Montour High Is Branded Racial Intimidation", Rishell, Grace, *Pittsburgh Post-Gazette,* October 7, 1986, page 23.

294 *Aliquippa's population ...:* *Census of 1980,* United States Census Bureau, Washington, D.C., 1980.

294 *And its football team's 70 percent ...:* "Cross Burning at Montour High Is Branded Racial Intimidation", Rishell, Grace, *Pittsburgh Post-Gazette,* October 7, 1986, page 23.

294 *"Growing up, we watched Pudgy Abercrombie" ...:* Gilbert, Sean, author interview, October 12, 2010.

294 *"I'm waiting for Uncle Sean" ...:* Gilbert, Diana, author interview.

295 *"I do think it's special", Aileen said of Aliquippa ...:* Gilbert, Aileen, author interview.

296 *"It just wasn't as noticeable" ...:* ibid.

296 *"It snowballed" ...:* Walker, Donald, author interview, November 10, 2011.

296 *"That's when everybody gave up" ...:* Brown, author interview.

297 *"I do think that history leaves its mark on a region" ...:* Leighton, Chris, Reverend, author interview, February 17, 2014.

297 *"When that mill went down" ...:* Law, Ty, author interview, August 19, 2013.

298 *In 1985, LTV's tax assessment ...:* "Aliquippa's Plight Mirrors That of Many Pa. Towns", Davidson, Tom, *Beaver County Times,* September 19, 2015.

298 *The 1988 budget ...:* "Better Budget: Aliquippa Sees Fiscal Recovery", Rishell, Grace, *Pittsburgh Post-Gazette,* April 8, 1989, page 4-B.

298 *On December 23, 1987 ...:* "Aliquippa Distressed; Can Obtain State Help", Byko, Jeff, *Beaver County Times,* December 24, 1987, page A1.

298 *"The best Christmas present"* . . . : ibid.

298 *Weeks later* . . . : "Aliquippa Adopts Two-Tiered Taxing Budget", *Pittsburgh Post-Gazette*, February 16, 1988, page 5-B.

298 *February of 1988* . . . : "7 Arrested on Weapons Charges in Aliquippa Gave Fake Names", Gigler, Rich, *Pittsburgh Press*, March 2, 1988, page B4.

299 *A year later, an estimated 80 percent of crime in the borough* . . . : "Officials Assess Status of Local Drug Trade", Skowron, Sandra, *Beaver County Times*, October 1, 1989, page A8.

299 *"You could see everything from Third Avenue"* . . . : Brown, author interview.

300 *But he missed four weeks that season* . . . : Baldwin, author interview.

301 *"Matter of fact, we started out, got hired part-time as Aliquippa police together"* . . . : Davis, Andre, author interview, November 7, 2011.

301 *Baldwin wasn't much of a cop* . . . : *"Informed me that he had a drug-dependency problem"* . . . : "Naim Case Headed to Jury: Suspects in Police Killing Decline to Testify; Closing Arguments Next", Simonovich, Milan, *Pittsburgh Post-Gazette*, May 7, 2002.

301 *Baldwin denied that on the stand* . . . : "Taylor, Brown Won't Testify", Vidonic, Bill, *Beaver County Times*, May 7, 2002. P.1.

301 *One night in 1986* . . . : Yannessa, author interview.

302 *"He got laid off"* . . . : McBride, Sherman, author interview, November 20, 2011.

303 *"I ate over there"* . . . : Short, Daniel, author interview, October 13, 2011.

303 *Two weeks later* . . . : Short, Daniel, Commonwealth of Pennsylvania criminal complaint against Grover McBride, Jr., August 6, 1988.

303 *One month later* . . . : Short, Daniel, Commonwealth of Pennsylvania criminal complaint against Grover McBride, Jr., September 6, 1988.

303 *"His first offense"* . . . : McBride, Sherman, author interview.

303 *All-American at Pitt* . . . : Beaver County Sports Hall of Fame, "Sean Gilbert", http://www.bcshof.org/halloffamers/gilbert2009.htm.

304 *That 13-0 defeat*...: "Beast of the East Berwick Knocks Off Best in West", Perrotto, John, *Beaver County Times*, December 11, 1988, page C1.

304 **USA Today** *had ranked Florida's Pine Forest*...: "Aliquippa Is No. 2 in National Poll", *Pittsburgh Post-Gazette*, December 2, 1988, page 20.

304 *Even the Berwick coach*...: "PIAA Dream Game Pits Aliquippa vs. Berwick", Perrotto, John, *Beaver County Times*, December 8, 1988, page C1.

304 *"Don't ever mention that one to him"*...: Gilbert, Diana, author interview.

304 *"You can't walk out here with no bullshit team"*...: Short, author interview.

305 *Little Mike Warfield*...: Warfield, Mike, author interview, October 12, 2011.

305 *"Art, hurry up!"*...: Patrick, Timmie, author interview, November 27, 2011.

306 *"The group of steel workers were arrested by local police"*...: "History of Aliquippa", Ireton, Gabriel, City of Aliquippa History Page, http://www.aliquippapa.gov/aliquippa_history.php.

307 *"It's just the way it is"*...: Yannessa, author interview.

308 *But now with that semifinal win*...: "Yannessa Reaches Milestone by Tying Aschman Win Mark", Perrotto, John, *Beaver County Times*, November 20, 1988, page C4.

308 *"You have to question the educational priorities at Baldwin High"*...: "Scorecard", *Sports Illustrated*, June 26, 1989.

308 *When Yannessa took the job*...: "'It's Time to Move On': Yannessa Era Ends in Aliquippa", Wolverton, Lee, *Beaver County Times*, June 4, 1989, page C1.

308 *"This is almost as big as J&L closing"*...: "Emotions High as Fans, Friends, Discuss Decision", Bires, Mike, *Beaver County Times*, June 4, 1989, page C1.

308 *"As far as having a good rapport with the blacks"*...: ibid, page C4.

309 *"Had a Sol's sporting goods downtown"*...: Walker, Dwan, author interview, September 24, 2010.

310 *"The first time I had sex: fourteen"*...: Baldwin, Tezmalita, author interview, November 10, 2011.

311 *Cleats got stuck in the mud*...: Law, author interview.

311 *And new head coach Frank Marocco* . . . : "Aliquippa's Football Team Wins Another WPIAL Title", Perrotto, John, *Beaver County Times*, November 26, 1989, page AI.

311 *Where Ty lived with his grandfather, Ray* . . . : Law, author interview.

314 *Named the city's Teacher of the Year* . . . : "Dedication-It Produces Results", Musala, Jane C., *Beaver County Times*, May 14, 1984, page A3.

314 *"I solved the major mystery"* . . . : Steals, Melvin, author interview, February 1, 2013.

314 *"By the time the kids had reached tenth grade"* . . . : ibid.

315 *Ty Law would go on to play big-time college ball* . . . : Beaver County Sports Hall of Fame, "Ty Law", http://www.bcshof.org/halloffamers/law2011.htm.

315 *"It's like you've lost everything"* . . . : Law, author interview.

316 *Law was named a Parade All-American* . . . : "Launching Pad: Quip Ty Law Makes Parade All-American", Starkey, Joe, *Pittsburgh Post-Gazette*, December 26, 1991, page W-7.

316 *First-ever state title* . . . : "A Shutout for Aliquippa; Rochester Falls Short", *Beaver County Times*, December 15, 1991, page AI.

316 *Marocco's boys avenged an early-season loss* . . . : "Looking at Quips Football, 1991: Ty Law & Co. Brought Home Aliquippa's First State Title", Barrickman, Bob, *Beaver County Times*, December 8, 2003, page B9.

316 *Rolled over Forest Hills* . . . : ibid.

316 *"I had to make it on this one"* . . . : Law, author interview.

316 *Law never had a chance to stretch* . . . : "STATE CHAMPS! Aliquippa Becomes King of the Hill in Class AA", Perrotto, John, *Beaver County Times*, December 15, 1991, page BI.

317 *"Crazy, crazy day"* . . . : ibid.

317 *"When we went to football games, we were going to wars"* . . . : Walker, Donald, author interview.

317 *"A 'Quip' is the heart of Aliquippa"* . . . : Marocco, Frank, author interview, January 4, 2012.

318 *"The coach for Hanover, he was very bitter about Aliquippa"*...: ibid.

318 *Having passed for nearly 7,000 yards*...: Catawba College Athletics, "Athletic Department: Mike Warfield", http://gocatawbaindians.com/profile.asp?playerID=1636.

318 *"Get in"*...: Short, author interview.

318 *"You would hear things"*...: Warfield, author interview.

319 *Another story Short tells himself*...: Short, author interview.

320 The **Pittsburgh Post-Gazette** *declared Short "Campbell's father"*...: "Quips' Campbell Was Best Among the Best", Adamski, Chris, *Pittsburgh Post-Gazette*, July 14, 2005, page W-9.

320 *"I don't know"*...: Campbell, Della Rae, author interview, February 24, 2014.

321 *"And if he wasn't crying he was fighting"*...: Short, author interview.

321 *"He thought I was going to do something with myself"*...: Law, author interview.

323 *But at 7:03 the night before*...: "USAirJet Crashes: 131 Aboard Die as Plane Goes Down Near Airport", *Pittsburgh Post-Gazette*, September 9, 1994, page 1.

323 *"I can't think of one accident"*...: Ivory, Karen. *Pennsylvania Disasters: True Stories of Tragedy and Survival*. Guilford, Conn.: Globe Pequot, 2007: 175.

324 *"The most horrible scene I've ever seen in my life"*...: "CRASH OF FLIGHT 427: THE CRASH SITE; 'A Horrifying Scene of Destruction' Leaves Emergency Crews Shaken", Kifner, John, *New York Times*, September 10, 1994.

324 *"We really needed this to take our minds off it"*...: "'We're All Looking for a Diversion': Despite Tragedy Nearby, the Game Goes on for Hopewell, Aliquippa", Allmann, Bill, *Beaver County Times*, September 11, 1994, page B8.

324 *"There's nothing here for them"*...: "Hard-Pressed Town Didn't Need Tragedy", Schaefer, Jim, *Detroit Free Press*, September 10, 1994, page 8.

324 *Aliquippa beat Hopewell that night*...: "Smashmouth Football: Quips Grind Out Marocco's 100th Victory", Allmann, Bill, *Beaver County Times*, September 11, 1994, page B8.

324 *Less than three miles away* ... : "Yannessa Gets Happy Homecoming with a Win In Ambridge", Equels, Jim, Jr., *Beaver County Times*, September 11, 1994, page B11.

326 *On April 22, 1995* ... : "Patriots Get Quips' No. 1 Man: Ty Law Ready to Go to Work for Parcells", Allmann, Bill, *Beaver County Times*, April 23, 1995, page B1.

327 *"I just made up my mind"* ... : Walker, Chedda, author interview, October 13, 2011.

327 *"I thought about it a thousand times"* ... : Walker, Chuckie, author interview, October 13, 2011.

327 *Between 1945 and 1978* ... : Gordon, Colin. *Growing Apart: A Political History of American Inequality.* Washington, D.C.: Institute for Policy Studies, 2013.

327 *By 2002, 72 percent of men over twenty-five with a diploma* ... : "American Manufacturing Is Coming Back. Manufacturing Jobs Aren't", Irwin, Neil, *Washington Post*, November 19, 2012.

327 *The family got by for a time* ... : Walker, Chuckie, author interview.

327 *Then Rockwell closed up* ... : "Rockwell Closing New Castle Plant; 530 Losing Jobs", Associated Press, *Beaver County Times*, October 16, 1991, page A5.

327 *And moved the plant to Mexico* ... : "Rockwell to Build Auto Parts Plant in Mexico: Expansion: Seal Beach Firm Cites a Growing Demand in That Country. It Says That No Jobs Will Be Lost at North American Factories.", Takahashi, Dean, *Los Angeles Times*, August 25, 1993.

328 *Together the two shops* ... : "J&L Deal Collapses; 115 Jobs Lost", Boselovic, Len, *Pittsburgh Post-Gazette*, August 9, 2002; "U.S. Steel 'Buys' LTV Tin Mill", *The Times of Northwest Indiana*, October 6, 2000.

328 *Chapter 11 bankruptcy* ... : "120-Year-Old North Side Company Dawar Changes with the Times", Reeves, Frank, *Pittsburgh Post-Gazette*, December 4, 2003.

328 *New, $112 million U.S. Gypsum plant* ... : "A Steel Town Finds Lost Jobs Tough to Replace", Ansberry, Claire, *Wall Street Journal*, May 27, 2004.

328 *George W. Bush, then running for president* ... : "Bush Outlines Environmental Cleanup Ideas", Mook, Jennifer, *Beaver County Times*, April 4, 2000, page A1.

328 *U.S. Steel shuttered the tin mill . . .* : "U.S. Steel-LTV Deal Will Shutter Aliquippa Plant", Lott, Ethan, *Pittsburgh Business Times,* October 6, 2000.

328 *"God blessed me" . . .* : Walker, Chuckie, author interview.

328 *In 1971 . . .* : *The Lost Decade of the Middle Class: Fewer, Poorer, Gloomier,* Pew Research Center, August 22, 2012.

329 *"Where I'm at?" . . .* : Walker, Chuckie, author interview.

329 *Then, just before 10 p.m. . . .* : "Police: Debt Led to Twin Murders", Ove, Torsten, *Beaver County Times,* April 14, 1996, page A1.

330 *And the outgoing "Hackensack" . . .* : "A Teen with Everything, Now Accused of Parents' Contract Hit: When an Outstate Pa. Couple Were Killed by Two Gunmen, Their Son's Reaction Was a Shopping Spree", Stark, Karl, *Philadelphia Inquirer,* April 21, 1996.

330 *"Friends, everybody, tried their best to break me" . . .* : Brown, author interview.

330 *But the arrests didn't hold . . .* : "Slain Parents' Son, Two Others Charged", Bauder, Bob, *Beaver County Times,* April 16, 1996, page A1.

331 *"I think why he told me what he told me is because of that relationship" . . .* : Short, author interview.

331 *As gruesome as the murder had been . . .* : "Murders: A Town in Shock", Ove, Torsten, *Beaver County Times,* April 18, 1996, page A1.

331 *"The father was like, You can't be one of them motherfuckers" . . .* : Short, author interview.

332 *"We forgive you, Brian" . . .* : David, George, author interview, January 6, 2012; Short, author interview.

332 *"We have been violated" . . .* : "A Teen with Everything, Now Accused of Parents' Contract Hit: When an Outstate Pa. Couple Were Killed by Two Gunmen, Their Son's Reaction Was a Shopping Spree", Stark, Karl, *Philadelphia Inquirer,* April 21, 1996.

332 *"I'm sixty-four years old" . . .* : ibid.

332 *At 7:51 p.m. . . .* : "Quips' Coach: Marocco's Out, Zmijanac Is In", Utterback, Bill, *Beaver County Times,* June 17, 1997, page A1.

332 *"It was the most ugly thing in the world"* . . . : Marocco, author interview.

333 *A week later, on June 27, he had a heart attack* . . . : ibid; "Dominic A. Iacobucci", *Beaver Valley Times,* June 29, 1997, page A5.

333 *"I hate a lot of people for that"* . . . : Marocco, author interview.

333 *To make the Aliquippa job more attractive* . . . : "Hiring, Not Firing, Time for Skepticism", *Beaver County Times,* June 19, 1997, page A6.

333 *"What's getting misinterpreted"* . . . : "Board, Marocco at Odds over Exit: Ex-Aliquippa Football Coach Calls It a Setup", White, Mike, *Pittsburgh Post-Gazette,* June 18, 1997, page C-1.

334 *Marocco's 73-25 record* . . . : "Players Irate, Confused by Marocco Ouster: School Board Releases Coach of Aliquippa Football Program", Fittipaldo, Ray, *Pittsburgh Post-Gazette,* June 19, 1997, page W-13.

334 *"We had a lot of gang activity"* . . . : Wytiaz, author interview.

334 *On April 2, 1998* . . . : "Woman, 45, Dies Trying to Get Away from Robber", Ehlers, Matt, April 3, 1998, page A1.

335 *"We saw young dudes walking around smoking weed"* . . . : Walker, Donald, author interview.

335 *In 1990* . . . : "Aliquippa Suspends Four Football Players After Fight", White, Mike, *Pittsburgh Post-Gazette,* November 13, 1990, page 19.

335 *"One of the most disgusting scenes you ever saw"* . . . : Wytiaz, author interview.

336 *"He'd gotten fired at Ambridge"* . . . : Zmijanac, Mike, author interview, September 23, 2010.

336 *"He was one of the few coaches who cared"* . . . : Law, author interview.

336 *"In my first year on the job"* . . . : Steals, Melvin. *Put Some Salt in the Water.* Baden, Pa.: Interlocking Visions, 2000: 1.

337 *"I told him that if man was going to be serving in that position"* . . . : Steals, author interview.

337 *"Remember, you're in a suburban inner city right here"* . . . : Zmijanac, author interview.

337 *"They didn't like him"*... : Yannessa, author interview.

337 *"From the outset they screwed Frank"*... : Short, author interview.

337 *"I loved that job"*... : Marocco, author interview.

338 *"That's not my domain"*... : Zmijanac, author interview.

339 *Aliquippa was facing $12 million in bond debts*... : "Learning a Lesson from Aliquippa Schools", Simonich, Milan, *Pittsburgh Post-Gazette*, December 21, 1997, page A-14.

339 *"They think they're better than we are"*... : LeDonne, Jon, author interview, November 18, 2011.

340 *Shutout loss*... : "Pendulum Swings Toward Jeannette at the Pit", Utterback, Bill, *Beaver County Times*, November 2, 1997, page B5.

340 *The next two years*... : *Aliquippa Quips 1910-2010*.

340 *"Well, this is my comeback for that"*... : Zmijanac, author interview.

341 *He brings up his basketball predecessor*... : "Aliquippa Hires Zmijanac as Boys' Basketball Coach", Perrotto, John, *Beaver County Times*, April 23, 1996, page B1.

341 *"Jimmy Deep won here"*... : Zmijanac, author interview.

342 *"And I mean aggressive tag"*... : Patrick, author interview.

343 *"That kid came back maybe a week later"*... : LeDonne, author interview.

344 *"Like watching two pit bulls go at it"*... : Patrick, author interview.

345 *"Words were exchanged"*... : Brown, author interview. Commonwealth of Pennsylvania, criminal complaint against Jeffrey Baldwin, June 28, 1999.

345 *"Oh, yeah!"*... : Baldwin, Jeff, author interview, November 1, 2011.

345 *"He was doing what I was selling"*... : Brown, author interview.

345. *Later that fall, Jeff was arrested and faced charges*... : Court of Common Pleas of Beaver County, Pennsylvania Criminal Division, Commonwealth of Pennsylvania vs. Jeffrey Baldwin, Case #1999-2353, December 15, 1999/ January 10, 2000.

345 *"Yeah, they got the guy"*... : Baldwin, Jeff, author interview.

346 *"It was so emotional"...*: LeDonne, author interview.

347 *The Quips steamrolled the competition*...: *Aliquippa Quips 1910–2010.*

347 *As a senior Weekley was listed at 6-foot-3 and 240 pounds*...: "Quips' Weekley Poised for Title Run", Equels, Jim, Jr., *Beaver County Times*, November 30, 2000, page B2.

348 *"A number one draft pick"...*: LeDonne, author interview.

348 *"Mo-Mo was unbelievable"...*: Peluso, Anthony, author interview, November 20, 2011.

348 *"I love hitting people"...*: "High School Athletes of the Week: Monroe Weekley/Aliquippa ~ Tanya McAnally/North Allegheny", White, Mike, *Pittsburgh Post-Gazette*, November 2, 2000.

348 *After Pitt flushed him*...: "Oh No, Monroe: Weekley Booted: Pitt's Harris Dismisses Ex-Quips Star", *Beaver County Times*, May 26, 2002, page B3.

348 *After the University of Kansas flushed him*...: "Jones, Weekley Leave KU", Caywood, Kurt, *Topeka Capital-Journal*, December 21, 2003.

348 *Killed a twenty-four-year-old*...: "Aliquippa Man Sentenced in Third-Degree Murder", O'Shea, Patrick, *Beaver County Times*, October 3, 2012.

348 *Avenged themselves on Washington*...: "Quips Lay It On: Nifty QB Leads Way as Aliquippa Advances to WPIAL AA Final with 43-28 Victory", White, Mike, *Pittsburgh Post-Gazette*, November 18, 2000, page 33.

349 *Held off Waynesburg*...: "Quips' Gaskin Tosses Winning Touchdown in Emergency QB Role", Utterback, Bill, *Beaver County Times*, November 26, 2000, page BI.

349 *When LeDonne's basketball Quips*...: *"Quips Falter Again: Poor Shooting Costly in 79-65 Loss to Trinity"*, White, Mike, *Pittsburgh Post-Gazette*, March 25, 2001.

349 *But when, three months earlier*...: "Mount Carmel Tops Aliquippa", Utterback, Bill, *Beaver County Times*, December 10, 2000, page BI.

349 *A photo of him*...: *Beaver County Times*, December 10, 2000, page AI.

349 *"Tears were coming down"...*: LeDonne, author interview.

350 *Then, just after 8:14 p.m* ...: "Aliquippa Policeman Shot to Death", Rosenblatt, Joel, *Pittsburgh Post-Gazette,* March 16, 2001, page 1.

350 *Earlier that afternoon* ...: Pennsylvania State Police Homicide Investigation Action Report, June 20, 2001, interview of Lee, Rayetta Jo, by Radatovich, Sgt. Paul on March 15, 2001.

351 *"They told us to be extra careful"*...: Carter, Sonya, author interview, March 25, 2012.

351 *On February 16* ...: *"Suspect issued police 'hit list':* Patterson, Scott A., Trooper, Homicide Investigation Action Report interview with J.D. Prose, April 1, 2001; "Second Man Arraigned in Police Killing", Musala, Jane C., Prose, J.D., Vidonic, Bill, *Beaver County Times,* March 18, 2001, page A1; "Slain Policeman Feared Killing Was Coming", Prose, J.D., *Beaver County Times,* March 18, 2001, page A1.

351 *Naim also told his mother and brother* ...: Radatovich, Sgt. Paul, Homicide Investigation Action Report interview with Paul Naim, April 11, 2001.

352 *William Alston* ...: "Naim's Killer Faces Life in Prison: Death, Probation Violation Could Bring Up to 60 Years", Simonich, Milan, *Pittsburgh Post-Gazette,* May 28, 2002.

352 *"I got rid of six policemen"*...: Battalini, Anthony, author interview, October 12, 2011.

352 *"This is one day before he got killed"*...: David, author interview.

353 *Average monthly rent*...: "Linmar Terrace Quiet in Wake of Killing", Ferguson-Tinley, M., *Pittsburgh Post-Gazette,* April 1, 2001.

353 *"My theory: Jamie Brown did do the shooting"*...: David, author interview.

353 *The second bullet*...: External examination by Pathologist James W. Smith, M.D., The Medical Center, Beaver, Pa., March 30, 2001.

353 *Naim was sprawled facedown* ...: officer statement by Young, Officer Shawn, Cassidy, Sgt. Daniel G., City of Aliquippa Bureau of Police.

354 *At one point* ...: Carter, author interview.

354 *"Do you know how many people called 911?"*...: Radatovich, author interview.

354 *The narrative later proved less provocative* . . . : "The Kitty Genovese Murder and the Social Psychology of Helping: The Parable of the 38 Witnesses", Manning, Rachel, Levine, Mark, Collins, Alan, *American Psychologist*, vol. 62 (6), September 2007, pages 555-562.

354 *"We're knocking at doors"* . . . : Radatovich, author interview.

355 *A manhunt was under way, too* . . . : "Suspect Questioned in Officer's Slaying", Vidonic, Bill, *Beaver County Times*, March 29, 2001, page A1.

355 *Once seventeen-year-old Acey Taylor was picked up on April 20* . . . : "Student, 17, Charged in Naim's Killing", Vidonic, Bill, Prose, J.D., *Beaver County Times*, April 22, 2001, page A1.

355 *"I thought this town was going to fall apart"* . . . : McBride, author interview.

355 *On the Saturday after* . . . : "Zmijanac Copes with Aliquippa's Perception, Pain", Cook, Ron, *Pittsburgh Post-Gazette*, March 21, 2001.

355 *"I'm sure there are people who think all of us are like the lowlifes"* . . . : ibid.

356 *On the morning of Tuesday, March 20, "Jimmy's Last Patrol"* . . . : " 'Jimmy's Last Patrol': Law Enforcers Bade Farewell to Slain Officer", Prose, J.D., *Beaver County Times*, March 21, 2001, page A1.

356 *"His funeral was beautiful"* . . . : Carter, author interview.

356 *The first to raise an alarm about Brown's hit list* . . . : Pennsylvania State Police Homicide Investigation Action Report, interview of Carter, Sonya Lynn, by Kokoski, Tpr. Michael L., June 28, 2001, page 410.

356–357 *Because Naim wasn't originally scheduled to work Linmar that Thursday night* . . . : Pennsylvania State Police Homicide Investigation Action Report, interview of Carter, Officer Sonya Lynn, Patrolman, by Melder, Raymond J., Cpl., March 19, 2001, page 121; . . . : Pennsylvania State Police Homicide Investigation Action Report, March 29, 2001, polygraph examination of Carter, Sonya Lynn, by Sherwin, Tpr. Thomas H. on March 22, 2001, pages 172-173.

357 *Seven days after the killing* . . . : Pennsylvania State Police Homicide Investigation Action Report, March 29, 2001, polygraph examination of Carter, Sonya Lynn, by Sherwin, Tpr. Thomas H. on March 22, 2001, pages 172-173.

357 *"I tried to do my job"...*: Carter, author interview.

357 *"It was crushing"...*: Patrick, author interview.

358 *"He's going to be an All-American"...*: Zmijanac, author interview.

358 *"My uncle was older"...*: Revis, Darrelle, author interview, October 21, 2010.

359 *"You don't know me well"...*: ibid; Zmijanac, author interview, September 23, 2010.

360 *"He's innocent and it's political"...*: Baldwin, Jeff, author interview.

361 *Police say they found a crack pipe...*: Receipt Inventory of Seized Property, Commonwealth of Pennsylvania, March 19, 2001.

361 *"Aww", Jeff said, when he recognized Radatovich...*: Radatovich, author interview.

362 *Nearly five months later...*: Short, Daniel, letter to Barr, Linda, August 2, 2001.

362 *Investigators doubled back...*: Pennsylvania State Police Homicide Investigation Action Report, Epps, Trp. Paul, August 7, 2001, pages 491–493.

362 *"I think they had to discredit what I wrote in that report"...*: Short, author interview.

362 *"I never seen a guy with a ponytail"...*: Walker, Connie, author interview, February 26, 2014.

363 *"They had to make someone the scapegoat"...*: Patrick, author interview.

363 *One fresh—and reported—allegation was a 1995 incident...*: "Eight Nabbed in Pittsburgh Probe of Prison Guards/Sheriffs", Bello, Marisol, *Pittsburgh Tribune-Review*, February 5, 2003.

364 *"Rick Hill is my father"...*: Campbell, Tommie, Jr., author interview, May 10, 2012.

364 *"With him getting me out of the way"...*: Hill, Rick, author interview, February 24, 2014.

364 *"Nothing that Rick and Della are saying"...*: Short, author interview.

364 *"Oh, yeah"*...: McBride, author interview.

365 *"Flip this"*...: Short, author interview.

365 *"I didn't want to lose Peep's friendship"*...: Warfield, Mike, author interview, October 12, 2011.

366 *"He loved that job"*...: Patrick, author interview.

366 *"Yeah," Tommie said*...: Campbell, author interview.

368 *"All those examples helped me"*...: Revis, author interview.

368 *The Quips went 8-3*...: *Aliquippa Quips 1910–2010.*

368 *"Quiet, always worked hard"*...: Zmijanac, author interview.

369 *In the state championship final*...: "Kings of the Hill: Quips Come from Behind to Reach Summit of PIAA", Utterback, Bill, *Beaver County Times*, December 8, 2003, page D1; "Revis' Performance One for the History Books", Perrotto, John, *Beaver County Times*, December 8, 2003, page D1.

369 *"He played like Jim Thorpe"*...: "Revis' Performance One for the History Books", Perrotto, John, *Beaver County Times*, December 8, 2003, page D1.

369 *"I don't know how I did that"*...: Revis, author interview.

370 *And despite just one basketball practice*...: "Having a Ball: Quips' Revis Scores 30 in Hoops, Too", Hall, Eric, *Beaver County Times*, December 10, 2003, page D1.

370 *"I remember telling my mom one time, 'We're going to make it out of here'"*...: Revis, author interview.

371 *Total population was heading south of 10,000*...: *Census of 2000*, United States Census Bureau, Washington, D.C.

371 *The Aliquippa school system*...: Pennsylvania Department of Education Bureau of Special Education, *Aliquippa School District Special Education Data Report 2010*, December 2010.

371 *"It's a national issue"*...: Wytiaz, author interview.

372 *"Half of them make it"*...: Zmijanac, author interview.

372 *"If he wants to come back"*...: McBride, author interview.

372 *More than 80 percent* . . . : Klink, Ron, child nutrition hearing, U.S. House of Representatives, Washington, D.C., March 22, 1995.

372 *"The football field was my sanctuary"* . . . : Walker, Willie, author interview, October 13, 2010.

374 *"Mike Lowe"* . . . : Peluso, author interview.

374 *"I still feel that sense of pride"* . . . : LeDonne, author interview.

375 *"Other than that? It's these hills"* . . . : McBride, author interview.

376 *Academic troubles and distractions* . . . : "Aliquippa Track Team Finds Way to Win, Even with Less Than Adequate Facilities", Emert, Rich, *Pittsburgh Post-Gazette*, May 17, 2005.

376 *WPIAL gold* . . . : "Quips' Star Is on Roll: Campbell Captures 100, 200 Crowns", White, Mike, *Pittsburgh Post-Gazette*, May 18, 2005, page F-8.

376 *"We didn't know how he was going to do"* . . . : Washington, Mike, author interview, September 25, 2010.

376 *"I ain't going to lie"* . . . : Campbell, author interview.

376 *"Quiet kid. Well dressed"* . . . : Davis, Andre, author interview, October 12, 2010.

377 *"It wasn't like Byron had technique"* . . . : Washington, author interview.

377 *Westmont Hilltop's Brad Kanuch* . . . : *Pittsburgh Post-Gazette*, May 29, 2005, page D-5.

377 *"The prettiest jump"* . . . : McBride, author interview.

377 *"If it wasn't for Byron winning that long jump"* . . . : Campbell, author interview.

377 *At 12:15 p.m* . . . : ibid; "Souped-Up Quips Win AA Title; Pitt-Bound Campbell Becomes Aliquippa's First Individual Winner in PIAA Running Event", White, Mike, *Pittsburgh Post-Gazette*, May 29, 2005, page D-4.

378 *"I ended up catching everybody"* . . . : Campbell, author interview.

378 *"If we had to run five more meters"* . . . : "Souped-Up Quips Win AA Title; Pitt-Bound Campbell Becomes Aliquippa's First Individual Winner in PIAA Running Event", White, Mike, *Pittsburgh Post-Gazette*, May 29, 2005, page D-4.

378 *"Byron's really why we won gold"* . . . : Washington, author interview.

378 *"It just showed us"* . . . : Campbell, author interview.

378 *"He couldn't believe it"* . . . : Davis, author interview.

378 *Now he'd just finished his freshman year at Pitt* . . . : "Darrelle Revis", Pitt Football, http://www.pittsburghpanthers.com/sports/m-footbl/mtt/revis_darrelle00.html.

379 *"He never got in trouble in high school"* . . . : Revis, author interview.

381 *Had been publicly honored* . . . : "Area Women Make the Grade from Welfare to Job Market", Ross, Virginia, *Beaver County Times*, June 5, 2002.

381 *"Forty inmates to one guard in the pod"* . . . : Gilbert, Diana, author interview, June 20, 2014.

381 *In 2005, Gilbert resigned* . . . : "Jail Report Revealed", Prose, J.D., *Beaver County Times*, February 28, 2007.

381 *"Expressed concern that the matter was not pursued criminally"* . . . : Gentile, Louis, Gentile-Meinert and Associates, Monaca, Pa., "Report of Investigation, Beaver County Jail, Conducted 2006", Beaver County Commissioners, 2007, page 75.

381 *"She was a good guard though"* . . . : David, author interview.

381 *"What Georgie David put out"* . . . : Gilbert, Diana, author interview.

381 *The 141–page report* . . . : "Jail Report Revealed", Prose, J.D., *Beaver County Times*, February 28, 2007.

382 *In 2007, he ran for sheriff* . . . : "Camp Holds Thin Lead for 3rd Seat", Silver, Jonathan D., *Pittsburgh Post-Gazette*, November 7, 2007, page A-12.

382 *"Me and her got along very well"* . . . : David, author interview.

382 *Years later* . . . : "Beaver County Sheriff George David Indicted on 11 Charges", Doerschner, Kristin, *Beaver County Times*, March 25, 2013.

382 *"Karma is a mother"* . . . : Gilbert, Diana, author interview.

384 *"When we first moved up here"* . . . : Baldwin, Tezmalita, author interview.

384 *"Someone drove past me and just started shooting recklessly"* . . . : Johnson, Kevin, author interview, November 9, 2010.

385 *On May 22 of that year* . . . : "Car Jumps Curb Killing 1; School Athlete Surrenders", Smydo, Joe, *Pittsburgh Post-Gazette*, May 24, 2009.

385 *"The car hit him straight-on"* . . . : Campbell, Della Rae, author interview.

385 *Immensely popular in Plan 12* . . . : "Car Jumps Curb Killing 1; School Athlete Surrenders", Smydo, Joe, *Pittsburgh Post-Gazette*, May 24, 2009.

386 *"That one-block section by the high school where Plan 12 Market is?"* . . . : Walker, Donald, author interview.

386 *"Go ahead", she said* . . . : Walker, Dwan, author interview, October 1, 2011.

387 *Wide receiver Deon Johnson* . . . : "Driver Named in Aliquippa Shooting Now Faces Homicide Charge", Vidonic, Bill, *Beaver County Times*, June 11, 2005.

387 *Defensive end Jordan "Ricky" Cain* . . . : "3 Inmates Charged in Aliquippa Slaying: Victim Shot Multiple Times in '06 Attack", Ove, Torsten, *Pittsburgh Post-Gazette*, March 2, 2011.

387 *Backup running back Darius Odom* . . . : "Aliquippa Man Convicted of Fatally Shooting Cousin", Associated Press, *Pittsburgh Post-Gazette*, May 1, 2010.

387 *Quarterback Stephen Hardy* . . . : "Murder Suspect Caught", O'Shea, Patrick, *Ellwood City Ledger*, September 1, 2010.

388 *Marquay Riggins* . . . : "Man, 18, Wanted in Aliquippa Killing", *Pittsburgh Post-Gazette*, July 31, 2012.

388 *Eddie Carter* . . . : "Eddie B. Carter III (Weedy)", *Beaver County Times*, September 14, 2012.

388 *"Seven of my high school teammates have died"* . . . : Revis, author interview, June 19, 2013.

388 *"He was sincerely apologetic"* . . . : Zmijanac, author interview.

388 *"What stopped me playing"* . . . : Gaskins, Tony, author interview, November 21, 2011.

389 *Gaskins, then eighteen* . . . : "Aliquippa Shootings: No One's Talking", Fontaine, Tom, *Beaver County Times*, November 21, 2009.

389 *"If I would've killed him"* . . . : Gaskins, author interview.

389 *Four years later* . . . : "Murder-Suicide Reported in Aliquippa", Bauder, Bob, *Beaver Valley Times*, September 5, 2009.

390 *"That's when the world opened up to me"* . . . : Walker, Dwan, author interview.

391 *And the other was a 6-foot-5 receiver* . . . : "Jon (yes, Jon) Baldwin Will Have Pitt Fans Dreaming and NFL Scouts Drooling This Fall", Fittipaldo, Ray, *Pittsburgh Post-Gazette*, August 15, 2010.

391 *"Every day we'd basically see each other"* . . . : Brown, author interview.

391 *"He started taking things more seriously"* . . . : Baldwin, Tezmalita, author interview.

391 *When, in May 2002, a jury convicted his half-brother* . . . : "Cop Killer to Prison: Judge Vows That He'll Serve the Maximum", Bauder, Bob, *Beaver County Times*, May 30, 2002, page A1.

392 *Seven months earlier* . . . : "Man Going to Prison for Attempted Robbery", Vidonic, Bill, *Beaver County Times*, October 24, 2002.

392 *"Mistaken identity"* . . . : Baldwin, Jeff, author interview.

392 *"First-degree miscalculation"* . . . : "A First-Degree Miscalculation", Roddy, Dennis, *Pittsburgh Post-Gazette*, May 11, 2002.

392 *"Innocent: a hundred percent"* . . . : Brown, author interview.

393. *Monica Horton faxed in a recantation . . . In 2005, Rayetta Lee* . . . : Horton, Monica L., letter to the attention of O'Neill, Trooper Donald, April 20, 2001. Notarized statement by Lee Green, Rayetta to Beaver County attorney Jeffrey Small, December 23, 2005.

393 *A staff psychologist at Aliquippa Middle School placed his reading* . . . : Pennsylvania State Police Homicide Investigation Action Report, interview of Walkney, Sarah Beth, by Lewis, Robert I., Tpr. on January 10, 2002.

393 *Heard and saw nothing that night* . . . : Pennsylvania State Police Homicide Investigation Action Report, interview of Hines, Darnell by Patterson, Tpr. Scott A., Melder, Raymond, Cpl. on March 16, 2001, pages 29–30.

393 *Just heard the gunshots*...: Pennsylvania State Police Homicide Investigation Action Report, interview of Hines, Darnell by Lewis, Robert I., Tpr. on March 16, 2001, page 31; "Witness: Suspect Pulled Trigger; Informant Testifies About Police Slaying", Simonich, Milan, *Pittsburgh Post-Gazette*, May 3, 2002.

393 *Complained that he was being pressured*...: Beaver County Department of Corrections Statement of Facts, April 6, 2001.

393 *He then passed a polygraph examination*...: Pennsylvania State Police Homicide Investigation Action Report, polygraph examination of Hines, Darnell by Sherwin, Thomas H., Tpr. on April 11, 2001, page 339.

393 *"I don't care what anybody says"*...: Hines, Darnell, author interview, March 29, 2012.

394 *"And it's going to be a wound"*...: Patrick, author interview.

394 *"Whether we got the right guy?"*...: Davis, author interview.

394 *"No", said Quips offensive coordinator Sherman McBride*...: McBride, author interview.

394 *"I just know the wrong guy's in jail"*...: Walker, Dwan, author interview.

394 *"Jamie Brown was involved with some real heavy hitters"*...: Short, author interview.

394 *Acey Taylor*...: "Cop Killer to Prison: Judge Vows That He'll Serve the Maximum", Bauder, Bob, *Beaver County Times*, May 30, 2002, page A1.

395 *"Can I rationally explain"*...: ibid, A6.

395 *"Great for me"*...: Baldwin, Jeff, author interview.

395 *Jonathan never played a proper game in pads*...: Baldwin, Jonathan, author interview, October 18, 2011.

396 *"The way I was raised"*...: Baldwin, Tezmalita, author interview.

396 *Jonathan became an All-State basketball star*...: "Chiefs Select WR Jonathan Baldwin with 1st Round Pick", Chiefs.com, http://www.chiefs.com/news/article-2/Chiefs-Select-WR-Jonathan-Baldwin-with-1st-Round-Pick/c94f740f-e362-4fa7-a08a-74425e4a051a.

396 *In any other game* . . . : "Jeannette Beats Quips, 70-48", White, Mike, *Pittsburgh Post-Gazette*, November 17, 2007.

397 *Followed his dad's trail* . . . : "Jonathan Baldwin", Pitt Football, http://www.pittsburghpanthers.com/sports/m-footbl/mtt/baldwin_jon00.html.

397 *Groping a girl's buttocks on a bus* . . . : "Pitt's Baldwin Cleared of Charges", Kerlik, Bobby, *Pittsburgh Tribune-Review*, January 12, 2010.

397 *"Purposely trying to disrupt my draft stock"* . . . : "Baldwin Works on 'Attitude'", Gorman, Kevin, *Pittsburgh Tribune-Review*, February 18, 2011.

397 *"That's why, when I'm in Aliquippa"* . . . : Baldwin, Jonathan, author interview.

398 *In 1980* . . . : "Myths of Post-Industrial America", Samuelson, Robert J., *Washington Post*, April 7, 2013.

399 *Manufacturing's* . . . : "A Revolution in the Making", Koten, John, *Wall Street Journal*, June 11, 2013, page R1.

399 *"Those types of jobs"* . . . : Briem, author interview.

399 *"I always think about: if the mill was still going"* . . . : Letteri, Gilda, author interview, May 11, 2012.

400 *"You came to the country with a brown bag with your clothes in it"* . . . : Betters, C.J. "Chuck", author interview, November 19, 2011.

400 *Long before his own grown sons, Mike and Mark began piling up drunk-driving arrests in Illinois* . . . : "Prosecutors: Ditka's Son Tests Positive for Opiates", Fuller, Ruth, *Chicago Tribune*, November 16, 2012; "Another of Mike Ditka's Sons Charged with DUI", *Chicago Tribune*, September 30, 2011; "Prosecutors Drop Felony DUI Case Against Son of Former Bears Coach Mike Ditka", *Chicago Tribune*, February 24, 2012; "Mike Ditka's Son Claims His Name Spurred DUI Charge", Ter Maat, Sue, *Chiacgo Tribune*, April 27, 2011.

400 *"I've had a big house and a lot of cars"* . . . : Ditka, Mike, author interview.

402 *"Aliquippa's in a weird place"* . . . : Briem, author interview.

402 *Gilbert started* . . . : "Amen! Sean Gilbert", *ESPN: The Magazine*, July 10, 2012.

402 *Law funded a Head Start program in Plan 12 . . .* : "Sports Stars Come Out to Support Head Start", *Beaver County Times,* May 29, 1998.

402 *And ran a charity golf tournament and basketball game . . .* : "Ty Law", Beaver County Sports Hall of Fame, http://www.bcshof.org/halloffamers/law2011.htm.

402 *Revis holds an occasional football camp . . .* : "Relaxed Revis Camps in Aliquippa on Way to Tampa", Chiapazzi, Andrew, *Beaver County Times,* June 20, 2013.

402 *"What are you going to do for us here in Aliquippa, Mr. Law?" . . .* : Law, author interview.

403 *"I love it to the utmost" . . .* : Revis, author interview.

403 *"Sit quiet, son" . . .* : Walker, Chuckie, author interview.

404 *"And I said 'I don't want you to give me anything'" . . .* : Walker, Dwan, author interview.

405 *"The selfish person's out there supporting himself" . . .* : Smith, Eugene "Salt", author interview, November 28, 2011.

405 *"Okay, Mr. Smith" . . .* : Walker, Dwan, author interview.

405 *"They're so fucking green" . . .* : Betters, author interview.

406 *"Like a lost little boy" . . .* : Campbell, Tommie, author interview.

406 *"Some of our guys have been struggling" . . .* : Wytiaz, author interview.

407 *Was arrested after being stopped near Sixth Avenue . . .* : "Former Aliquippa Football Star Facing Drug Charges", Utterback, Bill, *Ellwood City Ledger,* April 8, 2011.

407 *"He's as good or better than Revis" . . .* : Evasovich, author interview.

407 *Jonathan Baldwin became a first-round draft pick . . .* : "Pitt Standout WR Baldwin Signs with Chiefs", Associated Press, *Pittsburgh Tribune-Review,* July 30, 2011.

407 *"He was over some girl's house and they stuck a gun to his head" . . .* : Campbell, Della Rae, author interview.

408 *"It was a real scary moment, man"* . . . : Campbell, Tommie, author interview.

408 *By 2010, he had been kicked off the team* . . . : "Pitt Dismisses Fields from Team", Bennett, Brian, ESPN.com, February 19, 2010, http://espn.go.com/college-football/news/story?id=4921565.

409 *"There's a lot of time to think while you're mopping that floor"* . . . : Campbell, Tommie, author interview.

409 *Pulling up next to his Linmar enemies* . . . : "Two Charged in Aliquippa Shooting", Pound, Michael, *Beaver County Times*, September 4, 2007; Davis, Andre, author interview.

409 *In August 2009* . . . : "Ambridge Man Wanted in Aliquippa Bar Shooting", Vidonic, Bill, *Beaver County Times*, August 22, 2009.

409 *"He helped me in every aspect possible"* . . . : Campbell, Tommie, author interview.

410 *Finished with 29 tackles* . . . : "Tommie Campbell", Tennessee Titans, http://www.titansonline.com/team/roster/tommie-campbell/c9212fbc-6fba-4fdd-8015-064cb1c71b28/.

410 *"I quit putting blame on everything around me"* . . . : Campbell, Tommie, author interview.

410 *Lit up NFL scouts' eyes and stopwatches* . . . : "Campbell Isn't Going to Waste NFL Chance", Associated Press, *Paris Post-Intelligencer*, Paris, Tenn., August 30, 2011.

410 *He signed a four-year, $2.09 million contract* . . . : Spotrac, http://www.spotrac.com/nfl/jacksonville-jaguars/tommie-campbell/.

411 *On June 6, 2010* . . . : "Saving Steel: Salvagers Scoop Up What's Left to Tell Industry's Story", Nelson Jones, Diana, *Pittsburgh Post-Gazette*, June 6, 2010, page A-1.

411 *What remains on the seven-and-a-half-mile stretch* . . . : "USG Aliquippa Gives Tribute to Mill That Once Stood in Its Place", Cubbal, Kayleen, *Beaver County Times*, May 24, 2015.

411 *200 million tons of slag* . . . : Betters, author interview.

412 *"We bring 'em, we break 'em"* . . . : Betters, author interview.

413 *When, in 2008, bankruptcy claimed Aliquippa Community Hospital* . . . : "For Aliquippa Community Hospital, a 'Green' Demolition", Twedt, Steve, *Pittsburgh Post-Gazette*, March 15, 2011.

413 *There's something relative to my legacy"* . . . : Betters, author interview.

414 *The six-hundred-acre site* . . . : "DEP Begins 90-Day Review of Remediation of Old J&L Tin Mill Site", Stonesifer, Jared, *Beaver County Times*, January 20, 2015; Betters, author interview.

415 *"I've thought about it, don't get me wrong"* . . . : Gaskins, author interview.

415 *"It took a year to beat that jive-ass shit out of him"* . . . : Betters, author interview.

415 *"I stay there because I got things now in life that I thought I would never have"* . . . : Gaskins, author interview.

416 *The stadium in Hopewell that was renamed, in 2001, in his honor* . . . : "Hopewell Renaming Stadium for Dorsett", White, Mike, *Pittsburgh Post-Gazette*, September 6, 2001, page F-2.

416 *"The thing I'm disappointed in?"* . . . : Dorsett, Tony, author interview, September 24, 2010.

417 *The death at sixty-one* . . . : ibid.

417 *"Okay", Tony said* . . . : ibid.

418 *9,438 people still living there* . . . : "QuickFacts: Aliquippa City, Pennsylvania", United States Census Bureau, Washington, D.C., http://www.census.gov/quickfacts/table/PST045215/4200820.

418 *"To the workers of the Jones and Laughlin Steel Corporation"* . . . : "Memories of Steel", Theodore, Larissa, *Beaver County Times*, June 23, 2010.

418 *"Every time I come back"* . . . : Dorsett, author interview.

419 *"I did not contribute one cent to that campaign"* . . . : Betters, author interview.

419 *On May 17, 2011* . . . : "One Aliquippa Slate Surprises Incumbents", Prose, J.D., *Beaver County Times*, May 18, 2011.

419 *"This kid: I give him credit"* . . . : Battalini, author interview.

419 *It wasn't until election night* . . . : Walker, Dwan, author interview, November 8, 2011.

420 *"Twenty-five years?"* . . . : Battalini, author interview.

420 *Rejected by Royal Dutch Shell* . . . : "Aliquippa's First Black Mayor Walker Fights City's Stigma", Vidonic, Bill, *Pittsburgh Tribune-Review*, April 2, 2012.

421 *"I still think we're going to get some bounce-back"* . . . : Walker, Dwan, author interview, March 27, 2012.

421 *Meanwhile came this cosmic slap* . . . : "Instant Tickets Also Winning in the Region", O'Shea, Patrick, *Ellwood City Ledger*, December 26, 2012.

422 *"I was winning and he was getting mad"* . . . : Henry, Dravon, author interview, November 6, 2011.

422 *Aliquippa High would go on to win its fourteenth WPIAL football championship later that month* . . . : "Aliquippa Adds Another AA Crown to Collection", Schofield, Paul, *Pittsburgh Tribune-Review*, November 27, 2011.

422 *As Dravon racked up 5,454 career yards rushing* . . . : "Aliquippa's Henry Picks West Virginia over Pitt", DiPaola, Jerry, *Pittsburgh Tribune-Review*, December 9, 2013.

422 *Dravon's dad* . . . : Henry, Roland, author interview, November 6, 2011.

423 *"I didn't know what else to do"* . . . : Askew, Shanell, author interview, November 6, 2011.

423 *"I just stood there"* . . . : Henry, Dravon, author interview.

423 *Their grandfather, Ossie Foster* . . . : "Quips Could Be Too Hot for Seneca to Handle", Hecht, Steve, *Pittsburgh Post-Gazette*, October 4, 1979, page 12; "Mt. Lebo Rides KO to Title, Playoffs", Cuddy, Jim, Jr., *Pittsburgh Press*, November 2, 1979, page A-7.

423 *"No no", he laughed* . . . : Askew, David, author interview, November 6, 2011.

424 *In December 2002* . . . : "Two Confess to '99 Killings", Vidonic, Bill, *Beaver County Times*, December 19, 2002.

424 *"George . . . David"* . . . : David, author interview.

424 *"When the Naim case happened"* . . . : Patrick, author interview.

424 *"At first I tried blocking it out"* . . . : Askew, David, author interview.

425 *"He was different"* . . . : Gilbert, Diana, author interview, June 20, 2014.

425 *"Got caught in that spiderweb"* . . . : McBride, author interview.

425 *"The only thing I ask"* . . . : Gilbert, Diana, author interview.

425 *"Born with one foot to success and one in turmoil"* . . . : Askew, David, Askew, Shanell, Henry, Dravon, author interviews.

426 *"Franklin Avenue"* . . . : Betters, author interview.

427 *"I always tell people"* . . . : Walker, Dwan, author interview.

428 *160 boys* . . . : Jeter, Rod, author interview, September 25, 2010.

428 *40 percent of the boys* . . . : Gipson, Alvin B., author interview, October 1, 2015.

429 *"This is why I do what I do"* . . . : Zmijanac, author interview.

429 *Then again in 2012* . . . : "Aliquippa Routs Washington 34-7, for Class AA Crown", Wunderley, Ken, *Pittsburgh Post-Gazette*, November 24, 2012.

429 *"Football caused this"* . . . : "Pro Football Hall of Famer Tony Dorsett Says Settlement Is a Start, but Future Health Costs Still a Concern", Red, Christian, *New York Daily News*, August 31, 2013; "Hall of Famer Tony Dorsett, former NY Giants DT Leonard Marshall Diagnosed with CTE", Red, Christian, *New York Daily News*, November 8, 2013.

429 *A week later* . . . : "Youth Football Participation Drops", Fainaru, Steve, Fainaru-Wada, Mark, ESPN.com, November 14, 2013, http://espn.go.com/espn/otl/story/_/page/popwarner/pop-warner-youth-football-participation-drops-nfl-concussion-crisis-seen-causal-factor.

429 *"I wouldn't", Ditka said* . . . : "Monsters No More", *Real Sports with Bryan Gumbel*, Kronick, Jordan, produced by, HBO, January 20, 2015.

430 *People began carping again* . . . : "Quips Left to Wonder What Went Wrong", Bires, Mike, *Beaver County Times*, December 16, 2012.

430 *Then came back-to-back defeats* . . . : "South Fayette Beats Aliquippa, 34-28, in WPIAL Class AA Title Game", Everett, Brad, *Pittsburgh Post-Gazette*, November 23, 2013; "South Fayette Tops Aliquippa for WPIAL Class AA Football Title", Everett, Brad, *Pittsburgh Post-Gazette*, November 21, 2014.

430 *138 boys* . . . : "School Details: Aliquippa Senior High School", Pennsylvania Interscholatic Athletic Association, last updated on October 1, 2013, http://www.piaa.org/schools/directory/details.aspx?ID=11284.

430 *"I guarantee you"* . . . : Walker, Dwan, author interview.

431 *"They think they're fuckin' Vince Lombardi"* . . . : Zmijanac, author interview.

431 *In 2014, Henry was named a freshman all-American* . . . : "Trio of Big 12 Freshmen Earn Freshman All-American Honors", Chatmon, Brandon, ESPN. com, December 15, 2014, http://espn.go.com/blog/ncfnation/post/_/ id/105651/trio-of-big-12-freshmen-earn-freshman-all-american-honors.

431 *Swanson rushed for 732 yards* . . . : "Terry Swanson-2015 Football", University of Toledo Athletics, http://utrockets.com/roster.aspx?rp_id=4420.

431 *Darrelle Revis was back in uniform* . . . : "Darrelle Revis, New York Jets Agree to Terms on Deal", Rosenthal, Greg, NFL.com, March 10, 2015, http://www.nfl.com/news/story/0ap3000000477937/article/ darrelle-revis-new-york-jets-agree-to-terms-on-deal.

432 *"I guess I have a golden ticket"* . . . : Pugh, Kaezon, author interview, October 1, 2015.

432 *Pugh, a senior now, had rushed for 313 yards* . . . : "Aliquippa Survives Scare from Quaker Valley, Wins 35-14", Equels, Jim, *Beaver Valley Times,* September 25, 2015.

432 *At 6-foot-3* . . . : "100 Players in 100 Days-Day 91-Kaezon Pugh, Aliquippa", Splain, Billy, WesternPAFootball.net, August 26, 2015, http://www.westernpa-football.net/news/100-players-in-100-days-day-91-kaezon-pugh-aliquippa/.

432 *And though Pugh would soon become the fifth back in Aliquippa history to gain more than 4,000 yards* . . . : "WPIAL's 4,000-Yard Rushing Club Grows by Three", "from local dispatches", *Pittsburgh Post-Gazette,* October 31, 2015.

432 *"To be honest, I'm only in love with football because I think that's my only way out"* . . . : Pugh, author interview.

433 *Amassing 1,626 yards* . . . : "Goin' Campin' Stops at Aliquippa and Beaver Falls", White, Mike, *Pittsburgh Post-Gazette,* August 18, 2015.

434 *The* **Beaver County Times** *published a story* . . . : "Parents Accuse Quips Coach of Stalling Recruitment", Chiapazzi, Andrew, *Beaver County Times,* January 30, 2015.

434 *"That guy don't like me"* . . . : Askew, David, author interview.

434 *"Mike had been under fire"* . . . : Wytiaz, author interview, December 19, 2015.

434 *Four months later* . . . : "Goin' Campin' Stops at Aliquippa and Beaver Falls", White, Mike, *Pittsburgh Post-Gazette*, August 18, 2015.

435 *Then, a week before the first game* . . . : "Aliquippa RB Bronaugh to Miss Season After Cancer Diagnosis", Harlan, Chris, *Pittsburgh Tribune-Review*, August 31, 2015.

435 *Blood drives were held* . . . : Gordon, Anita, author interview, December 29, 2015.

435 *"The support has been overwhelming"* . . . : ibid.

435 *Romped for 253 yards* . . . : "Pugh, Quips Steamroll Seton-La Salle", Chiapazzi, Andrew, *Beaver County Times*, November 16, 2015.

435 *Ran for 237* . . . : "Aliquippa Routs Freeport to Return to Heinz Field", Beckner, Bill, Jr., *Pittsburgh Tribune-Review*, November 20, 2015.

436 *Pugh ground out another 179 yards* . . . : "Aliquippa Wins 16th WPIAL Title, Ends South Fayette's 44-Game Winning Streak", Price, Karen, *Pittsburgh Tribune-Review*, November 28, 2015.

436 *"Those are the kind of plays where if they don't work you look stupid"* . . . : ibid.

436 *The Quips came from behind in the fourth quarter* . . . : "Aliquippa Comes from Behind to Beat Karns City, Advances to PIAA Semifinals", Price, Karen, *Pittsburgh Tribune-Review*, December 4, 2015.

436 *Then trailed Central Martinsburg in the fourth in the semis* . . . : "Pugh's 3 Touchdowns Carry Aliquippa Back to PIAA Final", Harlan, Chris, *Pittsburgh Tribune-Review*, December 11, 2015.

436 *A bit below his playoff average of 192 yards per game* . . . : "Times Football Player of the Year: Kaezon Pugh Understands Place in Quips' History", Bires, Mike, *Beaver County Times*, December 13, 2015.

436 *"This is not a giving-up team"* . . . : "Pugh Pushes Through, Lifts Aliquippa to Hershey for First Time Since 2012", Chiappazzi, Andrew, *Beaver County Times*, December 11, 2015.

437 *"My plans?"* . . . : Pugh, author interview.

Index